The Selected Works of Eugene V. Debs

THE SELECTED WORKS OF EUGENE V. DEBS

This groundbreaking project by Haymarket Books will republish more than 1,000 of the articles, speeches, press statements, interviews, and open letters of labor leader and socialist activist Eugene Victor Debs. More than 1.5 million words will be reproduced in six thick volumes—the vast majority of which seeing print for the first time since the date of their first publication.

Eugene Victor Debs (1855–1926) was a trade union official, magazine editor, political opinion writer, and public orator widely regarded as one of the most important figures in the history of American socialism. Five times a candidate for president of the United States and twice imprisoned for his role as a strike leader and antiwar agitator, Debs remains today an esteemed and iconic figure of twentieth-century political history.

The Selected Works of Eugene V. Debs

Volume III: *The Path to a Socialist Party, 1897–1904*

edited by
Tim Davenport
and David Walters

Haymarket Books
Chicago, Illinois

Published in 2021 by
Haymarket Books
P.O. Box 180165
Chicago, IL 60618
773-583-7884
www.haymarketbooks.org
info@haymarketbooks.org

ISBNs: 978-1-64259-180-4 (hardcover)
978-1-64259-032-6 (paperback)

Trade distribution:
In the US, Consortium Book Sales and Distribution, www.cbsd.com
In Canada, Publishers Group Canada, www.pgcbooks.ca
In the UK, Turnaround Publisher Services, www.turnaround-uk.com
All other countries, Ingram Publisher Services International,
IPS_Intlsales@ingramcontent.com

This book was published with the generous support of Lannan Foundation and Wallace Action Fund.

Cover and text design by Eric Kerl.

Printed in Canada by union labor.

Library of Congress Cataloging-in-Publication data is available.

10 9 8 7 6 5 4 3 2 1

Contents

1898

1899

1900

1901

1902

1903

1904

Appendix

Introduction

This is the third of a six-volume series gathering the most important writings of American socialist and union organizer Eugene Victor Debs (1855–1926).

Volume 1: Building Solidarity on the Tracks, 1877–1892 followed the career path and intellectual development of a youthful Gene Debs, a boy who worked a year and a half as an unskilled engine maintenance worker before gaining promotion to the role of fireman for steam locomotives in the switchyard and aboard local trains. Attending business school during his free time, Debs dropped the scoop in 1874 to take a full-time job at a regional grocery wholesaler in Terre Haute, a large operation run by a family friend. Debs nevertheless managed to stay close to the railroad industry he loved as the founder and leading activist of Lodge No. 16 of the Brotherhood of Locomotive Firemen (B of LF) in February 1875.

Tireless work for the fledgling social benefit organization was rewarded in 1878 when young Gene was named assistant editor of *Locomotive Firemen's Magazine,* the brotherhood's official monthly, followed by promotion to editor and election as national secretary-treasurer in 1880, a well-remunerated and prestigious job. Debs would remain a top functionary of the B of LF for nearly 15 years. In his role as a national labor magazine editorialist, Debs closely observed the world and labor's place in it. Debs's worldview gradually evolved from an early paternalistic emphasis on sobriety, clean living, the Protestant work ethic, and active self-improvement to a radicalized perspective marked by class struggle and a ceaseless battle of workers for adequate wages, better working conditions, and social respect.

The bitter defeat of striking engineers, firemen, and switchmen in a landmark 1888 strike against the Burlington railroad system played a pivotal role in Debs's profound transformation. Seeing railroaders' division into a dozen craft-based railroad brotherhoods as an insurmountable weakness when arrayed against the united front of railway owners and managers, in 1889 Debs sought to unite the existing organizations in a centralized federation known as the Supreme Council of the United Orders of Railway Employees. Debs's hopes for this new structure were soon dashed, however, when the Supreme Council floundered and crashed in a bitter and dirty jurisdictional battle between two of its four affiliated member brotherhoods.[1] Debs was left even more firmly convinced of the need for unity among railway workers, feeling that a fundamental change in the form of labor organization in the railway industry was necessary for enduring success.

Volume 2: The Rise and Fall of the American Railway Union, 1892–1896 saw Debs quickly gravitate to the idea of a new industrial union encompassing all railway workers, abandoning the established system of craft-based brotherhoods altogether. While the original idea for such an industrial union originated with former railroad conductor George W. Howard, founder of a militant dual conductors' union, it was the charismatic Debs who rapidly became the top organizer and public face of the American Railway Union (ARU) from the time of its establishment in February 1893.

The ARU was fortunate to win a quick and widely publicized victory of an April 1894 strike against the Great Northern Railway via arbitration, but it came to grief the following year when delegates at the first and only "quadrennial convention" of the ARU voted to adopt an ongoing strike of railway-car assembly workers as their own. The union's boycott of trains attached to Pullman sleeper cars paralyzed much of America's railway system for more than a week, from Chicago westward, before being crushed by the one-two punch of legal action by the aggrieved railways and military intervention by the federal government. Debs and a half dozen other top ARU officials were jailed without trial for contempt of court for having refused to immediately terminate the Pullman strike following judicial injunction. Decapitated, the union floundered; facing the blacklist, its members scattered. Despite the crushing defeat delivered to his union, the six months spent in county jail and his triumphant emergence as an unsullied hero of the working class would prove to be a seminal event in Debs's life.

Upon his release in November 1895, Debs—convinced that lasting change was impossible through trade unionism alone—intensified his emphasis on politics, expanding his support of the independent "third party" politics of the fledgling People's Party ("Populists"). While this organization had real success in a number of western states, the movement proved short-lived, ultimately damaged beyond repair by the election of 1896 in which the Populists hitched their wagon to the candidacy of insurgent Democrat William Jennings Bryan.[2] Resisting an effort by radical elements in the People's Party to draft him as an alternative candidate for president, Debs instead campaigned for the half-hearted reformer Bryan, speaking dozens of times to labor audiences around the country on behalf of the Democratic-Populist fusion ticket.

Bryan's smashing defeat in November 1896 came as a severe blow to Debs and other earnest reformers. With the Populists discredited for their opportunism and the smallness of their intellectual horizons, the organization rapidly atrophied in size and influence. A new path was sought by those who sought fundamental economic change as a mechanism for building a better world.

ഗ

Home for Christmas 1896 from his relentless fall tour in support of the Bryan fusion ticket, Gene Debs found a surprise visitor to his Terre Haute home—Edward Boyce,[3] president of the radical Western Federation of Miners (WFM).[4] Boyce had a favor to ask of the ARU leader. A lengthy strike was underway in the booming mining town of Leadville, Colorado—a place where Boyce had himself toiled in the mines for four years previously. Wild fluctuations of the American economy had been the source of the trouble, with a partial recovery after the Panic of 1893 giving way to a new downturn in 1896. Unemployment escalated, and commodity prices, including those for silver and other metals, fell precipitously. Colorado mine operators used the bad economy and their weak bottom line as a pretext to cut wages, slashing the basic daily rate for a Leadville miner from $3 a day to $2.50. Feeling themselves unable to live on the reduced daily rate in the comparatively costly community of Leadville, then the second largest city in Colorado after Denver, miners had struck for a return to the former pay scale. The mine operators would not budge, and suspicions were rife that this intransigence was a mere pretext for an ulterior motive: busting the union. A massive strike had erupted, lasting for months. Boyce had come to Debs to ask for his help as a union activist and public orator in helping to bring the costly and violent Leadville strike to a reasonable conclusion. Debs promised his help early in the coming year.

The year 1897 would first begin with a profession of a new system of belief—a public declaration of allegiance to the doctrine of socialism. *Volume 3: Path to a Socialist Party, 1897–1904* opens with a lengthy and carefully crafted declaration of faith in socialism by Gene Debs, timed for effect for publication on New Year's Day. This was no casual announcement of support for an old cause, but rather a polished manifesto that attempted to build a groundswell for a new political movement to replace the discredited People's Party. In an interview granted one day prior to publication of his bold announcement, Debs acknowledged:

> I know that I will be criticized and berated by the press and especially by those persons who do not understand the true and better meaning of the term "socialist." But there is coming to be a better understanding of what enlightened socialism means. Some of the ablest men, in the pulpit, too,

> are beginning to sound the alarm, and they will be heeded before there is a violent explosion.[5]

Debs had already long been a socialist in all but name. Debs and his ARU cellmates in the McHenry County Jail at Woodstock, Illinois, had rather naively constituted themselves the "Cooperative Colony of Liberty Jail," news of which appeared in the press.[6] The small band spent three months reading, writing, discussing, and delivering formal lectures to one another on various social issues of the day, with Debs then spending an additional three months behind bars alone as a dubious reward for his leading role as ARU president. While Debs later retrospectively portrayed his conversion to socialism as the direct result of a volume by Karl Marx delivered to him in person at Woodstock jail by socialist propagandist Victor L. Berger,[7] in reality, Debs owed his evolving worldview more to ongoing discussions with his mates, the futuristic fiction of Edward Bellamy,[8] and the signature work of Laurence Gronlund[9] than he did to any alleged epiphany gained plowing through the ponderous *Das Kapital.*[10]

Early in January 1897, Debs made his way for the Mountain West, where he would spend about ten weeks on the road sharing the rostrum at public meetings with WFM president Edward Boyce. The Leadville strike had already been dragging on for months prior to Debs's appearance, with strikebreakers engaged in the mines, a dynamite attack and gunfight erupting between striking miners and strikebreakers, and National Guard troops inserted in an attempt to reestablish order.[11] A hefty $1 monthly tax had been imposed by the union upon every member of the Western Federation of Miners to provide financial support to the strikers. As fall turned to winter, the rank-and-file WFM had been drained not only of funds but also seemingly of the will to persevere. Debs was called upon to rally the flagging spirits of strikers and their union brethren in a speaking tour of mining cities across the region. Debs also sought, albeit with little success, to generate broad public support of the strike and to generate financial aid for picketing miners from the American labor movement as a whole. In addition, an unsuccessful attempt was made to insert Debs directly into the strike settlement process as a negotiator representing the miners.

The idea of a sliding wage scale based upon the market price of silver was floated, but the concept gained no traction, with mine owners clearly on the verge of victory and in no mood for compromise. Nor did the growing American Federation of Labor step up with the substantial financial support needed to keep the struggling miners away from work without their families starving. Despite the best eleventh-hour efforts of Debs and Boyce, the western hard-rock strike ended in total defeat in March 1897 when members of the Cloud

City Miners' Union voted overwhelmingly to return to work at the reduced wage scale.

One lasting token of Debs's commitment to the Cloud City Miners' Union was a literary contribution made after the fact, a series of seven articles on the Leadville strike and its lessons composed for *The Western Miner,* weekly newspaper of the union, during April and May 1897. The six most important of these articles are republished for the first time in this volume.[12]

ꟸ

Returning to Terre Haute from a trip to Salt Lake City in May 1897, where he had been the esteemed guest of the Western Federation of Miners at its fifth annual convention, Debs was greeted by Norman Lermond of Thomaston, Maine,[13] national secretary and leading spirit of a group of utopian socialist true believers known as the Brotherhood of the Cooperative Commonwealth (BCC). The BCC had been organized in September 1896 with the stated objective of educating the public in the principles of socialism and uniting them into a single "fraternal association" so that cooperative colonies and industries could be established "in one state until said state is socialized."[14] Lermond hoped to win over Debs—one of the most prominent American labor figures in the wake of the ARU's sensational 1894 strike—as a national organizer for his group.[15]

The BCC's strategy both paralleled and informed Debs's own manna-from-dirt-clods perspective,[16] which postulated that like-minded individuals could be banded together in cloistered, non-exploitative communities on the American frontier and cooperatively build successful local economies that would inspire widespread emulation. This growing network of colonists could then exert political muscle at the state level, winning control of state government via the ballot box and legislating tax policy that would drive wealthy exploiters out of business. Cooperative economy would then spread like wildfire from state to state, ending with the transformation of the national economy from "wage-slavery" to a system based upon higher, collaborative principles.

The BCC had previously focused on such states as Tennessee, Arkansas, and Utah—rural venues with economical land prices. Debs, on the other hand, had in mind the state of Washington, a newly minted 1889 addition to the United States on the Pacific coast that boasted not only affordable and exploitable land but a relatively small population who had already elected a Populist as governor and who therefore seemed potentially amenable to the ideas of socialism. Lermond agreed to postpone his group's Southeastern colonization plans pending the outcome of a convention of the moribund ARU, already scheduled for the middle of June in Chicago.[17]

The June 15, 1897 special convention of the American Railway Union would be its last, with the handful of delegates in attendance gaveled into session barely long enough to terminate their affairs. The gathering immediately reconvened in a larger hall under a new banner—the Social Democracy of America (SDA). Not coincidentally, the officers of this new organization would be the same as those of the old—a sort of Woodstock mafia consisting of jailed ARU functionaries Debs, Sylvester Keliher,[18] James Hogan,[19] Roy Goodwin,[20] and William E. Burns.[21] The weekly newspaper of the old ARU, *The Railway Times,* last vestige of the formerly active industrial union, was seamlessly repurposed with a new nameplate as *The Social Democrat.* The old union was transformed into a political party in a blink.

With public interest in the affairs of the self-proclaimed "labor agitator" Debs already high, an influx of observers and supporters made their way to Chicago to participate at the well-publicized founding session of the new political organization. The motley gathering would include a handful of loyalists to the Socialist Labor Party of America (SLP)—far and away the biggest and most influential Marxist political party in America.[22] Milwaukee newspaper publisher Victor L. Berger, long an enemy of the ultraorthodox SLP, would also be on hand, as well as independent radicals from Chicago such as Lucy Parsons,[23] a committed anarchist activist best known as the widow of Haymarket martyr Albert Parsons.[24]

The program of the new organization was eclectic; critics might call it muddled. On the one hand, it posited that the trade union struggle was ultimately fruitless, given the ready availability of armed force and the entire judicial system, waiting for the command of the real power behind the throne, capital. Only with the capture of the state through the ballot box and a revolutionary transformation of the entire political and judicial apparatus would just lasting change become possible.[25] Simultaneously, however, the new organization sought to pursue a parallel strategy of economic transformation through cloistered cooperative colonies, concentrated and connected in a single, sparsely-populated state in the West. Political transformation would start small, with the success of cooperative organization inspiring mass emulation and ultimately propelling the socialist cause to victory.

This dual political and economic scheme sounded reasonable in the abstract. Reality was more problematic. While plenty of people could be found to attend meetings, raising the massive funds needed to finance a large-scale program of land acquisition and colonization would prove more difficult. As a first step, the founding convention of the SDA elected a three-member

"Colonization Commission" consisting of prominent civil engineer and political activist Richard J. Hinton[26] of Washington, DC, and two important political journalists—the true fathers of the Bellamy political movement of the 1890s: Cyrus Field Willard of Boston,[27] and W. P. Borland[28] of Michigan. For his part, the Social Democracy's best-known adherent, Eugene V. Debs, would remain a giddy advocate of the colonization scheme throughout the summer of 1897, with his ardor only gradually attenuating as the price tag of colonization and the difficulty of uniting a diverse organization around a single location—or even tactic of colonies at all—became clear.[29]

Following the precedent of political parties and religious groups throughout history, the Social Democracy of America was an organization racked by factional disagreement. Beyond any disagreement over the tactic of colonization, the SDA faintly echoed a fundamental tension in the SLP of the 1880s, pitting a revolutionary socialist "anarchist" wing and the election-driven orientation of Debs and his fellows. This tension came to a head in September 1897 with news of the Lattimer Massacre in Pennsylvania, a premeditated bloodbath in which more than 20 striking immigrant coal miners marching on a public road were shot to death and dozens more wounded by a trigger-happy sheriff's posse. Debs railed against the butchery with a September 12 editorial in which he provocatively declared that had he not been "unalterably opposed to capital punishment I would say that the sheriff and his deputy assassins should be lynched."[30] However, when very similar sentiments were expressed at a meeting of Chicago Local Branch 2, SDA, a radical group that included the publicly known anarchist Lucy Parsons among its ranks, and the mainstream Chicago press caught wind, a harsh reaction followed. The moderate leadership of the SDA decided that, in order to quell the tempest, factional heads must roll. It was Debs himself who presided over the four-hour evening session of the SDA executive board that drummed the entire membership of Chicago Local Branch 2 out of the movement. These machinations foreshadowed the on-again, off-again factional war between radicals and moderates that periodically erupted within the future Socialist Party of America. In this first internecine battle, it should be emphasized, Debs was no wild-eyed leftist, nor were his hands clean.

∽

Following the expulsion of Chicago Local Branch 2, factional discord was briefly quieted. President Debs earned his $100 a month salary as a touring lecturer for the SDA, speaking on behalf of the party to crowds around the country. Debs even took his organizing campaign north of the border, making a series of appearances in the Canadian province of Ontario late in 1897 before returning home to Terre Haute for Christmas. From there he would depart on a more pleasant winter jaunt, touring the sunny states of Georgia, Alabama, and Louisiana early in 1898.

Debs's aggressive travel schedule as de facto national organizer for the SDA was duplicated by the group's independently financed Colonization Commission. Originally envisioned by the convention as a committee assigned in charge of hammering out details for a cooperative project in Washington or similar western state, the commission soon expanded its mission and around a broad section of the country investigating no fewer than four half-baked schemes.[31] First came a plan for the SDA to serve effectively as a general contractor for the construction of 75 miles of train track for the city of Nashville, a project that was to be funded by the sale of government bonds. This idea rapidly morphed into a grandiose proposal for the acquisition of 400,000 acres of rural Tennessee, underwritten by selling bonds to financial speculators backed by the value of the property. The commission visited Georgia because it was rumored that there might be a suitable place for a cooperative colony, then pondered land in Utah, before settling on the idea of selling 5-percent-interest-bearing bonds to purchase a working gold mine in Colorado. The precious metal extracted would be used to pay off investors and fund future efforts at agricultural colonization, the commission surmised.

In its first year of existence, the overmatched Colonization Commission accomplished nothing of value, frittering away on salaries, travel, and lodging expenses several thousand dollars that had been raised for the express purpose of establishing a model cooperative colony. With the political action faction of the SDA already running candidates in local elections in Milwaukee in 1897 with gratifying results, dissatisfaction with the fantasy and failure of the Colonization Commission grew as the scheduled date of the first national convention of the SDA drew nigh.

The June 1898 convention of the Social Democracy of America would prove to be the last public act by the group. While political action and colonization had been conceived as complementary strategies of an efficient and multi-pronged organization at the founding convention in 1897, after just twelve months it seemed clear that a small and underfunded group such as the SDA could barely pursue one, let alone both, of these antagonistic agendas. The committed advocates of each path came to see those favoring the other tactic in an adversarial light, and concrete factional organization was begun in an effort to capture the convention and control the future direction of the organization. Pro-colonization forces were particularly adept in their organizing efforts, hastily establishing 11 new Chicago local branches in the weeks preceding the convention, each barely meeting the minimum size requirement of five members.[32] These dubious newly-minted entities were nevertheless entitled to one voting delegate at the convention according to organizational rules. Smelling an attempt to pack the convention, national secretary Sylvester Keliher, a committed political actionist, attempted to block this foray by declining to issue charters for eight of the new local branches. This administrative action enraged the colonization faction, led by former ARU functionary James Hogan and Cyrus Field Willard of the Colonization Commission. The entire first day of the convention was spent in an acrimonious debate, arguing the case for seating these contested delegates. The colonization faction ultimately won the day, bolstering their delegate majority and indicating in no uncertain terms which way the convention would be turning.

The following morning, Vice President Hogan delivered a stinging two-hour report charging his former ARU brother Keliher with financial malfeasance, alleging that earmarked colonization funds had been improperly used to cover day-to-day operation of the national organization. Further debate over the party program devolved into a heated argument running late into the night, culminating in a 53–37 vote in the wee hours reaffirming the tactic of colonization, and approving the current scheme of establishing and operating a cooperative Colorado gold mine, financed by the sale of speculative shares to investors.[33]

Time was running out on the convention; some politically-oriented delegates had already left for home, with others needing to depart the next day.[34] Gene Debs was sick in bed, conveniently and not for the last time taking ill in the face of bitter factional conflict. Occupied with credentials fights, mutual recriminations of officers, and speechifying, four days had already been wasted. With new officers slated to be elected the following day and the colonization faction in decisive majority control of the convention, the time for a break had arrived.

At 2:30 a.m., the gavel of adjournment fell. Thirty-one members of the political action faction immediately proceeded across the street to the parlor of the Revere House to unanimously constitute themselves a new political organization, the Social Democratic Party of America.[35] With Gene's brother, friend, and top political advisor, Theodore, tapped as "temporary" national secretary of the new party at the pre-dawn founding conclave, there seemed little doubt where the elder Debs brother's allegiance would lie. But similar unity of purpose would not be shown by Gene's old ARU associates from Woodstock. The ambitious George Howard was first to split with his comrades back in their three months of joint internment. Then Louis W. Rogers[36] had stepped aside at the time of the 1897 transformation of the ARU into the SDA. Now, with the shattering of the SDA, three more ARU colleagues would part paths with Debs, with James Hogan and Roy Goodwin joining the nine-member National Executive Council of the restructured colonization group, and William Burns dealing himself out of national politics to return to the rank and file.

The split of the SDA was largely unexpected by the members and friends of the Social Democracy and drew sharp criticism from some quarters. Veteran Newark labor journalist Joseph Buchanan, investigating the situation just a few days after the breakup, revealed that he had previously warned Debs in no uncertain terms that any foray into politics would prove fatal for colonization efforts of his new organization, as the "many rich men who sympathized with the poor" and who gave generously to social reform causes would refuse aid if the industrial plan was attached to a partisan political scheme.[37] Now Debs and the political actionists were faced with the deceptively difficult task of developing a niche for the new political party in the narrow space between the People's Party on the reformist right and the Socialist Labor Party on the impossibilist left.[38] "He'll see, if he hasn't already seen . . . that there isn't any use trying just now to split between those two organizations," Buchanan warned. Revered godfather of American social democracy Laurence Gronlund was similarly displeased, taking to the pages of the penultimate issue of the official organ of the colonization wing to rebuke Victor Berger and the political actionists for an unrealizable extremist program that "would require a radical change in our national constitution."[39]

Debs seems to have been physically exhausted by two years of relentless touring and deeply demoralized by the death of his true intellectual child, the American Railway Union. He retreated to his home in Indiana for the summer of 1898, delivering just one public address in Terre Haute and a handful of hastily written contributions to the new weekly newspaper of the SDP, the *Social Democratic Herald.* By September, Debs was so far adrift personally and professionally that he was reportedly testing the water for an implausible return as a functionary of the Brotherhood of Locomotive Firemen. He traveled at his own expense to the organization's 1898 annual convention in Toronto, ostensibly to "see friends." A single speech in Erie, Pennsylvania, provided a suitable pretext for this journey, the results of which were otherwise barren.[40]

Only the coming of the fall election season shook Debs free from his torpor. Somewhat miraculously, the Social Democratic Party—taking over for and building upon a foundation laid in several previous local elections by the Socialist Labor Party—began to attract attention and support in a few industrial towns in Massachusetts, with shoe and textile operatives rallying to the red banner. Debs hurried to the scene of action, speaking nightly throughout October on behalf of the SDP in a series of Massachusetts engagements.[41] Night after night, he hammered home the SDP's message, appearing at Northampton, Holyoke, Worcester, Cambridge, Boston, and other locales. The SDP campaign was capped with success, with the party winning the election of Louis M. Scates[42] and James F. Carey[43] to the Massachusetts legislature, followed several weeks later by success at the city level in the towns of Haverhill and Brockton. Although modest and limited in scope, the victories of the SDP in the 1898 elections seemed to validate the strategy of the adherents of electoral politics, giving the tiny new party a reprieve for growth.

☙

With the elections having finished, Debs was once more left occupationally unmoored. Despite earlier misgivings that converting one's fame to fortune on the lecture circuit was somehow unseemly, in December 1898, Debs reversed course and embarked on a new career, shifting from organizational functionary of a fledgling political party to paid orator. Twenty dates were booked for 20 nights in the state of Iowa, with the "nonpartisan" Debs lecturing extemporaneously on "Labor and Liberty" before eclectic audiences in such rural enclaves as Eagle Grove (population 3,500), Creston (7,700), and Boone (8,500).[44] Turnout for this initial midwinter speaking tour was sparse, but the first steps of the learning curve were navigated, and lessons learned for the future. Debs dedicated a substantial percentage of the proceeds of his early paid speaking engagements to retirement of the ARU's five-figure debt for legal services incurred during the 1894 Pullman strike—a bill that he assumed personally following the union's termination in 1897 in an effort to preserve its good name.

Debs also sought to build a career as a publisher in this period, adding new socialist titles to the Debs Publishing Company's already substantial catalog of instructional books for railroad workers. A monthly series of socialist pamphlets under the series title "Progressive Thought" was launched in January 1899, with order fulfillment handled at home in Terre Haute by his wife, Kate. This fledgling operation was forced to battle for a place in a socialist publishing field already dominated by bigger rivals, including the former Unitarian publishing house of Charles H. Kerr in Chicago,[45] J. A. Wayland's expanding *Appeal to Reason* operation based in Southeastern Kansas, the Wilshire Publishing Company of Los Angeles, and John Spargo's Comrade Publishing Company of New York City.[46] Each of these friendly rivals published regular newspapers or magazines through which they promoted their wares, placing the Debs Publishing Company at a serious competitive disadvantage. Debs nevertheless continued to swim against the stream as a publisher through 1904, adding two short booklets from his own pen to the company's catalog—*The American Movement*[47] and *Unionism and Socialism.*[48] He would formally liquidate his publishing enterprise only in August 1905.[49]

Despite Debs's struggles as a publisher, his career as a paid public speaker began to flourish during the first half of 1899. Warming up with a couple of Indiana dates in January, Debs engaged his old ARU associate and current president of the Michigan Federation of Labor, former *Railway Times* editor L. W. Rogers, to manage a ten-day tour of the Wolverine State. Unlike many of his previous dates in Iowa, these Michigan events were attended by large and enthusiastic audiences who paid 25, 35, or even 50 cents for a ticket to hear the earnest and lively extemporaneous prose of the famous labor leader. A tour of Ohio and Indiana followed during late February, with Debs returning home for several weeks before catching a train to New York City for a long-anticipated speech at Delmonico's, one of the city's finest restaurants, at the invitation of the tony Nineteenth Century Club.[50] April saw a further tour of Indiana; a vast swath of territory was covered in May and June, with Debs speaking in such far-flung locales as Tennessee, Arkansas, Texas, Ohio, Pennsylvania, and Indiana. Touching base in Terre Haute from his massive tour barely long enough to sleep in his own bed, Debs immediately departed for Wisconsin, Minnesota, and South Dakota, before cracking back to Michigan and Illinois. Debs was much in demand as a public orator and willing to slake that thirst with political talks. Debs spoke earnestly and entertainingly for two hours a night on "Labor and Liberty" to audiences running into the thousands, in the meantime racking up honoraria with which he steadily chipped away at the ARU's standing legal debt.[51]

Factional discord had consumed the Social Democracy by the middle of 1898. One year later, a similar tension was festering in the rival Socialist Labor Party (SLP). In 1890, a talented Columbia University lecturer had been installed in the top echelon of party leadership, Daniel DeLeon.[52] As editor of the official English-language party weekly, *The People,* DeLeon would soon come to dominate the SLP through his masterful invective and political savvy, building a centralized faction of co-thinkers that included editor of the official *Vorwärts* (*Forward*), Hugo Vogt,[53] and the party's iron-jowled national secretary, Henry

Kuhn.[54] This leading group, enemies all of socialists making use of the tactic of "boring within" the established network of craft-based trade unions, had overplayed their hand by establishing a dual labor federation in 1895, the Socialist Trade and Labor Alliance (ST&LA). Marketed as a tool for organization of the unorganized, in practice the ST&LA did little more than initiate a series of bitter jurisdictional skirmishes with unions affiliated with the American Federation of Labor—a contest that accomplished nothing more than the utter destruction of carefully constructed bridges between socialist trade unionists and the established labor movement.

As a result of this trade union policy and an attempt to instill ideological uniformity, a first wave of defections began in 1897 when a number of the party's leading Yiddish-language journalists and activists, including Abraham Cahan,[55] Louis Miller,[56] and Morris Winchevsky,[57] exited amid insults and accusations. They chose to join forces with the fresh and unsullied Debs Social Democracy, participating in the founding convention of the SDA. This departure of the SLP's talented Yiddish leadership exacerbated an already tense internal situation inside the party. Despite the dwindling number of adherents of the new union, the SLP national leadership's support of the ST&LA continued unabated, while discontent at the state and local level grew. Criticism of party policy was stifled by the stranglehold on the press maintained by the New York leadership.

A factional explosion ripped apart the Socialist Labor Party in the summer of 1899, as an organized group of dissidents attempted to depose the DeLeon-Vogt-Kuhn leadership clique through regular party processes. The opposition faction was headed by attorneys Morris Hillquit[58] and Henry Slobodin,[59] as well as editors and staff of the *New Yorker Volkszeitung*, a semi-independent German-language SLP daily that had been sharply critical of the dual unionist ST&LA tactic.[60] The denouement came with the July 1899 election of the new General Committee of Section New York—the party unit that, under state and national party rules, was responsible for election of the National Executive Committee, which in turn appointed the party editors. DeLeon and *The People* accused the anti-ST&LA dissidents of duplicity, alleging that principle had been surrendered for the ephemeral support of the "labor fakirs" heading the constituent unions of the American Federation of Labor. Several outspoken opponents had been suspended.[61] The dissidents responded by publishing a new factional paper, a so-called monthly edition of the *Volkszeitung* that attempted to isolate the DeLeon-Vogt-Kuhn leadership and its trade union policies, making use of the party mailing list to place it in the hands of all subscribers of *The People* and *Vorwärts*.[62]

Rival slates were fielded for the General Committee elections, and the air was rife with accusations of election fraud and rumors of the establishment of phantom branches. The dissidents won the majority in the party election that followed. The newly elected delegates gathered for official reorganization on July 8, with unwavering DeLeon loyalist L. Abelson, organizer of Section New York, in the chair. An attempt to elect a temporary chair followed, with the nominee of the dissidents apparently receiving a majority of votes of those assembled before Hugo Vogt disrupted the proceedings by filibustering with an impromptu speech.[63] Recriminations about false credentials and violations of parliamentary procedure rapidly devolved into fisticuffs and, as one participant colorfully recounted,

> the delegates pummeled each other until blood was seen flowing from many wounds. Men were sprawling upon the floor, others were fighting in corners, upon the tables, chairs, and upon the piano, Hugo Vogt having climbed upon the latter yelling and fairly foaming from his mouth. Kuhn, Vogt, Fiebiger, and many others were bleeding, and when they saw that the majority were not willing to submit to mob law, they withdrew from the hall.[64]

With the first reorganizational meeting thoroughly disrupted, another session was called for July 10 at Laughut's Hall in the Bowery to elect a new General Committee of Section New York (and thereby the National Executive Committee). This session was boycotted by the pro-DeLeon faction, which alleged the gathering to have been illegally called. Free of obstructionist tactics by troublesome opponents, provisional organizer of Section New York Julius Gerber[65] called the meeting to order, and the dissident faction rapidly proceeded to take action to sweep away the old leadership of the party. In a first resolution passed by over 50 delegates duly assembled, organizer Abelson, secretary Kuhn, "and all other officers of Section New York, SLP" were suspended from their positions and temporary successors elected, with the decision to be ratified by referendum vote of the party membership.[66] In further resolutions, the seven members of the New York State Committee and five members of the National Executive Committee (NEC) were similarly suspended and replaced by new slates. Henry L. Slobodin was elected by the meeting as provisional national secretary, with top leaders of the dissidents Benjamin Feigenbaum and Morris Hillquit elected to the state committee and NEC, respectively.[67]

The administration faction refused to acknowledge the legitimacy of these suspensions and elections by the action of what they considered an illegally constituted "kangaroo court."[68] Following the conclusion of the meeting, national secretary pro tem Slobodin made his way with a handful of other delegates to take possession of the national office located at 184 William Street. They arrived to find locked doors, behind which sat Kuhn, Vogt, DeLeon, Abelson, and other administration loyalists. Yet another brawl ensued, this time with clubs and bottles being wielded as weapons. Slobodin and the dissidents were the losers in this pugilistic rematch, which drew to a premature conclusion with the arrival of the police.[69] Two rival political parties went forward, each wrapping themselves in the mantle of the Socialist Labor Party, each publishing editions of official organs under identical nameplates as *The People*.

Fist-fighting in the halls gave way to less sanguinary battlegrounds. First came a fight in the capitalist courts, with the DeLeonists awarded the valuable party logo and ballot line. The second battle, a fight for the hearts, minds, allegiance, and dues money of the local leaders and the rank and file, ended in a split decision, with some leaders and organizations, such as J. Mahlon Barnes[70] and Section Philadelphia, Tommy Morgan[71] of Section Chicago, Max S. Hayes[72] and Section Cleveland, and Job Harriman[73] in California decisively splitting with the DeLeon faction while others rallied to the cause of the charismatic political strategist, translator, and newspaper editor.[74]

∽

The dissident SLP remained as much a New York–centered organization as the official party; it held its organizing convention upstate in the city of Rochester from January 27 to February 2, 1900.[75] The split with the administrative faction had left the SLP dissidents—practical politicians all—feeling isolated and weak. A hunger grew to restore the strength and upward trajectory of the organization through unification with Midwestern-based organization of Debs and Berger. In addition to common antipathy to Daniel DeLeon and his cohorts, a substantial programmatic agreement was recognized. Volition for unity originated with the SLP dissidents. By an overwhelming vote of 55 to 1, their Rochester convention named a nine-member Unity Committee to negotiate merger terms with the Social Democratic Party. The same convention also nominated California attorney Job Harriman and Cleveland newspaper publisher Max S. Hayes as its respective candidates for president and vice president of the United States, with the understanding that this slate was subject to change should a new unified organization rapidly emerge.

The depth of the partisan antipathy still held by the top SDP leadership was grossly underestimated by the SLP dissidents. Good faith was in short supply; outright hostility or, at best, deep and poisonous suspicion was coin of the realm. For two years, Debs and his associates had been on the receiving end of a torrent of ridicule from the SLP, with party editor DeLeon and his co-thinkers pouring forth a thick layer of insults and mockery alleging the pseudosocialist nature of the weak-minded neophytes who comprised the thoroughly middle-class "Debserie." Although endured mostly in silence, this protracted attack was deeply resented by the top leadership of the SDP: Gene Debs and his brother, national secretary Theodore; grumpy and vain publisher Victor L. Berger of Milwaukee and his protégé, Frederic Heath; young Chicago attorney Seymour Stedman, a Debs acolyte from People's Party days; Chicago attorney Jesse Cox, an aging veteran of Chicago progressive politics; party editor Alfred Shenstone Edwards, a veteran of the failed Ruskin colony of Tennessee who had come to Jesus as a committed political actionist through personal experience with the dismal reality of communal living; and powerhouse organizer Margaret Haile of Massachusetts. These top leaders of the SDP saw the SLP dissidents as guilty by association with the worst excesses of the DeLeon–Kuhn regime. The protracted legal fight to retain the name and apparatus of the Socialist Labor Party waged by the breakaway dissidents had done nothing to calm the visceral loathing of the SDP leadership of the devil DeLeon.

Four members of the dissident SLP's unity committee were in attendance at the SDP's regularly scheduled nominating convention, held in Indianapolis from March 6–9, 1900. These four came cap in hand, respectfully, and were granted the floor at the convention. There they spoke positively for the idea of unity and were received warmly. This delegation consisted of multilingual Morris Hillquit, an urbane intellectual uniquely able to calm the most troubled waters with well-chosen words; both members of the dissidents' presidential slate of Job Harriman and Max Hayes, themselves very personable and affable individuals; and George B. Benham, editor of a San Francisco weekly, *The Class Struggle,* and a top socialist in the biggest city of the Pacific coast. Harriman graciously offered to stand aside for the famous Debs atop a unity ticket. Formal unification of the two kindred political organizations was envisioned to take place in the immediate future. In negotiations with SDP leaders, promises were made to continue using "Social Democratic Party" name in the new, unified party that was to follow.

Debs and the SDP leaders found themselves facing a veritable tidal wave of pro-merger sentiment at the March 1900 convention. Still wary of the SLP dissidents to the point of paranoia, they professed agnosticism on the unification question and bided their time. Berger, Heath, Haile, and Stedman were all elected to a nine-person joint unity committee by the gathering and given the task of meeting with their dissident SLP counterparts to hammer out a final unity proposal to be submitted to both organizations for ratification.[76] Debs, continuing his preference to be a party leader above the factional fray, did not participate in this SDP unity committee. Moreover, Debs initially resisted the entreaties of the SDP delegates to head the national ticket as candidate for president in 1900, repeating his refusal to run for office as a radical populist in the previous campaign. Only at the eleventh hour, amidst actual tears and figurative arm-twisting, was a recalcitrant Debs finally persuaded to put his hat into the presidential ring—thereby narrowly averting the deep organizational embarrassment that would have followed the SDP's endorsement of the full ticket of the dissident SLP, already in the field. It was decided: Debs of the SDP would be the nominee for president and Harriman of the dissident SLP the nominee for vice president. Even without a merger, the two parties would run a joint ticket under the banner of the Social Democratic Party. This hurried decision to coordinate national campaign efforts, made at a time when the prospect of organic unity burned most brightly, would prove fortuitous in later months, tamping down factional jealously and Machiavellian shenanigans and keeping differences between dissident SLP New York and SDP Chicago from spiraling to an irreconcilable split.

ᔕ

Seventeen of the 18 members of the two unity committees met in New York City from March 25–27, 1900.[77] Never was the old adage "the devil is in the details" more true. The division between the SLP-loathing leaders of Chicago and Milwaukee and the rest of the unity delegates became abundantly clear during discussions over the fundamental issues of party name, location of headquarters, and official publication. With Berger missing the trip due to the forthcoming birth of a child,[78] the SDP delegation split 5–3 on issue after issue at the conference, with the pro-unity majority led at the table by William Butscher of Brooklyn and Mayor John C. Chase[79] of Haverhill, Massachusetts.

Division within the Chicago SDP was bitter; factional war was brewing. The unity conference majority attempted without success to stifle publication of an unfavorable minority report by the three disgruntled opponents of the Chicago delegation. Margaret Haile returned home to Boston to begin rallying merger opponents in her home state while delegates Stedman and Heath raced back to Chicago to organize defeat of the formal unity proposal agreed upon by the other 14 delegates. Their joint effort, wrapped in the mantle of authority as a "Manifesto of the National Executive Board," was written on April 2 and rushed into print in the *Social Democratic Herald* later that week.[80] This rush to print effectively undercut the official majority report of the unity negotiators, which was only released for debate and a scheduled referendum vote in the subsequent weekly issue. The anti-unity manifesto was by four members of the five members of the National Executive Board (NEB), Debs alone declining to sign, and accused the dissident SLP of deception and duplicity, further asserting that the SDP's own unity delegation had exceeded the bounds of their authority granted to them by the convention. The specter of a takeover by the nefarious Socialist Labor Party was emphasized. An impromptu alternative referendum was rushed to vote by the Chicago NEB, polling the question of whether the membership felt any further unity discussions whatsoever were desirable in light of the shocking revelations of SLP double-dealing. An agitation campaign to discontinue the unity effort was begun in the party press.

Debs joined the anti-unity fray on April 21, urging in a lengthy and bitter article that the unity campaign should be halted and the merger plans of the unity negotiators defeated.[81] Debs contended that the breakaway SLP dissidents had continued to mock and criticize the SDP even after their split from DeLeon's organization, and that the entire effort to combine forces had been made in bad faith. Intimations in letters to the party press of the dissident SLP that "bossism" and "hero worship" were practiced by the Chicago organization—that is to say, anti-democratic behavior and a Debs personality cult—seem to have particularly touched a nerve. Although doing his part to feed the drama gods in the intraparty fight over unification, Debs nevertheless remained atop the joint presidential nominee of both organizations in 1900. With tightly pursed lips, the SDP fusion ticket of 1900 proceeded to the November election, backed by rival campaign committees, East and West, conducting activities with little or no coordination.

ൾ

On May 12 came the results of the snap referendum called by the Chicago leadership. The Social Democratic Party, it was announced, had decided to discontinue any further unity negotiations with the former SLP dissidents by a vote of 1,213 to 939. If Debs and the Chicago leadership believed that the drive for a unified socialist party had been effectively squelched with their rushed referendum, however, they badly miscalculated. The pro-unity majority of the SDP committee would continue to work with their SLP dissident counterparts as if no such resolution had been enacted. A second meeting of the joint unity committees, attended this time by Debs in an ex-officio capacity, had already been held in New York on April 20. After issuing demands that the meeting could only be unofficial in light of the ongoing party referendum, minority faction members Haile, Berger, Stedman, and Heath made their way to this second conference. They would stay just long enough to cause a commotion, stage a dramatic walkout, and take an early train ride home. The five-member majority of the Chicago SDP committee and the nine-member committee of SLP dissidents remained to proceed with unity preparations on their own. Through their work, a new joint organization was born, reusing the name "Social Democratic Party" in an effort to liquidate the red herring of party name featured in the anti-unity manifesto of the Chicago executive. New party headquarters were to be established in Springfield, Massachusetts, a choice made in an effort to reduce New York–Chicago rivalry by moving the party center to the hotbed of its political success. William Butscher, a veteran of the Debsian SDP organization from Brooklyn, was named the national secretary of the new organization.

As joint action by local activists continued during the 1900 campaign, pressure for unity by ordinary members of the Chicago-based organization steadily grew, effectively circumventing their anti-unity leaders. In the city of Chicago itself, a majority of local social democrats of all stripes joined forces in civic elections as an alliance presciently named the "Socialist Party." In May, a joint convention was held in Manchester, New Hampshire, called by the state affiliate of the Chicago SDP, with the gathering passing a resolution recognizing "the necessity of a union state ticket" and agreeing to meet in joint session without preconditions. Local branches were urged to establish "union caucuses in each locality" for joint city nominations.[82] In June, New York had its own convention, dominated by adherents of the dissident SLP but including a smattering of pro-unity members of the national organization based in Chicago.

Unity sentiment also burned strong in Massachusetts, the epicenter of SDP politics, when on June 12 the state committee voted—over the vehement objection of state secretary Margaret Haile—to open up its July 8 state convention to members of the Springfield group for participation on the basis of equality. This action preserved unity, bringing together the two most effective locals, the Springfield-allied Haverhill organization and the Chicago loyalists of Brockton. Haile was left to sputter that the cause of socialism had been "disgraced" when a joint program was agreed upon and a majority of former SLP members elected to the new Massachusetts State Committee.[83] Secretary Haile refused to accept this majority decision of the state convention, instead leading a split in September, enraged by the decision of the Massachusetts State Committee to end dues payments to the Chicago national office. In spite of this sectarian bitterness, the dueling Massachusetts SDP organizations continued to support the national unity ticket of Debs and Harriman as well as the mixed slate of state candidates named at the July joint convention in Boston. Neighboring Connecticut held a joint convention of its own in New Haven, bringing together "all socialists believing in social democratic principles" under one roof. The meeting went off without a hitch, passing a resolution that provided for unity between the SDP and the dissident SLP on "presidential, state, and local candidates, platform, and state campaign committee in the state of Connecticut."[84] Unity from below also appears to have been achieved in Ohio in which locals pledging allegiance to one or the other national organization jointly supported a unitary state committee with a portion of their dues.[85] Iowa socialists joined the unity parade in August, when it held a state convention in Oskaloosa delegated by representatives of either national organization.[86] On the Pacific coast, the Springfield SDP organization was predominant, with the radical Washington state organization particularly unified.

Only in Wisconsin did the executive officers of the Chicago SDP manage to effectively deflect the rank-and-file demand for unity. Victor Berger's powerful Milwaukee political machine continued to eschew organic unity so long as its eastern rival "holds on to its old stagnating, heresy-hunting, and narrow habits of agitation"—behavior that "would mean simply the turning over of the splendid social democratic movement into the control of men not at all in sympathy with its broadness, and put the American socialist movement back to where it was when the SLP was the only party and ruled despotically."[87]

Although it continued to control the party press and was thereby able to portray the ongoing factional situation in the rosiest of lights, the Chicago leadership could also count noses. It was clear to all that sentiment for unity had become a majority opinion among American socialists. Despite some timid saber-rattling by the Chicago NEB, no mass expulsions would follow, punishing its members for participating in "unionist" state conventions. The warlike official rhetoric emanating from Chicago proved toothless; the iron logic of a joint ticket pushed the Chicago and Springfield parties forward toward active collaboration. From the perspective of the ordinary member, similarities greatly exceeded differences between the two competing Social Democratic parties.

☙

Although the two rival organizations worked more or less effectively at the local level in support of their joint ticket, results from the polls in November 1900 were not edifying. The crown jewel of the Springfield SDP, the Haverhill, Massachusetts, organization, suffered a stinging loss when Mayor John C. Chase was defeated in his bid for reelection by a Republican–Democratic fusion ticket, as were two SDP aldermen seeking another term. The strong right hand of Victor Berger, Elizabeth H. Thomas, herself recently transplanted from Haverhill to Milwaukee, shamelessly crowed about the defeat, assigning blame to the decision of the Haverhill organization to sever itself from "moral and material aid" by cutting ties with Chicago party headquarters. "It has been disastrous for her and needs no comment," Thomas smugly noted, her confidence bolstered by news of the reelection of Brockton mayor Charles Coulter, a booster of the Chicago SDP, by a plurality of 35 votes in a three-way race.[88]

John C. Chase was not the only Social Democrat who failed to meet expectations in the November 1900 election. The biggest disappointment of all was the presidential ticket of Eugene V. Debs and Job Harriman. No amount of optimistic spin could conceal the fact that the SDP, in its first presidential effort, had been delivered a severe rebuke at the polls. Crowds had clambered to hear Debs during his six-week whirlwind of whistle-stops and evening lectures; halls were filled to capacity, and the level of enthusiasm was high. Yet when the ballots were counted (or not counted, as some contended), the results proved poor to the extreme in key electoral districts. A mere 12,869 votes were tallied for Debs in the state of New York, a dismal count barely topping the 12,622 ballots accorded Joseph F. Maloney, an obscure machinist from Massachusetts who stood as the presidential candidate of the DeLeonist SLP.[89] In Massachusetts, the Debs–Harriman ticket ran more than 3,500 votes behind the SDP's candidate for governor and failed to match the total delivered for any candidate on the statewide ticket.[90] Dreaming of a million votes, the Debs–Harriman ticket could not even achieve one-tenth of their vision.[91]

According to results published in the *Chicago Tribune* six weeks after the election, the Debs–Harriman ticket collected a mere 85,000 votes out of just under 14 million cast—just six-tenths of 1 percent.[92] Ballots cast for the Social Democratic Party's ticket were more than doubled by those delivered for the nominees of the Prohibition Party, third place finisher in the 1900 presidential race. In only one state did Debs and Harriman receive more than 2 percent of the vote: Massachusetts. In only six other states—Washington, Oregon, Wisconsin, Florida, New Jersey, and Montana—did the Social Democratic vote top 1 percent. Things got worse from there. The vote count in Pennsylvania and West Virginia, where Debs had invested so much time on behalf of striking coal miners in 1897, suffering a severe sunstroke in the process, was particularly dispiriting, with only 4,800 votes registered out of nearly 1.2 million cast in the Keystone State. In neighboring West Virginia just 220 votes out of 220,000 were tallied for the Debs–Harriman team.

Debs continued to present an optimistic face to the public; behind the scenes he was sullen and snippy. Immediately after the close of the election, Gene wrote his friend and consigliere, his brother Theo Debs, declaring:

> Thus closes the campaign—and the results show that we got everything *except votes.*
>
> I am serene for two reasons:
>
> First: I did the very best I could for the party that nominated me and for its principles.
>
> Second: The working class will get in full measure what they voted for.
>
> And so we begin the campaign for 1904.

With respect to potential unification with the Springfield SDP, Debs was even more bitter, writing:

> I am surprised at [NEB member and close ally Seymour] Stedman's intimation that we may have something to do with the other factions. Great heavens, haven't we got enough?
>
> If there is any attempt to harmonize or placate, *count me out.* We must go forward on our own lines and those who don't choose to fall in need not do so. There must be no *wobbling* at this time.
>
> I thought our plan of action was clearly understood and now I am overwhelmed with pleas to attend a conference etc etc etc etc.
>
> Hell! Don't we know what we want? Or are we crazy?
>
> We held a deliberate board meeting and went over the whole ground in detail and agreed to call a special convention within 30 days after election. I wrote the call and mailed it to you . . .
>
> I am well and in good spirits, but 30 hours a day for 6 weeks has told on me and I'm run down. I'll not go to Chicago, nor attend any conference till I'm rested. I would not be fit for service in my present condition. If the convention has been called *off* I feel as if I ought to pull out and let the whole thing go and attend to my own business, but I won't. I'll stick to the party, through the gates of hell, till it stands on rock and defies the thunderbolts of Jove.[93]

The surviving correspondence of Gene Debs is spotty and partial; he left neither a memoir nor unpublished manuscripts to reveal what he and the Chicago SDP leadership had in mind for their snap convention, which was planned for the month after the November 1900 general election. Nor does a stenographic report or official minutes exist for the gathering itself. We are left to read between the lines of the November 9 letter to Theodore above: *"We must go forward on our own lines and those who don't choose to fall in need not do so."*

The Debs brothers and the anti-unity Chicago leadership were now outnumbered on the unity question, but they were still spoiling for one more fight.

∽

As Debs suspected, the delay in publishing the convention call immediately after the November general election meant that no gathering could be held during December 1900. Belatedly, an announcement was issued for a conclave in Chicago, scheduled to open on January 15, 1901. This call rather fancifully asserted that demand for such a convention had sprung from individuals and local branches around the country and was made necessary to "meet the growing demands of the organization." The object of the special convention was thereby rendered as clear as mud. According to terms of the document, branches would be free to send as many delegates as they desired, with each paid member of the Chicago organization allotted one vote, assignable by written proxy to any individual able to attend.[94]

Despite the official rationale, the idea for the January convention clearly originated with Debs and the leadership, not the rank and file, and was called with factional intent—a last-ditch effort to build momentum for the existing Chicago-based organization and to halt the seemingly inexorable drift toward unification with the rival Springfield organization. Although originally scheduled for party headquarters, a larger venue was made necessary, and the 200 delegates were called to order by NEB secretary Seymour Stedman at Aldine Hall on Randolph Street.[95] Margaret Haile, one of the most fierce and uncompromising opponents of unity with the so-called "Kangaroos," was elected temporary secretary of the gathering.

A harsh anti-unity tone was orchestrated from the outset with the reading of an official message from the Springfield SDP objecting to Debs and the Chicago leadership's sudden and surprising decision to hold the special national convention, with the event portrayed as a new obstacle hastily constructed to impede unification. This message was poorly received, and protracted debate followed as to whether the communication should be demonstratively returned to Springfield or merely filed without action. Debs spoke with some hostility toward the Springfield group during the debate that followed, quoted by an unnamed reporter from the *Chicago Inter Ocean:*

> If the "Kangaroos" desire harmony, as they profess they do, why do they insult us in this manner? I am in favor of having the committee on resolutions give this letter the most considerate attention, but in their reply, let it be made manifest who is seeking to disrupt the socialistic movement in this country.
>
> Last summer I accepted the nomination for the office of president at their hands in the interests of harmony, because I felt it my duty to accept it. My experiences after that time were most humiliating. Instead of the expected harmony we took into our midst a lot of hissing snakes. However, for the sake of our principles I propose that every effort shall be made to conciliate the factions now at variance.[96]

Debs and party editor A. S. Edwards later both heatedly denied that the expression "hissing snakes" was ever used, thereby by the transitive property of political quote mutilation relegating the entire fascinating quotation above to the realm of apocrypha. Be that as it may, it seems indisputable that Debs went into the convention with a sharply negative attitude toward the Springfield organization and the question of unification.

Anti-unity NEB member Corrine Brown, a former chair of the industrial committee of the General Federation of Women's Clubs who had been tapped to replace attorney Jesse Cox on the board following his resignation,[97] then delivered the report of the executive, in which she lambasted the Springfield SDP as a "narrow, stagnating sect which harassed and obstructed in the hope of ruining the party." With that, working committees were elected and the delegates broke into small groups. A 16-member committee on organization was named, chaired by NEB member Seymour Stedman and including Debs, Berger, Haile, and other heavy hitters. This group was declared melodramatically by the unnamed *Inter Ocean* reporter to have been vested with "full power to outline the future policy of the Debs faction with reference to its enemies."[98]

Wednesday, January 16, the second day of the convention, was to be dedicated to committee work and was expected to be a maelstrom of conflict over party policy. Once again, however, when factional struggle reared its head, Eugene Debs was sick in bed—"confined to his room at the Tremont House" with "the grippe," leaving the other members of the organization committee all-stars to hammer out fundamental strategy without his input.[99] No account survives detailing the deliberations and backstage negotiations of the powerful organization committee.

On Thursday, a recovered Debs was back on the floor of the convention. By this time, however, a veritable sea change in organizational thinking had become evident. Unification was now accepted by a big majority of delegates as an inevitability; at issue were the terms of merger. A series of lengthy speeches unfolded as delegates expressed their hopes and misgivings. Tempers flared, with one pro-unity delegate nearly coming to blows with anti-unity delegate James Duggan.[100] Four greatly similar plans were offered for unity, with Debs stating the case for a general unity convention open to all organized socialists. In so doing, the venerated leader came under fire from at least one delegate, who accused Debs of having abruptly "changed his views" on the unity question and of offering the party nothing more than a choice of ropes with which to hang themselves.[101]

Following protracted debate, the Debs proposal was approved in slightly modified form on January 18, 1901, the fourth and final day of the convention. The final resolution called for a convention of all socialists to be held in Indianapolis, to open on the second Tuesday of September. Representatives of all socialist organizations were to be invited—including those of the hated Socialist Labor Party headed by DeLeon, Kuhn, and Vogt. Results of this unity conclave were then to be submitted to the participating organizations for formal ratification no later than January 1, 1902. Inclusion of the SLP in the call remains puzzling, perhaps best explainable as an attempt to ruin the recipe by introducing an incompatible ingredient. While participation in a single gathering by the hard-line SLP and those they mockingly named "Kangaroos" and "Debserie" would have made for entertaining political theater, fortunately for the cause of social democratic unity, the convention invitation was scornfully ignored by the Kuhn-DeLeon-Vogt organization and its 3,000 adherents. The SLP would boycott.

The unity path that was ultimately followed represented the least bad option for the leadership of the dwindling Chicago SDP, who no doubt had come to understand that a unity convention would be forthcoming in 1901, with or without their participation. By preemptively issuing the unity convention call themselves, the Chicago party was able to ensure a comparatively favorable Midwestern location for the assembly and preserve the possibility of vetoing the entire convention through membership referendum, should the end result be deemed politically offensive. Following the traditional voting system of the Chicago SDP, every member of any participating organization for at least 30 days prior to the opening of the convention was to be entitled to one vote, with these votes transferable by written proxy to any member able to attend the convention.

ஃ

Following negotiations with the Springfield SDP, a new date was agreed upon for a Socialist Unity Convention in Indianapolis designated to forge unity between the rival political organizations. William Butscher and the Springfield organization had quickly matched Chicago's January convention call with a call of their own, accelerating the timetable by setting July 29 as the date for the convention's opening, while conceding Indianapolis as the venue for the gathering as well as the basic form of delegate qualification and proxy voting. Seeking to minimize differences between the two convention calls, the Springfield call repeated the Chicago SDP's invitation to "all sections of the SLP," as well as "all other socialist organizations recognizing the class struggle and the necessity of independent political action."[102]

Even before the delegates gathered, it was clear that the Springfield organization retained a substantially larger paid membership than did Chicago, and thus the ability to control the outcome of crucial votes should its members act in a disciplined manner.[103] That they bent over backward to avoid exercising this power in actual convention assembled is a testament to the level heads in leadership positions in the Springfield organization.

While Victor Berger and Margaret Haile girded themselves for battle over organizational details, seeking to make sure the new organization would be a loose federation of largely independent state organizations with minimal central control, Gene Debs took an altogether different tack. He decided instead to remain at home, just 77 miles away from the Indianapolis convention, citing the illness of family members as an ostensible excuse.[104] Though no relative's survival depended upon Gene Debs's presence in Terre Haute, at no time during the four days of sessions of the founding convention of the Socialist Party of America did Debs make the short train trip to Indianapolis. Defeated in his effort to preserve the Chicago SDP as an independent organization, Debs chose to remain silent, leaving the outcome to the fates. Debs merely sent a telegram to the gathering, blandly asserting: "As I cannot be present, I send greetings to the convention and best wishes for the success of its deliberations."[105] One is challenged to imagine how he could have said less. Contrary to popular myth, the founder of the Supreme Council of the United Orders of Railway Employees, the American Railway Union, and Social Democracy of America did not directly participate in establishing the longest-lasting organization of them all, the Socialist Party of America (1901–1972).

Though pointedly absent, the Indianapolis convention was in Debs's thoughts. Asked for comment by a Philadelphia reporter about gossip in the *Indianapolis Sentinel* that he was being "shelved" by the united party, Debs responded with pique, declaring "they may shelve me if they like." Debs openly speculated that his being downgraded from top leadership was likely part of a plan by "the

Eastern faction to dictate to the Chicago faction, of which I am a member."[106] This misunderstanding of convention affairs was brief but provides an interesting window on Debs's thoughts. Debs was on the convention's mind as well, as it rushed to dispatch an urgent telegram to Terre Haute on the morning of July 30 denouncing such "false newspaper reports" and reassuring Debs that he retained "the esteem and love of all the comrades in this hall, as he always had."[107]

Gene's brother and confidante Theodore did attend the convention. He seems to have merely gone through the motions as dictated by decorum: delivering a short final report on behalf of the Chicago NEB as its national secretary and presenting a statement of Chicago's outstanding financial obligations for assumption by the new organization.[108] He gathered no voting proxies in advance of the event, made no speeches from the floor, and his presence would otherwise have gone undocumented had he not cast a recorded vote on the closing day of the gathering, August 1, voting in the minority for headquarters to be located in Chicago rather than St. Louis.[109]

Debs's journalistic contributions during the remainder of 1901, published in the *Social Democratic Herald*, the former official organ of the Chicago organization that was purchased and moved to Milwaukee by Victor Berger, were sparse, generally positive, and tepid. His public speecges were few.

ꟹ

Surviving coverage of Debs's 1902 speaking activities is very spotty. He had begun the year with a short tour of Michigan, traveled to St. Louis for May Day, and attended and addressed an important joint convention of the Western Federation of Miners, the Western Labor Union, and the Hotel and Restaurant Employees' Union at the end of May. He thereupon embarked on a tour of the West, traveling as far as Washington and British Columbia in July. Speaking to the public at opera houses under the auspices of women's groups, debating clubs, Socialist Party locals, church associations, and other groups, Debs was reinvigorated as a public speaker, his previous grave misgivings about liquidation through merger of his beloved Social Democratic Party having proven to be misplaced.

The Eugene V. Debs saga very nearly came to a premature end on August 2, 1902, when he was involved in a serious train crash in the middle of Alpine Tunnel in Colorado's Rocky Mountains—the highest railway tunnel in North America at 11,523 feet. Just after crossing the summit of the continental divide at 1 p.m. and beginning its descent, the train split into three pieces, with the car carrying Debs and four other passengers rolling ahead and crashing into the section of train in front of them. Debs fortunately suffered only bruises and a wrenched back in the derailment, although he and four others traveling in the same car were left mid-tunnel in pitch darkness. The party was able to hike out from whence they came before being suffocated by exhaust fumes, hiking back over the top of the tunnel before being transported to Buena Vista, Colorado, in time for Debs to deliver a speech scheduled for 7 p.m.[110]

Touring in 1903 began in the Midwest, followed by a short run in upstate New York in February. A quiet spring in the Midwest was followed by another major tour in June, this time running to Missouri and the unlikely socialist hotbed of Oklahoma. Speaking dates in the summer were few—Debs preferred to avoid touring and speaking during the sweltering heat—but included one-off speeches at major events, such as a massive annual picnic in Milwaukee in July, where an estimated 5,000 people gathered to hear him speak.

Two important speaking tours were conducted in the fall: another short stint to Oklahoma, followed by a longer journey in October, during which Debs traversed Arkansas, Texas, and Tennessee. The year was capped with a December 6 speech in Chicago under the auspices of the Socialist Party of Illinois, in which 10,000 people packed the Chicago Coliseum enraptured by the passionate orator from Indiana.

ᔕ

On May Day, 1904, socialists from around the United States descended upon Brand's Hall, located on North Clark Street in Chicago, to hold their first quadrennial national convention, called for the purpose of nominating a ticket for president and vice president of the United States. The venue was large and roomy, but poorly fit for purpose, with acoustics so poor that they "contributed greatly toward producing confusion and, at time, actual tumult." It was almost impossible to hear what the speakers were saying, one auditor complained, and "often when one delegate had the floor, his words were drowned by others calling out for the floor, in blissful ignorance that anyone already had it."[111]

Time had healed all wounds between the former Chicago and Springfield SDP organizations, with new *Social Democratic Herald* editor Fred Heath particularly enthusiastic about the New York delegation, deeming such former factional foes as Morris Hillquit, Frank Sieverman, Algernon Lee, and Henry Slobodin as "a bunch of thoroughbreds" and lauding the sound judgment of such seasoned socialist veterans.[112] Beneath the placid surface, factional difference loomed, however, with Victor Berger grousing in a front-page editorial in the May 21 issue of his *Social Democratic Herald* that there were also present "half-baked ex-Populist elements from the Far West, who, while very little acquainted with socialism, posed as extreme 'radicals,'" who joined "a few Chicago 'impossibilists'—former DeLeonites" in seeking to eliminate immediate demands from the platform in favor of an untenable all-or-nothing approach. Berger, the king of practical, ward-level politics, was adamant in his opposition to impossibilism, declaring that "to reject a working program altogether is to reject all political activity, and then there is no need of a political party at all."[113]

Debs attended the 1904 convention as a delegate, receiving tumultuous applause befitting a star when he dramatically entered the hall on the morning of May 1.[114] Together with eventual vice-presidential nominee Ben Hanford,[115] Victor Berger, and national secretary William Mailly, Debs was elected to the nine-member platform committee.

As a nominating convention, there was little drama to be mined—mainstream newspapers were unanimous in their belief that the second nomination of Eugene V. Debs for president was preordained. Such contrarian opinion as was offered was limited and half-hearted, with one or two papers speculating that perhaps Los Angeles publisher Gaylord Wilshire[116] might also be nominated. Anxious to create some sort of drama, eleventh-hour speculation was floated in the press that Debs might once again play coy and decline the nomination. Reality was not so dramatic; a straightforward nomination was made and a unanimous vote cast for a ticket headed by Debs, running with journalist and printer Ben Hanford of New York City.

If the Social Democratic Party's joint presidential campaign of 1900 was an electoral setback and disappointment packaged for public consumption as a mighty step forward for socialism, no rationalization or spin was necessary in 1904. The Socialist Party ticket of Debs and Hanford performed well, collecting nearly 403,000 votes, nearly 3 percent of all votes cast—an increase of more than fourfold from the 1900 Debs run. With this result, the Socialist Party of America emerged as the third party in American politics, handily topping the 259,000 votes cast for the ticket of Silas Swallow and George Carroll of the Prohibition Party, and dwarfing the 33,454 votes cast for the nominees of the rival Socialist Labor Party, consigned to the irrelevance of a sixth-place finish behind the moribund People's Party.

Perhaps no one was more optimistic about socialist prospects than Julius Augustus Wayland, proprietor and carnival barker of the weekly *Appeal to Reason,* its subscriber rolls quickly escalating toward the 300,000 mark. Even before the votes were tabulated, the mathematically challenged Wayland was regaling his readers with a tale of "an increase of several thousand percent in the Socialist vote" and a boast that the capitalist press could no longer "hide the fact from their dupes that the Socialist Party is the greatest political party on the face of the globe."[117] A front-page cartoon by Ryan Walker graced the first post-election issue of the *Appeal,* featuring a heroic socialist workman leading the charge on "Fort Capitalism," proudly waving a banner reading "Socialist President 1908."[118]

Socialist enthusiasm was growing; the next campaign was already in the wind.

General Series Notes

The *Eugene V. Debs Selected Works* will present his most important writings in six chronological volumes. Each book will include a brief introduction touching upon the major activities of Debs's life during the period of coverage and pointing toward key elements of his evolving thought. Archaic spelling, idiosyncratic punctuation, misspelled names, misquoted sources, and typographical errors appearing in the original published versions have not been treated as sacrosanct, but rather have been silently corrected and standardized for consistency and readability. A few words from defective source documents that had to be guessed from context are provided within square brackets, as are substantive clarifications provided by the editors. The inclusion of full articles rather than excerpts has been given high priority, although a few items have been shortened for reasons of space or clarity. These editorial alterations have been marked by ellipses (. . .) for very short deletions, and asterisks (* * *) for longer content removals. Debs himself periodically used a question mark inside parentheses to denote irony about the apparent misapplication of a word or phrase. This editorial oddity has been retained.

Titles of articles and speeches as they appeared in the press varied greatly from publication to publication. Those appearing in *Locomotive Firemen's Magazine* were written by Debs himself and have been generally retained without change unless the same title was used multiple times, as Debs was wont to do. A few Debs-generated titles that are particularly non-descriptive of actual content have been revised. The titles of articles and speeches appearing in publications edited by others have been either kept or rewritten for clarity as deemed most appropriate; those appearing previously in reprints of Debs's works have been retained to avoid confusion in almost every instance. Whenever titles have been changed, original names are also provided, together with other publication information.

Material has been chosen with a view to illustrating the evolution of Debs's thinking. Mundane contemporary affairs have been accorded low priority; matters touching on the events of the broader labor movement and society at large have been given closest attention. No material has been omitted or deleted for ideological reasons. We emphasize that Gene Debs was neither a saint nor a savant, but rather an evolving human being that was a product of his times, exhibiting at various times crassly individualistic aspirations; ethnic, racial, and gender biases; and ideological inconsistencies. We have attempted to chronicle these foibles and flaws rather than hide them through tendentious selection of content.

Debs never wrote a full-length book in his lifetime, nor did he attempt to compile his memoirs. All of his literary output was of an oratorical or journalistic nature, with the great majority of this material published as newspaper or magazine articles or speeches reproduced in pamphlet form. The editors attempted to review at least cursorily every known article, speech, or pamphlet by Debs for the time period covered by this volume. This goal was more or less successfully realized, with only three or four of the approximately 465 Debs items cataloged for the period of *Volume Three* escaping our grasp, of which none seem imperative.

While the editors have received no financial support from any individual or institution in the preparation of this volume, they have nevertheless benefited immensely from the activity of others in the world of Debs scholarship, whose work is listed in the footnotes below. The editors additionally wish to thank Benjamin Kite of the Eugene V. Debs Foundation and historians Paul Buhle, Micki Morahn, Steve Rossignnol, E. Philip Brown, and Bob Bills for their courtesy and assistance. Our friend Marty Goodman of the Riazanov Digital Library Project has aided in the investigation of certain rare publications. Similarly, the importance of radical booksellers to the cause of independent scholarship, with John Durham and Alexander Akin of Bolerium Books in San Francisco especially worthy of note. We also thank Nisha Bolsey, Amelia Ayrelan Iuvino, Rachel Cohen, and Eric Kerl, who skillfully handled the manuscript for Haymarket Books, as well as the entire Haymarket editorial board for their unflinching support of the Debs project.

The outstanding contribution to Debs scholarship was made by historian J. Robert Constantine and Tamiment Library archivist Gail Malmgreen, with their twenty-one-reel microfilm collection and printed guide, *The Papers of Eugene V. Debs, 1834–1945*. The editors note their debt to this pioneering effort to chronicle and collect the speeches, articles, and correspondence of Gene Debs—it is impossible to imagine the successful completion of this project without such an expert plowing of the field having previously been made. This material has already been harvested by Mr. Constantine for his outstanding three-volume collection, *Letters of Eugene V. Debs,* published by University of Illinois Press in 1990. The editors hope that these volumes edited by Mr. Constantine will occupy every shelf next to the volumes of the *Selected Works of Eugene V. Debs,* and that the two series will be viewed as integral parts of the same project.

It is a matter of regret that Bob Constantine, the dean of Debs studies, died in 2017 at the age of 93, before the editors were able to communicate news of this project to him. It is to his memory that this series is dedicated.

Notes

1. The Supreme Council of the United Orders of Railway Employees included the Brotherhood of Locomotive Firemen, the Brotherhood of Railroad Brakemen, the Switchmen's Mutual Aid Association, and the International Brotherhood of Railway Conductors—the latter a new dual union startup in rivalry with the conservative Order of Railway Conductors.
2. William Jennings Bryan (1860–1925) was a two-term Democratic member of Congress in the early 1890s. Appropriating the anti-capitalist "free silver" monetary rhetoric associated with the populist movement, Bryan ran as the nominee of a Democratic–People's Party fusion ticket for president in 1896 and as a straight Democrat in 1900, twice falling to defeat. Following Woodrow Wilson's victory in 1912, Bryan was appointed secretary of state, resigning in June 1915 over Wilson's increasingly bellicose actions toward Germany. In later years, he became an active religionist and anti-evolution activist.
3. Edward Boyce (1862–1941) was an Irish-born miner and trade union functionary. Boyce was president of the Coeur d'Alene Miners Union and was elected to the Idaho state legislature on the People's Party ticket in 1894. In 1895, he resigned his union position to become general organizer for the Western Federation of Miners (WFM). He was elected president of the WFM in 1896 and remained in that position until 1902. A committed socialist himself, Boyce played a vital role in the WFM, formally endorsing socialism in 1901.
4. We are accustomed to think of the WFM as a union. Rather, it was a federation of affiliated local miners' unions, akin to the role played by the American Federation of Labor as an umbrella organization of affiliated craft unions.
5. See "Present Conditions and Future Duties," January 1, 1897, this volume.
6. See, for example, "Debs's Busy Life in Jail: Interview with the *Chicago Chronicle,"* June 18, 1895, *Selected Works of Eugene Debs, Volume 2*, 635–40.
7. See "How I Became a Socialist," April 1902, *Selected Works of Eugene Debs, Volume 2,* 640–4. As the father and leading figure in the powerful Milwaukee socialist movement, Berger was already the second most prominent figure in the Socialist Party by the time this article was written.
8. Edward Bellamy, *Looking Backward, 2000–1887* (Boston: Ticknor & Co., 1888). Bellamy's novel inspired the formation of scores of "Nationalist clubs" around the country, many of whose members later found their way into the socialist movement.
9. Laurence Gronlund, *The Cooperative Commonwealth in its Outlines: An Exposition of Modern Socialism* (Boston: Lee and Shepard, 1884).
10. A series of journalists making a pilgrimage to Woodstock Jail to interview Debs made frequent note of the presence of books by Gronlund, Bellamy, Karl Kautsky, and other popular socialist and liberal reform writers, but no mention is made in any account of the presence of a copy of *Das Kapital.* By all accounts, Debs spent an enormous part of his time during his six months in jail dictating correspondence and writing articles for the press, not reading. Moreover, he emerged from jail energized to work for the reformist People's Party, not the Socialist Labor Party, the international socialist

political party in the United States. It seems doubtful that Debs curled up in jail with a thick volume by Karl Marx even if he did receive one from Berger.

11. For the best account of the Leadville strike of 1896–97, see William Philpott, *The Lessons of Leadville* (Denver: Colorado Historical Society, 1994).
12. See "Strike Lessons: A Dispassionate Review of the Great Leadville Struggle" (April 5, 1897); "Harmony and Unity—and Their Limits" (April 12); "Solidarity of Western Miners Essential" (April 17); "The Coronado Mine Attack" (April 27); "The Degradation of Mine Labor" (May 5); "An Anniversary Retrospective of the Great Leadville Strike" (May 31), this volume.
13. Norman Lermond (1861–1944) was an activist in the People's Party in Maine before turning to utopian socialism and establishing the Brotherhood of the Cooperative Commonwealth in 1896.
14. Quoted in Charles Pierce LeWarne, *Utopias on Puget Sound, 1885–1915* (Seattle: University of Washington Press, 1975), 58.
15. Although it is sometimes intimated that Debs accepted the post of national organizer of the BCC, it appears that he never did. His direct connection with the organization was certainly short lived.
16. One of Debs's close associates during his stint in the Mountain West on behalf of the hard-rock miners was Rev. Myron Reed of Denver, a leading advocate of the Brotherhood of the Cooperative Commonwealth. Debs knew Reed before he knew Lermond, and it seems logical that he was the conduit for the two meeting each other.
17. Though members of the two organizations would act in concert, no formal unity would be achieved, with the BCC putting its own program for the colonization of Washington state into practice in 1898. The official organ of the Brotherhood of the Cooperative Commonwealth, the newspaper *Industrial Freedom,* would be published in Washington state from 1898 to 1901.
18. Sylvester Keliher (1863–19XX) was secretary-treasurer of the Brotherhood of Railway Carmen of America from 1890 and editor of its monthly magazine, in which capacity he met Gene Debs, George Howard, and other leading advocates of railway federation. Together with Debs and Howard, Keliher helped draft the constitution of the American Railway Union in February and March 1893, serving as that union's secretary-treasurer. A staunch socialist, Keliher would later be elected national secretary by the Social Democracy of America in June 1897, in which capacity he would fight against the efforts of the colonization wing to take control of the organization. Keliher left in the 1898 split that formed the Social Democratic Party, declining to hold office in the new organization.
19. James Hogan (1867–19XX) was a railway brakeman who gained promotion to conductor in September 1890. He attended the first public meeting of the ARU in June 1893 and went to work for the union as an organizer that October. Hogan was jailed with Debs and other ARU officials for their part in the Pullman strike and served a three-month term. Following his release, Hogan was the chief western organizer for the ARU. In June 1897, he was elected vice president of

the Social Democracy of America, a salaried position. Hogan cast his lot with the colonizationists in the SDA split of 1898, breaking bitterly with Sylvester Keliher at the convention when he accused him of financial malfeasance and tendentious refusal to admit certain new local branches due to their opposition to political action. He was elected to the nine-person national executive council of the SDA.

20. Roy Goodwin (1863–19XX) left home at age 18 to become a switchman in Minnesota, soon gaining promotion to the supervisory role of yardmaster. During the April 1894 strike of the ARU against the Great Northern Railroad, Goodwin quit his position and went to work as an organizer for the union. Goodwin joined Debs, Sylvester Keliher, James Hogan, and William Burns on the five-member board of directors of the Social Democracy of America, apparently breaking with Debs and Keliher several weeks before the June 1898 convention. Goodwin was chosen as one of nine members of the newly established national executive council of the SDA following the departure of the political actionists.
21. William E. Burns (1856–19XX) worked for 15 years as a fireman and engineer on the Illinois Central Railroad. A delegate to 12 consecutive conventions of the Brotherhood of Locomotive Firemen, of which he was elected vice grand master in 1891, Burns followed Debs into the American Railway Union, serving on the board of directors. In June 1897, Burns was elected as general organizer of the Social Democracy of America, a salaried position.
22. The Socialist Labor Party of America (SLP) traced its roots to several local Marxist or Lassallean political parties that launched in the middle 1870s. The SLP was itself launched in 1876.
23. Lucy Parsons (c. 1853–1942) was a committed feminist and revolutionary socialist activist and newspaper publisher for the whole of her life. She edited and brought to publication the posthumously published memoir of her husband, Haymarket martyr Albert Parsons, and spoke widely for the anarchist cause throughout the 1890s. In addition to her early support of the Social Democracy of America, Parsons was a founding member of the Industrial Workers of the World in 1905 and wrote extensively through the 1930s.
24. Albert R. Parsons (1848–1887) was one of the leading American-born revolutionary socialists of the late nineteenth century. A newspaper editor and labor activist who turned away from electoral politics in 1880, Parsons launched an English-language anarchist weekly, *The Alarm*, in 1884. Beyond his ability as a journalist and political commentator, Parsons was regarded as the most effective English-speaking radical orator in Chicago. Parsons spoke at the Haymarket Square rally that was bombed in May 1886, and was sentenced to death for having allegedly inspired the bomber with his words. Parsons was hanged on November 11, 1887.
25. Note that this is the primary argument of Lassalleanism. Orthodox Marxists of the period believed in party organization through the trade union movement.
26. Richard J. Hinton (1830–1901) was an abolitionist who was active in several Kansas free state conventions during the 1850s. He was a dispatch rider for the Union army during the American Civil War and was mustered in to help lead the 1st Regiment

of the Kansas Colored Volunteers when it was founded in 1863. Hinton was active in the women's rights movement from the 1860s, participating in an 1869 National Women's Suffrage Convention with Elizabeth Cady Stanton, Susan B. Anthony, Clara Barton, and other feminist leaders. He was active in the Henry George movement in the 1880s and edited several newspapers in the East. A civil engineer by training with expertise in irrigation, Hinton worked for the US Department of Agriculture and US Geological Survey during the 1890s. As a member of the Social Democracy's three-person colonization commission, Hinton was the leading advocate of various railway and colonization schemes in the state of Tennessee.

27. Cyrus Field Willard (1858–1942) was a *Boston Globe* journalist and theosophy adherent who was won over to socialism through Edward Bellamy's utopian novel *Looking Backward.* Willard was a leading organizer and secretary of Nationalist Club No. 1 in Boston in 1888. He became active in the Social Democracy from its establishment in 1897 and was part of the SDA's three-person colonization commission. Willard was a bitter foe of the political action wing of the SDA, characterizing these as adherents of "armed revolution." Following the 1898 split of the SDA, Willard led the colonizationists in reorganizing as the Cooperative Brotherhood, of which he was secretary. In this capacity, he was closely involved in the establishment of the short-lived Equality colony in Washington state.
28. W. P. Borland was a journalist who was active in the People's Party in Michigan in the 1890s. He served as treasurer of the three-member colonization commission of the Social Democracy of America, although he was overshadowed by his compatriots Richard J. Hinton and Cyrus Field Willard. Borland remained with the colonizationists in the 1898 split of the SDP and was one of nine elected to the SDA's executive council. By the end of 1898, Borland had returned home to Bay City, Michigan, to launch a newspaper, *The Chronicle.*
29. A number of Debs's public statements on this topic appear in this volume. See especially "A Million Altruists Will Be Organized" (June 15, 1897), "Farmers Will Form the Vanguard" (June 18, 1897), "Open Letter to John D. Rockefeller" (June 19, 1897), "Statement on the Colonization of Washington" (June 21, 1897), and passim.
30. Debs, "The Lattimer Massacre," September 9, 1897, this volume, 152–4.
31. To wit: Nashville railroad building, Tennessee land speculation, Western colony establishment with a focus on Utah, Colorado gold mine.
32. Sylvester Keliher, "Withdrawal a Necessity," *Social Democratic Herald* [Chicago], vol. 1, no. 1 (July 9, 1898), 2.
33. Some delegates held proxies, allowing them to cast multiple votes. According to political actionist Margaret Haile of Boston, the pro-colonization forces included 26 delegates from the city of Chicago, five from other states casting single votes, a New Jersey delegate who held seven voting mandates, a New York delegate casting three votes, and two or three others holding multiple mandates—about 36 individuals in all. See: Margaret Haile, "Truth Coming Out," *Social Democratic Herald,* vol. 1, no. 2 (July 16, 1898), 1.
34. Haile, "Truth Coming Out."

35. Some sources indicate that 33 delegates attended the debut session of the SDP—the number of signatories of an official statement of delegates to the membership of the SDA published in the debut issue of the *Social Democratic Herald.* This count includes Gene Debs, who was sick in bed and unable to participate, as well as Theodore Debs, who, according to Margaret Haile, was sitting with him. See Haile, "Truth Coming Out."
36. Louis W. Rogers (1859–1953), a former schoolteacher, was a free-thought lecturer and publisher of several labor newspapers during the 1880s and 1890s. He was editor of *Railway Times* from its establishment in March 1894 and was nominated for Congress by the People's Party later that year. Rogers was sentenced to a three-month jail term in 1895 for contempt of court in conjunction with the Pullman strike. Upon his release, Rogers briefly remained a functionary of the American Railway Union, but, according to his own testimony in 1899, he did not follow his ARU compatriots Debs, Keliher, Hogan, Goodwin, and Burns into the Social Democracy of America in 1897, nor did he join the Social Democratic Party. In later years, Rogers was a prominent figure in the American theosophy movement.
37. Joseph R. Buchanan, "Social Democracy," *The Western Laborer,* July 2, 1898, 2.
38. Impossibilism is the belief that all ameliorative reform, even that ostensibly benefiting the working class, is a fetter upon the true resolution of social and economic problems through socialist revolution. It posits a program of education to pave the way for seizure of power and total economic transformation at a stroke, with political campaigns engaged for propaganda purposes only.
39. Laurence Gronlund, "Some Reforms," *The Social Democrat,* vol. 5, no. 25 (June 30, 1898), 1.
40. News of the prodigal son Debs's mysterious appearance at the B of LF convention appeared in the press. For his part, Debs explicitly denied that desire for reinstatement to the B of LF's good graces and payroll was the reason for his oddly timed visit to Toronto.
41. See, for example, Debs, "The Dollar Counts for Everything: Speech in Springfield, Massachusetts," October 23, 1898, this volume.
42. Louis M. Scates (1863–1954) was a former shoe worker who was elected to the Massachusetts state legislature on the Social Democratic Party ticket in 1899. Defeated in his bid for reelection, he became a functionary of the Boot and Shoe Workers' Union. He was expelled from the Socialist Party in 1907 for failing to follow party instructions at a convention of the Boot and Shoe Workers.
43. James F. Carey (1867–1938), a former shoe worker and newsstand operator, was elected to the common council of Haverhill, Massachusetts, in 1898, becoming the first member of the Social Democratic Party elected to office. He served two terms as a Social Democrat in the Massachusetts legislature from 1899 and was a prominent supporter of the Springfield SDP during the partisan squabble of 1900–01. He was later active in the Socialist Party.
44. Debs did deliver one lecture outside of Iowa state lines during this "non-partisan" speaking tour, appearing in Omaha, Nebraska, on December 22, 1898.

45. Charles H. Kerr (1860–1944) began as a publisher of liberal Unitarian and transcendentalist literature and poetry before turning to populism in the early 1890s and socialism in 1899. Kerr became increasingly radical during the first decade of the twentieth century, ousting *International Socialist Review* editor A. M. Simons in 1907 to take the publication in a more revolutionary and syndicalist direction. During the 1920s, Kerr sold the controlling stake in his publishing company to the Proletarian Party, an impossibilist offshoot of the Communist Party of America.
46. Also worthy of mention as a previous occupant in this specialized publishing field is the New York Labor News Company, publishing arm of the Socialist Labor Party.
47. Debs, *The American Movement* (Terre Haute: Standard Publishing Co., 1904). See this volume, 613–31.
48. Debs, *Unionism and Socialism: A Plea for Both* (Terre Haute: Standard Publishing Co., 1904). See this volume, 575–605.
49. The August 1905 letters of Thomas McGrady to EVD and EVD to Isador Ladoff provide minor details associated with the termination of this publishing effort. See: J. Robert Constantine (ed.), *Letters of Eugene V. Debs: Volume 1, 1874–1912* (Urbana, IL: University of Illinois Press, 1990), 209–11.
50. See Debs, "Prison Labor—Its Effects on Industry and Trade," March 21, 1899, this volume, 231–41.
51. No financial records detailing Debs's speaking engagements in this period have survived. Debs's business handlers apparently encouraged trade unions, lyceum societies, and other civic organizations to sponsor his appearances, handling hall arrangements and media advertisement, paying him a set honorarium, with the sponsor receiving the net proceeds of ticket sales. One contemporary news account of a speech in Rock Island, Illinois, estimates the cost of a Debs appearance at "about $200 including advertising"—a figure that implies a payment to Debs in the general vicinity of $50 to $100 for his evening's efforts, from which his traveling, lodging, and management costs must be deducted. In a letter to Frederic Heath dated August 6, 1900, Debs mentions the 1900 campaign as having "knocked me out of at least $2,000 financially"—which in round numbers for about 40 lost dates implies net income to Debs of about $50 per engagement.
52. Daniel DeLeon (1852–1914) was one of the most prominent American socialists of the 1890s and the first decade of the twentieth century. Born of Spanish-speaking Dutch Jewish parents on the island of Curaçao, DeLeon received a classical education in Germany beginning at the age of 14. He later attended Columbia University in New York City, receiving a bachelor of law degree. He briefly practiced law in Texas before serving a three-year stint as a lecturer of political science at Columbia. Active in the 1886 mayoral campaign of Henry George, DeLeon joined the Socialist Labor Party in 1890 and became editor of its English-language organ, *The People.* DeLeon ran for high political office several times on the SLP ticket but was primarily a newspaper editor, heading the staff of the *Daily People,* the first socialist daily in the English language, from its launch in 1900. Dogmatic in his interpretation of socialist theory and intolerant of dissent, vicious with his editorial invective, DeLeon and Debs were lifelong adversaries.

53. Hugo Vogt was perhaps the top German-speaking leader of the Socialist Labor Party in the period after an 1889 left-wing split that deposed the administrative faction of W. L. Rosenberg. As editor of the *Vorwärts,* official German organ of the SLP, Vogt worked closely with his factional allies Danial DeLeon and Henry Kuhn to control the political course of the party.
54. Henry Kuhn (18XX–1930) was executive secretary of the Socialist Labor Party from 1895 to 1906. A hard-line orthodox Marxist, Kuhn was the most important political figure in the party after English-press editor and factional leader Daniel DeLeon. Kuhn was perhaps the leading voice in the organization during the years of his executive tenure and did much to shape the character of the party organization during these factionally tumultous years.
55. Abraham Cahan (1860–1951) is regarded as one of the most important Yiddish novelists and journalists in the United States. Born of Jewish parents in today's Belarus, Cahan arrived in the United States in 1882, joining New York's fledgling socialist movement soon after the time of his arrival. Cahan was a contributor the Yiddish-language press of the Socialist Labor Party, editing the party's *Arbeiter Zeitung* (Workers' Newspaper) from 1891 to 1895. He helped launch the *Forverts* (Jewish Daily Forward) in 1897, at which time he broke with the SLP. Cahan worked full time at the *Forverts* from 1903, moving to the right wing of the Socialist Party as he grew older.
56. Louis Miller (née Efim Bandes, 1866–1927), a former sweatshop worker, was active in the Yiddish-language workers movement in New York City. Together with Abe Cahan, Miller was a cofounder of *Di Arbeiter Tsaytung* (Workers' News), the first Yiddish-language socialist newspaper in America, and the daily *Forverts* (Jewish Daily Forward). Miller, a staunch political actionist, was a delegate to the June 1898 convention of the SDA that established the Social Democratic Party.
57. Morris Winchevsky (née Leopold Novokhovich, 1856–1932), a poet and journalist, was the founder of the *Arbeter Fraynd* (Worker's Friend), a Yiddish-language anarchist paper. He joined Abe Cahan and Louis Miller in launching the daily *Forverts* in 1897. Winchevsky was a delegate to the June 1898 convention of the SDA that established the Social Democratic Party.
58. Morris Hillquit (née Moishe Hillkowitz, 1869–1933) grew up in a German-speaking Jewish home in Riga, Latvia, then part of the Russian empire. He attended Russian-language schools before immigrating to the United States in 1886, where he learned English and Yiddish and became active in the Jewish trade union movement of New York City. An international socialist from his teenage years, Hillquit joined the SLP and helped establish the *Arbeiter-Zeitung* (Workers' News), a Yiddish-language socialist newspaper. Hillquit graduated from New York University law school in 1893 and was a practicing attorney throughout his life. Hillquit is regarded by some as the unitary leader of the split of the so-called "Kangaroos" from the SLP in 1899, although this estimate seems inflated. A skilled negotiator with carefully measured emotions and an aptitude for planning, Hillquit played a major role in bringing the rival Springfield and Chicago Social Democratic Parties to a successful

unity convention in the summer of 1901. He was later a two-time Socialist mayoral candidate in New York City (1917, 1932) and served as national chairman of the Socialist Party after the death of Victor L. Berger in 1929.

59. Henry L. Slobodin was a New York City attorney and prominent socialist political activist. Together with Morris Hillquit, Alexander Jonas, and others, Slobodin was a leading figure in the 1899 Socialist Labor Party split. The pro-war Slobodin would ironically be expelled from the Socialist Party in January 1918 for arguing in favor of an opponent of Hillquit in the New York mayoral campaign the previous fall.
60. Ira Kipnis, *The American Socialist Movement, 1897–1912* (New York: Columbia University Press, 1952), 29–30.
61. Kipnis, *American Socialist Movement*, 31–2.
62. Kipnis, *American Socialist Movement*, 31.
63. According to the dissidents, the test vote for temporary chair was won by dissident candidate Richard Bock over administration candidate Henry Kuhn by a vote of somewhat more than 50 to 32, with Vogt beginning his "speech" to intentionally interrupt the vote counting. See "Latter Day History," *The People* [William Street version], vol. 9, no. 16 (July 16, 1899), 1.
64. "Latter Day History," 1.
65. Julius Gerber (1872–1956) was born in Riga, Latvia, and immigrated to the United States in 1890. He was an active participant in the 1899 split of the Socialist Labor Party and was named New York City organizer by the dissident general committee in July of that month. Gerber would play a leading role in New York Socialist Party politics for several decades afterward.
66. "Latter Day History," 2.
67. "Latter Day History," 2.
68. In the best tradition of their well-practiced invective style, the administration faction pejoratively named the dissidents "Kangaroos" to emphasize the pseudo-legality of their actions. The insult stuck. The insulting term was rejected by the dissidents themselves and is generally avoided here.
69. "Latter Day History," 2.
70. John Mahlon Barnes (1866–1934), a cigarmaker by trade, was active in the affairs of his union and the Socialist Labor Party. A former SLP candidate for governor of Pennsylvania, Barnes was the top leader of Philadelphia SLP dissidents during the split of 1899. Barnes was executive secretary of the Socialist Party from 1905 to 1911, when he was forced out in a sexual scandal involving office staff. Barnes is credited with originating the idea of the Debs Socialist Red Special campaign train of 1908.
71. Thomas J. "Tommy" Morgan (1847–1912) was one of the leading figures of the Chicago socialist community during the last two decades of the nineteenth century. The English-born attorney Morgan was the founder in 1884 of the Central Trade Union and of the International Association of Machinists in 1891. In 1895, he was one of those socialist activists who visited Gene Debs and his associates during their imprisonment at the McHenry County Jail in Woodstock. Morgan was the editor of the *Socialist Alliance*, official organ of the Socialist Trade & Labor Alliance from 1896

until his break with the SLP in 1900. Morgan was a founding member of the Socialist Party of America in 1901 and active in that organization for the rest of his life.

72. Max S. Hayes (1866–1945), a former member of the People's Party, was founding publisher and editor of the Cleveland *Citizen* in 1891. A member of the SLP, Hayes was a leader of socialist forces on the floor of conventions of the American Federation of Labor, earning the enmity of AF of L president Samuel Gompers. Hayes resigned from the Socialist Party in 1919; he was the nominee of the Farmer-Labor Party for vice president of the United States in 1920.
73. Job Harriman (1861–1929) was an ordained minister who came to socialism through the Bellamy movement, later turning to Marxism and joining the Socialist Labor Party. A leading figure in the Springfield Social Democratic Party, Harriman was nominated for the presidency by that organization at its 1900 convention, later agreeing to run for vice president with Gene Debs as part of a joint Springfield-Chicago unity ticket. Twice a Socialist candidate for mayor of Los Angeles in the 1910s, after his second defeat Harriman turned his back on electoral politics and returned to the ideals of Bellamyism, establishing a colony called Llano del Rio in Southern California in 1914.
74. Resolution of Section Chicago, July 18, 1899, in *The People* [William Street version], vol. 9, no. 18 (July 30, 1899), 4.
75. Keeping up with the confusing parallelism of recent months, this was denoted the Tenth Convention of the Socialist Labor Party—as would be the rival gathering held by DeLeonist regulars from June 2–8, 1900.
76. Each member of the SDP was entitled to one vote at the convention, the rights of which were assignable by proxy to the delegate of their choice if they were unable to attend the gathering themselves.
77. Victor L. Berger of the Chicago SDP was absent.
78 Edward John Muzik, *Victor L. Berger, A Biography*. PhD dissertation. (Northwestern University, 1960), 99.
79. John C. Chase (1870–1937) was a blacklisted shoe worker who established a cooperative grocery store in Haverhill, Massachusetts, and later ran a newsstand. He was elected mayor of Haverhill in 1898 and reelected the next year, but he was defeated by a Democratic-Republican fusion candidate in 1900. Chase was the Socialist candidate for governor of Massachusetts in 1902 and 1903 and for governor of New York in 1906. He also ran for Congress three times.
80. See: "Manifesto of the National Executive Board to the Members of the Social Democratic Party" (April 2, 1900), this volume, 695–702.
81. See Debs, "The Lessons of Unity," April 21, 1900, this volume.
82. "Socialists Unite!" *Haverhill Social Democrat,* May 19, 1900, 1.
83. Margaret Haile, "Cause of Socialism is Disgraced in Massachusetts," *Social Democratic Herald,* July 28, 1900, 3.
84. "Connecticut State Ticket," *Social Democratic Herald,* July 21, 1900, 1.
85. "Doesn't Like New Jersey Plan," *The Worker* [NYC], vol. 11, no. 13 (June 30, 1901), 4.
86. *Social Democratic Herald,* July 14, 1900, 3.

87. "Badger State Progress," *Social Democratic Herald,* July 14, 1900, 3.
88. Elizabeth H. Thomas, "The Haverhill Defeat," *Social Democratic Herald,* December 15, 1900, 4. Thomas would soon be elected state secretary of the Wisconsin organization, retaining that position for more than a decade.
89. *Social Democratic Herald,* December 22, 1900, 4, quoting the official count of the New York State board of canvassers.
90. *Social Democratic Herald,* December 22, 1900, 4.
91. Debs and Harriman were not on the ballot in 16 states, most notably California, Maine, and Virginia. Had they been on the ballot in all 46 states, the vote total would likely have topped 100,000. Even this would have represented a pallid underperformance. One prediction published early in the year by Massachusetts Rep. Frederic MacCartney declared that "if we had better organization in the different states, [Debs] would poll a million votes. As it is, we should be content if he polls 350,000." See MacCartney, "Eugene Debs for Candidate," *Social Democratic Herald,* vol. 2, no. 29, whole no. 79 (January 6, 1900), 4.
92. This number was gradually inched upward in various other official tallies as better results became available. Howard Quint has the final number of Social Democratic votes as 94,777. See Howard Quint, *The Forging of American Socialism: Origins of the Modern Movement* (Columbia, SC: University of South Carolina Press, 1953), 372.
93. EVD to Theodore, November 9, 1900, *Letters of Eugene V. Debs, Vol. 1,* 154–5.
94. "Special Convention: Official Call," *Social Democratic Herald,* vol. 3, no. 29, whole no. 131 (January 5, 1901), 4.
95. Ever the diplomat, Morris Hillquit helped Berger, Debs, and the Chicago leaders save face by neglecting to even mention this controversial convention in his pioneering *History of Socialism in the United States* (New York: Funk and Wagnalls, 1903).
96. "Debs for Harmony," *Chicago Inter Ocean,* vol. 29, no. 298 (January 16, 1901), 5.
97. The prosperous attorney Cox resigned in May 1900 in large measure due to his unwillingness to have anything further to do with unity discussions with the SLP.
98. "Debs for Harmony."
99. "Debs Has the Grip: Unable to Attend the Meeting of Social Democrats," *Chicago Inter Ocean,* vol. 29, no. 299 (January 17, 1901), 12.
100. "Fists on the Floor," *Chicago Inter Ocean,* vol. 29, no. 300 (January 18, 1901), 5.
101. "Fists on the Floor."
102. *Proceedings of Socialist Unity Convention Held at Indianapolis, Indiana, Beginning July 29, 1901* (St. Louis, MO: Socialist Party of America), n.d. [1901]. First day's session, 3. Multiple copies of this document exist on the Socialist Party Papers at Duke University microfilm edition.
103. Ultimately the Springfield SDP was represented by 68 delegates voting a total of 4,798 signed credentials, against 1,396 proxies borne by 48 delegates from the Chicago SDP. There were an additional eight delegates from other organizations, casting 352 votes. In all, 6,546 duly paid members of the various participating organizations signed proxies allocating their votes at the founding convention of the Socialist Party of America. As not all members signed proxies, total membership of

the new organization was optimistically estimated at approximately ten thousand. See "National Convention at Indianapolis," *The Worker* [New York], vol. 11, no. 18 (August 4, 1901), 1. By way of comparison, the Socialist Labor Party after its 1899 split counted approximately three thousand members.

104. According to a report in the *Philadelphia Times*, Debs was kept away by "the serious illness of his wife, his own mother, and his wife's mother." All would survive this veritable summertime epidemic. See "'They May Shelve Me if They Like': Statement to the *Philadelphia Times,*" this volume.
105. *Proceedings of Socialist Unity Convention*, first session, 15.
106. "'They May Shelve Me If They Like.'"
107. *Proceedings of Socialist Unity Convention*, third session, 1.
108. Both the Chicago and Springfield SDP had liabilities exceeding assets at the time of their merger to form the SPA.
109. *Proceedings of Socialist Unity Convention*, tenth session, 34.
110. For Debs's account of this August 1902 train wreck, see "A Narrow Escape: Letter to the *Social Democratic Herald*" (August 8, 1902) and "My Near Escape: Letter to Julius Wayland of the *Appeal to Reason*" (August 23, 1902), this volume.
111. Frederic Heath, "Lights and Shadows of the Chicago Convention," *Social Democratic Herald,* May 14, 1904, 4.
112. Heath, "Lights and Shadows of the Chicago Convention."
113. Victor L. Berger, "The National Convention," *Social Democratic Herald,* May 21, 1904, 1.
114. "National Convention of the Socialist Party," *The Worker,* vol. 14, no. 6 (May 8, 1904), 1.
115. Benjamin Hanford (1861–1910) was a New York City printer and writer who gained lasting fame for the creation of the fictional character "Jimmy Higgins," an unheralded Socialist Party gruntworker whose tireless efforts behind the scenes on behalf of the socialist cause made the well-publicized activity of prominent leaders possible. Hanford was twice tapped as the vice-presidential running mate of Eugene V. Debs, sharing the top of the ticket in 1904 and 1908. Hanford was active in the Socialist Labor Party in the 1890s and the Springfield Social Democratic Party that emerged from it. Hanford died after a protracted and agonizing gastric condition at the age of 48.
116. H. Gaylord Wilshire (1861–1927) was a real estate developer and magazine editor from Los Angeles. Wilshire was involved in the Belllamy-inspired Nationalist movement, running for Congress on the Nationalist Party ticket in 1890. He joined the Socialist Labor Party in 1891, running for attorney general of California in that year. He was a supporter of the Springfield SDP, running for Congress on that party's ticket in 1900 and was later active in the Socialist Party. His publication, *Wilshire's Magazine,* was regularly criticized by radicals for its ethically dubious advertising content.
117. *Appeal to Reason,* whole no. 467 (November 12, 1904), 1.
118. *Appeal to Reason,* whole no. 467 (November 12, 1904), 1.

Four hundred striking coal miners marched on September 10, 1897, in an attempt to shut down an anthracite mine in Lattimer, Pennsylvania. The Eastern European immigrants were met on a public road by a sheriff's posse and company guards, who opened fire without provocation. The resulting slaughter of 19 unarmed miners and wounding of 38 others would be the largest labor massacre of the nineteenth century in the United States. (Pennsylvania State Archives; *Philadelphia Inquirer*)

FIRING ON THE MINERS. AN ACCURATE VIEW OF THE FIELD WHERE THE TRAGEDY TOOK PLACE
Drawn by an Inquirer Staff Artist.

EUGENE V. DEBS ADDRESSING BRANCH NO. 1 OF THE SOCIAL DEMOCRACY.

Debs played an active role both in establishing Chicago Branch 1 of the Social Democracy of America in June 1897 and expelling Branch 2 in September. (*Chicago Tribune*, June 19, 1897.)

Gene Debs was depicted as the heroic physical embodiment of the Social Democracy and its liberating mission from the group's earliest days. (*Cincinnati Volks-Anwalt*, July 17, 1897.)

Former prisoner Debs was vilified by the right for alleged careerism. Here Debs leads the Tammany tiger, symbolizing Democratic corruption, as he begs for contributions. (*Judge*, July 17, 1897.)

National Executive Committee of the

SOCIAL DEMOCRATIC PARTY OF AMERICA.

Gene Debs was part of the five member national executive committee which directed daily operations of the Chicago Social Democratic Party in conjunction with national secretary Theodore Debs and party editor A.S. Edwards. This group opposed organic unity with the Springfield SDP and used skewed coverage of events in the party press to sabotage an early merger of the two organizations. It would be rank and file pressure that forced the unity convention that formed the Socialist Party in late August 1901.

FOR PRESIDENT

SOCIAL DEMOCRATIC PARTY

HEADQUARTERS 126 WASHINGTON ST. CHICAGO.

Eugene V. Debs

Surviving fragment of a poster from the 1900 Debs presidential campaign. Note how the poster prominently lists the full mailing address of the Chicago SDP headquarters to distinguish it from offices of the rival Springfield SDP.

(Debs scrapbooks, *Papers of Eugene V. Debs, 1834-1945* microfilm edition.)

Above: Pinback from Debs's first campaign for president in 1900 as the fusion candidate of the Social Democratic Party of Chicago and the Social Democratic Party of Springfield, Mass.

Right: The unexpected victory ot the SDP in the mill towns of Haverhill and Brockton, Massachusetts in city elections of 1898 gave the fledgling organization breathing space.

January, 1900. PROGRESSIVE THOUGHT. No. 10.
PUBLISHED QUARTERLY 25 CENTS A YEAR.

SOCIAL DEMOCRACY

SDP A STAR OF HOPE.

"A HISTORY OF SOCIALISM IN AMERICA."

"A TRIP TO GIRARD."

1900·

EDITED BY FREDERIC HEATH

RED BOOK·

10 Copies for $1.00. PRICE, 15 CENTS. 100 Copies for $6.00.

Debs Publishing Company, Terre Haute, Ind.
Entered at the Postoffice at Terre Haute, Ind., as second-class matter.

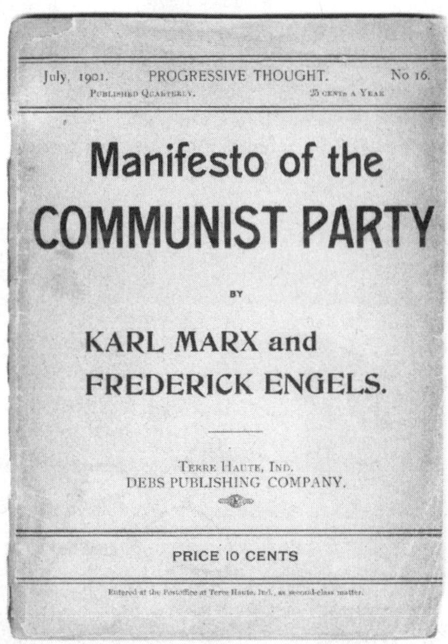

July, 1901. PROGRESSIVE THOUGHT. No 16.
PUBLISHED QUARTERLY. 25 CENTS A YEAR

Manifesto of the
COMMUNIST PARTY

BY

KARL MARX and
FREDERICK ENGELS.

TERRE HAUTE, IND.
DEBS PUBLISHING COMPANY.

PRICE 10 CENTS

Entered at the Postoffice at Terre Haute, Ind., as second-class matter.

From the time he left the Brotherhood of Locomotive Firemen as its well compensated secretary-treasurer in 1892 until 1904 Debs attempted to establish himself as a professional publisher of railroad and socialist literature. Titles published included Frederic Heath's pioneering history of the American socialist movement as part of the *Social Democracy Red Book* (January 1900) and an early American edition of *The Communist Manifesto* by Marx and Engels (July 1901).

Margaret Haile (18XX–19XX)

Frederic O. MacCartney (1864–1903)

Alfred S. Edwards (18XX–19XX)

Job Harriman (1861–1925)

Morris Hillquit (1869–1933)

John C. Chase (1870–1937)

Michael D. Ratchford (1860–1927)

John Mitchell (1870–1919)

Myron W. Reed (1836–1899)

The 1904 National Convention of the Socialist Party of America, which named Eugene V. Debs the party's nominee for president, was attended by 184 delegates from 35 different states and territories. The delegates were overwhelmingly white, male, middle-aged, and middle class. Only one black delegate appears in the official group photograph here, no. 46, George Washington Woodbey of California. Debs appears front and center in the insert (no. 207), together with Pennsylvania trade unionist James Maurer (205), Victor Berger (209), and Seymour Stedman (210). This was a rare occasion when Debs was actually an elected convention delegate, although his participation was limited to a speech of acceptance of the nomination on the closing day of the gathering (May 6).

The Double Headed Octopus

The 1904 Socialist Party presidential campaign was regarded as a rousing success, effectively pitting Debs and Hanford against big business-friendly Democratic and Republican tickets. Here is the iconic lithographed campaign poster featuring railroad and printer moiffs, a cartoon from the party press, and sheet music for a 1904 Socialist campaign song.

Eugene V. Debs as he appeared during the first few years of the twentieth century.

1897

Present Conditions and Future Duties: An Open Letter†

January 1, 1897

Terre Haute, Ind., Dec. 31 [1896]—Eugene V. Debs has come out for socialism and formally announces that he is no longer a member of the People's Party, for which he left the Democratic Party after the election of Cleveland in 1892.

It is his belief that, if Bryan had not been the candidate of the Democrats and Populists this year, the socialists would have cast a million votes. He says that Bryan at heart is a socialist, and that hundreds of thousands of voters who were ready to vote for an out-and-out socialist voted for Bryan because they looked upon him as one who would carry out their ideas so far as he could.

"I know," said Debs, "that I will be criticized and berated by the press, and especially by those persons who do not understand the true and better meaning of the term 'socialist.' But there is coming to be a better understanding of what enlightened socialism means. Some of the ablest men, in the pulpit, too, are beginning to sound the alarm, and they will be heeded before there is a violent explosion."

Following is his letter:

To Members of the American Railway Union and Other Toilers:—

Since the recent presidential election, I have received a large number of letters making urgent inquiries as to future efforts to emancipate wageworkers from their thralldoms, all couched in language which, properly interpreted, is the substance of the interrogatory, "What shall we do to be saved?"

As there is not time at my command to answer these numerous letters, I take this method of replying to my friends who have asked for my views upon present conditions and the outlook for the future. During the late campaign, I supported Mr. William J. Bryan and the platform upon which he stood, not because I regard the free coinage of silver as a panacea for our national ills, for I neither affirmed nor advocated such a principle, but because I believed that the triumph of Mr. Bryan and free silver would blunt the fangs of the money

---

† Published as "Debs Hails Socialism: Thinks It Is the Only Cure" in *Chicago Record,* January 1, 1897. Letter officially first published in *Railway Times* [Chicago], vol. 4, no. 1 (January 1, 1897), 1. Reprinted in expanded form in *The Coming Nation,* whole no. 191 (January 16, 1897), 1.

power; that it would extract the teeth of syndicate sharks; that it would banish from the highways of human endeavor, on the sea and on the land, many a black flag under which more piracies have been perpetrated during the last 25 years than the sum total of all the robberies by buccaneers on the high seas since the first corsair keel cleaved a wave. The free silver issue gave us not only a rallying cry, but afforded common ground upon which the common people could unite against the trusts, syndicates, corporations, monopolies—in a word, the money power—under whose sway the country has been well-nigh ruined, labor reduced to famine, and personal liberty banished; and, once united, could press forward in a solid phalanx in the crusade against social and industrial slavery, nor halt the advancing columns until the whole capitalistic system is abolished and the cooperative commonwealth has become an established fact.

That in this conclusion I was correct it is only required to point to the consternation everywhere manifested in the ranks of the shylocks and robbers which enabled Mark Hanna[1] to collect from them a fund of more than $16 million to prevent the election of Bryan and the success of his supporters. In this election, as in no other, the oppressors and plunderers of the people were united. This, in itself, caused a mighty mustering of the intelligent and progressive industrial forces of the country. It is safe to assume that 80 percent of the organized wageworkers supported Bryan and free silver. That the result of the election was not different was due largely, if not wholly, to the fact that unorganized workers overwhelmingly outnumbered those who were organized and who had been educated and drilled in the tactics of the enemy and could not be coerced, intimidated, or stampeded from voting their own convictions.

But the election is over, and, after mature deliberation, I am persuaded that it may be regarded as both a defeat and a victory. This affirmation may appear paradoxical, but it is true nevertheless. The result of the November election has convinced every intelligent wageworker that in politics, per se, there is no hope of emancipation from the degrading curse of wage-slavery.

In the late election they may read their doom as vividly outlined as if written in fire across the blue dome of the skies above them. The storm cloud of the campaign disappeared, bearing upon its frowning breast no bow of promise of better things. Cowering before the despotism of the money power—its injunctions, prisons, and standing armies—they were driven to the polls to vote for a system of wage piracy that they might hold their jobs, while sitting on the ragged edge of starvation, fearful that at any moment their famine wages might be withheld and they and their wives and children forced into an abyss of despair or death. It is, therefore, not surprising that they should ask: "What shall we do to be saved?"

And it is just here that the defeat which more than 6 million men sought to avert rises like "truth crushed to earth,"[2] and proclaims that what is called a defeat is like Nebuchadnezzar's fiery furnace,[3] made to stand by the genius of Justice, a flaming symbol of victory, because all over the broad land it served to arouse the mind forces of millions of men to hew out new departures to the goal of emancipation. The ballot, however much it has been eulogized, has been beaten to the earth by "boodle" wrung from unrequited toil, and as a weapon cannot be relied upon to execute the will of the people while they are in industrial bondage. An industrial slave cannot be expected to cast an independent ballot.

One John D. Rockefeller with his $200 million; one Cornelius Vanderbilt[4] with his $150 million; one Andrew Carnegie[5] with his $100 million; one C. P. Huntington[6] with his $75 million; one J. Pierpont Morgan[7] with his $60 million; one George M. Pullman[8] with his $50 million; and one Mark Hanna with his $40 million, alone or in alliance, can debauch the nation. Nine percent of our population having obtained possession of 71 percent, or $50 billion, of the nation's wealth, can and do poison every stream of knowledge, of truth, of justice, of love, of mercy, and make it run bank full of every vile contamination that human greed can devise and inflict upon suffering people.

It has passed into a proverb that the school of experience is a dear one, and it is as true as the aphorism that the wageworkers of America have an abundance of tuition in this school. They have worked and toiled down the declivities of poverty until they have reached the bottom, to find huts, rags, crusts, darkness, and despair. The palaces of those who have driven them downhill are on the highlands, ablaze with light. There is music and dancing, purple robes and fine linen; there is luxury beyond compare, and the robber barons, filled to the throat with wine, have their auction blocks where their daughters are offered in the market for titles, creating scenes as offensive and shocking as were the vices of Sodom.

Is there a way out of this labyrinth, this tortuous, blinding, and confusing maze? I believe there is. All that is required is a will on the part of wageworkers to find a place where they may extricate themselves from bondage and bask in the sunshine of prosperity. There are even now in the wilderness thousands of John the Baptists crying, "We will hew out a way for the oppressed toilers of the world, a highway of deliverance to new regions beyond the reach of Moloch maws and boodle beasts of prey."

These leaders of the socialistic army have thrown wide open the door of hope to the toiling masses and are inviting them to enter, and with a faith that is even now the substance of things hoped for, they can see a victory achieved for the producing masses in the late election, the full fruitions of which are now budding and are soon to bloom on the "thorny stem of time."[9]

Speaking for myself, I am a socialist. I have long since given expression to my socialistic convictions; they have grown with my growth and I am more strongly impressed with them at this hour than ever before since first I began the painful study of the progress and poverty of the race. Our competitive system is utterly cannibalistic. Human beings are set against one another, the strong devour the weak, and the heartless proceeding has to be done in self-defense. Crush and devour your neighbor, or he will you! Under this system, the few cunning and unscrupulous have been enabled to monopolize the earth and the fullness thereof, and they have used their ill-gotten possessions to enslave and degrade mankind. Private greed has been the controlling force, and it has been and is accounted as of vastly more importance than the public welfare. Under the regime of private capital, property has become sacred and human life has been reduced to a valueless commodity. A few men own and control the country. The producing many have been subjugated by degrees until millions work by permission and millions of others are tramping and starving to paupers' graves. And all of this amidst fabulous abundance! The theme invites to elaboration, but time and space forbid. I survey these frightful conditions, the ripened and rotting fruit of the capitalistic system, and I declare, with all the emphasis of which my words are capable, my implacable hostility to this system, and my determination to battle with all my power for its overthrow.

It is axiomatic that men have a right to work, the same inherent right to work that they have to breathe. And they have a right to all they produce, and if any part is taken from them without their express consent, it is robbery. The present system is founded, essentially, in the robbery of labor. No other word in the language properly describes the crime.

Every machine that is invented reduces labor to more desperate conditions. The whole system perverts and subverts and is fruitful of crimes beyond the power of language to catalog.

The issue is socialism vs. capitalism. I am for socialism because I am for humanity. We have been cursed by the reign of gold long enough. Money constitutes no proper basis of civilization. The time has come to regenerate society—we are on the eve of a universal change.

I am aware that socialism is a term little understood by the world at large, and that it is everywhere a target for denunciation by the plutocratic press. When analyzed, it means a more perfect and equitable distribution of the products of labor; cooperation instead of competition; collective ownership of land, capital, and all the means of production and distribution. It proclaims the coming of the cooperative commonwealth to take the place of wage-slavery. Under socialism there would be work and plenty for all, reasonable hours, and life would be something more and better than a prolonged agony or a continuous curse. Another panic would never curse the land. Crime would disappear, and suicide would cease to shock the public conscience.

The present industrial system is not only a failure, but a colossal aggregation of crime. It robs, it degrades, it starves; it is a foul blot upon the face of our civilization, indicative of poisoned blood flowing through the veins and arteries of the body social, industrial, and politic; it promises only an increase of the horrors which the world deplores, and which is leading nations, as well as individuals, into a decline and fall from which, as history teaches, there is no resurrection.

I confess no hope for the toiling masses of my countrymen except by the pathway mapped out by socialists, the advocates of the cooperative commonwealth.

I indulge in no illusions. As I contemplate conditions, productive of dismay and steadily growing worse, I am convinced that to continue in the old ruts and grooves is but to reach profounder depths of poverty and degradation, until, tagged, numbered, and branded, plutocrats, the managers of trusts, syndicates, and combines, will at no distant day call the roll of their white slaves, under the stars and stripes, in front of old Independence Hall, on Bunker Hill, and a thousand other places made sacred by patriotic bloodshed in the cause of liberty and independence.

Such being my convictions and conclusions after a careful survey of the field, I do not hesitate, with fealty born of hope in the ultimate triumph of the right, to enlist in the grand army of socialism, to do battle for the emancipation of those who toil from conditions and environments which shock humanity and tend inevitably to the degeneracy of the race.

Eugene V. Debs

"I Am with the Miners in their Present Trouble": Speech in Leadville, Colorado[†] [excerpt]

January 13, 1897

Mr. Chairman, Ladies and Gentlemen:—

I thank you from the depths of my heart for this manifestation of your good-will, which I appreciate far more than words of mine can express.

We have met this afternoon for the purpose of discussing some of the phases of the labor question, more particularly the situation here in Leadville. I am not unmindful of the fact that in every community there are those who are opposed to labor organizations. There are those who can see in them no good. Others can see in them only harm and believe they should be suppressed by law. This is born of misapprehension of their aims and objects.

The aims of organized labor, fairly and properly understood, appeal for the sympathetic support of every good citizen of this republic. I know it is unfortunate that now and then a strike occurs such as is now in progress in Leadville. I realize, as does every good man, that the strike is in the nature of a calamity. Sometimes it becomes a choice between a strike and degradation; then I am in favor of the strike. There is a condition, my friends, more to be deplored than that of being out of employment, and that is when a man submits to being stripped of his manhood and independence without protest. There are times under the present industrial system when a strike is not only justifiable but becomes an imperative duty. Labor organizations are born of oppressions of the employing classes.

I am not here to appeal to your prejudices, to arouse your passions, nor to oppose class against class, but I am here to bring about a better understanding of the causes and purposes of the strike.

In this connection, I do not discuss the individual employer, who, in these modern times, has been largely displaced by the corporations. The corporations perpetrate many wrongs upon the community which individual stockholders

† Published as "Debs' Great Speech" in the *Leadville Miner,* vol. 1, no. 16 (January 14, 1897), 1, 4. The speech was delivered at the Weston Opera House to a largely middle-class audience.

would not care to be responsible for. A corporation is a soulless thing. It has no feelings, no touch, no soul—it has only an appetite, and the more you feed a corporation, the hungrier it grows. Organizations of workingmen are of profound interest, not only to the wageworkers, but to all classes of citizens in every community. There are men who condemn labor organizations simply because they strike. Large bodies of workingmen do not voluntarily abandon their employment without good cause. They know by bitter experience that, if their organization can be broken down, it is only a question of time when they will be reduced to the condition of the Mexican peon.

I am with the miners in their present trouble for two reasons. In the first place, they are poor. In the next place, they are right. I do not countenance, nor do I attempt to justify violence. I am opposed to the destruction of life and property, but I maintain that the workmen have a perfect right to defend their rights along peaceful lines. They are fighting for wife and children and hearthstone; and the man who will not fight for wife and children is not fit to have either. *[Applause.]*

Workingmen are sometimes hasty when cool deliberation is required. But they do the very best they can when the conditions are considered; and they are willing to meet their employers halfway. They have never asked, nor do they now ask, anything more than arbitration. They are willing to submit their cause to fair and impartial arbitration. This has been denied them. The miners have faith in the sense of fair play of this community. But the mine owners refuse to make any concessions. It argues weakness for their claims. They declare, as Mr. Pullman did, that there is nothing to arbitrate. The miners say there is something to arbitrate. Let that question be examined into by all fair-minded men, when it will be found there is something to arbitrate. I want to say there is, or the present trouble would not be.

I would treat the mine owners in the controversy just as I would be treated were I in their place. I would not intentionally do a wrong to the mine owners, nor to anyone else. I believe in an appeal to reason, and there is nothing to be gained by this unfortunate strife. The mine owners and the miners are losing money, and all the interests of the state are suffering, not only here, but in other important centers. It seems to me that it ought to be the high purpose of every good citizen of this state to use his influence to have this strife cease, and to have the controversy settled satisfactorily to all the parties concerned. My friends, if the workingman is suffered to be impoverished, every business suffers. Every businessman is interested in keeping up a high standard of wages. If a miner gets only poor wages, he cannot meet his bills. Your prosperity as a community will disappear, never to return. The foundations of your prosperity are laid in the prosperity of the wageworkers of this community. Let the parties to this controversy be brought together, and let them meet in the true spirit of humanity. I venture to say that if this question shall be entertained by the mine owners as it has by the mine workers, the trouble will be decided in 24 hours.

There is much injustice done to the poor. My heart goes out to them, because I know something of the troubles that make their lives a curse. I have been in the centers of population where I have seen man's inhumanity to man. If we only had more of the golden rule, we could overcome the inequalities and, in a very short time, make this place fit for men to live in. *[Applause.]*

Put yourself in the place of the worker just a little while; think of the wage earner's struggle.

I am not unmindful of the fact that in every community there is a hatred for the tramp. The tramp is an abnormal product of this abnormal civilization. We have almost 4 million of them in this country. I approximated that there were 3 million but Carroll D. Wright,[10] the labor commissioner, said that there were 3.8 million. I remember when a tramp was a curiosity. He is now a vast army, whose *tramp-tramp* can be heard all over the country.

Mr. Debs then rapidly and eloquently portrayed the life of society's modern pariah, and showed how the introduction of labor-saving machinery had done its part in creating and fostering this incubus upon society. He painted the condition of a poor man who is obliged to look for employment. Mr. Debs continued:

He can find no work, but he does not lose courage. He says to his wife as he leaves home in the morning, "Mary, I believe I can find work today." He goes out through the country, but he does not travel in a Pullman palace car; he generally travels on the trucks of a freight. Let me subject you to that ordeal. Let me deny you the right to work. And if you save your self-respect and manhood, you are better than men generally are. If the present industrial condition continues, I, too, may find myself a tramp on the highway of life. Christ said in reference to his own unfortunate condition that "the foxes have holes and the birds have nests, but the son of man hath not where to lay his head."[11] The tramp is embittered against society, and who can blame him?

The middle classes are gradually disappearing, and men of small capital are gradually being driven to the wall. Last year was the most disastrous in the history of the republic—the failures aggregated $285 million. These represented the failures of the middle classes. Do you know there were 7,000 suicides and 14,000 murders last year? Do you know that insanity and prostitution have increased threefold? Have you thought of these frightful conditions that organized labor is trying to combat? We have deified the dollar in this country, and we call it the "almighty dollar." The standard by which we measure men's success or failure is the dollar. *[Applause.]*

I believe that American manhood and American womanhood are of infinitely more importance. I believe that the humblest miner in my hearing is of more consequence than all the hoarded millions of the plutocrats of the country. *[Applause.]* Money-getting has become the curse of the country and is eating out the heart of civilization. "Get money" is the motto of the age. With money you are a success; without it you are a failure. You tell me how much money a man has accumulated—I will not ask you by what method—and I will tell you the degree he marks on the social thermometer. Money is well enough, in its way, but I believe humanity is far, far above gold.

Do you know that a man who is grasping for money is almost as much to be pitied as the tramp on the highway? Jay Gould died 20 years before his time because he had too much money, or rather, because too much money had him.[12] A few people in this country have vastly too much, and the masses of the people are being subjected to impoverishment, and if this is ever reversed it will have to be done by organized labor. *[Applause.]*

It is a deplorable fact that the men who create all have nothing, and the men who create nothing have all. I believe there is something radically wrong with a system under which these injustices are possible. The time is not far distant when this system will be abolished. Workingmen are beginning to think; they will soon begin to act. They will not much longer supplicate for their rights but will take them. Not in lawlessness, not in crime, not in violence—but they will do it with the ballot.

* * *

Ladies and gentlemen, all the organized forces of society and all the powers of government are directed against the poor. It has been so since the dawn of creation. It has never been more so than now. As a general proposition, only the poor go to jail. You may commit almost any crime you choose and escape the consequences if you have money enough. But woe be to the moneyless man. This power that we call the money power dominates every department of the United States government. Do I hear objections? Let me say to you that even the United States Supreme Court has been invaded by the money power. Read the dissenting opinions of Justices White,[13] Harlan,[14] and Brown[15] in the decision on the income tax measure.[16] That law was declared unconstitutional.

I undertake to say, my friends, that if that law had taxed the poverty of this country, it would not have been declared unconstitutional. Three of the supreme judges gave dissenting opinions. What did they say?

The speaker here quoted the exact words of the dissenting judges in the income tax decision and continued:

This is not the language of wild-eyed anarchists or foam-flecked socialists, but it is the mature language of three of the members of the United States Supreme Court.

It is impossible for the people to have a measure enacted to relieve them. This money power has invaded the halls of Congress and even the pulpit. Now and then there is a magnificent exception, Myron W. Reed *[great applause]*, who preferred to preach the gospel of Jesus Christ and found himself out of a job. Some of these ministers, who are really the servants of mammon, have the audacity to advise workingmen to submit to wrongs rather than disturb the relations between themselves and their masters. When they say anything at all, it is to admonish working people to be law-abiding; but when they talk to the rich lawbreakers, there is not one word of rebuke. Only the poor are punished, but that does not signify that only the working classes are criminals. We have too many men in the public service who crook the knee. It is so popular to cater to the rich. I don't know why. They enjoy special privileges, and I don't know why.

The same judges who decided the case of myself and colleagues cited George M. Pullman to appear in court. He immediately ordered out his special car and took an eastern trip. What is the difference between George M. Pullman and my colleague Mr. Rogers?[17] Twenty million dollars.

The American people are now thinking more on these questions than at any time in the history of the country. They are beginning to investigate for themselves. They are no longer satisfied to follow the lead of others. They are beginning to represent themselves. *[Applause.]*

Let us have a little more real private character. Rely less upon others and more upon ourselves. I am sometimes called a leader, but I am nothing of the sort. Let us all be leaders. Let us cultivate self-reliance. Let us begin to depend upon ourselves. Workingmen could, if they would, improve conditions. If the working people would unite for their own interests, they would soon find a way to industrial emancipation. Have some interest in your fellow man. You have got to lift him, or he will lower you. While he is in ignorance, he keeps you down to his level. I would like to have every workingman understand the social question. I would like to have every lodge room a school and every assembly of labor a college. Why not? Workingmen have done all the toiling and have been satisfied for others to do all the thinking.

* * *

The World Is Not Right: Speech in Butte, Montana†

February 8, 1897

When a man gets up and talks in favor of his fellow man at large in this age, he is called a crank. Whenever a man has attempted to head any new movement that would be a blessing to mankind, he has always been known as a crank or a dreamer. The dreamer of one age, my friends, is the philosopher of the next. The man who stands up and says that a workman should be protected in his rights may be called an agitator and an anarchist, but he is nevertheless right.

The world is not right. Upon every hand there is evidence of cruelty. Men who work the hardest have the least, and men who work the least have all the wealth. Wall Street rules the American continent, and in some mysterious way it harnesses the American workingman, and while living and fattening upon his earnings compels him to pauperize himself.

In all ages there have been men who have had the courage to stand up for their rights and have even been crucified for it. Men who sought the improvement of mankind have always been maligned, persecuted, imprisoned, and even put to death, but the world is progressing, and even the workingmen are beginning to think and wonder why the men who build houses live outdoors and why their wives who make the fashionable garments are clothed in rags. Under our flag with 45 stars they begin to ask why they press their rags closer about their bodies so as not to brush against the silks they meet; why they

† Based primarily upon "Labor and Capital," *Anaconda Standard,* February 9, 1897, 6. Integrated with "Eugene V. Debs Talked," *Montana Standard* [Butte], February 9, 1897, 5; and "Labor's Leader," *Philipsburg [MT] Mail,* February 12, 1897, 1. The speech was delivered at the Murray Opera House in Butte.

cannot touch the food of the banquet hall they had to prepare, and why they walk in the shadows of the palaces which they had built but may not occupy. They are beginning to think, and when they think they will soon have their rights. They will no longer supplicate but will take their own—not by violence, but by the peaceful ballot. Shall not the workers come into their own? Let labor everywhere take hope, for the midnight is passing and joy cometh in the morning.

I am not here to appeal to the prejudices of men or to arraign man against man; would not if I could. But let us get close together and consider these things and see if we cannot devise some plan for overcoming the evils and distress we see around us. I have made up my mind that there is something wrong. Some men say I ought to have respect for public opinion. I don't hesitate to tell you that I have not the slightest respect for what is called public opinion. Public opinion has aided, abetted, and sanctioned every public wrong and outrage the world has ever known. Public opinion in this day is very often manufactured and expounded by a vicious and unprincipled press. Washington, Jefferson, Hancock, and Franklin stood almost alone when they said taxation without representation was not right. They held a little meeting, and the Tories called them agitators. The world has always held agitators in disrespect.

I take all the harsh terms that have been applied to that name and say that I am glad to be called an agitator. Washington was hated and vilified more than any president since his time, but he stood erect for what was right. With Franklin, Jefferson, and others he was called a rebel, a striker, and a revolutionist. The Tories cried, "Let us have peace," but the agitators stood together. They said, we may have to go to war, but they said, if we must, we will do so, that our children and our children's children may have peace. If there are any in this audience who are opposed to strikes, let them remember that we are under a striking government. The revolution, from Lexington to Yorktown, was a constant series of strikes—strikes against oppression, and but for those strikes we would still be under the British yoke.

If it was not for the oppression of laborers by the employers there would be no labor organizations today. Why do laborers organize? They combine through instincts of self-preservation. Before the individual employer was supplanted by the corporation, the employer was in touch with the laborer, but the corporation, a creation of law, cannot be reached by the laborer. It has no eyes, no ears, no soul, no conscience—only an appetite, and the more you feed it, the hungrier it grows. The workingman feels that he is oppressed, and there is a rankling in his breast. He cannot feed his wife and educate his children on the pittance he receives for his labor, and he does not know what to do. He goes to his fellow workmen and asks: "What shall we do?" "Let us strike," say his fellow laborers, but they decide to first see their employer. So they call on the superintendent with their grievance, but the superintendent is only an employee, and he orders them back to their work like quarry slaves.

Years ago, under individual employers, the coal miners of Pennsylvania were paid $5 a day, and they lived as a true type of American citizen. By and by, the corporation succeeded the individual employer, and schemes were planned for enriching its members at the expense of the miners. First, they went about to disrupt the organization and then to reduce wages, and when the men rebelled, the corporations imported Hungarians, Poles, and other cheap labor from Europe to take their places. The American miner was forced out of Pennsylvania, and today the coal miners in that state are paid 65 cents a day. They don't live; they simply exist and inhabit holes scarcely fit for wild beasts to inhabit. It is proposed to extend this condition to Montana. They have tried to establish it in Leadville—and their first effort is to destroy the organization of the miners.

It is to the interest of every good citizen to maintain the American standard of wages, for after the wages are reduced, they may also find themselves reduced. Only here in the backbone of the Rocky Mountains have laborers been able to maintain their wages. It is difficult to dislodge men who live in the mountains. William Tell lived in the mountains. The invigorating atmosphere seems to promote in each love of liberty.

This greed for money-getting has been the ruin of many lives as well as nations. Jay Gould died 20 years in advance of his time because of this disease. Very recently, a lot of glass manufacturers in Indiana got together and concluded they could make a few million dollars by closing their factories, forcing up the price of window glass, and forcing down the wages of the operatives. The plan was carried out, and 15,000 operatives were thrown out of employment. The manufacturers then fixed the price of window glass, which the people had to pay, and fixed the price of wages to which the employees had to submit, and from the decision there was no appeal.

The amassing of wealth and its centralization of wealth during the last quarter of a century is something not previously known in the history of the world. The money power has invaded the legislature; it has involved Congress. It has had its influence on the Supreme Court. It has even involved the pulpit and has sent forth the minister with the price of his defilement in his pocket. The Supreme Court declared unconstitutional the law taxing incomes. Do you believe that if a tax had been levied upon poverty it would have been declared unconstitutional? Three members of that Supreme Court declared it as their deliberate conclusion that the decision was an absolute surrender to the money power.

I have not the slightest prejudice against wealth. I do not hate the rich man, but there is such a thing as getting too much wealth for one's own good. The rich forget that shrouds have no pockets. The rich forget how insignificant they are and that there are only a few steps from the cradle to the grave. Death is a democrat. He is no respecter of persons. Only a short time ago, he entered the Fifth Avenue palace of a Vanderbilt, and in a second's time the multimillionaire was reduced to the level of the lowest vagabond that walks the highway.

The humblest child of the lowliest parents in Montana, in my opinion, outweighs all the gold and wealth in the universe. I believe in manhood and womanhood, such a manhood and womanhood as dignifies and uplifts humanity, which, but for this greed for wealth, might make of this country a paradise.

The cheapest commodity in the world is human flesh and blood. A railroad company would rather kill a brakeman than a hog. The hog has a commodity value, and the brakeman has not.

They speak to you about survival of the fittest. Who is the fittest—the man with the longest beak and the sharpest fangs, called a financial genius, whose only faculty is for money-getting? Or the man of superior intellect and mental endowment who cannot get a crust to eat and has a constant struggle for existence until death comes to his relief?

The mayor of Chicago, a few days ago, made an appeal, in the name of God, to save 50,000 of these wretches from starving and freezing in that city. A similar condition of affairs exists in New York, while the farmer freezes near his well-filled barns and granaries because there is no market for his grain—no one to buy it and no money to purchase clothing and fuel. Nature has abundantly supplied for the wants of all men, but man's devilish iniquity interferes with nature's plans.

The small businessman has a sharp, fierce struggle to make both ends meet, and I want to tell them that many of their brothers are on the highway to trampdom, for the business failures last year were something appalling. Who is the tramp? Let me tell you that he is your brother. I sympathize with a tramp for two reasons. The first is I cannot help it, and the second is that I am liable to be one myself someday.

The same conditions which have reduced the American workingman to the level of the Mexican peon is after the businessman who has $10,000 invested. They are also after lawyers and professional men, and sometimes the judge on the bench feels this power, not through his conscience, but through his pocket. Judges are not all that way, however, for there are some good men on the bench. I cannot speak the name of Judge Caldwell without taking my hat off, for he is one of the noblest and purest of men. The same court which cited me to appear and show cause why I should not be punished for contempt (and who would not be guilty of contempt for such a court?) also cited George M. Pullman. He came in his private car from New York, made an application to the court, and was excused. I explained and got six months. *[Great laughter.]* I am glad the people of Butte like it; I did not. Judge Jenkins[18] made an order reducing the wages of the employees on the Northern Pacific, and then made another order that if the men did not accept the reduction they would be sent to jail for contempt. The decision was so rank that even Congress ordered an investigation, but the committee soon exhausted the appropriation, and no investigation was ever made.

It is a poor rule that, like a locomotive engine, does not work both ways. If a judge has the right to reduce wages, he also has the power to raise wages, and if he has the power to compel to work, he also has the power to prevent a corporation from discharging its men. Did you ever hear of any such order? Jenkins should have been impeached, but he is a creature of wealth and was not molested. Wealth should not be a shield for rascality.

The man who takes a stand for right and for the interests of mankind is persecuted, maligned, and imprisoned. It has been so always. It has been the case from Socrates down to Coxey.[19] The experience of Christ was no exception. If Christ had a dollar, authentic history makes no mention of it. His face was always to the poor. He was utterly unfashionable, but his great throbbing heart always beat for the poor, and he was a friend of labor, too. We are all liable to make mistakes, and if there is a man who ought to be forgiven, it is he who makes a mistake. I have made so many myself that I feel the great need of the charity of forgiveness in the human breast.

When I see a man in jail, I feel like putting my arms around him and saying: "You have made a mistake, but come to me and I will help you overcome it." If I have one thing to thank Judge Woods[20] for in sending me to jail, it is for the opportunity it gave me to associate with the other unfortunates in prison and see the evidence of man's inhumanity to man. We are making criminals faster than we can incarcerate them, and when we get them in jail we don't forget or forgive. When they get out, the police keep them spotted; everybody points a finger at them and everyone avoids and shuns them; they may try ever so hard to obtain employment and reform, but their name and misfortune is a bar to all that, and soon they fall back into prison and we compel them to graduate from petty larceny to homicide. We should do something to prevent crime as well as to punish it. I would meet the man at the door as he came out of jail and say to him: "You have made a mistake and I'll help you, and we'll see if we can't forget." A helping hand, a word of encouragement and forgiveness, would redeem 95 percent of our criminals.

The jails are not for rich but for poor fellows who have not a cent to defend themselves. While in the Chicago jail, I met a poor fellow who was serving out 12 months for stealing an old cloak from in front of a secondhand store. He had been out of employment for a whole year; his wife needed a cloak to keep her rags together and her body warm, and, prompted by the purest motives that ever sprung up in a man's breast, he stole a cloak. It was not he who committed the crime; it was the other side that was wrong. He had no money, and it took the judge just five minutes to send him up for 12 months.

Some people who enlisted in this fight have given up. I never shall. Some people say: "Stop, there's no use." They said that to Columbus, and if he had heeded them, this continent might never have been discovered.

I wish to refer briefly to the Leadville troubles, regarding which the press has not spoken the truth. I don't want to criticize the press of your state, for I understand they have been very fair. When I went down to Leadville, I inquired into the situation as I wanted to act intelligently on the subject. I always want to find out both sides of a question. I am not one of those men who think labor organizations never make a mistake. We have made many a one, I am sorry to say, but in our principles we are right. Ella Wheeler Wilcox[21] said that no difficulty is settled until it is settled right. When I found out how matters stood in Colorado, I found that wages had been cut from $3 to $2.50 per day. The miners found that they could not live as white men on such wages, and they concluded to quit. They did so, and they are still out, and it looks like they will continue to remain on the outside.

The wages of the miners were reduced, but they protested and struck to prevent Pennsylvania conditions from being introduced in Colorado and Montana. They did not strike until they had made two efforts to settle the trouble peaceably. The men are united, but the mine owners are divided, and one of them said to me that when he could not pay $3 a day, he would shut down his mine.

After looking thoroughly into the matter, I talked to those 1,200 men who represented the striking miners of Leadville, and I told them what I thought.

I told them to give up everything but principle—to waive all past differences, to waive the new men imported to work, and to make every concession consistent with honor. They demanded $3 per day, and the mine owners offered $2.50. Now my proposal was to concede something on both sides and make the scale of wages $2.75 per day. Those 1,200 men, from whom nothing of the sort should be expected, for God knows the miner earns [his] $3 per day, those 1,200 men, I say, without a dissenting voice, agreed to make this sacrifice. They were right, but they were reasonable and were willing to concede anything in reason.

When I went to the mine owners with this offer of a compromise, which was indeed a concession of 50 percent, they said they would consider it. They did consider the proposition and soon returned with the message that it would not be accepted. What they wanted was unconditional surrender and a victory that would break the back of the miners' union.

I consulted with Governor Adams, who was there in hopes of settling the strike, and I told him of the very reasonable proposition of the miners. They were willing to leave their case in the hands of the people. Arbitration would be satisfactory to the miners in almost any form. They were willing to submit their case to a committee of five or any number of men and abide by the issue. In fact, all the advances were made by the miners and refused by the mine owners.

I proposed to Governor Adams[22] that the matter be submitted to arbitration, and he eagerly accepted the offer and said he was sure the mine owners would agree to it. The miners were unanimously in favor of it because they knew their course could not suffer before a committee of arbitration. Governor Adams himself drew up the plans and submitted them to the mine owners, but they, too, were rejected. The object of the mine owners is not so much to reduce wages at present as to break the band of union that binds the miners of Colorado together. Before I left Leadville, I advised the miners to never be unreasonable, but rather than submit to conditions that are attempted to be enforced on them to die and starve in their tracks, but never to give in, and every laboring man and woman in Montana should stand by them in this fight.

The mine owners may succeed in destroying the miners' union, but if they do, this republic is in danger. I don't say that labor organizations never make mistakes, for I am sorry to say they do. Here in Butte, you are splendidly organized and have great power, but beware how you abuse that power. I say it now that recent mistakes have been made and some of labor's best friends attacked by laboring men. Such things cannot help but weaken the cause of labor. When a labor union commences to persecute a man, it loses the moral support of the people, and it must lose its power and influence just as sure as right will prevail in the end. You are well organized and powerful, but such power must be used with discretion and judgment. To do otherwise is to help destroy the cause of the laboring man. Capital takes advantage of the mistakes of labor, and such a mistake is the worst that can be made.

I have been called a leader. I don't want to be a leader, and I don't want anyone to follow me. I want everyone to act for himself. If a few truths I tell you are of benefit to you, accept them and profit by them.

There are 4 million men and women in this country begging for employment and begging for the right to live. You are fortunate in your condition. The world is beginning to understand, and I see an improvement in the condition of mankind.

I want to see the time come when every woman can have the same right that I have. I want to see the time when man and woman can walk together in a land where there is not a single slave. Woman is entitled to all the rights possessed by man, and when a man questions that, I almost feel ashamed of my sex. If she has not the right to vote, where did we get that right? It has been said that every magnificent man had of necessity a magnificent mother; but probably any sort of man would do for a father. The idea of making women, who have more honesty and certainly as much intelligence as men, only equal politically to an Indian, an infant, or an idiot makes me ashamed of my own sex. Without woman's help, we would never have emerged from barbarism and darkness. She is entitled to walk side by side with man in the sunshine of light and should be politically his equal, as she is in any other way. She will purify politics. You cannot buy a woman's vote with a drink of whiskey as you can that of a man. She should be emancipated as she deserves.

Strike Lessons: A Dispassionate Review of the Great Leadville Struggle†

April 5, 1897

Terre Haute, Ind., April 5, 1897

The strike of the miners in the Leadville district has passed into history. It was one of the longest and most bitterly contested battles ever fought between organized labor and organized capital. Beginning June 19, 1896, and continuing until March 9, 1897, the strike extended over a period of eight months and 18 days.

It is a trite declaration that a strike is a war. This is more or less true of all strikes, but it applies with peculiar force to the prolonged strike of the Leadville miners. It was, indeed, war, and both sides so regarded it and made preparations accordingly. There are those who regard all strikes as unmixed evils. They are forever telling us about the losses entailed, the damage that has been done, the bitterness that has been aroused, and so on to the end of the chapter. It is admitted that in the great labor strikes of the past, many things occurred that were to be deplored, but it is safe to declare that there was not one but had its good results. And so, whatever there may be to regret in connection with the Leadville strike, it is certain to be productive of good and to have its lessons for those who are capable of profiting by observation and experience.

At the time of the strike, there were about 2,600 members in the local union, or about 97 percent of all the miners employed in the district. It will thus be observed that the miners were what may be called thoroughly organized, and it must be said to their credit that from first to last, through all the long and weary months, through good and evil report, they stood together, true to their organization, and only an insignificant number returned to work while the strike was in progress. Having been upon the ground and having had the opportunity of meeting and talking with these men, I speak advisedly when I say that they were impelled by pure and honest motives and that they conscientiously believed they were in the right, and this no doubt accounts

---

† Published as "Strike Lessons: A Dispassionate Review of the Great Struggle" in *The Western Miner,* vol. 1, no. 26 (April 10, 1897), 1. *The Western Miner* was the official organ of the Cloud City Miners' Union No. 33, WFM of A, the organization that conducted the Leadville strike.

for the facts that there were scarcely any deserters from the ranks and that the strike lasted so long a time.

What was the cause of the strike, and were the men justified in declaring it? In answering this question, as in all other matters which I shall discuss in these articles,[23] it will be my purpose to be fair and to state facts. I quote as follows from the official report of the joint special legislative committee by whom a thorough investigation of the strike was made. Under the head of "Grievances Before the Strike," the report says:

> It is in evidence that for some time, at least several months, before the strike was declared, the miners complained that a miner and his family could not live on $2.50 a day unless he worked every day, including Sundays, and that even then he would run in debt in case of sickness in his family or other temporary misfortunes and that these complaints were communicated to the mine managers from time to time in an informal way and the suggestion made that the scale be raised to $3; it is also in evidence that there was a fear on the part of some miners that some of the mines paying $3 per day would reduce the scale to $2.50, and two officers and a member of the union testified directly and unequivocally that one of the mine managers who was paying the $3 scale without discrimination had told them that unless the scale was raised to $3 throughout the camp, he would be compelled to reduce the scale to $2.50; this was unequivocally denied by the manager in question, but your committee is of the opinion that these officers of the union relied upon their understanding of the interview and entertained a fear that the general scale might be reduced to $2.50 . . .

It is not my purpose to enter into details, but simply to state the salient points in the causes that led up to the strike, and when the reader has these fixed in his mind he will be better able to determine whether or not the miners were justified in their subsequent action. It will hardly be disputed by fair-minded persons that a miner with a family at Leadville must live with rigid economy on a wage of $2.50 per day. Living expenses are perhaps higher than in any other city in the Union. Every item that enters into the household necessities, even to water, must be purchased. If sickness or injury falls to his lot, he is doomed. Wages cease and debt begins, and a workingman in debt is no longer a free man. I am aware that there are those who declare that $2.50 per day is a good wage and that a miner and his family should be able to get along comfortably at that rate, and for their benefit I quote again from the report of the legislative committee. In presenting the statement of the expenses of the soldiers who were quartered at Leadville during the strike, which amounted to almost $200,000 for a period of less than five months, or about $40,00 per month, the committee says:

> Taking the amount of the total expenses and dividing it by the number of days each man served, it appears that the average expense per man per day was $2.71.

This statement, considered in connection with the matter of living expenses, is in the nature of an "eye-opener." A wage of $2.50 per day of hard and hazardous work is sufficient for a miner to support his whole family, but the state is required to pay $2.71 per day to support a soldier who has nothing to do but kill time. In other words, it costs a soldier 21 cents per day more for his own expenses while doing nothing than is allowed a miner who works like a galley slave for the support of himself and wife and four or five children. Those who are interested in such affairs and are capable of fair play may ponder the proposition at their leisure.

Then again, there was a fear on the part of the miners, as reported by the legislative committee, that a general reduction to $2.50 would be made if the scale of the $2.50 miners was not raised to $3. The miners declare that the statement was made by a prominent mine manager; the fact remains that the miners were under that impression. They felt that their wages were in jeopardy. Some of them knew by experience that when reduction begins it does not usually stop until the bottom is reached. They had seen coal miners in Pennsylvania gradually reduced from $4 and $5 a day to 65 cents per day and at last driven from the mines as if they had been wild beasts to make room for the degraded creatures who had been imported to take their places. They were anxious to maintain, if possible, an American standard of living. They desired to preserve their own self-respect and independence. They thought of home and wife and children and resolved to defend their rights by such proper means as they had at their command. They perfected their organization, appointed and authorized committees to present their complaints to the mine managers, which was done, but as the concessions that were asked were refused, the strike was declared, and this by a unanimous vote of the miners in mass meeting assembled.

Much has been said about the strike having been caused by the "labor agitator," the "demagogue," etc., but nothing could be further from the truth. The abuse which was heaped upon President Boyce of the Western Federation of Miners and some of his associates was wholly unwarranted and grossly unjust. The miners themselves ordered the strike, and if a single one of them was opposed to it, he uttered no word to indicate his opposition. Neither have the miners at any time attempted to shirk the responsibilities of their acts. They have avowed again and again that the strike was their own voluntary action and that, win or lose, they had no regret for what they had done.

Harmony and Unity—and Their Limits†

April 12, 1897

Terre Haute, Ind., April 12, 1897

Rarely has so large a body of men as were engaged in the Leadville strike acted in all matters with such harmony and unanimity. I was particularly struck by this feature of the strike. During all the time I was at Leadville, I never heard a single complaint. There was confidence in the leaders and mutual confidence among the members; and, feeling that they were battling in a righteous cause, they stood by one another as if bound together by hoods of steel. There is in this a beautiful lesson for those who are capable of rising above selfish and sordid influences and appreciating an exhibition of devotion to principle and fidelity to fellow man.

As I write these lines, I remember the statements that were made and often repeated about the strike having been instigated by a few red-mouthed agitators. All the charge until the curtain fell upon the scene. A more flagrant falsehood was never uttered. It may be that those who made the charge repeated it so often that they themselves believed it, but there was not a scintilla of truth in it. In declaring the strike and carrying it forward, the men at all times *acted for themselves.* Whether the strike was wise or otherwise, the great body of the men ordered it by acclamation, and to this day not one of them can be found to avow the contrary, and to declare that it was precipitated by a few demagogues against the better judgment of the majority is to pervert the truth and insult the intelligence of men. I dwell particularly upon this point, for I know by bitter experience at what a disadvantage men are placed who are the victims of falsehood and misrepresentation at such a critical time. The "gullible public" is

† Published as "Debs on Strikes" in *The Western Miner,* vol. 1, no. 27 (April 17, 1897), 1.

led to believe that the strike was wholly uncalled for, that it was incited by a few irresponsible creatures who are enemies of society and monsters of depravity, and while, perhaps, they may express some sympathy for the strikers for being so easily misled, they are almost invariably against the strike and mass all their powers to crush it, not as much as dreaming that in so doing they are simply digging their own graves.

The agitator, the leader, the pathfinder has in every age paid the penalty imposed by the hosts of ignorance and superstition upon all self-sacrificing, sympathetic souls that ever sought to free and ennoble the race. Jesus Christ, the "Man of Sorrow," was nailed to the cross; Socrates was forced to drink the fatal hemlock; Columbus was chained in a dungeon as if he were a wild beast. Were it required, the list could be made as long as the track of the human race. Years, sometimes centuries after they are dust, monuments are reared above them in grateful memory of their service to mankind. Living, they are denounced as demagogues, and dead, they are metamorphosed into demigods, and the world pays them the tribute of its profoundest reverence. This has always been the way, and we have no reason to believe that a time will come when it will be otherwise. The only reason given why this should be so is that

> God moves in a mysterious way
> His wonders to perform.[24]

Taking a backward look, I am persuaded that the differences between the miners and the mine managers could have been easily adjusted had there been a mutual disposition to do so. It is safe to say, in the light of the fearful proportions to which the strike expanded and the loss of life and property, the paralysis of business and the suffering and distress which followed, that if it were to do over again the strike would not be called, and it is equally safe to assume that the mine managers, as well as the miners, would go liberally halfway to prevent it. And this is one of the important lessons of the strike, which it is to be hoped will be heeded by all.

From the testimony brought before the legislative committee,[25] and from the evidence which came to me personally, I am satisfied that the trouble had been "brewing" a long time, that from small beginnings the situation became more serious and the relations more strained until mutual ugliness developed and made anything like reasonable consideration of the existing differences next to impossible. The miners were organized. So were the mine managers, the latter letting the example. The mine managers, some of them at least, bought large numbers of guns and transformed their mines into forts and arsenals long before the strike was declared, while the miners made no purchase of arms until after the strike was on. The report of the legislative committee says:

> The evidence shows that, at the time of the strike, the manager of the Little Johnny had about twelve rifles and five shotguns at the mine and 150 rifles which had been purchased on a former occasion, but which were not then at the mine; that immediately after the Coronado affair, he purchased an additional 150 rifles and sent the 300 to the Little Johnny mine, and armed and drilled the non-union men he was importing from Missouri to work in the mine.
>
> That the Coronado mine, a year before the strike, had built an eight-foot fence of one-inch boards around its premises, which occupied an area of about 200 feet square; and that early in August the owners of the Coronado constructed inside of and about six feet from the fence; that some time before the Coronado attack, the Emmet and RAM built a fence around their premises, and the Emmet also covered the tramway crossing the road with boards containing portholes and made other preparations.

In such a struggle, workingmen are always at a disadvantage, and the odds are nearly always against them. They are so poor, and there are so many of them. Their surplus earnings, if any they have, are soon consumed. On the other hand, their employers are few in number and usually rich, or at least far above the "immediate want" line. They and their families can eat three times a day and fare comfortably for an indefinite period. They are shrewd, smart men. They meet in a small room and plan in secret, and there is no danger of a paid emissary from the other side getting into their council and betraying their secrets. They understand the conditions that confront the strikers: that it is entirely a question of the stomach and that starvation will determine the contest, and give them the victory, and so they simply . . . wait.

How different the situation with the workingmen? There is an army of them, and they are more or less poor and without resources. When their wages cease, hunger begins, and a hunger pang gnawing at his child will take the courage out of the strongest man, or drive him to desperation, one or the other. To feed and clothe and shelter this army, vastly augmented by the women and children who are dependent upon them, requires daily an enormous outlay. The organization under whose banner they are struggling responds nobly, but being composed wholly of wage laborers, most of whom have all they can do to provide for their own families, the drain severely taxes the resources of the order and soon their "relief," upon which the life of the strike depends, has to be suspended, and ignominious surrender is all that is left to the hapless strikers.

Another great disadvantage is that they make no plans that are not instantly communicated to the other side. They have got to take the whole big crowd into their confidence, and they might as well hold their meetings on the public square, for the spies, spotters, and sneaks of the corporations are always in their meetings and report fully everything that is done and every move that is contemplated. Many of their number are ignorant and suspicious and can be easily persuaded that their leaders are designing knaves and getting rich out of the strike; or they can be arrayed against one another, or, worse still, influenced to desert their brethren, return to work, and turn against their former comrades by aiding to defeat them, sink all to the depths of slavery and degradation.

Then, again, every violation of law, every criminal act committed during a strike is charged upon the strikers, no matter though they be totally innocent. The press grossly exaggerates every incident that is calculated to prejudice and influence the public, and often lies outright to accomplish this end. Labor, having no press that reaches the great public, must submit in silence. Thus "public sentiment," often brutally ignorant and misdirected, turns upon the struggling, suffering poor, smites them to the earth, and plants its remorseless heels in their emaciated, prostrate bodies.

In the Great Railroad Strike of 1894, the riots were incited, the fires were started, and innocent people were shot by the murderous minions of the railroad corporations, but all this was charged upon the strikers, and it lost them the strike and sent them to jail. The proof is simply overwhelming. Only a few days ago, William Bloom, who was arrested at Cleveland, Ohio, for arson, confessed that while serving as a militiaman at Chicago in 1894, during the Pullman strike, he set fire to a grain elevator and more than 50 railroad cars, and that he had committed similar atrocities under similar circumstances at a number of other points.

The New Commonwealth: Letter to the Editor of the *New York Journal*[26†]

April 16, 1897

Terre Haute, Ind., April 16 [1897]

Editor, the *New York Journal:*—

The approaching special convention of the American Railway Union, to be held at Chicago beginning the third Tuesday in June [June 15, 1897], promises to be one of the most interesting and important convocations of labor representatives held in recent years. There is no doubt that radical changes will be made, that the order will be vastly broadened in its scope, and that a progressive and up-to-date policy will be adopted. The members have long since realized that the old methods have been outgrown and that nothing more can be accomplished on present lines; and they have simply been waiting for the full effects of the great strike of 1894 to make themselves felt upon railroad employees, confident that it would result in ripening them for the great change which is now contemplated.

To Adopt New Tactics

To organize for another strike were worse than folly. At present, railroad corporations have things their own way so far as employees are concerned, and the latter might as well have no organization. If organizations are recognized or considered at all, it is only when they fully and unqualifiedly subscribe to the terms made by the corporations. Under such arrangements, "harmony prevails and the best of feelings exist between the companies and their employees." In the meantime, the capacity of all machinery is being increased, and more and more business is handled with less and less men. An army of idle employees, the federal and state soldiers, and a subservient federal judiciary would perpetuate this state of affairs indefinitely. Fortunately, however, such object lessons are not wholly in vain. Thousands of railway employees and all other kinds of workingmen who have been the victims of corporate supremacy have been

† Published in the *New York Journal,* unspecified date. Republished as "Debs' New Commonwealth" in *Appeal to Reason* [Girard, Kansas], whole no. 74 (May 1, 1897), 3.

using their brains, and as a result they propose to adopt new tactics, and by the application of commonsense methods overcome the selfish, sordid gang who have monopolized the country and the fullness thereof and place the people in possession of their own.

How is this to be done? By uniting the workers of the country in a grand cooperative scheme in which they shall work together in harmony in every branch of industry, virtually being their own employers and receiving the whole product of their labor. The country is ripe for such a movement, and I believe the coming convention of the American Railway Union will launch it. It is to be confined to no particular class of labor, but all who toil are to be admitted without regard to nationality, sex, color, or previous condition of servitude. The primary work will be largely educational. Every problem relating to our social, economic, political, and industrial life will be examined. Lecturers and organizers will take the field and enter upon a thorough canvass of every state of the Union. Some of the foremost men in the reform movement will head the crusade, and it is a foregone conclusion that it will grow more rapidly than any organization that has ever preceded it, and, being founded on the intelligence of its membership, the growth will be healthy and substantial, and it will not be long until the movement will be one of the determining factors in shaping the policy and destiny of the Republic.

Industrial Cooperation the Basis of the Project

Industrial cooperation as the basis of a higher type of civilization will be the principal object. It is impossible to enter into details so far in advance, but these will doubtless adjust themselves at the proper time. Upon fundamental, bedrock principles, a round million of us are agreed. We shall unite all our energies to destroy the present capitalistic system and establish the cooperative commonwealth. Under the former, which is now in the last stages of "consumption," the country has been brought to the verge of ruin, and humanity has been degraded beyond the power of language to describe. To one whose sensibilities are not wholly dead, a mere contemplation of the horror of our social life is sickening and shocking.

The time has come for social regeneration, and this is only possible through a new and worldwide change of system, and to inaugurate that change will be the purpose of the new movement to be launched soon in the great metropolis of the West.[27] Soon after the work is underway, it is proposed to begin active operations in some western state. The state will be colonized by our people, the leaders will converge there, a full ticket will be nominated, and we will undoubtedly have votes enough to secure complete possession and control of the state government. We will then establish the cooperative commonwealth, and the state government will be in harmony with it. The [jobless] thousands of the country will be invited to the state and will be given equal opportunities with all others to develop its resources and enjoy "life, liberty, and the pursuit of happiness."

There are several western states in any one of which all the unemployed of the country could, under sane conditions, not only provide for themselves, but attain a type of civilization compared with which the present would appear like cannibalism. From one state, the new life would rapidly overleap boundary lines and permeate others, and thus the tide will sweep in all directions until the old barbaric system has been destroyed and the Republic is redeemed and disenthralled, and is in fact the land of a free and happy people.

Eugene V. Debs,
President of the American Railway Union

Solidarity of Western Miners Essential†

April 17, 1897

Terre Haute, Ind., April 17, 1897

Solidarity is one of the principal lessons to miners in the Leadville strike. The engineers, being separately organized and having no immediate grievances, did not act with the miners, and in the course of developments became an important factor in their defeat. Had all been members of one organization, there would have been complete coöperation, and the cause of the strikers would have been indefinitely strengthened. The mine managers were not slow to see this opening and take advantage of it. They at once began to commend the organization of engineers for its "manly and conservative course" and to cultivate the goodwill of the members with the result that a wide and impassable gulf of hate was created between the miners and the engineers, and the latter became as zealous as the mine managers themselves in opposing the strike and defeating the miners.

The shrewd manager has always found a way of dividing workingmen at the critical time, when concert of action was required to win the day for labor. This has been all the easier because of the minute division of organized labor. If there is only a "corporal's guard" engaged in some given occupation and it varies just the slightest from some other occupation, a *grand international* and *independent* movement must be at once launched and in this way numberless organizations of every conceivable character have been set afloat, and these are not infrequently in conflict with one another. While disputing about questions of jurisdiction or other trifling matters, the ever-vigilant enemy is at work, and when the hour strikes for action, the corporation is in readiness to the minutest detail, while the workingmen find that from one cause or another they are in no shape for the contest. Then comes defeat, and another turn is given the wheel of oppression, and thus the process goes forward, day by day, while the lot of the toiler becomes steadily harder, until he is finally reduced to helpless, hopeless servitude.

Again and again has one branch of labor been used to accomplish the defeat of another, and this was a commanding feature of the Leadville strike.

---

† Published as "A Solid Phalanx" in *The Western Miner,* vol. 1, no. 28 (April 28, 1897), 1.

And when defeat comes, those who were "used" against their fellow workers are kicked for their thanks. While the strike is on and their services are needed, they are flattered and made to believe that they are the chosen people, but as soon as the strike is broken and they are no longer needed, they are treated with scorn and contempt. If they dare complain, they are promptly discharged. I have seen this very thing time and time again and could, were it required, cite any number of instances that came under my personal observation. Workingmen may set it down that employers have no use for those who can't be used for tools to do their dirty work, and when men consent to be so used, they are certain to receive the reward their cowardly and contemptible conduct invites.

The course to pursue to overcome these evils is so plain that scarcely a suggestion is required. Every man of whatever occupation who works about a western mine should be admitted to the Western Federation of Miners. All should be united in one and the same organization. Instead of having men grouped according to occupation and subdivided into various class organizations, "each for himself and the devil for the hindmost," I would have them all in one compact organization ready to act together in all things requiring concert of action, the grievance of one being made the grievance of all, and the shibboleth being "each for all and all for each."

The miners of Leadville, as elsewhere, should in my judgment adopt at once this plan of organization. Let the past be forgotten, or at least forgiven. To nurse hatred for those who were against us because, largely, the creatures of circumstances can do us no possible good, while the interminable hostility will create still further dissension in the ranks and ultimately disrupt the organization and make broad and smooth and downgrade the road to slavery. A wider scope for the organization, making it possible for all men who work in or about a mine to become members, a more liberal and progressive policy, is among the needs of the miners' union, and I do not doubt these matters will have the earnest and intelligent attention of the delegates to the approaching convention at Salt Lake City.[28]

Meantime every man must do his duty. Defeat in a hard-fought struggle is one of the severest tests to which men are subject. The weak give up in despair and lament about the "lost cause." The brave and strong, they who are made of "sterner stuff," buckle on their armor and fight again and again till finally victory crowns their cause. The Leadville miners have been temporarily overcome, but they are not vanquished any more than the revolutionary patriots were subdued at Bunker Hill.

The Coronado Mine Attack†

April 27, 1897

Terre Haute, Ind., April 27, 1897

The armed attack on the Coronado mine on the night of September 20 [1896] was fatal to the interests of the union and the striking miners, and removed all possibility of a settlement of the strike, if indeed any such possibility ever existed.[29] From that moment, the mine managers were triumphant and the strike was doomed. Had those who made the attack sought to play into the hands of the mine managers, they could not have done so more successfully. The provocation was, doubtless, very great. The union miners were exasperated in every conceivable manner. Foreign labor was to be imported to take their places and armed toughs taunted and insulted them.

Of course, it is not claimed that the miners were entirely innocent. That in some instances they acted with indiscretion goes without saying, and that a few of them were guilty of criminal conduct is also admitted. It would be strange, indeed, if under all the excitement incident to a strike of such magnitude there had been no breach of the peace. But, after all, the fact stands forth and should be given commanding prominence that as a body, as a union, the strikers were sober, peaceable, and law-abiding, and after the most searching scrutiny, the legislative committee was bound to exonerate them, as an organization, from any culpability for or in connection with any crime committed during the strike.

It was freely charged that the Coronado affair was instigated by the mine managers themselves. Whether this be true or not, I have no means of knowing, and in the absence of proper proof to sustain so grave an allegation, I shall certainly not make the charge. I am bound to admit, however, that from whatever source the attack was inspired, it was a master stroke for the mine managers. For them, it meant the protection and support of the militia and the civil power of the state and, if need be, of the nation. The strike was virtually taken off their hands, the state assuming control of the mine owners' interests and arraying all its forces against the strikers. It gave all their enemies the opportunity they longed for to open their batteries on the strike and hold up the strikers to public execration as criminals whose atrocities merited the

† Published as "Debs' Hot Shot" in *The Western Miner,* vol. 1, no. 29 (May 1, 1897), 1.

gibbet.[30] The mine managers were furnished by the Coronado incident with a strong pretext to reject all overtures looking to a settlement, and they used it to advantage to the very close of the strike.

In this connection, the conclusion of the legislative committee in reference to the attack on the Coronado is immensely significant. The committee says:

> On the evening of September 20, the owners of the Coronado and the Emmet received some intimation that an attack would that night be made at these mines; *they did not communicate these rumors to the civil authorities, nor to the committee of twenty*, and there is no evidence that the union of the committee of twenty had any knowledge of any rumored attack, *and the owners of the Coronado made no special preparations for defense*. (Italics mine. —EVD)

Here we find it in evidence that the mine owners were informed that the Coronado and the Emmet were to be attacked, and yet no special preparation was made for defense nor was any report of the intended attack made to the civil authorities. This strikes me, to put it mildly, as having been a most singular proceeding, and the conclusion can hardly be avoided that if the mine owners had nothing to do with instigating the attack, they at least did nothing to prevent it, and this in face of the fact that they knew it was coming and had ample time to at least make an effort to stop it. Doubtless they foresaw what the effect of it must be and simply let it come.

If the Coronado was not a shrewdly laid trap for the miners, it was at least providential for the mine owners, notwithstanding the deplorable incidents that attended it. It was to the Leadville miners what the "sunken road of Ohain" was to the French army on the field of Waterloo.[31]

I have intimated that even if the unfortunate attack had not been made on the Coronado, it is extremely doubtful if a settlement could have been effected by mutual concession or compromise.

The mine managers were not friendly to the union before the strike, and when it was declared, they avowed their hostility to the organization and determined to disrupt it. Upon this point there is no room for doubt. Two days after the strike had been declared, on June 22, they entered into a written agreement which, among other things, provided to "not recognize or treat in any manner or at any time with any labor organization."

This settled the matter. It was, in fact, an agreement not to treat with the miners at all and a declaration of war upon their organization. The miners struck, of course, as an organized body, and if they could not negotiate a settlement of their grievance as such, there was nothing left for them but unconditional surrender. This was the central, commanding issue, in fact the only issue, from the day the strike was inaugurated.

If the right of workingmen to organize be conceded—and the most implacable foe of labor dare not go before the American public in opposition to this right—can the arbitrary attitude of the mine managers be justified on any reasonable ground? This "agreement" not to treat with the miners, for that was the purport and import of the compact, was not prompted by the lawlessness or violence of the strikers, for none had been committed. It was entered into in the very beginning of the strike, it barred the door of conciliation and made "unconditional surrender" the only possible basis of settlement. This indisputable fact effectually silences the claim of the mine managers that during the early stage of the strike they proposed arbitration as a basis of settlement, and that their proposition was rejected by the strikers. The "agreement" and the alleged proposal to arbitrate are diametrically contradictory to each other, and hence the conclusion that the contention of the strikers that no proposal of arbitration was ever made by the mine managers was correct and must be admitted.

It is axiomatic that a rule, to be fair, must work both ways. Suppose that the miners, immediately upon declaring the strike, had entered into an agreement "not to recognize or treat in any manner or at any time" with any organization of mine managers? And suppose that in spite of all entreaties they had tenaciously adhered to this agreement and insisted upon the unconditional surrender and utter humiliation of the mine managers, even though such a policy meant misery to thousands, the loss of untold property interests, and the irretrievable ruin of the camp? In reviewing the Leadville strike, these interrogatories are in order and are well calculated to challenge thought and reflection in the minds of all men who love justice and fair play.

The Degradation of Mine Labor†

May 5, 1897

Terre Haute, Ind., May 5, 1897

In the article preceding this, I said that the paramount issue with the mine owners was the disruption of the miners' union. The question of wages could, and doubtless would, have been readily settled. Indeed, it is doubtful if upon this question alone the strike had ever been declared. The only effect of the question of wages was to speedily and thoroughly organize the miners. As soon as the matter of demanding increased wages was raised, men fairly flocked into the union, and it is in order to remark that if the increase had been secured, many of them would have been as prompt to flock out again.

There are workingmen who never join a union unless they have a personal grievance or want their pay raised, and then they rush into a union with a whoop and precipitate a strike, and when the strike is over, whether it succeeds or fails, their fit of unionism is ended, and they recede as unceremoniously as they appeared. Such men have no conception of union principles and are always a detriment to an organization. They are animated wholly by selfish motives. They do not join a union because they approve its principles or are in sympathy with its mission, or because of a desire to help their fellow men, but simply and solely to use it as emergency may require, to accomplish their own selfish ends. If the union happens to succeed, they pocket the benefits but never attend another meeting, nor pay another cent of dues. If failure results, they are the first to pour their denunciations upon the leaders for having "sold them out" and to condemn and renounce the union for having "beat them out of their jobs."

In this, of course, they have a chorus of sympathetic "amens" from plutocrats and their hirelings and parasites, generally including the press and often the pulpit, who, while feigning to commiserate with the poor "dupes," as they are termed, for having been led astray by designing agitators, proceed to traduce the leaders and misrepresent and vilify the union, and thus the organization is made to appear as a reprehensible conspiracy and is riven asunder, and the now defenseless employees settle down to their tasks, dismayed and

† Published as "How It Is Done" in *The Western Miner*, vol. 1, no. 30 (May 8, 1897), 1.

disheartened, while the screws are applied to them more vigorously than ever, and with accelerating rapidity they begin the downward course to degradation. I have neither time nor space to elucidate the point, but this is the outline of the process whereby the once-independent, self-respecting American workman has been reduced to mendicancy and servitude.

The state of Pennsylvania affords a humiliating illustration. The investigation just authorized by the state legislature has disclosed a most shocking state of affairs. Twenty years ago, the coal miners of that state could make from $4 to $6 per day. Now at the very best they cannot average to exceed $1 per day; in many cases they cannot make more than 50 cents, while others are only able to average 25 cents per day. What a tragic enactment on American soil, wet with the blood of the world's noblest martyrs, that liberty, equality, and justice might be the heritage of all, and this to gratify the insatiate lust for wealth and power.

Is the situation overdrawn? Do I hear it said that such talk is merely the gabble of a walking delegate, the raving of a lying agitator who is trying to stir up discontent? Listen, ye Americans, and especially ye who froth about organized labor and refuse to treat with it. Listen, I say, to what follows, for these workingmen are not organized. *Once they were.* They took the advice of some of our present-day employers, including certain mine managers. They abjured organized labor and "preserved their independence" and *relied upon the honor of their employers to do them justice,* and this has brought them to the 25 cents per day level, a rate of wages that an average Chinaman would scorn to work for.

Here is a brief extract from the report just issued in reference to the legislative investigation:

> The legislative committee that is investigating the condition of the miners of the Pittsburgh district completed its second day of personal inspection among the mines, and what the investigators witnessed would fill many large volumes. When the work was finished, the members of the committee made the statement that no such suffering was ever known by them to exist before, and they are well convinced that something must be done, and at once, to alleviate the condition of the unfortunate thousands who are in the district.
>
> The territory that was inspected today was in and about Banning on the P&LE Railroad,[32] about 40 miles above Pittsburgh.
>
> The mines are located at Banning station and are worked by about 100 miners. One half of that number could easily do the work, for the men do not get more than two or three days a week. When they do work,

> the cars are so scarce that no matter how hard they try, they are unable to make more than $1 a day at the outside, and very much more frequently their pay for the day is from 25 to 50 cents. The greater part of these employees are foreigners, there being but ten American-born families in the entire number.
>
> After leaving the settlement in and about Banning, the committee went to Jacobs Creek, about three miles below Banning, where the Darr mines of Osborne and Saeger are located. The condition of the miners here is worse, if anything, than at the mines at Banning. The men work from three to four days a week, but the wages they receive are so small that they can scarcely manage to exist. The greater part of the miners are foreigners, with a good sprinkling of Americans and Negroes.
>
> The company owns the miserable hovels which shelter the inhabitants. One of the most wretched is a shed about 18 x 12 feet. For this hovel the company received $4 per month, and it would cost about $25 to build it. The occupants of the house are Peter Jones, his wife and child, and eight "boarders." Where these eleven persons manage to find room enough to stretch out at night is a mystery. Inside there was a varied assortment of furniture, for the cooking, eating, and sleeping is all done in one room. "We just manage to live," said Mrs. Jones, "but if it was not for the boarders that we keep Peter could not make enough in the mines to keep us from starvation."

Here is food for a whole freight train of thought, and for none more than for western miners. Mine managers can also contemplate this appalling picture at their leisure, and if they are not destitute of heart and soul and conscience (and some, I know, are not), they will not only cease their antagonism to union labor but will encourage the men to organize and, with words of kindness and encouragement, do their best to secure and maintain harmonious relations and present a solid front against such Siberiazation of the western states. But aside from all ethical consideration, such a policy of degradation as reduced the once proud state of Pennsylvania to a plague spot is ruinous and destructive. The famishing miner is followed by the bankrupt operator. Read this dispatch, which I clip from this morning's paper:

> PITTSBURGH, April 29 [1897]. John M. Risher, the big coal operator, has confessed judgment to his wife for the sum of $115,376 on notes given to her at diverse times. Mr. Risher was supposed to be one of the wealthiest operators in the district. No reason for the judgment is given except the disastrous condition of the coal business.

Here we have an exhibition of the logical consequences of the intolerant, impoverishing policy of crushing labor.[33] This is the story briefly told: Organized capital—Organized labor—Strike—Nothing to arbitrate—Riots—Soldiers—Injunction—Labor vanquished—Reduced wages—Tramps—Bankruptcy—General demoralization and all-around ruin.

But fortunately such calamities are not unmixed evils. They are not only fruitful of lessons to observant men, but they are the means of shaking to their foundation and ultimately destroying old systems and decaying institutions and preparing the way for the new, and thus making possible the material progress and moral development of the world.

The Constitution Says People May Bear Arms: Statement to the Press in Salt Lake City†

May 11, 1897

Eugene V. Debs was seen at his room in the Grand Pacific Hotel yesterday afternoon [May 11, 1897] and, asked for an expression on President Boyce's inflammatory address, counseling workingmen to arm themselves.[34]

I am heartily in accord with Boyce's sentiments. The speech has no special significance. The Constitution says people may bear arms, so there is nothing unlawful about it. We see inoculated in every limb of the social makeup this idea of bearing arms. Every university and college has its military organizations in some form. Even Sunday schools resort to military drills. So I repeat that everywhere and all about us is being fostered a tendency toward militarism. Why should not the workingmen have their organizations, their rifle clubs?

Experience has taught us lately that on every occasion when force of arms has been invoked it has been to suppress labor. When appeals to arms have been made to the authorities, it has been at the behests of corporate capital and

---

† Published as "How Debs Views It" in *Salt Lake Herald,* vol. 27, no. 168 (May 12, 1897), 2.

always for the one purpose of overcoming the workingman. If no provocation exists, then it is a rank injustice.

Corporations do not hesitate to instigate lawlessness for the purpose of calling out the militia. Recalling the Cripple Creek strikes, we remember that 100 deputies were called out to shoot down the miners without provocation, and the governor of the state[35] took cognizance of this fact and at once ordered out the militia to suppress the deputies. Who suffered? Not the deputies, but the poor workingmen.

You must bear in mind labor has practically no rights when compared with capital. The latter controls everything. Why should not the working classes improve their condition in every way?

I see nothing in Mr. Boyce's attitude or in that of the organization he represents, in the event of his recommendations being carried out, that is not in perfect harmony with the constitution of our country. These men are all American citizens, animated by patriotic motives, and in taking this position the purpose is not to resist lawful authority, but to maintain it.

The Coming Republic†

May 30, 1897

The steady stream of earnest, anxious inquiry given rise by the recent announcement relative to the national cooperation movement proposed to be launched at Chicago next month [June 1897] indicates with unerring certainty the ardent and widespread interest in and approbation of the scheme. Thousands of struggling, suffering unemployed have hailed it as a benediction. It has revived their drooping spirits and restored some measure of their lost faith. Many professional and business people have volunteered their aid and encouragement; not a few well-to-do have expressed interest and sympathy, while others, including some of our most eminent citizens, have pledged their moral and material support.

Some opposition has, of course, been aroused. This is not only expected but is essential to success. Any project designed to alter the "existing order of

† Published in *New York Journal,* May 30, 1897, unspecified page.

things" which fails to provoke opposition must also fail to enlist support. Lack of vitality to offend in certain quarters means impotency and failure. The greatest blessings which have come to the world have had to force their way through the fiercest and most powerful opposition.

In presenting my views on this matter, it should be understood that I speak for myself alone. I have my own ideas as to what should be done in the present crisis by the approaching convention,[36] but what action the delegates may conclude to take cannot be foreshadowed. I am persuaded, however, from my intimate association with them, that they will respond to the great and growing demand and pronounce in favor of the national cooperative commonwealth and lay deep and strong the foundations of a mighty organization designed to accomplish this seemingly herculean task.

The most popular feature of the plan, especially with the unemployed, is that proposing the colonization of some western state presenting the best advantages, securing political control under forms of law, and establishing within the limitations of the federal jurisdiction the cooperative commonwealth. A singular spectacle is presented in the malevolent opposition to this part of the movement, which comes almost wholly from those who sneer at the unemployed as "tramps and loafers" and yet are now wrought into a frenzy at the mere suggestion that this element is to remove and sequestrate in some distant and uninhabited part of the country.

There are two social systems which have been in conflict since the human race began, and never more intensely so than at the present time. Under the one, the few enjoy and the many are doomed to serve as beasts of burden. The favored few, the beneficiaries of this beautiful system, honestly believe, for the most part, that it is ordained of God that a chosen few shall rule and that the masses shall toil and suffer and submit in silence, and any attempt to change or modify the situation they regard as dangerous and wicked and resent as an assault upon the very life of society. It is scarcely required to observe that this is the system under which we now live. Under the other system, the earth and the fullness thereof become the common heritage of *all* the people. There are no favored classes, no special privileges, but all have equal right to help themselves to nature's bounties and equal opportunity to enjoy the good things with which the earth abounds. This is the system that is to be, and all the evolutionary forces are pledged to achieve its triumph.

The former system is known as the competitive system and its motto is "survival of the fittest." It is a species of war which transforms mankind into a race of Ishmaelites.[37] The strong, keen, cunning, unscrupulous, merciless, and remorseless triumph. The weak, tender, sympathetic, conscientious, humane, and loving go to the wall. Murder, suicide, poverty, misery, prostitution, bankruptcy, fraud, insanity, and all their brood of woes tell the story of the cannibalistic conquest. Were this social state to continue forever, then, indeed, would Huxley's prayer that some stray comet might dash against this wretched earth and hurl it from existence become "a consummation devoutly to be wished."[38]

Now, as to the plans for establishing the new order of things. First of all, thorough organization on progressive lines will be required, and this is well under way in many sections. The movement to be launched in Chicago next month contemplates the unification of all workers, organized and unorganized, and all others, regardless of sex or color, who favor a change in our social and industrial affairs and believe it can be brought about only by a complete change of our social and industrial system. A constitution, brief and to the point, will be adopted and a declaration of principles issued. A corps of competent organizers will be at once placed in the field, and local branches will be instituted in every state of the union. A small admission fee will be charged and a small annual per capita tax levied, for which each member will receive a copy of the official paper of the organization, and it is proposed to make this the very best paper of its kind issued. Experience has taught that there is nothing weaker than organized ignorance. From the very beginning, powerful educational influences will be set in operation. In connection with the paper, which, as stated, will be first class in every particular, there will be established a book and pamphlet department and placed in charge of a competent manager, and every good work and treatise upon economics and kindred subjects can be here obtained at actual cost. A modern and well-equipped printing plant will be established and economic literature will be produced in cheap editions and large quantities, which will be freely distributed, especially among the poor, who lack the means to buy.

The various local branches will be duly chartered, and the membership will probably be limited to 500 members per branch. As members are enrolled, they are given the opportunity to place opposite their names the respective amounts of the voluntary monthly contributions which they are willing to make to advance the cause. Each will be expected to contribute in proportion to his or her means, while those who are poor or out of employment will be entirely exempt. The amounts so collected will be placed in the cooperative fund, and this will be in charge of a board of five or more careful, capable, and trustworthy persons under whose supervision it will be expended subject to such regulations as the organization may prescribe.

Before adjourning, the convention will name a board whose duty shall be to examine into the matter of selecting a state in which to begin operations. This board will make a thorough examination of the advantages presented by each state, as well as the objections, visiting the capital cities of the various states for the purpose and there holding meetings from day to day and hearing reports and testimony until a full and exhaustive showing has been made. That strong inducements will be offered by a number of western states is assured by the voluminous correspondence already on file. At the close of its investigation, the board will report to the executive board of the organization and the two boards in joint session will decide upon the state in which the beginning is to be made.

At the adjournment of the convention, or shortly afterward, a recruiting office will be established in connection with the general offices of the organization, and here will be recruited the bodies of men who, in such detachments as may be decided upon, will proceed to the state selected for their reception. The first of these pioneers will, no doubt, be required to march, but this will be done under perfect order and discipline. First of all, each applicant for enlistment must be examined and accepted by the recruiting officers. Only such will be accepted as comprehend fully the nature of the undertaking, the purpose sought to be accomplished, and whose hearts are thoroughly in the movement. Respect for discipline and obedience to regulations will be exacted. The advance bodies will probably consist wholly of unmarried men or men without families. That they may have to endure some privations is altogether probable, but they will be men of such fiber, and the conviction that they are the progenitors of a new humanity will burn and glow in their breasts with such intensity that come what may, they will have the courage and fidelity to stand and withstand until success is achieved. With these men, there will be something more than a principle involved. They will be animated by a fervor akin to religious zeal. The cause in which they enlist and to which they pledge devotion will be to them as sacred a cause as ever prompted men to action.

Those unduly excited persons who fear that there is to be an exodus of "bums and beats" may possess their souls in patience. Parenthetically, it may be here remarked that they who go into spasms at the mere mention of the Ragged Army of the Republic are the very ones who are responsible for its existence. Without pauperism there could be no plutocracy, and yet plutocracy has a horror of pauperism.

The men who will start west as the pioneers in the new movement will be neither mendicants nor highwaymen. They will be men, self-reliant and self-respecting; men "who know their rights, and knowing, dare to maintain them;" men, poor though they be, infinitely superior in heart and soul and conscience to the miserable creatures who at so much per line make them the subjects of stupid jokes, and attempt by falsehood and misrepresentation to surround them with odium and doom them to failure and disappointment. Such hirelings of corporate capital may do their worst, but they will never stay the march of this emancipating movement.

The question is now asked, how are these men to be supported? The answer is, from funds of the general organization, and only such members will be started as can be provided for until they are able to provide for themselves. The general organization should, and doubtless will, soon number 100,000 contributing members, and this number will steadily and rapidly increase. With such a membership, there will be no trouble in raising at least $25,000 per month. With this amount, the pioneers can be provided for, lands can be secured, agricultural machinery purchased, factories erected, and such productive enterprises established as the state may be best adapted to. All of this will be well underway prior to the next following state election. At the proper time, a complete ticket of cooperators will be placed in the field, and all the leaders of the movement will unite in a thorough canvass of the state. After achieving success at the polls, the legislature will be convened and a constitutional convention called. A new constitution compatible with the cooperative commonwealth will be adopted. This will be supplemented by suitable legislation. The public will acquire ownership and control of all the means of production and distribution, and there will be one state beneath the American flag in which a man, willing to work, will be able to secure employment. The work of developing the resources of the state, organizing industrial enterprises, building roads, canals, schoolhouses, public buildings, etc., will be vigorously prosecuted. The money question will be solved by the labor exchange system. The labor check will relegate the legal tender to the limbo of the obsolete.

The hours of labor will be shortened in proportion to the inventive progress and the number of able-bodied workers. There will be no idlers. They who will not work may not eat. All men will engage in useful occupation, and each will secure the full product of his toil.

All this will, of course, have to be carried forward within the limitations of the federal constitution. But in the meantime, the work of organizing will be carried forward with unabated energy in every part of the country. Other states will fall into line, for the success of the first will inspire others to emulation. In the national campaign of 1900, the new movement will be a factor in the election. Its political principles will be those of the Socialist Labor Party and its political battles will doubtless be fought under the banner of that party. In that election, 2 million votes should be polled, and in the national campaign following, in 1904, the great cooperative party, the party of equal rights and equal opportunities for all the people, should carry the country, and then the Cooperative Commonwealth will be fully established. Gaunt famine and the specter of failure will be remembered only as hideous nightmares. Humanity will then be emancipated from the horrible thralldoms which a soulless money oligarchy has forced upon it, and a free and happy people will march forward with majestic strides toward a diviner civilization.

Eugene V. Debs

An Anniversary Retrospective of the Great Leadville Strike†

May 31, 1897

Terre Haute, Ind., May 31, 1897

It was a year ago this month that the Leadville strike was declared. A world of history has been made since that time. The experience of the Leadville miners in encountering defeat after a long and weary struggle has been shared by hundreds of thousands of other workingmen, representing nearly all the trades known to modern industry. A few years ago, before the days of great combines, labor organizations were frequently able to not only prevent reductions but to secure increases in wages. They had a powerful restraining effect upon those who sought to reduce labor, for an organized strike was at best disastrous and a thing to be avoided. It is different now. The strike is now courted on the least provocation. It gives the corporation little or no inconvenience, for all it has to do is lay back until the government—municipal, state, or federal, as the case may be—suppresses the strike and starves or jails the strikers. *Capital has profited by the lessons taught by strikes, just as we want the miners at Leadville and elsewhere to do.*

† Published as "Lesson of the Great Strike" in *The Western Miner,* vol. 1, no. 34 (June 5, 1897), 1.

The Leadville strike cost the miners, in wages lost and in cash contributions, about $1.5 million. Think of this vast sum taken from the earnings of a comparatively small body of workingmen for the purchase of idleness and all the woes that follow in its train. I write in no spirit of lamentation or regret. In writing of labor's adversities, croaking is never in order. I simply call attention to certain facts as a basis to certain conclusions. The Leadville strike, if we are stupid and unreasoning, will be a total loss, but if we are wise, it will be worth every dollar it cost many times over.

The Leadville miners were as thoroughly organized as it was possible for them to be. They had the solid support of the Western Federation of Miners, the most aggressive and powerful labor organization in the West. They were able to hold their men together, practically without a break, for more than eight months, and yet they were defeated. Could they have won by holding out longer? No. Why? For several reasons.

First, the mine owners' and managers' association was composed in the main of very rich men, and they could afford to wait indefinitely. They had vast holdings elsewhere, and whether the mines at Leadville were in operation for a year or two or not did not prevent them from eating three square meals a day. Theirs was simply to *wait,* and as long as they were enduring no privations, they could afford to do that. The temporary loss thus entailed, whatever that might amount to, is always made good by reductions of wages after the strikers are starved back into submission.

Second, at the back (or in front) of the mine owners stood the state militia, the judicial guard, and all the resources of the state, and if this did not suffice, the president of the United States, the regular army, the navy, and all the organized forces of the national government. See? Organized capital is not only supported by the government, right or wrong, *it is* the government. They are synonymous terms.

Third, the country is swarming with idle men, miners as well as others, many of whom are verging on starvation. These are the product of the capitalistic system of production, and they constitute a factor in labor strikes which decrees inevitably the defeat of labor.

No labored argument is required to demonstrate that to strike under such conditions is wasteful, if not criminal folly. The contest is fearfully uneven. Labor is certain to be beaten and to have to foot the bill besides. What then? Let us reason together.

Suppose the miners now had the million and a half dollars the strike cost them, and suppose further that they concluded to go into the mining business themselves. Why not? Who dare say the proposition is not practicable? But it is not required to have so large a sum to begin with. A few thousand dollars would answer. The union could select three good members to supervise affairs and, by judicious management, cooperative mining could soon be established, and instead of miners working out their lives to enrich a few individuals, they would be doing something for themselves. This would not be all there is in cooperative industry, for this, to have the proper results, must be general, but it would end wage-slavery among the miners and at the same time be a ling stride in the right direction.

The wage system is at the foundation of labor's wrongs, and these will not be righted until the system is abolished. As long as thousands of workingmen depend for employment upon the assent of an individual, they are in fetters, and the Declaration of Independence is a falsehood and a mockery. There is no equality of men in such a situation. One is master in all the term implies, and the other are slaves. One commands and the others obey, and in these latter days even the opportunity to yield abject obedience has become a precious privilege.

This cruel, unnatural system cannot always prevail. Indeed, there are ten thousand evidences that it is even now in the grasp of dissolution. All that is required to send it tottering to its fall, never to rise again, is a little common sense among the common people.

That the Leadville miners and the western miners in general will profit by the lessons taught by the Leadville strike, I do not doubt. Already, the voices of the leaders are ringing out clearly in advocacy of more advanced ideas and more progressive policies, and when 12 months more have elapsed, the rank and file, remembering that a few mine owners had sufficient power to defy the governor, the legislature, and the entire commonwealth of Colorado, will take an inventory of their own resources of intelligence, courage, and independence and resolve to be free men, and thus the Leadville strike will have contributed its full share toward the emancipation of labor.

The Cooperative Commonwealth†

June 1, 1897

Terre Haute, Ind., June 1, 1897

The main purpose of the approaching special convention of the American Railway Union, to be held at Chicago beginning June 15 [1897], will be to declare in favor of the cooperative commonwealth, and to widen the scope of the organization so that all persons favorable to cooperative industry, regardless of color, sex, or occupation, can unite in one body for the promotion of this great object.[39]

It is conceded by practically all economic authorities that the present industrial system, in the light of modern progress in the methods of production and distribution, is not only a failure, but that it is fruitful of cruel injustice to labor, and utterly demoralizing to society, and that these ills cannot be remedied until the system which breeds them is abolished.

Uplifting of Humanity

In other words, the competitive wage system, under which labor has been reduced to a commodity and thousands of workingmen depend for employment upon the assent of an individual, is to be supplanted by the cooperative system, under which all may engage in useful occupation and work together in harmonious cooperation for the emancipation of labor, the uplifting of humanity, and the advancement of our civilization.

It is proposed to organize branches in all the villages, towns, and cities of all the states and territories in the Union, and by voluntary monthly contributions to provide sufficient means to colonize the unemployed in some western state, to be hereafter agreed upon, and to secure lands and establish industries upon a cooperative basis, in which they shall find employment and gradually build up their institutions, and thus prepare the way for the fraternal commonwealth.

† Written for the Scripps-McRae League. As published in the *Cincinnati Post,* June 3, 1897, unspecified page. Copy preserved in *Papers of Eugene V. Debs* microfilm edition, reel 9.

Million Supporters

It is believed that the time is propitious for the new movement, and that, within a short time after it is launched, it will have a million active supporters.

By uniting at the ballot box, political control of the state selected for colonization can be secured, and the organic law can then be modified so as to admit of the cooperative commonwealth being established, subject, of course, to the limitations of the federal jurisdiction.

This will be but the beginning, for the movement is national in its scope, and, as it is designed to emancipate labor from wage bondage and clothe American citizenship with its intended liberty, equality, and dignity, there is no doubt that the new life will spread from state to state until the Republic is redeemed and we are a nation of free and happy people.

Labor's New Eden: Interview with the *Chicago Chronicle*†

June 14, 1897

Bright and happy at the prospects of this, his crowning ambition, Eugene V. Debs stepped from a train at the Dearborn Station at 6:00 last night and warmly greeted a group of waiting friends. With him from Terre Haute came his brother, Theodore, Sylvester Keliher, and George P. Keeney. Showing little of the fatigue of recent work and travel, the president of the American Railway Union talked earnestly and animatedly of his project.

Never were the masses in America so badly off as at present. Menacing the happiness of the country and the continued freedom of its people from turbulence is an army of not less than 5 million persons out of employment. Every passing hour adds to their ranks. Introduction of new machinery, improvements on old appliances, the concentration of wealth, and other conditions are throwing people out of employment all the time. Millions are looking into a future that has

† Published as part of "Labor's New Eden" in *Chicago Chronicle,* vol. 3, no. 19 (June 15, 1897), 1.

no light, no hope. We propose to take them where they can, at the worst, find means of existence and may discover prosperity and have congenial occupation.

Trade unionism furnishes no adequate remedy for the terrible evils which confront the toilers. Organized labor, simply by the fact of its union, cannot hope to cope with organized capital. If all the workers in the country were organized at the present time and engaged in a concerted warfare with capital, they would be beaten. The people who have the money also hold all the means of production, of distribution, and of purchase. They could starve out their antagonists, who possess nothing. We offer a different solution of the labor problem and one which does not contemplate a battle with capital. Our ideas are endorsed by men of many classes and opposed by none.

Capitalists Approve It

Surely the capitalist who abhors socialism, the man who has money and whose secure interests are threatened by the imminence of an uprising of the starving millions will not object to the removal of this menacing multitude to a district thousands of miles away, where they will be industrious and contribute to the welfare of the country. He need not be philanthropic in order to endorse the movement; he need only consult his own interest. I have deep faith that our project will be successful and will exert a beneficial influence on all mankind. Even if it should fail, it may be the means of opening up an avenue that may yield the desired result.

[In this way,] revolution may be averted. It [*illegible*], but it is near enough [to be] threatening. The unrest and discontent of the idle, whom the ordinary citizen does not see, is like the seething of a giant subterranean cauldron. We seek to remove this condition, which is the result of want and inaction, by substituting for them occupation and opportunity of subsistence. I explain these circumstances to demonstrate that there are many sources, not apparent to one who does not reflect, from which will proceed abundant aid for the consummation of our scheme.

The plans which will be adopted by the convention have for their foundation the exodus of the cooperators to a western state. First of all, there are numerous places we can go. We have had invitations to settle in dozens of states. Governor Rogers[40] of Washington urges selection of that state, and places which have thus far been considered with most favor are Washington, Utah, Idaho, and Texas. Immense tracts of fertile land are there which can soon be irrigated and upon which can be built homes and stores and factories which will produce not only enough for the consumption of the community, but a surplus which can be sold to the outside world. For we do not contemplate isolating ourselves, but will keep in touch with the country and widen our propaganda until cooperation becomes the system of America.

The Advance Guard

A few thousand men will proceed within a few weeks to the location selected by the convention and will prepare abiding places for the great armies that will follow. Our only difficulty will be in transporting the advance guard. They may have to walk—orderly and peaceably, of course. But we are confident that, as our ideas become understood, we will have ample funds to start, given up not only by our friends and sympathizers in trade unions and schools of economic thought all over the country, but also from the capitalists, who will be glad to see the idle millions—the "tramps," as they are called—melt away from the cities and the byways like snow. Out of the small membership fee and per-capita tax that are charged, there will soon be a revenue of $25,000 a month. This will buy lands, procure agricultural implements, tools for building, machinery for factories, and such other articles as are needed at once.

Women will go. It will be a community of families and homes. The people will be educated. They will have newspapers and literature of the right kind, and they will represent organized intelligence and knowledge. They will develop the resources of the state, organize industrial enterprises, build roads, canals, schoolhouses, and public buildings.

We will have short hours of labor. Six hours a day for each man will be sufficient to produce enough for the community. The man who toils the hardest will work the fewest hours. The common store will supply all. The kitchen in the home will be abolished, and food will be distributed from a common kitchen. The general conduct of the colony will be such as the federal statutes will countenance, and it will be a happy, bright spot in civilization, where men will be brothers.

Opening Address at the Special Convention of the American Railway Union in Chicago†

June 15, 1897

Ladies and Gentlemen, Friends and Coworkers:—

We have assembled here in the paragon city of Chicago under the auspices of the American Railway Union to deliberate upon propositions which relate to industrial and economic affairs.

We are here as the representatives of labor, which, overleaping the narrower limits of unions, lodges, divisions, and guilds, inscribes upon its banner the conquering shibboleth, "Humanity," and goes forth to battle with one supreme, overmastering purpose in view, that of bettering the conditions of men and women who work and whose only capital is their brains and their hands.

The toilers of all enlightened nations, by which I mean those who comprehend their unalienable right to "life, liberty, and the pursuit of happiness," by processes of mind evolution, have arrived at the conclusion that their mission in the world is something superior to eternal servitude; that they were designed by their Creator to occupy positions superior to beasts of burden, to "dumb, driven cattle,"[41] superior to the coral insect which builds, and dies as it builds, superior to the worm that spins silk, lays its egg to perpetuate its toiling race, and dies.

But they find that after all the centuries of toil, servitude, and denigration, conditions remain essentially unchanged, except in those rare and widely separated instances when they have sought to achieve some measure of emancipation from their thralldoms by breaking the fetters which their masters had forged.

But history, that "register of the crimes, follies, and misfortunes of mankind,"[42] reveals the fact that the wage system, which is of necessity slavery, hoary with age and forever producing the same results, has created and perpetuated conditions at the mere mention of which humanity shudders.

But I should do violence to the truth and perpetuate the crime of ingratitude if I were to intimate that, amidst all the gloom of the centuries, the star of Hope had not held its place and cheered humanity to struggle for better conditions, and I should be untrue to my own convictions if I were to deny

† Published in *Railway Times,* vol. 4, no. 12 (June 15, 1897), 1–3.

that even now, as 1800 years ago, there is heard above all the sordid strife and tumult of the world the promise, "On earth peace, good will toward men."[43]

In the onward march of civilization and evolution, in the majestic mustering of the mind forces of the world, whose achievements make facts more wonderful than the creations of fancy, when the world, by the wires on which electricity travels with the speed of thought, is made a whispering gallery, when cities rise and flourish as if by magic, when in all the earth there is no *terra incognita,*[44] when steam and electricity on the land and on the sea are solving all the problems of commerce, and man stands forth by the fiat of his own genius the crowned conqueror of nature, I ask, in this period of sublime achievements, what benefits have come to the great family of toilers, without whose work the world would roll in space a wilderness? I answer, they are just where they were when the Pharaohs built the pyramids with their slaves and kings built cities for their own glory.

The wage system, in spite of all the refinements of sophistication, is the same in all ages, in all lands, and in all climes. Its victims work, propagate their species, bear all the burdens, and perish.

I am not here to denounce capital, nor am I here to expound my views of the rich, not even of that gentleman who discarded the beggar at his gate, and soon after "lifted up his eyes in hell."[45] Men, as a rule, are the product of conditions, circumstances, environments, and these are favorable or unfavorable, men become useful or useless, noble or ignoble, good or bad. It is, therefore, not with the individual that I have to do, but with the system of society that produces him and is responsible for him, and my purpose is to discuss conditions and aid as best I can in pointing out means of relief for those of my fellow toilers who believe that the time has come when better conditions for multiplied thousands can be secured.

I am not unmindful of the fact that there are those who disagree with us and who maintain that there can be no relief while any part of the wage system remains. They insist that the present competitive system must be completely overthrown and not a vestige of it left in any department of activity, on a foot of our soil, before permanent relief to the suffering masses can be provided. With these good people I have no quarrel. Indeed, among those who are pledged to the cooperative commonwealth and who differ as to method only, there is no occasion for unfriendly feeling and all I need to say is that while we propose to battle with all our energy and zeal to carry out our plans for immediate relief, there will be no abatement in our efforts to further the cause of socialism in general until its universal triumph is proclaimed—and we are impressed with the conviction that nothing heretofore attempted in our country is so well calculated to augment the hosts in the fraternal faith and hasten the divine day of deliverance as the work we are about to undertake.

It is well enough to extol the beauties of the ideal system, but in the presence of existing conditions, when millions are suffering, many of them tortured by hunger pangs and driven to desperation and despair, and all this in sight of fabulous resources, something should be done and done *now,* and though the whole world cried out in opposition, I should still favor immediate action on such lines as common sense commended and to such an extent as ceaseless effort and indomitable will made possible, in preference to serene contemplation of these horrors while awaiting the ushering in of the millennium by the ordinary processes in operation. Even though we fail—but we shall not fail, for our mission is sacred as ever aroused men to action, and tens of thousands will at once rally beneath our standard in every state of the Union, and cheered and sustained and reinforced by succeeding tens of thousands, press forward with the resistless ardor of a new crusade, nor will they be deflected from their course the breadth of a hair until slavery in every form has been abolished and humanity rises to exaltation, redeemed, regenerated, and disenthralled.

The fetters of the slave and the scourge of the master symbolize the reign of competitive commercialism, and while the barbarous system is suffered to endure, the Declaration of Independence is a meaningless platitude and our much-vaunted free institutions a delusion and a sham. Not until slave and master have both disappeared, and forever, and the equal freedom of all has been established, can we lay any proper claim to civilization.

No proposition will be accepted by the convention which will not withstand the severest criticism, which is fully expected. Neither the magnitude of the task we are about to undertake nor the power of the opposing forces is underestimated. You will observe when this convention is organized for business that only such propositions will be submitted as will have the endorsement of a host of the best thinkers in the land—students of affairs, men and women of large intellectual endowments, wide and varied knowledge and profoundly interested in the welfare of society. Some of these thinkers, interested in industrial, economic, and humanitarian affairs, will participate in the deliberations of the convention. They know, as Goldsmith knew, as we all know that

> Ill fares the land to hastening ills a prey,
> Where wealth accumulates and men decay [46]

and they know, as we all know, that the twin curse has long since reached the United States of America. Here, wealth has accumulated until individual fortunes deny computation; here, men by millions are decaying, and here the ills which the author of "The Deserted Village" so graphically portrayed are epidemic, and are spreading with alarming rapidity from the center, in every possible direction, over the land.

In certain quarters, it is esteemed a duty to indulge in criticisms designed to make any and every humanitarian enterprise the butt for ridicule and contempt, and to characterize their authors as vagarists, if nothing worse, and their schemes as senseless and impossible. But such a course, designed to work disaster and perpetuate wretchedness in the interest of those who profit by it, no longer intimidates those who, amidst storms and battles, have achieved so much self-emancipation as to dare to think for themselves, and have learned outside of optimistic and pessimistic schools that they must work out their own salvation and not trust the "ordering" of events relating to the emancipation of others, not even to that inscrutable "divinity" which is said to "shape our ends, rough-hew them how we will,"[47] nor supinely wait for that one "tide in the affairs of men that leads on to fortune,"[48] but with will and courage and self-reliance hew out for themselves new pathways to better conditions.

The past is not a sealed book. Whatever have been the trophies of our boasted civilization, the emancipation of wage-slavery does not appear in its list of victories. Nowhere on the face of the earth has a monument been erected as a memorial of such an event. The combined forces of religion, education, science, and civilization have been unequal to the task of so shaping affairs as to permit men who toil to own themselves. The wage system has held them with unrelaxing grasp in perpetual bondage.

We have had the declaration from an inspired apostle of the Christian religion that "God is no respecter of persons."[49] We have it incorporated in our Declaration of Independence that "all men are created equal," and we have constitutions and statutes in consonance with the declaration, but it is held that the cruelty of the wage system can in no wise be modified; that while "men may come and men may go," the system, like the brook in the poem, must flow on forever; that wage-slavery is the one curse for which there is no redress, and that labor must forever be the creator of wealth in which its share is bare subsistence and, all too often, a cipher at the right hand of a decimal point.

But the "thorny stem of Time" is even now budding with cheering indications that a new dispensation is at hand.

What is this new dispensation, and what does it signify?

In the presence of this audience, made up of workers and thinkers, I would not, even if I had the tongue of an angel, seek to encourage delusive hopes.

My experience and observation teach me that we live at a time in the history of our country when industrial conditions are of a character which everywhere excite unrest and alarm. Business prostration is universal. "Confidence" seems to have taken to itself wings and flown away, and so far as the most penetrating vision can discern there is no indication that it will ever return. In the meantime, the gloom that has settled down upon the country deepens into darkness, nor would relief come to the disemployed millions if confidence were to return tomorrow, simply because there are more workers by far than can find employment under the most favorable conditions possible under the present system, and because the number of enforced idlers is steadily and rapidly increasing by reason of the labor-displacing machine which, under the capitalist system of production, has doomed labor to fathomless depths of servitude, suffering, and degradation.

Statistics relating to the vast army of men, women, and children who toil for a living in all our centers of population constitute a picture of poverty which cannot be contemplated without the most painful forebodings of ills which affright courageous men. Hunger and squalor in a land of fabulous plenty is a condition which, whatever else may be said, demonstrates beyond controversy that the Almighty does not rule in the councils of nations and if, in the onward march of mind evolution, men are at last convinced that they must emancipate themselves from bondage, it is all that can be hoped for. No miracles will be wrought to supply men with food, clothing, and shelter. No northern blast will be tempered to a southern zephyr in response to the bleatings of the shorn lamb. No "five thousand men, besides women and children" will be "fed with five loaves and two fishes." No ravens will feed the lone tramp in the fence corner or under a haystack. No widow's "barrel of mean" and "cruse of oil" will be replenished by an Elijah. What then?

If the new dispensation is to continue the wage-slave system, eulogies are out of order and the tongue of Hope may rest from its labors.

Not so, however. The new dispensation is not ushered in by heralds proclaiming that man shall work no more, but it does come promulgating the new and divine gospel that man may work for himself, that the chains which bind him to wage-slavery shall be broken, and that unfettered, disenthralled, and emancipated, he may expand to the full stature of a free man, receiving, by right divine, the proceeds of his toil.

It is a dispensation that ushers in the Cooperative Commonwealth, not at once in its full orbed noon, but more properly its sunrise, its morning, its beginning.

Cooperation is not a word newly coined. It is as old as the tower of Babel, erected by the tribes in the plain of Shinar, when men believed they could build a tower whose top might reach into heaven, a majestic folly, but demonstrating, nevertheless, what may be accomplished by cooperative effort.[50] These cooperative workers did complete their tower, they did lay the foundations of Babylon and their tower, though its top did not reach the skies, stood for a thousand years one of the great wonders of a great city. And men now, as then, are interdependent and the term "cooperation" illustrates the idea, and debate upon the law of mutual dependence is not required. It is a fundamental law, an axiomatic truth, the only question to be debated being, is the purpose of cooperative effort wise or otherwise? Is it a vagary or a verity? No scientist, no philosopher, no statesman, no philanthropist ever has in the past, does in the present, or will in the future pronounce cooperation a vagary, a hallucination unworthy of consideration. Cooperation presupposes a condition, as applied to industrial affairs, in which men work together in harmony for one another's property, happiness, and independence, a condition in which no man is master and no man a slave, a condition in which a man's brain and brawn and soul are all his own and not, as under the wage system, another's.

I would have no one deceived. Here, in this presence, should be mindful of the practical. The *ultima Thule*[51] of cooperation, the Cooperative Commonwealth, is perhaps in the distant future, not, however, in the dreamland of the enthusiast, but entirely within the realm of the possible.

We are here to deal with initials and, among other things, to find a location, a spot favored by nature, in climate salubrious and a soil which will yield abundant harvests of food products for man and beast. Any one of several western states, which are sparsely settled and where the people are very largely in sympathy with the enterprise can be selected for the beginning. Invitations, cordial and heartfelt, have been extended by thousands of citizens, including governors of states and others eminent in public affairs. The state decided upon, we propose to colonize it with men and women thoroughly imbued with a knowledge of economics as applied to industrial affairs, men and women whose philosophy has taught them to deal with the knowable and the attainable, men and women of profound convictions who point to the ten thousand monuments of cooperative success that line all the pathways of civilization, the profits of which have been snatched from the builders to enrich those who owned the wage-slave, while the toilers, despoiled of their rights, lived on as they are living today, by permission of those who control all opportunities and dictate all conditions.

There are those who believe, and I am one of the number, that it is practicable to inaugurate a change of program and that the time is ripe for a beginning.

There may be those within the sound of my voice who expect the Cooperative Commonwealth to advance and reach maturity by some inscrutable power, without the aid of human endeavor. Not so, my friends. It means hard work. It involves moral and physical courage of the highest order. It presupposes earnest convictions. Its goal is industrial independence, an independence the world has never known and can never know until cooperative labor, solving every problem and surmounting every obstacle in industrial affairs, achieves emancipation for its votaries.

I need not be told that the term "independence" is a much-used and a much-abused word. It may stand for much or for practically nothing at all. Under the operation of the wage system, there is no independence for those who toil, because independence means exemption from control by others, the direction of one's own affairs without interference. Dealing with the subject from this point of view, there is not in the United States a wageworker who is independent. He must not only work to live, but always under conditions dictated by another person. His life and the lives of those dependent upon his work are absolutely under the control of others.

True it is, borne down by the exactions of masters, the toilers have struck in the hope of securing emancipation, but when the struggles are over they found themselves in the grasp of the same old system, more heavily manacled than before. The chains which bound them, unbroken, gnawed deeper into their flesh—into their very souls—and the contest has served to deepen the impression that the fight for independence has made them still more dependent and that they are pariahs in their much-vaunted "land of the free and the home of the brave."

Such conditions have aroused thoughtful men within and without the ranks of labor, and the consensus of opinion is that there is one way out of the labyrinthian pathways in which toilers have traveled for centuries, in which poverty has kept abreast of progress and is now so far in advance that a remedy must be found and applied without delay. The antidote is believed to be cooperative effort on the part of all toilers. By cooperation they can work out their own salvation, their redemption and independence. By cooperation they can burst through every enthrallment, break every fetter, rise superior to present environments, and produce such a change as shall challenge the admiration of the world.

I have referred to the building of the tower of Babel, not to approve the folly of the workers in the construction of a monument to perpetuate a delusion, but to demonstrate the possibilities of cooperative effort. But we have in our own land and within a period of living witnesses a far more stupendous cooperative enterprise carried forward to the acme of success. I refer to the achievements of the Mormons in Utah, not to condone persecution, but simply to demonstrate that cooperative effort possesses those essential qualities of success that achieve victories over the most obstinate impediments. In the case of Utah, it made "the desert rejoice and blossom as the rose." It made "the wilderness and the solitary places glad."[52] It touched the mountain streams which, in their flow, awakened the fertility of a generous soil and filled the land with harvest-home melodies. It built a city and adorned it with a temple equal to any of the seven wonders of the world, and Utah and Salt Lake City are enduring monuments of what cooperative effort may accomplish.

"Work for the unemployed" is the first call to duty and demands immediate action. To rescue these from tenements and hovels, from streets and slums, from charity's degrading bondage and give them the opportunity of applying their labor to the natural resources is the initial and commanding duty of the present hour.

When carping critics say our scheme is not feasible, let the answer be "work for the unemployed." These words must burn and glow on the first banner thrown to the breeze in the new crusade. "Work for the unemployed" must be the battle cry, and it must be taken up and echoed and re-echoed until it reverberates in tones of thunder throughout the land. Here and now, I declare myself enlisted in the cause of "work for the unemployed." Nature provides the means and, in the words of "Old Hickory,"[53] "by the eternal," we will provide the places. No excuse or evasion, no compliment or criticism will deflect us from our course. Nothing less than "work for the unemployed" will answer the demand.

An organization of a million workers whose hearts are with us is the first thing in order. We must at once press the work of organizing until every village, hamlet, town, and city of every state and territory in the union is voiced the demand and command, "Work for the unemployed."

In the new organization, there will be no division lines. All whose hearts are attuned to the symphonies of humanity will be welcomed, totally regardless of race, color, nationality, occupation, or sex. It will be an organization of equals pledged to the sublime work of giving effect to the Declaration of Independence on American soil.

Each will contribute according to his ability to the support of the new movement, and the monthly installments will soon be sufficient to start the pioneers westward, and by that time the state will have been selected. Under the supervision of able and experienced persons, the foundation of the new order will be laid, lands will be secured, machinery and tools will be provided, the soil will be cultivated and industrial enterprises will be established, and thus will begin the work which will not end until the Cooperative Commonwealth has become a realized fact. Gradually we will develop along cooperative lines, withdrawing, wherever and whenever possible, all patronage and support, commercial and political, from the decaying old competitive system, until "innocuous desuetude"[54] opens its vaults to receive it.

The theme is inspiring and invites to elaboration, but time forbids detail. The convention will mature plans and devise ways and means to proceed, and the day of adjournment will mark the first day's campaign. Not one day nor hour is to be lost. Action, here and now, is the supreme demand, and this convention will respond in a spirit to dispel all doubt as to ultimate success.

The fruits of cooperative industry are benedictions. Plenty banishes poverty. Free men, the possessors of free homes, are not scourged to their tasks by hunger pangs. Work is no longer a curse to be deplored, and life, emancipated from despair, is worth the living. Wifehood becomes a thing of beauty—motherhood a joy forever, and home a type of heaven.

I felicitate you upon this auspicious beginning of a great and philanthropic work. If wisdom prevails in our councils, we are destined to see thriving cooperative colonies planted in this country which, growing, as success crowns earnest endeavor, will ripen at last into a national Cooperative Commonwealth in which men shall be brothers and shall enjoy emancipation and all the fruitions of independence.

A Million Altruists Will Be Organized: Letter to the Editor of the *New York World*†

June 15, 1897

Chicago, June 15 [1897]

To the Editor of *The World*:—

To find work for the unemployed is the immediate purpose of the new movement. Tens of thousands of men are in distress, many of them actually verging on starvation.

There is no hope of relief in sight. Congress will do nothing. The constant improvement in machinery is increasing the army of unemployed at an alarming rate, and as their condition becomes more precarious, the very peace and order of society will be menaced.

In this supreme crisis, something must be done at once. The American Railway Union has a remedy and will proceed to apply it. It will be along peaceable, constitutional, and patriotic lines.

The boundless West is sparsely settled and has fabulous resources. Land can be procured, machinery purchased, and the unemployed set to work and enabled to provide themselves and dependent ones with clothing, food, and shelter.

A million altruists will be organized to provide the means, each voluntarily making a monthly contribution, according to his means. The work will be carried forward under the supervision of a board composed of men and women of the highest integrity and unquestioned business capacity.

The colonies to be established will be cooperative, and the whole movement will be carried forward on the same lines. The brotherhood of man is recognized as a fact in nature, and in obedience to natural law will form the basis of the new life, from which, it is confidently believed, there will spring a higher, nobler civilization.

Eugene V. Debs

---

† Telegraphic dispatch, published as "Labor's Land of Promise" in *New York World*, vol. 37, whole no. 13,084 (June 16, 1897), 1.

Farmers Will Form the Vanguard: Statement to the *Chicago Chronicle*†

June 18, 1897

* * *

Such is the outline of the constitution [said Eugene V. Debs after giving a summary]. Changes may be made by the convention, but the ideas of the delegates have been substantially set forth. There are many minutiae to be discussed and adopted, and these are being drawn up with a view to having everything done with precision and by specification. The foundation of the cooperative community will be carefully laid, and the structure will be built solidly.

First, the farmers, who will form the vanguard, will clear the forests, cultivate the soil, and prepare land for habitation. They will be supported by funds from the organizations and will, of course, live in primitive houses. Stock ranches will be built, and crops will be grown. Then the carpenters, bricklayers, plasterers, and other builders will follow, and they will erect substantial dwellings and structures for factories, workshops, and stores. Then will come the pilgrimage of artisans.

We will take these starving garment workers from Chicago. They will have every comfort given them. They will make the clothes for the community. And we do not contemplate that wages shall be paid, but that products shall be interchangeable and that everything shall be free to everyone. Each shall be given according to his needs and each shall produce according to his capabilities. Such is our ideal.

Recruiting headquarters will be established as soon after the convention adjourns as possible. The transporting of the first regiment will follow as quickly as sufficient funds have been raised. In addition to the constitutional sources of revenue, we have been promised financial aid from a great number of people. Communications are received daily from professional men, among them preachers, and from small merchants and working people, pledging their sympathy and support. As the preliminary work progresses and people are more thoroughly informed as to its practicability and beneficence, we shall not want for encouragement from all kinds and conditions of people.

† Published as part of "Making Laws for Utopia" in the *Chicago Chronicle,* vol. 3, no. 23 (June 19, 1897), 2.

Open Letter to John D. Rockefeller†[55]

June 19, 1897

McCoy's Hotel, Chicago, June 19, 1897

John D. Rockefeller,
New York City

Dear Sir:—

I take the liberty to inform you that we have this day organized the Social Democracy of America, an organization designed to rescue the oppressed and suffering of our land from the grasp of industrial conditions which they did not create and which they are powerless to control or modify.

The purpose of the organization is, briefly stated, to supplant the present cruel, immoral, and destructive system by the Cooperative Commonwealth, under which millionaires and mendicants, the abnormal products of an abnormal civilization, will disappear together and the brotherhood of man will be ushered in to bless and beautify the world.

In this city alone, in which the university which bears your name stands monumental of the triumphs of labor and the fabulous wealth of the country, 8,000 families are practically homeless, and 40,000 workingmen are verging on starvation.

If you think this statement an exaggeration, I beg that you may come here and I will arrange to have them assembled on the lakefront, and there, under the common sky, their only shelter, their emaciated faces and tattered garments may bear testimony to the haggard truth of man's inhumanity to man.

The picture is well calculated to appeal to men and angels, and, as you are a Christian gentleman and are widely known for benefactions, perhaps you might deem it proper, no less than dutiful, to give your support to an organization whose high purpose it is, not to fool and humiliate these suffering fellow beings with the paltry crumbs of charity, to perpetuate conditions which make their lives a continuous curse, but to strive for a more exalted humanity, a diviner civilization, such as the Master taught when he said: "On earth peace, good will toward men."

---

† Wire service report, as published in "Will He Accept?" *Logansport [IN] Pharos,* vol. 22, no. 208 (June 21, 1897), 1.

The immediate object will be the relief of the unemployed by colonizing a western state where they may cooperate in the application of their labor to the resources of nature, to provide for themselves and their dependent ones and manfully discharge the duties of an emancipated citizenship.

In this movement, there are no class distinctions. Rich and poor are equally welcome to aid in dethroning gold and exalting humanity. Then the strong shall help the weak, the weak shall love the strong, and the brotherhood of man shall transform the earth into a veritable paradise.

To consecrate one's self to such a work is my highest conception to duty to myself and my fellow men, and trusting that you may find it consistent with your own sense of social and patriotic obligation to join hands with us in our emancipating and ennobling mission, I subscribe myself yours

Very truly,
Eugene V. Debs

Closing Speech at the Founding Convention of the Social Democracy of America[†] [excerpt]

June 21, 1897

The times are ripe for a change. There are five million men in the country without employment. In Alabama, little girls work in factories 14 hours a day for 35 cents a week. In Sheboygan, men work ten hours for 50 cents. Manhood is reduced to merchandise, and even so it is not worth quoting on the exchange. Negro slaves were worth $1,500 apiece, but the white slaves of this country are not worth 15 cents a cord.[56]

I hate riches, but not the rich. I pity the poor man who has $20 million and cannot let go. I believe in helping him to let go. I cannot understand how a man can cling to $5 million when men around him are going insane through starvation.

---

† Wire service report, as published in *Huntington [IN] Daily News-Democrat,* new series vol. 1, no. 71 (June 22, 1897), 1. The speech was delivered at Uhlich's Hall, Chicago.

Last winter, the mayor of Chicago[57] had to address a proclamation to the people informing them that thousands of men and women were in danger of freezing to death. Yet there was plenty of coal in Chicago. What kept those freezing thousands from helping themselves? I cannot tell. Man is the only animal I know of that has not sense enough to feed himself. Take, for instance, the Kansas jackrabbits. If you kill one of them and you find him, fat you may be sure all the other jackrabbits are fat, too. There are no plutocrats among them who corner the crops and get fat while the others starve. No jackrabbit is stupid enough to allow a thing like that.

Coming through Nebraska not long ago, I traveled for miles and miles between rows of corncribs bursting with the corn crop of last year. Most of them had on them the mark of the Chicago Produce Company. There was no demand for this corn. The jackrabbits helped themselves, and why did not starving men and women do the same?

In Chicago, there are 50,000 starving people, starving in full view of food. Nature has provided an abundance for every creature, and it is stored mountain high in Chicago, before the very eyes of these sufferers. Why do they not help themselves? I cannot tell.

Statement on the Colonization of Washington†

June 21, 1897

The first thing we would do after getting control would be to call a special session of the legislature.[58] Then we would call a convention to revise the constitution and get all the rot out of it. We will have control of the taxing power and can tax syndicates and land sharks out of the state. Persons shall be taxed according to their means and shall have according to needs. We will have trusts, nothing but trusts, in our state, but we will all be in the trust.

The operatives will not work 12 or 14 hours a day, but four or five. We will be in the field in 1900 with a new party. These men who represent the new life

† Published as "Nothing But Trusts" in *St. Paul Globe,* vol. 20, no. 173 (June 22, 1897), 5.

are going to unite as if by magic for the overthrow of commercialism and the establishment of the Cooperative Commonwealth, by which the brotherhood of man will become a fact.

I do not know whether this question will be solved peaceably or otherwise. I hope peaceably. But I am one of those who believe in getting ready for any solution that may be necessary.

Mr. Debs said that in settling up the Cooperative Commonwealth in Washington, the colonists might be running against the Supreme Court. He would consult good lawyers and learn just what were the rights of the colonists.

We want to know our rights and make them rebels. If they send the military to invade our rights, then there will be an army of 300,000 patriots on the state line to meet them on that issue.

The Social Democracy Is a Political Movement: Statement to the *Milwaukee Daily News*†

circa July 7, 1897[59]

The colonization scheme is very much misunderstood, even by my best friends. As a matter of fact, this is but one feature of the Social Democracy. But it can be made an important one in vitalizing and developing the general movement.

The Social Democracy is not a colonization scheme. It is a political movement. Were the colonization plan to prove a failure, it would not stop the social democratic movement.

As I conceive it, the colonization scheme is an incidental plan to relieve the present distress all about us as much as possible. It is not a vital portion of the movement, though it may prove a great help.

The Social Democracy is a party, a political party, as much so as the Republican or Populist[60] parties. It is a reform party and has a most radical reform program. It aims to do away with the present economic system and substitute

† Published in *Milwaukee Daily News,* date unspecified. Reprinted as "A Political Movement" in *The Social Democrat* [Chicago], vol. 4, no. 14 (July 15, 1897), 4.

collective ownership and cooperative operation of all means of production and distribution. As the Republican Party was organized to abolish chattel slavery, so the Social Democratic Party is organized to do away with industrial slavery. One is no more revolutionary than the other. The only way to abolish industrial slavery is to abolish the competitive system.

A strike settles nothing permanently. It does not go to the root of the evil. It does not remove the cause of the trouble. The two parties to the dispute are certain to renew it sooner or later, and if labor wins one time, capital will win another time.

The strike of the miners now on is somewhat different. In this case, the miners are not getting work because they cannot live on the wages now paid. They are striking against starvation. Nor are the operators better off. They are making nothing. Profits have ceased.

In the district where I live, there is an operator who formerly was a miner himself. He has struggled for years against the reduction of wages, but the pitiless law of competition has forced him to cut his men down to starvation rates in order to operate his property at all. For some time, he has operated at no profit and has given the men the benefit in wages.

A few days ago, his men decided to go out [on strike] with the others, and the employer said to them, "Boys, I don't blame you! I advise you to quit. I would pay you more if I could, but I can't. I have sympathy for you, but I can't help you. I am powerless."

In the coal-mining business, rock bottom has been reached, and there is, in my opinion, but one escape from the heartrending conditions which now prevail in this business. That is the collective ownership of the coal mines and cooperative operation.

As to the Social Democracy, I have boundless faith in the future. Every day, hundreds of letters from the very best people of the country come to us. The organization will expand with magical spontaneity. It will be a revelation even to the most sanguine. Mark it. It is not an experiment, but an actuality. My whole soul throbs and surges with it, and I feel that I cannot be mistaken.

In 12 months, it will be the most important factor in our social and economic affairs, and in two years it will lead the world.

To those who lack faith in the intelligence of the people to carry out the plans of the Social Democracy, I would earnestly point out the fact that the people are being educated on these questions more rapidly than ever before. They have learned more in the past year along these lines than they learned in ten years previous.

"Sweet are the uses of adversity"[61] and the hard times have brought along with suffering and misery, thought of as knowledge. The people are waking up.

Why, if you give workmen $1.25 a day, tomorrow they would as a whole settle down under the present conditions, satisfied. At least, they would have done so a year ago. But there are a constantly increasing number now who see that the present system is wrong and would never be satisfied under it again under any circumstances.

I have a firm, unwavering faith that right is eternal, that truth must triumph, and I believe no man who has self-respect should ever despair. He dare not despair. He is bound by every atom of nobility in his nature to fight to the death for the truth, and to never, never surrender.

Men may betray. I have been betrayed by supposed friends, persecuted, blacklisted, maligned, misrepresented, and abandoned. But the knowledge of my own uprightness of purpose and the serene faith in the power of truth has so far upheld me, and I believe always will.

I have faith in the right. I have faith that the principles of social democracy are right. I have faith that the people are awakening to the truth. Victory will come.

Women in the Movement: Interview with Dorothy Richardson†

circa July 8, 1897[62]

* * *

"But you have not said one word about women or what part they will take in this great Cooperative Commonwealth that you are about to establish. Do you expect to adopt any specific measures toward the emancipation and advancement of wage-earning women?"

† Published as "Women in Debs' Colony" in *Milwaukee Sentinel,* July 25, 1897, unspecified page. Copy preserved in the *Papers of Eugene V. Debs* microfilm edition, reel 9.

Women? What part will women play in the Social Democracy? Well, that question is sort of a riddle. To tell you the truth, I cannot exactly define the attitude which the Social Democracy will assume toward women, further than they will stand according to our constitution on a perfect political equality with men, sharing with them all those privileges that have heretofore been considered man's sole prerogative. Women in the Social Democracy will be entitled to cast their ballots and vote in all municipal and state elections, as well as to hold office. The Social Democracy will ultimately be the realization of the woman suffragist's dream and the special boon of the new woman, but we have as yet given the woman question only a minimum share of attention which has been bestowed on the Social Democracy as a unit.

"But what about women in the colony you propose establishing in Washington? Have there not been any definite plans laid for giving employment as soon as the colony is established to at least a few of the tens of thousands of unemployed, self-supporting women to be found in the populous cities?"

Oh, yes, to be sure, but you must remember that Rome was not built in a day; neither can the Cooperative Commonwealth be established by a wish. In the beginning, there will not be any work that would be at all suited to women, not even to the most advanced of her sex. What we shall require there will be a force of rugged, able-bodied men, whose mission will be to get the colony into running order and make it a habitable place for their families. The work will be arduous, and you will pardon my frankness, but there will be no room for women, nor do we care to be bothered with them. By and by, however, when things are brought into shape, and system and order is established out of chaos, we will then turn our attention to women and their establishment in the colony. Indeed, to say the least, I think our colony will receive its first great impetus toward speedy success only when we can open the gate to the trammeled wage-earning woman and bid her welcome to the privileges of the Cooperative Commonwealth. When this time arrives, and my hope is that it will not be far off, we expect to have established diverse occupations in which women may engage without jeopardy to either the physical or moral nature. We have an appropriation of $50,000 from the state of Washington which amount is to be expended for irrigation purposes, agricultural implements, and other necessary things, and which will constitute the monetary nucleus of the colony.[63]

There are tens of thousands of women who are today working in Eastern sweatshops for a mere pittance. Of all the downtrodden working women in America, I think the lot of the sweatshop slaves is the worst. Now, it is our intention, just as soon as possible, to begin the manufacture of men's clothing in the colony, which will necessitate the importation of skilled operators, which I propose to bring from Chicago. Of course, we cannot furnish work to very many at first, but as the movement strengthens and spreads out, we will be able to increase the capacity of the establishment. The manufacture of shirtwaists[64] and of women's and children's wraps and dresses will also give employment in time to a large force of women and girls, as will also the making of shoes, slippers, and notions. These industries that I have named are only a few of the many that we hope to establish. These will be inaugurated first, however, for the reason that they do not entail any great expenditure of money for buildings or machinery, and because they will give employment almost immediately to women.

"How do you regard the new woman, Mr. Debs, and will she be allowed as many privileges in your colony as she assumes elsewhere?"

How do I regard the new woman? Why, I think she is the noblest kind of woman God ever made, and if I have my way, she shall continue her course unhindered when she reaches the new colony. God never intended that any woman should be denied any innocent pleasure or recreation that she desires or craves, and as one of the watchwords of the Social Democracy is freedom, that freedom shall be allowed the new woman in overflowing measure.

"But are you not afraid that this unbounded freedom you propose giving women will be in time abused and prove a detriment to her higher moral development?"

Not a bit of it! Not a bit of it! I have too much faith in the new woman ever to fear that unbounded freedom as to the selection of dress, amusements, and occupation and to the expression of thought will ever be abused.

"Then I presume you would encourage rather than discourage the wearing of bloomers by the women in your colony?"

No; I will always remain perfectly neutral on that point. I say that if a woman wants to wear bloomers, let her wear them, but if she does not show any such inclination, so much the better. No; although the new woman shall do just as she pleases in this matter in our colony, I hope she will not entirely discard petticoats and the thousand-and-one lace befrilled odds and ends that constitute so much of the charm of femininity.

"And how do the prominent philanthropic women of the nation regard the movement? Have you sought to interest them in the plans, and have you succeeded?"

Many of the great and good women of America, as well as of Great Britain, have come forward to extend their goodwill, money, and influence toward the success of the Social Democracy. The women are taking more interest in the movement than my most sanguine dreams ever anticipated. I have received communications from many leading club women wishing me Godspeed, while leading advocates of dress reform, temperance, and social purity have declared their intention to cooperate with us.

"Speaking of social purity, will there be any specific measures taken to preserve it in the plan of the Social Democracy?"

Well, no, no specific measures. Social impurity, like all other evils existing in society, is the outcome of a diseased industrial system. What makes nine-tenths of these poor abandoned wretches go wrong? Is it from choice? No. It is hunger—oftener starvation. You know that a proud, honest man will steal before he will beg or accept cold charity. I contend that a starving woman is not a responsible guardian of her honor.

"But do you think the people oppressed and trampled upon as they are will have the courage to assist you in carrying out this project to completion?"

Yes, I do, indeed. The people are ripe for it, and the organization will grow as no organization ever grew before. The work of organizing has already begun, and in earnest. Fully 300 applications for charters for local councils are now on file, while thousands of letters are pouring in from every quarter, and with scarcely an exception they contain messages of greeting and good cheer. Never was a movement more favorably received by the common people. From every source comes the tidings that the Social Democracy is just what is wanted. The movement must go to the front with majestic stride. Its mission is the emancipation of labor from wage bondage and the inauguration of the Cooperative Commonwealth. Nothing can save the existing social and industrial system. Cooperation is inevitable. The cooperation that I advocate is so wide in its application, so general in its nature, so all-prevailing in its scope, that altogether different conditions would surround human life and human effort under its control. Cooperation cannot fail to perform its mission and to perform it quickly.

Take the Mormons, for instance. Was not cooperation there a success? Had it not been for the undermining influence of the institution of polygamy, might they not have been a power in the land today? Cooperation knit together and made strong a nomadic little band of people driven from pillar to post.

Cooperation raised a splendid acropolis by the shores of the Great Salt Lake and made a veritable Egypt out of an arid waste. If cooperation did so much for the Mormons, will it not do more, infinitely more, for us?

The Coal Miners' Strike†

July 15, 1897

The strike of the coal miners is without a parallel in the annals of labor struggles. It is a strike of both employees and employers, the former against starvation and the latter against bankruptcy and ruin.

From the black mouth of the mine issues the wail of famishing miner and from his hovel habitation comes in accents sad and clear the refrain from the despairing wife and suffering child.

The mine is no longer profitable to the operator, nor yields up a living wage for the miner, and so the mine, once the source of untold wealth to the owner and of high wages to the miner, is abandoned by both until in some mysterious way the pall is lifted and some measure of the former prosperity comes back again.

Will it come? Let time answer.

In this sad struggle to save the child from the wolf of want, the miner has the sympathy, the tears of the country, but these will not help him. He is battling against cruel conditions which are as inexorable as fate, and all we can do is to stand by him as best we can and hope for the best.

In contemplating this strange and tragic struggle, but one conclusion is possible. The competitive commercial system has done its worst, and in the mining industry, the rock bottom has been reached. The trust alone is triumphant.

In the competitive war which raged long and fiercely, profits have been reduced to nil and wages to starvation. Both employer and employee are exhausted. Under the system that leveled them down to ruin and starvation, they can never build up again.

† Published as "Debs on the Miners' Strike" in *The Social Democrat,* vol. 4, no. 14 (July 15, 1897), 2.

What is the remedy? There is but one. It is the collective ownership of mines, so that instead of being operated for "profit" in the interest of the individual, they shall be operated by the whole people for their common welfare.

Plea for a New Order: Speech at Ferris Wheel Park, Chicago†

July 17, 1897

There are two social and economic systems which have been conflicting since the morning stars sang together and the son of God shouted forth their joy. Under one system the few have enjoyed the fruits of the earth and the masses have been doomed to serve as beasts of burden. The beneficiaries of this system believe, for the most part, and honestly, that a system under which the few rule and the masses toil and submit to their masters in silence is on the whole a good system. It is a system, however, which has filled the world with unspeakable woe, and it is needless to say that it is under this system we now live. There is another system under which there is no favored class, no special privileges, where the earth and the fullness thereof becomes the heritage of the common people. *[Applause.]*

Under this system, economic freedom will be established and the brotherhood of man will be inaugurated. The most ardent supporters of the present system are bound to admit that it is a disastrous failure. On the one hand it has produced thousands of millionaires, and upon the other its millions of mendicants, and this process is in operation during all the circling hours of the day, the week, the month, and the year. There are those who believe, and I am among them, that the time has come to supplant this system with the cooperative system under which men shall work together for the common uplifting of our common humanity. *[Cheers.]*

I am not unmindful of the fact that there are a great many excellent people

---

† Published as "Debs' Plea for a New Order" in *Appeal to Reason,* whole no. 87 (July 31, 1897), 2. Reprinted as "Arouse, Ye Slaves!" in *Social Democratic Herald* [Chicago], vol. 1, no. 17 (Oct. 29, 1898), 4.

who look upon every agitator as a dangerous man. It is a fact that it has always been unpopular to attack the existing order of things, but thank God in every age there have been men who had the courage of their convictions, men who have been true to themselves, men who stood erect and braved all the storms of persecution, and were it not for those men we would never have emerged from savagery and barbarism. *[Applause.]* This world has always crucified its saviors and crowned its Satans. *[Cries of "That's right!"]* It has always been so in the past and may always be so in the future. There are a great many men who cannot possibly conceive of a man engaging in a work unless he has some personal, selfish motive to gratify. They cannot rise above themselves. They estimate others by their own standard, and he who attacks the system under which we live and the beneficiaries of crimes perpetrated upon others becomes in their eyes perfectly infamous.

A little while ago the term "socialism" was exceedingly offensive to our people. There was deep-seated hostility against it on the part of those that had no rational conception of the meaning of the term. Socialism is the direct opposite of competition. We are now living under the competitive system, a system that puts a premium not upon men who are good and virtuous, but upon men who are cunning, shrewd, and unscrupulous, men who use their brain power for the oppression and plunder of their fellow beings. Under the competitive system, the best men go into bankruptcy, the men who are scrupulous and honest and conscientious in modern commercialism fail, and they are failing, my friends, at the rate of about 45 a day. In 1896, there were in this country 13,197 failures, aggregating $225 million, an increase of 12 percent over 1895, or an increase of $50 million.

But that is not all, nor the worst of all. During 1896, 6,520 suicides were committed. In proportion, as millionaires and mendicants increase and multiply, suicides and murders increase, and they have increased threefold since the year 1890. Only the other day, Barney Barnato, one of the richest men in the world, a product of the competitive commercial system, committed suicide. At one end of this system is produced insanity and suicide; at the other starvation and crime. *[Cries of "That's right!"]* At one end multimillionaires, at the other mendicants and paupers. Both, as I have said, are the abnormal product of an abnormal civilization.

I make no attack upon the rich man. I do not deal with individuals. I realize that, to a very large extent, he is the product of his surroundings. Some men naturally become rich. The capacity for acquiring money is inherent in them; others naturally remain poor. In this mad strife for the accumulation of money, it sometimes seems to me the heart has been eaten out of our civilization. Men have no other object in life except material success. Fail in business, and your life is a failure. That is the way the world looks at it. The chief aim is to become wealthy, and in these days we are not very particular as to the means we employ in accumulating our wealth. The man who has money is the master of the world, and in his presence the people debase themselves.

The concentration of money in a few has developed the money power in this country, and this money power now dominates every department of our government. Even our Supreme Court has been tainted and polluted by its influence. It was only a little while ago that our Supreme Court was one of the most august judicial bodies in the world. Now it is assuming the legislative functions of our government. That body returned a decision the other day which nullified the 13th amendment of our federal constitution and reestablished involuntary servitude in the United States. With that body, only the money power has influence, and the same is true to a very large extent with the Congress of the United States. *[Cries of "That's right!"]*

That power maintains an organized lobby not only at the national capital but at the capitals of all the states in this nation, and no one knows this deplorable fact better than the people of the state of Illinois. [*Loud applause.*] It is the power of money that rules the country. They who have it are the rulers of the country. The wealth of the country is concentrated in the hands of the few, and the few dictate the destinies of the republic.

Mr. Vanderbilt will soon own the railroads of the country, and Mr. Havemeyer all the sugar.[65] Mr. Carnegie will own the coal, Mr. Rockefeller the oil, and Mr. Yerkes the street railways,[66] and so on through the list, while, under the present drift of things, the people will become as helpless as an individual labor agitator. *[Applause.]*

There are those who say this system is right; that it is the only system that will develop individuality and individual incentive to accumulate wealth. Shrouds have no pockets. Death is no respecter of persons. What is the object of this much-talked-about incentive? What sense is there in accumulating more than one can use? Jay Gould died because he had too much money. If he had remained poor, he would have been alive today. If he had been poor, he would never have suffered as he did the fear of an assassin's knife. His brain was wrought with perplexing problems, and life to him was a weary burden, despite his immense fortune. He had as much too much, as millions have too little.

The present tendency is to do away with all competition, as the captains of industry realize that competition is destructive of business. Mr. Rockefeller realized this and set out to tear down all concerns competing in the oil business. Now he is the monarch of the country. He fixes prices and wages while the American people are obliged to pay the prices he fixes for oil, as his slaves are obliged to take the wages he give them. Seventy million people stand by and watch these big corporations slowly secure their grip on the great national industries. Here in Cook County, railroad property is estimated to be worth from $300 million to $500 million. Examine your tax duplicates and you will find that the railroads pay taxes on $1,250,000 worth of property. This great railroad power is in politics and spends $50 million annually for the purpose of debauching the representatives of the people. This great power dominates the country and dictates legislation so far as its own interests are concerned.

The people pay the rates fixed by the roads and have absolutely nothing to say in the direction and management of these enormous properties. There are those who say that the people in their collective capacity could not operate the railroads. That is a very unfortunate condition. I should like to know why not. If Mr. Vanderbilt can operate the railroads in his own interests, why cannot the people of the country operate them in their own interests? *[Applause and cheering.]* To assert to the contrary means that Mr. Vanderbilt is more intelligent than all the people in the country combined.

We are the only civilized nation on the face of the globe that doesn't own its own telegraph system. If I send a message to California, I must pay ten cents a word for it. In Great Britain, you can send a message to any part of the kingdom for a cent a word. This great monopoly has plundered the American people of millions of dollars. Our people ought to own and operate not only the telegraph, but they ought to control all the public utilities. *[Loud applause.]*

In order to bring about these changes, an organization known as the Social Democracy of America has been launched. Through this organization we propose to appeal to the intelligence and to the patriotism of the common people. It is an organization designed to rescue this republic from the chosen few who have despoiled it and restore it to the common people. This organization proposes to supplant the present commercial competitive system. A little while ago, a prominent paper in discussing this matter said that the competitive system was the only rational system, and a little further along it added that the Supreme Court had attacked this system by rendering a decision against the pooling bill, allowing railroads to pool their interests and fix rates. This paper charged that the Supreme Court had aimed at the most fundamental and vital necessities of trade. It declared that the railroads could not exist under the present system of cutthroat competition. Of course not. Neither can the workingmen exist under cutthroat capitalism. "By their fruits ye shall know them."[67]

We have before us the fruits of the competitive system. There are more than 5 million American workers who are looking for work and are unable to obtain it. But the people say, "Wait until the tariff bill has been passed. *[Applause and laughter.]* That will solve all our evils, and prosperity will return to the people." How foolish and absurd! How ridiculous! The workingmen are paupers now, and yet by adding to their taxes these reformers are going to tax them back into prosperity? Others say you must solve the currency question. They insist there is no real difficulty in this country and there ought to be no agitation. As for socialism, they say it is well enough for Germany and Italy, those king-cursed countries, but that it has no place in the land of the free and the home of the brave, where the poor man has the same chances as any other man, and where the poor man's boy may become the president of the United States. But let me tell you that there are 5 million people in this country who would be willing to swap their chances for the presidency for a good square meal.

What avails it if a man be a political freeman and an industrial serf, enslaved by his material wants and by his economic necessities? He is compelled to work for the wages offered to him by his master. He has the alternative of starving or accepting the wages offered him. He has the choice between slavery and starvation, and there are many who prefer slavery to starvation because they have families depending upon them for support. The obligations to take care of their loved ones become the occasion for their slavery and degradation.

I know there are those who say this is a good system. It may be a good system for its beneficiaries, but it is not a good system for the people at large. Nor is it in any proper sense a good system for its beneficiaries, for if a man were perfectly civilized, he would scorn to be the downfall of his brother and his brother's family. A man is endowed with a brain, but after all, this is merely an incident so far as he is concerned, and if he uses his brain for the oppression of his fellows, he is perfectly infamous in my judgment. I admire, I respect, I love a superior man who uses his superiority for the uplifting of his less fortunate fellow men *[applause]*, but I despise a man who makes it the means of his own selfish aggrandizement.

A great many people say that men are classified and graded by nature, and that they are separated as widely as the poles. Men and women are separated because they do not have equal opportunities. If men and women enjoyed economic freedom, if they had equal opportunities, this would be a different world—it would be a veritable paradise. There is many a poet in the coal mines, and many an artist is doing hard labor because he has not had a fair start in life. The difference between men is not a natural one. It is due to the fact that a few people have monopolized the earth and the fullness thereof. It is due to the fact that people have been denied their best rights and the opportunity to develop their higher faculties. I believe human nature is not inherently vicious. I believe there is good in every human heart. I believe that people are naturally good, but they can be perverted under the present industrial system. Greed is the dominating motive. Every man for himself, and every man against every other man not working in his interests. You have got to knock down your fellow man under our system in self-defense. It is a fight for self-preservation, and in the fight the honest, conscientious, and scrupulous man goes down. There is no longer anything like conscience in our commercial system. Absolute honesty is impossible. I know it from observation and experience. Everything is fair in business, and business is war.

The Social Democracy proposes that there shall be one capitalist in the country and that capitalist shall be the collective people. Then there shall be employment for every man in the republic; then there will be a reduction in the hours of labor proportionate with the improvements in the mechanical arts. This will settle the hour-day question. Today there are millions of people in this country who are without work, and other millions who are working from 10 to 14 hours a day for a bare subsistence. Professor Hertz, of the University of Vienna, estimates that the working population of Austria who are over 16 and under 50 years of age could, under a condition of socialism, produce the necessaries and comforts of the kingdom at the rate of one hour and 27 minutes work per day. Our machinery is idle seven months in the year, and one-third of our working population is looking for work. Fifty years ago, these things were unheard of. Then tools were simple, and every man could own the means of production. Now, the primitive implements of industry have been superseded by costly and ponderous machines which only corporations or a combination of corporations can afford to purchase.

The Social Democracy proposes that this machinery, which is doing the work of the country, shall become the property of the people. The machinery that was designed to bless the world is, under its present management, the curse of the country. The machine displaces labor, the machine starves labor. These conditions are due to the fact that we have not changed our systems of production and distribution. Think of it, there are 20 million people on the verge of starvation in this country. This statement will be contradicted, but it is a haggard fact. Miners in Ohio and Pennsylvania have been working for 42 cents a day. There was not a tramp in this country 35 years ago. Today, those who work the longest and the hardest get the least, and those who work the least get the most. A little while ago, eight men sat at table in George Vanderbilt's Carolina residence[68] representing $350 million, yet not one of them ever produced a dollar or its equivalent. Fifty years ago, a workingman could support his family decently and educate his children. A little later the wife was compelled to go to work, and now the children are forced to contribute to the support of the family. During a recent visit to Sheboygan, I learned that a cane factory in that city was employing little children eight and nine years of age for nine cents a week. To my mind, this is barbarous in a free country.

While in the McHenry County Jail, one of my fellow prisoners told me he had been sent up for 12 months for stealing a $2 cloak, which he gave to his wife, who was perishing with the winter's cold. Mr. Spalding will not go to jail.[69] *[Loud applause.]* It is only the poor that are punished for wrongs which their right brethren escape. The great criminals go scot-free, but the poor and unfortunate, those who constitute the submerged tenth,[70] they are entitled to no consideration when they are out of work. A human being is the only creature that has no market value. A slave in antebellum days was worth between $1,500 and $3,000, and when he was sick, he was given good care, the same as we would care for a good horse, but the white slave receives no consideration when he is confined to his bed. No physician counts his pulse or watches at his bedside. He must work at given wages or starve, and it is my belief that there are a great many people who would secretly rejoice if 4 million or 5 million idle men could be swept into the ocean and buried out of sight forever.

I am not a pessimist. I believe there is a future for this country, but I have often marveled at the great patience of the American people and have wondered that this country has not been thrown into revolution long ago. The new movement may be retarded, but it is sure to win success. This industrial question is up and will not be settled [until it is resolved] in accordance with the eternal principles that make for justice and the solidarity of mankind. Sometimes I think I can catch a faint glimpse of the promised land, but, whether the good time comes sooner or later, it will come, and the common people, who have long and patiently borne the burdens of their oppressors, will be restored to the rights and opportunities which an all-wise providence intended should be their portion.

No Hope but through the Back Door of Suicide: Speech on the Coal Miners' Strike, Wheeling, West Virginia†

July 26, 1897

Ladies and Gentlemen and Fellow Citizens of West Virginia:—

Such a meeting as this is unusually significant.[71] It bears testimony to the fact that the people in every walk of life are aroused, and that there is on every hand an increasing interest in the labor question and that it has expanded to such proportions that it is taking precedence over all other matters. I shall not appeal to your prejudices. I would not if I could arouse your passions or incite the populace. I appeal to your sense of justice and to your patriotism, and I ask you to examine the conditions under which millions of your fellow beings are dragging out of a wretched existence, and to ask you to get closer together—so close that you can hear one another's heart throbs.

In the words of Paul, let us reason together. A great strike is in existence. More than 180,000 miners are engaged in a struggle for enough wages to keep soul and body together. With their families, they represent nearly 1 million people. There are a great many excellent people who are opposed to strikes under all circumstances. Let me admit in all candor that I, too, am opposed to strikes. Most of the time, strikes are of little avail, but now and then there comes a time when men must choose between a strike and starvation and slavery, and such a time is upon us now. *[Applause.]*

I understand perfectly the misfortune of being out of employment. But there is a condition infinitely worse—that of the American workingman degraded and reduced to a point where he can no longer resist oppression. Then it is a duty to strike. I would remind you that we live under a strike government. *[Applause.]* Every stripe and star that dignifies and glorifies the flag is the result of a strike. Our forefathers struck at Lexington, and again at Concord, and so on in a succession of strikes. And against what? Tyranny and oppression and for liberty and independence, and had it not been for those striking forefathers, you and I would today be subjects of Great Britain

† Published as part of "The Debs Meeting Was a Monster" in *Wheeling Register,* vol. 36, no. 16 (July 27, 1897), 1, 5.

instead of sovereign American citizens. *[Applause.]*

It is sometimes charged that my colleagues and myself are agitators. I plead guilty to the indictment. *[Laughter.]* I accept the compliment. *[Laughter.]*

The progress of the world has been made possible only by agitators. *[Applause.]* Moses was an agitator. *[Laughter.]* So was Socrates. So was Jesus Christ. *[Applause.]* And the scribes and Pharisees nailed him to the cross. The world has the happy habit of crucifying its saviors and crowning its oppressors. *[Applause.]*

The trouble is, we have too little consideration in this world. So far, we are creatures of circumstances. *[A voice: "That's the stuff!"]* I believe in speaking the truth at all times, though the stars fall. You tell me to respect public opinion. Let me admit to you that I have no faith in public opinion, as either counselor or guide. Public opinion, as a general rule, has been and is wrong. The few have always led the world, and finally the minority becomes the majority, and this is the right view. It is not always popular to speak the truth, and no one understands that more perfectly than the ordinary politician. *[Laughter, and a voice: "Hit 'em again, Debs!]* I'll get around to them before I get through. *[Laughter.]*

There are some people who are perfectly honest, who are inclined to tell the truth about the labor question, yet they say they are with us. If you are with us, why not speak out? The man who is right ought to speak openly. I believe in keeping on good terms with myself, and if I am afraid to do so, I am dishonest. Self-respect is a great thing. I don't want to be in the predicament of the man who jumped out of bed in the middle of the night and exclaimed: "There is nobody in this room!" *[Laughter.]* I propose to walk with my self-respect and go to bed with my manhood. *[Applause.]*

Now I come to a discussion of the question of this great mining strike. It is not a strike in the usual acceptance of the term. It is not a strike for recognition or position, but a strike about starvation and rags. It was only yesterday I saw a miner in the Fairmont region. He had worked for three months, and he was in debt to the company $2.77. *[Applause.]* Nor is that an extreme instance. I have in my possession the time sheets of the men out there, and I know whereof I speak, and I am prepared to substantiate every statement I make by the documentary evidence.

In the first place, the Fairmont miner is robbed by fraudulent measurement. It is a notorious fact. It has been ascertained by the correspondent of the *New York Journal,* who made a full and impartial investigation, and reported the facts to that great paper, that cars which were supposed to hold two tons of coal actually held two and a half tons and two and three-quarters tons. *[A voice: "Right you are."]* And not only that, but after deducting his supplies—that is, the powder and oil and tools, and 50 cents a month for the company doctor, whether one is sick or not, the miner nets but 18 or 19 cents a ton. But this is not all, nor the worst of it all. The miner is not paid in money. He is given a check, or a book of checks, and is compelled to deal at the company store, and the farmers in that vicinity will tell you that the miner is compelled to pay from 20 to 30 percent more for his goods than the other customers. *[A voice: "Right you are, old man."]* All the miner has is his labor, and he is compelled to sell that at the cheapest, and to buy at the dearest rates. Under that system, every right of the individual is hopelessly lost. How would you citizens like someone else to draw your pay and spend it for you? *[Laughter.]*

That is the lot of the West Virginia miner. His wife goes to the store where the checkbook is kept, and buys what she wants and the checks are taken out, and although her husband works every day, at the end of the month he is in debt and has not a dollar to show for what he has done. Thus the miner is an abject slave, with no hope for him except through the back door of suicide. *[Sensation.]* I appeal to you to put yourself in their places. Would you be satisfied? *[A voice: "No."]* I am sure you would not be. If the people of the United States could be put in that position for one week, this strike would be settled in favor of the men—that is to say, it would be in favor of the right and in favor of honesty.

But they say that Debs and Rea[72] came here to make a contest. That is the fact. If men are contented in such a state of degradation, then there is no hope for the future. But in this contest, every American citizen should be an organizer. *[Applause and cries of "Good."]* If you could spend one day out there in the mining region, you would stand as I do, holding that conditions are a disgrace and an outrage.

We are making a little progress—just a little progress every day, and I have faith in the future, because I have faith in the people. They are coming around to believe in the necessity of acting. The miners and garment workers have sunk to soulless depths of degradation. I remember when the miner made $5 a day, and he could live like a white man and educate his children. But his wages have been gradually reduced until, in my own state, the miners, on an average, before this strike make 42 and a half cents a day. I am familiar with their condition.

At this point, Mr. Debs spoke in detail of the condition of the miners in some sections of the country, particularly citing Brookdale, Alabama, where the men, although working hard, never see any money, and just manage to get enough clothes to make them presentable on the streets. Proceeding, he said:

John Bright[73] once said that the nation lived in a cottage. It was a beautiful and poetic idea. But a large proportion of the wage earners among our citizens no longer live in a cottage, for the cottage implies a home. Byron said: "When falls the Coliseum, Rome shall fall; and when Rome falls—the world."[74] Here and now, we say that when the American home falls, then falls America; and when America falls, there falls the greatest country in the world. I do not say the American home is to fall; but I do say the American home is in jeopardy when a man has to work for 42 and a half cents a day. *[Applause.]*

The average miner does not live in a cottage. He lives in a hut, a hovel, sometimes in a hole in the ground hardly fit for wild beasts. He works hard, yet his return is little. His habitation cannot be a happy one. His wife is discouraged—she has been trying to live on 15 or 20 cents a day—the children are half naked, ignorant, and all is wretched. And after ignorance comes crime, and after crime punishment, in the shape of the prison or the life strangled out on the gallows. These are the products of conditions. Under proper conditions, we have true manhood and virtuous womanhood; under vicious conditions, humanity sinks to the level of the beast. Go to the large centers of population—to New York and Chicago—and you will see hundreds of thousands of people huddled together, ignorant, vicious, and depraved, and as a natural result of these conditions there is not a state at present with adequate capacity for the punishment of its criminals. This question appeals to the patriotism of every honest citizen of the Republic.

And I want the ear of the businessmen of this community for a little while. I want to say to them that they are just as much interested in this matter as the miners. If they are defeated, you will suffer to a corresponding degree. If the miner gets but 42 cents a day, he must live on it somehow. He cannot buy good, wholesome food. He can't pay a grocery bill. He can't wear good clothes. He cannot become a factor as a consumer. If he has children and they are sick, he cannot pay the doctor; and if he is wronged, he cannot employ a lawyer; and so it is all around. The entire superstructure of our system rests upon labor—labor is the representative and all-important thing. Labor is the foundation, and if the foundation is weak, the superstructure cannot be strong. *[Applause.]*

Who is to be benefited by the defeat of the strikers? Will it be the businessman? No! Then who will it be? I will tell you: it will be the few millionaires who traffic in the misery of the common people. *[Applause.]* A fair standard of labor should be secured, in the interests of capital, of labor, and of the country at large. No country can prosper where labor is impoverished. That is an axiom in economics. Labor produces everything; it pays all the revenues, and it ought to be able to maintain a living wage.

But they say, "What have the miners of West Virginia got to do with it?" I will tell you. West Virginians are mining coal and sending it to the western markets. They might just as well send their miners there and put them to work in place of the strikers. *[Applause.]* But they say, "West Virginia miners ought to be given a fair shot now." But suppose the strike is defeated, and western prices go down, do you think that West Virginia prices will not follow suit? You can't send West Virginia coal there then. *[Applause.]* But you say, "The West Virginia operators are paying their men living wages." How long have they been paying them, and how long will they continue to pay them if the strike is a failure? *[Applause.]* Four years ago, your wages increased. *[A voice: "Nit."]* You were deceived all along the line. *[Applause.]*

You are enjoying a boom at present, but it will be a short-lived one. They are willing to pay big wages now, but they are speculating on the empty stomachs of the miners, and every dollar gotten in that way is blood money and represents the misery of your fellow citizens. The workingmen of the country are not benefited. The consumers who buy in small quantities are compelled to pay the price. The real benefit goes to the big men. I declare it to be the duty of the miners of West Virginia to drop his tools until living wages are paid to all. *[Applause.]*

You have become disorganized and therefore demoralized. The strike is clearly right, and will prevail, but if it shall fail through the West Virginia miners, and after that happens and the men are scourged back at starvation wages, you here will be helpless, and you will not dare to strike, and no one knows that fact better than the operators. The result will be that you, having worked until the other miners were defeated, they will work in turn until you are defeated. The thing to do is to stand together, and see that a uniform scale is made in each district that will do justice to each, and then all can go back to work in a body, and you will all be earning living wages, with no more strikes in sight. *[Applause.]* But as long as the miners of one state can be used against the miners of another, wages will go down until the bedrock of degradation is reached. *[Applause.]*

I do not think we will fail. I am not in the habit of looking on the dark side of things. I believe we are making a little progress. *[Applause.]* The most hopeful thing is that workingmen are beginning to think, and as they think they are wondering why they must draw their rags a little closer so as not to touch the silks they have woven, why they must walk in the shadow of the palaces they have built but may not enter. And when they see these things properly, they will take their own—not by force, nor by violence, but by the ballot, which falls lightly as a snowflake, which works the will of man as lightning does the will of God. *[Applause.]*

Labor is the creator of all that is useful and beautiful in this world, and shall not labor come into its own? Who shall doubt it? As the mariner plowing Southern seas turns his eyes to the Southern cross blazing in the sky, as a beacon to guide him on his way, let labor everywhere take heart of hope, for the cross is bending and the midnight is passing,[75] and "joy cometh in the morning."[76]

Mr. Debs then turned his attention to the courts in their acts against labor and in favor of capital, and after discussing this in a most interesting manner, to the delight of his audience, concluded at half past ten, the crowd greeting him with three cheers.

The Social Democracy†

August 1897

The public press has had much to say about the Social Democracy since its organization a few weeks ago. Most of the comment and criticism, both favorable and unfavorable, has been inspired by a total misapprehension of the organization, its principles, its plans, and its purposes. Columns have been written about the failures of colonization schemes of the past. Other columns have been written about the impossibility of establishing a new social system outside the existing one. The time and space given to such discussion have been simply wasted.

That some of our critics know better, but persist in misrepresentation, from motives of their own, is a fact too well understood to admit of doubt;

† Published in *The New Time* [Chicago], vol. 1, no. 2 (August 1897), 78–79.

and although some of these pretend to laugh the "scheme" to scorn, the large amount of space they devote to it makes it apparent that they are not blind to its immense possibilities.

The Social Democracy is a great social, economic, and political organization. It is at once national and international. Politically speaking, it is a party within and for itself, and within 12 months its national representatives will have formulated a national political platform. Similarly, the various state representatives will have adopted state platforms and the municipal representatives local platforms.

The unit of organization is the local branch. These are organized in each ward and township. Five or more persons can organize a local branch, and the membership is limited to 500.

The local branches have local or municipal jurisdiction. From these are chosen annually, in April, representatives to the state union, who meet annually in May at the capital of the state to prepare a platform, nominate candidates, and transact other business pertaining to the state. The several state unions elect representatives to the national council, and this body meets annually, in June, to adopt a national platform, choose officers, nominate candidates, and transact other business pertaining to the national organization.

The National Council annually elects an executive board of five members, which constitutes the executive department of the organization. The declaration of principles adopted by the late convention is too long to be introduced in full, and I will therefore only give two paragraphs, as follows:

> We hold that all men are born free, and are endowed with certain natural rights, among which are life, liberty, and happiness. In the light of experience we find that while all citizens are equal in theory, they are not so in fact. While all citizens have the same rights politically, this political equality is useless under the present system of economic inequality, which is essentially destructive of life, liberty, and happiness. In spite of our political equality, labor is robbed of the wealth it produces. By the development of this system it is denied the means of self-government, and by enforced idleness, through lack of employment, is even deprived of the necessaries of life.

* * *

> We therefore call upon all honest citizens to unite under the banner of the Social Democracy of America, so that we may be ready to conquer capitalism by making use of our political liberty and by taking possession

> of the public power, so that we may put an end to the present barbarous struggle, by the abolition of capitalism, the restoration of the land, and of all the means of production, transportation, and distribution, to the people as a collective body, and the substitution of the Cooperative Commonwealth for the present state of planless production, industrial war, and social disorder—a commonwealth which, although it will not make every man equal physically or mentally, will give to every worker the free exercise and the full benefit of his faculties, multiplied by all the modern factors of civilization and ultimately inaugurate the universal brotherhood of man. The Social Democracy of America will make democracy, "the rule of the people," a truth, by ending the economic subjugation of the overwhelmingly great majority of the people.

By far the greater part of the criticism has been directed against the "colonization scheme," and there are those who still insist that this is all there is to the movement, or, at least, that this is its chief purpose.

To all of these be it said that the proposed colonization scheme is simply one of the features of the movement and has been assigned a special department known as the "Colonization Department."

There has never been any intention to organize isolated colonies, and they who have worked themselves up in describing the fate of other "colonies" and predicting calamity have been wasting their time. They have been attacking the phantoms of newspaper reporters.

The purpose has been, and is, to mass a sufficient number of our supporters in a state to secure political control, and then another state, and so on. Meanwhile everything possible will be done to provide employment for the unemployed. At worst, they will be no worse off than they now are. It is believed that with such financial support as can be given by the general organization, the soil of the state chosen can be put under cultivation, certain industries can be established, and work provided for the unemployed, while at the same time much can be done on this line to promote the national Cooperative Commonwealth.

Those who so violently oppose our "colonization scheme" will not give the real reason for their opposition. Why are they opposed to our carrying a state for the Social Democracy?

The magnitude of our undertaking is not underestimated. Of course, there are thousands who look sad and say, "It can't be done." They mean well but are helpless and cannot help it. We say it can be done, and what is more, it will be done. The program adopted at Chicago will be carried out in full. No part of it has been or will be abandoned.

The Colonization Commission will soon be appointed and will work in conjunction with a similar commission of the Brotherhood of the Cooperative Commonwealth[77] in carrying out that part of the program. Meanwhile, the work of organizing the general movement will be carried on with unceasing energy. Applications for charters are already pouring in from every quarter. It is safe to predict that the Social Democracy will grow more rapidly than any other organization ever started, and that its spontaneous development and expansion will be a revelation to the people.

The Social Democrat, the official paper of the organization, will be published weekly for the present, and on January 1 [1898], a daily paper will be issued.[78] In addition to this, a literary bureau will be established for the printing and distribution of social, economic, and political literature.

In this brief article to *The New Time,*[79] hurriedly written, I have no time for detail, and I have not attempted anything beyond the statement of the scope and general purposes of the movement.

The success of the Social Democracy is assured from the very beginning. Its reception by the masses is proof positive that the people are ripe for it and that it will rapidly grow in favor until it fulfills its emancipating mission.

Press Release on the Forthcoming St. Louis Conference of Labor Leaders[†]

August 28, 1897

Terre Haute, Ind., August 28 [1897]

From information I have, it is safe to predict that the St. Louis meeting next Monday [August 30] will be the most important convention of labor this country has ever witnessed.[80] I am no alarmist, but I do not hesitate to say that if the people do not take cognizance of the awful and widespread suffering of the miners and their families, and adopt prompt and effective measures for their

† Wire service report, as published as "Debs Talks" in *Paris [KY] Bourbon News,* vol. 17, no. 70 (August 31, 1897), 3.

relief, something will occur to shock them into a realization of their obligations to their fellow beings.

What will be the result of the St. Louis meeting I am not prepared to say. I may venture the prediction that the injunction and its free and indiscriminate use in relation to organized labor will be the engaging theme. The injunction is the deadly bludgeon of corporate capital, and labor throughout the country is aroused to this fact. The heart of all labor is with the miner. From end to end of the country, workingmen demand relief for their suffering fellows, and it will require little effort to precipitate a sympathetic strike that will simply paralyze the country.

Eugene V. Debs

To the Hosts of the Social Democracy: A Message for Labor Day†

August 30, 1897

Terre Haute, Ind., August 30, 1897

There are periods of time in the course of human events when every sentiment of fealty to humanity prompts men to make declarations involving new departures from the old beaten pathways in which men have tramped and wrought and starved and died, and left as an inheritance to their children the same deplorable condition—lives in which the agony of trial, beginning in the cradle, pursues its victim until death closes the scene; a condition in which high aspirations and noble ambitions live for a time to allure their possessors and then

> Like Dead Sea fruits that tempt the eye,
> Turn to ashes on the lip.[81]

a condition which tells by the wounds and bruises which afflict the victims how deep has penetrated the steel of oppression when selfishness and greed directed the blow.

† Published as "To the Hosts of the Social Democracy" in *The Social Democrat*, vol. 4, no. 19 (September 2, 1897), 2.

I would not, if I could, exaggerate conditions. I know of no words in the lexicons of our language which, though they were pigment and brush in the hands of a Raphael, could be made to paint a darker picture than the unadorned facts present for our contemplation. Nor could words, though wielded by the matchless imagination of a Dante or a Milton, whether describing Hell or Paradise Lost, be made to exaggerate the distress of the poor in the United States of America.

It is told of Parrhasius,[82] an Athenian painter, that his ambition was to "paint a groan," and for the purpose subjected a slave to torture. If groans extorted by torture in the United States could be painted and hung in the corridors of Inferno, Satan could appoint a jubilee day for the delectation of his hosts, and if Heaven could but catch a glimpse of them, the saints would rend their white robes and tear off their crowns, and all the harps in the Celestial City would be tuneless and silent.

Labor Day has come again, and the sons and daughters of toil are to celebrate its coming. Is it to be an old-time celebration, with music and dancing and feasting, a day of revelry? When the rising sun that ushers in Labor Day sends forth his *avant-couriers* of streaming light and gilds all the horizon in ineffable glory, had he, like a monster of mythology, 50 ears, or, like a fabled Argus, 100 eyes, what would he see and hear as in his sublime march he mounts to the meridian? Shedding his light on the fairest and most fruitful land from Orient to Occident and once the freest, he would see an army of 150,000 coal miners, who with their wives and children swell the number to a million, struggling for bread, and his ears would be saluted with prayers, imprecations, and wails, blending in one long agonizing lament over conditions forced upon them by an accursed wage system that has reduced them to peons and pariahs, for which under that system there is no relief but in death.

One hundred and fifty thousand begrimed men coming up out of the bowels of the earth to assert their right to live is enough to make the "dry bones" Ezekiel saw in his vision stand up and swing their skeleton arms in approval of the crusade[83]—a crusade not like that of Peter the Hermit for the sacred shrines of Palestine, but to wrench from the grasp of a soulless plutocracy the sacred shrines of homes despoiled by pirates who build palaces of poor men's skulls and cement them with workingmen's life blood.

I do not care at this time to discuss strikes as a means of securing better conditions for working people. To a limited extent, in some instances, strikes have succeeded, but in almost every instance the victory won has been ephemeral. Defeated capitalism has found a way to regain its lost ground and make another strike a necessity, and in practically every effort upon a large scale in industrial enterprises involving public interests, failure has been written with an "iron pen and lead in a rock forever."[84]

Why is this fact woven into strikes which involve public convenience? It is because the public will not be inconvenienced for any length of time, though every toiler is found dead in his hut, and wives and children become the victims of conditions in the description of which all language is meaningless.

Nevertheless, those whose blood is not warmed in seeing Americans strike against tyranny of any and of every description would have had, had they lived when Washington and his compatriots were leading and fighting forlorn hopes, on the side of the enemies of liberty and independence—traitors to country and humanity.

I know it is the old, old story, the old song, the old refrain, but God pity us all when the old story of the struggle for liberty and independence no longer inspires us to deeds of valor and sacrifice; when Patrick Henry's defiant words, "Give me liberty or give me death," cease to thrill the American heart; for when that time comes, and its ominous shadows, black as Plutonian darkness, are even now lying athwart our pathway, the Republic will have been divided into two classes—brigands and beggars, masters and slaves—and the glory of the nation will have departed to return no more forever.

Present conditions startle the most apathetic. If there are those who can discern emancipation from spoliation by nursing into a more vigorous life the schemes of robbery now rife and growing in strength and ferocity, the theory must be that poverty is a crime to be denounced and punished, while wealth is a virtue to be protected and applauded. That this is the view taken by the federal judiciary has long since passed beyond the realm of debate and no longer admits of controversy.

To arraign federal judges, the pampered menials of corporations, trusts, and every other combine, separately or in the aggregate known as the "money power," has become an American duty as sacred as was ever imposed upon sons whose sires, in the days that "tried men's souls," placed in peril "life, liberty, and sacred honor" for the priceless boon of liberty.

I need not recite the malign decrees of judicial caitiffs in the recent past, the Woodses, Jenkinses, Tafts, et al., who, to placate corporations, perpetuated crimes in the name of law which, had they been committed in tsar-cursed Russia, would have multiplied nihilists, though they knew that every rod of the road from St. Petersburg to the penal mines in Siberia would be adorned by their skeletons, monumental of the glory of dying in the pangs of a struggle for emancipation. But Russia, with its absolute ruler, is as free as the United States under the sway of judges, who, having a lease of office running parallel with their lives, are growing more violent and virulent as the months go by.

Here we have a written constitution, ordained by "We the people," in which certain invaluable rights are guaranteed, but which the judges of the federal judiciary treat with contempt, and issue their injunctions with an abandon which discloses the most flagrant usurpations of power known to any land or nation, and in almost every instance for the protection of capitalism and the spoliation of workingmen.

The coal miners were adjured to "keep the peace," to perpetuate no "act of violence." Betrayed, robbed, degraded, and enslaved by corporate capital, half fed and half clothed, feeling the deep damnation of their wrongs—women wailing and children crying, but still obedient to law, they simply exercised the right of free speech. Wielding but one weapon, that of persuasion to call out men to join the army fighting for bread, they found themselves confronted by injunctions issued by judicial fleas rioting in the hair of corporation dogs, striking down the right to march and hushing to silence, as if by a mandate of Jehovah, every voice that had been pleading for the suffering poor. The judicial satraps—Jackson,[85] Mason,[86] Collier, Goff,[87] et al.—as if ambitious to win an immortality of ignominy, hesitated at nothing. No constitutional barrier impeded their despotic career. Relentless as pirates, and with the tenacity of sleuth hounds, they pursued the miners through every lane and avenue of high and holy endeavor to obtain living wages until drums ceased to beat and flags were furled. The miners were scattered, and once more so-called freemen by the thousands were reduced to slavery and must begin anew their life work of starvation and death.

In my own state of Indiana, there recently occurred an instance of the exercise of judicial power which I mention to show to what lengths and heights and depths of infamy a federal judge will go to aid a corporation to rob the people.

The capital city of Indiana has a corporation known as the "Citizens' Street Railway," which has issued $9 million in stocks and bonds on an investment of $2 million, upon which it has by exorbitant charges of transportation compelled the people to pay dividends.

The legislature of Indiana enacted a law requiring the corporation to charge three instead of five cents fare, and the Supreme Court of the state decided the act constitutional. In this emergency, the corporation took its case into the federal court before one Showalter,[88] a despot of regulation make and mind, who issued an injunction forbidding the governor from executing the laws of the state, and he promptly obeyed. Disrobed and degraded, the governor of a once-sovereign state, without a word of protest, pockets the insult without an effort to meet the obligations imposed by the sanctity of his oath of office that he would execute the laws of the state. Surely if the governor of a state can stand such a humiliation, it is not surprising that coal miners should yield to the mandates of a judge.

In view of such facts, what will there be in connection with the annual holiday of labor to rejoice over? What one fact looms aloft which presages for labor better conditions in the immediate and remote future?

On the deck of the storm-tossed ship of Labor millions of eyes are seeking to penetrate the surrounding gloom. Millions of voices, listening to what the billows say, would, if they could, interpret the message and point to a haven of safety and repose.

In this supreme hour, when hope is giving way to despair, and stout-hearted men are yielding to what they term the "decree of fate," the star of the Social Democracy, like that which the wise men saw when Christ was born, blazes above the horizon, and hope revives and again is heard by ears attuned to the minstrelsy of humanity, "Peace on earth, goodwill toward men."

Once more comes into view the "brotherhood of man," and the old-time shibboleth "Each for all and all for each" is vital with new significance and power.

It is no utopian dream, not an *ignis fatuus,*[89] not the product of imagination, not a mirage of the desert to allure and vanish, but a theory of life and labor in which the humblest individual owns himself and by his labor secures life, liberty, and happiness.

The Social Democracy deals with the possible, with the practical, with axiomatic propositions in the everyday affairs of life. It lays hold upon fundamental principles with unrelaxing grasp and challenges criticism. It makes humanity the focal, converging, and animating idea, and proposes to lift it above chicanery into the clear, serene, and unbefogged realm of common sense. It beholds Labor a mendicant, half fed and half clothed, inhabiting hovels, forever doomed to play its part in the tragedy of toil, to die at last unknelled and uncoffined, destined to a hold in the potter's field, and proposes to lift it up and out of its degrading environments, not by pathways decked with the flowers of fancy, but along the lines of practical endeavor, where mind, muscle, skill, humanity, and home, in holy alliance, in well adjusted, cooperative effort liberates the enslaved, gives a new birth to hope, aspiration, and ambition, and makes the desert blossom and the waste places glad—a condition in which, when a man earns a dollar, he is not compelled to divide it with a capitalist, who, as now, scourges him to his task as if he were a galley slave, but takes to himself all the fruits of his labor, and thus emancipated by industrial and economic laws which elevate, bless, and adorn humanity, the devotee of social democracy advances by degrees until the fangs and pangs of poverty disappear, until in his own home fears of eviction no longer breed despair, until wife and children, the recipients of the benedictions of cooperative prosperity, enjoy the fruitions of peace and prosperity, and under their own vine and fig tree live as free from carking care as the songbirds of the woodlands.

Here is a theme for Labor Day worthy of the genius of orator and poet. Fancy may plume its wings for flights to where the "universe spreads its flaming walls," but will find no object more worthy of its powers than a home where love and contentment reign supreme—a home beyond the reach of an injunction—a home amidst pathways of peace and prosperity—a home where the call to labor has no note of degradation, but is attuned to life and liberty and joy, as when a Switzer[90] salutes the rising sun with his Alpine horn, and from peak to peak and crag to crag the shout is heard, "Praise God!"

In writing this message to Labor and to the Social Democracy of America, I would emphasize the fact that a new departure has been inaugurated in response to a demand voiced by conditions in which calamities are forever treading upon the heels of preceding disasters and, like the tracks of animals to slaughter pens, no footprint indicates the escape of the doomed victims. It is a new departure based upon the immutable laws of love for the emancipation of humanity from degradation. The principle, ancient as creation, lives for the purpose of being applied whenever and wherever humanity lifts its bowed head and wails forth its cry for help. This it is now doing. The winds are burdened with moans, and the Social Democracy, with hope and help in alliance, comes to the front with an invitation to all who would escape from the grinding curse of wage-slavery, who would place themselves beyond the reach of the jaws and paws of plutocratic tigers, to break loose from their degrading environments and come within the ramparts which the Social Democracy is building for the safety of those who have suffered long for an opportunity to work out their salvation, not with "fear and trembling," but with a faith "that is the substance of things hoped for" and willing to consecrate all their mental and physical faculties to the work of rescuing their fellow men from the grasp of a system which has enslaved them and help them to realize the full measure of happiness that comes to free and independent men.

Nearly a hundred years ago, Shelley, one of England's great poets, sounded the tocsin of the Social Democracy when he wrote an "Appeal to the Men of

England," which I transcribe, because it rings out an appeal to the men of America today:

Men of England, wherefore plough
For the lords who lay ye low?
Wherefore weave with toil and care
The rich robes your tyrants wear?

Wherefore feed, and clothe and save,
From the cradle to the grave,
Those ungrateful drones who would
Drain your sweat—nay, drink your blood?

Wherefore, bees of England, forge
Many a weapon, chain, and scourge
That these stingless drones may spoil
The forced produce of your toil?

Have ye leisure, comfort, calm,
Shelter, food, love's gentle balm?
Or what is it ye buy so dear
With your pain and with your fear?

The seed ye sow, another reaps;
The wealth ye find, another keeps;
The robes ye weave, another wears;
The arms ye forge, another bears.

Sow seed—but let no tyrant reap:
Find wealth—let no imposter keep:
Weave robes—let not the idle wear:
Forge arms—in your defense to bear.

Shrink to your cellars, holes and cells—
In halls ye deck another dwells;
Why shake the chains ye wrought? Ye see
The steel ye tempered glance on ye.

With plough and spade, and hoe and loom,
Trace your grave, and build your tomb,
And weave your winding sheet—till fair
England be your Sepulchre.[91]

"I Plead Guilty to the Charge of Being Radical": Speech to the St. Louis Labor Conference†

August 31, 1897

Gentlemen of the Convention and Ladies:—

I believe the gravity of the industrial situation is fully understood by every delegate here, and you gentlemen are aware that liberty is dead on American soil.

I wish to state, in support of what I say, that I have appealed to all the courts in this country, from the lowest to the highest, and have failed to get justice. I shall appeal no more. The federal judges of this country are but the creatures of plutocracy. The American Railway Union raised $40,000[92] to test this question, only to be told in the end that we had no rights in this country which corporate wealth is bound to respect.

There have been combinations of wealth for a long time, and the time has now come, my friends, for a combination of the common people to rise up in their might and beat back to their native hell the allied forces of plutocracy.

It will not be long before Labor Day, and it is a sad thing to think that on that day, when labor should celebrate its independence, we should still see labor rattling its chains to the music of its own groans.

Labor is the cheapest commodity on God's earth, and yet there are those who would have it at a lower price. Only the other day, the united voice of labor was raised against the appointment of Mr. Powderly to a federal position,[93] and I notice that he was promptly put into the place. *[Mingled cheers and hisses.]* From Justice of the Peace to Justice of the Supreme Court of the United States, all the judicial powers of the United States are directed against labor. All the organized forces of society are against labor, and if labor expects to emancipate itself, labor must do it.

In my own state, there are today almost 8,000 men and their families starving. Think of it! Do you realize what I mean when I say starving? In the presence of the awful facts and ghastly misery in the mining districts, description sits down powerless to draw pictures of the scene.

† Published as "E.V. Debs' Great Speech" in *Brauer-Zeitung* [St. Louis], vol. 12, no. 37 (September 11, 1897), 1; checked to and amended with additional material from "Gravity of Labor's Condition" in *Facts* [Denver], vol. 3, no. 22 (September 11, 1897), 1–2.

The time has not yet quite come to incite the populace to arise in their might, but I want to serve notice to the plutocracy that we are to hold a meeting next month in Chicago to keep these questions alive,[94] and one meeting shall follow another to keep these questions alive till there shall be such an uprising as the world has never seen.

I have been called a demagogue by the newspapers, and I accept the title, if being a demagogue means a man who stood in the front ranks with his colleagues in Chicago in 1894 and braved the dangers of that hour.

I did not come here for the purpose of furthering the Social Democracy or any other movement. There is no division among us. If your heart is touched with the scene of human suffering, I care not what you are, we can stand shoulder to shoulder in this fight. I am myself a unionist and a socialist, and I am ready at all times to fight their battles.

I am no pessimist. I do not stand with those who cannot see a single star of hope in the heavens. I am not a prophet, either, but I can see the beginning of the end.

Another meeting is to follow this. It is called for in the resolutions. Another meeting will follow that, and another, until there is an uprising that will sweep away the Supreme Court and change the entire complexion of Congress, and when that time shall come American freemen shall have their rights. We will then suppress the injunction, and the issuer of the injunction with it.

The last quarter of a century has so degraded American workingmen that there is hardly any spirit left in them. I have read that we are reaching a point where all troubles in civilized countries will be settled without the aid of the sword or the bullet, but I want to say, should it be necessary in defense of American liberty, I shall be found in the time of [crisis] not in the rear, saying "go," but in the lead, calling on you to come. It may, in the course of human events, become necessary that blood shall be shed, and I may go down to my grave a slave, but at the resurrection I do not want to hear the clanking of chains on my children.

What little brain I may have is not for sale. It is not on the market, and the plutocracy has not enough money to buy it. They may exile me and those I love, but I will not part with my manhood. The judiciary has put a padlock on my lips and has forbidden me to walk on the highway, but it is of no avail; the liberties of a free people cry aloud for protection, and my voice shall not be still. What I am doing is not for humanity, but to still the cry of my own conscience. The duty we owe is first to ourselves. Let me say to you that with unity of purpose there is power enough in this convention to revolutionize the country in 12 months.

Not long ago I was with Mr. [W. D. Mahan][95] in the mining districts of West Virginia. Everything there is owned by corporations, and the miners have become so fearful of their power that they do not know whether they own their own souls. A miner started to tell me of the misery I could see they were suffering, and when I asked him his name he slipped away. He was afraid.

The mining companies employ preachers by the year to preach to the miners, and in their sermons to tell chance visitors of how fatherly the care of the company for the miner is. Fatherly care in paying him off in checks on the truck store which belongs to the company, where the miner is swindled in the prices he pays and always kept in debt to the company. They have a schoolhouse there, too—a schoolhouse where there have been no children across its threshold for five years. And it is right that there should be none—in the name of God, why do they want to educate the children in order to make the realities of their life more horrible to them than it is now? The more ignorant they are, the better it is for them while condemned to such abject misery.

Did you ever notice that whenever the plutocracy have any real dirty work to do they always employ a preacher to do it for them, and the preacher never finds a case so bad but what he is able to excuse it on some text built from the life of the Man of Sorrows who was acquainted with grief? I saw a procession of hungry children in West Virginia, and at their head was an American flag, and I said if the American flag typified such poverty and misery, its color should be as black as the raven's wing.

This movement has attained tremendous impetus and will go ahead with a rush. When the people are ready, and that day is not far off, my friends, there will be a spontaneous uprising, the Supreme Court will be abolished, Congress dispersed, and the sacred rights of American citizens and American freedmen will be enthroned. *[Great applause.]*

I plead guilty to the charge of being radical. I only wish you would allow me to be more radical still. Support us, gentlemen of the convention, and I promise you we will support the attempt to abolish government by injunction and the judges who issue them.

I hope in the march of common intelligence we will reach a point where we will be able to settle these questions without appealing to the sword or bullet. But I cannot tell. Certain it is there are thousands of our citizens who are suffering, and certain it is this cannot last. The time will come to incite the populace. When this time comes, you can depend on me. *[Cheers.]* I will not stand in the rear and ask you to go ahead. I will be in front and say to you: "Come on." *[Renewed cheering.]*

I shrink from that bloodshed. But if this is necessary to preserve liberty and our rights, in that event I will shed the last drop of blood that courses through my veins. [*Outbreak of cheering.*]

Plutocracy cannot buy me. They may send me to jail; may ostracize or hang me; but, in the language of the revolutionary heroes, I do not propose to part company with my self-respect, independence, and manhood.

We no longer have a republic—there is not a vestige of it left. The people are ripe for a great change. All they lack is direction and leadership. Let this conference supply it. Let this conference set the pace. Announce to the world that it will temporarily adjourn for three weeks to renew preparations. Ask every man to pledge himself to be there.

Let us do our duty, one and all. Be true to yourself; be true to your family; be true to your country.

The Lattimer Massacre[†]

September 11, 1897

Terre Haute, Ind., September 11 [1897]

Now that he realized the enormity of his crime and the popular indignation it has aroused, Sheriff Martin[96] is beginning to explain how he and his deputies came to fire upon a body of peaceable and defenseless miners on the road leading to Lattimer and committing wholesale murder.[97]

The sheriff's explanation simply does not explain, and such of it as would furnish a shadow of a justification is proven to be false. Instead of preserving the peace and upholding the law, the sheriff and his murderous deputies provoked disorder and then deliberately shot down the victims of their conspiracy.

Were I not unalterably opposed to capital punishment, I would say that the sheriff and his deputy assassins should be lynched. Each of them is guilty of murder in the first degree, and as they totally defied the law they were sworn

† Published as "Calls It Murder" in the *Chicago Chronicle,* September 12, 1897, unspecified page. Republished as "Massacred Miners" in *The Railway Times,* September 16, 1897.

to uphold in striking down their victims, they have forfeited all rights to protection under the law.

Robbed for Years

The men who have been shot down in cold blood are Pennsylvania miners. For years, they have been robbed in countless ways by the combines and companies which employed them, and now that they have been reduced to famine and rags, they are murdered in the public highway, as if they were so many rabid dogs.

I have been among them and know by personal observation all about their wretched condition. Even now, I can see the marching miners pursuing their endless journey. They are hungry, and the hot sands blister their shoeless feet. Their hovel habitations are the abodes of despair. Wives and half-naked children are in the grasp of starvation.

If by some magic the American people could look upon the scenes in some of the Pennsylvania mining regions, the bloody incident at Hazleton would precipitate a revolution.

The responsibility does not rest entirely with the sheriff and his deputies, as they are but tools in the hands of the real murderers, for whom we must look higher. As a general rule, the public functionaries in the mining regions are spineless and subservient creatures of companies. They issue proclamations, read riot acts, and commit murder when ordered to do so by their masters.

Men Were Peaceable

The miners who were murdered yesterday in the name of law and order were perfectly peaceable. They were quietly walking on the highway, when the assassin authorities stopped and bullied and attacked them.

Suppose a man of wealth, a coal operator, were stopped and killed under the same circumstances. The whole country would be around in an instant and the newspapers, supported by the Christian clergy, would demand in thunder tones that all the powers of the government be invoked to crush out the whole body of workingmen.

Wholesale murder has been committed at the behest of corporate capital by the public authorities in the name of law and order. No amount of jugglery or sophistication can obscure the indictment.

Is this an attack on government, or is it government?

Is it an assault on "Old Glory," as they declared when the Pullman strike was on, or is it what the old flag now symbolizes?

Governor Hastings[98] has ordered out the troops. Is it for the purpose of shooting the murderers or murdering more miners?

The crime is so revolting that it is difficult to keep within the bounds of moderate statement.

Text for Ministers

The 20 or more bloody graves of these murdered workingmen loom up before us.[99] What a text for the Christian ministry!

Will they raise their voices in a solemn protest as if the strikers were the murderers instead of the victims of the authorities?

When I think of these hard-worked, half-starved coal miners lying in the dirt of the highway, the blood coming from their ragged bodies, and then think of the hovels in which wives and children are awaiting their return, my heart melts in compassion and my whole being revolts against the satanic crime.

It is worthy of remark that the massacre occurred in a state that boasts of a majority of 280,000 in favor of protection of American labor.[100]

Government by injunction is bearing fruit. We will soon have government by murder.

The Pennsylvania horror is a blot upon the state, a disgrace to the Republic, and a blistering reproach to our civilization. It is sufficient to shock all Christendom, and it is to be hoped that the American people will wake up.

Statement to the Press Regarding the Suspension of Chicago Local Branch No. 2†

September 19, 1897

Our action in suspending the charter of this branch shows as plain as words can do that we will not be held responsible for utterances like the resolutions of last Sunday [September 12, 1897].[101] At the same time, we did not desire to take hasty action. We wish to discover how matters stand in this branch, and to see if the statement is well founded that the majority of its members are opposed to incendiary declarations. Until we take further action, the Social Democracy will have nothing to do with this branch.

As said, we do not wish to be harsh, but there is no connecting link between the platform of the Social Democracy and anarchy. If any of the members of Branch 2 hold sentiments incompatible with our program, there is nothing for them to do but withdraw, or, if they do not, the only course for us to take is to sever their connection with the organization.

Ours is a peaceable organization which seeks to educate the people to the use of peaceful means of reform. We believe in the ballot, not in bullets.

I do not deny that the provocation offered by the Hazleton affair was great, and that an excitable young man like Fitzgerald Murphy[102] may have been led away, as he now declares. However, our leaders should not allow themselves to be led by their feelings.

† Published as part of "Toss Out the Rabid," *Chicago Tribune,* vol. 56, no. 262 (September 19, 1897), 1.

We Cannot Hope to Succeed by Violence: Speech to Local Branch 1 SDA, Chicago† [excerpt]

September 19, 1897

You have political liberty now, and if you have not intelligence enough to enforce your demands by peaceful methods, can you do so by force?

This is not a contest between individuals. It is a clash of principles, a struggle between classes. If you want to make sympathy for the millionaires and strengthen their cause, go out and shoot one down or burn a block of buildings. That is the easiest way to destroy the Social Democracy.

The crime of Hazleton was not an unmixed evil.[103] It has opened the eyes of tens of thousands, and a New York paper's defense of the sheriff of Luzerne County will do us infinite good.

We must organize. We cannot be enjoined from organizing, but if speeches and resolutions like those of last Sunday [September 12, 1897] are repeated, the police will stop your meetings. *[Voice: "They've got the right to stop them, too, mister."]*

Well, we will not discuss the right. They will stop them. They have done it before. It isn't necessary to give our enemies this advantage. We cannot hope to succeed by violence. The powers against us are entrenched, and it will take time and organization and education to dislodge them.

Danger of Revolution

Some of you do not wish to wait. You want a revolution. I want to say that there is no man living that can bring on a revolution. Revolutions come in the fullness of time, and those who try to incite them get themselves killed.

If people have not intelligence enough to make use of the ballot to remedy their evils, they are dangerous materials to make revolutions with. In 1894, 200,000 workingmen in Illinois volunteered to shoot us down. We must reach these men.

One thing as to Hazleton. The deputies are nearly all former miners, whose places were taken by the imported laborers. They used to get living wages. They

---

† Published as part of "Debs Not for Bloodshed" in *Chicago Tribune,* vol. 56, no. 263 (September 20, 1897), 2.

resisted a cut and were displaced. They have been waiting for revenge. They did not wait for a second order to fire. We want to abolish these hellish conditions where labor is pitted against labor.

A man in the rear row asked in broken English what Mr. Debs proposed to do in case the demands of the Social Democracy should be refused.

We will make no demands until we have the power to enforce them. *[A voice: "You mean until you can take what you want?"]*

Yes, but no corporal's guard can take anything, and when you are able to take by force what you want, you will not need to take anything. If you should undertake to carry out last Sunday's program, you would be hanged. *[Voices: "No" and "Yes."]*

All Must Make Sacrifices

No man has a right in this organization who is unwilling to make sacrifices. We must be prepared to yield our lives if necessary. But I do not want senseless sacrifices. We need our men in the ranks, not in the grave. I am opposed to violence, bloodshed, and retaliation on principle. I do not believe in the eye-for-an-eye policy. I say it is barbarous. I do not want to take any man's life, because I object personally to being killed. I hold every man's life as sacred as my own. No man can say I ever sanctioned anything that savored of assassination. If revolution comes, of course blood will flow, but let the capitalists make it, not us. They are hastening it very fast now.

The program of violence is not only wrong, it is disruptive. It would destroy this entire movement. Do not think I am here to dictate. I believe our movement is the only one that promises anything. We shall gain in numbers and respect and influence, day by day and month by month and year by year, until we have the majority on our side, not so much by reason of what we do as by virtue of what we forbear to do. Every trust formed hastens the end of the competitive system. The big fish swallows the little one until there is left only the shark. I sympathize with the suffering this process entails, but all progress seems to be through suffering.

Without organization, nothing can be accomplished. Capital is organized. Touch it at one point and see how the entire mass responds. In 1894, we did not attack the newspapers, but they attacked us. See how the newspapers have denounced the United States Supreme Court for its ruling against railway pools.[104] They say that no roads can live in murderous competition. No, and neither can labor thrive in the competitive environment. We must educate.

Keynote Speech to the Chicago Conference of Labor Leaders† [excerpt]

September 27, 1897

I want it understood I was not to blame for the announcement that the convention was called off.[105] The Social Democracy does not wish to shoulder the blame of this action. We have been consistent; the others have not. I want it understood we are not opposed to trades unions. We are with trades unions always in a fight against organized capital.

The American Federation of Labor is solely to blame for calling off the convention. And right here I want to say, if we have a few more such victories as the Federation of Labor claims credit for in settling the coal miners' strike, the workingmen of the country will be starved to death. The settlement of the coal miners' strike as the executive board of the Federation of Labor arranged it left West Virginia and Illinois out in the cold.[106] Those labor leaders have said that the ordering of a strike would settle a difficulty, but my experience has taught me that the more we strike, the worse we are off. All the strikes of the last few years have been flat failures.

I am of the opinion that the workingmen will never get relief until they have sense enough to go to the ballot box in one body and vote for their own interests.

† Published as part of "Frost for E.V. Debs" in the *Chicago Tribune,* vol. 56, no. 271 (September 28, 1897), 10.

The Approaching Elections†

October 16, 1897

New York City, October 16, 1897

Since coming east,[107] I have been asked by many members of the Social Democracy what ticket, if any, I consider it advisable to support this fall in New York, Pennsylvania, and other states, in view of the fact that the Social Democracy has no ticket in the field. I answer, unhesitatingly, the ticket of the Socialist Labor Party, the only anti-capitalistic party in the field. At this juncture in the evolution of socialism, the supreme demand is to support principles. The personality of the candidates, especially as there is little or no prospect of electing a single one of them, is of little moment. In any event, personal prejudice should not influence any member to either vote against a socialist candidate or, which amounts to the same thing, not vote at all and thereby give support directly or indirectly to the capitalistic power that keeps him in fetters.

There are those who are embittered against the Socialist Labor Party on account of alleged persecution. Show that you are a true socialist by returning good for evil.

Above all parties, we are socialists, and in due course of time we shall find common ground and unite in one great party. What party that shall be, time will determine.

In the meanwhile, we must continue to bear in mind that there is no logic in abuse, and that ridicule and slander are not accepted as argument among intelligent and reputable men.

We are entirely pleased with the outlook for the Social Democracy. In June next, our national council will hold its first annual session. We are already organized in 26 states, and the rest will be in line in the next 90 days, so that our first national convention will see every state and territory represented. A national political platform will then be formulated, and the Social Democracy will be formally launched on the waters of American politics. Then we can support our own candidates as well as the principles of socialism.

To those who declare we are not "scientific" enough, we have only to say that we stand for the complete overthrow of capitalism, the abolition of the

† Published in *The Social Democrat,* vol. 4, no. 26 (October 21, 1897), 1.

wage system, and the collective ownership of all the means of production and distribution; and the Social Democracy of America, as a national and international political and economic organization, will fight along that line without a shadow of fusion or compromise, either as to principles or candidates (except in case of an honorable alliance with another socialist organization), until victory is achieved and the Cooperative Commonwealth is established.

Workingmen and the Social Democracy†

October 28, 1897

Boston, October 28, 1897

Never since history gives any account of man has the struggle for universal liberty and justice been carried forward with so much earnestness and determination as at the present time. Discontent and unrest have wide sway. To the most superficial observer, it is evident that there is something wrong in our social and economic life, and ignore it as we may, the question is daily expanding in proportions and will not down until it has arrested the public attention and has been settled in accordance with the principles of justice.

At the bottom of this widespread unrest is the grievance of the laboring class. The marvelous inventions and discoveries which were hailed with joyous acclaim because designed to lift the burden from the bowed form of toil have not only brought no relief to workingmen, but the machine, under the control of the private capitalist, has driven thousands from employment and forced the wages of other thousands to the starvation point.

In the days of the handicraftsman, the workingmen, as a rule, were far better off than they are today. The young man mastered a trade and was then sure of steady employment at fair wages. He worked a reasonable number of hours, had some leisure for reading and recreation, and was able to lay by something for a rainy day. In that day, there were no great employers of labor as we now understand that term. The modern "captain of industry" was unknown. The millionaire manufacturer had not yet made his appearance, nor

† Published as "His View of the Workingmen" in *Boston Journal,* (October 31, 1897), 10.

had his corollary, the tramp. They came together, after the machine appeared upon the scene, and the minute subdivision of labor which followed. Then it was no longer necessary to be a skilled mechanic, for the machine did the work; production was indefinitely increased and cheapened, and the process of making millionaires upon the one hand and mendicants upon the other was begun in earnest, and we have today the results before us and can contemplate the picture at our leisure.

The system which has thus been evolved is known as the capitalist system. That is to say, a comparatively few individuals own the capital, including land, factories, mines, railroads, and machinery of production, and by virtue of such private ownership control the destinies and the very lives of the toiling millions of our population Without this capital, labor is helpless. The workingman is denied access to the land, and machinery of production, unless he will agree to the terms fixed by capitalists, and as they invest their capital solely to make profits, the wage allowed the workingman is, as a general proposition, no larger than is required to maintain his subsistence. And even were the capitalist disposed to allow a liberal wage, he is in competition with other capitalists, and the wage of the worker tends irresistibly downward to the point of subsistence.

To give it still further power, capital combines and centralizes, and having crushed out competition, it enjoys a monopoly which makes it the master of the industrial no less than the commercial situation. The great body of wage-workers, the active producers of wealth, are at its mercy. They are essentially slaves under this system. They are compelled to accept what is allowed them, and must work under such conditions as capital imposes or pay the penalty of idleness, starvation, and death. There is no possible escape from economic servitude under this system.

It is true that workingmen still have their political rights, but these are largely infringed, if not destroyed, by their economic dependence. Thousands of employees of corporations know that their employment depends upon their voting as their employers want them to vote, and their political independence is thus extinguished and they become the unresisting serfs of the capitalist class.

It is thus that workingmen are reduced. From this social condition flows all the vice and crime that curse the world, and the stream will widen and deepen as long as we have a commercial system which traffics in the lives of human beings and reduces all men who labor to the level of merchandise to be bought and sold in the ever-cheapening markets of the world.

I need not for the purpose of this article show how, upon the other hand, corporate capital debauches public morals by the corrupt use of a large share of its ill-gotten gains in controlling legislation and other sources of power that perpetuate its supremacy at the expense of the people and to the utter subversion of the free institutions of our country.

Let it be borne in mind that it was Jefferson who said: "We want to establish a government under which there shall be no extremely rich and no extremely poor, and under which there shall be an equitable distribution of property."[108]

Who will be bold enough to aver that there is anything like an equitable distribution of property in this country? The laboring class, which alone produces, is poor, often to the verge of want and suffering, and the capitalist class, which does not live by useful labor, but by its cunning, riots in luxury and wealth.

The two hideous extremes mar and scar our civilization. They are widely separated by a yawning chasm of hate. Under such a condition there can be no social peace, and such a condition cannot be a permanent one.

To meet this social disintegration, the Social Democracy of America has been organized. Its motto is "Peace on earth, good will toward men."

The following is its declaration of principles and specific demands for relief:

Declaration of Principles

> We hold that all men are born free, and are endowed with certain natural rights, among which are life, liberty, and happiness. In the light of experience, we find that while all citizens are equal in theory, they are not so in fact. While all citizens have the same rights politically, this political equality is useless under the present system of economic inequity, which is essentially destructive of life, liberty, and happiness. In spite of our political equality, labor is robbed of the wealth it produces. By the development of this system, it is denied the means of self-employment, and by enforced idleness, through lack of employment, is even deprived of the necessities of life.
>
> To the obvious fact that our despotic system of economics is the direct opposite of our democratic system of politics can be plainly traced the existence of a class that corrupts the government, alienates public property, public franchises, and public functions, and holds this, the mightiest of nations, in abject dependence.
>
> Labor, manual and mental, being the creator of all wealth and all civilization, it rightfully follows that those who perform all labor and

create all wealth should enjoy the fruit of their efforts. But this is rendered impossible by the modern system of production. Since the discovery and application of steam and electric powers and the general introduction of machinery in all branches of industry, the industrial operations are carried on by such gigantic means that but few are now able to possess them, and thus the producer is separated from his products.

While in former times the individual worker labored on his own account, with his own tools, and was the master of his products, now dozens, hundreds, and thousands of men work together in shops, mines, factories, etc., cooperating according to the most efficient division of labor, but they are not the masters of their products. The fruits of this cooperative labor are in a great measure appropriated by the owners of the means of production, to wit: by the owners of machines, mines, land, and the means of transportation.

This system, by gradually extinguishing the middle class, necessarily leaves but two classes in our country: the large class of workers and the small class of great employers and capitalists.

Human power and natural forces are wasted by this system, which makes "profit" the only object in business.

Ignorance and misery, with all concomitant evils, are perpetuated by this system, which makes human labor a ware to be bought in the open market and places no real value on human life.

Science and invention are diverted from their humane purposes and made instruments for the enslavement of men and the starvation of women and children.

We, therefore, hold that in the natural course of social evolution, this system, through the destructive action of its failures and crises on the one hand, and the constructive tendencies of its trusts and other capitalistic combinations on the other, will annihilate the middle class, the basis upon which the system rests, and thereby work out its own downfall.

We therefore call upon all honest citizens to unite under the banner of the Social Democracy of America, so that we may be ready to conquer capitalism by making use of our political liberty and by taking possession of the public power, so that we may put an end to the present barbarous struggle, by the abolition of capitalism, the restoration of the land, and of all the means of production, transportation, and distribution, to the people as a collective body, and the substitution of the Cooperative Commonwealth for the present state of planless production, industrial war, and social disorder—a commonwealth which, although it will not make every man equal physically or mentally, will give to every worker the free exercise and the full benefit of his faculties, multiplied by all the modern factors of civilization and ultimately inaugurate the universal brotherhood of man. The Social Democracy of America will make democracy, "the rule of the people," a truth by ending the economic subjugation of the overwhelmingly great majority of the people.

With a view to the immediate relief of the people, all our efforts shall be put forth to secure to the unemployed self-supporting employment, using all proper ways and means to that end. For such purpose, one of the states of the Union, to be hereafter determined, shall be selected for the concentration of our supporters and the introduction of cooperative industry, and then gradually extending the sphere of our operations until the national Cooperative Commonwealth shall be established.

We also make the following specific demands for relief.

Demands for Relief

1. The public ownership of all industries controlled by monopolies, trusts, and combines.

2. The public ownership of all railroads, telegraph, telephone, all means of transportation, communication, waterworks, gas and electric plants, and all other public utilities.

3. The public ownership of all gold, silver, copper, lead, coal, iron, and all other mines; also all oil and gas wells.

4. Reduction of the hours of labor in proportion to the progress of production.

5. The inauguration of a system of public works and improvements for the employment of the unemployed, the public credit to be utilized for that purpose.

6. All useful inventions to be free to all, the inventor to be remunerated by the public.

7. The establishment of postal savings banks.

8. The adoption of the initiative and referendum, the imperative mandate, and proportional representation.

The organization is national and international, and is political as well as economic in character. No organization ever launched has met with such spontaneous and widespread favor. Less than four months old, it is already organized in 26 states in the Union.

The first national convention will be held at Chicago in June 1898. Every state and territory in the Republic will be represented. A national political platform will then be formulated, and the organization will be formally launched on the waters of national politics.

The main object will be economic emancipation, that is to say, the abolition of the capitalist system of production and distribution and the substitution of the Cooperative Commonwealth. In a word, economic democracy. Then "all men will be born equal" and the Declaration of Independence will become a realized fact. Then poverty, the prolific parent of crime, will disappear. Then all men will have equal right to labor, and they will receive the full product of their toil. Then production will be carried forward for the use and comfort of man, and not for the gratification of private greed. Then we shall have industry organized, and work, being scientifically done, will be relieved of all drudgery and the hours of labor reduced in proportion to the progress of invention—and it is then that we shall begin the march to a diviner civilization.

The Indiana Coal Miners†

circa November 30, 1897

The statement from Judge Terhune,[109] special agent for Governor Mount, of Indiana, that 8,000 families are literally starving to death in Indiana coal fields, is not overdrawn.

It is the haggard truth. The trouble is, the people will not believe it. They refuse to realize the appalling calamity, even though the groaning victims are at their very doors. The miners have been steadily ground down until the starvation point has been reached. This condition prevails over the entire mining region.

† Published in an undetermined Chicago evening newspaper. Reprinted in the *Kansas Agitator* [Garnet, KS], vol. 8, no. 29 (December 3, 1897).

It has been suggested that the governor compel the operators to concede living wages. This cannot be done. While the mines are private property, the owners will insist on operating them to suit themselves. Nor would any good result from a settlement in Indiana. The men must cover the whole competitive field.

The greed of the large operators will eventuate in the collective ownership of the mines. Man has no more right to private ownership of the coal mines than of the sea or the sun.

But something should be done now. There is a condition akin to war upon the country. The nation's defenses are going down in the battle against starvation. War measures are in order. The president of the United States can act. Let him issue a proclamation calling on the operators to meet and allow the miners living wages within 48 hours, under penalty of having their mines seized by the government and operated in the interest of the people.

That would settle the matter in an instant. Something has got to be done, and done quickly. If Indiana allows the families of 8,000 luckless laborers to be tortured by starvation, she will not escape the penalty, and the same is true of all other states and the country at large.

Notes

1. Mark Hanna (1837–1904) was a prominent businessman and political boss of the Republican Party. He was elected to the US Senate as a representative of Ohio in 1896.
2. From "The Battle-Field" (1839), by William Cullen Bryant (1794–1828).
3. Nebuchadnezzar II (634–562 BC) was the king of Babylonia. Daniel 3:1–7 tells a tale of Nebuchadnezzar decreeing that those subjects who failed to worship a golden statue of him would be immediately killed by being thrown into a blazing furnace.
4. Cornelius Vanderbilt (1794–1877) was one of the most prominent American transportation tycoons, becoming one of the richest people in the world through his ownership of various steamship and railway operations. Some of Vanderbilt's railroad lines included the New York Central, Michigan Central, and New York, Chicago & St. Louis Railroad.
5. Andrew Carnegie (1835–1919) was a Scottish-born steel magnate known for his Homestead works, site of a violent and bloody 1892 strike, as well as for his sponsorship of museums and public libraries.
6. Collis Potter Huntington (1821–1900) was a railway magnate associated with the formation of the Southern Pacific Railroad.
7. J. Pierpont Morgan (1837–1913) was a wealthy financier and banker. Morgan was instrumental in financing the corporate acquisitions that led to the establishment of the massive US Steel Corporation in 1901.
8. George M. Pullman (1831–1897) was the New York–born son of a building mover who made his fortune manufacturing and operating posh sleeping and dining cars for intercontinental railway traffic. The founder and namesake of a for-profit model city near Chicago that was to serve as his base of operations, Pullman crossed swords with striking workers backed by the American Railway Union in a sensational strike in the summer of 1894.
9. From "The Present Crisis" (1845), by James Russell Lowell (1819–1891).
10. Carroll D. Wright (1840–1909) was a statistician from New England who pioneered the field of labor statistics. Wright served as the first US commissioner of labor, holding that post from 1885 to 1905.
11. Luke 9:58 and Matthew 8:20.
12. Jay Gould (1836–1892) was a financial speculator who controlled the Union Pacific railroad. Through crooked and ruthless tactics, Gould managed to amass a fortune of nearly $80 million. He died of tuberculosis in 1892.
13. Edward Douglas White, Jr. (1845–1921), a former Confederate soldier from Louisiana, was appointed to the Supreme Court by President Grover Cleveland in 1894. He helped to establish the legal basis for racial segregation as part of the majority in the 1896 case of *Plessy v. Ferguson.* He was promoted to the post of chief justice by Republican William Howard Taft in 1910.
14. John Marshall Harlan (1833–1911) was appointed to the Supreme Court by Republican Rutherford B. Hayes in 1877. Harlan was the sole dissenter in the landmark 1896 case of *Plessy v. Ferguson,* which provided the legal rationale for racial segregation.

15. Henry Billings Brown (1836–1913) was appointed to the Supreme Court in 1890 by conservative Republican Benjamin Harrison. Brown wrote the majority opinion in the 1896 case of *Plessy v. Ferguson.*
16. The income tax was ruled unconstitutional by a split decision of the Supreme Court on April 8, 1895. This decision was ultimately overcome with the passage of the Sixteenth Amendment to the US Constitution in 1913.
17. Reference is to Louis W. Rogers (1859–1953), editor of *The Railway Times,* who drew a three-month sentence for contempt of court in the aftermath of the 1894 Pullman strike.
18. James Graham Jenkins (1834–1921) was a Democratic politician who became US District Court judge for the District of Wisconsin in 1888. In 1893, he was named to a seat on the US Circuit Court for the Seventh Circuit. In December 1893, Jenkins issued an injunction against employees of the Northern Pacific Railroad from combining together to strike against a reduction of wages.
19. Jacob S. Coxey, Sr. (1854–1951) was a progressive politician from Massillon, Ohio, who led an "army" of unemployed in a sensational cross-country march on Washington. A two-time nominee for governor of Ohio atop the ticket of the People's Party, in 1932 Coxey ran a campaign for president of the United States under the banner of the Farmer-Labor Party.
20. William A. Woods (1837–1901) was appointed to the US District Court for the District of Indiana by Chester A. Arthur in 1883. He was appointed to the US Court of Appeals by Benjamin Harrison in 1891, a position that brought him into contact with Eugene V. Debs.
21. Ella Wheeler Wilcox (1850–1919) was a poet and author from rural Wisconsin. As a poet, Wilcox attained a substantial popular following in her day, but she is not well regarded by historians of early-twentieth-century verse.
22. Alva Adams (1850–1922) was a Democratic governor of Colorado, elected to three non-consecutive terms.
23. This was the first of a series of seven articles by Debs in *The Western Miner,* official organ of the Cloud City Miners' Union No. 33, Western Federation of Miners of America, the organization that conducted the Leadville strike of 1896–97.
24. Opening lines of the hymn "God Moves in a Mysterious Way" (1774) by William Cowper (1731–1800).
25. A special committee was named by the 11th Colorado Legislative Assembly to investigate the circumstances of the Leadville strike. It published its findings as *Report of the Joint Special Legislative Committee of the Eleven General Assembly on the Leadville Strike* (1897).
26. The *New York Journal,* a newspaper that was part of William Randolph Hearst's stable, was initially styled as a publication friendly to radical discourse. It included on its staff as writers and editorialists at various times such luminaries as socialist author Laurence Gronlund, Albert Brisbane (son of prominent Fourierite Arthur Brisbane), and Herbert Casson.
27. That is, Chicago.

28. Reference is to the 5th Annual Convention of the Western Federation of Miners, held in Salt Lake City from May 10–19, 1897. The last eight days of the gathering were held in non-public session, which reelected Edward Boyce of Warner, Idaho, as president.
29. At 12:30 a.m. during the night of September 20–21, 1896, a mob of armed strikers attacked the Coronado mine, a facility reopened during the Leadville labor stoppage through the use of strikebreakers. A gun battle lasting almost an hour erupted between strikers and armed strikebreakers inside the mine, during which three dynamite bombs were thrown. At 1:45 a.m., an oil tank ruptured and exploded into flames, engulfing the mine buildings and forcing the strikebreakers to retreat. During the battle and its aftermath, three members of the Cloud City Miners' Union and a Leadville fireman who refused mob demands not to attempt to put out the fire were killed; the surface structures of the Coronado mine were completely destroyed. A similar assault was conducted against the Robert Emmet mine, located about a mile away, although no fatalities resulted from that protracted gun battle. The attacks caused Governor Robert McIntire to reconsider his previous refusal to accede to mine owners' requests for deployment of the state militia to protect their property interests. The first troops arrived the very next night.
30. *Gallows.*
31. The Chemin d'Ohain was a deeply sunken lane that bisected the battlefield at Waterloo and that enabled field marshal Arthur Wellesley, the duke of Wellington, to conceal his forces and entrap and defeat the advancing French army of Napoleon Bonaparte on June 18, 1815.
32. The Pittsburgh & Lake Erie Railroad, established in May 1875.
33. While the economic condition of coal operators may well have been disastrous in this period, the example Debs cites here is far from prototypical. It involves financial machinations that were part of a dispute among siblings over disposition of the $450,000 estate of coal operator John C. Risher, who died in 1889, leaving his mining operation and various real estate holdings in trust to his children. One of these children, John M. Risher, drew out more than his share from the trust fund, prompting legal action. The John M. Risher Coal Co. was liquidated in the summer of 1898, retaining a positive cash balance.
34. Edward Boyce (1862–1941) was president of the Western Federation of Miners. Debs was called to Leadville by Boyce in January 1897, and the pair toured the West together during the first quarter of 1897, sharing the stage at public meetings and smaller sessions of organized workers. On May 10, Boyce—still traveling with Debs—delivered a speech in Salt Lake City that included a call for the WFM to "devise ways and means to provide every member with the latest improved rifles" with a view to arming 25,000 men within two years, which brought about the request for this statement.
35. The governor of Colorado during the bitter Cripple Creek miners' strike of 1894 was Davis H. Waite (1825–1901), a Populist. The five-month strike was led by the Western Federation of Miners.

36. The American Railway Union had earlier called a special convention to be held in Chicago on June 15, 1897.
37. The term derives from Genesis, chapter 16, with Ishmael being the son of Abraham and the slave Hagar who, in turn, sired a great tribe. In this context, "outcasts at war with society."
38. From *Hamlet,* Act III, Scene 1 (c. 1600), by William Shakespeare (1564–1616).
39. Note that this marks an expansion on all three fronts—race, gender, and occupation—from the previous membership requirements of the ARU, which was constitutionally limited to white railway workers, and thus was essentially all male.
40. John Rogers (1838–1901) was elected governor of Washington in 1896 on the ticket of the People's Party, becoming the third chief executive of the new state. Rogers jumped to the Democratic Party in 1900.
41. From "A Psalm of Life" (1838), by Henry Wadsworth Longfellow (1807–1882).
42. From *The Decline and Fall of the Roman Empire* (1776), by Edward Gibbon (1737–1794).
43. From Luke 2:14.
44. "Unexplored place."
45. Adapted from Luke 16:23, part of the story of Lazarus.
46. From *The Deserted Village* (1770), by Oliver Goldsmith (1728–1774).
47. From *Hamlet,* Act V, Scene 2.
48. From Julius Caesar (1599), Act IV, Scene 3, by William Shakespeare.
49. From Acts 10:34.
50. Allusion to the Tower of Babel, from Genesis 11:1–9.
51. "Furthest limit."
52. Adapted from Isaiah 35:1.
53. President Andrew Jackson.
54. The expression is a construct of Grover Cleveland (1807–1908).
55. This open letter to Standard Oil tycoon John D. Rockefeller, variously interpreted as a publicity stunt made for political effect or a bizarre plea for financial assistance, was apparently spurred by an interview conducted a few days previously by prominent journalist James Creelman (1859–1915). Creelman, a critic of the colonization scheme, had named Rockefeller among a short list of "men of power and genius." He pointedly asked Debs, "How are you going to dispose of them? What are you going to do with the wealth they have gathered?" Creelman indicates this prompted a moment of reflection before Debs replied, "Their wealth will be gradually absorbed into the common ownership of products. We offer them a glorious field for their energy and genius. A man like Mr. Rockefeller could organize and direct the oil industries of the country for the benefit of the people. He would live comfortably, and, I believe, happily, and would not have to lie awake at night racked with the responsibilities of too great wealth." (See Creelman, *New York Journal and Advertiser,* June 19, 1897, 1–2.) It seems that Debs sought to make this public offer in good faith to affirm his statement made to Creelman, while certainly not expecting for a moment that anything would actually come of it.

56. A cord is a unit of measure of firewood, defined as a stack measuring four feet wide, four feet high, and eight feet long.
57. The mayor of Chicago in 1897 was George Bell Swift (1845–1912), a Republican.
58. This statement to the press was made in Chicago following the close of the founding convention of the Social Democracy of America.
59. Debs was in Milwaukee from July 7–11, 1897. The main speech delivered during his visit was held at West Side Turner Hall in the evening of July 7. This statement was probably issued that day or the day after.
60. That is, the People's Party.
61. From *As You Like It* (1599), Act II, Scene 1, by William Shakespeare.
62. Debs arrived in Milwaukee to speak on July 7, 1897, with one published report still having him in town until leaving for Oshkosh on July 12.
63. Details of this alleged $50,000 appropriation remain unclear.
64. Women's blouses.
65. Henry Osborne Havemeyer (1847–1907) was president of the American Sugar Refining Company and founder of a sugar trust bringing together most of the country's refiners to regulate production and prices.
66. Charles Yerkes (1837–1905) was a financier that controlled most of Chicago's street railway lines following a series of takeovers of independent lines during the 1880s and 1890s.
67. From Matthew 7:20.
68. George Washington Vanderbilt II (1862–1914) was the youngest son and an heir of railroad magnate William Henry Vanderbilt (1821–1885). The younger Vanderbilt had constructed for himself the largest country estate in America, a 179,000-square-foot mansion located on more than ten square miles of land near Asheville, North Carolina.
69. Charles Warren Spalding was the president of the Globe Savings Bank and treasurer of the University of Illinois board of directors. After being acquitted in two previous bank embezzlement trials, Spalding was charged with misappropriation of $25,000 in state funds in connection with the bank's failure. Spalding ultimately served six years in the state penitentiary at Joliet following a July 1897 conviction.
70. Apparently a reference to the country's unemployment rate, which exceeded 10 percent from the onset of the Panic of 1893 until 1899.
71. This speech was delivered outside the Wheeling City Building to a crowd of 3,000.
72. J. W. Rea of Chicago was second vice president of the Brotherhood of Painters, Decorators, and Paperhangers of America and shared the podium with Debs at Wheeling.
73. John Bright (1811–1889) was a British Liberal politician.
74. From *Childe Harold's Pilgrimage* (c. 1812) by George Gordon Noel Byron (1788–1824).
75. Historian Richard Oestreicher has noted that the same metaphor of the "bending cross" was effectively used in Debs's final speech at time of sentencing September 14, 1918 and subsequently repurposed by Ray Ginger as the title of his 1949 Debs

biography. Oestreicher attributes the origin of the phrase to an 1890 keynote address at the annual convention of the Brotherhood of Locomotive Firemen by Tom Fitch. See Oestreicher, "A Note on the Origins of Eugene V. Debs' 'Bending Cross' Speech," *Indiana Journal of History,* vol. 76, no. 1 (March 1980), 54–6. Dr. Oestreicher's research from the pre-internet era misses Fitch's own likely source of inspiration and the true origin of the metaphor, an anonymous July 1863 poem from Roxbury, Massachusetts, entitled "Midnight is Past—The Cross Begins to Bend," which also invokes imagery of a mariner sailing the Southern seas. See *The Living Age,* whole no. 1,000 (August 1, 1863), 194.

76. From Psalms 30:5.
77. For background on the Brotherhood of the Cooperative Commonwealth, see the introduction to this volume, p. 5.
78. As was the case with a previous forecast of a future daily newspaper for the American Railway Union, this prediction by Debs proved unrealistic and was unrealized.
79. *The New Time* was a self-described "reform magazine" published by Charles H. Kerr & Co. of Chicago from 1893 to 1898. The magazine was populist in political orientation and was succeeded in 1899 by the *International Socialist Review.*
80. The St. Louis labor conference was held from September 28–30, 1897. The meeting was called in response to judicial repression of an ongoing coal miners' strike and was attended by about 200 delegates from various unions affiliated with the American Federation of Labor. Leading roles were played by Michael D. Ratchford, head of the United Mine Workers of America, and James Sovereign of the Knights of Labor. AF of L president Samuel Gompers boycotted the event. The conclave was dominated from the podium by Debs, who delivered a speech that electrified the delegates. Debs attempted unsuccessfully to parlay the event into a more permanent organization, with a follow-up convention organized by him failing miserably.
81. From *Lalla Rookh* (1817) by Thomas Moore (1779–1852).
82. Little is known of the biography of Parrhasius, regarded as one of the greatest painters of ancient Greece, who gained renown sometime prior to 399 BC.
83. Allusion to Ezekiel 37.
84. From Job 19:24.
85. John Jay Jackson, Jr. (1824–1907) was a judge for the US District Court for the District of West Virginia, sitting more than four decades on the bench. Known as the "Iron Judge," Jackson issued an injunction against Debs in July 1897 prohibiting him from speaking in the state on behalf of striking coal miners.
86. John W. Mason was a judge of the Marion County [WV] Court. He issued an injunction against Debs in July 1897 prohibiting him from interfering with a strike taking place at the West Fairmont Coal and Coke Company, alleging a conspiracy to "induce and coerce" employees from working in the mines.
87. Nathan Goff, Jr. (1843–1920), a former secretary of the Navy during the Rutherford B. Hayes administration. He served as a judge of the US Court of Appeals for the Fourth Circuit from 1892 to 1913, having been appointed to the bench by President Benjamin Harrison.

88. John William Showalter (1844–1898) was a judge of the US Circuit Court of Appeals for the Seventh Circuit in Indianapolis. He was appointed to the post in 1895 by conservative Democrat Grover Cleveland.
89. Foolish idea.
90. A person from Switzerland.
91. "Men of England" (1819), by Percy Bysshe Shelley (1792–1822).
92. The stenographer of the *St. Joseph Herald*, which published a tendentious alternative verbatim report of the speech, has this as "$45,000."
93. Terence V. Powderly (1849–1924), former general master workman of the Knights of Labor, was appointed commissioner general of immigration by Republican president William McKinley in July 1897.
94. Debs was co-signatory of a call for a conference of labor leaders to be held in Chicago on September 27.
95. The original reads "Mr. Martin," likely a transcription error. W. D. Mahan was the president of the International Union of Carmen and is known to have joined Debs on the platform to address striking West Virginia miners in the summer of 1897.
96. James F. Martin (18XX–1951) was the sheriff of Luzerne County, Pennsylvania.
97. On September 10, 1897, the Luzerne County sheriff's posse, under the authority of Sheriff James F. Martin, fired on a crowd of striking immigrant coal miners outside the Lattimer mine near Hazleton, Pennsylvania, after they refused orders to disperse. The strikers, mostly Slavic and Baltic immigrants, were marching in the hot summer sun from their village of Harwood to the Latimer mines, located on the northeast side of the neighboring town of Hazleton, about six miles away. Twenty-one of the strikers were killed and scores more injured in the bloodbath, many of whom were shot in the back. Although a trial resulted, no member of the posse was convicted of any crime.
98. Daniel H. Hastings (1849–1903), a Republican, was governor of Pennsylvania. Hastings was formerly a high-ranking officer in the Pennsylvania State Militia.
99. The official death count was 19.
100. Reference is to the majority of Pennsylvania voters casting ballots in favor of the Republican Party and its "protective" tariff.
101. In the aftermath of the Lattimer Massacre of September 10, in which 19 unarmed striking coal miners were shot to death near Hazleton, Pennsylvania, by a county sheriff's posse, with dozens of others wounded, Chicago Branch 2 passed inflammatory resolutions calling for retaliatory violence against the capitalist class, provoking this reaction by the executive council of the SDA. Among the officers of Branch 2 was Lucy Parsons, widow of revolutionary socialist activist and Haymarket martyr Albert R. Parsons. After a four-hour closed meeting during the night of September 18–19 between the national executive council and the five-member executive board of Local 2, the Local Branch No. 2 was suspended, and Debs made this statement to the Chicago press.
102. Fitzgerald Murphy (1869–1906), a journalist, playwright, actor, and the president of Chicago SDA Local Branch No. 1, was quoted as saying, "If I had my way, I

would kill 20 millionaires today to pay for the poor fellows who were shot down in Pennsylvania." See *Chicago Tribune,* September 14, 1897, 6. Murphy speedily retracted the statement after it made print.

103. Reference is to the Lattimer Massacre of September 10, 1897, in which 19 unarmed immigrant coal miners in a crowd of strikers were shot down by a Luzerne County sheriff's posse. In response, SDA Branch 2 issued inflammatory resolutions calling for armed struggle, which moved Debs and the Board of the SDA to revoke the branch's charter for violating the constitution of the national organization.
104. Earlier in 1897, the United States Supreme Court ruled that pooling—agreements between railroads systematically dividing traffic on competitive routes to thereby maintain high prices—was a violation of the Sherman Antitrust Act.
105. At the conference of labor leaders held in St. Louis on August 30, 1897, Gene Debs lit up the room with a sensational radical speech. Intending to build upon the momentum of the gathering, he joined Knights of Labor general master workman James Sovereign and others in calling a follow-up convention, to be held in Chicago on September 27. AF of L president Samuel Gompers and other top officials of the federation seem not to have been amused with Debs's agitation on behalf of the Social Democracy of America and the tactic of political action, however, and efforts were made to scuttle the Chicago gathering, with the AF of L releasing a statement indicating "We can see no need for the labor convention in Chicago . . . We advise our unions not to be represented there . . . It is not by conventions, with irresponsible talk, inflammatory declamation, and revolutionary buncombe that the cause of labor can be advanced." (See *Chicago Tribune,* September 27, 1897, 3. As a result, only an eclectic band of 65 delegates made their way to Chicago for the September 27 gathering—a major black eye for Debs and the Social Democracy.
106. While the recent coal strike was settled with significant improvements for the Pennsylvania miners, those from outside the state were excluded from the settlement.
107. Debs began an East Coast speaking tour on October 7 with the first of six appearances in New York City on behalf of the SDA. His tour, which lasted more than five weeks, took him to various points in New York, Pennsylvania, Connecticut, Massachusetts, Maryland, and New Jersey before returning home by way of Cleveland.
108. While not themselves Jefferson scholars, the editors have been unable to connect this quotation directly with Thomas Jefferson (1843–1826). It seems likely that this is a fabricated chestnut that was circulated in slightly changed variants among many progressive orators and writers of the 1890s, with one writer quoting another who had quoted another.
109. Thomas J. Terhune (1848–1926) was an ex-circuit court judge from Boone County, Indiana. In July 1897, he was appointed by Governor James A. Mount as a special commissioner to investigate the conditions and grievances of striking coal miners in Indiana.

1898

The Martyred Apostles of Labor†

February 1898

The century now closing is luminous with great achievements. In every department of human endeavor, marvelous progress has been made. By the magic of the machine which sprang from the inventive genius of man, wealth has been created in fabulous abundance. But, alas, this wealth, instead of blessing the race, has been the means of enslaving it. The few have come in possession of all, and the many have been reduced to the extremity of living by permission.

A few have had the courage to protest. To silence these so that the dead-level of slavery could be maintained has been the demand and command of capital-blown power. Press and pulpit responded with alacrity. All the forces of society were directed against these pioneers of industrial liberty, these brave defenders of oppressed humanity—and against them the crime of the century has been committed.

Albert R. Parsons, August Spies, George Engel, Adolph Fischer, Louis Lingg, Samuel Fielden, Michael Schwab, and Oscar Neebe paid the cruel penalty in prison cell and on the gallows.[1]

They were the first martyrs in the cause of industrial freedom, and one of the supreme duties of our civilization, if indeed we may boast of having been redeemed from savagery, is to rescue their names from calumny and do justice to their memory.

The crime with which these men were charged was never proven against them. The trial which resulted in their conviction was not only a disgrace to all judicial proceedings, but a foul, black, indelible, and damning stigma upon the nation.

It was a trial organized and conducted to convict—a conspiracy to murder innocent men, and hence had not one redeeming feature.

It was a plot, satanic in all its conception, to wreak vengeance upon defenseless men, who, not being found guilty of the crime charged in the indictment, were found guilty of exercising the inalienable right of free speech in the interest of the toiling and groaning masses, and thus they became the first martyrs to a cause which, fertilized by their blood, has grown in strength and sweep and influence from the day they yielded up their lives and liberty in its defense.

---

† Published in *The New Time*, vol. 6, no. 2 (February 1898), 79–82.

As the years go by and the history of that infamous trial is read and considered by men of thought and who are capable of wrenching themselves from the grasp of prejudice and giving reason its rightful supremacy, the stronger the conviction becomes that the present generation of workingmen should erect an enduring memorial to the men who had the courage to denounce and oppose wage-slavery and seek for methods of emancipation.

The vision of the judicially murdered men was prescient. They saw the dark and hideous shadows of coming events. They spoke words of warning, not too soon, not too emphatic, not too trumpet-toned—for even in 1886, when the Haymarket meetings were held, the capitalistic grasp was upon the throats of workingmen and its fetters upon their limbs.

There was even then idleness, poverty, squalor, the rattling of skeleton bones, the sunken eye, the pallor, the living death of famine, the crushing and the grinding of the relentless wills of the plutocracy, which more rapidly than the mills of the gods grind their victims to dust.

The men who went to their death upon a verdict of a jury, I have said, were judicially murdered—not only because the jury was packed for the express purpose of finding them guilty, not only because the crime for which they suffered was never proven against them, not only because the judge before whom they were arraigned was unjust and bloodthirsty, but because they had, in the exercise of free speech, declared that men who subjected their fellow men to conditions often worse than death were unfit to live.

In all lands and in all ages where the victims of injustice have bowed their bodies to the earth, bearing grievous burdens laid upon them by cruel taskmasters, and have lifted their eyes starward in the hope of finding some orb whose light inspired hope, 10 million times the anathema has been uttered and will be uttered until a day shall dawn upon the world when the emancipation of those who toil is achieved by the brave, self-sacrificing few who, like the Chicago martyrs, have the courage of crusaders and the spirit of iconoclasts and dare champion the cause of the oppressed and demand in the name of an avenging God and of an outraged humanity that infernalism shall be eliminated from our civilization.

And as the struggle for justice proceeds and the battlefields are covered with the slain, as Mother Earth drinks their blood, the stones are given tongues with which to denounce man's inhumanity to man—aye, to women and children, whose moanings from hovel and sweatshop, garret, and cellar arraign our civilization, our religion, and our judiciary—whose wailings and lamentations, hushing to silence every sound the Creator designed to make the world a paradise of harmonies, transform it into an inferno where the demons of greed plot and scheme to consign their victims to lower depths of degradation and despair.

The men who were judicially murdered in Chicago in 1887, in the name of the great state of Illinois, were the *avant-couriers* of a better day. They were called anarchists, but at their trial it was not proven that they had committed any crime or violated any law. They had protested against unjust laws and their brutal administration. They stood between oppressor and oppressed, and they dared, in a free (?) country, to exercise the divine right of free speech; and the records of their trial, as if written with an "iron pen and lead in the rock forever,"[2] proclaim the truth of the declaration.

I would rescue their names from slander. The slanderers of the dead are the oppressors of the living. I would, if I could, restore them to their rightful positions as evangelists, the proclaimers of good news to their fellow men—crusaders, to rescue the sacred shrines of justice from the profanations of the capitalistic defilers who have made them more repulsive than Augean stables. Aye, I would take them, if I could, from peaceful slumber in their martyr graves; I would place joint to joint in their dislocated necks; I would make the halter the symbol of redemption; I would restore the flesh to their skeleton bones—their eyes should again flash defiance to the enemies of humanity, and their tongues, again, more eloquent than all the heroes of oratory, should speak the truth to a gainsaying world. Alas, this cannot be done—but something can be done. The stigma fixed upon their names by an outrageous trial can be forever obliterated and their fame be made to shine with resplendent glory on the pages of history.

Until the time shall come, as come it will, when the parks of Chicago shall be adorned with their statues, and with holy acclaim, men, women, and children, pointing to these monuments as testimonials of gratitude, shall honor the men who dared to be true to humanity and paid the penalty of their heroism with their lives, the preliminary work of setting forth their virtues devolves upon those who are capable of gratitude to men who suffered death that they might live.

They were the men who, like Al-Hassen, the minstrel of the king, went forth to find themes of mirth and joy with which to gladden the ears of his master, but returned disappointed, and, instead of themes to awaken the gladness and joyous echoes, found scenes which dried up all the fountains of joy. Touching his golden harp, Al-Hassen sang to the king, as Parsons, Spies, Engel, Fielden, Fischer, Lingg, Schwab, and Neebe proclaimed to the people:

O king, at thy
Command I went into the world of men;
I sought full earnestly the thing which I
Might weave into the gay and lightsome song.
I found it, king; 'twas there. Had I the art
To look but on the fair outside I nothing
Else had found. That art not mine, I saw what
Lay beneath. And seeing thus I could not sing;
For there, in dens more vile than wolf or jackal
Ever sought, were herded, stifling, foul, the
Writhing, crawling masses of mankind. Man!
Ground down beneath oppression's iron heel
Till God in him was crushed and driven back,
And only that which with the brute he shares
Finds room to upward grow.

Such pictures of horror our martyrs saw in Chicago, as others have seen them in all the great centers of population in the country. But, like the noble minstrel, they proceeded to recite their discoveries and with him moaned:

And in this world
I saw how womanhood's fair flower had
Never space its petals to unfold. How
Childhood's tender bud was crushed and trampled
Down in mire and filth too evil, foul, for beasts
To be partakers in. For gold I saw
The virgin sold, and motherhood was made
A mock and scorn.

I saw the fruit of labor
Torn away from him who toiled, to further
Swell the bursting coffers of the rich, while
Babes and mothers pined and died of want.
I saw dishonor and injustice thrive. I saw
The wicked, ignorant, greedy, and unclean,
By means of bribes and baseness, raised to seats
Of power, from whence with lashes, pitiless
And keen, they scourged the hungry, naked throng
Whom first they robbed and then enslaved.[3]

Such were the scenes that the Chicago martyrs had witnessed and which may still be seen, and for reciting them and protesting against them they were judicially murdered.

It was not strange that the hearts of the martyrs "grew into one with the great moaning, throbbing heart" of the oppressed; not strange that the nerves of the martyrs grew "tense and quivering with the throes of mortal pain"; not strange that they should pity and plead and protest.[4] The strange part of it is that in our high noon of civilization, a damnable judicial conspiracy should have been concocted to murder them under the forms of law.

That such is the truth of history, no honest man will attempt to deny; and hence the demand, growing more pronounced every day, to snatch the names of the martyred evangelists of labor emancipation from dishonor and add them to the roll of the most illustrious dead of the nation.

Words of Old Coinage[†]

February 1898

The terms "social" and "democracy" are of old coinage. They have come down to us from a former generation. But they live in pristine strength and are as available now for legitimate use as when they received the stamp of the mint and were sent forth on that mission of war or peace as fate might determine in the interest of humanity.

In the first place, I would have my readers comprehend exactly the significance of the words used as the title of a great movement in the United States and throughout the civilized world, which is progressing at a rapid pace for the reconstruction of government, the regeneration of society, and the elimination of antiquated errors productive of modern miseries so numerous as to challenge calculation, so degrading as to defy exaggeration, and so monstrous as to create widespread horror and alarm.

Need it be said that the term "social" relates to society, and in the connection used, to the entire social body, "to the public as an aggregate body;" or that the term "democracy" relates to government by the people, that is to say, self-government. Hence "social democracy" is a movement embodying the best sentiments of the times in which we live to improve social, economic,

† Published in *Democratic Magazine,* February 1898, unspecified pages. Reprinted in *The Social Democrat,* vol. 5, no. 9 (March 3, 1898), 1.

and political conditions, which, while the main idea is the emancipation of the poor from poverty and the ten thousand ills which poverty breeds, is also in the interest of every other class that goes to make up the body social and politic—the ignorant and the learned, the virtuous and the vicious, all, of every name and grade, constituting the vast and motley population—because this vast aggregation, touched anywhere by disease, involves the whole mass, and there is no hope for society while we live under a capitalistic system that exalts the few and degrades the many, makes one man fabulously rich and ten thousand despairingly poor. Such conditions are unnatural—they are violative of every conception of justice and righteousness. They create two classes—masters and slaves, monarchs and menials. They arraign "divine providence," make the "brotherhood of man" a myth, the Declaration of Independence a sham, economic equality a vagary, and social peace an impossibility.

Under this monstrous system, millions of the struggling, staggering, suffering poor have been reduced to slavery, and their homes (?) are no better than the lairs of wild beasts.

All social and political equilibrium is destroyed. The "scales of justice," manipulated by robed rascals for pelf, have destroyed all respect for courts, until all over this fair land, from center to circumference, he whose ears are attuned to the notes of despair may hear the whispered maledictions of millions of victims whose words should be those of satisfaction and contentment.

In the midst of such conditions, the Social Democracy strides to the front and offers its services to ameliorate the woes of which the poor complain.

It proposes to put an end to the rule of capital by abolishing the capitalist class and transferring the means of production and distribution from private hands for personal gain to public ownership for the common welfare.

The profit system will thus cease to exist, and all industry will be owned and controlled by the people in their collective capacity, organized on a scientific basis, operating with the most improved machinery, and carried forward cooperatively for the promotion of the welfare of the whole people. This will mean economic equality, the basis of the only real civilization the world can ever know.

All men will enjoy the inalienable right to work and the full product of their toil. Wage-slavery will cease. The towering capitalistic master and the cowering wage-menial will disappear together. Both will reappear as men, and free from the perverting, callousing, and degrading influences of the old system, they will be united as brothers, and with their faces toward the economic sunrise, they will begin the march to ideal, all-embracing civilization.

This is the supreme purpose of the great national and international social democracy. It is composed of a progressive and intelligent membership, and is equipped for action on both political and economic lines. It comprehends the present chaotic conditions and their cause, and proposes to move forward, direct as a rifle ball, upon the works of the enemy. Its weapon is the ballot. It will not turn backward, nor move aside the breadth of a hair. It will not fuse nor compromise. Its numbers will steadily increase, for it is composed of a class-conscious membership who cannot be bribed, nor intimidated, nor stampeded.

The battle royal is now on. It is between capitalism and socialism; there is no middle ground and there can be no compromise. The issue is the collective instead of the individual ownership of the earth, and the freedom instead of the slavery of mankind.

In June [1898] the first national convention of the Social Democracy will be held. Every state in the union will be represented. The work of the organization will then be prosecuted with all the ardor of crusaders. The colonization department, organized under an efficient commission, to enter upon the work of colonizing the unemployed and establishing a system of cooperative industry, is one of the strong features of the organization, and gives promise not only of practical and beneficent results in the near future, but of being a powerful factor in promoting the general movement and hastening its triumph.

What a noble and ennobling spirit animates the Social Democracy!

It would strike the fetters from the millions of victims of wage-slavery. It would enthrone manhood.

It would inaugurate independence where now crouching, crawling, slaving dependence exists.

It would give to every toiler a home in his own right, make it light and bright and joyous; a fit place for mothers to expand in all the loveliness of womanhood, where children may be reared and lisp in song and praise their thankfulness for blessings to which millions of them are now strangers.

In seeking to accomplish the work in which the Social Democracy is now engaged, there is no departure from the severest demands of common sense. The Social Democracy is as free from vagary, as far from the impracticable, as the science of mathematics.

It uses words and terms which are signs of emancipating ideas—lifting, building ideas. It sees in social democracy the certainty of man owing himself, of receiving and enjoying all he earns, giving no part of it to an exploiter who poses as his benefactor. It sees cooperative workingmen in control of their own factories, their own machinery and tools, regulating their own hours of labor and conditions of employment, working for themselves and their loved ones, owning their homes, and knowing no master excepting the law which, as a "rule of action," liberates instead of crushes and dwarfs their energies.

Contrast this program with what is transpiring around us today, and men of thought must be satisfied that there is a demand growing every day more imperative for the Social Democracy.

The unseemly wranglings in Congress over civil service, indicative of inordinate greed for spoils, mantles the face of the nation with a blush of shame, emphasizing the fact that political baseness and corruption have reached fathomless depths, and demonstrating that under the rule of capitalism the political waters, foul beyond conception, are breeding stenches more numerous than Coleridge found at Cologne,[5] and that the minds of Republican politicians, the avowed champions of "protection of labor" and "civil service reform," are as contaminating as the exudations of a pestilence.

While the Social Democracy is putting forth its energies to solve problems of interest to the toiling masses, the operations of the Dingley tariff are multiplying and strengthening the trusts of the country,[6] and these are tightening their grasp upon the throats of the people and commanding obedience by extortion. While there is neither war nor pestilence, failures, bankruptcy, insanity, suicide, murder, larceny, and prostitution increase at a rate to threaten the country with wreck and ruin; and while this appalling program is being carried out, national banker and Secretary of the Treasury Gage is formulating a currency plan that will deliver the people to the tender mercies of four thousand or more national banks,[7] whose rapacity is equal to as many man-eating tigers in the jungles of Bengal.

What prospect is there that things can be improved under this system? None whatever, and the more prudent men contemplate the outlook, the more satisfied they become that the lines mapped out by the Social Democracy are the ones to be followed if the hopes of the poor are not finally to go down in black despair.

But I do not doubt the triumph of the Social Democracy.

It is founded on established economic principles. It is philanthropic without one departure from axiomatic truth, and it is growing because the more it is investigated, the more it is found to embody those principles of life and growth and expansion which meet the approval of thoughtful men.

That the capitalist class, their politicians and parsons, their press and judiciary, oppose it with all their power is a sign of the times full of promise.

Labor will not be "fooled all the time." There must come a time when labor will arouse from its lethargy, when workingmen will no longer submit to being sheared like so many sheep, nor tagged and branded like so many cattle, when, grasping in the fullness of its emancipating power, the Social Democracy movement, they will rush to its standard and bear it to victory.

The Social Democracy is moving onward and upward. It is gathering momentum each day. It is in the interest of humanity, and never, in all the ages, has humanity awakened a profounder interest than now; so marked, so deep, so vivid are the lines of impression that it would be treason to truth to doubt ultimate results.

I am not only filled with hope, but with confidence, and this confidence grows in strength as from the East and the West, from the North and the South, advanced thinkers, students of affairs, men and women of action, great and good, with "thoughts that breathe and words that burn,"[8] flock to our standard with words of cheer.

When the first campaign of the Social Democracy has been fought, the United States will marvel at the progress of the movement, and the millions of social democrats throughout the world will join in generous applause.

"I Love Humanity Better than I Do Gold": Speech at Coliseum Hall, Denver† [excerpt]

February 6, 1898

I welcome you all to the temple of the Social Democracy. For a little while this afternoon, we will dismiss all thoughts of caste and condition and discuss the greatest question of the age. It touches a vital point, if not reaching to every portion of society. In this modern contest between the alley and the avenue, the rags and the riches, I stand for the alley and the rags. I stand here today as a socialist because I love humanity better than I do gold. It makes

† Published as "Debs Day in Denver" in *Rocky Mountain News* [Denver], vol. 39, no. 38 (February 7, 1898), 1, 10.

no matter what the future may have in store for me, for I propose to stand by my colors.

My friends, in these latter days we have seen the dollar deified above all things. When we consider that the man who works the longest and the hardest is the poorest, we think there is something radically wrong in the financial and commercial system in this country. In the march of the money system, the poor but honest man is no longer able to do his duties as an American citizen. In this country, there are millions of the victims of man's inhumanity to man. We have unlimited abundance, but there is also unspeakable poverty. It is the development of an abnormal system, and when it disappears, we will see the millionaire and the tramp go together as men. I am opposed to a system which makes the poor inferior to the lapdogs of the rich.

During the past 25 years, wages have steadily tended downward. Wages have not gone down so greatly, however, but the men do sometimes four times the work they formerly were required to do. But in the aggregate, the wage has been decidedly reduced, and in this the machine has been a potential factor. In the days of hand work the boy who learned the trade and followed it was reasonably sure of being able to make a living. With the coming of the machine passed the industry to the capitalist. The employee no longer looks forward to the time when he will be the employer. He now works by permission of his capitalistic employer alone.

The woman displaced the man to a great extent but helped support the family. But the machine grew to reproduce itself, and then the children were called in. Thus, it is the man who was reduced to vagrancy, the woman to penury, and the child to machine oil. In partnership with the machine, the capitalist is enabled to reduce wages and labor. The question of what wages a man is entitled to is no longer asked of him.

Workingman's Share is Too Small

The average workingman receives one-fifth of what he produces. Production is limited by consumption, and as the remaining one-fourth of the world cannot use the four-fifths' production, an overproduction follows. When the great strike of the miners occurred last year, it was found that they were receiving on an average 42½ cents a day. The tramp was formerly a curiosity. Now he is a product of this system. Labor is the root of the social and commercial tree, and the roots have not been nourished.

In the year 1896, nearly one-fifth of the concerns doing business in the United States disappeared, either voluntarily closed up or went into bankruptcy. There is a moral phase to this of as much importance as the ethical side—there were over 5,000 suicides and over 10,000 murders. In the short space of six years, the number of murders and suicides has increased threefold. I know that the press and others call those who present the situation as it is a "calamity howler." I take it from what I hear that there are none out of employment in Denver. *[Cries of "Oh, no!" "One-fifth," etc.]*

All of the social forces of the present system operate against the unfortunate. You wonder that men become criminal, and I wonder that they don't. Take it on our railroads: a man if he has influence gets a pass; if he has some money, he purchases mileage; if he is poor, he pays full fare. With the smallest wage, he pays the highest price.

One person in 757 is in jail. I speak from experience as well as observation. *[Uproarious applause.]* Don't laugh too much, you may be next.

Child Slaves in Georgia

Recently I found children working in the cotton mills of Georgia at 57 cents a week. I was refused admittance when I wished to investigate. If all have not equal rights, none have. If I am in any respect superior to any human being, I am under obligations to that person and should help raise him to my plane.

No single workingman in this country is employed except that he parts with almost all of what he produces. We have not risen above the beasts of the jungle. The greater fish eats the smaller, and so on until finally only the sharks remain.

Philip D. Armour[9] was once asked what he thought about the social question. He answered: "I have not had time to think about it. If you want to know how to make sausages, I can tell you." Think of it! With all his millions, he has not risen above the sausage level.

We propose the abolition of the system that produces these conditions under which one man is gorged to suffocation and another dies of want. The time will come when people will wonder at such places as New York City.

Realize that this is a conflict between socialism and capitalism, a contest for the collective ownership of the world for the benefit of man.

The trust is the inevitable outgrowth of the competitive system, and you cannot legislate against it.

Our modern social state would not be what it is without the railroads. Read the opinions of the Supreme Court in the Arago case, whereby the 13th Amendment to the constitution was abolished, annulled, and slavery reestablished in this country.[10]

We will operate the railroads and the telephone and telegraphs for the people. We will reduce the rates and give the railway men the protections that they were ordered by the national Congress, but which they have not received as yet. For this we are organizing every city and village and hamlet in the country, until we reach the height of emancipation. I am confident of this, I can strain my eyes and see the first dawn of the Cooperative Commonwealth. It means the social regeneration of the world. It means that every human being shall do the work that nature intended him to do.

I believe with Lowell that "he is true to man who is true to God."[11] To the banner of the Social Democracy we welcome those who want to leave this world a little better than they found it. *[Tremendous applause.]*

Against Fusion†

May 14, 1898

Spring Valley, Ill., May 14, 1898

Notwithstanding our repeated declarations as to the attitude of the Social Democracy in respect to fusion with other political parties, there are still those who persist in misunderstanding our position.

The Social Democracy is a socialist party and is pledged to the principles of socialism. It cannot and will not fuse with any capitalist party, by whatever name it may be called. As special allusion to the Populist Party[12] is made by our inquirers, let it be said that the Populist Party is a capitalist party and the Social Democracy will not fuse with it any more than it will with the Republican or Democratic Party.

It is urged by some that we should encourage alliance with the Populist Party because it inclines in our direction. Their advice, if followed, would wreck our party. If socialism is right, Populists should become socialists and join the Social Democracy. If they are not ready to do this, they are not socialists, and hence opposed to socialism, and fusion with their party would result in inevitable disaster.

† Published in *The Social Democrat,* vol. 5, no. 20 (May 19, 1898), 1.

The only object of such fusion would be the securing of office—the loaves and fishes. We are not after office, we want socialism. We care nothing about office except insofar as it represents the triumph of socialism.

Therefore, be it understood once and for all that the Social Democracy will not fuse with any party that does not stand for pure socialism, and there will be no departure from this policy.

There are thousands who are not swept from their feet by the war craze.[13] They realize that war is national murder, that the poor furnish the victims, and that whatever the outcome may be, the effect is always the same upon the toiling class.

In 1894, the press denounced us [American Railroad Union] for the alleged reason that we were murderous and bloodthirsty, and now the same press denounce us [Social Democracy of America] because we are not.

We are opposed to war, but if it ever becomes necessary for us to enlist in the murderous business, it will be to wipe out capitalism, the common enemy of the oppressed and downtrodden in all countries.

We are not afflicted with the kind of patriotism which makes the slaves of our nation itch to murder the slaves of another nation in the interest of a plutocracy that wields the same lash over them all.

It seems not a little singular that thousands are so patriotic (!) in a country in which the only interest they have is six feet in a potter's field.

Workingmen of America, do not be deceived. Do not permit the booming of the cannon to silence your agitation. Beneath it all, the real warfare for humanity is being waged. The millions of suffering poor in America appeal just as strongly for emancipation from the hellish conditions inflicted by capitalism as do the starving *reconcentrados*[14] on the ill-fated island of Cuba.

A splendid branch with a charter membership of 34 was organized here last night. They are all bright and active young fellows and will give a creditable account of themselves. Other branches will follow rapidly until we have the whole mining district solidly organized.

Our first national convention meets June 7. It is hoped that each branch will be represented. A national platform will be adopted, and the constitution will be amended to meet demands. We confidently look forward to our first national convention as a socialist convention of such character and proportion as to immensely strengthen the movement and inspire the whole membership with fresh zeal in the cause.

Letter to Victor L. Berger about the Forthcoming Convention of the SDA[†]

May 27, 1898

Terre Haute, Ind., May 27, 1898

My Dear Victor:—

You will be a delegate to convention, will you not? You must arrange to be there at the beginning and remain there through the session. We should be able to get through by Saturday at the latest.[15] It will be an important meeting, and *everything* depends upon what action is taken there. I will rely upon your being on hand and hope [Frederic] Heath will also be there.

Love to you and Mrs. Berger from Mrs. Debs and

Yours always,
E. V. Debs

† Handwritten letter on letterhead of the "National Council, Social Democracy of America," listing Debs as "chairman." Published in *Victor L. Berger Papers,* microfilm edition, reel 14, frame 0005. Not included in J. Robert Constantine (ed.), *Letters of Eugene V. Debs: Volume 1, 1874–1912.*

Edward Bellamy Was a Friend of Mine†

May 28, 1898

It was with the most sincere regret that I learned of the death of Edward Bellamy.[16] He was a very warm friend of mine.

When in 1888 the first edition of *Looking Backward* appeared, the name of Edward Bellamy flashed around the world. Of this epoch-making book it is estimated that fully 200,000 copies have been sold, and it has been translated into German, French, Italian, Russian, and many other languages.

Rarely has a book created such a profound impression on the popular mind. For years there has been agitation of the social question in other countries, especially in Germany and France, where a mighty international socialist movement was developing at a rate to arouse apprehension among the ruling class. *Looking Backward* was the first popular exposition of socialism in this country. Thousands read it with keen delight without being aware that it undermined the existing social order and paved the way for the social commonwealth.

From that time to this, there has been a worldwide interest in Edward Bellamy, and he has been classed with the great men of the country. There are those who, while admiring the brilliant achievement of the man, esteem him wholly impractical and place him in the category of visionaries and dreamers. They are less than just to themselves. A careful study of Mr. Bellamy's later works, especially *Equality*,[17] will convince any fair-minded person that the author was eminently practical in his views and theories. As a matter of course, he was an idealist, but this only developed the practical side of the man and made it possible for him to present his theories so admirably and effectively as to captivate the mass of the people in all civilized lands.

The fame of this distinguished author, reformer, and humanitarian will rest upon *Equality*, the book that may be said to have sapped his life currents and hurried him to a premature grave.

He foresaw the death of the present competitive system with prophetic vision, and how clearly he indicated the revolutionary processes by which the economic world is being revolutionized and the new social order established

† Published as "Mr. Debs on Bellamy" in *Terre Haute Express*, May 29, 1898, unspecified page.

will be realized only long after his earthly labors ended.

Edward Bellamy died in the very prime of his manhood. He was but 48 when the summons came. Personally, he was one of the gentlest and most lovable of me. He was in the truest sense a friend of suffering humanity. Touched and shocked by the daily exhibition of social wrong he encountered, he gave his whole heart and head to the task of finding a way to ameliorate the ills of *Les Misérables,* not by dispensing charity, but by the development of a social system, the basis of which should be economic equality, and in which industry should be organized and carried forward cooperatively, not for profit, but for the common and equal good of all.

It is yet too early for the world to form an estimate of the work and worth of this great and able man. Future generations will know him better than this, and when history is fairly and impartially written, his name will appear among the most illustrious of the ages.

The Coming Nation: Speech at the Grand Opera House, Terre Haute† [excerpt]

May 31, 1898

For the first time in the record of the ages, the inalienable rights of man—life, liberty, and the pursuit of happiness—have been usurped.

On July 4, 1776, our forefathers signed the Declaration of Independence, by which the ruler descended from his sceptered throne, the gem of liberty was planted in eternal truth, and the workingman stood erect in his heaven-decreed prerogative, freed from his bonds.

It was decreed by the infinite that man should stand forth the coronated sovereign of the world. The song of liberty is the song of the stars. There is no more appropriate theme than to wave the banner of freedom. No matter how nature may be decked with beauty, no matter if she sends forth a succession of

† Published as "Debs' Lecture on 'The Coming Nation'" in *Terre Haute Gazette,* June 1, 1898, unspecified page.

glorious melodies, if liberty is ostracized and expelled, the world wheels round the sun a gilded prison, a blot to the Siberian sphere of the heavens.

Strike down liberty, no matter by what subtle art, and the world becomes paralyzed by an indescribable power. Strike down the fetters of the plain, and it becomes a new world through the almighty genius of liberty. Its works redeem the poor man from animal suspense and make of him a new being. In our courts, the product of our political liberty is being realized to a gratifying extent. I believe in a few years woman will be franchised, and we will elect the officers of our country by direct vote. The political democracy will be complete.

The social problem today has grown to such an extent that it reaches all branches of life, it touches the vital parts of all society. Let us, friends, set aside all prejudice and think not of class, caste, or condition in consideration of this great question. We are all citizens of a common country and are all interested in the great problems engaging our people.

According to the Declaration of Independence, all men are created equal, and are entitled to certain rights, among which are included life, liberty, and the pursuit of happiness. If a man has a right to live—and no one will attempt to contradict this proposition—he has the right to work, and any system that deprives him of the right to work, deprives him of the right to live.

Carroll D. Wright, in speaking of the labor conditions in 1890, says that there were 3.2 million men who had no work at some time during the year, and 2.8 million who had no work at all. Something is wrong if this is true—something appears wrong to the true and patriotic citizen. Years ago, there was not a single millionaire in this country and not a single tramp. Now there are 4,000 millionaires and 4 million tramps.

In the infancy of our country, a workingman could earn honest wages and was able to support a family as was becoming for an American citizen, and the woman was queen of the little home. In the march of this system, the man has been reduced to vagrancy, the wife to rags and tears, and the child to machine oil.

The machine sprang from the brain of the laborer and, instead of becoming a blessing, it was monopolized and made the means of enslaving the workingman. Formerly the workingman controlled his tool, and then he was master of the situation and had a certainty of an honest living. With the march began the formation of associations of labor. The employer and employee worked side by side at the same bench. There was no upper class, no lower class. If the workman had a grievance, he brought it to the attention of the employer, and the matter was speedily adjusted. If the workman made a pair of shoes worth $5, his wages were perhaps $4, the difference representing the running expense of the shop. By this plan, consumption and supply were balanced, and the workman could buy back the equivalent of what he produced. Since the introduction of the machine, one man can produce ten times as much as half a century ago. Why does he not then enjoy ten times as much? Or why does he not do his work in one-tenth of the time?

The machines were at first crude in construction, but as the process became more and more perfect, man was pushed into the street. The tramp was at first a curious thing, but now the poor vagabonds wander from the Atlantic to the Pacific in countless numbers. Machines after a while became so perfect the men were not needed to operate them. Women tramped from their homes to the factories and there took their seats before the machines. Finally, the touch of a child was sufficient to produce from another machine, and now we find the child brought into competition with woman, and woman with man.

Take the reports of the great Indiana Labor Commission, which show the average wage of the workman to be but 58 cents a day. Statistics show that the wage of workmen has steadily declined until now they receive one-fourth of what they produce. This brings the cause of overproduction. It is because we have too many shoes that we go half-shod, it is because we have too much wheat that we starve, it is because the store is overstocked that the merchant fails in trade.

The consumptive capacity of the workingman is not considered. Competition springs up, and competition is war. The aim of trade is to get, to underbid, to reduce wages. Under the present system, the employer is as helpless as the employee. Some are generous, some are just, and some would be good in treatment of employees if they could, but they are helpless. A prominent coal operator told me not long ago that he wanted to give his miners better wages, but he could not do so and remain in the field against fierce competition.

This system is now in the throes of dissolution. A new order is evolving from the social chaos. Bear in mind, production should be limited by consumption, and consumption by wages. When one man quits canvassing, one quits producing.

Edison has said that in a few years, machinery will do the work of the world, and men hope for better times. Better times will not come with this. Private profit has become of more consequence than personal life, and the great institution of labor ceases to be profitable and is thrown out.

Labor is the foundation of the social fabric, the root of the social tree, but labor is thrown out and wages reduced. Twenty-five years ago, the miner received $5 a day. Now the average wage is 75 cents a day. Still he can spend

$5 a day more easily than he could before. As labor has been impoverished, the middle class has been in a process of extinction. In 1897, there were 13,197 commercial collapses, aggregating $215 million—12 percent greater than those of the preceding year. Of 1.15 million firms, according to Bradstreet, 224,534, or one-fifth, withdrew from business. In 1897, 6,520 firms succumbed against 2,040 in 1890—an increase of 300 percent.

In the constant turmoil of this commercial war, man is not in his normal condition. He is not in his natural mind. The laboring man, the small businessman, all are in competition. Thoughts of strife and gain throng through their busy heads, while expense increases and frantic efforts are made to drum up business. The busy toiler works 24 hours a day. Visions of failure and poverty haunt his sleep, and his footsteps are dragged by the black phantom, poverty.

This drives to suicide and insanity. In 1890, there were 4,290 suicides. In seven years, this number increased 250 percent, to 10,562. Now there are in the United States 180,000 insane persons, 184,000 in poor houses, 83,000 in jails. Every year 800,000 persons die, and of this number 500,000 are children under five years of age. Children who perish for lack of food and fresh air. Think of it! Perish in multiplied thousands.

How does this speak for our private charity and Christian commissions? As I said, personal gain has become of more consequence than private life.

When Thomas Jefferson helped found this government, his ideal was a country where there would be no excessively rich men and no excessively poor, where there would be an equal division of property. Man was of more consequence than property in those days. Man was before the dollar—and this is true today, but it is on bended knee.

* * *

Take the power of wealth in our national capital and in our state capitals, where money power has organized lobbies to defeat the will of the people. While developing a free political institution, we have allowed it to become a despotism. As Horace Mann says, "I may as well depend on another for my head, as for my bread."[18] Today the industrial master owns both. He owns the industrial slave.

Under the present system, labor has been reduced to the level of a commodity, and that commodity has no market value. In some respects, the American citizen is in a worse condition than was the chattel slave of 40 years ago. The slave was placed on the auction block and sold to the highest bidder. The modern wage-slave is placed in the labor market and sold to the lowest bidder. In the march of this system, the wage of the workingman has been reduced so that, in thousands of instances, it no longer suffices to keep a protesting soul in a half-clad body. The slave was sure of steady employment, he was not afraid of losing his situation; he was well fed and comfortably clothed. He was cared for as well as his master's house, for he had a certain economic value. Upon the auction block, he was sold to the highest bidder. The workman today is sold to the lowest bidder. By the system of contracts and underbidding, his wages are reduced, and he is made helpless in factory, mine, and shop.

When a man buys any commodity, he pays what he is asked for it. This rule is true for all but one commodity—labor. The workman does not get what he asks for his toil, he cannot sell it, it is not capital in his hand. He must stay in the grasp of suffering until he gives his work for what he can get. He is forced to sell.

A short time ago, I spent 30 days in West Virginia investigating the conditions of the miners. It is impossible to describe the conditions. Words fail. Men are there who have worked a year and never had the sight of any money. When payday came, they ever found themselves in the debt of the company, when they should have had something coming. From this slavery, there was no escape but the back door of suicide. Their lives were a constant curse from the cradle to the grave.

Like these poor wretches, there are in our country thousands of victims of man's inhumanity to man. One man's success is only possible by failure of others. There was a time when success was possible without failure. When a failure did occur, it was not to bury forever the unfortunate man in ruin and poverty. His failure assisted him to rise again and carry on his trade.

Today it is different—he fails to rise any more, and competitors rush on over his prostrate body. The strife goes on, and the victim does not last long. They invade commerce. They destroy each other. In modern competitive systems, there is no industrial harmony, no social peace. The outgrowth is the castes and unnatural artificial classes of society. At the Astor House, in New York, I saw lately some representatives of the extremely rich. I said, they are hothouse plants, they are not reared in nature's garden. They were artificial, pale, and bloodless beings.

I read in a paper a column article about a lapdog for which a wealthy woman paid $30,000. I read how three of her dogs were quartered in a fine hotel, how they wore collars worth $10,000, how they were bathed three times a day in perfume water, how they were attended by two footmen and two maids. I do not object to property, but I do object to the lapdogs of the rich being treated as superior to the children of the poor. The excessively rich have no real warm blood, they have no sympathy for the common people. With overwrought stomachs and exhausted natural desires and exhausted unnatural desires, they are not live enough to live and not dead enough to bury.

> Life is a mystery,
> Life is a doubt,
> Where men be dead
> Who walk about.[19]

There is a small class of people who have tons of food but no appetite, and another class who have tons of appetite but no food. The trouble is in the proper distribution.

The man who works the hardest and longest receives the least pay, while he who works the least is overpaid. The cheaper bread becomes, the harder it is to get. The men who build houses live in hovels. The men who support the government are suppressed by it. As a general rule, only the poor go to jail.

This system will kill itself. A short time ago, there occurred 245 failures in one week—40 failures a day, or one every 15 minutes. All represented the businessmen of smaller means who could not compete successfully with the great combines. Centralization and combination have been made the master spirit of the age. Competition goes forward to a certain point. In the process, the smaller men are crushed, the trust is formed, expenses are decreased, and enormous profits made possible. John D. Rockefeller is not in favor of competition. It is because he has destroyed it by the power of wealth and bribes. He fixes the price of his product and the world has to accept it.

What is true of the oil product will be true of every other product in a few years. Other gigantic monopolies will be formed, a few economic masters made and the weaker crushed. The goal of this system will never be reached. In itself, it contains the germ of decay. The excessive property ownership is slowly failing and is being supplanted by the cooperative system.

The forces of nature move under the cooperative system. Think, in the majestic [cosmic] system, what a crash of worlds there would be should each [body] circle about independent of all others. Think of the cooperative action in the stomach. When I take food into the stomach, it is not for the stomach alone. If it is not transformed for the use of all, it is soon in decay. But in the system in which we live, it is each one for himself and his satanic majesty take the hindmost—and also the foremost.

We need a little something to uplift every day and help in the inevitable dissolution of the system by which the workman is deprived of the product of his own industry. What right has any man to gain out of the industry of another man? It is but a question of time till the oppressive system will melt and flow away, and in its place will be the cooperative commonwealth. And, like Columbus the great explorer, as pictured in the poem of Joaquin Miller, it will "sail on."

Behind him lay the gray Azores,
  Behind the Gates of Hercules;
Before him not the ghost of shores,
  Before him only shoreless seas.
The good mate said: "Now we must pray,
  For lo! the very stars are gone.
Brave Admiral, speak, what shall I say?"
  "Why, say, 'Sail on! sail on! and on!'"

"My men grow mutinous day by day;
  My men grow ghastly wan and weak."
The stout mate thought of home; a spray
  Of salt wave washed his swarthy cheek.
"What shall I say, brave Admiral, say,
  If we sight naught but seas at dawn?"
"Why, you shall say at break of day,
  'Sail on! sail on! and on!'"

They sailed and sailed, as winds might blow,
  Until at last the blanched mate said:
"Why, now not even God would know
  Should I and all my men fall dead.
These very winds forget their way,
  For God from these dead seas is gone.
Now speak, brave Admiral, speak and say"—
  He said, "Sail on! sail on! and on!"

They sailed. They sailed. Then spake the mate:
  "This mad sea shows his teeth tonight.
He curls his lip, he lies in wait,
  With lifted teeth, as if to bite!
Brave Admiral, say but one good word:
  What shall we do when hope is gone?"
The words leapt like a leaping sword:
  "Sail on! sail on! sail on! and on!"

Then pale and worn, he kept his deck,
  And peered through darkness. Ah, that night
Of all dark nights! And then a speck—

A light! a light! at last a light!
It grew, a starlit flag unfurled!
It grew to be Time's burst of dawn.
He gained a world; he gave that world
Its grandest lesson: "On! sail on!"[20]

In every age, there have been men and women of conviction and courage who have dared to express their views as to the right; who also have defied all the storms of detraction. But for such people the world would never have emerged from savagery or barbarism. And the great crusade is now being led against other forms of wrong. The question is: "Is it right?" If it is, then, in the spirit of Andrew Jackson, let them take the consequences of their acts.

At times, I will admit, the outlook appears gloomy, but let us remember that our work is an inspiration and that this is a great movement in the industrial world. It will give us a new nation in which there will be not one master and not one slave. I know it is said this is impossible, that it is but a dream. The dreams of one age are the realized facts of the next age. This change is coming whether we will it or not. It is coming as certainly as that the rivers find their ways to the seas. I have great hopes that right will be enthroned; that the competitive system will be dissolved and that the cooperative system will supplant it. I want a social democracy as well as a political democracy.

There are multiplied thousands who cannot get work. I know it is denied, but I can prove it. In Chicago today, there are 50,000 men who cannot get employment. In Indiana, during the coal strike, to use the language of Gov. Mount,[21] "Six thousand miners and their families are literally starving to death." This is to increase as long as the system endures.

Workingmen are not always true to themselves. They do not always take advantage of the opportunities presented. What is their duty? It is to read, to think, and to study. Shakespeare says there is no darkness but ignorance.[22] There is no better picture than a workingman, after he gets home from work and has his supper, going to his library and taking down a book on some economic subject. This is an economic battle.

Workingmen should organize. They should move on the ballot box and vote in the cooperative system and vote out the competitive system. *[Applause.]* Even the rich men fear the present system. What assurance has he under it that he will not be penniless within a month? Do you not see cases around us of rich men who, through reverses in some unfortunate speculation, lose all they possess? Have we not had such cases in our midst? Why does the rich man insure his life? Is it not because he wants to provide for reverses that come under the present system? It is not a rational system. Work must be for the equal good of all.

George M. Pullman had solved the problem of how to accumulate wealth. He accumulated millions. What good did it do him after all? He came into the world without a dollar and he went out without a dollar. Yet Pullman was an economic monarch. Death is a social democrat. He went up into that mansion on Prairie Avenue and, pointing his body finger at that palpitating heart, said: "Stop!"—and it stopped.

It does not pay to be selfish and sordid. It is better to help than to hinder. Some people who do not agree with us tell us we are entitled to what we can get. Suppose we carry out that argument to its logical conclusion. If I possess abnormal physical strength, have I the right to go out into the street and because of this strength overpower my weaker brother and take away from him such as I wish? Or suppose I possess abnormal mental ability. Have I the right to play the part of an intellectual highwayman any more than a physical highwayman?

I believe all the children of the earth have equal rights. Rockefeller with his $200 million is not a free man. He is a spiritual vagrant. He is afraid of the danger of the assassin, and his position is not to be envied. Under our system, we would say to Rockefeller, "You have great organizing ability and we will have you use that ability in the interest of the people at large. *[Applause.]*

No great action was ever done purely for money. The Declaration of Independence was not written for pay. No great painting was painted solely for money. The approbation of the public was the thing most desired.

Life will be lengthened under our plan. It will be a world for good men and good women to live in. There will be social peace, perfect harmony, economic equality—a march to the highest type of civilization ever known. [*Loud applause.*]

This Is Not a War of Humanity: Floor Speech at the First National Convention of the Social Democracy†

June 7, 1898

So far as I know, not one of the ten thousand members of the Social Democracy has enlisted to fight in this war.[23] Social Democrats are against war. The socialists of America have friendly relations with those of Spain, and do not cherish the slightest enmity toward them. Communications of friendship have passed between them, not officially, but as individuals.

This is not a war of humanity—far from it. It is true that people have been starving in Cuba by the thousands, but why? The original cause is because the capitalists of Spain and of this country ground them down and enslaved them to add to their wealth. We pitied them and declared war ostensibly to save them from starvation. What do we do? Do we send food to relieve them, and do we kill off the capitalists who are responsible for the condition?

No; we establish a blockade so that more of the *reconcentrados* are starved than ever, leaving scarcely any by the time we get down into Cuba to do anything for them. We send over a fleet to capture the Philippines, and we give a lot of contractors a chance to grow richer than ever equipping the army.

We send a lot of workingmen down to kill a lot of Spanish workingmen who had nothing to do with creating the conditions and are in no way responsible for them. Meanwhile, the capitalists grow fat on the situation. They lend money, secure valuable concessions, and altogether have a pleasant time out of it all.

If the people want to relieve the starving, why don't they begin at home? I can show them thousands of men in the coal camps and in other parts of America who lack food for themselves and their families. Why don't the people take care of them?

There is only one remedy, and that is social democracy. I don't believe in taking a man's personal property, but I do believe that all the means of production should be used for the common good—each man doing his share of the work and receiving his share of the returns.

---

† Published as "Debs Opposes War: Social Democracy Friendly to Spain" in *Buffalo Express,* vol. 53, no. 123 (June 8, 1898), 3.

Declination of Office in the Social Democracy of America at the First National Convention†

June 8, 1898

I have been in this work a long time, and I want a rest.[24] The Social Democracy can get on just as well, and I shall work as a private in the ranks. But before that I shall have a vacation—perhaps go to Europe. It is not consistent with our ideas to elect a president and other officers. The government will probably be left to an executive board. But I shall not even belong to that. I shall accept no office of any kind.

The Only Thing I Fear Is Ignorance: Speech at the First National Convention of the Social Democracy of America at Chicago‡ [excerpt]

June 9, 1898

At one time, I thought that if a man could not pay 15 cents per month [SDA dues], he was not worth having. But I have found that thousands of men in this country have not got 15 cents, and in many cases, they have not got 15 cents because they are men. I have it on good authority that there is not ten cents in the South, wages being paid in merchandise. We must make Social Democracy broad enough to reach these men. The problem that confronts the world today is the economic problem. The Southern people are rapidly being disfranchised. They are being robbed of the power of the ballot. If we are equal to the trust imposed in us, we can carry on the economic action in harmony

† Published in *Chicago Tribune,* vol. 57, no. 160 (June 9, 1898), 9.

‡ Published as "Speech to the First Convention of the SD of A" in *The Social Democrat,* vol. 5, no. 12 (June 16, 1898), 4.

with the political action. The economic situation in the United States appeals to the stomach, heart, and brain.

I give the Socialist Labor Party great credit for what it has done, but it is too narrow to appeal to the great broad spirit of American socialists. When they find a downtrodden toiler that has just enough conscience left to realize that he belongs to the working class, down comes the class-conscious club and knocks him into unconsciousness entirely.

The great difficulty is that the workingmen are cowards; their courage has been crushed out, and unionism has done more than anything else to awaken them to class-consciousness or a realization that the producers' interests are identical the world over.

The mission of social democracy is to awaken the producer to a consciousness that he is a socialist and to give him courage by changing his conditions. I have not changed in regard to our procedure. Give me ten thousand men, aye, one thousand in a western state, with access to the sources of production, and we will change the economic conditions and we will convince the people of that state, win their hearts and their intelligence. We will lay hold upon the reins of government and plant the flag of socialism on the state house. The state government in this offers us an advantage that is not found in any European country. We can take possession of one state and not wait until we get the whole United States. We must get one state at a time. In a movement such as this, there is always some friction. We are in the birth throes of a new movement, the most responsible movement the world ever saw, and it demands the most careful consideration of honest men and women.

We may wreck social democracy today, but the movement is evolutionary. If there is a Judas among us, like Judas of old, he will hang himself. Don't deceive yourselves. I don't fear the man that says I don't agree with you. The only thing in this world that I fear is ignorance. I am mortally afraid of an ignorant supporter. I have faith that this body will obliterate those dividing lines before we adjourn. Think for yourself, would be my last word. If you oppose and defeat me, I have infinitely more respect for you than if you support me without thinking for yourself.

The Future: An Open Letter†

July 16, 1898

To the Social Democratic Party.

Comrades:—

That I have not earlier sent greeting to my comrades is due to prolonged indisposition. The incessant work and travel of more than 20 years have temporarily placed me *hors de combat.*[25] But only temporarily. With returning health and strength, my work will be continued. It is not a little disquieting to have to "let go," even for a little while, when there is such urgent need for action.

The separation at the late convention was inevitable. It had to come. The contemplation of division was painful, as only those can fully realize who were party to it. But painful as it was, the operation had to be performed. And it was a success, for the Social Democratic Party of America lives. All the members are full-fledged socialists. They are in accord with the program of international socialism. There is not only in the number opposed to independent political action, not one that asks or expects anything from any old capitalist party, by whatever name it may be called.

There is harmony. There is oneness of purpose, there is true-hearted fidelity to principle, there is unrelaxing energy, and these qualities in alliance presage success. So I contemplate the course of events with serenity.

Had there not been division now, there would have been disaster later. The proceedings demonstrated beyond all question that conciliation was not possible and, had there not been absolute divorce of the antagonistic elements, the organization would have gone to certain destruction.

There are those in the Social Democracy who yet believe that it is possible to "harmonize" and conquer. They are welcome to all the success their efforts may achieve. I have had all the experience along that line my constitution will stand.

I am with and for the Social Democratic Party of America. As a socialist, it pleases me to make this avowal of my faith in the new organization. The branch of which I am a member has unanimously taken the same action, and this fall a complete SDP ticket will be placed in the field.

† Published as "The Future" in *Social Democratic Herald,* whole no. 2 (July 16, 1898), 1.

The hundreds of kind communications I have received since my illness are appreciated more than words can express, and appeal to every fiber of my being for renewed efforts in the noble cause of socialism.

Eugene V. Debs

Socialism Advances into the Arena†

October 1898

In the outset, and to "clear the deck" for action, some attention should be paid to definitions. What is meant by the term "social democracy"? The term "social" as applied to "democracy" means, simply, a society of democrats, the members of which believe in the equal right of all to manage and control it. Reading this definition, men are likely to say, "There is nothing new in that," and they speak understandingly. The men and women who are engaged in organizing the Social Democratic Party of America are not pluming themselves upon the novelty of their scheme for the improvement of social, industrial, and political conditions. They claim for their movement a commonsense basis, free from the taint of vagary and in all regards preeminently practical.

The wise man is credited with saying, "The thing that hath been, it is that which shall be; and that which is done is that which shall be done: and there is no new thing under the sun."[26] Crediting the declaration of Solomon as conclusive, there must have been a time before he lived when something like "social democracy" of which I write existed in the earth, the germ idea of which, though latent for centuries, has aroused men from their lethargy from time to time in the processes of evolution, to find its most potent expression in the present era of "progress and poverty,"[27] civilization and savagery, wealth and war, charity and greed, aroused them to an interest in socialism, which, with the chivalric courage of crusaders and the revolutionizing zeal of iconoclasts, has appeared to do battle for the regeneration of society.

---

† Published as "Social Democracy" in *The National Magazine,* vol. 9, no. 1 (October 1898), 54–6. Reprinted in *Social Democratic Herald,* vol. 1, no. 14 (October 8, 1898), 2.

No one hesitates to admit that the task is herculean; no one underestimates the power of opposing forces. Their name is legion, and they are organized forces—close, compact, resourceful, and defiant. They do not propose to surrender, compromise, nor arbitrate. They have the masses in the dust, their claws upon their throats and their hooves upon their prostrate forms. In the face of all the verified facts that startle thinking men, there is no requirement for extravagant speech.

But conditions as they exist are artificial, not natural. They were created by men, and may be changed by men, since it is a truth "that where there is a will there is a way" to elevate humanity as certainly as where there is a will there is a way to degrade it, and social democracy has one central pivotal purpose, the amelioration of social conditions and the emancipation of the victims of a vast brood of wrongs, all of which converge and consolidate in one great and overmastering wrong of robbing them under the forms of law, of the fruits of their toil, and thereby reducing them to a condition where men dispose of their manhood and women of their chastity for the means of continuing lives that are a ceaseless horror. No well-informed honest man either doubts or attempts to controvert the proposition. It is as self-evident as the law of gravitation. It is the crime of the ages, the one great curse resulting from "man's inhumanity to man," the ever-present and threatening calamity which wage earners are required to face and provide against as best they may.

Capitalism is running riot throughout the land. The private ownership of the means of production, that is to say, the means of life, is doing its deadly work. The trusts, syndicates, and corporations, with more eyes and hands than any mythological monster ever possessed, concoct new schemes of spoliation, and the masses sink to lower depths of poverty, want, woe, and degradation.

The picture is not overdrawn. A Hogarth's hand would relax its hold upon its pencil in tracing the horrors of a sweatshop or the agonies of the lives of tramps.[28] Dante would look in vain throughout the realms of the infernal for incidents more horrifying than are found in the deep, dark, mining hells where miners work and famish. Only a Milton would be equal to the task of depicting the wreck and ruin wrought by the capitalist system in a land which should be a paradise, but which has been transformed into an arena more horrible than those where Roman emperors delighted to torture the victims of their vengeance.

All over this fair land, in every center of population, in mine and factory and shop, and spreading out into the forest, field, and farm, where bird and bee and brook make merry music and the winds transform leaf and spray into harps, where the flowers vie with the stars in making the earth as beautiful as the sky above, iron-tongued and iron-handed monsters of greed and lust, conscienceless as a Moloch and as relentless as death, have inaugurated wretchedness and poverty until from ocean to ocean, from valley to mountaintop, rises one unceasing complaint, touching every note in the scale of discontent and anger, while statesmen and students, philosophers and philanthropists, amazed and aghast, contemplate environments and await developments.

The millions of wage earners do not own themselves, they are wage-slaves, and their masters control their lives and subject them to conditions as degrading as those which existed in times of chattel slavery. True it is that the united forces of labor could make themselves masters of the situation and change conditions to their liking, but, divided on lines of political partisanship, intimidated, bulldozed, and bribed, they have done the bidding of the capitalist class, have been misled and betrayed by ignorant and dishonest leaders until hope has all but perished.

At this supreme juncture, socialism has come into view and advances to the arena. It offers a remedy for social ills which must be mitigated if peace and prosperity are to come to the land. It strikes at the very root of capitalism by proposing to transfer the means of production and distribution, i.e., the land, mines, factories, railroads, machinery, etc., from private capitalists to the whole people to be operated by them in their collective capacity for the good of all, and this it proposes to do by the ballot of a triumphant majority of awakened, class-conscious supporters. The revolution is to be complete, but it is to be achieved by the ballot.

From the date of the introduction of chattel slavery into the British colonies of America to the time when the shackles fell from the limbs of 4 million slaves by the proclamation of Abraham Lincoln, 243 years had elapsed. But it was amidst the smoke and carnage of war, when a thousand streams ran red to the sea, that chattel slavery with its blocks and whips and pens disappeared from the land.

Wage-slavery has now in the United States a firmer standing than was ever secured by chattel slavery. For two centuries and a half, no gleam of hope flashed upon the darkness in which the chattel slave lived and wrought and died, but along all the years, forces were being evolved to secure his rescue, culminating in a war of calamities unparalleled in the history of the world.

Socialism would work out the redemption of the wage-slave without a sanguinary conflict. Its emancipating program includes no bloody ordeals. It unfurls to the winds no battle banners except those inscribed with peace and goodwill to man. Its first great proposition is to educate workingmen and, by an act which requires an exercise of willpower, to stand forth, redeemed and disenthralled, from the domination of any other man or set of men under heaven. This can be done. It is the initial step to a higher plane of existence and a nobler life, where men grow and expand to their full stature. It is a step which evinces the beginning of wisdom. He who takes it plucks for his own behoof and those dependent upon him the richest fruit that has grown on the tree of knowledge of all the ages.

Thousands are doing their own thinking and are conscious of their class interests in the economic struggle. They are organizing everywhere. The movement is international.

The following is from the declaration of principles of the Social Democratic Party of America:

> The control of political power by the Social Democratic Party will be tantamount to the abolition of capitalism and of all class rule.
>
> The solidarity of labor connecting us with millions of class-conscious fellow workers throughout the civilized world will lead to international socialism, the brotherhood of man.

Capitalism is to culminate in socialism. The scepter it has wielded so long and so mercilessly in the interest of its class is soon to fall from its nerveless grasp. It is destroying itself, and from its ruins will rise the Cooperative Commonwealth.

The Dollar Counts for Everything: Speech in Springfield, Massachusetts†[29] [excerpt]

October 23, 1898

Nothing is more certain than that the social and economic system under which we live is undergoing a process of evolution. A new social order is to be evolved out of the present chaos.

Any system under which a man is deprived of the fruit of his labor is unjust. The present system divides men into two classes, the capitalist and the laboring man. If there is to be a class struggle, it is the trouble of the system.

Men are endowed by the Creator with certain natural rights, among which is the right to live. If men have a right to live, they have a right to work, and any system that deprives them of the right to work deprives them of the right to live. Does the present system do this? I answer that in all your cities you can hear the tramp of thousands of the unemployed.

We are told that prosperity has returned to the country. I deny it. I do not deny that in some parts of the country conditions are better, but I do deny any general prosperity.

Examine the official report of the mine inspector of the state of Illinois and you will find that the average wage of the average miner during 1897 was $16 per month. While men labor for this amount, there is no general prosperity.

My friends, I am not here to appeal to your passions. I am here to appeal to your reason. I propose to tell you the exact truth and to open up to you my opinions and views.

We live under the capitalist system. It is founded upon the principle that money is of more value than men. Abraham Lincoln once said, "The man before the dollar." We see this literally today, but it is the man on bended knee before the dollar. The dollar counts for everything, men for nothing.

I do not attack individuals. I oppose the system. A few men collect together property which they can never use, while the many suffer. No workingman can

---

† Published as "Debs Was Cheerful" in the *Springfield Union,* October 24, 1898, unspecified page. Merged with additional content published as "Coming Doom of Capitalism" in the *Springfield Daily Republican,* October 24, 1898, unspecified page. Articles preserved on *The Papers of Eugene V. Debs* microfilm edition, reel 15.

obtain employment unless he is willing to part with nearly all he produces.

In the final analysis the competitive system ruins all, including the capitalist. The socialist system is complained of as attacking property. It is not so. It is the capitalist system that attacks property. A hardware dealer said to me after attending one of my meetings: "You might be a useful man, but your work is in the wrong direction." At that time, his business was prosperous. Within two years, a competitor came into town, and he was gradually driven into bankruptcy. I held another meeting there and at the close the same man came to me and said, "I am with you." He had seen the result of the working of this system.

Under such a plan, you must either be a millionaire or a mendicant, and the chances are ten to one that you will be the mendicant. Under it, the brotherhood of man on earth can never be attained. You know all the time that your neighbor is doing all he can to injure you.

There are many things of importance in the world, but at present the whole thought is to get money. The parent says to his son, "Get money. Get it honestly if you can—if not, dishonestly." Tell me how much money any of your citizens has, and I will tell you how he stands on the social thermometer of Springfield.

There are many workmen who envy businessmen. They have no cause for envy. Take the ordinary businessman with no large capital. He fights against men with ten times as much. Gradually his expenses exceed his profits. He goes home at night with his brain filled with problems. He wakes in the morning tired and careworn, the specter of bankruptcy in his eyes. At 50, when he ought to be in possession of his best powers, he is in decay. What is such a life worth to him? Business is war, and a man engaged in it is engaged for life. As Burns says, until death, who is sometimes man's best friend, comes to his rescue.

You tell me you propose to destroy monopoly, and I tell you that it is absolutely impossible. It is the direct result of the system, and you can no more destroy it than you can stop the water from flowing.

It is possible for persons with resources to dictate opinions to judges. I do not say that judges are dishonest, but that the judiciary is a little partial to capitalist interests. I speak not only from observation, but also from experience.

Mr. [George M.] Pullman was cited to appear before the same court as my colleagues and myself. Mr. Pullman took his private car to New York. When he returned, he had a whispered conversation with the judge [Peter S. Grosscup], and that ended it. I also tried to explain to the judge, and I got six months. What was the difference between Mr. Pullman and myself? Only $20 million.

Human life is not taken into account by capitalism. Wages have been reduced because of the economic revolution that has followed the introduction of machinery. A workingman can produce five times as much as he could 40 years ago, and he ought to have five times as much. The machine was designed to be a blessing to labor, to give better homes, but it actually enslaves men. Forty years ago, we had no millionaire and no mendicant. The millionaire and the tramp came together. The latter is the corollary of the former.

In the old days, the employer and employee worked side by side. There was a reasonable degree of economic equality. Today, the same forces have produced 4,000 millionaires and 4 million tramps. Society is being split in twain. A few have become millionaires, and the rest have been reduced to poverty. Formerly employers and employed were friends and visited one another. They do not do so now.

We had little shops in our communities. Then the machine appeared, and the subdivision of labor began. One man makes the 72nd part of a shoe, and the machine begins to push the men out in the street. The tramp army is recruited.

Gradually, the machine pushed the laborer out. Meanwhile, competition came in between employers and began to force wages down. Finally, the women were summoned to take the place of men at lower wages. There came a Saturday evening when the foreman said to some of the men, "You need not come back, but we can give your wife work, she will work cheaper than you."

The manufacturers began to import the cheapest labor in the world. They used to pay good American labor $5 in the mines, now they pay 42 cents. The necessity of selling lower and lower to beat their neighbors embitters the struggle, and soon the child is brought into the factory, so that it now takes the whole family to support the family. The result is men are thrown out of employment, the demand for the products of labor is restricted, the store of merchandise are full of goods which the laboring people cannot buy because they have no work and no money.

According to Carroll D. Wright's statistics of a recent year, there are 2.8 million people who have not worked at all during the year. There are 3 million more who work for 60 or 75 cents a day. In the cotton fields of the South, they are picking cotton for 15 cents a day. There has been a reduction of every department of industry. One-fourth of the workingmen are out of work, and a half are reduced to the bare necessities of life. The cheapest commodity in the world is flesh and blood.

The most favored wage earner of today does not know but that he will be a tramp tomorrow. If he loses his job, he probably cannot get another. The workingman is no better than the slave, who at least was sure of his job. He was placed on the auction block and sold to the highest bidder. You are placed in the labor market and sold to the lowest bidder. Labor is the only commodity the price of which is fixed by the buyer. Many a man submits to the most glaring injustice because of his wife and his children.

The competitive system is steadily destroying the consuming capacity of the people. They have not the money to buy from the businessman, he cancels his orders to the factory, the shops close, a panic comes, and they call it overproduction.

What do we propose to do about it? I stand before your presence a socialist. I believe in socialism as the only salvation. Socialism is coming as certain as the stars shine above you, whether you will it or not. The capitalistic system teaches men to regard each other as scoundrels, the socialistic system teaches men to regard each other as brothers. The capitalistic system is called survival of the fittest. It is not; it is survival of the slickest, the shrewdest.

If you rob a man and are sent to jail, you are at last given a chance to work. If the state can give you a chance to work after you commit crime, it can give you a chance before. Capitalism makes criminals of citizens, socialism makes citizens of criminals. When the means of production are owned by the people, industry will be carried on for the good of all, and the production of tramps and paupers and criminals will cease.

Men will work because it will be disreputable not to work. Now there is no incentive to work. The politicians talk about the dignity of labor. That disappears on election night. When the inauguration ball comes off, there is no place for the horny-handed son of toil. Under socialism, a man can be a workingman and be a gentleman; he cannot be a gentleman unless he is a workingman.

They say all men are equal, that any boy may be president. I am sure there are 5 million people who would swap their chance of the presidency for a square meal.

Many people oppose socialism, but it is generally because they know nothing about it. Socialism is industrial democracy. Socialism contemplates economic as well as political equality. If people are fit to be political equals, are they not fit to be economic equals? What good does it do a man to have political freedom and be a slave under the economic system? As long as one babe is born the possessor of untold wealth, and one on the next street to an inheritance of rags and misery and agony, as long as one is born master and the other servant, there can be no peace on earth and goodwill to men. They say you must change human nature. I say change the conditions, and you will change human nature.

A change is coming. We are on the eve of the greatest change the world has ever seen. We are about to solve the problems. The great capitalists are unconsciously paving the way to socialism by centralizing industry. They are combining all industry in the hands of a few men. It is either combination or destruction. They combine, organize, fix the price of products and the price of wages. They are socialists for revenue only.

We do not object to the trust, because it is but the means for the accomplishment of our end. We propose to let the capitalists go on and form their combinations. Soon they will absorb all the capital. When they have reared this splendid fabric of centralization, we will take possession of it and direct it for the good of the people.

The capitalist says, "You attack my property and take away my business." It is not the socialist, but your own coworker that destroys you. The large fish swallow the small fish, and ultimately in the capitalistic waters there will be only a few devilfish left.

The working classes are beginning to ask why they who build the houses are in the cold, why they must walk weary and shelterless in the shadow of palaces they have built but cannot enter. It is labor that rolls and beats out the red-hot iron for the use of man; that grows all the fleeces and makes therefrom a thousand fabrics; that feeds and drive the black cavalry of commerce. Shall not labor come into its own? Who shall doubt it? As the mariner in southern seas looks at the southern cross bending to the South, and knows that the midnight has passed, as the Almighty marks the hour on the stars, so let labor take heart, for the cross is bending, and joy cometh in the morning.

The man who is engaged in this competitive struggle becomes mentally diseased. He sets out that he wants a moderate fortune; if he is successful, he wants more, he is never satisfied, his ambition becomes perverted. Money is not worth all this struggle, which deadens one's desire for the better things in life. It is better to help humanity than to hinder it in its struggles. With this faith, we are organizing this movement in every village and city in the Union, organizing men who shall without compromise vote out the last remnant of capitalism and vote in the Cooperative Commonwealth.

An End to War—A Start to Militarism†

circa November 15, 1898

Now that the [Spanish-American] war has been practically terminated, a multiplicity of new questions are budding on the "thorny stem of time."[30] Among these the central, commanding proposition is, "What shall be done with the army?" and upon the answer depends the character and to a large extent the perpetuity of the Republic.

Stripped of all verbiage designed to confuse the mind and obscure the issue, the question is, "Shall the United States of America succumb to the rule of militarism which dominates the old world?"

Back of this interrogatory, in shadowy outline, looms the "man on horseback" awaiting the answer, not of the American people, but of the select few to whom, under our benign representative system, they have surrendered their sovereign prerogatives.

Militarism is defined by Webster as "reliance on military force in administrating government." For years, especially since great labor strikes have alarmed capitalists and incidentally disturbed the country, the way has been quietly, gradually cleared for the introduction of legislation into Congress providing for a substantial and permanent increase in the standing army. Every conceivable reason, except the right one, was put forth in justification of the demand. General Miles caught the spirit long before the war with Spain or any other country was ever dreamed of. He boldly made the recommendation and in support of the proposition ventured nearer than any other in disclosing its true purpose by putting it upon the ground that the country should be "prepared against internal dissension."

The matter was taken up by the press, and large and influential papers were moved to give hearty endorsement to the project. But, somehow, it would not take with the people. They were uniformly and emphatically against it. They were instinctively opposed to a large standing army. They felt that it was in conflict with the spirit of democratic institutions and in violence of American doctrine and traditions. The spirit that prompted Washington in his "Farewell"

---

† Published in the *Cincinnati Post,* title, date, and page unspecified. Reprinted as "Eugene V. Debs on the Army Question" in *Social Democratic Herald,* vol. 1, no. 20 (November 18, 1898), 4.

to warn his countrymen against "overgrown military establishments, which, under any form of government, are inauspicious to liberty, and which are to be regarded as particularly hostile to republican liberty," still burned and glowed in their breasts. They knew that a large standing army is inimical to liberty; and that they cannot dwell together is a fact attested by all history.

At this conjuncture, the Cuban question began to agitate the country, culminating in the declaration of war. Legislation by Congress to organize and equip an army followed in rapid order. In the excitement incident to the wave of patriotic sentiment which swept over the country, all objection to increase of the army disappeared, but now that the war is ended, the question of a standing army, its size, distribution, pay, and the general policy of the government relative thereto, again appeals to the calm and thoughtful consideration of the American people.

Speaking for myself, I am of the opinion that the army should as speedily as possible be reduced to its former peace footing. That there is any probability of this being done, I do not believe. The opening came, the army expanded under the necessities of war, and it will never be reduced to its former limits and limitations. The commercial spirit, born of the capitalist system, requires a large standing army to maintain its regime and enforce its edicts, and as Congress is subservient to its will, the army will remain a fixed and permanent, if not the central and controlling factor, in our government. There are many and cogent reasons for opposition to a large standing army in the United States. These are mainly geographical and historical.

In a historical sense, the main point of difference between a despotism and a democracy is the standing army. Where there is a despotism, there is a standing army, and where there is a standing army, there is a despotism. Henry Labouchère,[31] the famous editor of the London *Truth,* in discussing the effect of a standing army in the United States, said in a recent issue of his paper:

> This army would soon crush out democracy at home and in the end some popular general would feel it his duty to save society by making himself such a president as the Constitution never contemplated.

He is right. The democratic spirit would soon decline and wither in an atmosphere charged with militarism, and if any trace of it survived, it would be speedily stamped out.

A century of national progress has been achieved with but the nucleus of a regular army, and in all the exigencies which have arisen. The volunteer army, the citizen-soldiery have been found equal to every demand of the country.

Most conclusively were the readiness and efficiency of the volunteer host demonstrated in the war just closed. Why, then, should there be any departure from our national policy at this time, and a standing army maintained in time of peace? The answer readily suggests itself. They who favor a strong military arm are not much concerned about a foreign foe. They know that the people can always be relied upon to defend the country against aggressions from the outside. The secret of their anxiety is that they do not trust the people—their own countrymen.

The fearful poverty to which tens of thousands of workingmen have been ground in the merciless mill of capitalistic competition has created discontent and anger which portend resistance on an everlasting scale, and it is to force and keep in subjection these victims of capitalistic conquest that the standing army is demanded.

Judicial decrees, issued at the behest of the "power behind the throne" and subversive of every vestige of liberty, will command obedience when served with the gleam of bayonet upon them. Every federal judge will be a tsar, and, ex-officio, commander of the forces in his jurisdiction.

The standing army is a ceaseless and stupendous burden upon the people. It gnaws at their vitals in all the circling hours of the day and night. It produces nothing. It simply devours. Viewed in its most favorable light, it is a necessary evil, and should be reduced to the minimum.

Will a large standing army add to our moral strength at home or abroad? On the contrary, it will serve as a demoralizing factor. We are strong and we are respected in proportion as we trust the people and cultivate fraternal relations among them. We become weak and invite contempt in proportion as we seek to dominate them by brute force.

I maintain, therefore, that an increased regular army would weaken, not strengthen, the nation, and that it would provoke, rather than allay, hostilities with other countries.

The immediate reduction of the army to its former footing would, in the moral effect it would have, add immeasurably to the strength of the country at home and its security against other nations.

Washington laid great stress on "our detached and distant situation" and the fact that it "enables us to pursue a different course" from that followed by European countries.

Let it be borne in mind that the march of progress cannot be arrested by armed force. All the armies of the world cannot restrain the silent, invisible evolutionary forces which are in operation, and these are tending steadily away from war and toward peace. Slowly but steadily, we are emerging from the savagery of war. Its horrors are still glorified in the name of civilization, but the clarion words of Douglas Jerrold,[32] "War is murder in uniform," are not entirely drowned in the huzzahs inspired by the death and desolation wrought upon the vanquished foe.

Not all our people participated in thanksgiving to the Almighty, in obedience to the president's proclamation, for having enabled our soldiers to overwhelm and crush and mangle the soldiers of Spain and make widows of their wives and orphans of their children.[33]

Every consideration of civilization, every interest of humanity, commands us to cultivate the arts of peace and to discourage the horrors of war, and thus fulfill our national destiny by furnishing a model for the emulation of other nations of the earth.

What has here been said has, of course, reference only to our own country. The disposition of the countries which came into our possession in consequence of the war is another question. Spanish authority has been driven out of these countries, and that was the sole issue of the war. A reasonable protectorate should be exercised by the government over the islands she has conquered until their domestic affairs are organized, and for this purpose an army sufficient for garrison service should be maintained, which can be gradually withdrawn as this object is accomplished.[34] Then let the inhabitants govern themselves as they see fit, and in due course of time they will work out their own destiny.

Of course, there are those who see, or imagine they see, great complications in the near future, and, therefore, insist that our country should be armed to the teeth, ready for war with other great nations at the word of command. They are not close students of the course of events. There is a movement, silent and spontaneous as the dawn, which they omit from their calculations.

Socialism, quickened into life in the womb of capitalism, is spreading over the civilized world. Its growth during the past few years has been phenomenal. The late elections in Germany, France, and other European countries were a revelation. In a few years more, probably sooner, socialism will have wrested these countries from the grasp of capitalism, and their armies will disappear as if by magic, and war will be no more. Socialism is precisely the same the wide world over. In its march, hate ceases and love begins.

The German soldiers and the French soldiers who riddled each other with balls in 1870, since touched by the magic of socialism, now stand beneath the same emancipating banner and mingle their voices in the inspiring strains of "La Marseillaise."

War, all war, is the result of the conquest of capitalism. Cuba was exploited and all the cruel atrocities she suffered were inflicted by capitalism—the ruling class, the world over, here as elsewhere. With the end of capitalism, war will cease. Then it will be in order to "beat swords into plowshares and spears into pruning hooks,"[35] and the nations of the earth will dwell together in peace forevermore.

Gratifying Results: An Open Letter to Local Branches of the SDP†

November 20, 1898

Marquette, Mich., November 20, 1898

Comrades:—

The recent election had gratifying results for us, but these results are of permanent value to our cause only to the extent that we follow them up with renewed vigor and determination. Each branch should at once prepare for the work of the future. In this work, each member should enlist with heart and hand. There is not a moment to be lost. Henceforth we are in the field to press our claims and advocate our principles in municipal, state, and national campaigns until we have swept the country and the cause of socialism in triumphant.

The national headquarters of our party should have its resources strengthened in order that organizers may be placed in the field and the work of propaganda pressed with all possible vigor. The admission fees of new members and quarterly dues should therefore be promptly remitted, and the returns should be full and complete.

Besides this, a thorough canvass should be made for subscribers to the *Social Democratic Herald.* Each branch should appoint an agent, and each member should assist in securing subscribers. Let this work be taken in hand at once and our subscription enlarged, so that in the near future the size of our paper can be increased to meet the growing demands of the organization.

† Published as "To Local Branches" in *Social Democratic Herald,* vol. 1, no. 21 (November 26, 1898), 1.

Comrades, action only will determine your interest in our cause. Words, promises, professions will not do. The time to act is now, and you, each of you, is expected to do his duty. Will there be any who fail to respond?

Notes

1. Those listed are the anarchists who were victimized in the Haymarket Affair of May 4, 1886, during which a terrorist hurled a bomb at police lines. After the smoke cleared from the blast and the storm of gunfire that followed, seven police officers and four civilians lay dead. The public was enraged against the bomber. Top leaders of the Chicago radical movement were blamed for having inspired the blast and were prosecuted on that basis. After a sensational seven-week trial, seven death sentences and one 15-year prison term were handed down by the hostile jury. Two of these death sentences were later commuted, and one defendant committed suicide to cheat the hangman, but on November 11, 1887, Parsons, Spies, Fischer, and Engel were hanged. The revolutionary movement in Chicago was set back for years as a result of the bombing and retaliatory judicial murder of the prominent journalists and orators Spies and Parsons.
2. Allusion to Job 19:24.
3. The source of this quoted material has not been located.
4. The source of these quotations is unclear.
5. Reference to the poem "Cologne" (1828), by Samuel Taylor Coleridge (1772–1834), in which the author denigrated the city of Köln, Germany, as a town of "two and seventy stenches, / All well defined, and several stinks!" The city was the birthplace of its namesake distilled fragrances, invented there by an Italian chemist early in the eighteenth century.
6. The Dingley Act of 1897, initiated under the new administration of Republican William McKinley, was the highest tariff in American history. It placed heavy new taxes on hides and raw wool and dramatically increased existing tax rates on imported sugar, woolen goods, linen, silk, and other products.
7. Lyman J. Gage (1836–1927), named secretary of the treasury by President William McKinley, was instrumental in winning passage of the Gold Standard Act of 1900, which placed the United States on a monometallic gold-based monetary system.
8. Definition of poetry by Thomas Gray (1716–1771).
9. Philip D. Armour (1832–1901) was the founder of the Chicago-based Armour & Co., one of the largest meatpacking companies in the country. He was one of the wealthiest industrialists of the American Gilded Age.
10. On July 7, 1895, the merchant ship *Arago* arrived in San Francisco with four of its crew in irons. The four had signed contracts to work aboard the ship on a round trip to Chile but, owing to bad conditions, had attempted to jump ship in Astoria, Oregon. Although arrested, the four had subsequently refused to return to work, which led to their being disembarked in chains in California. The four argued that their arrest and forced labor constituted a form of involuntary servitude, violating the 13th Amendment's prohibition against slavery. The court case that resulted, *Robertson v. Baldwin*, was decided by the Supreme Court in January 1897 rejecting the sailors' claim. The case outraged the nation and led to the passage of ameliorative legislation in 1898 and 1915.
11. From "On the Capture of Fugitive Slaves Near Washington" (1845), by James Russell Lowell (1819–1891).

12. That is, the People's Party.
13. The congressional declaration that launched the Spanish-American War was passed April 25, 1898. Hostilities ended on August 12 of that same year.
14. *Reconcentrados,* a name given by the Spanish military occupation to those members the non-combatant Cuban rural population who were forcibly moved to new locations clustered around fortified cities during the 1895–1898 armed struggle for Cuban liberation. The reconcentration campaign, an effort to isolate anti-Spanish guerrilla forces in the countryside, resulted in the death of 30 percent of those so relocated due to inadequate food and bad sanitation .
15. The Social Democracy of America split in the early morning hours of Saturday, June 11, 1898, with Berger, Heath, and Debs leaving the organization to form a new Social Democratic Party of America.
16. Bellamy died of tuberculosis on May 22, 1898 at his home in Chicopee Falls, Massachusetts. This statement to a representative of the *Terre Haute Express* was made by Debs the evening of May 28 from his own home.
17. Edward Bellamy, *Equality* (New York: D. Appleton & Co., 1897).
18. From "Superfluous Riches," by Horace Mann (1796–1859).
19. The source of this snippet of doggerel could not be traced.
20. There follows "Columbus" (1892), by Joaquin Miller (1837–1913).
21. James A. Mount (1843–1901) was governor of Indiana from 1897 to 1901. Mount, a Republican farmer, was something of an unwilling politician and was physically exhausted at the end of his gubernatorial term. He died of a heart attack at the age of 58 just two days after leaving office.
22. From *Twelfth Night* (c. 1601), Act IV, Scene 2, by William Shakespeare.
23. These comments were apparently part of Debs's introductory remarks to the approximately 125 people who gathered for the opening of the first national convention of the Social Democracy of America. Debs's mention of a membership size for the organization is a rare exception to the group's silence on the matter and almost certainly represents a significant exaggeration.
24. This statement was made after a morning session marked by what one observer characterized as "considerable violent argument" over the matter of seating of 11 delegates contested by SDA secretary Sylvester Keliher and the ability of delegates to vote proxies for local branches not in attendance—two propositions that were passed by the convention over Debs's opposition.
25. "Out of the fight."
26. Ecclesiastes 1:9.
27. Allusion to the 1879 book of the same title by Henry George (1839–1897).
28. Reference to William Hogarth (1697–1764), an English illustrator remembered for realistic depictions of the cruelty and depravity of daily life.
29. This speech, part of a Massachusetts tour in advance of the November 1898 general election, was delivered at Springfield Turn Hall under the auspices of the Social Democratic Party.
30. From "The Present Crisis," by James Russell Lowell (1819–1891).

31. Henry Labouchère (1831–1912) was a British Liberal Party politician, writer, publisher, and theater owner.
32. Douglas Jerrold (1803–1857) was an English playwright and novelist. A prolific author, Jerrold was a personal friend of Charles Dickens, who served as a pallbearer in his funeral.
33. President William McKinley gave thanks to God for bringing about a speedy end to the Spanish-American War in his Thanksgiving message of October 28, 1898.
34. The United States forced Spain out of Cuba and took possession of Guam, Puerto Rico, and the Philippine Islands as a result of the Spanish-American War.
35. Allusion to Isaiah 2:4.

1899

Labor and Liberty: Speech in Saginaw, Michigan†

February 5, 1899

There are those who view with widespread alarm the proposition of self-government. There are those who fear the sun of the Republic is to set in universal gloom. But I am persuaded that the grand old ship of state will breast all the storms and billows and safely reach the haven port. The social system is in the process of dissolution. A new system of order is evolving from competitive chaos. We stand upon the eve of the greatest change the world has ever seen.

Lamentable is the fact that the man who works longest and hardest has the least to show for his labors. The trouble is with the distribution of wealth. Those whose labor creates do not enjoy its benefits. Espouse his cause for him and you are denounced as an agitator and a demagogue; you are charged with trying to uproot and overthrow the institutions of the people. This has already been the case with those who paved the way for better conditions for the human family. Socrates was compelled to drink the fatal hemlock. The savior of mankind perished on the cross. This has been so true of our own country. No president was ever so vilified as was George Washington. Samuel Adams, who organized the American Revolution, was an agitator. Yet he it was who inspired the revolution which led to the independence of the country. He was denounced by the Tory press as an arch-rebel. Fortunate it was that at that time there was no government by injunction.

All progress is made possible through agitators. By them is given the choice between agitation and stagnation. The insufferable crime of chattel slavery polluted the soil of our country. It controlled the president, the houses of Congress, and the Supreme Court. It ruled the ministers of the gospel and controlled the press. All the forces of organized government and processes of law upheld it. It was founded on iniquity, as was the present wage system, under which men work and endure the ills and hardships of the competitive system.

Among the first to pay the penalty of this iniquity was Lovejoy, of Illinois, whose interest in the right of free speech caused him to be mobbed and

† Published as "Labor and Liberty" in *Saginaw News,* February 6, 1899, unspecified page. Content checked to "Debs" in *Saginaw Exponent,* February 10, 1899, unspecified page. Copies preserved on *Papers of Eugene V. Debs* microfilm edition, reel 9.

murdered. In his day there was still another—William Lloyd Garrison. A short time ago I was at Newburyport, Massachusetts, where he protested against this institution. I followed him, in fancy, to Boston and saw him pursued by another and larger mob. I saw him there face his pursuers and say to them that he would not retract. Then there was Wendell Phillips, the aristocrat, yet the greatest combination of heart and brain. He was hated because he rebelled against the degenerate, demoralizing institution of slavery. Gerrit Smith[1] and Harriet Beecher Stowe, too, are remembered. While writing *Uncle Tom's Cabin,* the author was visited by friends, who pleaded with her not to give her book to the world, telling her that she would make herself infamous. Had she been stopped by the felling of the public pulse, the book would never have dignified the literature of the world.

Such men and such women have made it possible for me to enjoy what little liberty is left to me, and I propose to do what lies in my power to increase the liberty of every man, woman, and child to come. The world is not just, and it is a long way from generous, but it is getting better every day. The problem of the day is the economic condition of the country. Some imagine it can be solved by overwhelming force, that a standing army will silence the protests of the workingman. But the industrial problem will not be settled until it is settled by the great principle of justice.

There are two social systems. Under the one, only a few are to enjoy the wealth and the others are to serve as the hewers of wood and drawers of water. Under the other, all are equal and all are to be recognized as entitled to life, liberty, and the pursuit of happiness. I believe the spiritual truths now being voiced are to prevail throughout the civilized world. Only a few are cultured, and the great mass of the people is ignorant. But civilization is awakening to the system under which this condition arises, and the time is coming when men will stand together for the good of all the children of the civilized world. The times are cheering. Never has there been a time when men and women have been thinking so seriously. Most prominent is it that woman is enlisting for a higher humanity and civilization. Go where you will—counting room, banking house, editorial room, or the church—and you find women are taking an active part in the discussion of the great economic and industrial question.

I believe I shall live long enough to at least see the promise of a Cooperative Commonwealth. The laboring man will not much longer think about the conditions, but he will act. He will not act in violence, but through the ballot.

There has been an industrial evolution during the past years. Many, especially the businessmen in the struggle of competition, are oblivious to the change. They fail to realize that the conditions are no longer as they were. In former years, work was done almost exclusively by hand—by a simple tool under the control of the man who used it, and no being could doom him to industrial degradation and slavery. The tool was touched by the spirit of invention and began to expand into the machine. Little shops grew into factories, growing larger and larger. But the capitalist operates the machine for individual profit, not for the benefit of labor. There may be a generous employer who would pay good wages to his men, but they are not fixed by him. Rates are fixed by competition, which forces wages down until the final point of subsistence is reached.

Some claim that wages have not declined. But the coal miner in Pennsylvania who formerly got $4 or $5 a day is getting 50 cents a day. It is the same with the textile factories of the East and the cotton mills of the South. Machinery is being operated by women and children. In the day of hand work, the man supported the family; there was no tramp then, the word had not been coined; but under the competitive system man has been reduced to a hunger pang, his wife to a machine, and his child to machine oil. In those old days, there were no trusts to close the doors of opportunity against the man. The laborer could look forward to laying aside his tools and becoming the employer; the clerk could look forward to becoming the proprietor. Now the clerk in the great department store is grateful if he is permitted to work even for $6 or $7 a week. There is no longer the opportunity to advance.

In the days of hand labor, there was no overproduction. The results of labor were meager, and it has been called a slow age, but there were no slums in the center of our population. There was no submerged one-tenth of the population.[2] There was a chance for all, but this is no longer true. Then a boy could learn a trade, but what avails him now to learn one? The machine invades the territory, and after he has just learned the trade, the machine comes in to do his work faster. Skill is eliminated by the machine. The machine is becoming more perfect, and labor is becoming more common. The competition for work is becoming sharper every day. The more workers, the less the wages, and the tendency of wages is to go down but with a temporary rise. Under the present system, they must go down until they will just suffice to keep him. If we could work without food or shelter, wages would be nil.

They tell us that railroad engineers are getting the same wages they did years ago. But they are hauling three times as many cars. One crew of five men is now doing the work of three crews of 15 men. The same thing has happened to the printers. The linotype machine has thrown hundreds of typesetters out of employment, and there is now being perfected a machine which will do the work of 20 operators.[3] What is to become of the printer? Enter some other occupation? The machine is there, too, for the machine has entered every department of life. But there has been no betterment of the laboring man. The machine was evolved from his brain to allow him to devote hours to the improvement of the mind, but under the present system it has worked out simply to enslave the man.

Crime and suicide are directly traceable in a large measure to idleness of the rich as well as the poor. Excessive wealth is just as degenerating, just as degrading, and just as demoralizing as abject poverty. One gets more than he can use, while another is in a constant struggle from the cradle to the grave.

They say our system is rational, and they quote the words, "the poor always ye have with you,"[4] and go along satisfied, never recalling that those words were uttered in rebuke. I don't wonder men don't want to work under this system. Who wants to be a coal miner? How would you like to go down into the earth 200 feet and occupy a cell for life for 60 cents a day? That is human slavery, and in some ways worse than our old system of chattel slavery. [The chattel slave] had his animal wants supplied, was housed and fed and clothed, because he had a commercial value. The modern slave does not. He has his wages squeezed out of him. If sick, there is none to send a doctor; if out of employment, he must get along as best he can. The chattel slave had steady employment and didn't have to beg from door to door for permission to work. The chattel slave was sold to the highest bidder, but the wage earner has to go into the market and sell his work to the lowest bidder.

Work is becoming more precarious every day. All of the forces of nature, all her materials are ready for the application of hands and brains, but men are not permitted to work, for between them and labor stands the capitalist, who has organized labor for personal gain, no matter what becomes of the laborer. When the man sells his labor, he sells himself, and the purchaser becomes the master, the seller the slave. This system is undermining the American home, and when the American home falls, the Republic falls, and the brightest light that ever gloated across the heavens of the nations goes out.

The system is rapidly reaching concentrated cooperation. Man no longer makes a shoe, but 70 men with machines make thousands of pairs of shoes. But we have this paradox: that the easier it is to make them, the harder it is to get them. Competitive devices take from him the reward of his production. Formerly, when a man made a shoe, he could buy it back, but now the average worker receives one-quarter in wages of what he has produced. The worker and his dependents form two-thirds of the population, and the remaining one-third cannot absorb the other three-fourths of his product, and so we have overproduction. Two years will see us struggling under the results of overproduction again. Panics are becoming longer and the intervals between them shorter. Politicians want to open new markets across the Pacific, and they want to send to them the very goods our own people are suffering for. If the people of this country had the purchasing capacity equal to their productive power, there would be no overproduction. We would shorten the labor day and instead of struggling through on the animal plane would develop the real man, have labor not competitive but cooperative, and make this the greatest civilization the world has ever known.

I have no sympathy with the expansion policy.[5] I personally was not in favor of the war. I recall the words of Victor Hugo, "Peace is the virtue of civilization; war is the crime." We claimed that this war was commenced in the name of humanity. The first thing we did was take Puerto Rico without the consent of the governed, and yet that is the great principle underlying our own government. The inhabitants of Cuba had been the victims of tyranny and exploitation for centuries. It was not of the ruling class of Spain alone, but of the United States. It was not the common people of Spain. But it was the common people of both countries that had to enter the war; it was the workman who had to fight workman. If we are in complete control of Cuba, it will not be five years before it will be Mark Hanna's plantation. What will we have done for Cuba? Simply given them a new set of masters. I believe it possible to settle all questions without war. At the first call, the workman hastens to the front. In the rebellion, he rushed to the front to save the Republic, and how much of it belongs to him today? All war is degrading and demoralizing, and I hope to see the time when workingmen will cease to fly at each other's throats at the behest of their masters.

Competition is cornering herself. The corporation is being absorbed by the trust and the next stage will be a trust of trusts; combination is coming to be master of the age. People are becoming aroused and will learn that capitalism is but one link in the chain. As capitalism is the outgrowth of feudalism, so socialism is the outgrowth of capitalism. The change will come naturally. Socialism is still offensive because people do not understand it. It is only a cooperative industry in which every man receives the equivalent of this production. Work will then be a pleasure. Why shouldn't we be coal miners if by so doing we can work three hours a day under the best conditions and have hours for the improvement of the intellectual and moral life?

We are not opposed to private property, but to private property in the means of life. The basis of industry is to be cooperative. But no human being shall have private property in the means of production, and the economic problem shall be solved; there will be economic as well as political freedom, and the declaration of independence shall be realized.

In this country, we still have the ballot. A revolution can be brought about by this method. For this purpose, we are organizing the people. To this we must come and to it we are coming. The signs of the times are cheering. Men are being impoverished, the businessmen are being crowded out by the big department stores, and when at last the time comes, they will vote out competition and vote in cooperation. As competition declines, cooperation increases. If not for cooperation, the government wouldn't hold together five minutes. The railroads, which are now operated for private profit, will then be managed by the people. I would take possession in the name of the people. You say it is confiscation. How did these men now in control get the property? They froze out the smaller stockholder. His property was confiscated by the large holders. The large corporations absorbed the individual, the trust the corporations, and the people in time will absorb the trusts.

If we are fit for political equality, we are fit for economic equality. If one man is an economic slave, the other will be the economic millionaire. The failures of the past year represent the disintegration of the middle classes. It is either become a millionaire or a mendicant—with the chances one to a million in favor of the latter.

In the humanizing process, I want to see woman have every right that man enjoys. Some say that woman should not have the right to vote. I believe if she did, many of the ills which we claim would disappear. Woman has more integrity, more honesty, than man. You could not buy her vote for a drink of whiskey.

I can only outline the work we should do, not complete it in detail. Arouse the workingman to the consciousness of this true power and brush from his knees the dust of servitude. Have faith in yourselves and the justice of the great cause of labor. Brush jealousy and envy aside and stand together in one great brotherhood. Every man should be a missionary in the field of labor. Disseminate intelligence. There is no darkness but ignorance and slavery. Reach down and light up the men who can't read or he will drag you down. Books are better than beer. Under the new system, you will become a man. The people collectively can do all things. I can sum it up in the three words—read, think, and study.

We are not going to extend the powers of government, but to limit them. At present it is coercive—a huge police system; under the new it will be perfectly administrative. We shall have the initiative and referendum. When a law becomes oppressive, we will repeal it. Corruption will be unknown, because you can't corrupt the whole people. Then will we have an industrial, economic, and political republic, and liberty shall triumph.

Socialism or Capitalism? Open Letter to R. S. Thompson, Chairman of the Union Reform Party†

February 16, 1899

[Terre Haute, IN], February 16, 1899

R. S. Thompson, Esq.
Chairman, Union Reform Party
Springfield, Ohio

Dear Sir:—

Your favor of the 8th inst. [February 8, 1899] with enclosure has been received. I thank you for the courtesy of the invitation to attend the conference of the Union Reform Party with a view to organizing a new national party, but being a socialist and a member of the Social Democratic Party and being profoundly impressed with conviction that only through socialism is there relief from the ills of capitalism, I am not in favor of such a party as is proposed, which, in the nature of things, must be founded in compromise and cannot long survive the internal dissensions which swept its predecessors from the field and are bound to overwhelm and destroy the new party. It is either socialism or capitalism—complete freedom or total slavery. I am a socialist without a shadow of concession or compromise.

Socialism is founded on the rock of truth, and while its growth is slower than that of "reform" movements that spring up spontaneously and disappear

---

† Published in *Social Democratic Herald,* vol. 1, no. 34 (February 25, 1899), 1.

likewise, it is a sound and permanent development, and no power on earth can resist its march to victory.

Apart from socialism, the initiative and referendum has little, if any, value. Under capitalism, the ignorance of the mass makes it even a dangerous weapon. Had my fate been decided by it in 1894, I would have been hanged for the crime of trying to help humanity.

For these reasons, I am a social democrat and will give my support to a straight socialist party to the exclusion of all other parties, especially those that make concessions and compromises to secure a union of forces.

Yours very truly,
Eugene V. Debs

Prison Labor—Its Effects on Industry and Trade: Address to the Nineteenth Century Club in New York City†

March 21, 1899

In my early years, I stood before the open door of a blazing furnace and piled in the fuel to create steam to speed a locomotive along the iron track of progress and civilization. In the costume of the craft, through the grime of mingled sweat and smoke and dust, I was initiated into the great brotherhood of labor. The locomotive was my alma mater. I mastered the curriculum and graduated with the degree of DD, not, as the lexicons interpret the letters, "Doctor of Divinity," but that better signification, "Do and Dare"—a higher degree than Aristotle conferred in his lyceum or Plato thundered from his academy. I am not in the habit of telling how little I know about Latin to those who have slaked their thirst for learning at the Pierian springs,[6] but there is a proverb that

† Published as part of the pamphlet *Prison Labor: Address Delivered Before the Nineteenth Century Club at Delmonico's, New York City*, March 21, 1899 (Terre Haute, IN: Debs Publishing Co., 1899), 1–12. Reprinted in *Appeal to Reason,* whole no. 225 (March 24, 1900), 2.

has come down to us from the dim past which reads *"Omnia vincit labor"* and which has been adopted as the shibboleth of the American labor movement because, when reduced to English, it reads "Labor overcomes all things." In a certain sense, this is true. Labor has built this great metropolis of the new world, built it as coral insects build the foundations of islands—build and die; build from the fathomless depths of the ocean until the mountain billows are dashed into spray as they beat against the fortifications beneath which the builders are forever entombed and forgotten. Here in this proud city where wealth has built its monuments grander and more imposing than any of the seven wonders of the world named in classic lore, if you will excavate for facts, you will find the remains, the bones of the toilers, buried and embedded in their foundations. They lived, they wrought, they died. In their time, they may have laughed and sung and danced to the music of their clanking chains. They married, propagated their species, and perpetuated conditions which, growing steadily worse, are today the foulest blots the imagination can conceive upon our much-vaunted civilization.

And from these conditions there flow a thousand streams of vice and crime which have broadened and deepened until they constitute a perpetual menace to the peace and security of society. Jails, workhouses, reformatories, and penitentiaries have been crowded with victims, and the question how to control these institutions and their unfortunate inmates is challenging the most serious thought of the most advanced nations on the globe.

The particular phase of this grave and melancholy question which we are to consider this evening is embodied in the subject assigned the speakers: "Prison Labor, Its Effects on Industry and Trade."[7]

I must confess that it would have suited my purpose better had the subject been transposed so as to read: "Industry and Trade, Their Effect on Labor," for, as a socialist, I am convinced that the prison problem is rooted in the present system of industry and trade, carried forward, as it is, purely for private profit without the slightest regard to the effect upon those engaged in it, especially the men, women, and children who perform the useful, productive labor which has created all wealth and all civilization.

Serious as is the problem presented in the subject of our discussion, it is yet insignificant when compared with the vastly greater question of the effect of our social and economic system upon industry and trade.

The pernicious effect of prison contract labor upon "free labor," so called, when brought into competition with it in the open market, is universally conceded, but it should not be overlooked that prison labor is itself an effect and not a cause, and that convict labor is recruited almost wholly from the propertyless, wage-working class, and that the inhuman system which has reduced a comparative few from enforced idleness to crime has sunk the whole mass of labor to the dead level of industrial servitude.

It is therefore with the economic system, which is responsible for not only prison labor, but for the gradual enslavement and degradation of all labor, that we must deal before there can be any solution of the prison labor problem or any permanent relief from its demoralizing influences. But we will briefly consider the effect of prison labor upon industry and then pass to the larger question of the cause of prison labor and its appalling increase, to which the discussion logically leads.

From the earliest ages, there has been a prison problem. The ancients had their bastilles and their dungeons. Most of the pioneers of progress, the haters of oppression, the lovers of liberty, whose names now glorify the pantheon of the world, made such institutions a necessity in their day. But civilization advances, however slowly, and there has been some progress. It required five hundred years to travel from the inquisition to the injunction.

In the earlier days, punishment was the sole purpose of imprisonment. Offenders against the ruling class must pay the penalty in prison cell, which, not infrequently, was equipped with instruments of torture. With the civilizing process came the idea of the reformation of the culprit, and this idea prompts every investigation made of the latter-day problem. The inmates must be set to work for their own good, no less than for the good of the state.

It was at this point that the convict labor problem began,, and it has steadily expanded from that time to this and while there have been some temporary modifications of the evil, it is still an unmitigated curse from which there can be no escape while an economic system endures in which labor, that is to say the laborer, man, woman, and child, is sold to the lowest bidder in the markets of the world.

More than thirty years ago, Professor E. C. Wines and Professor Theodore W. Dwight, then commissioners of the Prison Association of New York, made a report to the legislature of the state on prison industry in which they said:

> Upon the whole, it is our settled conviction that the contract system of convict labor, added to the system of political appointments, which necessarily involves a low grade of official qualification and constant changes in the prison staff, renders nugatory, to a great extent, the whole theory of our penitentiary system. Inspection may correct isolated abuses; philanthropy may relieve isolated cases of distress; and religion may effect

> isolated moral cures; but genuine, radical, comprehensive, systematic improvement is impossible.

The lapse of 30 years has not affected the wisdom or logic of the conclusion. It is as true now as it was then. Considered in his most favorable light, the convict is a scourge to himself, a menace to society, and a burden to industry, and whatever system of convict labor may be tried, it will ultimately fail of its purpose at reformation of the criminal or the relief of industry as long as thousands of "free laborers" who have committed no crime are unable to get work and make an honest living. Not long ago, I visited a penitentiary in which a convict expressed regret that his sentence was soon to expire. Where was he to go, and what was he to do? And how long before he would be sentenced to a longer term for a greater crime?

The commission which investigated the matter in Ohio in 1877 reported to the legislature as follows:

> The contract system interferes in an undue manner with the honest industry of the state. It has been the cause of crippling the business of many of our manufacturers; it has been the cause of driving many of them out of business; it has been the cause of a large percentage of reductions which have taken place in the wages of our mechanics; it has been the cause of pauperizing a large portion of our laborers and increasing crime in a corresponding degree; it has been no benefit to the state; as a reformatory measure, it has been a complete, total, and miserable failure; it has hardened more criminals than any other cause; it has made total wrecks morally of thousands and thousands who would have been reclaimed from the paths of vice and crime under a proper system of prison management, but who have resigned their fate to a life of hopeless degradation; it has not a single commendable feature. Its tendency is pernicious in the extreme. In short, it is an insurmountable barrier in the way of the reformation of the unfortunates who are compelled to live and labor under its evil influences; it enables a class of men to get rich out of the crimes committed by others; it leaves upon the fair escutcheon of the state a relic of the very worst form of human slavery; it is a bone of ceaseless contention between the state and its mechanical and industrial interests; it is abhorred by all and respected by none except those, perhaps, who make profit and gain out of it. It should be tolerated no longer but abolished at once.

And yet this same system is still in effect in many of the states of the Union. The most revolting outrages have been perpetrated upon prison laborers under this diabolical system. Read the official reports and stand aghast at the atrocities committed against these morally deformed and perverted human creatures, your brothers and my brothers, for the private profit of capitalistic exploiters and the advancement of Christian civilization.

What a commentary on the capitalist competitive system! First, men are forced into idleness. Gradually they are driven to the extremity of begging or stealing. Having still a spark of pride and self-respect, they steal and are sent to jail. The first sentence seals their doom. The brand of Cain is upon them.[8] They are identified with the criminal class. Society, whose victims they are, has exiled them forever, and with this curse ringing in their ears they proceed on their downward career, sounding every note in the scale of depravity until at last, having graduated in crime all the way from petit larceny to homicide, their last despairing sigh is wrung from them by the hangman's halter. From first to last these unfortunates, the victims of social malformation, are made the subject of speculation and traffic. The barbed iron of the prison contractor is plunged into their quivering hearts that their tortures may be coined into private profit for their exploiters.

In the investigation in South Carolina, where the convicts had been leased to railroad companies, the most shocking disclosures were made. Out of 285 prisoners employed by one company, 128—or more than 40 percent—died as the result, largely, of brutal treatment.

It is popular to say that society must be protected against its criminals. I prefer to believe that criminals should be protected against society, at least while we live under a system that makes the commission of crime necessary to secure employment.

The Tennessee tragedy is still fresh in the public memory.[9] Here, as elsewhere, the convicts, themselves brutally treated, were used as a means of dragging the whole mine-working class down to their crime-cursed condition, the Tennessee Coal and Iron Co. leased the convicts for the express purpose of forcing the wages of miners down to the point of subsistence. Says the official report: "The miners were compelled to work in competition with low-priced convict labor, the presence of which was used by the company as a scourge to force free laborers to its terms." Then the miners, locked out, their families suffering, driven to desperation, appealed to force and in a twinkling the laws of the state were trampled down, the authorities overpowered and defied, and almost five hundred convicts set at liberty.

Fortunately, the system of leasing and contracting prison labor for private exploitation is being exposed and its monster iniquities laid bare. Thanks to organized labor and to the spirit of prison reform, this horrifying phase of the evil is doomed to disappear before an enlightened public sentiment.

The public account system, though subject to serious criticism, is far less objectionable than either the lease, the contract, or the piece-price system. At least the prisoner's infirmities cease to be the prey of speculative greed and conscienceless rapacity.

The system of manufacturing for the use of state, county, and municipal institutions, adopted by the state of New York, is an improvement upon those hitherto in effect, but it is certain to develop serious objections in course of time. With the use of modern machinery, the limited demand will soon be supplied, and then what? It may be in order to suggest that the prisoners could be employed in making shoes and clothes for the destitute poor and schoolbooks for their children and many other articles which the poor sorely need but are unable to buy.

Developing along this line, it would be only a question of time until the state would be manufacturing all things for the use of the people, and then perhaps the inquiry would be pertinent: If the state can give men steady employment after they commit crime, and manufacturing can be carried forward successfully by their labor, why can it not give them employment before they are driven to that extremity, thereby preventing them from becoming criminals?

All useful labor is honest labor, even if performed in a prison. Only the labor of exploiters, such as speculators, stock gamblers, beef-embalmers, and their mercenary politicians, lawyers, and other parasites—only such is dishonest labor. A thief making shoes in a penitentiary is engaged in more useful and therefore more honest labor than a "free" stonemason at work on a palace whose foundations are laid in the skulls and bones, and cemented in the sweat and blood of ten thousand victims of capitalistic exploitation. In both cases, the labor is compulsory. The stonemason would not work for the trust-magnate were he not compelled to.

In ancient times, only slaves labored. And, as a matter of fact, only slaves labor now. The millions are made by the magic of manipulation. The coal miners of West Virginia, Pennsylvania, Ohio, Indiana, and Illinois receive an average wage of less than 75 cents a day. They perform the most useful and necessary labor, without which your homes, if possible at all, would be cheerless as caves and the great heart of industry would cease to throb. Are they free men, or are they slaves? And what is the effect of their labor on trade and industry? And upon themselves and their families? Dante would search the realms of inferno in vain for such pictures of horror and despair as are to be found in the mining regions of free America.

To the student of social science, the haggard fact stands forth that, under the competitive system of production and distribution, the prison problem will never be solved—and its effect upon trade and industry will never be greatly modified. The fact will remain that whatever labor is performed by prison labor could and should be performed by free labor, and when in the march of economic progress the capitalist system of industry for private profit succumbs to the socialist system of industry for human happiness, when the factory, which is now a penitentiary crowded with life convicts, among whom children often constitute the majority—when this factory is transformed into a temple of science, and the machine, myriad-armed and tireless, is the only slave, there will be no prison labor and the problem will cease to vex the world, and to this it is coming in obedience to the economic law, as unerring in its operation as the law of gravitation.

That prison labor is demoralizing in its effect on trade and industry whenever and wherever brought into competition with it, especially under the various forms of the contract system, is of course conceded, but that it has been, or is at present, a great factor in such demoralization is not admitted. There is a tendency to exaggerate the blighting effects of prison labor for the purpose of obscuring the one overshadowing cause of demoralized trade and impoverished industry.

Prison labor did not reduce the miner to a walking hunger pang, his wife to a tear-stained rag, and his home to a lair. Prison labor is not responsible for the squares of squalor and miles of misery in New York, Chicago, and all other centers of population. Prison labor is not chargeable with the sweating dens in which the victims of capitalistic competition crouch in dread and fear until death comes to their rescue. Prison labor had no hand in Coeur d'Alene, Tennessee, Homestead, Hazleton, Virden, Pana, that suburb of hell called Pullman, and other ensanguined industrial battlefields where thousands of workingmen, after being oppressed and robbed, were imprisoned like felons and shot down like vagabond dogs; where venal judges issued infamous injunctions and despotic orders at the behest of their masters, enforcing them with deputy marshals armed with pistols and clubs and supported by troops with gleaming bayonets and shotted guns to drain the veins of workingmen of blood, but for whose labor this continent would be a wilderness. Only the tortures of hunger and nakedness provoked protest, and this was silenced by the bayonet and bullet; by the club and the blood that followed the blow.

Prison labor is not accountable for the appalling increase in insanity, in suicide, in murder, in prostitution, and a thousand other forms of vice and crime which pollute every fountain and contaminate every stream designed to bless the world.

Prison labor did not create our army of unemployed, but has been recruited from its ranks, and both owe their existence to the same social and economic system.

Nor are the evil effects confined exclusively to the poor working class. There is an aspect of the case in which the rich are as unfortunate as the poor. The destiny of the capitalist class is irrevocably linked with the working class. Fichte,[10] the great German philosopher, said, "Wickedness increases in proportion to the elevation of rank."[11]

Prison labor is but one of the manifestations of our economic development and indicates its trend. The same cause that demoralized industry has crowded our prisons. Industry has not been impoverished by prison labor, but prison labor is the result of impoverished industry. The limited time at my command will not permit an analysis of the process.

The real question which confronts us is our industrial system and its effects upon labor. One of these effects is, as I have intimated, prison labor. What is its cause? What makes it necessary? The answer is, the competitive system, which creates wage-slavery, throws thousands out of employment and reduces the wages of thousands more to the point of bare subsistence.

Why is prison labor preferred to "free labor?" Simply because it is cheaper; it yields more profit to the man who buys, exploits, and sells it. But this has its limitations. Capitalist competition that throngs the streets with idle workers, capitalist production that reduces human labor to a commodity and ultimately to crime—this system produces another kind of prison labor in the form of child labor, which is being utilized more and more to complete the subjugation of the working class. There is this difference: The prison laborers are clothed and housed and fed. The child laborers, whose wage is a dollar a week, or even less, must take care of themselves.

Prison labor is preferred because it is cheap. So with child labor. It is not a question of prison labor, or of child labor, but of cheap labor.

Tenement house labor is another form of prison labor.

The effects of cheap labor on trade and industry must be the same, whether such labor is done by prisoners, tenement house slaves, children, or starving "hobos."

The prison laborer produces by machinery in abundance but does not consume. The child likewise produces, but owing to its small wages, does not consume. So with the vast army of workers whose wage grows smaller as the productive capacity of labor increases, and then we are afflicted with overproduction, the result of underconsumption. What follows? The panic. Factories close down, wageworkers are idle and suffer, middle-class businessmen are forced into bankruptcy, the army of tramps is increased, vice and crime are rampant, and prisons and workhouses are filled to overflowing, as are sewers when the streets of cities are deluged with floods.

Prison labor, like all cheap labor, is at first a source of profit to the capitalist, but finally it turns into a two-edged sword that cuts into and destroys the system that produced it.

First, the capitalist pocket is filled by the employment of cheap labor—and then the bottom drops out of it.

In the cheapening process, the pauperized masses have lost their consuming power.

The case may now be summed up as follows:

First. Prison labor is bad; it has a demoralizing effect on capitalist trade and industry.

Second. Child labor, tenement house, and every other form of cheap labor is bad; it is destructive to trade and industry.

Third. Capitalist competition is bad; it creates a demand for cheap labor.

Fourth. Capitalist production is bad; it creates millionaires and mendicants, economic masters and slaves, thus intensifying the class struggle.

This indicates that the present capitalist system has outlived its usefulness, and that it is in the throes of dissolution. Capitalism is but a link in the chain of economic development. Just as feudalism developed capitalism and then disappeared, so capitalism is now developing socialism, and when the new social system has been completely evolved, the last vestige of capitalism will fade into history.

The gigantic trust marks the change in production. It is no longer competitive, but cooperative. The same mode of distribution, which must inevitably follow, will complete the process. Cooperative labor will be the basis of the new social system, and this will be done for use and not for profit. Labor will no longer be bought and sold. Industrial slavery will cease. For every man, there will be the equal right to work with every other man, and each will receive the fruit of his labor. Then we shall have economic equality. Involuntary idleness will be a horror of the past. Poverty will relax its grasp. The army of tramps will be disbanded because the prolific womb which now warms these unfortunates into life will become barren. Prisons will be depopulated, and the prison labor problem will be solved. Each labor-saving machine will lighten the burden and decrease the hours of toil. The soul will no longer be subordinated to the stomach. Man will live a complete life, and the march will then begin to an ideal civilization.

There is a proverb which the Latin race sent ringing down the centuries which reads, *"Omnia vincit amor,"* or "Love conquers all things." Love and labor in alliance, working together, have transforming, redeeming, and emancipating power. Under their benign sway, the world can be made better and brighter.

Isaiah saw in prophetic vision a time when nations should war no more—when swords should be transformed into plowshares and spears into pruning hooks. The fulfillment of the prophecy only awaits an era when Love and Labor, in holy alliance, shall solve the economic problem.

Here, on this occasion, in this great metropolis with its thousand spires pointing heavenward, where opulence riots in luxury which challenges hyperbole, and poverty rots in sweatshops which only a Shakespeare or a Victor Hugo could describe, and the transfer to canvas would palsy the hand of a Michelangelo—here, where wealth and want and woe bear irrefutable testimony of deplorable conditions, I stand as a socialist, protesting against the wrongs perpetrated upon *Les Misérables,* and pleading as best I can for a higher civilization.

The army of begging Lazaruses, with the dogs licking their sores at the gates of palaces, where the rich are clothed in purple and fine linen with their tables groaning beneath the luxuries of all climes, make the palaces on the highland where fashion holds sway and music lends it charms, a picture in the landscape which, in illustrating disparity, brings into bolder relief the hut and the hovel in the hollow where want, gaunt and haggard, sits at the door, and where light and plenty, cheerfulness and hope are forever exiled by the despotic decree of conditions as cruel as when the tsar of Russia orders to his penal mines in Siberia the hapless subjects who dare whisper the sacred word "liberty"—as cruel as when this boasted land of freedom commands that a faraway, innocent people shall be shot down in jungle and lagoon, in their bamboo huts, because they dream of freedom and independence.

These conditions are as fruitful of danger to the opulent as they are of degradation to the poor. It is neither folly nor fanaticism to assert that the country cannot exist under such conditions. The higher law of righteousness, of love and labor will prevail. It is a law which commends itself to reasoning men, a primal law enacted long before Jehovah wrote the Decalogue[12] amidst the thunders and lightnings of Sinai. It is a law written upon the tablets of every man's heart and conscience. It is a law infinitely above the creeds and dogmas and tangled disquisitions of the churches—the one law which in its operations will level humanity upward until men, redeemed from greed and every debasing ambition, shall obey its mandates and glory in its triumph.

Love and labor will give us the economic republic—the industrial democracy—the equal rights of all men and women, and the emancipation of all from the vicious thralldoms of the centuries.[13]

Tribute to Robert G. Ingersoll†

July 22, 1899

Numberless tributes will be paid to Robert G. Ingersoll.[14] Not one of them all, however great the love that may inspire it, will be as tender and touching, as beautiful and poetic, as his own enchanting words in the presence of death. His tribute over the remains of his brother, Ebon C., in Washington [DC] in 1879, moved by its exquisite tenderness the whole country to tears. Almost every line of it has become classic. What a pity that there is not one, with tongue inspired, to speak such noble words above his pulseless clay. Howe truly these words, spoken of his brother, apply to himself:

> The record of a generous life runs like a vine around the memory of our dead, and every sweet, unselfish act is now a perfumed flower. * * * There was, there is, no gentler, stronger, manlier man.

In the same oration he said:

---

† Published as part of the article "Local Views on Ingersoll" in the *Terre Haute Gazette,* July 22, 1899. Reprinted in *Social Democratic Herald,* vol. 2, no. 6 (July 28, 1899), 4.

> He who sleeps here, when dying, mistaking the approach of death for the return of health, whispered with his last breath, "I am better now." Let us believe, in spite of doubts and dogmas, of fears and tears, that these dear words are true of all the countless dead.

What a strange and beautiful coincidence that his own latest words were the same as those of his brother! Asked by his devoted wife how he felt, he answered with a smile, "Oh, better!" and in the same second his great soul winged its way to the farther shore. He died as he wished to die, and again his own words must be quoted:

> When the duties of life have all been nobly done; when the sun touches the horizon; when the purple twilight falls upon the past, the present, and the future—then, surrounded by kindred and by friends, death comes like a strain of music. The day has been long, the road weary, and the traveler gladly stops at the welcome inn.

For 23 years it has been my privilege to know Colonel Ingersoll, and the announcement of his sudden death is so touching and shocking to me that I can hardly bring myself to realize the awful calamity. Like thousands of others who personally knew Colonel Ingersoll, I loved him as if he had been my elder brother. He was, without doubt, the most lovable character, the tenderest and greatest soul I have ever known. His heart went out to all who suffered, and his purse went with it. Scores of incidents of his sympathetic, generous nature came under my own observation, though he was extremely modest and gave without ostentation. He used both hands in scattering his benefactions, but always, when possible, in secret.

A young woman once called at his office in New York. Her father had been rich, but failed. She was a member of an influential church, but her friends deserted her. The church authorities "promised" repeatedly to see what could be done for her. At last she went to Ingersoll and told her story. He gave her a $20 gold piece and requested her to call at the same hour the next day. She was there at the appointed time, and was then informed that arrangements had been made to give her a course of instruction in stenography and typewriting; that all the expense incident thereto had been paid, and that in the meantime any means she would require would be furnished here, and, furthermore, that when she had completed her course, a position at a good salary awaited her.

Such incidents of kindness to the distressed and help to the needy might be multiplied indefinitely, for Colonel Ingersoll's whole life was replete with them, and they constitute a religion compared with which all creeds and dogmas become meaningless and empty phrases.

The Ingersoll home in New York is a true type of a rational conception of heaven. Four generations dwell together there, and within that charmed circle, Love has autocratic sway. In my visits to this sweet home I felt as if I had become an inhabitant of a new world. Such kindness and such gentleness! And never a harsh word nor an unkind thought. The colonel was, of course, the central figure in the beautiful group. How eagerly all waited for his homecoming, and how he was surrounded and embraced when he came! He was at once husband, father, brother, lover, companion, and friend, and in each relation his life was truly ideal. I can see the picture yet, and it will remain in memory's gallery forever.

The home he filled with love and light is now dark, indeed. The very soul has gone out from it, and where but a few hours ago there was song and laughter, there is now grief and lamentation beyond the power of all language to express. The hearts of millions throb sympathetically with the stricken ones in their awful bereavement.

To paraphrase Victor Hugo, in his estimate of Voltaire, "There has died a man. He died immortal." The name of Robert G. Ingersoll is in the pantheon of the world. More than any other who ever lived, he destroyed religious superstition. Like an electric storm, he purified the religious atmosphere. With dauntless courage and transcendent ability, he applied himself to his mission and won an immortality of gratitude and glory.

He was the Shakespeare of oratory—the greatest the world has ever known. Henry Ward Beecher[15] called him "the Golden-Mouthed American," and once said of him: "Robert Ingersoll is the most brilliant speaker of the English language on the globe."

His metaphor was marvelous. Here is a specimen, of which there are hundreds in his writings, equal to Shakespeare: "Wit is the lightning of the soul." Speaking of the Bard of Avon, in a strain of poetic rapture, he said: "From his brain there poured a Niagara of gems."

Robert G. Ingersoll lived and died far in advance of his time. He wrought nobly for the transformation of this earth into a habitable globe, and long after the last echo of detraction has been silenced, his name will be loved and honored and his fame will shine resplendent, for his immortality is fixed and glorious.

The National Convention†

August 5, 1899

Comrade Chase is not in favor of the recommendations made by the late conference,[16] especially that relating to the basis of representation.[17] He was opposed to the conference being held on account of the useless expenditure of money. Let me say to Comrade Chase that there has been no expenditure of money, so far as the party is concerned, for we who attended paid our own expenses, as we have done for the last year.

Comrade Chase is opposed to branch representation and urges state representation instead. On the basis he proposed, there will be no national convention next year. It is doubtful if five states would be represented.

The conference took a careful survey of the situation, present and prospective, and decided upon a basis that will make possible a representative national gathering, qualified to adopt a platform and nominate candidates.

Branches have eight months in which to raise money to send a delegate, and most of them will do it. No branch need send more than one delegate, he having votes proportioned to the membership he represents. Our present constitution may not be "fit for use," and it would be easy to say the same of that proposed by the comrades from Massachusetts. The conference, be it said, was influenced in its action by financial considerations. A new constitution, though effective but a few months, would have cost money. Is Comrade Chase prepared to go down in his pocket and furnish it, as the rest of us have done and are doing to keep the national party going?

Massachusetts comes to the front promptly with a big "kick" at the slightest provocation. This is good and I like it. But Massachusetts should also be in when the coin is needed. If other states had done as little as Massachusetts for the national party since it was organized a year ago, we would not have a sign of a national party in existence. I admire Massachusetts, glory in her progress, and rejoice in the victory of her comrades, but she and they are all wrapped up in Massachusetts, and although strongest in membership, have done scarcely nothing for the party at large. They have met every appeal for finance (and these have been made in an extremity) with a deaf ear, or, as one comrade put it: "We don't like your appeals for money; they are humiliating to the party!"

† Published in *Social Democratic Herald,* vol. 2, no. 7 (August 5, 1899), 3.

We want the advice and suggestions of our Massachusetts comrades, and we also want them to bear their share of the party's burden. The paltry dues for which the *Herald* is given will not establish a political party. In addition to what is due for the local branch and for the state, something is due the party at large, and this is the point I seek to impress upon Comrade Chase and those for whom he speaks.

I have been candid, but what I have said is prompted in no other spirit than that of comradeship.

In closing, I hope the basis of branch representation proposed by the conference will be adopted by the referendum vote.[18]

The Workers and the Trusts[†]

August 31, 1899

Labor, at least that part not reduced to the dullness and servility of "the man with the hoe," will arouse and unify in the next year or two and take cognizance of the trend of the economic development from which there is even now evolving a new and progressive trades unionism, which will be arrayed against capitalism, not alone on the industrial but also on the political field.

Such alleged leaders as [Peter M.] Arthur and other high officials who are on terms of intimacy with the oppressors of labor, and whose leadership consists in keeping labor in chains, will be ignominiously retired.

Labor will realize that its only means of salvation lies through united political action along class-conscious lines, and then, in spite of the protestations of fools and knaves, labor will mass its forces beneath the emancipating banner of the Social Democratic Party, whose platform declares its object to be "the establishment of a system of cooperative production and distribution through the restoration to the people of all the means of production and distribution, to be administered by organized society in the interest of the whole people, and the complete emancipation of society from the domination of capitalism."

---

† Part of a syndicated symposium featuring four prominent labor leaders on the same topic, as published, for example, in the *Jamestown [ND] Weekly Alert,* vol. 23, no. 6 (August 31, 1899), 6.

In the campaign of 1900, this party, by the support of that part of labor that can be fooled and bunkoed no longer, will surprise the country; in 1904, if it does not carry the country, it will take second place, and in 1908, when it will sweep into power in spite of hell and all its furies, what will it do to the trusts? In the language of the Bowery, "Oh, not a thing!"

Labor (and I am talking about intelligent labor) will take no hand in "smashing the trusts." Labor's voice will not be heard in the political pick-pockets' clamor to "down the trusts." They have sense enough to know that they might as well attempt to force the waters of the Mississippi back into the millions of tributaries when they come.

Labor will meet the "swift and intense concentration of capital" by the "swift and intense concentration of labor." The swifter and intenser the concentration the better. The trust is the final manifestation of this concentration before labor has its inning. Here is the order of development: the individual, the firm, the trust, the *people.*

As a socialist, therefore, I hail the trust. I view its development and expansion with supreme satisfaction, and I would not, if I could, check its growth by laying so much as a straw in its way. The socialists want the trusts. When they are ripe, the people will be ready, and then there will be a change of ownership and operation.

The people will come into possession of their own. No man will then labor, but all men will work. Wage-slavery will disappear, the machine will be the only slave, economic equality will prevail, and labor, for the first time since the earth was flung into space, will be free.

Scattered Topics[†19]

September 2, 1899

We have heard a great deal about the "glorious victories" won for miners during the last two years. It is a ghastly lie. The only victory I know of is the $3,600 job snatched from the enemy by Ratchford, the understudy of Mark Hanna.[20]

Here in Indiana, hundreds of them are idle and suffering. In Illinois, according to the official report of [UMWA] State Secretary Ryan,[21] they are on strike at 14 different points. At Girard [Kansas] the other day, they issued an appeal for charity, declaring that they were homeless and hungry. The "glorious victories" have reduced them to common beggars—and they belong to the union to a man.

Oh, miners, will you not open your eyes, and will you not use your brains and see and think for yourselves?

You have won no victories worthy the name. You are slaves, every last one of you, the victims of the wage system, and as long as the mines you work in are privately owned, you will be robbed while at work and clubbed and shot like dogs when you quit.

Arouse from your slavery, join the Social Democratic Party, and vote with us to take possession of the mines of the country and operate them in the interest of the people, as well as the railroads, factories, and all the means of production and distribution, and then, and only then, will "glorious victories" have been achieved and you and your comrades be free and our families happy.

Patriotism

The American "patriot" is the biggest humbug on earth. Under pretense of loving his country, he struts and swaggers, prates about the "flag" and the "glories of war," and makes a spectacle of himself generally. This "patriot" is never so ready to respond to the call of "his country" as when half-famished working slaves are to be shot at—at so much per shot.

The boss "patriots" are the plutocrats. They do their share of the fighting in sumptuous banqueting halls where amidst the roar of champagne corks they glorify the "flag," while the poor fool "patriots" murder one another, according to the ethics of "civilized warfare," for $13 a month.[22]

† Published as "Current Events Passed in Review" in *Social Democratic Herald,* vol. 2, no. 11, whole no. 61 (September 2, 1899), 1.

Roosevelt of New York may be held up as the typical American patriot. He has the face of a bulldog and a heart to match. That such a savage is elected governor of the leading state in the Union is proof enough that we are yet a million miles from civilization. According to the capitalist program this ideal "patriot" is to be made president in 1904, but he will hear something "strenuous" drop by that time, and when he takes a second look, he will see a socialist president in the seat his "patriotic" pantaloons yearned to warm.

The "patriotic" war in the Philippines blackens the blackest page in the nineteenth century. It is fiendish without a redeeming feature. All war is murder, and I am opposed to the shedding of human blood, but since this war is forced upon the Filipinos, I regret that they lack the power and means to blow up every battleship that lands there. I am with and for the Filipinos, and hope with all my heart that they may yet repel the invaders and achieve their independence.

I am not a "patriot," as that term is defined by the lexicon of capitalism. "All the world is my country and all mankind are my countrymen."[23]

Not being a fetish-worshiper, I see no difference between a flag and any other piece of cotton goods. All flags look alike to me, but since we have not yet outgrown this fetish, mine is the blood-red flag of socialism.

Idaho

The "bull pen" of Idaho is the joint product of Republican, Democratic, and Populistic administration. The pictures drawn of this hellhole by reliable correspondents are enough to make decent devils blush with shame. The Democratic-Populistic governor Steunenberg and the Republican general Merriam,[24] monsters of degeneracy, constitute the tsars of this domain. Here hundreds of honest workingmen, without a charge against them, are corralled like cattle, starved like outlaws, and shot like mad dogs, and while the outrages are being perpetrated in the name of "law and order," their wives are made victims of the lust of their brutal keepers.

We often hear that violent revolution is close upon us, but this is only bluster, for if there were but the faintest revolutionary spirit abroad, the Idaho "Bull pen" would fan it into flame like a cyclone, and such fiends as Steunenberg, Merriam, and other degenerate tools of the Standard Oil Company would be hung higher than Haman.[25]

Some of these miners may remember what I told them nearly three years ago about coming events, about voting with the old parties and about socialism. They were not ready for socialism then, but now that their unions are broken up, their homes desolate, and themselves prisoners or exiles, and all this by the capitalist system which they have supported by their own votes, they will be compelled to realize that through socialism alone is there escape from the tyranny of capitalist rule and the atrocities of the wage system.

Dreyfus

It requires no accurate observer to discover that Dreyfus, the victim of the foulest conspiracy ever conceived, is not being given a fair trial.[26] The refusal of the court to adjourn when his counsel was stricken down by an assassin shows clearly enough which way the wind blows. But whether he is tried fairly or not, one thing is certain, and that is that the French people are wide awake, and sooner or later justice will be meted out in spite of hell and the French army. For the epauletted conspirators, from first to last, there is a day of retribution, and when it comes there will be such an accounting as even the people of France have never witnessed.

It is not Dreyfus alone that is on trial. Militarism, honeycombed with rottenness, is also arraigned before the high court of the French nation, and when the final verdict of the French people shall have been reversed, militarism in France will have been crushed out of existence forever. Through it all there is a mighty mustering of the forces of socialism, and, out of it all there is certain to emerge the socialist republic.

The Cleveland Boycott

The Street Railway Employees of Cleveland and their sympathizers are putting up a brave fight, and we can only hope that victory may perch upon their banner. But they are fighting, barehanded, a powerful foe, backed by municipal clubs and state bayonets.

The attitude of [Peter M.] Arthur, the renegade chief of the Brotherhood of Engineers, is refreshing, but not at all surprising. The rich old labor leader is simply true to his base record. He is against the Cleveland strikers and against labor generally. He is the pliant tool of the railroads and in 1894 made a record black as a crow's wing. The Brotherhood of Engineers knows all this and has known it for years and still, to satisfy the general managers, who are the real rulers of the brotherhood, they continue to crown this traitor to labor "grand chief," and for such a brotherhood, honest men should have only unmitigated contempt.

The SDP

The progress our party is making must be a source of gratification to every member. We now have an unbroken chain of branches stretching across the continent, from New England to the Golden Gate. Day by day there are new accessions to our ranks, and in 1900 the party will be in superb fighting form.

The carbuncle at New York has come to a head, and the pus is flowing freely.[27] Purification is bound to follow, but in the meantime the olfactory nerves will be put to the severest test.

Private advices give assurance that our party stands high with the leaders of the European socialist movement. We have every reason to take courage and put forth the mightiest efforts at our command.

There is a united socialist party just ahead, and its initials will be SDP.[†]

---

† This line is a subtle potshot at the SLP dissidents, who in referendum voted for "United Socialist Party" as the name for a forthcoming unified organization. Debs is here reaffirming an unwillingness to budge on the name and independence of the Chicago-based Social Democratic Party.

Signs of Social Revolution†

September 2, 1899

That the capitalist system is rushing to its doom is apparent to the most casual observer, and as this system declines, the new social order develops, and all the signs indicate a speedy and complete change.

It is impossible to contemplate the horrors of capitalism and remain neutral or passive unless, indeed, one be dead to every sentiment of humanity. When I think of the working class, their hovels, their rags, and their crusts, and of the class out of work, patiently pleading for permission to do some menial service to enable them to relieve the hunger pangs of loved ones; when I think of the wretchedness of the coal miners and the millions of others who do the world's most useful work—the poverty of the toiler, the despair of his wife, the hopeless future of his children; the filth and groans and cursings, the lewdness and squalor, the prostitution and drunkenness, the suicide and murder, and the ten thousand other forms of evil that afflict society in the twilight of the nineteenth century, I conclude that our vaunted civilization is a sham and that in spite of our mental achievements and material progress, the earth we live on is not yet a habitable globe.

But I would not have it understood that I am pessimistic, that I have lost faith in the ultimate triumph of humanity. Oh, no; I was never more cheerful and never more confident, for like millions of other socialists in all lands beneath the bending skies, I am reading the signs of social revolution, and, therefore, I know beyond all question that capitalism is wearing out, and that from the chaos with which its competitive conquests have filled the world, there is evolving a new social order, universal in scope and based upon cooperative industry of every field of human activity.

Can the day of change be hastened? Without a doubt. Every socialist who spreads the light according to his opportunity, who helps the propaganda, votes the socialist ticket, and encourages others to do likewise is doing his share to speed the day of the new commonwealth.

The Social Democratic Party now extends across the continent, and new branches are being instituted with gratifying rapidity. In 1900 a presidential ticket will be placed in the field upon an uncompromising socialist platform,

† Published in *The Coming Nation* [Ruskin, TN], whole no. 328 (September 2, 1899), 1.

and we confidently expect to poll a vote that will surprise the country.

Permit me to assure the comrades of Ruskin Commonwealth of my best wishes in their new field of operation.[28] I have always had a keen interest in Ruskin and have followed the comrades in their trials and privations with deep sympathy, hoping that at last they might overcome every obstacle and realize their laudable ambitions.

I have not forgotten, nor shall I forget, how kind and helpful our Ruskin comrades were to my colleagues and myself and how loyally *The Coming Nation* supported us in the dark days of '94, and so I say: All luck to Ruskin Commonwealth.

The Future Is Bright†

September 2, 1899

Those who read aright the signs of the times are not discouraged because of delays in accomplishment of great undertakings in matters pertaining to human advancement. A great wrong, however remote its antiquity, cannot survive the ceaseless attacks of the right. Truth, justice, and right, since the time when the morning and the evening announced one day complete in the building of the universe, have formed a holy alliance, and the compact is as vital today as when humanity began, and in no voice of nature, from the rippling laughter of brooks to the thunderings of cataracts, from the melodies of birds to the music of the spheres, from the lullaby accents of the zephyr to the wrathful tones of the tornado, has there ever been recorded a sound in justification of error.

It is only as men reckon time that the advance of truth appears tardy. The sublimating process by which the nations of the earth, with grand acclaim, are to acknowledge and practice right and justice, are apparently slow in their operation, but the work is going steadily forward. There has been no century that the life of some man did not witness its beginning and close—hence, the lives of four men have encompassed all the years since Columbus discovered a new world, and the lives of 19 men since the day that Christ was born.

† Published in *Duluth Labor News,* vol. 5, no. 18 (September 2, 1899), 1.

Such reflections may serve to inculcate lessons of patience and give assurance that in due time the right is to be enthroned, that ignorance and superstition are to disappear, and that men, everywhere, disenthralled and emancipated, are to be crowned sovereigns by inherent and, therefore, divine right.

Intellectual development—mind culture—which enables the masses to grasp ideas possessed by lifting power, is one of the signs which betoken the triumph of the right, the coming day when Truth will be coronated the presiding genius, the controlling and governing power of the world.

What are the signs to those who look abroad for indications which presage man's emancipation from capitalization? Do men now, as in the faraway past, accept the lash uncomplainingly? Do they crawl with their faces in the dust as in the days of the Pharaohs? Do they now regard their oppressors as divinities ordained of heaven to rule? The answer comes back like an electric flash from its cloud—No! The sublime truth that all men are created equal is germinating in millions of brains, and its vitalizing roots are taking strong hold upon heart and soul. It is irrigated with blood and tears, but it is growing. Men are feeling its power. They are looking up and they are demanding emancipation, enfranchisement, citizenship. Rulers are seeking to perpetuate the bondage of the working class, but the decree of socialism has gone forth, and kings and thrones and crowns and scepters of every form are to disappear. The ruling class is to give place to the ruling mass, and the acknowledgment of the sovereignty of all will be the sublimest triumph in human history.

In the grand march of socialism, there are indications of triumphs in the near future which refresh like the shower and cheer like the sunshine. In the Social Democratic Party, a vast body of practical men and women are laboring for practical results and, inspired by courage, born of perfect faith in their cause, they are moving forward to certain and glorious victory.

The National Labor Party: Interview with the *St. Louis Post-Dispatch*†

September 9, 1899

I have been addressing big meetings in the East and Central West, and I am very much encouraged by the apparent interest taken by wage earners in the pressing questions of the day. I am now on my way west and expect to cover the entire country before spring. On the first Tuesday in March, a new political party will be born. At Indianapolis, we will meet in regular delegated national convention to choose candidates for president and vice president of the United States.[29] Our party will be formed from the nucleus already in the field under the name of the Social Democracy.[30] The name of the new party will probably be the National Labor Party. We will carry the organization of the party into the states and cities, and nominate state and city tickets wherever possible.

One very encouraging sign is the awakening of interest among the farmers. Heretofore, agitation has been effectual only among the laboring classes in the cities, but my meetings have been largely attended by farmers, and I predict that there will be a combination of the agricultural and industrial elements. When this alliance comes, victory will be near.

One of the great troubles with movements like ours is lack of cohesiveness. This is the result of so many shadings of opinion. It has been the history of all great movements. In Germany, the socialists were divided into several groups for many years, but they have now become homogeneous, and at the last elections cast 2.4 million votes and elected 56 representatives to the Reichstag. Now they move as one man. In France, they are divided into groups, but they work in harmony on all great issues. We in America must pass this stage of development, but we will emerge in the end a united party.

This is the era of concentration. The capitalist is doing the preliminary work of combination and organization, but at the proper time the people will take possession. Do not make the mistake made by so many and suppose that we propose to interfere with private property. Under our system of government, private property will be for the first time truly sacred. We want the people to take charge of the means of production and distribution—the means of life.

---

† Published as "Debs on the Trusts" in *St. Louis Post-Dispatch,* vol. 51, no. 20 (September 9, 1899), 2.

The machine was the first step in the development toward the end we desire. In the beginning, the tool was controlled by the artisan; now it has passed completely from his control to that of the capitalist. I believe in the machine, because I want to see labor of all kinds reduced to the minimum and leisure increased. The second step in the evolution toward socialism is the so-called trust. It is simply a monopolization of the machine, a concentration in the control of a few of the means of production and distribution, the means of life. The next step is socialism. The capitalist, in serving his selfish ends, is simply an instrument. He is the forerunner. He is preparing the way for an easy transition from what we have now to the supremacy of the people. It is useless to oppose this evolution. We should rather help it along.

Every department of industry is coming under the sway of concentrated capital. Even the farmers are becoming victims. The great syndicate farm is driving the small farmer off the land. We need not wonder why farm products have so rapidly depreciated in value. The syndicate farm has done it. The department store is doing the same thing to the small dealers in the cities. It is foolish to try to protect and hold up the small dealer. We can get what we want better and cheaper from the department stores, and we should patronize them for that reason.

The traveling man is disappearing. He is doomed. I was much interested in watching the tobacco situation when Liggett & Myers were holding out against the trust. I met a man who traveled for them in Indiana. He told me they would never surrender. I told him they would surrender within six months. Next morning the paper announced that they had gone into the trust. I met another St. Louis man who used to travel for Drummond. He was in the East looking over the situation, and in search of work. I told him he was on a fruitless mission; that his avenues were closing, never to reopen. Three years ago, the traveling man abused us agitators, calling us a dangerous class. Now the traveling man has become an agitator.

The revolution, which will surely come, will be peaceful. Not a drop of blood will be shed provided the socialists are allowed to control the situation. We will win by the ballot. We realize that we can do nothing until we have complete control of the government. We must have the presidency and Congress before we can accomplish anything, and we will attempt nothing until we control these offices. Then we will simply take, in the name of the people, the means of production and distribution. They have been paid for, over and over again, by the people, and are ours by every moral right.

"I Will Not Be a Candidate for President": Interview in LaPorte, Indiana[†] [excerpt]

November 13, 1899

Though I am doing all in my power to further the cause of the Social Democratic Party, and may be said to have been the "father" of the movement, I will not be a candidate for president before the national convention which meets at Indianapolis in March [1900]. The slogan of the party will be "No Fusion, No Compromise," and the platform will advocate the collective ownership of the means of production and distribution.

A full ticket will be put in the field, and a great vote will record the socialistic strength of the nation. I look for the heaviest returns from Massachusetts, Washington, Oregon, and California. In Washington, I believe our party will win out. The enthusiasm on the Pacific coast, from which I have just returned, is phenomenal.

† Published in *La Porte Herald,* title, date, and page unspecified. Reprinted as "Crowded House at LaPorte" in *Social Democratic Herald,* vol. 2, no. 23, whole no. 73 (November 25, 1899), 3.

More Than a Municipal Campaign: Speech in Haverhill, Massachusetts†

November 27, 1899

Ladies and Gentlemen, Citizens of Haverhill:—

A year ago, the name of Haverhill was flashed around the world. On Wednesday next [December 6, 1899] the magnificent victory achieved then will have been ratified by an increased majority.

This is something more than a municipal campaign. There are issues involved that are of vital and commanding interest to every man, woman, and child in Haverhill, in Massachusetts, throughout the length and breadth of the land.

The competitive system, with its extreme wealth upon the one hand, its abject and widespread poverty upon the other, its political corruption, its economic servitude, its social demoralization is on trial. What pen or tongue, from primeval man to the dullest intellect, can describe the effect of this struggle upon the great mass of the working people? Multiplied millions of them answer to the description of the embruted peasant in the poem of Edwin Markham, a poem fraught with such significance that it blazed the immortality of the author on wings of lightning around the world:

> Bowed by the weight of centuries he leans
> Upon his hoe and gazes on the ground,
> The emptiness of ages in his face,
> And on his back the burden of the world.
> Who made him dead to rapture and despair,
> A thing that grieves not and that never hopes.
> Stolid and stunned, a brother to the ox?
> Who loosened and let down this brutal jaw?
> Whose was the hand that slanted back this brow?
> Whose breath blew out the light within this brain?[31]

The capitalist system must answer for this appalling indictment at the bar of humanity. This is the real issue involved in the campaign now in progress in the city of Haverhill, Massachusetts.

---

† Published as "Debs' Speech" in *Haverhill Social Democrat,* vol. 1, no. 9 (December 2, 1899), 3, 6. Excerpt reprinted as "Debs at Haverhill" in *Social Democratic Herald,* vol. 2, no. 26, whole no. 76 (December 16, 1899), 2.

It is no part of my purpose this evening to appeal to your prejudice, to incite your passion. In the little time which is my privilege to spend in your presence, I propose to address myself to your reason. Were this simply a contest to secure office, I should have no mission here. I realize the far-reaching effect of the result of this campaign. But few of those who live in Haverhill have any proper conception of the effect the result a year ago had upon the country. It was in the nature of an inspiration to the downtrodden and oppressed everywhere. The man with the hoe for the first time stood erect, brushed the dust of servitude from his knees, took hope, looked upward, began to move everywhere, and from that day to this, men and women in every village and town of every state and territory in this country have been massing their forces beneath the conquering banner of economic equality.

Since coming here, my attention has been called to an attack in the public press upon the local Social Democratic Party because of its alleged hostility to private property. It has declared that the Social Democratic Party is opposed to private property. It is not true. The present system is opposed to private property. Centralization and combination are the conquering forces of this age. Competition must culminate in combination. In manufacture, it is the great factory that is steadily crushing out the smaller establishment. What becomes of the property of the small manufacturer? Is it confiscated in the socialist program? Not at all. The small manufacturer is engaged in a very unequal struggle. He cannot successfully compete against the great corporation or the trust. He begins to lose ground. In due course of time, his profits have been completely destroyed. He closes his doors. The sheriff succeeds him in business. His trade has been usurped. His property has been confiscated. At the end of his life, perhaps in the very sunset, he finds himself confronted by the poorhouse. What has become of his property? It is gone. He has absolutely nothing to show for it. Did the socialist get it? Did the socialist attempt to get it? Oh, no; it was his larger competitor of his own class, and the small manufacturer who is supporting the system that is going to force him into bankruptcy and ruin.

In distribution, the great department store is bringing about the same result. In the smaller cities, its influence is not yet completely felt. It is on its way to Haverhill. It will be here in due time. It will not be sidetracked. You may rest assured that it will put in its appearance. There will be a million or two [dollars], or more, at the back of it, and the owners of this great department store can and will sell more cheaply than a smaller dealer can buy. That is the beginning of the end. In a little while, he will close his doors. He will cease to be a businessman. What becomes of him? What becomes of his private property?

Is it the socialist party that has expropriated him, ruined him, put him on the street and reduced his family to want? Not at all. It is the present system. In this system we are going to become millionaires or mendicants, with chances a million to one that we become mendicants.

The trust is a very conspicuous issue in this local campaign. What do you propose to do about the trust? The people as a rule are opposed to the trust. We make the contention that the position of the socialist is the only logical position with reference to the trust. The trust cannot be dissolved. Monopoly cannot be abolished. The trust is the product of the ages. The individual first, in small business, the firm, the company, the corporation, the trust. The trust is simply the latest phase of the development of industry. It represents concentrated capital, the dismissal of every superfluous man, modern machinery, the discharge of the traveling man, and here let me say that the traveling man as a factor in business will soon be a thing of the past. He is about 40 years old now. He will not live to celebrate his fiftieth birthday. It is not the socialist that is after him. In proportion as the trust is perfected, the traveling man disappears. He came with competition; he goes with competition.

The trust is absolutely the economic master in the fields of economic activity. There is but one dealer in the goods that you must have, and if you want those goods, you are required to pay the price fixed by the trust. Did you read the dispatches from Chicago three or four days ago announcing the fact that in the city of Chicago every evening after the Board of Trade adjourns, five men meet and fix the price that is to be paid the farmers of the entire country for their grain next day? They hold the power of life and death. The people are at their mercy, absolutely so. And they represent a very great trust. They have millions of dollars. They levy taxation upon the people; they fix the price of every loaf of bread consumed by the people. What do you propose to do about it? Dissolve the trusts? I am looking for the man that will tell me how he is going to dissolve them. By law? You have been trying to control the corporation by law for the last 30 years, and to what extent have you succeeded? If you have been unable to control the corporation by law, how do you expect to control a trust, a vastly greater aggregation of wealth and power, by law? You propose to harness this great elephant with cobwebs. The trust simply laughs at the statutory enactment.

President Stickney, of the Great Western Railroad, testified before the Industrial Commission at Chicago just a week ago that the interstate commerce law, so far as it attempted to regulate rates on railroads, was a roaring farce; and he added after this that every other law that was designed to curb the rapacity of railroad corporations was likewise a farce. You have not been able, you never will be able, to control corporate capital by law.

We are confronted by one of two conditions. First of all, let it be said that no power on earth can prevent the complete concentration of industries. One industry after another is being completely monopolized. The middle class is disappearing. They are struggling to get into the small capitalist class. About one in a thousand will succeed. The others will be forced down into the overcrowded ranks of the working class, and this process will continue until all the capital of the country is concentrated in the hands of a single syndicate or trust so that we will finally have a trust of trusts. We will have an economic oligarchy. We will not be ruled by a king, by an emperor or a tsar, we will be ruled by economic potentates that will control the people because they control their necessities.

Either this, or the collective ownership of trusts and the operation of all industry in the interest of the whole people. That is to say: capitalism or socialism, slavery or freedom. You will have a chance to vote upon these alternatives next Tuesday.[32] You may forge your chains still stronger; you may vote to strike the last fetter from the last economic slave on this continent.

There is very much involved in this municipal campaign. I would, if it were in my power, impress upon you its importance and its significance. I have just returned from the Far West. I spent a week in California and was asked again and again in that coast state, "What about Haverhill?" They understand out there that there has been a very strong combination perfected in Haverhill for the overthrow of the Social Democratic Party. They are as familiar with the situation as most of your citizens are. I said: "I feel quite confident that this combination will succeed—in destroying itself." It represents absolutely no principle, and I challenge contradiction. By some strange magic, the Republican here finds himself in the embrace of a lifelong enemy—the Democrat. Waking up in the morning, they find themselves in the same camp. All of the hostility has been declared off. They stand revealed as one party, or, to speak more properly, no party at all—for you could not find a trace of the Republican Party with a magnifying glass. The Democratic Party has totally lost its identity, if it ever had any. A citizens' party, they call it. The corporations are very profoundly interested in the success of this citizens' party. The professional politicians are also profoundly interested in its success. It is a new party, for a new and very strange purpose.

You are a Democrat, perhaps. You have been in the Democratic Party for a long while. What purpose have you in forming an alliance with a lifelong enemy at this time? What is the purpose? Does not the answer suggest itself? A combination of these two parties to defeat the Social Democratic Party—that is the purpose, and the only purpose. The "party," so called, has no other program. How strangely its nominations were made! We live in a republic. Governments derive their just powers from the consent of the governed. Whence they derive their unjust powers is not stated. These nominations were made, but the rank and file had no voice in the making of them. The program has been made in caucus, and the nominations announced—not, however, subject to the approval of the constituents of these nominees. The contract has been made. The votes are to be delivered, and the question for every self-respecting Republican and Democrat to ask himself is whether he proposes to deliver the goods in fulfillment of the contract made by the politicians. I do believe that when the votes have been deposited and the last ballot has been counted, the announcement will go forth that this unholy compact has been rebuked by such an overwhelming vote that the repetition of it will never again be attempted in Haverhill.

And just here let me say that the Social Democratic Party enters into this campaign with absolute confidence of success. It was never more certain of the absolute justice of its underlying principles. The party is harmonious. It stands before the people without a blemish upon its name. What about its candidate? John C. Chase has held the office of mayor for one year. There has not been one breath of scandal in connection with his administration. His official integrity is as spotless as a star. So with his personal character. In all of the severity of criticism, no one has ventured to impugn his honesty of purpose. And what is true of John C. Chase, the first socialist mayor in the United States, is likewise true of his colleagues. They stand before you, asking for your support purely upon the principles embodied in their platform, and upon the record they have made as representatives of their party.

What is true of the local representatives is likewise true of those who represented you at the capital while the legislature was in session. That brilliant young man, James F. Carey, made a record there well calculated to challenge the admiration and respect, not only of his constituents, but of every citizen of the state. His speech upon "child labor" will win for him immortality. His colleague, Louis M. Scates, true to every obligation as the needle to the pole, temporarily defeated—but sometimes defeat is victory, and it is victory in his case, for he largely increased his vote, and he is stronger in the confidence of his fellow citizens than he was before the election;[33] and when he stands again, as stand he will, he will be triumphantly elected by the people.

But a single week remains. There remains a week for serious thought, for sober reflection. What is the actual condition with which we have to deal today? We cannot determine these questions by mere local conditions. We must take the general condition of the country at large into account. It is admitted that a few more men are employed, that there is a little more activity than there was. It is also admitted that there never was a time when there was as much centralization, such rapid growth of trusts, and centralization of political and economic power to correspond as there is today. The condition of the workingman, in the grasp of this stupendous power, grows more precarious day by day. He sells his labor in the cheapest market. The small dealer, confronted by the same power, feels himself steadily losing ground.

In the West, they told me that there was unusual activity in New England, especially in Boston. I was much interested in the testimony given by Samuel M. Price, president of the whiskey trust in the city of Washington before the Industrial Commission last week. Mr. Price, who ought to be an authority on the subject, stated that the city of Boston consumed more whiskey than any other city in the United States in proportion to its population. It may be that this has some influence in stimulating the situation. There is unparalleled prosperity—but it is confined to very limited circles; on the one hand, the fortunes mounting skyward.

A certain chosen few are growing enormously rich, Mr. Rockefeller, for example, worth $350 million. Compared with him, the richest man in this audience is a beggar on the highway. He has the power to gradually confiscate the holdings of the small dealer in every department of trade. It is said that we socialists are envious of the success of such men as Mr. Rockefeller; that we would, if we could, destroy him, or, what is worse still, drag him down to our level. We do not envy him. We realize that no man fails so completely in this system as the man who succeeds. John D. Rockefeller is a prisoner for life. He is enslaved by his possessions. He lives on the eighth floor of a big building, in the care of a bodyguard. When he walks abroad, he conceals his identity. He is not on terms of peace with his fellow men. He has millions of dollars, but he is not living a complete life. He is said to be a beneficiary of this system. He is bearing a very heavy burden in the care of his enormous possessions; and he has expressed himself as being willing to pay a million dollars a year if he can find the right man to take care of them for him. There's an opening for some of you—a million dollars a year! Would you change places with him? Who is there to envy him? He is simply trying to find some way of relieving himself from the fruit of his success. The Social Democratic Party would like to help him. It would relieve him of his burden, and it proposes to do so for his benefit as well as for the benefit of the country at large. He has as much too much as others have too little. His life is a complete failure from that standpoint.

Take one of those men who have solved the problem of success. He is 40 years of age, or 50. He ought to be approaching his prime. His hair is white; he is physically infirm; he is in the grasp of decline because he has succeeded under this system. If you are fortunate enough to have succeeded in raising yourself upon the shoulders and backs of your fellow men, your success is not to be envied. You do not hear the melody in the voice of your wife. You do not hear the prattle of our children. You are engaged in this competitive struggle with all your faculties and ability, and the springs of kindness are dried up within your breast. In this competitive strife, all that is selfish and hard has been developed in your nature. You are unconscious of it. You are a perverted human being. You have millions, perhaps, and yet you are, from every proper standpoint, a pauper on the highway of life. You are spiritually dead. You are morally petrified. You are intellectually bankrupt.

When I was in New York recently, I went to the Waldorf-Astoria to see some of the beneficiaries of this system. I went there at midnight because I knew they had reversed the order of nature and turned day into night; and I saw them under the influence of electric light, men and women whose fathers amassed millions, who themselves never did a day's work; and they seemed entirely artificial to me—waxen images. I said to myself: "Under this social system, they have become reduced to a state that makes it impossible for them to enjoy life."

In Boston last night, I told them of the great dog festival that was held in New York a short time ago, where one lady had three pet dogs, each with a $40,000 collar around its neck; and those three dogs were lodged at the Gilsey House, a very select hotel, had spacious apartments and special servants to attend to them, and were bathed in perfume three times a day; and when I read about it, I said, "My heart goes out to the dogs." I concluded it was a case that appealed to the Society for the Prevention of Cruelty to Animals. And then I reflected upon the fact that just a dozen blocks from there, in the Bowery, in Mott Street, in those narrow, filthy streets, the rows of tenements, the miles of misery, the squares of squalor, were thousands of children in wretchedness and rags. I thought about this, and I said to myself that with all the energy at my command, I propose to wage war on the social system in which the lapdogs of the rich are the social superiors of the children of the poor.

This also is involved in this campaign—great moral issues that appeal with ever increasing force to every voter here and elsewhere. There are those to whom it seems to be impossible to rise above self-interest. They do not know to what extent they have been influenced and improperly influenced under the system in which they live. They do not realize that in the march of the great economic force, the time has come when a great change in human affairs is about to take place—a change as wide as humanity. This movement is organizing for the purpose of rescuing humanity from the thralldom of all the ages. What an awakening there is everywhere! How completely the people are aroused! But a little while ago it was the working class who met on the third or fourth floor of some building. The busy world was utterly ignorant of their existence. It was scarcely possible for them to get their movements before the public. Today we find men and women in every walk of life who are interested and vitally interested in the solution of this great economic problem.

There is a cause for it. It is not a mere matter of accident. People are beginning to inquire into the whys and wherefores of things. They are beginning to ask some questions, and they are insisting that these questions shall be intelligently answered.

This movement is an abolition movement, vastly larger and more important than that which had its origin three-quarters of a century ago. In the inception of that great abolition movement, there were thousands of excellent people everywhere who were intensely hostile to it. I have but a dim recollection of it, but I remember that in my childhood, an abolitionist was regarded as a very vicious human being who ought to be suppressed by law. The great mass, then as now, did not express their honest convictions. This was reserved for a few. There was a Lovejoy who had moral courage enough to stand boldly for the right of free speech. He was hooted, dragged through the streets, and murdered; and the state of Illinois applauded. If you go down the Mississippi River today you will see a magnificent monument bearing the inscription "To the Memory of Lovejoy, a Martyr in the Cause of Human Freedom."

There was another champion of the rights of man who began to assert his convictions with wondrous power. His name was Wendell Phillips. He did not ask, "Is this movement popular? Can I afford it?" He had the moral courage to be hissed by the professors and the students at Ann Arbor University. He had convictions. He had courage equal to them. He stood magnificently erect, just as the representatives of this noble abolition movement stand today. He won an immortality of gratitude and glory. Just a little while before his eloquent lips were silenced in death, I heard some of the story of his persecution. The world was against him, but he had faith in himself and he had faith in his conquering mission. He knew that he was right. He had the spirit of that reformer who, when told the whole world was against him, said: "Then, thank God, I am against the whole world."

So it was with William Lloyd Garrison. Not long ago I was in Newburyport, Massachusetts. My attention was called to the fact that it was there that he was first attacked. The whole community was against him. The abolition movement was intensely unpopular, as unpopular as it was righteous. And then I had imagination enough to pursue William Lloyd Garrison as he went to the city of Boston, the center of culture and intelligence and refinement. I had imagination enough to see the greater mob that pursued and attacked him there. Then I saw him, in all his glory, expand to the proportions of magnificent manhood in the presence of the angry mob. He stood erect, and he said: "I will not equivocate. I will not excuse. I will not retract a single inch. I will be heard." And these words are inscribed upon his monument today.

So with Gerrit Smith;[34] so with John Greenleaf Whittier; so with Harriet Beecher Stowe. An abolitionist informs us that in her day friends called upon Harriet Beecher Stowe in the city of Hartford, and sought by all the influences at their command to prevent her from giving *Uncle Tom's Cabin* to the world. Had she been one of the moral cowards that are so numerous, had she trimmed her sails to catch the popular breeze, *Uncle Tom's Cabin* would never have dignified and glorified the emancipating literature of the world.

This movement is not yet popular. It is founded in the principles of eternal justice. It is in harmony with the perpetual growth of society. Socialism is not a dream. It is not the product of the visionary socialist. It is the next inevitable stage in the eternal march of evolution. It means a higher humanity, a nobler civilization. Competition means war. Society in a competitive state consists simply of a mass of warring units. Take care of yourself. Be absolutely selfish, no matter what becomes of your fellow man. Build up, if you have got to do it on the ruin of your weaker neighbor. And the only attempt at justification of this capitalistic condition is that it results in the survival of the fittest. If this is to continue forever, there is no difference between the human being and the beast in the jungle. They devour each other; so do we. We differ simply in methods.

The poor miner, toiling 600 feet underground, day after day, to earn a miserable 80 or 90 cents a day that scarcely serves to keep his rebellious soul within his protesting body, is being devoured. The poor girl who works in the sweatshops of Boston or Chicago or New York, in the basement or the attic of a tenement where there is scarcely any light, no ventilation, filth and rags, is being devoured, and her sunken cheeks and hollow eyes bear testimony to the barbarity of the competitive system.

Is this to continue forever? Fortunate it is that this system carries within itself the seeds of its own dissolution, the elements of its own overthrow. We are on the eve of the crisis. We are approaching the beginning of the end. The transition is very painful.

When I was in San Francisco, I picked up a daily paper and read that a boy, 19 years of age, had committed suicide because, after three weeks of continuous search, he was unable to find employment. He had some self-respect. He had destroyed himself. How many are there who have any proper conception of the enormity of this social crime? Suicide has increased 300 percent in the United States during the past six years. A man in a normal state of mind and heart does not commit suicide. It is the wretched workingman who is driven to despair; it is the small struggling businessman, who is fighting against his impending ruin, that commits suicide. Why is it that all our jails, reformatories, almshouses, and asylums are crowded to their utmost capacities? There is reason for it. And every student of sociology knows the process is: first, idleness; and then degradation and then despair, and then—desperation. Poverty is the most prolific parent of all the vices and the crime that curse this world.

"The poor you have always with you." When the man of Galilee, the carpenter of Nazareth, uttered those words, he uttered them in rebuke and not in commendation. There is absolutely no excuse for enforced poverty in this day. The average producing capacity of the worker has increased about twentyfold in the last 40 years. The worker today produces 20 times as much as he did 40 years ago. Why doesn't he have 20 times as much? Why doesn't he enjoy 20 times as much? Why is he not relieved of 19/20ths of his burden? The reason is self-evident. He does not produce for himself. He produces for a master; and he can only work when it is profitable to his master that he should work. He has nothing but his labor, and he is compelled to sell that for what he can get for it, and is thus reduced to the position of a slave.

The same struggle is going on in the middle class—each trying to ruin and destroy the other. We are told to love our neighbor as ourselves, but it is hard to love the man who tries to swallow you. Talk about Christian nations, about the golden rule, about brotherly love! These things are absolutely impossible in a state of society in which each man's interests are diametrically opposed to each other's.

We have classes in this country. The one class owns the machinery and the other the labor. The owners of the machinery have got to have cheap labor, and the owners of the labor have got to have high wages; and here they stand arrayed against each other in irrepressible conflict. It is this that constitutes the class struggle. Let me call your attention to the fact that these classes were not created under socialism, nor by socialist agitation. These classes are the product of the competitive system, in which a man must be a master or he must be a slave. I can sell to a corporation my labor-power, and if I do, I sell to that corporation what else? I traffic in my intellect. I can get what is called a higher situation, become a professional man. I can be employed by some great capitalistic newspaper. I can prostitute my intellectual faculties. I can write columns of editorials that are repugnant to my sense of justice. But I scorn to do it. I would not be an instrument of the oppression and the degradation of my fellow men.

Lincoln said: "For the reason that I object to being a slave, I protest against being a master."[35] The one is just as immoral, just as degrading as the other. Were I compelled to make my choice, I would rather be a slave than a master, upon the principle that I would rather be the victim than the beneficiary of a wrong. I stand, therefore, in your presence a socialist, and a member of the Social Democratic Party, because I believe that the earth is the equal heritage of every human being who inhabits it. I understand perfectly, as does every other social democrat, that if I succeed in this competitive system it is because I have destroyed my weaker brother; that he who amasses the largest fortune has simply succeeded in ruining and destroying the largest number of his fellow creatures. If you succeed, somebody else fails. Success is the fruit of failure A perfectly sane, self-respecting man does not want to succeed in that way.

This struggle to secure the means of life makes anything like security an impossibility. You may be worth $30,000 or $40,000 today, and you may die in the poorhouse. You do not know. You cannot guess. Everything is insecure and in doubt; and when you fail and fall, your successful competitor rushes in over your prostrate body, and what becomes of you?

But even if you do reach your destination in safety, what is to become of your son? Carry this question home with you, and answer it to yourselves at your leisure. This is also one of the issues involved in this campaign. What do you propose to do with your son, or rather, what is he going to be able to do for himself? When you were young, a boy could learn a trade. He could build up gradually. He could go into business with a capital of $500 and build up gradually. There were no trusts in the country, capitalized at $8 million. But your son? Is he going to learn a trade? What trade? Every trade is crowded to overflowing. Whatever trade he learns, he will find that the machine is there in advance of him. The machine is to take full possession. Skilled labor will become common labor. In this system of private ownership, the man will be under the machine. The machine, instead of being a blessing, becomes an instrument to enslave humanity.

Perhaps you want your son to take up some profession. What profession? In Boston, there are scores of doctors that are not making a respectable living; lawyers without number, picking their teeth, waiting for a victim. In New York, they have actually had to pass a law restraining lawyers from questionable practices to create cases for themselves. There is no chance for a lawyer except in exceptional cases, unless he becomes a corporation lawyer; and he must sacrifice all the scruples of the profession, if it has any nowadays to find ways for evading the laws that were enacted for the interest of the people. In this day, a lawyer will work for one side or the other, if there is enough money in it, entirely irrespective of the right or justice of the case. If you are a criminal, if there is money enough in it, he will work to clear you; and if you are innocent, he will work to convict you, if there is money enough in it.

The avenues for making a living are rapidly closing up. I advise you to invest what little you have in socialist propaganda; stand by the representatives of the Social Democratic Party. It is going to triumph. You will add your name to the roll of honor. Vote to achieve this victory, and the sons who bear your name will be proud of it to their last breath.

We appeal to you only upon the ground that our principles are eternally right; that our candidates are above reproach; that our principles being right and our candidates having acquitted themselves to your unqualified satisfaction, it is to your interest of your wives, of your children, of your firesides, of your city and your country to vote with us, to achieve this victory that shall give heart of hope to the struggling masses throughout the whole civilized world.

I thank you all for the patience with which you have listened to me, and my heart from now until Tuesday next, will be attuned to the harmonious notes of certain victory.

Notes

1. Gerrit Smith (1797–1874), an anti-slavery activist and politician from New York, was elected to a single term of Congress in 1852 on the ticket of the Free Soil Party. Smith was a financial angel of the abolitionist movement.
2. Allusion to the ranks of the unemployed.
3. Invented in the mid-1880s, the linotype machine allowed an operator sitting at a typewriter-like keyboard to generate finished sections of lead type line by line, eliminating the need to place letters of type individually.
4. From John 12:8.
5. That is, the broadening of national control over foreign colonies and their markets.
6. The Pierian spring was a sacred rivulet in Greek mythology, said to provide knowledge and inspiration to those who drank from it.
7. This speech marked a bit of a departure for Debs, an address delivered at the invitation of an elite New York City social club at Delmonico's, regarded as the finest restaurant in New York City. This appearance by Debs had been arranged several months in advance, and he was one of three speakers to deliver 40-minute discussions on the same assigned topic. Sharing the podium with Debs were Clare de Graffenried and Charlton T. Lewis.
8. Allusion to the curse of Cain recounted in Genesis 4:11–16, in which the fratricidal Cain was punished by God by having placed upon him a mark that would cause him to be killed should anyone find him, thereby condemning him to life as a solitary vagabond.
9. The Tennessee Convict Lease Wars were a series of skirmishes between striking coal miners and convict strikebreakers leased by the Tennessee Coal and Iron Co. during the second half of 1891 and the summer of 1892, during which shots were exchanged, prisoners were released, and stockades were burned.
10. Johann Gottlieb Fichte (1762–1814) was a founding figure in the German idealist movement, building upon ideas originated by Immanuel Kant.
11. Where Fichte first said this is unclear; Debs appears to have borrowed the quote from a pamphlet by Ferdinand Lassalle, *The Working Man's Programme (Arbeiter-Programm): An Address* (London: Modern Press, 1884), 48.
12. The Ten Commandments.
13. A friend of Debs who attended the speech indicated that "the audience was completely disarmed of prejudice" by Debs's performance, interrupting him several times with applause, culminating in an ovation at the conclusion of the address. (See "E.V. Debs at Delmonico's," *Labor Advocate* [Birmingham, AL], vol. 10, no. 15 (April 15, 1899), 1.)
14. Rationalist orator Robert G. Ingersoll (1833-1899) died of heart disease on July 21.<< I think that will fit on the line without impacting pagination. If not, lose the word "rationalist" and add the year 1899 at the end of July 21.
15. Henry Ward Beecher (1813–1887) was a Congregationalist minister and prominent abolitionist orator.
16. On July 6, 1899, a conference committee met in Chicago, which decided to send

out a five-question referendum to the membership of the Social Democratic Party (1) querying whether the constitution should continue until the next convention; (2) querying whether the "demands for farmers" should be eliminated; (3) seeking approval of Indianapolis as the location of the next national convention; (4) setting the date for opening the convention as Tuesday, March 6, 1900; (5) basing representation at the convention as one delegate for each branch established for at least 45 days prior to the convention, plus one additional delegate for every 50 members.

17. Announcement of the referendum brought forth a lengthy response, published in the July 29 issue of *Social Democratic Herald* by Haverhill, Massachusets, mayor John C. Chase, who declared the conference committee a waste of party funds, the existing constitution "not fit for use," the demand for farmers "out of place in our platform," and who sought a convention location closer to Massachusetts, which was at that time the key center of SDP activity. Chase also called for a smaller convention delegated on the basis of states rather than local branches, suggesting apportionment of five delegates per state. "So long as we are a small party, and poor financially, we will be unable to get a representative convention by branch representation," Chase argued, provoking Debs's ire.
18. While the first four propositions passed by overwhelming margins, the fifth proposal, calling for delegation on the basis of local branches, failed by a vote of 210–316, with Massachusetts responsible for about 45 percent of these negative votes, and the distant states of Connecticut, Maryland, and New York also contributing substantially to the negative result. With 35 branches chartered in Massachusetts alone by August 1899, the paying of rail fare of even one delegate per branch represented a potentially massive expense to the Massachusetts organization—a cost that would be substantially alleviated under a system with fewer delegates, each allotted multiple votes.
19. Many of the articles Debs wrote for the *Social Democratic Herald* in this period took the form of this piece—short opinion essays on sundry contemporary news topics. As much of this content is transitory, it has been generally excluded from this volume. Interested scholars are referred to back issues of that newspaper, which have been digitized by the editors and presented on the Marxists Internet Archive, www.marxists.org, in conjunction with this project.
20. M. D. Ratchford, president of the United Mine Workers' Union during the 1897 coal strike, did not seek reelection in 1899. Later that year, he joined the Federal Industrial Commission as its token labor representative—apparently the reference made here.
21. William D. Ryan was secretary-treasurer of District 12 (Illinois) of the United Mine Workers of America from 1897 to 1908.
22. Rate of pay for a soldier.
23. Slight misquotation of a line of William Lloyd Garrison (1805–1879): "My country is the world; my countrymen are mankind."
24. General Henry Clay Merriam (1837–1912), based in Denver, was the commander of federal forces which intervened in the 1899 Coeur d'Alene miners' strike.

25. Allusion to Esther 7: 6–10.
26. Captain Alfred Dreyfus (1859–1935) was a French military officer of Jewish-Alsatian ethnicity who was wrongly convicted of providing military secrets to the Germans. He would spend five years imprisoned on Devil's Island in French Guiana before his final exoneration in 1906.
27. Allusion to the Socialist Labor Party, tightly controlled by a New York City faction headed by party editor Daniel DeLeon.
28. The Ruskin Commonwealth Association was a utopian socialist colony established near Tennessee City, Tennessee, in 1894. The group's financial angel was land-developer-turned-socialist-evangelist J. A. Wayland (1854–1912), who gifted his socialist weekly, *The Coming Nation,* to the new cooperative enterprise. Wayland soon became disgruntled with rural pioneering and departed the colony in 1895, moving to Kansas City to launch a new weekly newspaper, *Appeal to Reason.* Internal dissension was rife and the colony's primitive industry unsuccessful; after a move to Georgia, the group disbanded in the fall of 1901.
29. Reference is to the regularly scheduled 1900 convention of the Social Democratic Party.
30. This is likely a transcription error, as Debs had previously been consistent in referring to the Social Democratic Party by its correct name.
31. Opening lines from "The Man with the Hoe" (1898), by C. Edwin Markham (1852–1940).
32. The Haverhill city election that reelected Social Democrat John C. Chase as mayor was held December 6, 1899.
33. The 1899 Massachusetts state election was held on November 7, 1899, one month prior to the Haverhill city election. In it, Social Democrat Louis M. Scates was defeated by a Democratic-Republican fusion candidate, managing to simultaneously increase his vote and lose the race. In the second election, Scates ran successfully for Haverhill City Council, winning a seat in ward 6.
34. Gerrit Smith (1797–1874) was an abolitionist and politician from New York.
35. Lincoln's line was actually: "As I would not be a *slave,* so I would not be a *master.* This expresses my idea of democracy. Whatever differs from this, to the extent of the difference, is no democracy." From "Fragment on Democracy," circa August 1, 1858.

1900

The Hour for Unity Has Not Yet Arrived: Letter to the *Social Democratic Herald*†

January 14, 1900

Kansas City, Mo., January 14 [1900]

Editor of the *Herald:*—

For some time, I have been asked to declare myself through the *Herald* in reference to the proposed union between the anti-DeLeon element of the SLP and our party. I have delayed doing so until I had the opportunity to examine the situation in various parts of the country.

First, let me say that while no one can be more desirous for a united party of socialists than I, it is my settled conviction that the hour for such a consummation has not yet arrived.

There are hundreds of SLP comrades of the faction named whom I have met and love and honor, and would be proud to greet as party comrades; but there is also an element in that faction, by no means insignificant in proportion to the whole, with whom we can have no affiliation without inviting disruption. A union with this element will simply not unite, or, if it does, it can result only in a dissension, and, sooner or later, a split, and we have had quite enough experience along that line.

Barring such papers as the *Cleveland Citizen* and *The Class Struggle,* I am not satisfied with the tone or temper of the press of the anti-DeLeon SLP and particularly with the official organ, *The People,*[1] which continues to retail malicious libels respecting our party and our comrades.[2]

The People knows that in the past our party, from its very inception, has been foully maligned and our comrades vilely slandered by the promoters of the party of which, since its so-called expurgation, it is now the official organ. Has it ever uttered one word to atone for such shocking indecency or to make restitution for the outrages intended, if not committed? If it has done itself such a manifestly plain duty in its regenerated capacity, it has not come to my notice. Could honorable men have done less? For my own part, I have always ignored these petty detractors, and

† Published as "Debs on Unity" in *Social Democratic Herald,* vol. 2, no. 31, whole no. 81 (January 20, 1900), 3.

I do not want any apology now or at any time, but were I in the attitude *The People* maintains to the Social Democratic Party, I know what the plain and unmistakable dictates of conscience must prompt me to say and do in mitigation of wrongs with which I had been at least identified in perpetrating.

When *The People,* as the official organ of the party, honestly and courageously clears its skirts, then we can and will accept its professions that it is in favor of a united party.

Not only this, but *The People* continues to be the vehicle of libel and detraction of our comrades. In a recent issue, it permits us to be charged with not yet having "cut loose from Bryanites," and our officers, especially myself, with drawing exorbitant salaries for party service. *The People* knows, or can know if it wishes to, that these statements and their like are bald-faced lies, and yet it continues to inoculate its readers with their poison. I care nothing about these lies, nor their craven authors, but I want no affiliation with such serpents of defamation.

As a matter of fact, I have never drawn a dollar of salary in any capacity in the Social Democracy or the Social Democratic Party. During the year I served as chairman of the National Executive Board of the Social Democracy and gave the party my whole time, I worked without a cent of compensation from the party, and during the past 18 months that I have served on the executive board and as general organizer for the Social Democratic Party, I have never been paid a cent, and I have met all my official expenses from my private means, and the same is true of every other member of the executive board. We are not making this statement by way of explanation, or to elicit credit, for none is due, but to emphasize the conviction that if *The People* is sincere in its professions, it will at least stop circulating lies and libels about those with whom it seeks affiliation.

The anti-DeLeon party has not yet had its last purging. They hated DeLeon, not because of his principles or lack of principles, but because he was their master at their own game. I am confident that our members stand for a united party and also that they will not rush rashly forward to what seems to be such a party, to find themselves the victims of deception. We are not egotistical when we say there will soon be a united party, and that without taking any chances. The Social Democratic Party has proved its right to live. It has emerged unscathed from all the assaults that have been made upon it and is moving majestically to the front. No odium attaches to its name, and no stain is upon its honor. The election of 1900 will indicate its standing and establish its supremacy.

Eugene V. Debs

A Revolutionary Party†

March 6, 1900

Indianapolis, March 6 [1900]

The Social Democratic Party is not a reform party, but a revolutionary party.[3] It does not propose to modify the competitive system, but abolish it. An examination of its platform shows that it stands unequivocally for the collective ownership and control of all the means of wealth production and distribution—in a word, socialism.

The modern tendency is toward centralization and cooperation. This has given us the trust, and there has been a great hue and cry about this latest phase of economic development. The Republican and Democratic parties, yielding to the popular outcry, will declare in favor of destroying or restraining the trust, but just how puerile and dishonest such declarations are every member of the Social Democratic Party knows too well to be deceived into voting for either of said parties. As a matter of fact, the trust is the inevitable outgrowth of the competitive system, and to declare against the private ownership of the trust is to declare against the system itself. That neither the large capitalists, who own the trusts, nor the small capitalists, who are opposed to them because they do not own them, favor the overthrow of the capitalist system of production and distribution is a foregone conclusion.

The Republican Party represents the former class and the Democratic Party the latter class. Both stand for essentially the same system of exploitation, and the socialist wageworker realizes that it makes precious little difference to

† Published as "Eugene V. Debs Says: The Social Democracy Convention Will Emphasize Startling Truths" in *New York Journal,* March 7, 1900, unspecified page. Reprinted as "The Social Democratic Convention Has Emphasized Startling Truths," *Appeal to Reason,* whole no. 225 (March 24, 1900), 3.

him and his class whether they are exploited by a few great capitalists or an innumerable brood of small ones. They propose to put an end to exploitation entirely by abolishing the system and transferring the means of production from private hands to the collectivity and having them operated in the interest of all alike. To carry out this program the first step necessary is political organization, and this step has been taken by the Social Democratic Party. It is now organized in 25 different states and is spreading rapidly over the entire country. Its progress has been greatest in the states of Massachusetts, Wisconsin, and Washington. These three states are marked for early conquest. California has also proved hospitable soil, and it is confidently expected that the Golden Gate State will develop a phenomenal increase of strength in the near future.

Just what the party declarations will be is, of course, a matter of conjecture, but so far as the essential principles of socialism are concerned, they will be avowed in clear and commanding terms. The party will stand squarely upon the principles of international, revolutionary socialism. There will be not so much as a hint or a squint at compromise. It is safe to predict that the agents of fusion will not venture into that class-conscious convocation.

So far as I know, there is as yet not a single candidate for either president or vice president. There will be no lobbying for office. The convention will be entirely free to choose its most available representatives, and they will accept from considerations not of greed or glory, but of duty to the cause.

The Social Democratic Party is necessarily an international party. It is as wide as the domain of capitalism. It is everywhere and always the same. It takes no backward step. The reins of government are its goal. It refuses to be flattered, bribed, stampeded, or otherwise deflected from the straight course mapped out for it by Marx and Engels, its founders, and pursued with unflagging fidelity by their millions of followers. Before its conquering march, every throne in Europe is beginning to tremble. The last one of them will fall to the earth while the century is still in its swaddling clothes. The socialist hosts of Germany give confident assurance that the day of deliverance for the people will soon dawn. In France, Belgium, England, Austria, Italy, Russia, and other countries, the same principles animating the proletarian class are finding expression in great parties, all linked together in the indissoluble bonds of international socialism. The battle cry of Marx is heard around the world: "Workingmen of all countries, unite; you have a world to gain! You have nothing to lose but your chains!"[4]

Among the last countries to organize, for reasons so generally understood that they need not be discussed here, is the United States,[5] but the conditions which develop socialism have come upon us so rapidly during the past few years that it now seems certain that the American movement will soon become the most formidable of them all, and that here, where political democracy was first achieved, industrial democracy will gain its first triumph.

The Social Democratic Party has no interest in any of the so-called issues over which capitalist politicians fight sham battles. They care nothing about the currency question, the tariff, or imperialism.[6] They stand first, last, and always for the collective ownership of all the means of production and distribution, and they will press forward unceasingly until they secure them, thereby liberating the race and resolving the problem of the centuries.

Speech Accepting the Nomination for President of the United States[†7]

March 9, 1900

Mr. Chairman and Comrades:—

A few moments ago, your committee advised me of the great honor conferred upon me by this convention in making me one of the standard-bearers of the party in the great campaign upon which we are now entering. Never in all of my life was I so profoundly impressed with the conviction that there is a divinity that shapes our ends, rough-hew them how we will. Yesterday [March 8] I left this hall under the solemn belief that I could not, under any possible circumstances, accept the nomination tendered me with such enthusiastic unanimity. But with your united voices ringing in my ears, and your impassioned appeals burning and glowing in my breast, and your eyes searching the very depths of my soul, I was soon brought to realize that in your voice on behalf of socialism there was the supreme command of duty—that I could not disregard it and decline the nomination without proving myself wholly unworthy of the confidence which inspired it. I felt that I could not decline the nomination,

† Short excerpt first published as "Eugene V. Debs Accepts" in *Indianapolis Journal,* vol. 50, no. 69 (March 10, 1900), 8. Full version published as "Debs' Speech of Acceptance" in *Social Democratic Herald,* vol. 2, no. 40, whole no. 90 (March 24, 1900), 1.

tendered me under such circumstances, without being guilty of treason to the cause we all love so well; and so I come to you this afternoon, obedient to the call voiced by your committee, to say that I accept your nomination, and with it all of the responsibilities that the great trust imposes; and with my heart trembling upon my lips, I thank the comrades, one and all, for the great honor you have conferred upon me.

I also thank you for having nominated as my associate and colleague so true a socialist, so manly a man, as Comrade Job Harriman, and let me assure you that we will stand together, side by side, in the true spirit of socialism and, joining hands, will bear aloft the conquering banner of the Social Democratic Party of America.[8]

The ordeal through which we passed yesterday was indeed painful and trying to us, but perhaps it was necessary to completely consecrate us to our great task.[9] Standing in your presence this afternoon the standard-bearer of a united socialist party, so long a cherished hope and now practically a realized fact, all the skies of the future are bright, and I do not hesitate to believe that in the great campaign upon which we are now entering that we are to achieve results that will mark the real beginning of socialism in America, as also the real end of capitalism. The line is to be sharply drawn. The issue is to be clearly understood. We are to move forward side by side, a united party, a solid indivisible phalanx. We are to move forward with steady step, our eyes on the goal. No backward step is taken. We are not to be deflected from our course the breadth of a hair; and in the first battle, whatever the outcome, a great victory will have to be achieved to be followed by others until, at last, socialism is triumphant in the United States, capitalism falls, never to rise again, and the working class, bruised, degraded, and plundered through all the centuries of the past, for the first time in the history of all the ages will stand forth redeemed and disenthralled, the coronated sovereigns of the world.

I congratulate my comrades, one and all, upon the very happy outcome of this historic convention. I would be less than just to myself if I failed to make some proper acknowledgment of the invaluable services rendered us by the committee representing the Socialist Labor Party.[10] During the trying hours of yesterday, I was more than impressed with their noble bearing, with their manly conduct. They appeared before us in the spirit of socialism. Fortunately for you and me, and for the party, they were met with the same spirit; and now, instead of being in hostile camps, with divided forces, we stand before the world in a united body that is to move forward until it wrests this government from the grasp of capitalism and restores it to the people at large.

Comrades, we invoke your united aid and cooperation. We should be remiss in no single obligation that has been imposed upon us. We shall, to the extent of our ability, serve you and those you represent in this great cause. There is no mistake as to the ultimate outcome. Speaking for myself, I am not only hopeful, I am confident. The new crusade is now thoroughly organized, and when the message goes forth, it will send joy and hope and enthusiasm to the heart of every socialist in the land.

Allow me to say, in closing, that I am deeply sensible of the great honor that you have conferred upon me—that when I attempt to express the gratitude with which my heart is overflowing, all language is meaningless. I am proud to be a socialist. I believe with all my heart in the conquering and emancipating power of socialism. With me, it is something more than a conviction. It throbs in my heart; it surges in my soul; it is my very life. Without it, every star that blazes in the horizon would go out forever. Without it, this earth were simply a jungle and we wild beasts devouring each other. With it, this earth becomes transformed into a veritable paradise, and we are almost gods. Again and again, I thank you. All hail to the united socialists of America![11]

Trade Unions and Politics†

April 5, 1900

Terre Haute, Ind., April 5, 1900

Greater activity has marked the work of organizing labor during the past year than the world has ever known. It is in the air. It is irresistible. Every brand of the industrial army, skilled and unskilled, is wheeling into line. It overleaps all color lines and wipes out all sex discriminations. The movement is universal, and it foreshadows the emancipation of the working class from wage-slavery.

Most heartily do I approve the work and commend the mission of organized labor. I would have the workers of all kinds thoroughly organized and then cooperate harmoniously under the supervision of a central body. The agitation incident to organizing is healthful and vitalizing. It is educational. In

† Published in *Appeal to Reason,* whole no. 230 (April 28, 1900), 2.

the breast of despondency, the heart of hope begins to throb, and the bowed form begins to rise.

Let the good work go forward and let all unite in it! In the trade unions, the workers are being fitted to take possession of, and manage, their trades when the time comes for the great change toward which the world is irresistibly tending, when the workers will own and operate the means of production in their own interest.

The trade union, as such, should not go into politics. It is an economic and not a political institution. When it is made to endorse candidates and other political service, disruption follows. The members should keep their eyes on the political heelers and henchmen who join the union to swing it their way in payment of a recognition in the form of a cheap political job to some member of the organization.

While trade unionists should keep their union out of politics, they should put themselves into politics in a solid, united body and stand together at the polls as they do in the strike and lockout. As their interests are identical, they should vote together to turn out the class that oppresses and exploits them and put their own class in control of the government.

The trade union, properly directed, becomes a mighty factor in the emancipation of the working class, and every man and woman in the land should support the trade union movement.

The Issues of Unity†

April 16, 1900

Terre Haute, Ind., April 16, 1900

Comrades:—

A crisis is upon us. The very life of our party is threatened. Shall it emerge from the ordeal in glory or perish in ignominy? If we be men, fit and worthy to have

† Published in *Social Democratic Herald,* vol. 2, no. 33, whole no. 94 (April 21, 1900), 1.

custody of a party to which the working class are turning with a last hope, the issue is not in doubt for a single instant.

Shall the SDP and the SLP unite upon the basis agreed to and recommended by the majority of the New York conference?[12]

I have read the report of the conference,[13] the manifesto of the executive board of the SDP,[14] the replies thereto by comrades Harriman, Hillquit,[15] Hayes,[16] and Benham,[17] the current issues of the press of both parties, as also a vast number of personal communications relative to the unity proceedings. After a careful survey of the entire situation and the maturest deliberation of which I am capable, I have arrived at a conclusion, and I now propose to meet the responsibilities that rest upon me in my triple capacity as member, official, and candidate, by declaring my position in clear and unequivocal terms and facing without fear all its consequences, be they what they may.

As I write, I see the blanched faces, the appealing eyes of the working class, to whom alone, and my own conscience, I am finally accountable for my acts. Rather than betray them and turn their hope into despair, I would destroy myself, and if in what I now have to say I write a word not dictated by my conscience and approved by my best judgment, I hope the hand that pens it may be palsied at its task.

Dismissing all personal prejudice and all partisan predilection, and viewing the matter solely from the standpoint of a socialist to whom the cause is dearer far than his own life, I take my stand against union of the parties on the basis proposed by the New York conference, and until our party has been rescued from the maelstrom which threatens to engulf it, against union on any terms. I say this with the fullest realization of what it means to break with comrades loved and true, yet sustained by the conviction that duty demands it, that time will triumphantly vindicate the action and that the odium of today will be the honor of the future.

Lest I be misunderstood, let me write it in plain words. I am opposed to union because I favor unity. In the present strained situation, there can be unity without union, but there can be none with it; and as certain as it is effected, if such should be the verdict of the ballot, the Social Democratic Party will be disrupted and there will be no unity in the united party.

In arriving at my conclusions, I have been guided largely by my intuitions, but I shall try to make the reasons which actuated me as clear as I can to my comrades of both parties.

It will be remembered that a short time previous to the convention, I wrote an article for the *Herald* stating that in my opinion the time for union had not yet arrived, which article provoked considerable criticism.[18] For months I had been doing all I consistently could to harmonize the two parties and to pave the way to unification. There were many obstacles in the way. For years, the official organ of the SLP had drilled it into their members that the SDP consisted of a lot of freaks, frauds, and fakirs without redeeming feature. They were fairly saturated with the virus of hate and contempt. Hundreds of them, members of the anti-DeLeon party, and I speak advisedly, still rankle with that feeling which, to even the superficial observer, is but ill-concealed. It is this sort of training in the school of intolerance, fanaticism, and hate which have given the party a spirit irreconcilably in conflict with that of the Social Democratic Party, which by its high-minded toleration has appealed so successfully to the American people on behalf of socialism that its complete supremacy as the socialist party was only a question of months, while at every step of its progress its members were derided as "half-baked socialists" by the very men who now, we are assured, insist upon union. The spirit is still there, whatever may be said to the contrary, and it is this that, in my opinion, prevented the SLP representatives from even temporarily accepting our name, even though they had to change their own, even though some of them assured us it would be done, and even though our identity be totally obliterated on the eve of a national campaign. It is this spirit with which I have to deal, and it is this that largely forms the basis of my opposition to union.

I shall not attempt to follow the unity proceedings through their torturous windings. I care nothing about quibbles and hair-splitting technicalities. There are those who are schooled in artifice, in word jugglery, in the legerdemain of smooth and cunning phrase which can be made to mean anything or nothing, and they are proud of it. I am not an adept in such practice and have no desire to be.

When the representatives of the SLP appeared at our convention and assured us that they wanted unity, I unqualifiedly accepted their word and persuaded myself that my misgivings had been exaggerated, nor shall I now charge them with violating their pledges, although it seems clear to me in the light of subsequent proceedings that in their zeal to effect union they exceeded the scope of their authority and went counter to the wishes of their party.[19]

Comrade Harriman will doubtless recall the conversation he and I had as we walked to the convention hall to attend the closing session at which I accepted the nomination. Without any reservation whatever, he assured me that the name "Social Democratic Party" was entirely acceptable to him and that he was confident that his party felt as he did, and that there would be no opposition upon that point. He also added that on the eve of a campaign was no time to make a change, and that whatever change might seem desirable could be made after the national election by the united party.

Now I admit that the name in itself amounts to little and should not stand in the way of union one instant, but it is what the name stands for, the spirit, the morale, the party identity, that amounts to everything and—let us not be deceived—it is this that inspired the labored arguments in opposition to the name, so that while the name itself is of no consequence, it covers the central, controlling issue between the two parties and in rejecting it, the SLP representatives, inadvertently perhaps, struck the proposed union a fatal blow, and as I now view it, fortunately so for the cause of socialism.

To what extent did this conflict of party spirit actually dominate the conference?

Referring to the name, the attitude of the SLP amounted to this: "We are going to change our name, but will not have yours."[20] In the matter of headquarters, each party said in effect: "I can't have it and therefore you shan't," and made a selection ridiculously unsuitable for a national party.[21]

Without going further, it is perfectly obvious that in all of this the SLP shrewdly yielded little or nothing, while our party surrendered practically everything, and the adoption of the majority report would simply mean the swallowing up of the Social Democratic Party and its domination by an element composed largely of men who had despised and ridiculed it and who would today scorn the suggestion of union did they not see the handwriting on the wall; and this perfectly plain and evident fact many of our own comrades who are clamoring for unconditional union seem utterly unable to see.

If unity was possible when the conference met, it was no longer possible when it closed. It is admitted that they had a complicated situation to deal with, and if they did the best they could, they were simply unequal to the task, and so far as failure is chargeable to the conference I have no more fault to find with the SLP representatives than with our own. From first to last, there was sparring for party advantage instead of an honest, controlling desire for unification, and this in itself, conspicuous in every important feature of the negotiations, proves beyond cavil the conflict of party spirit.

Some of our own comrades will deny this, for while they are members of the SDP, they have the spirit of the SLP, just as there are members of the latter who are in accord with the spirit of our party.

The National Executive Board has been severely censured for issuing its manifesto in advance of the majority report. My name is not attached to it, but I am equally responsible with my four associates for what it contains. If it is "criminal" and "malicious," as charged, I claim my full share of the odium, not from any sense of self-sacrifice, but because I endorse, if not the specific grounds, the action, and am prepared to answer for my share of it.

The purport of the report had gone out. It had struck the party with the effect of a lightning stroke, and revolt threatened instantaneously. Prompt action was required in the emergency, and the board took it and will stand by it until time vindicates their fealty and turns denunciation into praise. Had they not acted as they did, the party would ere this be deserted by hundreds of loyal comrades, the very ones who worked and sacrificed, and put up the money, too, to make the national party what it is today.[22] I am not now discussing the justice of revolt. They do occur and, unless the executive board had taken prompt action, the SDP would have been disrupted, and even though part of it had united with the SLP, we would not more have a united socialist party than we had before.

I have said that the spirit of the two parties, as a whole, is totally dissimilar, and it is this fact rather than the incidents to it that is responsible for the failure of the union. The SLP was trained in the bitter school of bigotry and intolerance. It must preserve an air frigidly scientific. Emotion and sentiment must be banished. Hard and stern are the party methods, and it must be confined strictly to the working class. Tolerance is a crime. Members must suspicion each other, and rows must occur at intervals as to prevent the party from getting beyond the bounds of a mere faction. It has taken years to cultivate and intensify this spirit that has dwarfed socialism in America, and it cannot be overcome in a day nor by resolutions passed in a conference.

Diametrically opposite to this is the spirit of the SDP. It has from the beginning been tolerant and hospitable. It pursued the even tenor of its way through showers of abuse. Its dignified policy, its spirit of toleration appealed to the people, while its comrades loved and trusted each other and worked with inexpressible zeal for its success.

I cheerfully admit that in some places the spirit of the parties has so modified as to make union entirely feasible. But this is not true of the parties at large. Take Chicago, for example. We are told the SLP have 600 comrades there. Not [six] of them all told have ever been at our headquarters, even since the unity negotiations have been in progress. At heart, they have no use for our comrades and hold them in contempt, and it should also be said that our comrades have no use for them. This is the fact, and there is no use trying to conceal it.[23] Taken as a whole, they will not work together, and all the resolutions that can be passed will not unite them in their present spirit toward each other. To put them into one party at this time means simply disruption and disaster. Better far to keep them in separate parties until the logic of events has ripened them for union.

In discussing the spirit of the SLP, I am struck by the exhibition of it in Comrade Benham's letter, which I wish every one of our comrades to read with care, especially the paragraphs in which he charges our executive board, in innuendo so direct that specific averment could add nothing to its force, with being in the pay of capitalism. I confess to being greatly surprised in the source in which that spirit had found expression. Comrade Benham's letter must furnish its own comment so far as I am concerned. After reading what he has to say, and the manner in which he says it, I am satisfied that he and I are not ready to belong to the same socialist party.

It seems hardly possible that this is the same comrade who in the convention made the touching plea to me to accept the nomination for president, inviting me to his California home to have my health and vigor restored by the balmy breezes of the tropics; and yet, was it not that same evening at the "peace conference" that he took the ground that if I were given the nomination, he would insist upon our party giving up its name? Just why my nomination should be at the expense of my party's name I will leave others to explain.

It has been charged that Victor Berger knew that I would accept the nomination before he went into the "peace conference."[24] This is not true. Up to the time the convention adjourned, I had steadfastly refused the nomination. I left the hall with my brother alone, and after a long struggle with myself concluded to accept the nomination. I did not know a conference was held and did not see Berger until after it adjourned. He could not have known that I would accept the nomination, for I had not at that time communicated the fact to anyone.

For the reasons herein imperfectly stated, I am opposed to union at this time, and I shall vote against it and also against the report of the majority and use my best efforts to defeat both. I propose to stand by the Social Democratic Party until conditions favor a united party; and my judgment is that this consummation will not be deferred long after the national election. In the meantime, I stand ready to work in harmony with the SLP, and so far as I am concerned, we shall go into the national campaign with a united front.

I shall not resign the nomination at this time unless the party desires it. I did not want the nomination at the convention, but I shall not desert when the party needs me. Nor can I be neutral, as some of my best loved comrades insist, without feeling myself guilty of cowardice. The effect upon myself personally is of no consequence, and I am not concerned upon that point. It has been intimated that the reason I did not want the nomination this year was because I wished to nurse my chances till the party becomes strong enough to elect. All I have to say is that the presidency and all other offices are alike to me, and I do not think there is a man living who has a stronger aversion than I to public office; and that I am a candidate at all is simply because of an overwhelming sense of party duty.

And now I respectfully propose the following line of action:

First, let us decide against union at this time and reject the majority report.

Second, elect a National Executive Board of nine members by referendum vote. Upon this board, women should be represented by their own sex.

Third, elect a national secretary and treasurer and editor of the official organ.

Fourth, elect a national campaign committee.

This program can be carried out in short order, and then we will be ready to cooperate with the SLP in moving on the enemy with a united front. If they are willing to unite on candidates, that can be readily arranged, and if not, we will go into the campaign with our own.[25] We will lose no time in attacking the common enemy. Whenever it is possible, let the two parties unite on candidates and otherwise cooperate, and where this cannot be done, there need at least be no friction. Separately organized, the parties can move forward on parallel lines and accomplish the substantial objects of unity; while these must certainly be defeated by an enforced union of elements that are fundamentally dissimilar and inharmonious.

Such cooperation as is herein indicated would be in the nature of a preparatory stage for final union and would inevitably lead to such a result.

And now a closing word to our comrades. How far you may agree or disagree with me I do not know. I have given you as accurately as I could a transcript of my head and heart. I have written without malice toward anyone and with the cause of socialism the guiding influence in reaching my decisions. You are to decide this important question, and I have no wish to control your action. Having faith in your judgment and your loyalty, I have no fear of the verdict you will render.

I hope that each of you will carefully read all the testimony presented by both sides before you cast your vote. Read the New York *People,*[26] the *Cleveland Citizen,* and other SLP papers as well as the *Social Democratic Herald* and then vote as your conscience may dictate, and the party we love and which has been such a shining success will emerge from the fire unscathed, and, tempered by the heat and passion of conflict, will be better than ever fitted to enter upon the glorious future that awaits it.

Yours fraternally,
Eugene V. Debs

Union Must Be a Mutual Affair: Remarks at the Second Unity Conference, New York City†[27] [excerpt]

May 20, 1900

To be successful, union must be a mutual affair, entered into freely by both parties. Our party has by an emphatic majority decided that it wants no organic union at this time, and were the vote taken again, that majority would be so overwhelming as to silence all controversy upon that point.

It has been freely charged that the manifesto of the executive board is responsible for all the trouble; that but for this a united party would have been assured. This is wholly untrue. The real mischief was done, and our comrades were up in arms before the manifesto was even thought of. Following the actions and conclusions of the conference, a condition of affairs developed spontaneously which made union an impossibility. I, with others, recognize this absolute fact. I took up my stand against union under such conditions, not because I was, or am, opposed to union, but because I was, and am, opposed to the wrecking of our party. I assume full responsibility for my action, and I have no apology to make for it.

Let it be distinctly understood that I know my comrades are not responsible for the conditions which made union impossible. These had their origin long ago, and the controlling purpose was to capture and secure control of our organization. Had this plan succeeded, our party would have been destroyed,

† Published as part of Margaret Haile, "The Fusionists Reject Political Cooperation" in *Social Democratic Herald,* vol. 2, no. 50 (June 2, 1900), 2.

and the united party built upon its ruins would have been farther from a *united* party than ever before.

Enforced union under such conditions would prove abortive. There is no shadow of doubt about it. The party has expressed itself after hearing all the testimony, and it cannot be denied that the other side had a full hearing, for our branches were fairly deluged with their papers, circulars, and letters.[28]

While denying that organic union is possible at this time, I am in favor of cooperation. If it is claimed that this is not possible, then it must be conceded that organic union is out of the question, for certainly if we are unable to co-operate, we are not ready to unite.

For the moment some of our members, in their eagerness to see a united party, have been misled and deceived; but their sober second thought will soon bring them into line with the Social Democratic Party, which will, in good time, give the country a truly united socialist party.

Social Democrats, Stand Pat![†]

June 30, 1900

The unprecedented growth of the Social Democratic Party during the last few months is a vindication of the past and a guarantee of the future.[29] The showing is most remarkable; it is extraordinary and must extort exclamations of surprise and delight from the most pessimistic.

Since January 1 [1900], 144 new branches have been organized—an average of 24 per month. Since the first day of the present month, 29 branches have been instituted—the largest number in the same space of time in the history of our party.

In view of these facts, it is evident that the "manifesto," the referendum vote thereon, and the comment and controversy that followed have not checked the growth of the party. Indeed, it is more rapid at this hour than ever before, and will continue at an accelerating rate, all predictions to the contrary notwithstanding.

† Published as "Social Democrats, Stand Pat! Review Our Splendid Progress" in *Social Democratic Herald*, vol. 3, no. 2, whole no. 104 (June 30, 1900), 1.

The plain meaning of this progress in the face of all kinds of opposition, from within as well as without, is approval of the policy and tactics of the party and endorsement of the administration of its affairs.

Through all these weeks of controversy, at times violent and acrimonious, the party has expanded with undiminished vigor, and promises even better for the future. There is, therefore, all reason for Social Democrats to be serene, hopeful, and confident—not the slightest for despondency or despair. The storm has been weathered—the gale has spent its force, the waves are receding, and the skies are brightening.

Comrades, stand pat!

The socialist movement is having its trials. This is to be expected. The transition from capitalism to socialism will be tempestuous at times. It would be folly to even hope for all smooth sailing. The storm is as necessary as the calm. It is a part, an essential part, of the development.

Let no comrade despair of the future. Above all the quibbles and quarrels of individuals, the movement sweeps on.

The Social Democratic Party has struck root in American soil. Its general course has appealed to the American people, and its propaganda has quickened the heart-pulse of the American proletariat. It has made mistakes enough to demonstrate that it is a human institution.

The cry of "bossism" heard in certain quarters can safely be ignored. The work accomplished, the results achieved, the progress made, which none can dispute, proclaim the truth and defy denial.

Karl Marx and Ferdinand Lassalle were violently denounced as dictators and usurpers by their own followers. The "bosses" are sometimes those who in wind and wave hold the party true to its desired course.

It is the storm that makes the sailor, the battle that makes the soldier, and it takes them both to make a socialist.

Comrades, stand pat!

The question of "union" need worry us no more. Let those of our comrades who desire to join with the SLP do so.[30] That is their unquestioned privilege. Let the rest remain where they are. That is their absolute right. A united party is "a consummation devoutly to be wished," but it is a matter of growth and not compulsion. When conditions favor a united party, no power can prevent it. As long as cause exists for separate parties, no power can unite them. The matter will in time automatically adjust itself, and all the sooner if wrangling ceases and sense has sway.

Others may act as they choose, but I do not propose to be a party to an attempt to force men out of a party that suits them into a party that does not.

Whether we have one socialist party or a dozen, we can fight capitalism, the common enemy, as one, if we only will, and he who seeks to prevent this is the real enemy of socialism. Union of parties is of small consequence compared with union of action; and those who imagine that compulsory union would ensure united action have something yet to learn about human nature.

Political cooperation has gone forward splendidly thus far without organic union. What has been done in some states can be done in all states. The question of party allegiance need not interfere with harmonious cooperation and vigorous action. Besides, only an insignificant part of the socialists are members of any party. They are not interested in our imbroglio; they are only disgusted with our kindergarten contentions.

Let us rise above the level of bickering and strife and vituperation. The columns and pages of accusations, insinuation, denial, and counter-charges alter nothing. I can better afford to permit a hundred falsehoods to go unchallenged than descend to the plane where they have their origin.

For the national and state campaigns, each state can act for itself. The national candidates are already nominated. In each state, a united ticket can be placed in the field by joint convention or otherwise, and this is the supreme demand at this time. The question of organic union is settled as far as it can be for the present.

This is the sane, sensible course to pursue, and will lead up to the highlands. We can then appeal to the hundreds of thousands of American socialists and multiply them into a million or more at the ballot box in November.

Comrades, once again, stand pat!

No Organic Union Has Been Effected†

July 21, 1900

Silence seems to give acquiescence to misrepresentation regarding the "unity" question. It is important enough that we should have a clear understanding about it. There has been no organic union of the SDP and SLP. The issue was placed squarely before our party by the manifesto of the National Executive Board and defeated by a decided majority. Nor is this all. The second vote taken upon the committee report by those who took exception to the manifesto simply verified the first vote and emphasized the decision of the party. But a small minority of members in good standing voted on the report at all. Repeated extensions of time and the most vigilant drumming of votes could not alter the result.

The two parties are therefore separate and distinct organizations as they were before the question of union was raised. This is the fact, and no amount of misrepresentation can change it. Yet there are those who insist that the two parties are now one.[31] Defeated by the general vote of the party at large, they have appealed to the states to secede from the party, and we have heard that one state after another has effected organizations in defiance of, if not renouncing allegiance to, the national party.[32] These reports are in nearly every case false and misleading.

Take New York, for example. Four bona fide SDP delegates attended the "joint" convention. Sixteen branches refused to participate on the ground that they were opposed to organic union, yet these four delegates, representing but about 10 percent of our membership in New York, acting with the delegates of the SLP, declared the two parties a "united" party. Such actions are not calculated to promote union sentiment. They simply inaugurate strife. And yet those who object to such methods are denounced for opposing union.

The national party decided against organic union, and I maintain that no state convention has any authority to commit the party to such an alliance and that those who take such a step in defiance of the party's mandate secede from and sever their relations with the party. I have no fault to find with comrades for joining the Kangaroo SLP, but I object to the assumption that their action is that of the party of which they are but a very small minority. The National

---

† Published in *Social Democratic Herald,* vol. 3, no. 5, whole no. 107 (July 21, 1900), 2.

Executive Board has been and is unanimous upon this question.[33] When they issued their manifesto, it was charged that they, and they alone, were opposed to union, and it was freely predicted that the board and its action would be repudiated by an overwhelming majority. Instead of this, the board has been twice sustained by the party, once by the vote on the manifesto and again by the negative action of the report of the "unity" committee.

We have been told over and over again that the rank and file demand "union" and that only the "leaders" stand in the way. Then why do not the "rank and file" remove the "leaders" and unite? Nothing is easier or simpler. Our constitution provides the power of recall, and 5 percent of the members can initiate the demand. The fact is that a large majority of our comrades are opposed to joining the SLP. They are satisfied with their party as it is; and in spite of all that has been said about their NEB, they know that no one of its members sought or desired official position, that not one of them has ever received a cent of salary, that every one of them has served the party to his personal loss and inconvenience, and that every cent of their official expenses from first to last has been paid from their own private income. Can the same be said of their accusers and traducers?

There has been no opposition to "union" in any proper sense of that term. We have resisted an alliance which, under the circumstances, was fraught with dissension and strife, not union and harmony. We do not quarrel with those who differ from us. They have all the rights we claim for ourselves. Let them unite with the SLP if they choose to, and we will have nothing mean to say about them.[34] Time will show which of us is right.

Since there has been some question about my status as a candidate, I wish it understood that I am the candidate of the Social Democratic Party, whose convention nominated me at Indianapolis and whose national headquarters are located at Chicago.

I do not doubt the time will come when we shall have a united party. Until then we yield to the inexorable logic of facts.

We do not claim that we are better than others. We may not be as good. That is not the question. We differ from them, and we are simply standing by our convictions.

But be these differences among socialists what they may, they can and should in every battle unite against capitalism and to such a policy of united action we stand pledged until we have a truly united party.

Letter of Acceptance of the Nomination for President by the Springfield Social Democratic Party†

July 31, 1900

Terre Haute, Ind., July 31, 1900.

William Butscher, Esq.
National Secretary, Social Democratic Party
Springfield, Mass.

My Dear Comrade:—

Your communication of the 18th inst. [July 18, 1900] has been received, and I note that by the action of the unity committee elected at the Rochester and Indianapolis conventions, approved by referendum vote, my nomination has been ratified as candidate of the Social Democratic Party for the office of president of the United States.[35]

Permit me to return my thanks to the committee and the comrades they represent for the ratification of my nomination, which I esteem a signal honor.

Having responded to the call of my comrades in accepting the nomination of their confidence and partially bestowed upon me, I am deeply sensible of the responsibilities which rest upon me as a socialist candidate for the office of president of the United States. Fully imbued with the philosophy of socialism, I seek no personal preferment, and I claim consideration as a representative of the principles of international, class-conscious socialism. In that capacity and that alone, I appeal to the working class and my countrymen for their support. The confidence implied by the unanimous action of my comrades moves me to regret my limitations and to wish myself a worthier representative of the principles so sacred to them because fraught with such grave import to the countless victims struggling in the grasp of economic bondage.

But all the strength and ability I have are at their service. Long since I consecrated myself to the cause, and all I have laid with joy on the altar of socialism.

† Published as "Accepts the Nomination," in *The Workers' Call,* vol 2, whole no. 75 (August 11, 1900), 1. Reprinted as part of "'Unionists' Endorse the Social Democratic Ticket," *Social Democratic Herald,* vol. 3, no. 8, whole no. 110 (August 11, 1900), 2.

As we look abroad, we behold the steady and stately march of transformation. Capitalism, which has written its record in the tears and blood of the human race, is staggering to its doom, while socialism, herald of light and freedom, quickened by the spirit of the new revolution, is sweeping over all the world.

Here in the United States of America, we are on the eve of our first great battle. Let us gird on our armor and press forward to meet the enemies of freedom, the oppressors of the people, the exploiters of the working class, and the foes of all humanity.

Let us dismiss all minor considerations and unite in every state and territory, from end to end of the land, in one mighty effort to hasten the end of capitalism and the inauguration of the Cooperative Commonwealth.

Thanking you again and through you the members of your committee and all your comrades for the honor conferred upon me, I remain

Yours fraternally,
Eugene V. Debs

Letter to Frederic Heath in Milwaukee† [excerpt]

August 6, 1900

* * *

Returning from Danville, I find your telegram asking if I accepted [the nomination] to [Springfield SDP national secretary William] Butscher and announcing that your boys are wild.[36] I am sorry to hear this, and all I have to say is that they will simply have to get tame again. There are fools and fanatics on our side as well as the other who would sacrifice the ticket and sink the movement to gratify their miserable 2x4 spite and resentment. It has been said that war is hell, and the same is true of the man who is the candidate of such

† Published in Howard H. Quint, *The Forging of American Socialism: Origins of the Modern Movement: The Impact of Socialism on American Thought, 1886–1901* (Columbia, SC: University of South Carolina Press, 1953), 366–7. Not included in J. Robert Constantine (ed.), *The Letters of Eugene V. Debs: Volume 1, 1874–1912.*

dwarfish creatures. You know under what circumstances I accepted the nomination.[37] Besides a thousand other objections I had to it, it knocked me out of at least $2,000 financially, and from that day to this, hell has been popping around my ears in token of grateful appreciation.[38]

I have made up my mind to do as I please, that is to say, as I think right, and if the wild men who nominated me do not like it, all they have to do is nominate somebody else to dance on with hobnail shoes.

I have accepted the ratification of my nomination by the Springfield party. I did it in the interest of the socialist movement, compared with which all parties so far developed in this country amount to less than nothing. Had I done otherwise, I would have been as small and contemptible and as unworthy of the position I occupy as those in the other party our people are making so much fuss about.

* * *

Declination of Nomination for the National Executive Board of the SDP†

August 18, 1900

To the Social Democratic Party.
Comrades:—

I respectfully decline nomination as a member of the National Executive Board.[39] I have served my time in that capacity and now step aside to make room for another. My decision is unalterable, and the secretary [Theodore Debs] will please strike my name from the list of nominees.

In severing my relations with the board, it is due my colleagues to say that during the two years of our incumbency I found them always loyal to the party, steadfast in their devotion to socialism, and true to every obligation, official and personal. Each of them has my thanks, and all of them I hold in affectionate esteem.

---

† Published as "Debs Declines" in *Social Democratic Herald,* vol. 3, no. 9, whole no. 111 (August 18, 1900), 4

The new board will have my unqualified allegiance and support. After the campaign, to which I owe, and shall contribute, my best energies, I shall have time and opportunity to organize and otherwise work in the interest of the party, and this I shall do, although in an unofficial capacity, with all the zeal and ability I can command.

Thanking my comrades for the honor intended, which is appreciated quite as much as if it had been accepted, I remain,

Yours fraternally,
Eugene V. Debs

Wilhelm Liebknecht, the People's Tribune†

August 18, 1900

A titan has fallen. Liebknecht, the scarred warrior of the social revolution, lies pulseless on the field of battle. He fell in full charge, his face to the retreating enemy. For 40 years he fought with dauntless valor, and where the fight was thickest, the plume of Liebknecht, like a banner, waved defiant. Great captain of the revolutionary hosts, his only title was the divine right of genius to lead, and the only arms he bore were truth and justice.

This immortal man was not Germany's alone. He fought for and belonged to all mankind. His name was known and honored in all the zones that belt the globe, and 7 million socialists uncover and unite as one in reverent tribute to his memory.

With Marx, Lassalle, and Engels, he plucked from fate the fadeless laurels of immortality.

> Thou art Freedom's now, and Fame's;
> One of the few, the immortal names
> That were not born to die.[40]

At the bier of Liebknecht, socialism bows and weeps. For her he was bruised by the contumelious stone; for her he languished long in prison cell;

---

† Published in *Social Democratic Herald,* vol. 3, no. 9, whole no. 111 (August 18, 1900), 2.

for her he bore the sacrificial cross.

Bismarck, in the zenith of his autocratic power, could not daunt him. With resolute mien and flashing eye, he stood erect; he dared to challenge the king himself though death had been the penalty.

Intrepid soul, thou coulds't proudly say:

> Out of the night that covers me,
> Black as the Pit from pole to pole,
> I thank whatever gods there be
> For my unconquerable soul.[41]

When the Wilhelms, Bismarcks, and all the titled tyrants of all times have passed to dust, or are remembered only for their crimes, our Liebknecht's name will shine with luster in the firmament of the ages.

Of Wilhelm Liebknecht, too, some Hugo of the future may say, "He disappeared, but left us his soul, the Revolution." And when socialism is triumphant, "I affirm it up there, in the stars, Liebknecht will smile."[42]

The worn and weary children of toil scarce know their benefactor. But their children and their children's children, emancipated by the genius of socialism he so truly typified, will weave garlands for his grave and sing sweet anthems to his memory.

And we who follow him will seize the standard he held aloft unsullied through all the years, until death relaxed his hold, and bear it on and on until it symbolizes humanity disenthralled, the universal commonwealth.

Socialist Sentiment is Spreading: The Program of the Social Democratic Party†

August 23, 1900

In the presidential election of 1892, the socialist candidate received 21,512 votes; in the election of 1896, the vote was increased to 36,275 votes.[43] The following two years witnessed an unprecedented spread of socialist sentiment and, in the congressional and state elections of 1898 the socialist candidates received 91,749 votes, an increase of almost 200 percent, in two years. But it must not be assumed that this vote represented the entire political strength of socialists in the United States. In a number of states, the election laws were such that the socialist ticket could not be placed upon the official ballot, while in many districts the number of socialists was so small and they were so widely scattered that no nominations were made and the socialist vote was not polled.

The figures given are sufficient to indicate that in the United States, as in other countries, international socialism is making tremendous strides, and that its 7 million supporters, spread over all the belts and zones of the globe, and the most active propagandists ever known, will in the next few years be multiplied into controlling majorities in all lands which have modern industry as the basis of their civilization. Socialism being wholly a question of economic development, this will mean the end of the present capitalist competitive system and the introduction of its economic successor, the Cooperative Commonwealth.

The movement is international because it is born of and follows the development of the capitalist system, which in its operation is confined to no country, but by the stimulus of modern agencies of production, exchange, communication, and transportation, has overleaped all boundary lines and made the world the theater of its activities. By this process, all the nations of the earth must finally be drawn into relations of industrial and commercial cooperation as the economic basis of human brotherhood.

This is the goal of modern socialism, and it is this that inspires its disciples with the zeal and ardor of crusaders.

So much has been said and written of socialism by persons who have no

† Published as "The Social Democratic Party" in *The Independent* [New York], vol. 52, whole no. 2699 (August 23, 1900), 2018–21. Reprinted in *Social Democratic Herald*, vol. 3, no. 12, whole no. 114 (September 8, 1900), 1–2.

proper conception of its origin, its philosophy, and its mission, or who, for reasons of their own, have resorted to willful misrepresentation, that it is not strange that a great many people instinctively shrink from the merest mention of it, and look upon those who advocate this perfectly sane and scientific doctrine as the enemies of society, maliciously plotting to overthrow its cherished institutions.

What is socialism? To answer in a single sentence, it means the collective ownership by all the people of all the means of wealth production and distribution. It is purely an economic question; the evolution of industry has developed socialism. Man can only work, produce wealth, with tools. The mere hand tools of former times have become ponderous and very costly machines. These machines, socialists contend, represent progressive social conceptions. These and the factories, mills, and shops in which they are housed, as well as the lands and mines from which the raw materials are drawn, are used in common by the workers, and in their very nature are marked for common ownership and control. Socialism does not propose the collective ownership of property, but of capital; that is to say. the instruments of wealth production, which, in the form of private property, enable a few capitalists to exploit vast numbers of workers, thus creating millionaires and mendicants and inaugurating class rule and all its odious and undemocratic distinctions.

At this point I deem it proper to introduce the platform of the Social Democratic Party, adopted at its recent national convention, held at Indianapolis:

> The Social Democratic Party of America declares that life, liberty, and happiness depend upon equal political and economic rights.
>
> In our economic development, an industrial revolution has taken place, the individual tool of former years having become the social tool of the present. The individual tool was owned by the worker who employed himself and was master of his product. The social tool, the machine, is owned by the capitalist, and the worker is dependent upon him for employment. The capitalist thus becomes the master of the worker and is able to appropriate to himself a large share of the product of his labor.
>
> Capitalism, the private ownership of the means of production, is responsible for the insecurity of subsistence, the poverty, misery, and degradation of the ever-growing majority of our people; but the same economic forces which have produced and now intensify the capitalist system will necessitate the adoption of socialism, the collective ownership of the means of production for the common good and welfare.

The present system of social production and private ownership is rapidly converting society into two antagonistic classes—i.e., the capitalist class and the propertyless class. The middle class, once the most powerful of this great nation, is disappearing in the mill of competition. The issue is now between the two classes first named. Our political liberty is now of little value to the masses unless used to acquire economic liberty.

Independent political action and the trade union movement are the chief emancipating factors of the working class, the one representing its political, the other its economic wing, and both must cooperate to abolish the capitalist system.

Therefore, the Social Democratic Party of America declares its object to be:

1. The organization of the working class into a political party to conquer the public powers now controlled by capitalists.

2. The abolition of wage-slavery by the establishment of a national system of cooperative industry, based upon the social or common ownership of the means of production and distribution, to be administered by society in the common interest of all its members, and the complete emancipation of the socially useful classes from the domination of capitalism.

The working class and all those in sympathy with their historic mission to realize a higher civilization should sever connection with all capitalist and reform parties and unite with the Social Democratic Party of America.

The control of political power by the Social Democratic Party will be tantamount to the abolition of all class rule.

The solidarity of labor connecting the millions of class-conscious fellow workers throughout the civilized world will lead to international socialism, the brotherhood of man.

As steps in that direction, we make the following demands:

1. Revision of our federal constitution in order to remove the obstacles to complete control of government by the people irrespective of sex.

2. The public ownership of all industries controlled by monopolies, trusts, and combines.

3. The public ownership of all railroads, telegraphs, and telephones; all means of transportation, and communication: all waterworks, gas and electric plants, and other public utilities.

4. The public ownership of all gold, silver, copper, lead, iron, coal, and other mines, and all oil and gas wells.

5. The reduction of the hours of labor in proportion to the increasing facilities of production.

6. The inauguration of a system of public works and improvements for the employment of the unemployed, the public credit to be utilized for that purpose.

7. Useful inventions to be free, the inventor to be remunerated by the public.

8. Labor legislation to be national, instead of local, and international when possible.

9. National insurance of working people against accidents, lack of employment, and want in old age.

10. Equal civil and political rights for men and women, and the abolition of all laws discriminating against women.

11. The adoption of the initiative and referendum, proportional representation, and the right of recall of representatives by the voters.

12. Abolition of war and the introduction of international arbitration.

It will be observed that the Social Democratic Party is pledged to equal rights for all without reference to sex, color, or other conditions. Equality of rights and opportunities for all human beings is the vital fundamental principle of socialism. It aims to establish economic equality by making all equal proprietors of the means upon which all depend for employment, and without which there can be no "life, liberty, and pursuit of happiness." This ensures economic freedom for every human being. As no one would have private property in that upon which another depended for employment, industrial mastery and slavery would disappear together, and competition for profit would give way to cooperation for use.

The rapidly changing economic conditions are paving the way for the transition from competitive capitalism to cooperative socialism. Socialists are simply indicating the trend of the evolution and seeking to prepare the way for its orderly reception. The coming of socialism is with them not a debatable question. That is not a matter of doubt or conjecture, but of scientific calculation.

The evolution of the social organism is a fact in nature. In the ceaseless process, one state of society follows another in the sequence of succession. Capitalism, the present system, was warmed into life in the womb of feudalism and sprang from that medieval system. Within the span of two centuries, this system has practically reached the climax of its development, and the marvelous material progress of that period exceeds the achievements of all the centuries since the slaves of Pharaoh built the pyramids.

The rapid centralization of capital and the extensive cooperation of labor mark the high state of our economic development. Individual initiative and competitive effort are becoming less and less possible. The day of small production has passed, never to return. Notwithstanding the outcry, trusts and department stores, these great modern agencies, increase in number and power. They are the inevitable outgrowth of the competitive system. The efforts of small capitalists to destroy trusts will prove as fruitless as the efforts of workingmen to destroy labor-saving machines when first introduced in the last century.

Socialists take the ground that the trust in itself is not an evil, that the evil lies wholly in the private ownership and its operation for private profit. The remedy is collective ownership, and they propose to transfer all such agencies from private hands to the collectivity, to be managed and operated for the good of all.

Ignoring all such alleged issues as "expansion," "imperialism," "free silver," "gold standard," "protection," "free trade," etc., the Social Democratic Party declares that economic freedom is the supreme question that confronts the people. A century and a quarter ago the revolution settled the question of political equality in the United States. But since then an industrial revolution has taken place, and political equality exists in name only, while the great mass struggle in economic servitude. The working class are dependent upon the capitalist class, who own the machines and other means of production; and the latter class, by virtue of their economic mastery, are the ruling class of the nation, and it is idle under such conditions to claim that men are equal and that all are sovereign citizens. No man is free in any just sense who has to rely upon the arbitrary will of another for the opportunity to work. Such a man works, and therefore lives, by permission, and this is the economic relation of the working class to the capitalist class in the present system.

In the last century, millions of workers were exploited of the fruit of their labor under the institution of chattel slavery. Work being done by hand, ownership of the slave was a condition necessary to his exploitation. But chattel slavery disappeared before the march of industrial evolution, and today would be an economic impossibility. It is no longer necessary to own the body of the workingman in order to appropriate the fruit of his labor; it is only necessary to own the tool with which he works, and without which he is helpless. This tool, in its modem form, is a vast machine which the worker cannot afford to buy, and against which he cannot compete with his bare hands, and in the very nature of the situation, he is at the mercy of the owner of the machine, his employment is precarious, and his very life is suspended by a slender thread.

Then, again, the factory and mine are operated for profit only, and the owner can, and often does, close it down at will, throwing hundreds, perhaps thousands, out of employment who, with their families, are as helpless as if in the desert wastes of Sahara. The recent shutdown of the American Wire and Steel trust in the interest of stock jobbery presented a startling object lesson of economic dependence of the working class.

The few who own the machines do not use them. The many who use them do not own them. The few who own them are enabled to exploit the many who use them; hence a few millionaires and many mendicants, extreme opulence and abject poverty, princely palaces and hideous huts, riotous extravagance and haggard want, constituting social scenes sickening to contemplate, and in the presence of which the master hand of Hugo or Dickens is palsied and has no mission.

The Social Democratic Party is organizing in every village and hamlet, every town and city of every state and territory of the union. It has held its national convention, its candidates are in the field, and it is appealing to the American people. It will neither fuse nor compromise. It proposes to press forward, step by step, until it conquers the political power and secures control of government. This will mark the end of the capitalist system. The factories and mills and mines, the railroads and telegraph and telephone, and all other means of production and distribution will be transferred to the people in their collective capacity, industry will be operated cooperatively, and every human being will have the "inalienable right" to work and to enjoy the fruit of his labor. The hours of labor will be reduced according to the progress of invention. Rent, interest, and profit will be no more. The sordid spirit of commercial conquest will be dead. War and its ravages will pass into history. Economic equality will have triumphed, labor will stand forth emancipated, and the sons and daughters of men will glorify the triumphs of social democracy.

Outlook for Socialism in the United States[†]

September 1900

The sun of the passing century is setting upon scenes of extraordinary activity in almost every part of our capitalistic old planet. Wars and rumors of wars are of universal prevalence. In the Philippines, our soldiers are civilizing and Christianizing the natives in the latest and most approved styles of the art, and at prices ($13 per month) which commend the blessing to the prayerful consideration of the lowly and oppressed everywhere.

In South Africa, the British legions are overwhelming the Boers with volleys of benedictions inspired by the same beautiful philanthropy in the name of the meek and lowly Nazarene; while in China the heathen hordes, fanned into frenzy by the sordid spirit of modern commercial conquest, are presenting to the world a carnival of crime almost equaling the "refined" exhibitions of the world's "civilized" nations.

And through all the flame and furor of the fray can be heard the savage snarlings of the Christian "dogs of war" as they fiercely glare about them, and with jealous fury threaten to fly at one another's throats to settle the question of supremacy and the spoil and plunder of conquest.

The picture, lurid as a "chamber of horrors," becomes complete in its gruesome ghastliness when robed ministers of Christ solemnly declare that it is all for the glory of God and the advancement of Christian civilization.

This, then, is the closing scene of the century as the curtain slowly descends upon the bloodstained stage—the central figure, the pious Wilhelm, Germany's sceptered savage, issuing his imperial "spare none" decree in the sangfroid of an Apache chief—a fitting climax to the rapacious regime of the capitalist system. Cheerless indeed would be the contemplation of such sanguinary scenes were the light of socialism not breaking upon mankind. The skies of the East are even now aglow with the dawn; its coming is heralded by the dispelling of shadows, of darkness and gloom. From the first tremulous scintillation that gilds the horizon to the sublime march to meridian splendor, the light increases till in mighty flood it pours upon the world.

From out of the midnight of superstition, ignorance, and slavery the

† Published in *International Socialist Review* [Chicago], vol. 1, no. 3 (September 1900), 129–35.

disenthralling, emancipating sun is rising. I am not gifted with prophetic vision, and yet I see the shadows vanishing. I behold near and far prostrate men lifting their bowed forms from the dust. I see thrones in the grasp of decay; despots relaxing their hold upon scepters, and shackles falling, not only from the limbs but from the souls of men.

It is therefore with pleasure that I respond to the invitation of the editor of the *International Socialist Review* to present my views upon the "Outlook for Socialism in the United States."[44] Socialists generally will agree that the past year has been marked with a propaganda of unprecedented activity and that the sentiment of the American people in respect to socialism has undergone a most remarkable change. It would be difficult to imagine a more ignorant, bitter, and unreasoning prejudice than that of the American people against socialism during the early years of its introduction by the propagandists from the other side. I never think of these despised and persecuted "foreign invaders" without a feeling of profound obligation, akin to reverence, for their noble work in laying the foundations deep and strong, under the most trying conditions, of the American movement. The ignorant mass, wholly incapable of grasping their splendid teachings or appreciating their lofty motives, reviled against them. The press inoculated the public sentiment with intolerance and malice which not infrequently found expression through the policeman's club when a few of the pioneers gathered to engraft the class-conscious doctrine upon their inhospitable "freeborn" American fellow citizens. Socialism was cunningly associated with "anarchy and bloodshed" and denounced as a "foul foreign importation" to pollute the fair, free soil of America, and every outrage to which the early agitators were subjected won the plaudits of the people. But they persevered in their task; they could not be silenced or suppressed. Slowly they increased in number and gradually the movement began to take root and spread over the country. The industrial conditions consequent upon the development of capitalist production were now making themselves felt, and socialism became a fixed and increasing factor in the economic and political affairs of the nation.

The same difficulties which other countries had experienced in the process of party organization have attended the development of the movement here, but these differences, which relate mainly to tactics and methods of propaganda, are bound to disappear as the friction of the jarring factions smoothens out the rough edges and adjusts them to a concrete body—a powerful section in the great international army of militant socialism.

In the general elections of 1898, upwards of 91,000 votes were cast for the socialist candidates in the United States, an increase in this "off year" of almost

200 percent over the general elections of two years previous, the presidential year of 1896. Since the congressional elections of 1898, and more particularly since the municipal and state elections following, which resulted in such signal victories in Massachusetts, two members of the legislature and a mayor, the first in America, being elected by decided majorities—since then, socialism has made rapid strides in all directions, and the old politicians no longer reckon it as a negative quantity in making their forecasts and calculating their pluralities and majorities.

The subject has passed entirely beyond the domain of sneer and ridicule and now commands serious treatment. Of course it is violently denounced by the capitalist press and by all the brood of subsidized contributors to magazine literature, but this only confirms the view that the advance of socialism is very properly recognized by the capitalist class as the one cloud upon the horizon which portends an end to the system in which they have waxed fat, insolent, and despotic through the exploitation of their countless wage-working slaves.

In school and college and church, in clubs and public halls everywhere, socialism is the central theme of discussion, and its advocates, inspired by its noble principles, are to be found here, there, and in all places ready to give or accept challenge to battle. In the cities, the corner meetings are popular and effective. But rarely is such a gathering now molested by the "authorities," and then only where they have just been inaugurated. They are too numerously attended by serious, intelligent, and self-reliant men and women to invite interference.

Agitation is followed by organization, and the increase of branches, sections, and clubs goes forward with extraordinary activity in every part of the land.

In New England, the agitation has resulted in quite a general organization among the states, with Massachusetts in the lead; and the indications are that, with the vigorous prosecution of the campaign already inaugurated, a tremendous increase in the vote will be polled in the approaching national elections. New York and Pennsylvania will show surprising socialist returns, while Ohio, Michigan, Indiana, Illinois, Missouri, and Kentucky will all round up with a large vote. Wisconsin has already a great vote to her credit and will increase it largely this year. In the West and Northwest, Kansas, Iowa, and Minnesota will forge to the front, and so also will Nebraska, the Dakotas, Montana, Oregon, Washington, Idaho, and Colorado. California is expected to show an immense increase, and the returns from there will not disappoint the most sanguine. In the Southwest, Texas is making a stirring campaign, and several papers, heretofore Populist, will support our candidates and swell the Socialist vote, which will be an eye-opener when announced.

On the whole, the situation could scarcely be more favorable, and the final returns will more than justify our sanguine expectations.

It must not be overlooked, however, when calculations are made, that this is a presidential year and that the general results will not be so favorable as if the elections were in an "off year." Both the Republican and Democratic parties will, as usual, strain every nerve to whip the "voting kings" into line, and every conceivable influence will be exerted to that end. These vast machines operate with marvelous precision, and the wheels are already in motion. Corruption funds, national, state, and municipal, will flow out like lava tides; promises will be as plentiful as autumn leaves; from ten thousand platforms, the Columbian orator will agitate the atmosphere, while brass bands, torchlight processions, glittering uniforms and free whiskey, dispensed by the "ward-heeler," will lend their combined influence to steer the "patriots" to the capitalist chute that empties into the ballot box.

The campaign this year will be unusually spectacular. The Republican Party "points with pride" to the "prosperity" of the country, the beneficent results of the "gold standard" and the "war record" of the administration. The Democratic Party declares that "imperialism" is the "paramount" issue and that the country is certain to go to the "demnition bowwows"[45] if Democratic officeholders are not elected instead of the Republicans. The Democratic slogan is "The Republic vs. the Empire," accompanied in a very minor key by 16 to 1[46] and "direct legislation where practical."

Both these capitalist parties are fiercely opposed to trusts, though what they propose to do with them is not of sufficient importance to require even a hint in their platforms.

Needless is it for me to say to the thinking workingman that he has no choice between these two capitalist parties, that they are both pledged to the same system and that whether the one or the other succeeds, he will still remain the wage-working slave he is today.

What but meaningless phrases are "imperialism," "expansion," "free silver," "gold standard," etc., to the wageworker? The large capitalists represented by Mr. McKinley and the small capitalists represented by Mr. Bryan are interested in these "issues," but they do not concern the working class. What the workingmen of the country are profoundly interested in is the private ownership of the means of production and distribution, the enslaving and degrading wage system in which they toil for a pittance at the pleasure of their masters and are bludgeoned, jailed, or shot when they protest—this is the central, controlling, vital issue of the hour, and neither of the old party platforms has a word or even a hint about it.

As a rule, large capitalists are Republicans and small capitalists are Democrats, but workingmen must remember that they are all capitalists and that the many small ones, like the fewer large ones, are all politically supporting their class interests, and this is always and everywhere the capitalist class.

Whether the means of production, that is to say, the land, mines, factories, machinery, etc., are owned by a few large Republican capitalists, who organize a trust, or whether they be owned by a lot of small Democratic capitalists, who are opposed to the trust, is all the same to the working class. Let the capitalists, large and small, fight this out among themselves.

The working class must get rid of the whole brood of masters and exploiters and put themselves in possession and control of the means of production, that they may have steady employment without consulting a capitalist employer, large or small, and that they may get the wealth their labor produces, every bit of it, and enjoy with their families the fruits of their industry in comfortable and happy homes, abundant and wholesome food, proper clothing, and all other things necessary to "life, liberty, and the pursuit of happiness." It is therefore a question, not of "reform," the mask of fraud, but of revolution. The capitalist system must be overthrown, class rule abolished, and wage-slavery supplanted by cooperative industry.

We hear it frequently urged that the Democratic Party is the "poor man's party," "the friend of labor." There is but one way to relieve poverty and to free labor, and that is by making common property of the tools of labor.

Is the Democratic Party, which we are assured has "strong socialistic tendencies," in favor of collective ownership of the means of production? Is it opposed to the wage system, from which flows in a ceaseless stream the poverty, misery, and wretchedness of the children of toil? If the Democratic Party is the "friend of labor" any more than the Republican Party, why is its platform dumb in the presence of Coeur d'Alene?[47] It knows the truth about these shocking outrages—crimes upon workingmen, their wives and children, which would blacken the pages of Siberia—why does it not speak out?

What has the Democratic Party to say about the "property and educational qualification" in North Carolina and Louisiana, and the proposed general disfranchisement of the Negro race in the Southern states?

The differences between the Republican and Democratic parties involve no issue, no principle in which the working class have any interest, and whether the spoils be distributed by Hanna and Platt,[48] or by Croker and Tammany Hall[49] is all the same to them.

Between these parties, socialists have no choice, no preference. They are one in their opposition to socialism, that is to say, the emancipation of the working class from wage-slavery, and every workingman who has intelligence enough to understand the interest of his class and the nature of the struggle in which it is involved will once and for all time sever his relations with them both; and, recognizing the class struggle which is being waged between producing workers and non-producing capitalists, cast his lot with the class-conscious, revolutionary, socialist party, which is pledged to abolish the capitalist system, class rule, and wage-slavery—a party which does not compromise or fuse, but, preserving inviolate the principles which quickened it into life and now give it vitality and force, moves forward with dauntless determination to the goal of economic freedom.

The political trend is steadily toward socialism. The old parties are held together only by the cohesive power of spoils, and in spite of this they are steadily disintegrating. Again and again, they have been tried with the same results, and thousands upon thousands, awake to their duplicity, are deserting them and turning toward socialism as the only refuge and security. Republicans, Democrats, Populists, Prohibitionists, Single-Taxers are having their eyes opened to the true nature of the struggle, and they are beginning to

> Come as the winds come, when
> Forests are rended;
> Come as the waves come, when
> Navies are stranded.[50]

For a time, the Populist Party[51] had a mission, but it is practically ended. The Democratic Party has "fused" it out of existence. The "middle of the road" element will be sorely disappointed when the votes are counted, and they will probably never figure in another national campaign.[52] Not many of them will go back to the old parties. Many of them have already come to socialism, and the rest are sure to follow.

There is no longer any room for a Populist Party, and progressive populists realize it, and hence the "strongholds" of populism are becoming the "hotbeds" of socialism.

It is simply a question of capitalism or socialism, of despotism or democracy, and they who are not wholly with us are wholly against us.

Another source of strength to socialism, steadily increasing, is the trade union movement. The spread of socialist doctrine among the labor organizations of the country during the past year exceeds the most extravagant estimates. No one has had better opportunities than the writer to note the transition to socialism among trade unionists, and the approaching election will abundantly verify it.

Promising, indeed, is the outlook for socialism in the United States. The very contemplation of the prospect is a wellspring of inspiration.

Oh, that all the working class could and would use their eyes and see; their ears and hear; their brains and think. How soon this earth could be transformed and by the alchemy of social order made to blossom with beauty and joy.

No sane man can be satisfied with the present system. If a poor man is happy, said Victor Hugo, "he is the pickpocket of happiness. Only the rich and noble are happy by right. The rich man is he who, being young, has the rights of old age; being old, the lucky chances of youth; vicious, the respect of good people; a coward, the command of the stouthearted; doing nothing, the fruits of labor."[53]

The great Frenchman also propounded this interrogatory which every workingman will do well to contemplate: "Can you fancy a city directed by the men who built it?"

With pride and joy, we watch each advancing step of our comrades in socialism in all other lands. Our hearts are with them in their varying fortunes as the battle proceeds, and we applaud each telling blow delivered and cheer each victory achieved.

The wire has just brought the tidings of Liebknecht's death. The hearts of American socialists will be touched and shocked by the calamity. The brave old warrior succumbed at last, but not until he heard the tramp of international socialism, for which he labored with all his loving, loyal heart; not until he saw the thrones of Europe, one by one, begin to totter, not until he had achieved a glorious immortality.

The Essence of Social Democracy†

September 3, 1900

Terre Haute, Ind., September 3, 1900

The economic basis of society is changing more rapidly today than ever before in human history, and as the character of society and all social institutions change unerringly to correspond to their economic formation, this is preeminently an age of social evolution.

In swift succession, change follows upon change in the mode of production and distribution. Cheaper and cheaper production, more rapid and still more rapid methods of communication and transportation are demanded to supply the world's elusive and shifting markets.

Everything must be done on a gigantic scale to be done successfully, or even at all, for in the operation of the remorseless law of competition the weak, the aged, infirm, and all who lack the latest modern equipment are driven from the arena by the more powerful rivals with as little compunction as a champion of the prize ring experiences when he sees his "opening" and administers the "knockout" blow which determines the fate of his ill-starred competitor.

At this very hour—believed by many to mark an era of unparalleled prosperity—commercial collapses are occurring at the rate of a thousand or more a month, 40 for each business day in the round year, in the United States.

Concentration, swift and irresistible, is a part—an inevitable part—of the economic development. The individual businessman has long since been supplanted by the firm, the firm by the company, the company by the still more powerful corporation, and latterly the corporation has been swallowed up by the trust. And this concentration not only continues in spite of threat and protest, uttered by the thousands ruined or menaced by it, but is steadily accelerated as each revolution increases the momentum of a train rushing downward on a heavy grade.

† Published as "Eugene V. Debs Predicts a Social Revolution" in *St. Louis Chronicle,* September 3, 1900, unspecified page. Copy preserved on *Papers of Eugene V. Debs* microfilm edition, reel 9.

Victims More Numerous

McKinley thinks it isn't right, and Bryan is certain it ought to be stopped.

Why? Because evolution is a crime? No; because the victims are more numerous than the beneficiaries, and they have votes.

This accounts for the opposition (?) of McKinley to the trusts; likewise that of Croker. The rapidly declining middle class is still powerful; not nearly so large as the working class, but very much larger than the big capitalist class, and hence a potential factor in the control of elections.

Totally oblivious, seemingly, of the plain and unmistakable trend of the economic transformation in progress, the middle class is easily made victim of the illusion that, Joshua-like, the politicians can halt not only the sun but make the whole world stand still.[54]

Concentration and cooperation are supplanting diffusion and competition. Scattered small property is being absorbed and concentrated in colossal enterprises. Every failure, every bankruptcy hastens the end. The propertyless class grows large in inverse ratio.

Here are some approximate estimates: Of our total population, 6 percent are in the capitalist class, 19 percent are in the middle class, and 75 percent are in the working class. Of our nation's wealth, 82 percent is owned by the capitalist class, 15 percent by the middle class, and 3 percent by the working class.

The day of small production and competition is passing, and the state of society it developed is passing with it.

The Era of Socialism

Socialism, the new (and destined to be the controlling) force in the social and economic progress of mankind, is evolving steadily from the existing capitalist system, which has reached the climax of its development and bears increasing signs of decline and decay.

One state of society succeeds another in the ceaseless process of evolution, by virtue of which mankind reaches higher elevations in the scale of being, and each period is so distinctive, so clearly marked that it is readily distinguishable from all others which preceded or succeeded it.

The present capitalist system was quickened into life in the womb of feudalism and sprang from that system. In its early stages, it was received with ridicule and contempt, and the incipient capitalist was treated with the same lofty scorn by the feudal baron and subjected to the same social ostracism that the modern capitalist has decreed for the socialist "agitator."

The progenitor of the full-blown capitalist was the socialist of his day and generation. Capitalism has had its day; it has served its time, run its course, fulfilled its mission, and must now give way, by the inexorable law of economic evolution, to its successor, which already appears upon the arena, and those with ears attuned can hear the lusty urchin shouting with imperious authority his decrees to clear the road for socialism, which henceforward has the right of way on the track of the centuries.

Social democracy is revolutionary in character and international in scope. The machine has been the germ of the transformation which is annihilating space and drawing all the nations of the earth into the socialist bands of harmonious cooperation. The struggle for the world's markets will determine the period of transition.

Death Rattle of Capitalism

The massacre in the Philippines, the conquest in South Africa, the invasion of China are the death rattles in the throat of capitalism.

These civilized crimes are, at bottom, economic and not political issues.

The fierce international struggle for control of the world's markets makes wars of conquest inevitable. The large capitalist class have the surplus products they must get rid of, or their fate is sealed. These are the "patriots" who wage wars for "humanity" and "civilization."

The small capitalist class have no surplus products to dispose of, and they are fiercely opposed to these wars on "high moral grounds."

As a matter of history and of fact, the ethical follows the economic development, and is fashioned and molded by it.

Chattel slavery only became immoral by the popular verdict when it became economically impossible. It can be easily demonstrated that chattel slavery could not exist in highly developed capitalist society.

Capitalism is rushing to its doom. Every new machine abridges its reign, every competitor crusted limits its regime, and every workingman displaced hastens its downfall.

As already intimated, the machine is the vital force in the transformation of the social organism. The machine increases production, displaces workers, intensifies competition, and lowers wages. Production increases, while consumption, determined by wages, diminishes. There is bound to be a surplus.

One nation after another is becoming a manufacturing nation. The customers of yesterday are the competitors of today. How long will it be before the crisis, international in scope, is reached?

Social democracy solves the problem. There is no escape from it. Retarded it may be, and is, by ignorance and prejudice, but its triumphant consummation cannot be prevented. All the laws of social and economic evolution are pledged to its supremacy, and the gates of hell cannot prevail against it.

Social democracy is the only democracy. Our politics are not chainless so long as industry is in fetters.

To Disenthrall Industry

Politics in our country have been nominally democratized, but until industry is disenthralled, there can be no true freedom in the land.

One man used to manage our politics. This was the king, and he declared by all that was holy that the people were not fit to govern themselves. But they finally concluded otherwise, overthrew the king, and declared the republic. Since then the people themselves have managed their politics, and, although they may not have made a glittering success of it, they will never go back to king rule. Just so with our industrial system. It must be rescued from one-man rule, notwithstanding the ancient blasphemy that the people are not fit to manage their own affairs.

If the people are fit for political equality, why not for economic equality?

Politics concerns the liberty of the citizen—industry involves his very life. Without employment he cannot live, and the individual who controls that is his king.

Social democracy proposes the collective ownership of all the means of production and distribution, the operation of industry in the interest of the whole people, the utilization of every machine and every worker in reducing the hours of daily labor, the equality of all races and sexes in respect to rights and opportunities, the elimination of rent, interest, and profit, the full product of labor to the producer, the abolition of poverty, the end of war, the economic freedom of every human being—and thus emancipated from the cruel and degrading thralldom of the capitalist system, the twentieth century will be, as Victor Hugo prophesied, "the century of humanity."

Seven million men and women are marching proudly beneath the banner of international socialism. Almost 100,000 voters were registered for socialism in the United States in 1898.

What shall be the poll in 1900? Wait and watch!

Working Together in Unison: An Open Letter to J. B. Smiley of Chicago†

September 17, 1900

Terre Haute, Ind., September 17, 1900

J. B. Smiley, Esq.[55]
Chicago, Ill.

My Dear Comrade:—

Your favor of the 14th advising me of the demonstration to be held at Chicago on the 29th inst. [September 29, 1900] has been received, and it gives me pleasure to say that I shall be in attendance as requested by the committee.[56]

I am gratified to note that the socialists of Illinois are working together in unison and harmony, and I do not doubt that the results in November will vindicate the wisdom and fealty to wisdom of our comrades in deciding upon a policy of united action.

Wishing your committee all possible success in the prosecution of its arduous labors, I remain

Yours fraternally,
E. V. Debs

---

† Published as "E.V. Debs Accepts" in *Workers' Call* [Chicago], vol. 2, whole no. 81 (September 22, 1900), 2.

Warning Notice†

September 21, 1900

Terre Haute, Ind., September 21, 1900

To our Comrades and Friends:—

The persistence with which the report is circulated that I have resigned, or intend to resign, in favor of the Democratic candidate,[57] impels me to issue this denial of the falsehood originated by the capitalist press to deceive and mislead our friends and supporters.

Comrade Harriman and I have been nominated as candidates for vice-president and president, respectively, of the Social Democratic Party, and we shall stand as candidates to be voted for on election day, all reports and rumors to the contrary notwithstanding.

It is not at all improbable that this report may be sprung afresh on the very eve of the election, too late to be met and contradicted by the weekly socialist press of the country, and for this reason I take the liberty to request all socialist papers, and any other that may be friendly to our party, to publish this statement and keep it standing in the last three or four issues preceding the election.

To resign at such a time would be rank betrayal, of which no honorable man would be guilty; but if from any inconceivable reason such a step became necessary, I would not under any possible circumstances resign in favor of the Republican or Democratic Party. They are alike the representatives of the capitalist system; they are one in the support of private property in the means of production; they are agreed as to wage-slavery; they do not differ in their hostility to socialism, and I would as readily think of resigning in favor of one as the other of these parties.

Our party comrades understand this and cannot be misled; but there is danger that some of our friends may be deceived, and hence this warning note.

The Republican papers declare that socialists will vote for Bryan, while the Democratic press charges that socialists are in the pay of Mark Hanna. These old campaign liars know better, but they understand each other. This fall they

---

† Published in *Social Democratic Herald,* vol. 3, no. 15, whole no. 117 (September 29, 1900), 1.

will be made to realize that, with all the corruption funds at their command, there is no private property in socialists.

Others may prefer capitalism and slavery. We stand unyielding as a wall of granite for *socialism and freedom.*

Eugene V. Debs

[Friendly papers please copy.]

The Democratic Party Will Not Destroy Us: An Open Letter to Lewis A. Russell of Cleveland†

September 29, 1900

My Dear Mr. Russell:—

The action of Mayor [Samuel M.] Jones[58] in voting for capitalism, while avowing himself a socialist, will, in my judgment, end his political career. I have not time to discuss the matter further than to say that Mr. Jones has made a mistake, and, unless I am wholly in error about its consequences, he will never again be elected to public office.[59] This may be in accordance with his desire, and, if so, his action in supporting a capitalist party will serve the purpose intended.

As for the Democratic Party as such, I have no faith in it, nor have I any use for it. It professes to oppose private monopoly, but does it suggest public monopoly? It declares that it will break up the trusts, but it knows such a proposition is idiotic, to put it mildly.

All the old bloated leaders that were supposed to have been kicked out in 1896 are coming back, one by one. Cleveland will probably be the next to declare for the Democratic Party to preserve the Republic (?), as against the empire. Perhaps the kind of a republic Cleveland, Croker, Olney, Whitney,[60] Gorman,[61] Steunenberg,[62] Van Wyck,[63] Belmont,[64] et al., believe in may suit you, but it will not suit me. We have an industrial empire here, and whether

---

† Published as "Debs on Bryanism" in *Social Democratic Herald,* vol. 3, no. 15, whole no. 117 (September 29, 1900), 2.

McKinley or Bryan is elected will not alter the situation, for the means of production will still be private property, and the miners of Pennsylvania and the workers generally will still be slaves.

I am a socialist, and my face is set uncompromisingly against capitalism. You say that I should be practical. I am intensely so, and that is the trouble.

Let me remind you that four years ago, just after the election, and just after I had made almost 100 speeches for Bryan and the Democratic Party, the leaders of the party met at Chicago and solemnly declared through the press that such socialists and anarchists as Debs (and others that were named), were responsible for the defeat of the party, and must be gotten rid of, as they had driven out the reputable elements.

Please bear this in mind, Mr. Russell: the Democratic party has chloroformed the Greenback Party, the Union Labor Party, and the Populist Party, but I will guarantee that it will not deceive and destroy the Social Democratic Party.

I have not the least fear of an empire, for socialism is coming. I have not one moment to waste on the miserable makeshifts under which the millions are groaning. The total abolition of the capitalistic system is our uncompromising demand, and with that as our controlling purpose, we are marching direct as a rifle ball to the goal of emancipation. That march may be slow, but it is sure and free from pitfalls.

Eugene V. Debs

Competition vs. Cooperation: Speech at Central Music Hall, Chicago†

September 29, 1900

Ladies and Gentlemen:—

No words of mine can possibly express my appreciation of this beautiful testimonial of the esteem and love of my old comrades, the members of the

† Published as part of "National Campaign Opened," *Social Democratic Herald,* vol. 3, no. 16, whole no. 118 (October 6, 1900), 1–2. Reprinted as "Competition vs. Cooperation" in *Appeal to Reason,* whole no. 254 (October 13, 1900), 3.

American Railway Union.[65] I can only say that, like the rosebud under the influence of sunshine and shower, my heart opens to receive their benediction.

The only vital issue in the present campaign springs from the private ownership of the means of production, and it involves the whole question of political equality, economic freedom, and social progress. This fundamental issue has been studiously ignored by both the Republican and Democratic parties; it has been clearly stated and squarely met by the Social Democratic Party. The alleged issues of the old parties are well rooted in the existing economic system, which system they are pledged to preserve and perpetuate and which the Social Democratic Party is pledged to abolish.

The contest today is for the control of government by three separate classes, with conflicting interests, into which modern society has been divided in the development of the competitive system. The capitalist class is represented by the Republican Party; the middle class is represented by the Democratic Party; the working class is represented by the Social Democratic Party. Each of these parties is committed to the economic interests of the class it represents.

The Republican platform is a self-congratulation of the dominant capitalist class. "Prosperity galore, give us four years more." The Democratic platform is the wail and cry of the perishing middle class; calamity without end. The Social Democratic platform is an indictment of the capitalist system; it is the call to class consciousness and political action of the exploited working class; and it is a ringing declaration in favor of collective ownership of all the means of production and distribution, as the clarion voice of economic freedom.

Parties, like individuals, act from motives of self-interest. The platform of a party is simply the political expression of the economic interests of the class it represents. The Democratic Party differs from the Republican Party as the small capitalist differs from the large capitalist; it is a difference in degree only. The Socialist Party differs from them both as the exploited wageworker differs from his exploiter; the difference here is not in degree but in kind. The Republican Party is in favor of expansion, the acquisition of foreign territory; a colonial policy. Why? Senator Beveridge says, "because we are the trustees of Jehovah."[66] But Senator Depew,[67] who is a man somewhat older, may be permitted to answer. Mr. Depew says:

> The markets for the products of our farms and factories accessible by the Atlantic Ocean will soon be filled, but across the Pacific are numberless opportunities. Within a distance from Manila not much greater than Havana is from New York, live 900 million people, purchasing now annually

> from all nations of the things which they produce to the sum of $1 billion, of which we furnish 5 percent; that 5 percent should be 50 percent.

The getting of the 45 percent constitutes "The White Man's Burden." Mr. Depew also says:

> What is the tendency of the future? Why this war in South Africa? Why this hammering at the gates of Peking? Why this marching of troops from Asia to Africa? Why? It is because the surplus production of civilized countries of modern times is greater than civilization can consume; it is because this overproduction comes back to stagnation and poverty. The American people produce $2 billion more than they can consume.

The Democratic Party is flatly opposed to this policy; it denounces it as imperialism and declares that is the paramount issue of the campaign. The difference between these two capitalist parties upon so-called paramount issues is so clear as to be self-evident. The small capitalists, represented by the Democratic Party, lack the modern economic equipment necessary in the struggle for the control of foreign markets. They have none of the surplus products which must be disposed of to avoid stagnation. Upon the other hand, the expanding markets for which the large capitalists are struggling will extend their lease of power and greatly augment it. The vast foreign trade will develop their resources, increase their economic power, and enable them the more easily to crush out their small competitors in the middle class. This is the bone of contention between the two capitalist parties, and what is called the burning issue of the campaign.

In the Republican convention, the national convention that was held in the city of Philadelphia [June 19–21, 1900], a most remarkable address was delivered by Senator Wolcott,[68] the temporary chairman. Among other things, this gentleman, eminent in the council of that party, said: "There is not an idle mill in the country today." This, in the face of the fact that at that very time there were scores of idle mills in the country, and multiplied thousands of working men seeking in vain for employment. It is my judgment that the man who makes such a statement as this in the face of existing facts ought to be sentenced to serve a term in the anthracite coal region.

He furthermore says: "There is no man who labors with his hands in all our broad domain who cannot find work, and the scale of wages was never so high in the history of our country." Another absolute falsehood. The Republican Party touches this economic question at a vital point, but as you will observe, does not attempt to grapple with it. In their platform, we find this statement: "We recognize the necessity and propriety of the honest cooperation of capital to meet new business conditions, and especially to extend our rapidly increasing foreign trade, but we condemn all conspiracies and combinations intended to restrict business, to create monopolies, to limit production, or to control prices, and favor such legislation as will effectively restrain and prevent all such abuses." If the Republican Party favors legislation restricting such abuses, why has it not enacted such legislation when it has been in absolute control of every department of the government during the past three years? "Wages in every department of labor have been maintained at high rates, higher than before."

In Mr. McKinley's letter of acceptance, we find this statement: "Prosperity abound everywhere throughout the Republic." The worst that can be said about the president is that he has been absolutely true to the party that elected him. He says:

> Combinations of capital which control the market in commodities necessary to the general use of the people by suppressing natural and ordinary competition, thus enhancing prices to the general consumer, are obnoxious to the common law and the public welfare. They are dangerous conspiracies against the public good, and ought to be made the subject of prohibitory or penal legislation. Publicity will be a helpful influence to check this evil.
>
> Honest cooperation of capital is necessary to meet new business conditions and extend our rapidly increasing foreign trade, but conspiracies and combinations intended to restrict business, create monopolies, and control classes, should be effectively restrained.

Just where the line is drawn between honest combinations and vicious combinations he does not attempt to say. All combinations and monopolies privately owned and controlled by the people, in the interests of the people, are good combinations.

We find by an examination of the Democratic platform that substantially the same statements are made upon this question: "Private monopolies are indefensible and intolerable. They destroy competition." Observe that both the Republican Party and the Democratic Party are in favor of competition, the existing system. They condemn its tendencies, its fraud, but they still favor the system itself.

> They destroy competition, control the price of all material and of the finished product, thus robbing both the purchaser and consumer, they lessen the employment of labor, arbitrarily fix the terms and conditions thereof, and deprive individual energy and small capital of their opportunity for

> betterment. They are the most efficient agent yet devised for appropriating the fruits of industry to the benefit of the few at the expense of the many. They are fostered by Republican laws and they are protected by the Republican administration in return for campaign subscriptions and political support. Corporations should be protected in all their rights, and their legitimate interests should be respected.

Corporations are organized purely for private profit; the rights of the corporations to exploit the working class and exact tribute from the people are to be respected, according to the Democratic platform.

In Mr. Bryan's letter of acceptance, it is stated that "private monopoly is an outlaw," and private monopoly is built absolutely on private ownership. If Mr. Bryan is opposed to private monopoly, why doesn't he propose a public monopoly in its place? A public monopoly, built upon collective ownership, which converts a curse into a blessing to society. He says: "I shall recommend such legislation as may be necessary to dissolve every private monopoly which does business outside the state of its origin." He might as well attempt by legislation to prevent a river flowing outside the country in which it has its source. "The Democratic Party does not seek to embarrass capitalists engaged in a legitimate business, but it does protest against capitalists entering politics and attempting to assume control of the instrumentalities of government."

Now, my friends, we observe after examining both these platforms that both the Republican and Democratic parties are in favor of the private ownership of the means of production and distribution. They are in favor of the existing wage system. There is absolutely no difference between them. Upon the other hand, the Social Democratic Party, standing upon a platform declaring in favor of collective ownership of the means of production, declares to the world that there is no other solution of this economic problem.

There is an economic revolution in this and other countries in which modern industry has been developed in the past century. We have been so completely engaged in competitive labor that we are utterly oblivious of the fact. A century ago, work was done by hand very largely, or with simple primitive tools. How to make a living was an easy question. A boy learned a trade, served his apprenticeship, and the skill inherent in the trade secured steady employment for him at fair wages, by virtue of which he could provide for his family, educate his children, and discharge the duties of good citizenship. In that day, the workingman owned and controlled the tools with which he worked and was virtually his own employer. Not only this, he was the master of what his labor produced. It was a very slow age, meager of results; it required 10 to 16 hours daily labor to enable the workingman to supply his material wants. It was then the machine emanated from the brain of labor; it was designed to aid the laboring man, so that he could provide for his social, moral, and intellectual improvement.

At this point an industrial revolution began. The machine, the new tool of production, passed from the control of the workingman who used it into that of the newly developed class. The small employer became a capitalist, and the employed became a wage worker, and they began to grow apart. The machine was crude and imperfect at first; it increased production, it began to displace the workingman, it pushed him out of the shop and into the street. The workingman forced into idleness became a tramp. I have said again and again that I am with the tramp, and against the system of society that made him a tramp.

The machine became more perfect day by day; it lowered the wage of the worker, but in due course of time it became so perfect that it could be operated by the unskilled labor of the woman, and she became a factor in industry. The owners of these machines were in competition with each other for trade in the market; it was war; cheaper and cheaper production was demanded. In the march of time, it became necessary to withdraw the children from school, and these machines came to be operated by the deft touch of the fingers of the child. In the first stage, machine was in competition with man, in the next, man in competition with both, and in the next, the child in competition with the whole combination. Today there are more than 3 million women engaged in industrial pursuits in the United States and more than 2 million children. It is not a question of white labor or black labor, or male labor or female labor or child labor in this system; it is solely a question of cheap labor, without reference to the effect upon mankind.

The simple tool of production became an excellent machine; it necessitated the cooperation and concentration of capital. The tool of production was no longer owned and controlled by the workingman who used it. It was owned by the class who didn't use it and was used by a class who didn't own it. The owners of the machine want profit, and the users of the machine want wages. Their economic interests are absolutely in conflict, diametrically opposite. What is good for one is not good for the other.

It is this conflict of interest which has given rise to the modern class struggle which finds expression in strikes, lockouts, boycotts, and deep-seated discontent. But I am not looking on the dark side of things. I am in no sense a pessimist. I am observing the trend of economic development. I realize it is only a question of time until this concentration of industry will be completed. One department after another is being monopolized in this march of concentration; the interests of the trusts are so completely international that in the near future there will be a trust of trusts. In this trust the middle class, representing the small capitalists, is being crushed and ground beneath the upper millstone of concentration of capital and the nether millstone of vanishing patronage.

The workingman has been impoverished. Examining the reports, I find that during the past 50 years of the age of the machine, his producing capacity has steadily increased, but upon the other hand, in the competitive pressure, his wage has steadily diminished. The more he produces, the worse he is off. He cannot consume what he produces. The more he produces, the more there is an overproduction based upon underconsumption. The factories close down and he finds himself out of employment and the reason suggests itself; he no longer works for himself, he works for another, for a wage that represents but a small share of what he produces. This accounts for the fact that periodically the country is affected with overproduction; this accounts for the fact that the large capitalists are struggling to open new markets for the sale of surplus goods, the very goods our own people here at home are suffering for want of. In this great competitive system, the mammoth department store is sapping the life currents of the small shopkeeper; the great bonanza farm is driving the small farmer to bankruptcy and ruin.

No power on earth can arrest this concentration. It is paving the way for a new economic system, a new social order. Socialists understand its trend; they are beginning to organize in every village and every hamlet, every town and every city, of every state and territory in the country. They are organizing their forces beneath the conquering banner of economic reality.

A century and a quarter ago, this country witnessed a mighty struggle for political equality, the right of men to govern this country, and the formation of this republic was the crowning glory of the century. Today there is another struggle going forward for economic equality. If men are fit to be political equals, they are also fit to be economic equals. If they are economic equals, they will be social equals; class distinctions will disappear from human society forever.

Look over in the direction of Europe: We observe that the socialists there are organizing day by day; that before their conquering march the thrones are beginning to tremble and will, within the next few years, totter to their fall. The same movement is spreading over the United States. Its progress has not been so rapid here for the reason that we have had a new country, and until recently there has been some opportunity for individual initiative. But no country on the face of the globe has been so completely exploited within so short a space of time as the United States of America.

Socialists are organizing for the purpose of securing control of the government. Having conquered the political power upon the platform that declares in favor of collective ownership in the name of the people, they will take possession of industry. It will already have been organized to meet cooperation, that is to say, self-operation, in the development of the capitalistic system. Industry will be rescued from cupidity; it will be cooperative in every department of human industry. The badge of labor will no longer be the badge of servitude. Every man will gladly do his share of the world's useful work. Every man can then honestly enjoy his share of the world's blessings. Every machine will be a blessing to mankind because it will serve to reduce the number of hours constituting a day's work, and the workday will be shortened in exact proportion to the progress of invention. Labor will no longer be bought and sold in the markets of the world. We will not make things for sale, but will make things to use. We will fill the world with wealth, and every man can have all that he can rationally use. Rent, interest, and profit, three forces of exploitation, will disappear forever.

Every man will have the same inherent right to work that he has to live; he will receive the full product of his labor. The soul will no longer be dominated by the stomach. Men and women will be economically free; life will no longer be a struggle for bread; then the children of men can begin the march to the highest type of civilization that this world has ever known.

The abolishing of the capitalistic system does not merely mean the emancipation of the working class, but of all society. It will level upward to higher and nobler elevation. This earth, for the first time since it was flung into space, will be a habitable globe; it will be fit for good men and good women to live in.

The existing system is unspeakably cruel; the life currents of old age and childhood are the tributaries of the bottomless reservoir of private profit. The face of capitalist society is blotched with the effects of a diseased organism. What is the state of Christendom today? We boast of our civilization and yet every Christian nation on the face of the globe is armed to the teeth. Against whom? Against heathens, barbarians, savages? No, against other Christian nations. And the world pays its highest tribute in that form of ingenuity that enables us to destroy the most human lives in the shortest space of time. Go to the city of Washington today with a device that will enable you to destroy 100,000 lives in a second, and your fame and your fortune are made. Is that civilization in the proper sense of the term? We must bear in mind, my friends, that competition is war; that war is the normal state of capitalism.

If there were no gold in the Transvaal, there would be no British soldiers there. If there were no prospect of acquiring material wealth in the Philippines, we would not worry ourselves into premature graves because the Filipinos lack capacity for self-government. Those wars were declared by the spirit of commercial conquest. They are necessary to the development of the capitalist system. With the end of capitalism comes the end of war and the inauguration of peace.

In the march of invention, space has almost been annihilated; the nations of the earth are being drawn into closer relations with each other. In the new social order, each nation will have its place in the sisterhood of nations, just as every man will have his place in the brotherhood of men.

I will do what little I can to hasten the coming of the day when war shall curse this earth no more. I am not a patriot in the sense in which that term is defined in the lexicon of capitalism. I have no ambition to kill my fellow man, and I am quite certain that I have no ambition to be killed. When I think of a cold, glittering steel bayonet being pushed into the soft, white, quivering flesh of a human body, I recoil with horror.

All hail to socialism! You may retard it, you can hasten its coming by your actions; but you cannot defeat it; you cannot prevent it. It is coming just as certain as the rivers find their way to the sea. It is not yet a popular institution. It is right. A half century ago the institution of chattel slavery was very popular in the United States. It was doomed to disappear. There were thousands who believed that it was criminal and unjust; that it ought to be overthrown; but they did not have the courage of their convictions; they dared not speak out. There were a few, however, who stood erect. They were agitators to their day, and they were covered with odium. William Lloyd Garrison was one of them. Not a great while ago in Newburyport in Massachusetts, I saw a little church where the bells rung to assemble a mob to attack him when he attempted to make a speech against slavery. Wendell Phillips was another. Elijah Lovejoy was another. In 1837, in Alton, Illinois, Elijah Lovejoy published the *Alton Observer;* a committee of friends called on him and said: "You will have to stop these attacks on slavery; our people believe in it." Mr. Lovejoy said: "I have sworn eternal opposition to it, and I will not turn back." They called on him again. He said: "I can die at my post, but I will not desert." His printing office was attacked, and he was mobbed and murdered. The state of Illinois applauded the crime. Sixty years after, the grandchildren of the men who murdered him erected a monument above his self-sacrificed dust in memory of his name. These men were great men, because they dared to be true to themselves and to their convictions of right and duty. They didn't ask, "Is it popular, can I afford it, does it pay?" They simply asked: "Is it right?" and satisfying themselves that it was right, they stood by it without fear of consequences.

Ah, my friends, this movement of socialism will be popular in the next few years. It is moving forward in all directions; every man, woman, and child in the land is vitally interested in it. Such a meeting as this is immensely suggestive, immensely significant; it bears testimony to the fact that men and women are thinking upon this great question as they have never thought before; they realize that the world is trembling on the verge of the greatest organic change in human history. And the socialists realize that the next ruling class of the world will be the working class. So they are pressing forward step by step until the minority they represent becomes the majority and seizes the reins of government and inaugurates the system of the Cooperative Commonwealth. If you believe in these conquering principles, we ask you to join the new crusade and stand side by side with us and cast your lot with socialism and cast your votes for the Social Democratic Party and hasten the day of its triumph.

I would address a few words to those who are in sympathy with the Social Democratic Party, but who hesitate to vote for it for fear they may lose their votes. Let me say to you: It is infinitely better to vote for freedom and fail than to vote for slavery and succeed. The Social Democratic Party also appeals to the considerate judgment and the common sense of the middle class of the country. This class is doomed to disappear in the march of the capitalist system; it is only a question of a short time until the middle class will be in the working class. And the sooner the better. For the middle class, the best investment of the little capital that still remains for you is to put it into socialistic propaganda. It is possible that you may reach your journey's end in safety, but how will it be with your son? You have a boy 12 or 13 or 14 years of age; if you have that solicitude for him a good parent should have for his child, this question can cause you no little concern. He can no longer learn a trade; there is not a trade but that is crowded to overflowing. If he spends three or four years learning a trade, he will find that a machine has arrived there in advance of him. He has no capital. He has simply his bare hands that represent his labor-power. He cannot buy a factor; he is compelled from the very nature of the situation to offer his labor-power, that is to say himself, for sale. If he is fortunate, he becomes a wage-slave. But even the privilege of selling himself into bondage may be denied him, and he may become a tramp. We cannot tell, for in this system everything is insecure, in doubt, uncertain; you may be worth $40,000 or $50,000 today and a bankrupt next week or next month, and in the very sunset of your life, the poorhouse looms in your vision.

Is it not possible to improve upon such a condition as this? Yes, by the intelligent application of the principles of socialism. We live in the most favored land beneath the bending sky. We have all the raw materials and the most marvelous machinery; millions of eager inhabitants seeking employment. Nothing is so easily produced as wealth, and no man should suffer for the need of it; and in a rational economic system, poverty will be a horror of the past; the penitentiaries will be depopulated, and the shadow of the gallows will no longer fall upon the land. Cooperative industry carried forward in the interest of all the people—that is the foundation of the new social order; economic freedom for every human being on earth; no man compelled to depend on the arbitrary will of another for the right or opportunity to create enough to supply his material wants. There will still be competition among men; but it will not be for bread, it will be to excel in good works. Every man will work for the society in which he lives, and society will work in the interests of those who compose it.

I look into the future with absolute confidence. When I strain my vision the slightest, I can see the first rising rays of the sun of the Cooperative Commonwealth; it will look down on a nation in which men and women—I say men and women, because in the new social order, women will stand side by side with men, the badge of inferiority will be taken from her brow—and we will enjoy the enraptured vision of a land without a master, a land without a slave.

Three Classes, Three Parties: Campaign Speech in Cincinnati, Ohio†

October 4, 1900

Ladies, Gentlemen, and Comrades:—

The only vital issue in this campaign, as the chairman has intimated, springs from the private ownership of the means of production. It involves the whole question of political equality, economic freedom, and social progress. The alleged issues of the old parties are all rooted in the existing economic system, a

† Published as "In Roars" in *Cincinnati Enquirer,* October 4, 1900, unspecified page. Copy preserved in *Papers of Eugene V. Debs* microfilm edition, reel 12.

system which they are obliged to preserve and perpetuate, and a system which the Social Democratic Party is pledged to abolish.

The contest today is for the control of government by three separate classes, with conflicting interests, into which modern society has been mainly divided in the development of the competitive system. The dominant capitalist class is represented by the Republican Party. The middle class is represented by the Democratic Party. The working class is represented by the Social Democratic Party, and each of these parties is committed to the economic interests of the class it represents. The Republican Party is the representative of the capitalist class. "Prosperity galore—give us four years more." The Democratic Party is the wailing cry of the perishing middle class; calamity without end. The socialist platform is an indictment of the capitalistic system by the exploited working class, and its ringing declaration in favor of collective ownership of the means of production is the clarion voice of economic freedom. Parties, like individuals, act from motives of self-interest. The platform of a party is simply the political expression of the economic interests of the class it represents.

What Beveridge Says

The Republican Party is in favor of expansion—acquisition of foreign territory—colonial policy. Why? Senator Beveridge says, "Because they are the trustees of Jehovah," but Senator Depew of New York is somewhat older, and we will permit him to answer the question. In his speech at the Republican National Convention in the city of Philadelphia, he said,

> We produce $2 billion more than we can consume and must find a market for the surplus, or we can go back to poverty and stagnation. The Atlantic markets have been largely closed up. We must now turn our eyes to the Pacific. There are 900 million inhabitants, who furnish a market for our products.

The Democratic Party is violently opposed to this policy. It is denounced as imperialism and declares that it is the burning issue of the campaign. The expanding market for which the large capitalists are struggling will extend the lease of power and greatly augment it. The middle class, represented by the Democratic Party, have no surplus products to dispose of. They are not interested in expanding the markets. If the Republican Party succeeds in opening these markets, the vast foreign trade thus secured will develop their resources more rapidly, increase their economic power, and enable them the more easily to crush out their small competitors in the middle class, and this is the bone of contention between the Republican Party and the Democratic Party in respect to what is called the burning issue of imperialism.

Workingman Was Master

My friends, there has been a complete economic revolution in our country during the past 50 years. A great many well-meaning people have been so completely engaged in this competitive struggle that they are utterly oblivious of the fact that half a century ago, and even less, work was done by the hand, and a simple tool was used, and the workman who used it owned it. He could employ himself. He did not rely upon the arbitrary will upon the permission of another for the opportunity to work.

Not only this, but he was the master of what he produced; he was, in a large sense, an economic free man. The more industrious he is, the more he produces, the worse he is off. The market is flooded, there is overproduction and underconsumption, and when the consumption of the product ceases, the factory closes down and he is out of employment. Half a century ago, he worked for himself; today he works for another for a profit that represents but a small share of what he produces. If we examine the official reports issued by our national commission, we find that production has increased from 20 to 44 percent during the last 50 years. Upon the other hand, the consuming capacity has rapidly diminished, because at that time the labor was performed by the hand of man, whereas at the present time, on the other hand, the same articles are turned out by means of modern machinery in fabulous abundance, the public is not able to consume what is produced, and therefore there is a lack of market. There is a surplus product every now and then. We produce so much of everything that we suffer for the want of everything; consequently, there is a universal stop, a stagnation.

Examine the reports again and we find the workingmen received in wages about $2 billion during the past 12 months; we find during the same period of time the capitalists received in products about the same amount; under the present development of the wage system, the workingman is compelled to produce a dollar for the capitalist before he is able to produce one for himself. Then the goods he produces filter through the middle class, they are sold to him at retail prices, and we find that he is only able to buy back about 20 percent, or one-fifth, of what his labor produces.

Half a Century Ago

Compare this condition with the condition that existed half a century ago. If a man were a skilled shoemaker and he received orders for more shoes than he could make, he hired a shoemaker to help him, but he was compelled to pay that shoemaker the full equivalent of the value of his work, or, if he failed to do this, the shoemaker could quit and, with a few dollars that he had saved, he could buy a small stock and open up a little shop of his own and make shoes for himself. It is true that it was a very slow age, meager of results, involving long hours of toil, but each man was his own master.

At this time, the tool was touched by the magic wand of genius, and the revolution began in full force. This tool expanded to the proportions of a ponderous machine which necessitated the cooperative labor of men. This tool, which supplanted the labor done by the hand of the laboring man, became costlier step by step as it increased in size and capacity, and was the price of the workman's independence, and the man who first owned the machine in its simple form and acted in the capacity of an employer emerged into that of the capitalist, the employee became the wageworker; the division between the classes began to grow apace, and the division has been steadily widening from that day to this, until today we find that we have a class that represents a sixth part of our population who have about 85 percent of the wealth.

We find that 75 percent—that percentage of our population that creates all the wealth by its labor—in other words, a very small capitalistic class and a very large working class. The capitalist class owns the machinery of production, they don't use it. The wage-working class use it, but they don't own it. The capitalist class demands that they reap the profits. The greater the wage, the smaller the profit; the smaller the wage, the greater the profit.

Conflict Between Interests

You will find between these two classes a decided conflict of interest; their interests are diametrically opposite. What is good for one is not good for the other, and it is this conflict that finds expression in the strikes. When work was done by hand, every workingman could look forward to the time that he would be an employer instead of an employee; there was some future for him; there was some incentive for him to apply himself; but today all those doors of advancement have been closed and barred against him.

The modern wageworker remains the wageworker, and there is no possible escape for him except through the back door of suicide. A department clerk is always a department clerk; he is never foolish enough to imagine, even under the influence of Democratic or Republican oratory, that the day will down when he will be anything more than a wageworker. Is there a clerk in one of the large department stores or bazaars or emporiums who is silly enough to imagine that he or she is to be anything but a clerk? I admit that it is possible that some exceptional young man might rise above his environments and reach a greater height, but he would be an exception who only serves to prove the rule. The fruit of this system is before us.

No Real Prosperity

We are told that the country is prosperous. I do not hesitate to say that it is a ghastly farce; that there is no real prosperity in the land. Rockefeller is prosperous; Russell Sage[69] is equally so, so is Gould, so are some of the rest of the owners of the means of production, but, so far as the middle class, so far as the wage-working class is concerned, there is no prosperity in any proper sense of the term.

I said in the beginning of my address that the Social Democratic Party was essentially the party of the working class, but it also appeals to the principles and judgment of the middle class, if not to the immediate interest of the middle class. The small production upon which the middle class was reared has been revolutionized. This is an era of large production carried forward on a gigantic scale, a scale of tremendous proportions, in which the middle class is doomed to be crushed and ground between the upper millstone of capitalism and the nether millstone of great poverty. The great factory crushes out the life of the small producer exactly as the large department store absorbs the smaller merchant and saps his life.

The large farm is equipped with improved machinery and is operated on a scale with which the small farm cannot compete; it crowds out and obliterates the crude implements of a quarter of a century ago, and this course of events is going steadily forward. If, in spite of the protest of the Republican Party and the objection of the Democratic Party, the Social Democratic Party would push this evolution to its logical and inevitable termination, the Republican Party would have the sun stand still, and the Democratic Party would force it backward on its shining track, but the socialists contemplate with serenity the exit of capitalism and with equal serenity the rise of socialism.

The Trust Problem

The Republican Party declares that there are certain vicious combinations in the country that ought to be regulated, restrained, suppressed, if necessary, by law. The letter of acceptance of President McKinley says substantially the same thing, but do you know of a Republican who has ever drawn the line between combinations that are vicious and combinations that are otherwise? Let me draw the line. Every privately owned monopoly or combination is a vicious combination. Every publicly owned combination is a good combination. The Democratic Party charges that all these combinations have gone forward under the Republican administration. It is a matter of economic development. As well legislate the ebb and flow of the tide or the rising and setting of the sun. If the Republican Party is opposed to trusts—I don't know whether it be or not, for, according to Mark Hanna, there are no trusts in the country—but, if the Republican Party is opposed to the trusts, why has it not legislated against trusts? It has been in control of every department of the government for the last three years.

The Democratic Party charges all of these evils to the Republican Party. Seven hundred trusts have been developed within the last three years. Now comes the Democratic Party and says, when we get into power we will dissolve these monopolies. We will revive competition and then the country will be overwhelmed with prosperity. But they don't tell us how it will be done. Competition is orderly. It goes forward to a certain point; the smaller and weaker is crushed out by the larger; it is driven to the side by an opponent, and it is swallowed by the combinations. They are the economic masters of the situation. Can the world be forced backward? The world moves forward, not backward; therefore, in the course of competition, the smaller is absorbed by the larger and stronger. These are the great forces of the age economically.

Centralization Inevitable

Those of you who have studied the economic development of the world know that when the machine first appeared, a little over a century ago, that there was an outcry against it on the part of the working class. It displaced the workingman, forced him into the street, made a tramp of him. The weavers and spinners of England organized and violently took the cotton-spinning machinery from the factory, feeling that if they could destroy the machinery, they could regain their former employment. They did not know enough to know that the machine had come in obedience to an economic law; that it was a mere factor in the industrial development of the world. They were doomed to disappointment. It is precisely the same with the attempt of today to destroy the trusts. No power on this earth can arrest the force of centralization. Those who attempt to are doomed to failure and disappointment.

Individuals who were competitors against each other have concluded that cooperation is better than competition; that in increasing each other's labor and expenses they decreased each other's profits, and therefore resolved to combine in a partnership; from an individual enterprise, partnerships have been formed; partnerships have merged into corporations, and the corporation has been finally swallowed up and absorbed into the trust or combination, as a result of economic conditions and development.

Doomed to Disappointment: An Open Letter to Samuel M. Jones†

October 8, 1900

Terre Haute, Ind., October 8, 1900

Mr. Samuel M. Jones,
Mayor, Toledo, Ohio

My Dear Mr. Jones:—

Your communication of the 25th ult. [September 25, 1900] was received some days ago, but I have been too busy to make earlier reply.[70] In all you say you are kind and gentle, and I trust that there may be no lack of the same spirit in my answer, although I shall be perfectly candid in the expression of my views touching your recent action in allying yourself with the Democratic Party and doing battle against the cause of socialism.

Do not, I pray you, tell me that you have not "joined" the Democratic Party. That is puerile, if not disingenuous, for it implies evasion of responsibility for an action from which your own conscience would seem to shrink in disapproval. With David B. Hill,[71] you have declared, if not in words, in deed, which is more conclusive, "I am a Democrat," and you are today as much a part of the Democratic Party as Croker and his Christless gang who are levying blackmail upon moral affliction to save (!) our republic (?) from "imperialism."

† Published as "E.V. Debs to Mayor Jones" in *Social Democratic Herald,* vol. 3, no. 17, whole no. 119 (October 13, 1900), 1. Not published in J. Robert Constantine (ed.), *Letters of Eugene V. Debs: Volume 1, 1874–1912.*

You sign yourself "a man without a party." Permit me to observe that you are not that now, but when the Democratic Party gets through with you, you will indeed be "a man without a party."

Let me now quote briefly from your letter. You say, "Suppose I am never again elected to office," etc. You must know it is not the office, per se, that is in question, and yet to a man with whom serving the people is a consuming passion, I imagine that if my prediction proves true, you are doomed to be a sorely disappointed man.

As for the implied spirit of martyrdom which characterized your action, it should be said that no great self-sacrifice is required to join the majority, the strong, in crushing the minority, the weak. Had you, as a professed socialist, taken your stand on the side of socialism, instead of joining hands with its avowed enemies, the case would be different, and your contention might be urged with some degree of consistency.

You say you are for "all the people." Do you think you are for the poor Negroes of the South who have been disfranchised by your party, the party you are supporting with pen and speech? Do you really think you are for the working class, the prisoners of private property and competitive conquest which your party is pledged to perpetuate? If you really think so, then I say for these voiceless victims, deliver us from such a friend.

Are you for the exploiters as well as the exploited, the masters as well as the slaves?

Moses was not for all the people; Jesus Christ was not for all the people; Jehovah himself, if he is correctly quoted, was not for "all the people." They smote their enemies and they smote them hard. Only Mr. Jones of Toledo is for "all the people," and being for "all the people," as a matter of fact, he is for none of the people.

Ultimately, I am for "all the people," but not now. Till the fight is fought and won, I am for the working class and against their exploiters, the capitalist class. In your effort to perform the miraculous feat of being upon both sides of the class struggle, you have somehow gotten on the side that represents your class interests. I will not accuse you of capitalist class consciousness, but simply observe in a spirit of charity that you have committed political suicide, and this you have done, not for a principle, but against a principle; and that you are conscientious in the matter makes your demise all the more pitiable.

You may remember what I said in a previous letter about your alleged socialism, and your extreme popularity with such papers as the *New York Journal* and *Cincinnati Enquirer.*[72] When these papers are entirely through with you, they will relegate you to obscurity only equaled by the prominence into which they boosted you to serve their own capitalistic designs.

All the popularity and influence these papers developed in you have been cast with the exploiting class and against the working class. The workingmen and women of the country will never forget that in a critical hour of the contest, you, their professed and trusted friend, joined the enemy and turned against them.

The only ground upon which you attempt to justify your attitude is your pretended fear of "imperialism." Is it possible? Did I not know you as I do, I would openly question your sincerity. You certainly cannot be in ignorance of the fact that this so-called issue is simply an effect of private ownership and of competitive warfare inherent in the capitalist system. You are opposed to the fruit of the system, but you have joined the party pledged to perpetuate the system, and such influence as you still have you are now using to prolong the barbarous struggle which in the past you denounced with such passionate severity and condemned as void of a single redeeming feature.

You may still be esteemed as the modern apostle of the "golden rule," at least until the election is over, but I cannot imagine how you can enjoy mental serenity when you contemplate your connection with, and your activity for, a party explicitly committed by its own platform to revive and renew and intensify and continue forever the competitive strife you have so fervently denounced, as with tears streaming from your eyes you recited its agonizing woes for the listening multitude. In what I have had to say, I have not questioned your motive. I leave that entirely with your own conscience. I have simply discussed your action from my point of view, and this, I trust, I have done in all kindness consistent with perfect candor. Since you have seen proper to give your letter to the press, I may avail myself of the same privilege.

With the strength of all my being pledged to socialism, come it soon or come it late, socialism as uncompromising as truth, I remain

Most truly yours,
Eugene V. Debs,
A Man with a Party[73]

A Final Word†

November 3, 1900

Comrades and Fellow Workingmen:—

By your unanimous vote of confidence, I was designated as one of the standard bearers of the Social Democratic Party in the political campaign now in progress throughout the country.

The responsibilities of the position are appreciated in no small degree, and I am doing all that lies in my power to achieve success for the party.

The vast assemblages of people we are daily addressing bear eloquent testimony, not only to the righteousness of the principles of socialism, but demonstrate beyond cavil that wisdom, truth, and justice were in holy alliance when the Social Democratic Party was organized and sent forth on its class-conscious mission.

But we cannot be in a hundred, nor even in two places at the same time, nor are we able to respond to one in 20 of the calls made upon us, and this must be my apology, if one is required, for resorting to this method of addressing the many thousands I cannot otherwise reach.

The thronging multitudes of earnest men and women who press to the meetings held under the auspices of the Social Democratic Party, and the inspiring and tumultuous applause which greets the announcement of its principles, bears trumpet-toned appreciation of the cause in which we are engaged and of its ultimate triumph.

Comrades, there is a mighty wave of thought, of intense interest sweeping over the country. Workingmen and women, everywhere in our broad land, are aroused as never before to the woeful condition of the working class in the capitalist system. They have tried the Republican and Democratic parties again and again with the same results. They are beginning to realize that they are but two sections of the same party of the capitalist class, two wings of the same unclean capitalist bird, and that what is required is a change not merely of parties, but of systems, and hence they are coming to the Social Democratic Party, which stands committed to abolish wage-slavery by making common property of all the means of wealth production.

† Published as "Debs' Final Word" in *Social Democratic Herald*, vol. 3, no. 20, whole no. 122 (November 3, 1900), 1.

A wide field of observation enables me to say that the outlook for our party is inspiring and that, all things considered, it could scarcely be more hopeful or animating.

The Social Democratic Party in its youth is developing the stature of a giant. It has torn off its swaddling garments and, with startling strides of self-contained strength, already menaces the reign and rule of capitalism and the two old parties which do its bidding like trained monkeys in a circus ring. It has created consternation in their ranks, and as they see the pedestaled gods of crime which they worship with pagan devotion tumbled down by the iconoclastic attacks of the Social Democratic Party, they know their doom is sealed.

If but yesterday the light of the Social Democratic Party flashed upon the country was that of the glowworm in the meadow, it is today as effulgent as that of a fixed star in the realm of political activity.

Comrades, a vote cast for the Social Democratic Party in this campaign is to be, by the fiat of history, a landmark—aye, a mind mark—better still, an emancipation mark in the onward and upward march of socialism, of the working class, until they reach the highlands of that rightful freedom where a man owns himself, works for himself, and enjoys all the fruitions of that liberty that knows no master, where fetters of the mind and shackles of the body disappear and he stands free and disenthralled by the overmastering power of the genius of socialism.

Comrades, the battle is on. The serried host of capitalism confront us on every hand. They are as numerous as the sands and have money beyond the dreams of avarice. They ride in special trains provided with all the appliances of luxury and repose that plundered wealth can provide. They flash their shining blades in the faces of the working class upon which are engraved the texts from the sacred Koran of capitalism, and the wires flash the exultant boast, "We have smiled upon the working class and they are ours."

Comrades, now is the time for men to do and dare. Now is the time for the workingman to show that he is the equal of the capitalist. Are we ready for the fray? Is our courage equal to our conviction?

Comrades, my faith in your integrity is abounding. I take your hand and feel the thrill of comradeship. I catch the gleam of victory that flashes in your eye and hope takes on a warmer glow. I hear your resounding battle cry as if coming from the throat of a cyclone: "Lead on, we are with you to the end." It is enough.

Progress of the Social Revolution†

November 26, 1900

The returns of the national election are still indefinite and incomplete. It seems certain, however, that our vote is over 100,000 and it may reach 150,000.[74] The figures are smaller than most of us expected, but we are satisfied. Under all the circumstances, the party did all that could have been reasonably expected and the showing, if not inspiring, has at least nothing discouraging in it.

From private advices received, I am convinced that a large percentage of our vote was counted against us or cast out upon technical grounds. We were not represented upon the election boards, and it was an easy matter to discredit our vote.[75] In some of the southern states, the Social Democratic vote was counted in the Democratic vote and there was none present to object. We must expect all such difficulties until we are strong enough as a party to protect our interests and have our votes fairly counted.

If all the votes cast and meant to be cast for our party had been counted in our favor, it is safe to assume that the Social Democratic Party would stand credited with 200,000 votes.

But we accept the logic of facts and prepare for the next battle. We are too busy getting ready for what is to be to waste any time over what might have been. The vote cast for our ticket measures the progress of the social revolution and, taking note of this, we press forward with renewed energy, vitalized by the first encounter with the enemy upon the national battlefield.

The old parties, with whom a campaign is simply a contest for spoils, have folded their flags and stored away their torches for four years more.

The Republican Party has triumphed, and the trusts will riot in the spoils of conquest. With such an overwhelming endorsement, the dominant capitalist class will throw off all restraint and trustify everything in sight. The centralization of large capital and expropriation of small capital will proceed as never before. The development of capitalism will reach its greatest momentum. Consumption will not be able to keep pace with production, and before McKinley's "prosperity" administration closes, the crash will come and then the working class will get in full measure what they voted for.

---

† Published in *Social Democratic Herald*, vol. 3, no. 24, whole no. 126 (December 1, 1900), 1.

Overproduction, glutted markets, paralyzed factories, silent mills, deserted mines, enforced idleness, reduced wages, strikes, lockouts, injunctions, soldiers, and the funerals of workingmen will follow in rapid succession. There will be no work for the hands, and the brain will have a chance. Workingmen will have ample time for reflection. When their ambition for this sort of thing is fully satisfied, they will cease voting robes to their masters and rags to themselves; they will stand with their class for the abolition of the capitalist system. Meantime the country will dance to the music of capitalist prosperity.

The Democratic Party presents a picture never before exhibited in the political gallery. Its platform looks as if a cyclone had revised it and its demoralization is complete. Its reactionary, cowardly, and dishonest policy has been spurned with merited contempt and repudiation. There is no longer room for a party that seeks to ride into office by straddling the class issue and engaging, or pretending to engage, on both sides of the class struggle. It is one side or the other, and with the double-dealing Democratic Party doomed, the political atmosphere will clear up and the working class will be able to see the class contest, and they will then rally with the Social Democratic Party, the party of the working class in the struggle for emancipation.

Disintegration is already preying upon the Democratic Party. Its leaders are unable to "point with pride" to a single thing. They have not yet recovered sufficiently to even "view with alarm" or "deplore," or "condemn as un-American" anything, not even the "paramount issue" of "throwing away" their votes. The Eastern leaders, who are Republicans in fact, are scrutinizing the wreck, but they can hardly make up their minds that it is worth raising. And yet the capitalist class cannot afford to allow the Democratic Party to retire from business. It must be used to arrest the progress of socialism, and so it is entirely probable that the "radical" element will be given full permission to galvanize the corpse with an injection of "public ownership."

A great many of the rank and file, however, know when they have enough. This is shown by the fact that the tide is already setting in the direction of the Social Democratic Party. A week at headquarters enables me to perceive the drift. Never since we have been a party have the inquiries for party literature, for organizers and speakers, equaled the present demand. Never have the branches increased in number and in membership as now. The party has entered upon an era of development hitherto unequaled and unknown, and it is spreading over the entire country, including the Southern states, and I feel not only confident but absolutely certain that within 12 months our party will have an effective organization in every state in the union.

We are not discussing the "cause" of the recent Republican victory and Democratic defeat. We have no time for that. Ours is a part of the future and not of the past; we are looking forward and not backward; let others linger with the slain on yesterday's field of action, we must gird afresh our armor and move on the enemy again and again, and yet again, until he is overthrown and routed and driven from the field.

The approaching convention of our party will be an event of special interest and importance.[76] The representatives who will assemble at Chicago will be familiar with the trials of the past and equal to the demands of the future, and we can confidently look forward to the most progressive and prosperous year in the history of the party.

I cannot close without reference to the loyal support of comrades in the recent presidential contest. Other candidates may boast a larger vote, but not one dare claim more steadfast devotion. It was born of fidelity to principle and was and will be faithful even unto death.

In the name of the Social Democratic Party which honored me, I thank all comrades for their loyal support.

A Word About the "Independent"†

December 8, 1900

A great many men and women who call themselves socialists do not affiliate with the national party. They hold aloof while the struggle is progressing and the party is evolving. They watch the struggle instead of being in it, with the result that the struggle is prolonged and the development of the party delayed. These "independents" may understand socialism, but whatever they may conceive themselves to be, they are not socialists.

The real struggle of socialism is to establish the Cooperative Commonwealth. Once the party is perfected, the rest follows as a natural sequence and is comparatively easy.

† Published in *Social Democratic Herald,* vol. 3, no. 25, whole no. 127 (December 8, 1900), 1.

Note the struggle in Germany, for example, for over a third of a century to build up the national party. Who shall tell of the patience, self-denial, anxiety, suffering, the strife and turmoil, the jealousy, suspicion, anger and hate, the factional discord, friendships made and broken, the period of temporary harmony shattered by dissension and disruption entailed by the herculean task? But out of it all came the magnificent Social Democratic Party, the wonder and admiration of the socialist world. Such a party could only have been forged and tempered and molded and fashioned in the flame of passion, the lightning of treachery, the tempest of hate, the sunshine of hope, the tide of economic necessity, the torrent of determination. This is evolution. Did the Titans who were its instruments sit on the fence and "wait" until the party was "made" and presented to them on a silver platter? No, they plunged into the struggle and "made" the party. They did not wait for it to "be made."

Suppose Liebknecht had been one of the "waiters" who are so numerous in this country. Would he have become the social colossus of his day? Would his funeral procession have shaken all Europe? Would the millions of the earth build monuments of flowers, watered by their tears, where the old warrior sleeps? No! If Liebknecht had been an "independent," if he had spent his time on the fence instead of in the fray, if remembered at all, it would be as a time-server and a coward, of whom there has been an overproduction ever since man began his tramp from savagery to civilization.

Marx, Engels, and Lassalle were not "independent" factors in the social struggle. They shared in all the trials and privations incident to, and inseparable from, the building of a great political movement, and the world will forever remember them with gratitude and love.

Those who become members of clubs and leagues, and those who are connected with "independent" and "unattached" bodies for fear that their sensitive organisms may be shocked in the clash of the party struggle, may become socialists, but they are not such in their present capacity.

Only those are socialists who are in the national and international party; and if the national party has not yet fully developed, only those have correct conception of socialist duties who are in and of the struggle, however fierce, of which the party is born, and from which it derives its strength and power.

Martin Irons, Martyr†

December 9, 1900

It was in 1886 that Martin Irons, as chairman of the executive board of the Knights of Labor of the Gould Southwestern Railway system, defied capitalist tyranny, and from that hour he was doomed. All the powers of capitalism combined to crush him, and when at last he succumbed to overwhelming odds, he was hounded from place to place until he was ragged and footsore and the pangs of hunger gnawed at his vitals.

For 14 long years, he fought singlehanded the battle against persecution. He tramped far, and among strangers, under an assumed name, sought to earn enough to get bread. But he was tracked like a beast and driven from shelter. For this "poor wanderer of a stormy day," there was no pity. He had stood between his class and their oppressors—he was brave, and he would not flinch; he was honest, and he would not sell; this was his crime, and he must die.

Martin Irons came to this country from Scotland as a child. He was friendless, penniless, alone. At an early age, he became a machinist. For years he worked at his trade. He had a clear head and a warm heart. He saw and felt the injustice suffered by his class. Three reductions in wages in rapid succession fired his blood. He resolved to resist. He appealed to his fellow workers. When the great strike came, Martin Irons was its central figure. The men felt they could trust him. They were not mistaken.

When at the darkest hour Jay Gould sent word to Martin Irons that he wished to see him, the answer came, "I am in Kansas City." Gould did not have gold enough to buy Irons. This was the greatest crime of labor's honest leader. The press united in fiercest denunciation. Every lie that malignity could conceive was circulated. In the popular mind, Martin Irons was the blackest-hearted villain that ever went unhung. Pinkerton bloodhounds tracked him night and day. But through it all this loyal, fearless, high-minded workingman stood steadfast.

† Published as "Tribute to Martin Irons" in *Social Democratic Herald,* vol. 3, no. 26, whole no. 128 (December 15, 1900), 2 and as "Nailed to the Cross for Fourteen Years," *Appeal to Reason,* December 17, 1904. Reprinted as "Martin Irons, Martyr" in *Debs: His Life, Writings, and Speeches* (Girard, KS: Appeal to Reason, 1908), 273–5.

The courts and soldiers responded to the command of their masters, the railroads; the strike was crushed, and the workingmen were beaten.

Martin Irons had served, suffered for, and honored his class. But he had lost. His class now turned against him and joined in the execration of the enemy. This pained him more than all else. But he bore even this without a murmur, and if ever a despairing sigh was wrung from him, it was when he was alone.

And thus it has been all along the highway of the centuries, from Jesus Christ to Martin Irons.

Let it not be said that Irons was not crucified. For 14 years he was nailed to the cross, and no martyr to humanity ever bore his crucifixion with finer fortitude.

He endured the taunts and jeers and all the bitter mockery of fate with patient heroism; and even when the poor dumb brutes whose wounds and bruises he would have swathed with his own heartstrings turned upon and rent him, pity sealed his lips, and silent suffering wrought for him a martyr's crown.

Martin Irons was hated by all who were too base or ignorant to understand him. He died despised, yet shall he live beloved.

No president of the United States gave or tendered him a public office in testimony of his service to the working class. The kind of service he rendered was too honest to be respectable, too aggressive and uncompromising to be popular.

The blow he struck for his class will preserve his memory. In the great struggle for emancipation he nobly did his share, and the history of labor cannot be written without his name.

He was an agitator, and as such shared the common fate of all. Jesus Christ, Joan of Arc, Elijah Lovejoy, John Brown, Albert Parsons, and many others set the same example and paid the same penalty.

For the reason that he was a despised agitator and shunned of men too mean and sordid to comprehend the lofty motive that inspired him, he will be remembered with tenderness and love long after the last of his detractors shall have moldered in a forgotten grave.

It was in April 1899, in Waco, Texas, that I last pressed this comrade's hand. He bore the traces of poverty and broken health, but his spirit was as intrepid as when he struck the shield of Hoxie 13 years before;[77] and when he spoke of socialism he seemed transfigured, and all the smoldering fires within his soul blazed from his sunken eyes once more.

I was pained, but not surprised, when I read that he had "died penniless in an obscure Texas town." It is his glory and society's shame that he died that way.

His weary body has at last found rest, and the grandchildren of the men and women he struggled, suffered, and died for will weave chaplets where he sleeps.

His epitaph might read: "For standing bravely in defense of the working class, he was put to death by slow torture."

Martin Irons was an honest, courageous, manly man. The world numbers one less since he has left it.

Brave comrade, love, and farewell!

Notes

1. Following the 1899 split of the SLP, both factions for a time produced rival editions of *The People,* making use of the same volume numbers and identical front page banners. Debs was a regular reader of the dissident edition of *The People,* a fact illustrated by the partial run of intact issues retained in his newspaper files and preserved on reel 15 of *The Papers of Eugene V. Debs* microfilm edition.
2. It is unclear what set Debs off so severely against the dissident edition of *The People,* which in general did not take an aggressive line against the SDP.
3. This piece was written specifically for the *New York Journal* from the location of the First National Convention of the Social Democratic Party of America, which was held in Reichwein's Hall in Indianapolis from March 6–9, 1900.
4. A slight variation of the last three lines of *The Communist Manifesto* (1848) by Marx and Engels: "The proletarians have nothing to lose but their chains. They have a world to win. *Workingmen of all countries, unite!*"
5. This neatly ignores a quarter century of history of the Socialist Labor Party of America and its Lassallean forerunners of the middle 1870s.
6. Debs's reduction of the question of imperialism to a mundane controversy of contemporary bourgeois politics, rather than placing emphasis upon it as a fundamental structural feature of modern capitalist development, is worthy of notice. Marxist thinking on the question of imperialism was only in its infancy at this juncture, and Debs was not a theoretician, but a popularizer and publicist. See Richard B. Day and Daniel Gaido (eds.), *Discovering Imperialism: Social Democracy to World War I.* [2011] (Chicago: Haymarket Books, 2012).
7. This speech was delivered shortly after noon at Reichwein's Hall in Indianapolis, site of the SDP convention.
8. Job Harriman had previously been nominated for president in January by the convention of the Social Democratic Party with headquarters in Springfield, Massachusetts. The nomination of Debs and Harriman for president and vice president thus was an act of political fusion between two erstwhile rival organizations.
9. Thursday, March 8, the third day of the convention, had been one of acrimony. A decision was made to name a nine-member committee to negotiate unity with the Socialist Labor Party dissidents who had met in convention in January and named the ticket of Job Harriman for president and Max S. Hayes for vice president. Things had gone downhill in the afternoon, however, when Gene Debs declined the convention's nomination, citing reasons of health. In a scramble to fill the gap, SDP national secretary Theodore Debs had been nominated, but he also declined, this time for reasons of age. Job Harriman was then nominated, but he too declined, and a discussion about whether to endorse the SLP ticket of Harriman and Hayes degenerated into acrimonious debate that lasted into the night. Only after multiple visits to his room at the Occidental Hotel was Debs finally persuaded to accept the nomination of his party.
10. Four representatives of the Socialist Labor Party's nine-member unity committee elected at Rochester were in attendance, including Morris Hillquit, Job Harriman, G. B. Benham, and Max Hayes.

11. In its generally accurate stenographic report, the *Indianapolis Journal* has this final line as "All hail to the United Socialist Party of America."
12. The first conference of the Joint Unity Committee of 18 met in New York City from March 25–27, 1900. One committee member of the SDP, Victor Berger, did not attend. The eight SDP delegates split 5–3 in favor of a majority report outlining the program, constitution, and terms of unity between the SDP and the dissident SLP organization, which split from the party after failing to depose Daniel DeLeon and the party leadership in 1899. The three SDP unity committee members voting in the minority—Frederic Heath, Seymour Stedman, and Margaret Haile—then successfully sabotaged a vote on the majority report with a barrage including a front-page "Manifesto" of the National Executive Board, written April 2 and published in the *Social Democratic Herald* of April 7, accusing the SLP of double-dealing and negotiation in bad faith, as well as this piece by Debs attacking the agreement as an individual. Unity between the two organizations would be delayed until August 1901.
13. "The Union Conference," *Social Democratic Herald,* April 7, 1900, 2. Minutes and a lengthy negative commentary on the proceeding by Margaret Haile, secretary of the SDP delegation to the March 25–27 conference.
14. See "Manifesto of the National Executive Board to the Members of the Social Democratic Party," April 2, 1900, this volume. This document was signed by National Executive Board members Jesse Cox, Victor Berger, Frederic Heath, and Seymour Stedman, but not by Debs, who, largely for matters of form, awaited release of the majority report before offering his negative opinion. The majority report was itself published in the *Social Democratic Herald,* April 14, 1900, 1, 4.
15. Job Harriman and Morris Hillquit replied with a joint letter in *Social Democratic Herald,* April 21, 1900, 4.
16. The letter of Max S. Hayes, dated April 7, was published in *Social Democratic Herald,* April 14, 1900, 3.
17. A long letter by San Francisco SLP activist G. B. Benham was published in *Social Democratic Herald,* April 21, 1900, 1, 4.
18. "On Unity," January 14, 1900, published in *Social Democratic Herald,* January 20, 1900, 3. Republished in this volume.
19. The Social Democratic Party convention of March 6–9, 1900, was attended by Morris Hillquit, Job Harriman, Max S. Hayes, and G. B. Benham on behalf of the SLP dissident faction.
20. The SLP dissidents favored the name "United Socialist Party of America."
21. The SDP was based in Chicago and the SLP dissidents in New York City; the latter favored Springfield, Massachusetts, as the new national headquarters of the united party. Massachusetts was a hotbed of social democratic activity during the late 1890s and was removed by distance from both metropolises, making it a logical location as a neutral site for party headquarters.
22. According to the official report of Theodore Debs published in the *Social Democratic Herald,* issue of March 24, 1900, as of the first of that month the Social Democratic Party had liabilities $751.44 in excess of assets, with three creditors accounting for

this amount: Eugene Dietzgen for $225, with editor A. S. Edwards and national secretary Theodore Debs representing the balance, presumably in the form of unpaid wages. The party's total disbursements from its formation in June 1898 through the end of February 1900 totaled $8,245.74, a majority of which related to costs of publication of the organization's weekly newspaper.

23. The organ of the SLP dissidents in Chicago was *The Workers' Call,* edited by Algie M. Simons, a weekly launched in March 1899.
24. The source of this alleged charge is unclear.
25. This is a plain call for "political fusion," regarded as anathema by many socialists of the day after the People's Party's William Jennings Bryan debacle of 1896.
26. That is, the forerunner to *The Worker* published at William Street in New York as the official organ of the SLP dissidents, not the established newspaper also published in New York City and edited by Daniel DeLeon.
27. The March 1900 convention of the Social Democratic Party named a nine-member unity committee to meet with a similar group chosen by the January 1900 Rochester convention of the Socialist Labor Party's dissident faction, which had split from the DeLeon organization the previous year. This so-called "Committee of 18" met in New York City from March 25–27 to hammer out terms of union, including name, headquarters city, constitution, and party press. The SDP delegation divided at this time with a 5–3 vote (Victor L. Berger not attending due to his wife's maternity), with Frederic Heath, Seymour Stedman, and Margaret Haile dissenting. Despite a majority of the unity committee voting to support a referendum on union, the formal proposal was scuttled by the National Executive Board (NEB)—a body that included Heath, Stedman, Berger, bitter unity foe Jesse Cox, and Debs. The NEB rushed an anti-unity "manifesto" into print one week before the majority report on unity was released for a vote and preempted its presentation and a vote with a substitute referendum on the question "Is union between the Social Democratic Party and the Socialist Labor Party faction desirable?" With the waters muddied by well-publicized charges of bad faith, the NEB's substitute proposition failed by a vote of 939 to 1,213.

    Thoroughly alienated by the dirty tactics of the NEB in sabotaging the work of the unity committee, the majority of Chicago SDP negotiators continued forward with their dialogue, meeting the SLP dissidents a second time in New York City on May 20, with Debs in attendance by request. The Chicago SDP leadership took the position that the unity committee had been liquidated by the snap referendum of the NEB, a position supported by Debs in this speech. Instead, an agreement on unity was hammered out by the majority of the Chicago unity committee and their counterparts from the dissident SLP and a new "Social Democratic Party" with headquarters in Springfield, Massachusetts, was born.
28. In fact, debate in the *Social Democratic Herald* was significantly skewed, with unsigned anti-unity editorials by editor A. S. Edwards running each week in the party voice, certain pro-unity or anti-NEB resolutions truncated or delayed, anti-unity affidavits run twice, and letters titled tendentiously—tactics straight out of the DeLeonist playbook.

29. In the aftermath of the May 1900 rejection of the concept of organic unity between the SDP and the SLP dissidents, an intervention by the National Executive Board ostensibly to prevent a split of anti-unity elements, the SDP found itself in the midst of a split of its pro-unity elements, who continued and completed merger negotiations. A united party also named the "Social Democratic Party" was thereby launched, the name chosen to avoid electoral cataclysm in Massachusetts in the forthcoming November election. In July 1900, headquarters for the new organization were established in Springfield, Massachusetts, and William Butscher of New York, a former member of the Chicago SDP, was elected as national secretary. The Massachusetts socialist movement divided itself between the rival party organizations, with the Haverhill organization going with Springfield and the Brockton organization going with Chicago. In this article, Debs cheers on the Chicago-based SDP's course of action and attempts to find a middle ground between all-out partisan warfare and merger of these two organizations, the latter of which Debs continues to refer to here as "SLP."
30. Debs refers here to the dissident SLP faction, which broke with the established party leadership in July 1899.
31. Headed by the majority of the Chicago SDP's unity committee, negotiations continued between pro-unity elements of the SDP and the SLP dissidents headed by Henry Slobodin, Job Harriman, and Morris Hillquit. These negotiations ended with the establishment of a joint organization also calling itself the Social Democratic Party, with headquarters established in Springfield, Massachusetts.
32. At the time of this writing, joint state conventions of the SDP and SLP on a more equal basis of representation and delegate authority were held in New York (June 16), Connecticut (July 4), and Massachusetts (July 8). A further convention was scheduled for Iowa (August 10). The New York convention was called by dissident elements that would become the Springfield SDP; the other three gatherings were regular annual conventions called by the state committees of the SDP loyal to Chicago.
33. Members of the National Executive Board at this juncture were Frederic Heath (chairman), Seymour Stedman (secretary), Eugene V. Debs, Victor L. Berger, and Corinne S. Brown. National secretary was Theodore Debs, and editor of the official organ was A. S. Edwards. This statement was not long true, with Stedman changing his position as a result of the 1900 election campaign, during which members of both parties worked together on behalf of a joint statewide ticket in Illinois.
34. This article ran on the same page of *Social Democratic Herald* as did a hatchet job editorial by A. S. Edwards entitled "Harriman's Propaganda in Behalf of 'Socialism': Infamous Tactics Resorted to by the Managers of the So-called United Party," in which Debs's running mate was intimated to have spread "smooth and well-chosen palaver" at the March 1900 convention in Indianapolis and characterized as a leader of "party-wreckers, masquerading as the guardians of the cause of human freedom" who was "stabbing the party, vilifying the organization, and getting pay for doing it."
35. William Butscher, formerly from Brooklyn, was the secretary of the nine-member

joint unity committee elected at the March 1900 convention of the SDP and a leading voice for continuing to pursue unity with the SLP dissidents even after the majority report of his committee had been sabotaged by the April 2 "Manifesto of the National Executive Board." Nearly two weeks were allowed to pass between the writing of Butscher's brief notice that the new joint organization formed by "the treaty of union formulated by the unity committees elected at the Rochester and Indianapolis conventions" had endorsed Debs as its nominee for president of the United States. Shortly after Butscher's letter was written, the *Social Democratic Herald* published Debs's article "No Organic Union Has Been Effected," which warned that any organization that, through joint action with the "Kangaroo SLP," acted in "defiance" of the National Executive Board did thereby "secede from and sever their relations with the party." This open letter in reply to Butscher, released to the mainstream press, toned down that rhetoric greatly.

36. Heath was a key figure in the Milwaukee organization affiliated with the Chicago SDP. He would later become editor of the *Social Democratic Herald* following the merger establishing the Socialist Party of America, when that publication was added to publisher Victor L. Berger's Milwaukee stable.
37. Since he would be campaigning on behalf of the SDP rather than conducting paid lectures for about six weeks, a promise had been made to assist Debs with the outstanding legal debt of the American Railway Union, which he had been in the process of repaying through speaking fees.
38. In round numbers, 40 lost speaking dates to generate $2,000 would indicate an average net to Debs of $50 per speech.
39. The March 1900 convention of the Social Democratic Party approved a new constitution, subsequently ratified by referendum vote of the membership with the final tally of 801–50 announced on July 7. The new document called for replacement of the five-member National Executive Board (NEB) with a nine-member body, which was to include five members within commuting distance of headquarters (Chicago) and four others, hopefully from other areas of the country. On July 21, the outgoing NEB formally opened nominations. Outgoing board members Seymour Stedman and Debs both declined nomination, the former making the decision ostensibly to better dedicate himself as secretary of the campaign committee of the latter.
40. Concluding lines of "Marco Bozzaris" (1825), by Fitz-Greene Halleck (1790–1867).
41. First stanza of "Invictus" (1888), by William Ernest Henley (1849–1903).
42. Adapted from "Oration on Voltaire" (1878), by Victor Hugo (1802–1885).
43. This refers to votes cast for the presidential nominees of the Socialist Labor Party of America, Simon Wing (1892) and Charles Matchett (1896).
44. The *International Socialist Review,* edited by Chicago Socialist Labor Party dissident A. M. Simons (1870–1950), was launched in July 1900 by publisher Charles H. Kerr (1860–1944). It followed a pro-SDP unity political line.
45. "Damned dogs." The unusual phrasing is lifted from *Nicholas Nickleby* (1839), by Charles Dickens (1812–1870).
46. Allusion to the unlimited coinage of silver at the value ratio of 16:1 to gold.

47. The Coeur d'Alene strike of 1899 pitted hard rock miners affiliated with the Western Federation of Miners against mine operators intent upon rolling back wages and terminating union miners. The battle was a violent one, including gun battles, the dynamiting of a mill, intervention of federal troops, and the confinement of a thousand miners in a crude temporary prison called "the bull pen." Several years later, Democratic governor of Idaho Frank Steunenberg was assassinated in a bombing, for which WFM officials were blamed.
48. Thomas C. Platt (1833–1910) was a United States senator from New York and a recognized kingmaker of the Republican Party, as was his senatorial colleague, Mark Hanna of Ohio.
49. Richard W. Croker, Sr. (1843–1922) was the boss of the Democratic political machine headquartered at Tammany Hall in New York City.
50. From "Gathering Song of Donald the Black," by Walter Scott (1771–1832).
51. That is, the People's Party.
52. Counterintuitively, the "middle of the road" faction was the left wing of the People's Party, who distrusted William Jennings Bryan and the policy of cooperation with the Democratic Party.
53. From an appeal to the poor made by Victor Hugo shortly before his death in 1885.
54. Allusion to Joshua 10:12–13.
55. J. B. Smiley was a member of the arrangements committee for the appearance of Debs for an address at Central Music Hall in Chicago. The event was jointly arranged by adherents of both of the rival SDP organizations working in concert despite the animosity and mistrust of many in the Chicago-based Debs organization. *The Workers' Call,* edited by *International Socialist Review* editor A. M. Simons, was allied with the Social Democratic Party with headquarters in Springfield, Massachusetts.
56. See Debs, "Competition vs. Cooperation: Speech at Central Music Hall, Chicago," September 29, 1900, this volume.
57. William Jennings Bryan, for whom Debs campaigned actively in 1896, was again the nominee of the Democratic Party in 1900.
58. Samuel M. "Golden Rule" Jones (1846–1904) was a self-styled Christian socialist who served as mayor of Toledo, Ohio, from 1897 until the time of his death. In 1886, he established the Ohio Oil Company, which was later sold to John D. Rockefeller's Standard Oil Company, making Jones a wealthy man. He used the proceeds of the sale to establish the Acme Sucker Rod Company, which manufactured equipment for oil drilling, enacting the eight-hour day and a liberal wage scale for his employees as a manifestation of his belief in the "golden rule." Jones characterized himself as a "non-partisan believer in all the people"; his refusal to support the class-based Social Democratic Party frustrated Debs greatly.
59. After unsuccessfully campaigning for the election of William Jennings Bryan in 1900, the following year Samuel M. Jones won reelection with 57 percent of the vote. He was elected to a third term in 1903, receiving a plurality of 48 percent in a three-way race.
60. Edward B. Whitney (1857–1911) was a prominent figure in New York Democratic politics. He served as an assistant attorney general under Grover Cleveland.

61. Arthur P. Gorman (1839–1906) was a US senator from Maryland. Defeated in an 1898 reelection bid, he was returned to office by the Maryland legislature in 1902. Gorman was a white supremacist who worked to disenfranchise black voters, who tended to vote Republican, and was a supporter of the Republican policy of high tariffs.
62. Frank Steunenberg (1881–1905) was the Democratic governor of Idaho, serving in that capacity from 1897 to 1901. Steunenberg gained the enmity of the organized labor movement when he asked President William McKinley to send in federal troops to quell a violent strike by the Western Federation of Miners in April 1899. He was assassinated by a bomb outside his home in Caldwell, Idaho, on December 30, 1905.
63. Robert A. Van Wyck (1849–1918) was the Democratic mayor of New York City from 1898 to 1901.
64. Oliver Belmont (1858–1908) was a socialite and Democratic politician from New York, elected to Congress in the general election of November 1900.
65. Debs was given a bouquet of roses at the start of this speech, which formally launched his 1900 campaign for president of the United States.
66. Albert J. Beveridge (1862–1927) was a progressive Republican from Indiana who served in the US Senate from 1899 to 1911.
67. Debs's old nemesis Chauncey Depew (1834–1928), head of the New York Central Railroad, was elected to the first of two terms in the US Senate in 1898.
68. Edward O. Wolcott (1848–1905) of Colorado was first elected to the US Senate in 1888. He was not renominated by the Republicans in 1900, effectively ending his political career.
69. Russell Sage (1816–1906) was a New York financier and railroad executive who amassed a fortune through speculative investment.
70. Jones's letter to Debs of September 25, 1900 is reprinted in full in J. Robert Constantine (ed.), *Letters of Eugene V. Debs: Volume 1,* 149–52. This open letter published in response is not.
71. David Bennett Hill (1843–1910) was a Democratic US senator from New York from 1892 to 1897. He had previously served as governor of that state, following Grover Cleveland in holding that office.
72. The letter has not been preserved.
73. This signature parodies Jones's signature to his September 25 letter, "A man without a party."
74. Several "official totals" exist for the vote received by the 1900 Social Democratic ticket, none of which reach the 100,000 mark. The party ultimately received fewer than half of the more than 208,000 votes cast for the ticket of the Prohibition Party, the third-place finisher in the election. The result failed to meet the most cautious predictions of a vote and was deeply disappointing to Debs, a fact he makes clear in his letter to his most trusted political associate, his brother, Theodore, in a letter of November 9, 1900. In it, Debs lamented "the results show that we got everything—*except votes,* while remaining upbeat by the level of enthusiasm demonstrated by the crowds to which he spoke. (See: Constantine, *Letters of Eugene V. Debs: Vol. 1,* 154.)

75. The vote total of barely over 10,000 in New York State, in the wake of a march and mass meeting on the eve of the election at Madison Square Garden that drew an estimated 5,000 participants, is particularly suspect.
76. The call of the National Executive Board of the Chicago SDP for a January 15, 1901 special convention was published next to this article in the same issue of the *Social Democratic Herald.*
77. Herbert M. "Hub" Hoxie (1839–1886) was Jay Gould's first vice president of the Southwestern system from 1883.

1901

The Approaching Convention†

January 12, 1901

The special convention which meets at Chicago on the 15th [January 1901] promises to mark an important era in the progress of the party. It is called by members of the party, the "rank and file," of whom we hear so much these days, and they will have entire control of its deliberations.[1] Every member of the party is entitled to a seat in the convention with full rights as a delegate; and if unable to attend in person he may sign the credential of some other comrade, thus being represented by a delegate of his own personal choice. This will make the convention as democratic as such a body can possibly be.

And yet it is not doubted that we will hear about "boss rule" and "hero worship."[2] This sort of talk is not strange to us. We have heard it all along the route. It comes from the throat of envy and is inspired in the heart of failure.[3]

When you hear this cry, turn your dark lantern in the direction whence it comes, and you will see—not always, but generally—a very small man, or two or three of them, in fear of losing their occupation. They are desperately opposed to "bosses"—other than themselves. They are greatly alarmed lest their own service be dispensed with, and hence their lilliputian assaults upon "leaders" and "bosses" and "hero worshippers." Artemus Ward[4] would probably have classed them with his "amoosin kusses,"[5] and as such we dismiss them.[6]

The convention will be well attended, but I write to urge every comrade who can possibly do so to answer the roll call in person.

I heartily concur in the call for a national meeting at this time. Matters of great importance demand consideration and action. Delay would simply impede progress.

It is generally admitted that the party has outgrown its present form of organization. Certain changes are necessary that the party may keep pace with the progress of events.

There will be both opportunities and responsibilities for the delegates. They should and doubtless will be actuated by the loftiest motives. The party must be made the best expression of the socialist movement. If less than this, the defects must be remedied and the weak points strengthened.

---

† Published in *Social Democratic Herald*, vol. 3, no. 30, whole no. 132 (January 12, 1901), 2.

There is not one who does not wish to see all factions merged into one united party, but it is time wasted to try to force a union of inharmonious elements. The growth of the movement will do the work. The unifying process will go forward with the infusion of new blood.

It is not a question of uniting two antagonistic factions, but of bringing all the socialists of the country into harmonious alliance that there may be one united party which can summon to its aid all the strength of the socialist movement in grappling with the capitalist parties for the overthrow of capitalism.

The delegates must, if true to themselves and equal to their responsibilities, take advanced ground. Great strides have been taken since the last convention,[7] and the party must be adapted to the conditions now existing, and be prepared to face the future with not only a clear comprehension of its demands and necessities, but the required ability and power to successfully meet them as they come.

Tens of thousands stand ready to join us. Our policy must be such as to appeal to them, as well as to other thousands that are being rapidly prepared for socialism by the economic development.

Wisely directed, the coming convention will pave the way from the bogs and fens of factional strife to the highland of party supremacy.

As to "Hissing Snakes": Letter to the Editor of *The People*[†]

February 10, 1901

Comrade:—

In your issued of the 27th ult. [January 27, 1901] you have an editorial captioned "The Chicago Convention," from which the following is an excerpt.

† Published in *The People* [New York; dissident], February 10, 1901, original title and page unknown. Reprinted as "A Calumny Noticed," *Social Democratic Herald,* vol. 3, no. 35, whole no. 137 (February 16, 1901), 2. *The Papers of Eugene V. Debs* microfilm edition wrongly attributes this letter to 1900.

> We hope for an authoritative denial of the widely published report that Comrade Debs said that, after accepting the nomination of the comrades represented by the Springfield executive, he found himself in contact with a nest of hissing snakes.

For obvious reasons I break over a rule not to notice calumny. Every delegate who sat in the Chicago convention knows that the statement above quoted is an unmitigated falsehood, and so does the anonymous person who penned it. How "widely published" it has been I do not know, as your paper is the first and only one in which I have seen it.[8]

In a capitalist paper, such a paragraph would be perfectly becoming, but in a socialist paper, it is quite inexcusable. The editor is satisfied the statement is false, practically admits it, then proceeds to circulate it as widely as possible, and finally, in all charity, pleads with the victim to exculpate himself from the calumny he helped to fasten upon him.

Mr. Editor, it is easy to guess what party your informant belongs to, and it is safe to assume that he is an evangel of "unity." This is of small consequence, but allow me to suggest that the next time that such a palpable slander comes under your eye, you give the victim a chance to explain before, instead of after, crucifying him.

The recent Chicago convention in its clearly defined attitude voiced my sentiments in regard to socialists of all parties. I rejoice that my comrades went on record by acclamation and am confident that they will labor with becoming zeal to have the joint convention accomplish fully the purpose for which it is intended.

Yours fraternally,
Eugene V. Debs

Fraud and Imposture at Modern Funerals[†]

March 30, 1901

Two funerals of international interest have recently occurred. Queen Victoria of England and ex-president Harrison of the United States furnished the subjects, and their subjects furnished the funerals. The pomp and panegyric of these occasions dominated for days the columns of nearly every newspaper in Christendom. The amount of sham and hypocrisy that characterizes the burial of a modern ruler, no matter how useless, corrupt, or cruel, seems incredible to a sane person. The dead are always great as gods and immaculate as virgins. The press gushes with all its reserve force, and a mighty flood of fulsome flatulency inundates the country. Thousands vie with each other to honor (?) the dead, and all the adjectives are strained to give *éclat* to the grave occasion.

Queen Victoria lived and preyed upon her subjects as long as she could. She did not surrender the scepter until death wrung it from her nerveless grasp. All her long life she had been a parasite. She held the working class in sovereign contempt. They were only fit to labor, propagate their species, and die. This is the estimate all royalty places upon the working animals of the world. The queen was entitled to no special credit for dying. She simply could not help it.

Thousands of women, immeasurably her superior in all the qualities that distinguish true womanhood, die in England every year, but they go to their graves unhonored and unsung. Only a titled parasite excites the adulation of all mankind. We have traveled but little beyond the chattel slave who bowed in the dust before his master and poured out his gratitude for his chains.

The burial of General Harrison was equal in pomp and display to that of the English queen. The funeral pageant was gorgeous with military trappings, and this was its distinguishing feature. The report says: "The military display has not been equaled in Indiana since the breaking out of the Spanish-American War, when the state troops were mobilized. The entire National Guard was ordered out to escort the body of Indiana's distinguished citizen from the family residence to the state house."

In our capitalist society, the military establishment is growing steadily in power and popularity. Whether it be an inauguration, a funeral, or a labor

---

† Published in *Social Democratic Herald*, vol. 3, no. 41, whole no. 143 (March 30, 1901), 1.

strike, the soldiers are at the head of the procession and give military supremacy to the occasion. There is significance in this which reveals the tendency and design of capitalist development.

Benjamin Harrison was in some respects a superior man, while in some essential qualities he fell far short, and yet the press, in solemn accord, held him up as a paragon of virtue, a flawless model, a composite Lincoln, Washington, and Jesus Christ; and the multitude would scarcely have been astonished had the heavens opened wide to receive the dead president amidst the acclamation of angels. Why this exaggeration, hypocrisy, sham, flattery, fraud, and colossal lying when a public man dies? He is no better dead than living, and living or dead, the truth should be spoken.

"The Nation Mourns" is one of the favorite figures. It is the veriest balderdash. The nation mourns for nobody. Of course, the crowds gather, the bands turn out, and the "mourners" parade, but they do all that on very slight provocation, whether the occasion be a funeral or a picnic.

The great crowd at Indianapolis would have been on hand had the occasion been an inauguration, a prize fight, or a lynching, and from much of the same sense of patriotic duty.

General Harrison was held up as the loftiest of patriots, when in fact he never rendered his country a service which he was not well paid for.

Tens of thousands are yearning to sacrifice themselves upon the altar of their country at the same price. In all his ambitions, he served himself first, and whether as lawyer, soldier, or statesman, he demanded and received all the compensation his service would command.

But that is not what prompted the writing of this letter.[9] The biography of the ex-president has not been completed by his admirers of the capitalist press. Several incidents of consequence have been overlooked, and in the interest of truth I propose supplying them.

Benjamin Harrison was first and last in the service of the capitalist class. He was the enemy of workingmen. The capitalist press may deny it, but his record proves it.

When the great railroad strikes of 1877 reached Indianapolis, Harrison made his way into a meeting of strikers and in a speech proceeded to insult and discredit them. Among other things, he denounced them as a mob of lawbreakers, declaring that if he were in authority, he would put them back to work if he had to do it at the point of a bayonet. He was roundly hissed by the striking railroad employees and they left the hall in a body. The *Indianapolis News* said at the time, in reporting the speech, ". . . at this point the railroad portion of the audience rose en masse and made a break for the door."

Scores of men who attended that meeting, many of whom I personally knew, testified that Harrison declared in the same speech that a workingman could live on a dollar a day and that he ought to be willing to do it. Following the meeting, talk of mobbing the speaker was freely indulged in by the enraged strikers and their friends.

It was at this time that Benjamin Harrison organized Company C, consisting of 111 men, and had them armed with Springfield rifles for the purpose of shooting down the half-starved and unoffending strikers, and he had personal command of the company. Mayor Cavin had a different feeling toward the strikers and had 300 of them sworn in to protect railroad property and keep the peace, and it was thus that bloodshed was averted.

At this time, Harrison was a railroad attorney, and when the strike was over, he followed up and prosecuted the strikers. Innocent men were arrested and jailed, and Harrison succeeded in sending four of them to prison. The railroads paid him liberally for his infamous services, the records showing that he received $21,000 from the Ohio & Mississippi company.

The ex-president once made a speech in which he described his observation of a gang of street cleaners at work. He told about watching the poor devils who receive about $1.25 per day and how much time they waste during the day, reciting in detail how they first stop to take a chew of tobacco, then a drink of water, then to spit on their hands and so on, minutely, to the discredit and ridicule of the poor street workers, who, to a man with a heart in his breast, would appeal to the sympathy and a desire to aid, and could only extort a contemptuous sneer from a nature coldblooded and callous as a graven image.

When Grover Cleveland, while president, in 1894, ordered out the federal troops to murder workingmen at the command of the railroad companies, Benjamin Harrison heartily approved the action and publicly declared that, had he been president at the time, he would have pursued precisely the same course.

These are a few plain facts that should not be overlooked when the record is made up. Mr. Harrison has gone to his rest. I would do his memory no injustice, but out of respect for the truth, I would have the record read just as he made it.

In all this, there is a lesson for the workingmen. As long as they elect corporation attorneys and other hirelings of the capitalist class to rule them, the same consequences will follow, and they will be responsible for them. But gradually they are beginning to see. The glamour of imposture will not forever blind them. They are opening their eyes to the true meaning of military display and the "old soldier" fraud upon the government. The class conflict is appealing to them as never before; they are grasping the class-conscious doctrine and are filled and thrilled with the spirit of the coming revolution. The capitalist system must go, and with it all its shams, hypocrisies, and frauds, to make way for the socialist commonwealth and the reign of man.

Carnegie Libraries—Monuments of Degeneracy[†]

March 30, 1901

March 30, 1901

Many thousands of misguided people are applauding the alleged philanthropy of Andrew Carnegie and of these by far the larger number are workingmen. Manifestly they have forgotten, or they have never heard of the horrors of Homestead—or perhaps they are too ignorant to understand or too cowardly to profit by the bloody lesson.[10]

The reckless prodigality of Carnegie with the plunder of his victims brings into boldest prominence the crimes he committed when they protested against his monstrous rapacity. Then what? An army of 300 Pinkerton mercenaries were hired by this bloody benefactor to kill the men whose labor had made him a millionaire. He did not have the courage to execute his own murderous designs, so he commissioned another monster, Frick, by name, with bloodless veins and a heart of steel, to commit the crimes while he went to Europe and held high carnival with the titled snobs there until the ghastly work was done. It was one of the foulest conspiracies ever concocted against the working class, and the very thought of its atrocities, after nearly ten years, fires the blood and crimsons the cheek with righteous indignation. Not only were the Pinkerton murderers hired by Carnegie to kill his employees, but he had his steelworks surrounded by wires charged with deadly electric currents and by pipes filled with boiling water so that in the event of a strike or

† Published as "Crimes of Carnegie" in *The People* [New York, dissident], April 7, 1901, unspecified page. Reprinted in *The Missouri Socialist* [St. Louis], vol. 1, no. 15 (April 13, 1901), 2.

lockout he could shock the life out of their wretched bodies or scald the flesh from their miserable bones.

And this is the man who proposes to erect libraries for the benefit of the working class—and incidentally for the glory of Carnegie.

Will the workingmen of this country accept any gift from the hands of Andrew Carnegie, red with the blood of their slain comrades? That some of them have already done so is to their everlasting shame. The employees who a few days ago received, with expressions of gratitude, the bonded booty, to be held in trust for them until they become paupers, have debased themselves beyond expression. They may have to work for Carnegie, but they are not compelled to recognize as a gift the pennies he throws them in return for the dollars he stole from them, and when they do, they are guilty of treason to their murdered brothers, and are better described as spineless poltroons than as self-respecting workingmen.

Some years ago, when Carnegie endowed the first library for the alleged benefit of workingmen, I objected. And I object now with increased emphasis. Such a library is monumental of the degeneracy of the working class. It is a lasting rebuke to their intelligence and their integrity.

The workingmen of New Castle have led the revolt.[11] Let their splendid example be followed wherever a Carnegie library is suggested. Let mass meetings of workingmen be held, and let the horrifying scenes of the Homestead massacre be presented to stir them to a sense of indignation at the vulgar and insulting display of the spoil exploited from their class.

Let honest workingmen everywhere protest against the acceptance of a gift which condones crime in the name of philanthropy. Let them put themselves upon record in terms that appeal to the honor of their class and the respect of all mankind.

We want libraries and we will have them in glorious abundance when capitalism is abolished and the workingmen are no longer robbed by the philanthropic pirates of the Carnegie class. Then the library will be as it should be, a noble temple dedicated to culture and symbolizing the virtues of the people.

Socialists Who Would Emasculate Socialism and Other Matters†[12]

April 20, 1901

Socialism has been a long time on its journey from the past to the present. The truths it magnifies and the justice it demands have been in all the centuries in abeyance. The battles it has fought and the defeats it has sustained have not diminished, but increased its vigor. They were

> . . . [B]ut the prelude Fate's orchestra plays,
> To the strains that shall come in the fullness of days;
> For the age-lengthened rhythm beat out by the Fates
> In the building of cities, the founding of states,
> In the earthquakes of war, in its thunder and groans,
> In the battle of kings and the crumbling of thrones,
> Is but prelude that's written by Destiny's pen
> To herald an epoch of masterful men.
> And socialist heroes from the hills to the sea
> Have sent forth this call to the years yet to be.[13]

Yes, socialism calls for men. The fields are ripening for the harvest of great deeds, the fruitage of centuries; and reapers are wanted—men of courage, dauntless men, men who dare and men who do, men of brains, men of vision, men of ideas and ideals:

> Men with empires in their purpose,
> And new eras in their brains;
> Men whose thought shall pave new highways
> Up to ampler destinies.[14]

And such men—and women, too—are filling the ranks of socialism. The thrill of class-conscious solidarity is in their breasts. They defy defeat. The handwriting of destiny is on their banners.

ꟹ

The *Social Unity*, organ of the Social Reform Union, has an editorial on "A New Party" in its April [1901] issue. It is a curious mixture, the product of a disordered vision and confused mind.[15] Brief extracts follow:

---

† Published in *Social Democratic Herald*, vol. 3, no. 45, whole no. 147 (April 27, 1901), 1.

> One of the main functions of *Social Unity* is to find out what people think by instituting referendums. We held a referendum on the class consciousness question and found out that among the 2,500 people to whom this magazine goes, no great interest is taken in that special question, but that of those who did take the trouble to express an opinion, a large majority was opposed to the class-conscious position. We are now glad to institute a referendum on the question whether or not there should be a new political party formed for the campaign of 1901. We shall be curious to see how people vote on this question. * * *
>
> Eventually, we believe, we can do away with parties, but it may be that for the present we cannot and that it is necessary and possible, without being partisan, for the reform forces to establish and make use of a new party.

These people, mostly honest, imagine themselves socialists—that is, in a mild, not a malignant form. They have decided that there is no class struggle, and now they propose to determine whether or not to organize a new party—that is to say, whether or not capitalism will abolish itself. If a new party should be decided upon, it must not be partisan. Can any sane person conceive of such a monstrosity? Think of the wolf and the lamb in loving embrace, the fox and the pullet dancing a two-step, and the lion and the ox scouting the class-conscious doctrine over peaches and cream, while the ass mused, "I have long been waiting for this party of 'all the people.'"

Socialism was born of the class antagonisms of capitalist society, without which it would never have been heard of; and in the present state of its development, it is a struggle of the working class to free themselves from their capitalist exploiters by wresting from them the tools with which modern work is done. This conflict for mastery of the tools is necessarily a class conflict. It can be nothing else, and only he is a socialist who perceives clearly the nature of the struggle and takes his stand squarely and uncompromisingly with the working class in the struggle which can end only with the utter annihilation of the capitalist system and the total abolition of class rule.

We count everyone against us who is not with us and opposed to the capitalist class, especially those "reformers" of chicken hearts who are for everybody, especially themselves, and against nobody.

While I believe that most of these "reformers" are honest and well-meaning, I know that some of them, by no means inconspicuous, are charlatans and frauds. They are the representatives of middle-class interests, and the shrewd old politicians of the capitalist parties are not slow to perceive and take advantage of their influence. They are "socialists" for no other purpose than to emasculate socialism. Beaten in the capitalist game by better shufflers, dealers, and players, they have turned "reformers" and are playing that for what there is in it. They were failures as preachers and lawyers and politicians and capitalists. In their new role as "reformers," they dare not offend the capitalist exploiters, for their revenue depends upon their treason to the exploited slaves over whom they mourn dolefully and shed crocodile tears.

I respect the honest effort of any man or set of men, however misguided, to better social conditions, but I have no patience with the frauds and quacks who wear the masks of meekness and in the name of "brotherhood" betray their trusting victims to the class that robs them without pity and riots in the proceeds without shame.

On the very eve of the last national election, some of these "socialists" sprung a petition on me to withdraw in favor of Bryan. The Associated Press was cocked and primed, and the petition was flashed all over all the wires and appeared in all the capitalist papers. It was a political sandbagging conspiracy that would have done violence to the code of Hinky Dink.[16] The reports were freely published that the socialists had turned me down and would support Bryan. I tried to put the truth on the wires, but it would not go. The wires had their orders, my denial was refused, and the disreputable trick served the miserable purpose of its reptilian instigators.

This element will be conspicuously in evidence at the Detroit conference, and the capitalist press will accord them patient and respectful consideration.[17]

∽

Read this dispatch:

> UNION CITY, IND., April 20—Charles Penny of Greenville, O., a bricklayer, 30 years old, deadheading his way on a Panhandle train, was ordered off by a brakeman, and in jumping he fell under the wheels. His leg was crushed from the knee to the foot. In this condition, he crawled nearly a quarter of a mile, spending the night in a barn. He was brought here today and the limb amputated.

It is enough to make one's heart stand still. Looking for work, no doubt, and no money to pay fare. Probably has wife and children. It is horrible beyond description, and yet the chances are 99 in 100 that he votes with the Republican or Democratic Party, both of which support the existing system in which workingmen's lives are no more consequence than if they were vagabond dogs, and this is proclaimed to be the triumph of Christian civilization.

ꕤ

It is unquestionably true that Prof. Ross of the Leland Stanford University of California was dismissed for utterances along economic lines which the widow of the dead millionaire objected to, and, as she is the reigning queen of the institution, her will is law.[18] Free speech is not tolerated in the Stanford University, nor in any other university, and whatever may be the boast of the educators in such institutions, the fact remains that they are as certainly the wage-slaves of capitalism as are the coal diggers in the anthracite mines of Pennsylvania.

The Climax of Capitalism[†19]

April 27, 1901

At the present rate of industrial and commercial concentration it will not be long before competition in the realm of production will practically be a thing of the past. The great capitalists of the world, through their agents and promoters, are engineering gigantic deals and schemes to absorb or crush out all competition, thus giving them substantial and undisputed control of the situation, and enabling them to exploit the people at their own sweet will and exercise despotic authority over their countless victims.

So completely are these capitalists absorbed in their manipulations that it is doubtful if a single one of them realizes that they are working with might and main for their own financial undoing and that at the climax of capitalism they will be "hoist by their own petard," and socialism, which they affect to despise and dread, will relieve them of their crowns and scepters, abolish their despotic functions, and give them equal opportunities with others to earn an honest living and enjoy "life, liberty, and the pursuit of happiness."

When the glorious day dawns, the capitalists will work for what they get, and the workers will get what they work for. The hideous inequalities which now mock civilization and deform society will be known no more forever, except in the historic annals of the "dark ages" of capitalism.

In this terrific rush toward the climax, which may be spelled cataclysm,

---

† Published in *Advance* [San Francisco], whole no. 351 (April 27, 1901), 1.

Andrew Carnegie, whose income is a million a month, is having a desperate time resisting the surplus value that is forced upon and threatens to engulf him. The other day he made a gift of $4 million in charities for the benefit of his disabled and superannuated employees. He scatters libraries as the wind scatters leaves in autumn. It may be that the Scotch-American multimillionaire sees some writing on the wall, or that in his advancing years, as the horrors of Homestead come back to his memory, and he sees the streets slippery with the blood of workingmen he robbed and then hired Pinkerton thugs to murder, his conscience festers with accusation and he hopes to blot out the awful tragedy by tapping the vast reservoir of blood which his cupidity prompted him to drain by force and crime from the veins of his helpless wage-slaves.

The tragedy of Homestead is fresh in our memory. The wound in the body of labor, "poor dumb mouth," is mutely crying for vengeance. Carnegie the philanthropist, who went to Europe and left Frick, the monster, in charge, cannot escape responsibility for the infamous crime of the 300 Pinkerton thugs who murdered workingmen in 1892. He was deaf to every appeal, and upon his soul the bloodstains are as ineffaceable as the spots on the skin of a leopard, and though he build ten thousand libraries, the ghosts of his victims will surmount them all and point their fleshless fingers of guilt at the rankest Pharisee in Christiandom.

The days in which we live are indeed pregnant with great possibilities. The working class is charged with the gravest responsibility of the ages, and the day of action draweth nigh. What a privilege to have a part in the closing acts of this stupendous drama! The slavery of all the centuries is to be blotted from the earth forever, and it is for this sublimest of achievements that the socialists of all lands are marshaling their hosts to do and to dare until capitalism is overthrown and the working class seizes the scepter of authority and rules the world.

Workingmen of America, do not forget for an instant that the great struggle in which you are engaged is a class conflict, and that the lines must be sharply drawn in every battle, whether on the economic or the political field. The slavery of your class is responsible for your chains, rags, and crusts, and never until your entire class is emancipated can you escape from the iron grasp of your capitalistic masters.

So far as this struggle is concerned, there is no good capitalist and no bad workingman. Every capitalist is your enemy, and every workingman is your friend. You have got to stand and act as one. Solidarity is your salvation, and socialism points unerringly the way.

Day by day, the class-conscious socialist movement increases in power. It scorns all compromise. It firmly holds every inch it conquers. It cannot be intimidated by frowns nor frightened by threats. It is pursuing its historic course and come what may, it will press on and on until the goal is reached and labor rules the world.

The July Convention†

June 15, 1901

The convention for unifying socialists and converting jarring factions into a united party is now a certainty. The Socialist Labor Party alone declines to participate.[20] This is to be regretted—and yet, perhaps, it may be better so. Time will tell. Whatever may be said about the policy of the Socialist Labor Party in hoeing its own row, it must be admitted that more or less danger attends the converging of factions which have long been divided and are still, being human, influenced by their prejudices and their antipathies.

But the very fact that the convention was agreed to by practical unanimity would seem to indicate that the separate columns are ready to unite into a grand army, and that henceforth factional strife is to be silenced and the combined resources of the party are to be brought into concerted action upon the enemy.

As one who earnestly hopes that the convention may accomplish the object for which it has been called, I wish to address a few words to the members of our own party, urging that as many of them as possible be in attendance. The wholesome effect of the commingling and intercourse of the rank and file of the various factions will serve not only to check any tendency on the part of the leaders to yield to their former antipathies, but also to hold the convention true to its course until its mission shall have been accomplished.

It is also important that our delegates should enter the convention hall representing a party free from encumbrance, and as our debt is but small, each branch should cheerfully contribute the trifle necessary to discharge the indebtedness to the last farthing, so that we shall be able to close an honorable

† Published in *Social Democratic Herald*, vol. 3, no. 52, whole no. 154 (June 15, 1901), 1.

record, if that is necessary, and transfer to our successors a clear and clean set of books.

I shall not venture to discuss prospects and probable results further than to say that I confidently believe a united party is inevitable. The bitter experiences of the past were perhaps necessary to a more thorough compact and disciplined party, and if we shall profit by it, a new era in the socialist movement of the United States will date from the Indianapolis convention.

The one thing necessary is that we shall have a sound socialist party, with a platform that will bear the test of critical analysis. By this I do not mean that we shall quibble and split hairs, but that so far as the fundamental principles of socialism are concerned, they shall be stated with such clearness as to silence all reasonable question as to our party being free from the taint of compromise and in harmonious alliance with the socialist movement of the world.

The convention need not last long. The sooner it settles the question and adjourns, the better. A day would suffice, though I have no expectation that we shall have such luck. Still, I hope some of the long-winded vocal efforts which seem necessary to all conventions—socialist like the rest—will be postponed or abbreviated.

What we want to do is to get together and down to business. A provisional committee could handle affairs until a permanent one is chosen by the several states, and I am in favor of having every state absolutely control its own affairs, thus leaving little for the national party to do except in years of presidential campaigns. In this particular, we can safely follow the methods of the old parties, whose leaders are adepts at organization.

There will be no trouble to organize after the convention. Rapid growth is what we shall have to guard against, and that is a danger which will threaten the socialist movement more and more as it advances to political prominence.

If I am permitted to attend the convention, I shall have but one object there. I shall have no friends to favor and no enemies to punish. The scalps I am after do not grown in socialist timber.

The Mission of Socialism Is as Big as the World: Speech to Third Annual SDP Picnic, Chicago[†21]

July 4, 1901

Ladies, Gentlemen, and Comrades:—

It is our good fortune, if we can boast no other, to live in the most marvelous age of all the centuries, not contemplating the material progress of our time, which overwhelms and bewilders by its extraordinary achievements. Improvements have been accomplished as if by magic, and we behold with wonder and awe the march of human conquest. The forces of nature which terrified primitive man, and before which the ancient world bent in superstition, have to a large extent been conquered and are the subject servants of man's desire. In this march of progress, the brain and heart have been expanded, the one shedding light and the other life, without which civilization would turn back upon its axis. Fortunately for man, everything is subject to change, and all change tends to the development of the race and the advancement of human institutions. Institutions crumble in this march of time. All of them have their periods of gestation, of birth, of development, maturity, decline, decay, and death. All of them come in their order. They fulfill their mission, they give birth to their offspring, and they pass away.

A little over a century ago, the inhabitants of this country were not citizens. They were ruled by a foreign king. They petitioned for relief. Their petitions were disregarded. They objected to taxation without representation. Their protests were scorned. Finally, they revolted. They issued the Declaration of Independence and enunciated the proposition that men are created equal. But the founders of this republic had only vague conceptions of democracy. The working class as we understand it today were not represented in the Constitutional Convention. The founders of the Republic, in declaring that men were created equal, evidently meant themselves alone. They did not include the Negro, who had been brought here against his will and had been reduced to a state of abject slavery. The institution of chattel slavery was already securely established at that time. It was founded in iniquity, yet it did not seemingly

---

† Published in *Social Democratic Herald,* vol. 4, no. 4, whole no. 158 (July 13, 1901), 1, 4.

disturb the consciences of the founders of the Republic. This institution was in conflict with the spirit of the Declaration, with the genius of free institutions, and yet it was incorporated in them. It steadily grew in power, and in course of time it controlled the country and the courts and the life of the people.

On this day, commemorating the Fourth of July, 1776, the Declaration of Independence was issued. Thousands of orators all over this broad land will glorify the institutions under which we live. In pride, they will point toward Old Glory and declare that it is a flag that waves over a free country. In these modern days, we hear very much about that flag and about the institutions over which it waves. I am not of those who worship the flag. I have no respect for the stars and stripes, or for any other flag that symbolizes slavery. It does not matter to me what others may think, say, or do. I propose to preserve the integrity of my soul. I will give you a transcript of my mind and tell you precisely what I think. Not very long ago, the president of the country [William McKinley], in the attitude of mock heroics, asked who would haul down the flag. I will tell him. Triumphant socialism will haul down that flag and every other that symbolizes capitalist class rule and wage slavery.

I am a patriot, but in the sense that I love all countries. I love the sentiment of William L. Garrison: "All the world is my country and all mankind are my countrymen." Thomas Jefferson once said: "Where liberty is, is my country." That is good. Thomas Paine said: "Where liberty is honored, that is my country." That is better. Where liberty is not, socialism has a mission, and, therefore, the mission of socialism is as wide as the world.

ᴒ

The framers of the Constitution of this country had no faith in the people. They did not suffer them to see the proceedings of the convention. The insufferable institution of chattel slavery was compromised in the American Constitution. It was at this time a perfectly legal institution, but it was founded in iniquity. It was doomed to finally disappear, and the agitation against it began in a feeble way. Lovejoy was one of the pioneers of the revolt. He went to New England and then to Illinois, and with all the vigor of his intellect began to attack slavery. A committee called upon him. He said to them, "I can afford to die at my post, but I cannot afford to desert it." I take pride in paying to such a man the humble tribute of my gratitude and love. It is such men as he who have made it possible for me to enjoy some degree of liberty. I can only discharge my duty to him and to them to try to do something for those who are to come after me. In 1837, the mob took his office and destroyed it by fire, his printing press was thrown in the Mississippi River, and he was murdered.

But to the greatest and noblest figure among those early pioneers was reserved the final act which culminated in the rule in which the institution of slavery disappeared from American soil. I need only mention his name, and although it is a very common one, you will at once recognize it—John Brown. He was educated in no college, he graduated from no university—he was simply a child of the people. He knew that his part in that struggle required the sacrifice of his life, and with a dozen men he attacked the so-called Commonwealth of Virginia. He struck the immortal blow. He was dragged through a mob trial, he was sentenced to death. On his way to the gallows, he begged for a Negro child and pressed a kiss upon its black face.

He was strangled to death. His soul went its way to that borne from which no traveler returns. John Brown was branded a traitor, a scoundrel, and a monster of iniquity. The whole country applauded the crime. In just ten years, with the mellowing wings of time, John Brown was the hero of the people; enshrined in their hearts—he had won immortality.

Chattel slavery disappeared because in the development of machinery an improved form of slavery was required, and this new slavery must not be confined to the black race alone, but must embrace within its mighty folds all of the toiling children of men. Slavery in that form only became extinct, and the people as such only rose against it when it became impossible; and just here it is in order to say that the development in every form is dependent upon economic conditions.

We live today under a system that has the best code of morals and the best instruments of production and distribution. It has also the most destructive weapons of warfare. Commercialism not only requires the cheapest possible production, but it also requires the most murderous instruments of death, and in the full development of this system, the world pays its highest tribute to that man who can devise ways and means that can murder the most men in the smallest space of time. If you go to the city of Washington tomorrow with some device that will enable you to kill 1 million human beings in the twinkling of an eye, your name will become famous.

ᔕ

When the [Civil] war closed, modern machinery was developing very rapidly, the small workshop was beginning to disappear, being supplanted by the larger factory. The individual worked no longer by himself, for his tool had been touched by the magic of industrial evolution; the shop began to expand, and the modern industrial revolution was on. Up to this time, production was carried on largely for use in separate communities. There was no demand for a foreign market because there was no surplus production, and the worker's ability to consume was equal to his producing capacity. But with the advent of machinery, conditions were changed. If the workers had had intelligence enough to have retained the ownership and control of the tool—that is to say, of the means of production, there would have been no such problems as now confront us.

The women were formerly the queens of the homes, and the children were being sent to school and equipped for the battle of life. When labor began to supply so abundantly and the machine could be operated by the finger of a little child, we had an intensification of the struggle—women competing with men and the child competing with all. No workingman is given employment that he may provide for himself and his family. It is only on condition that a profit can be extracted from his labor. If there is no profit, he is discharged. His wife may suffer, his children may be on the street; no matter what the results, he cannot work.

I have said again and again, in this system, there is nothing quite so cheap as human flesh and blood. It is in the power of a single individual sitting in New York to press a button that will send a message over the wire that will doom 50,000 willing men, women, and children. Concentration and cooperation are the master forces of this age. In the conflict that is going forward among the capitalists, the capital of the country is held in the hands of a few, and these few, though untitled and uncrowned, wield greater power than crowned kings and despots. The owners of the means of production are the real rulers of the American people and of all other people of other nations. Those who control the means of production, land, and capital, control all human institutions.

൭

Now, there are a great many men who believe that they have a voice in government. You workingmen have as much to do with the control of this government as if you inhabited Mars or some other planet. *[Cheers.]* You regularly deposit your ballot and suppose it to be counted. The will of the people is supposed to be registered. But what your votes register is the will of the capitalist class. The capitalist class rules absolutely in every department of our government. It controls every legislature. It controls both branches of Congress, and the Supreme Court is simply its convenience. Why, it is not possible for a lawyer, whatever his attainments, to find his way to the bench of the Supreme Court unless he has given overwhelming evidence of his capacity to serve the capitalist class and his willingness to crook the pregnant hinges of the knee that thrift may follow fawning. Every judge who sits on the bench of the Supreme Court today is a tool of the capitalist class. I had an experience. *[Great applause.]* I think it was a good thing. I ought to have known better. The working class have no rights.

☙

I am not fond of denouncing the capitalist class. I am more inclined to find fault with the working class. Now, do you know that for every capitalist, large and small, in the United States, there are about ten workingmen? That is to say, you workingmen are in the majority, are in the clear majority of ten to one, and as long as you suffer the capitalist class to rule, you do not deserve to fare better. As Lincoln said: "If that is what you want, that is what you want," and as long as you are satisfied with the capitalist rule or misrule, you will have to submit to it.

Now, a few workingmen realize that the old parties are simply two wings of the same capitalist vulture, and that every reform party is a straggling tail feather in that same bird. Socialism is after that bird, and if you look at it, you can see the light between the wings. Some of that light is beginning to reach gradually the working class. They are beginning to realize, first, that their interests as workingmen are absolutely identical, that what is good for one is good for all, what is equal for one is equal for all. They are beginning to realize that there are trade unions in the year 1901 which fall short of requirements; that while organization is a necessity upon the economic field, it is vastly more important on the political field. There was a time when there was some efficiency in the strike. What difference does it make to you to go out on strike, even if you win a raise in your wages of 15, 20, or 25 cents per day, if the same class that employs and pays your wages has also the power to raise the cost of the commodities?

In the wage system, you and your children, and your children's children, if capitalism shall prevail until they are born, are condemned to slavery, and there is no possible hope unless by throwing over the capitalist and voting for socialism. Now, what you want to do is quit every capitalist party of every name whatsoever. What you want to do is to organize your class and assert your class interests as capitalists do the interests of the class that is robbing you. It will not do for you to go to the polls and vote for some good men on some of the tickets and expect relief in that way. What can a good man do if he should happen to get to Congress? What could he do? Why, he simply would be polluted or helpless, or both. What we want is not to reform the capitalist system. We want to get rid of it. *[Tremendous cheers.]*

☙

Now, it is a curious thing to me that a great many workingmen will vote for a thing that will do them no good, a thing that they do not want, because they are dead sure of getting it; and they will vote against the thing they need, against the thing they want, because they reason that if they all vote for it, they might get it. Every workingman in every community should assert himself on election day, totally regardless of what others do.

Suppose you are the only socialist in the community. Now, that might require a little more courage on your part, and if you lack it, we cannot win. But if you have a little more courage, and if you cast a socialist vote, you will give some evidence of the final redemption of your community. If you cast that vote, someday you and your children will be proud of it; you will make a beginning, and you will soon have company. Now, I would rather vote my convictions and vote alone than to vote against my convictions and be with the majority. What good is it to be with the majority of cowards, anyway? As a matter of fact, in the history of great principles, men everywhere have been wrong outside the minority. All of these great changes depend upon minorities, and in the march of time a minority becomes a majority, and everyone applauds. In ten years from now, it will be very difficult in the city of Chicago to find a man who was not a socialist 25 years ago.

There has never been any democracy in the world. Political democracy in the United States, so called, is a myth. A single capitalist, upon whom 25 workingmen depend, has political power more than equal to the slaves in his employ, simply because he owns and controls the means upon which their lives depend, without which they are doomed to idleness and starvation. What good would it do if it were in my power to shut off the supply of life and heat; you would all vote my ticket, would you not? Your lives depend upon the control and ownership of the means of production and distribution.

The owner of the slaves had to provide for them, he had to feed them, and he had to care for them in a way. It is not necessary to own slaves bodily today in order to exploit their labor. You simply have to own the tool, then they are completely at your mercy. To begin with, a slave cannot buy the modern tool. They are gigantic machines of great cost. The great mass of workingmen cannot buy them. They are compelled to present themselves at the door of the giant and humbly petition him for the privilege of using the tools they made for a share of what their labor produces. They are at his mercy, and not only this, but in the regular periods of depression that always follow periods of activity, it is even a privilege to be a slave, and thousands of so-called free Americans are denied that privilege. *[Cheers.]* If they go on voting the Republican ticket and the Democratic ticket, either party perpetuates the system that keeps them in fetters and their wives in rags and their children in hunger.

Arouse, ye slaves! Declare war, not on the capitalist, but on the capitalist system, and if it should be your fate or your fortune to suffer in years to come, that suffering will not be the result of your own deliberate act. I am for the freedom of the working class. Though my heart yearns for the freedom of men, I am powerless. Only the working class itself can achieve its emancipation. The workingman who is not yet awakened, who has not yet realized all his class interests, is a blind tool, the willing instrument of his own degradation, and thousands of them on the Fourth of July, when reference is made to the capitalist flag that symbolizes the triumph of capitalism only, thousands of these wage-slaves will applaud their own degradation. What is wanted is not a reform of the capitalist system, but its entire abolition.

ℒ

Notwithstanding the boast that is often made that this is an era of prosperity, notwithstanding the statement that is made by capitalist politicians that the wages of workingmen are higher than ever in the history of the country, I do not hesitate to declare, and I challenge refutation, that there never was a time when wages were so small in proportion to the products as now. Politicians assure us that we are extremely prosperous because our exports exceed the exports of all other nations of the world. What have you got to do with the exports? I think if you held a little interview with your stomach, you are more interested with import than export. Much money goes into the pockets of the capitalist class out of the product of your labor. You never receive notice from the government to get your share of the dividends, and, as a matter of fact, in this system the more you produce the worse you are off. If you could produce as much tomorrow as you could in the next six months, you would be out of a job the day after tomorrow. *[Loud applause.]*

I wonder how many of the workingmen of Chicago are enjoying today at the sea coast this summer, or how many of them are toying with icicles in the arctic region, and next September how many will go down to Florida and stop at the Palmetto Hotel? Not many of them. Only the man can afford these luxuries, can afford these enjoyments, who has nothing to do with the production of them. No man that has anything to do with building a Pullman car can ride in it. You show me a man who has to make a Pullman car, and I will show you a man who walks when he travels.

If you have calloused hands, I will show you precisely what degree you mark on the social thermometer. I will locate you close to the zero point.

A man has to be a master or a slave. He will have to either wield a lash or hold the plow. Socialism proposes to free them both and level them both up to the plane of manhood. Whatever walk of life, constant struggle is going forward, man is arrayed against man, nation against nation, and all due to the capitalist system. The survival of the fittest is a survival of cunning over conscience. Business means doing somebody else, and in the struggle, the middle class loses in economic power. Men are driven to dishonesty in the system; they suspect each other, not because they do not know each other, but because they do. It is a mock civilization. Socialism will give humanity a new world. *[Great cheer.]*

Businessmen attend the same prayer meeting, but they keep a business eye on each other. Business is business, and each one knows that the other is trying to do him. In the capitalist system, we cannot give expression to the noblest sentiments of humanity; all success is born of failure and he who achieves the largest success succeeds in destroying the largest number of his fellow men.

ᔓ

The revolution is underway, but, like all revolutions, it is totally blind. It is in the nature of great social forces that they sometimes sweep humanity down. Let us work so that this revolution may come in peace. Socialists are organized to pave the way for its peaceful culmination.

We appeal first to the working class to come together in one class-conscious solidarity. We likewise appeal to the middle class who will day by day be forced down in the crowded ranks of the working class. We are asking them to open their eyes and see the new light. Their class is doomed, and this debauched civilization is doomed to disappear with them. If I were in the middle class today, I would be a socialist. I would be a socialist from a perfectly selfish motive. I would say to myself: "My class is to be crowded out, and my only hope is in the new social order; and although I may not live to see it, I may be doomed to die a slave, I will cast my lot with the man that proposes to make it possible for my children and the children of my children to enjoy life."

But there are a great many who say that is all well enough, but we will not see it in our time. When a man talks so to me, I am inclined to think that there is something seriously wrong with him. Very often the case is that it is impossible to reach the intellect of such a man as this. It is questionable whether he has a thing that we can properly call by that name.

So far as I am concerned, it does not matter in the slightest whether it comes next year or next century, or in a thousand centuries—that is not a question that concerns me. I simply know that the change is bound to come sometime, and I know that it is my duty to do all I can to hasten its coming; and although I feel and indeed, I know, that I will be here to help celebrate its coming, to ratify its triumph, whether I am or not is a matter of the slightest consequence. I simply say that the capitalist system has almost fulfilled its mission. On every hand, we behold the signs of change. It is disintegrating. It is to dissolve and pass away, and you can prolong it if you wish, and that is what you are doing if you are supporting the old parties.

❧

There are two fundamental principles that are in conflict with each other—individualism and cooperation. Now, there is perfect individualism among the beasts of the jungle. They do not cooperate, they compete, and the stronger competitor devours the weaker. You see a girl in the sweatshop only able to earn enough to keep her wretched soul within her shrunken body. Her pulled cheeks, her sunken eyes, her emaciated body testify to the poverty and horror of the competitive system. Hail the coming of socialism!

But in every nation, in every civilized nation, men and women are massing beneath the banner of socialism, men and women, for in socialism woman stands side by side with man, she has all the rights that he enjoys.

We declare, then, that the time has come when workingmen should open their eyes to the economic struggle, when they should have an intelligent understanding of socialism and pave the way for its triumph and the abolishment of capitalism from the face of the world.

Now, I have a right to get rich if I can in this system. I scorn to get rich. I could get rich only by making someone else poor. Suppose I have sharper claws and keener fangs than some of the rest of you, am I justified in using them to prey upon your vitals? If I have any ability whatever, I can only prove it by using it for the benefit of my fellow man. John Rockefeller is as completely a slave as any coal miner in the anthracite region of Pennsylvania. He lives in a gilded cell, but he is serving a life sentence. He does not mingle with his fellow men, he does not enjoy the fellowship of the class he robs. He rules by the power of private ownership, and he tries to ease the pangs of conscience by endowing universities. We do not want educational institutions in that way, and when socialism supplants capitalism, and when the wealth that is created is in the possession of the men who created it, when every man has not only plenty of what is required to supply his physical wants, but has leisure to enjoy, we will fill this country with educational institutions, we will make education universal; not only that, we will rescue industry from its cupidity. Then man shall stand erect in touch with his fellow man. He will be the monarch of his work. It will not be possible for one man to enslave another without forging fetters for himself. There is no release, there is no relief on any other line. It is socialism or capitalism; as capitalism declines, socialism follows it, so it is only a question of time.

ဢ

I like the Fourth of July. It breathes a spirit of revolution. On this day, we reaffirm the ultimate triumph of socialism. It is coming as certain as I stand in your presence. Trials are not to be regretted. They are a part, and a necessary part, of the development. We may disagree. We may divide. It is possible that we shall quarrel and still be perfectly honest. The development demands it all. We are all subscribers to the same fundamental principles. We all stand upon the same uncompromising platform. We all have our faces turned toward the economic dawn. We are battling for the triumph of the producers of the world. We are in touch with the international socialists of the world—with our ears turned down, we can hear the thrones totter before the great march of the international hosts of socialism.

So do not be discouraged for a single instant. If you have the courage of your convictions, you can face the universe. So far as I am concerned, if there were a million, I would be one of the million. If they should be reduced to a thousand, I would be one of a thousand; if reduced to a hundred, I would be one of the hundred; if a single one survive, I would be that one against the world. I want every one of you to be that one, and if you find that you are not so constituted that you can be that one against the world, you have no place in the socialist movement, but go to the old parties and stay there until you get ripe.

We are educating, we are agitating, we are organizing, that is to say, we are preparing for the inevitable. It is only a question of time when socialists will be in the majority. They will succeed on a platform declaring for the social ownership of the means of production and distribution. Then the factory will no longer be a dismal den thronged with industrial convicts. Then for a' that and a' that, man to man the world o'er, shall brothers be for a' that.

Telegrams to the Joint Unity Convention Founding the Socialist Party of America†

July 29 and 30, 1901

I.

Terre Haute, Ind. [July 29, 1901]

As I cannot be present, I send greetings to the convention, and best wishes for the success of its deliberations.

Eugene V. Debs

II.

Terre Haute, Ind. [July 30, 1901]

The expression of the convention is gratifying to the extreme.[22] May a united and harmonious party crown your labors. Press reports do not disturb me. I am a socialist. A thousand thanks to the delegates for their personal expression. But for illness in my family, I would be with you.

Eugene V. Debs

† Published in *Proceedings of Socialist Unity Convention Held at Indianapolis, Indiana Beginning on July 29, 1901*. Mimeographed typescript published in St. Louis by the Socialist Party of America, 1904. First day's session, 15; third session, 29.

"They May Shelve Me If They Like": Statement to the *Philadelphia Times*†

July 30, 1901

Eugene V. Debs was not unprepared for the story from Indianapolis that the Springfield faction of the socialists' unity convention was in the majority and sought to repudiate him as a leader.[23] *He is kept at home by the serious illness of his wife, his own mother, and his wife's mother. He said when he read the press report that he was to be shelved:*

They may shelve me if they like. It is simply an effort on the part of the Eastern faction to dictate to the Chicago faction, of which I am a member.[24] But they cannot dictate socialism's future. It is clear to me that if the Indianapolis convention does not act in harmony that the time for socialism's debut as a strong, active party is not here.

When the time comes, it will sweep into power. It needs no leader. No leader can make socialism, and no would-be leader can unmake it. There must be men to head the movement, but no leader can dictate its course. It is a party of men, and not of a man.

I have no desire to be a leader. If I had been politically ambitious, I could have found a profitable home in one of the old parties. No man can truthfully accuse me of being of a grasping disposition. If I had been, I would not today be striving to upbuild socialism.

† Published as "Future of Socialism" in *Philadelphia Times,* whole no. 9433 (August 1, 1901), 2.

A United, Harmonious, and Enthusiastic Party: Letter to the Editor of *The Worker*†

August 5, 1901

Terre Haute, Ind., August 5 [1901]

Editor of *The Worker*:—

The Socialist delegates who met at Indianapolis last week and by their wise counsel, patient effort, and fidelity to principle converted rival factions into a united, harmonious, and enthusiastic party, are entitled to the thanks and congratulations of every socialist in the country.

Considering the strained relations of the past, and many other difficulties under which the delegates assembled, they accomplished all, and even more, than could reasonably have been expected, and it is with special satisfaction that I voice my approval of the results of their labor. There may be those who will use a magnifying glass in seeking points of objection, but I am confident that hearty concurrence will mark the verdict of the membership at large.

Only our friends, the enemy, have cause for chagrin and disappointment. Most assiduously did their emissaries scatter the seed of dissension and strife, but it failed to germinate. The soil and climate were not congenial to it, and the crop was a total failure. In the severity of debate, it may have seemed at times as if the convention was doomed to failure, but as passion subsided, the delegates were brought nearer and nearer together until, at last, all differences were hammered into forms of harmony and strength, and the stirring strains of "The Marseillaise" burst from the throat of the delegation and proclaimed the triumph of the convention.

The platform is a sound and practical expression of the principle and program of the party; the name is free from objection; the general plan of organization meets the demand, and the national headquarters have been wisely located.

For national secretary, the convention could not have made a better choice than Leon Greenbaum.[25] Knowing the comrade personally, I can with pleasure bear testimony to his honesty, efficiency, and unflagging devotion to socialist principles.

---

† Published as "Comrade Debs is Pleased" in *The Worker* [New York], vol. 11, no. 19 (August 11, 1901), 1.

Through *The Worker,* I extend a hand of cordial congratulation to every comrade.[26] Let the dead past bury its dead. Let the convention stand as a monument above internal dissension and factional strife.

The proletariat is to be organized for the great class struggle, and the task appeals for our united and unflinching efforts. Hail the Socialist Party of America and the Social Revolution!

The Indianapolis Convention: Letter to the Editor of the *Social Democratic Herald*[†27]

August 6, 1901

It is not to find fault, but to commend and approve, that I write [of the] socialist convention held at Indianapolis. While I could wish results [differed in] some particulars, in the main, the work accomplished by the delegates [meets with un]qualified approval. The best was done that could have been expected [under the] circumstances, and now it remains for us to ratify the labors of the [convention in] a united and determined effort to make the socialist party *the* Socialist Party of America.

The general plan of organization adopted by the delegates makes it [possible] for all hands to work in harmony in building the party, and if the energy hitherto exerted in factional strife is now employed in the right direction, [we shall] soon have a socialist party that will make its influence felt in the [politics of the] country and strike terror to the exploiters of the working class.

The convention, while providing for an efficient national organization, left the states and territories free and untrammeled in their own jurisdictions, and [each] of them is the master of its own propaganda and can proceed with the work of organization according to its peculiar conditions and tendencies, provided only that the fundamental principles of the party are kept inviolate.

The platform, as finally adopted, is a clear and forceful expression of the principles and purposes of the party. While uncompromisingly socialistic in

---

† Published in *Social Democratic Herald* [Milwaukee], vol. 4, no. 7, whole no. 159 (August 17, 1901), 3.

every plank, it is broad enough as a whole for all socialists to stand upon. The party is not the less revolutionary because of the "demands" attached to the platform, [as] these clearly explain themselves and furnish a working program that will rally many to the party's standard who otherwise would keep aloof from it.

It is possible to make a platform all "science" and no sense. The one adopted at Indianapolis has both. It is the socialist conception of present political and economic conditions and tendencies and is so clearly expressed as to compel conviction.

The new name of the party is more suitable than the old, for the present at least, and until socialism has disinfected the term "democrat" from the foul pestilence of capitalist politics which clings to it like the garment of a leper.

The national headquarters are well located in St. Louis, and Leon Greenbaum will make an efficient national secretary.

For the rest, I am entirely satisfied to trust to the logic of events. The broad field of socialist activity spreads out before us, and there is ample work and opportunity for all.

The enemies of the party relied on the efficacy of falsehood and misinformation to disrupt the convention and defeat unity.

From the opening to the closing day, they had the writer turned down with the heel of the convention on him to keep him there. All of which is very [*illegible*], or would be if it had not been otherwise. The convention had other business and transacted it with fidelity and earned the respect and gratitude of its constituents; and, as for the writer, he will "turn up" often enough before he gets through to relieve all anxiety on that score.

I feel as if a special word is due our own delegates. They represented the party ably and faithfully from first to last, and contributed in full measure to the success of the convention. In the debates, in the counsels, and on the committees they won honorable distinction, and their work should be ratified by [every] member of the party.

I rejoice that the *Herald* is not only to live but to expand. It was our only light during many dark days, and I feel for it the attachment of an old comrade. In Milwaukee, it has a future. With Comrades Edwards, Berger, Heath, Thomas, and others in control, it will be heard from as the battle proceeds.

All success to the Socialist Party of America!

Statement to the Press on the Shooting of President William McKinley†

September 7, 1901

I cannot imagine anything so deplorable. I cannot conceive the motive for an attack on a man who is so universally admired as is President McKinley.[28] Misery and poverty must have caused it. The deed was not that of a madman. The method he pursued shows that the act was coolly and deliberately planned. It is one of the periodical outbreaks of a festering society. One cannot imagine the mental status of a man so mean, so cowardly, so brutal as to join in the throng that was pressing forward to greet the president and have the murder of the one whose hand he sought to grasp in his heart.

Under pretense of greeting him as an admirer, he shot the president to give to the world the definition of his own misery. It was because he represented the great American people as their chief executive, and he thought that by ending the president's life he would give solace to his own aching heart. It is just a chapter in life's story. The poor miner is borne to his cabin in the throes of death. His wife falls at his side with the same kind grief as that felt by Mrs. McKinley, one of the noblest and best women that ever lived. The miner dies, and the world knows nothing of it. The sorrow does not go beyond the circle of his own household and friends. The world would feel McKinley's loss, yet the sorrow of his own family would not be more profound than that of the poor miners.

This is an echo of Lattimer and Homestead. Men are being driven into desperate straits, and they cannot fail to make an outcry or to offend the higher realm of society. Ground to a merciless poverty, there cannot fail to be an uprising. That spirit of love for justice cannot be suppressed. The lower walks of life must and will cry out. When men who fought for a principle are shot down because they dare to assert their rights, the mutterings of those oppressed must have redress, and it is just such deplorable outbreaks as this attack on the president that cowardly seekers after vengeance find solace in.

† Published as "Eugene V. Debs on Buffalo Tragedy" in *The Star and Muncie Morning News* [Muncie, IN], vol. 3, no. 103, extra edition (September 8, 1901), 5. Reprinted as "Debs on Assassination" in *Social Democratic Herald,* whole no. 163 (September 14, 1901), 4.

As long as the world lasts, there will be this disgruntled, festering, degrading class of peace disturbers who believe justice can be obtained only by such acts as that of yesterday.

Vice President Roosevelt would not be assassinated. Strange to say, anarchy does not assert itself against a military man. It is always the man from the civic walks that is attacked. True, McKinley had a Civil War record, but that is forgotten since the Spanish-American War has been added to history. Grant went without bodyguards and was not molested. He was worshipped as a military hero. Roosevelt could do the same without being molested.[29]

As long as this lasts, however, there will be mutterings from those who are oppressed or think they are oppressed, and such murderous attacks as the one on President McKinley will be made by demons who can find revenge only in blood.

The War for Freedom†

December 11, 1901

Terre Haute, Ind., December 11, 1901

The country we inhabit is generally supposed to have been in a state of peace since the close of the Civil War, excepting the brief period required to push the Spaniards off the western continent. And yet during this reign of so-called peace, more than a score of bloody battles have been fought on American soil, in every one of which the working class were beaten to the earth, notwithstanding they outnumber their conquerors and despoilers at least ten to one, and notwithstanding in each case they asked but a modest concession that represented but a tithe of what they were justly entitled to.

To recall the bloody scenes in the Tennessee mountains, the horrors of Idaho, the tragedies of Virden, Pana, Buffalo, Chicago, Homestead, Lattimer, Leadville, and many others, is quite enough to chill the heart of a man who has such an organ, and yet, above the cloud and smoke of battle, there shines forever the bow of promise, and however fierce the struggle and gloomy the

† Published in *Miners' Magazine,* January 1902, 32–4. Reprinted in *Social Democratic Herald,* vol. 4, no 28, whole no. 180 (January 11, 1902), 2.

outlook, it is never obscured to the brave, self-reliant soul who knows that victory at last must crown the cause of labor.

Thousands have fallen before the fire of the enemy, and thousands more are doubtless doomed to share the same fate, but

> Freedom's battle once begun,
> Bequeathed from bleeding sire to son,
> Though baffled oft, Is ever won.[30]

The struggle in this and other lands by the children of toil is a struggle between classes which in some form or other has been waged since primitive man first captured and enslaved his weaker fellow being. Through the long, dark night of history, the man who toiled has been in fetters, and though today they are invisible, yet they bind him as securely in wage-slavery as if they were forged of steel.

How the millions toil and produce! How they suffer and are despised! Is the earth forever to be a dungeon to them? Are their offspring always to be food for misery?

These are questions that confront the workingmen of our day, and a few of them at least understand the nature of the struggle, are conscious of their class interests, and are striving with all their energy to close up the ranks and conquer their freedom by the solidarity of labor.

In this war for freedom, the organized men in the western states have borne a conspicuous and honorable part. They have, in fact, maintained better conditions on the whole than generally prevail, and this they have done under fire that would have reduced less courageous and determined men. But, notwithstanding their organized resistance, they must perceive that, in common with all others who work for wages, they are losing ground before the march of capitalism.

It requires no specially sensitive nature to feel the tightening of the coils, nor prophetic vision to see the doom of labor if the government is suffered to continue in control of the capitalist class. In every crisis, the shotted guns of the government are aimed at the working class. They point in but one direction. In no other way could the capitalists maintain their class supremacy. Court injunctions paralyze but one class. In fact, the government of the ruling class today has but one vital function, and that is to keep the exploited class in subjection.

Labor unions, most of them with antiquated methods, are inadequate to cope with the situation in any crisis, and when the smoke of battle clears away, their members lie stark and dead on the field, or languish in prison, or are forced to leave wife and child and tramp among strangers in quest of a job.

Every battle that has been fought teaches the one lesson, that the workers must unite upon class-conscious ground, that they must vote as one against every capitalist candidate even though he be their best personal friend; that they must nominate their own candidates upon a platform that recognizes clearly and declares unequivocally in favor of their interests and stand by them until they make their own class the governing class and abolish the wage system and the countless crimes that follow in its train.

Let the labor unions staunchly contend with all their power for such concessions as are possible under the present system, but at the same time let the members who compose them open their eyes to the fact that an industrial revolution is in progress, and that to secure inestimable blessings they must make their class, the only class essential to modern society, the governing class, which means the abolition of class rule and wage-slavery and the inauguration of the reign of freedom.

Notes

1. Ascribing the volition for the January 1901 Special Convention to the rank and file rather than the leadership of the Chicago SDP is disingenuous. In his letter of November 9, 1900 to his brother, Theodore, Debs reminded him that "we held a deliberate [national executive] board meeting and agreed to call a special convention within 30 days after election. I wrote the call and mailed it to you." (See Constantine, *Letters of Eugene V. Debs: Vol. 1,* 154–6.)
2. Debs was deeply sensitive to charges made by the Springfield SDP that the Chicago SDP tended toward Debs hero worship and that its anti-unity National Executive Board was a political machine out of touch with the actual views of the rank-and-file membership. In reality, both of these criticisms had a basis in fact.
3. This braggadocio obscures the fact that the paid membership of the Springfield organization greatly exceeded that of the Chicago organization.
4. Artemus Ward was the pseudonym of Charles Farrar Browne (1834–1867), a humorist writer and public speaker who was a contemporary and personal friend of Mark Twain (1835–1910).
5. "Amusing cusses."
6. This seems to be a matter of projection, as it was the Chicago NEB, holders of position and privilege, that blocked the 1900 drive for socialist unity. For its entire existence, paid positions in Debs's social democracy had been dominated by the trusted old circle of American Railway Union functionaries. None would retain their positions by the end of the merger.
7. The first national convention of the Chicago SDP was held in Indianapolis from March 6–9, 1900.
8. The line was from the Chicago *Inter Ocean,* one of the leading conservative dailies of the city, which quoted Debs on the floor of the Chicago SDP's January convention as saying: "Last summer I accepted the nomination for the office of president at their hands in the interests of harmony, because I felt it my duty to accept it. My experiences after that time were most humiliating. Instead of the expected harmony we took into our midst a lot of hissing snakes. However, for the sake of our principles I propose that every effort shall be made to conciliate the factions now at variance." (See "Debs for Harmony," *Inter Ocean,* January 16, 1901, 5.) This quotation was disavowed by *Social Democratic Herald* editor and Chicago NEB insider A. S. Edwards, who, in a February 2 editorial, upbraided the Springfield SDP for republishing this line, declaring "this language was not used by Comrade Debs or any other speaker, and since there was no justification for printing it in *The People* we hope that paper will correct the false impression its incomplete and erroneous report may have created."
9. Apparently written as a letter to the editor of the *Social Democratic Herald* but published as a lead article.
10. Debs was a close observer and active commentator on the bloody Homestead Steel Strike of 1892. See *Selected Works of Eugene Debs, Vol. 2.*
11. In March 1901, the city of New Castle, Pennsylvania, approached Andrew

Carnegie for $75,000 for the construction of a public library. Local members of the Amalgamated Association of Iron, Steel, and Tin Workers made a public objection to the campaign, citing lack of justice with respect to wages, hours, and working conditions in Carnegie's mills and calling the proposal "an insult to labor."

12. A number of the columns written by Debs for the *Social Democratic Herald* in this period took the form of short snippets of commentary about contemporary issues, as exemplified by this piece.
13. Adapted from "The Coming American" (1894), by Sam Walter Foss (1858–1911). The next-to-last line is one of Debs's own creation.
14. Adapted from "The Coming American." Debs silently omits two lines and tweaks another, his version presented here unaltered.
15. The editor of *The Social Unity* was W. D. P. Bliss (1856–1926), a prominent Christian socialist and editor of the massive *Encyclopedia of Social Reform* (Funk and Wagnall Co., 1897).
16. Michael "Hinky Dink" Kenna (1858–1946) was a saloon owner and city alderman whose name epitomized political corruption in early-twentieth-century Chicago.
17. The National Social and Political Conference was held in Detroit from June 28 to July 4, 1901, bringing together activists from various branches of the progressive social reform movement. Despite Debs's disdain, the gathering was addressed on July 1 by Seymour Stedman, chair of the National Executive Board of the Chicago SDP, as well as A. M. Simons, editor of the *Workers' Call,* weekly Chicago newspaper of the Springfield SDP.
18. Dr. Edward Alsworth Ross (1866–1951), a professor of sociology at Stanford University, was fired by President David Starr Jordan (1851–1931) at the behest of Jane Stanford (1828–1905) in November 1900 for public expression of anti-Japanese sentiments. The Ross incident was among the first major academic freedom cases at Stanford.
19. This article was written for *Advance,* the most important organ of the Springfield Social Democratic Party in the western United States. Originally known as *The Class Struggle,* the San Francisco broadsheet had been the most important Socialist Labor Party weekly in the West, allying itself with the so-called "Kangaroo" dissidents in the party split of 1899. The paper did not long survive the founding of the Socialist Party, apparently terminating at the end of 1902.
20. Debs means the New York City–based Socialist Labor Party dominated by party editor Daniel DeLeon, not the so-called "Kangaroos" of the Springfield SDP.
21. This speech was delivered at Hoerdt's Park, located at Western, Belmont, and Clybourne avenues in Chicago. The advertised title of Debs's speech was "Progress."
22. Reference is to the telegram dispatched to Debs by the convention on the morning of July 30 denying a report in that day's edition of the *Indianapolis Sentinel* that Debs was being "shelved" by the unified organization.
23. Debs's perplexing absence from the joint unity convention in Indianapolis fueled a speculative and false story in the July 30 morning edition of the *Indianapolis Sentinel* that he was being pointedly reduced in stature by the newly unified organization.

This article drew the ire of the convention, which ordered a telegram dispatched to Terre Haute immediately upon opening its July 30 session telling Debs to "be not deceived by false newspaper reports . . . Comrade Debs has the esteem and love of all the comrades in this hall, as he always had." Debs replied in the afternoon that "Press reports do not disturb me." This statement was made in the interim.

24. Despite public pronouncements of support for unification, Debs clearly still had misgivings about the Springfield SDP.
25 Leon Greenbaum (1866-19XX) was a regional organizer for the American Federation of Labor who became involved in socialist politics late in the 1890s. He was the candidate of the Social Democratic Party for lieutenant governor of Missouri in 1900 and for mayor of St. Louis in 1901. When the 1901 Indianapolis convention named St. Louis the headquarters city of the Socialist Party of America, Greenbaum was tapped as the first national secretary of the new organization. An ineffectual leader, Greenbaum was removed from party office by the January 1903 meeting of the national committee, ostensibly over his public support of the Socialist Party of California's political coordination with the Union Labor Party, reckoned as a form of prohibited political fusion. In later years he became deeply involved in the Christian Scientist movement.
26. *The Worker*, formerly the dissident version of *The People* published at a William Street address in New York City, was the official organ of the Springfield SDP prior to the 1901 Socialist Unity Convention. This letter by Debs was effectively a post-unification olive branch offered to these former rivals of his Chicago SDP organization.
27. This letter to the *Social Democratic Herald* after its acquisition by publisher Victor L. Berger and move to Milwaukee, was extremely poorly microfilmed from a slightly damaged copy. Words in brackets are the best guesses of the editors from context after examination on state-of-the-art microfilm equipment. In 1945, the *Herald* was believed by one prominent librarian to have "suspended publication April 6 to August 8, 1901," with this erroneous message left on the leader of master negative microfilm. In actuality the paper was suspended in Chicago effective July 27, 1901, whole no. 160, and restarted in Milwaukee on August 17, erroneously whole numbered 159.
28. On September 6, 1901, President William McKinley was shot twice in the abdomen at close range with a .32-caliber revolver by Leon Czolgosz, a Michigan-born Polish-American anarchist who formerly worked as a steelworker. McKinley died eight days later from an infection. The 28-year-old Czolgosz was executed by electric chair on October 29 of that same year.
29. Ironically, presidential candidate Theodore Roosevelt would be the victim of an attempted political assassination when he was shot in the chest in Milwaukee on October 14, 1912.
30. From *The Giaour* (1813), by George Gordon Byron (1788–1824).

1902

Peace, Peace, There Is No Peace![†]

January 24, 1902[1]

There is nothing specially startling about the proceedings or results of the late "Industrial Peace Conference" in New York.[2] The captains of industry are now in practical control of their organized vassals. This has been the tendency during the past five years. The powwow at New York was simply the climax of "keep out of politics" trade unionism, and while things may run smoothly for a while, when the break comes, the organized workers will find that they have their necks in the noose and that the hand of "arbitration" has a good grip at the other end. They are now committed to arbitration, and they'll be damned if they don't, they'll be skinned if they do, and they'll be both anyway.

Grover Cleveland is the keystone in the arch of peace.[3] He has the final word. Ex-officio, he is now president of the American Federation of Labor, and Brother Gompers has simply to look wise, occasionally knit his brow, and draw his salary.

The Republican papers now apotheosize Cleveland, and in a steady stream their eulogy pours upon his massive majesty in his new role of "dove of peace."

Cleveland! Gods! Look upon his puffed and purple jowl, his bulging veins, his bloodshot eyes, his flabby neck, his sideshow girth of vulgar fat—in every feature, Nature has marked him as the coarsest cormorant that ever defiled the executive seat of the nation. Look at him, you workers, and then take off your hats and bow in the dust at his feet. All hail the great Arbiter of Labor. The black slave lifting his eyes to Lincoln may now dissolve from view. Great Grover is the mighty Moses of all races.

In 1894, he traced his love for labor in crimson characters—he commanded the United States regulars to shoot the working class into submission to their pirate masters. This was his glory. He entered the White House poor and emerged a millionaire. This was his evil crown. Well qualified, indeed, is he to sit in supreme judgment between the sleek coyote of Capital and the bleating lambs of Labor.

Archbishop Ireland is another "neutral" gentleman—a priest to match the politician, and they constitute a charming pair. When an exceptional job of

† Published in *The Toiler* [Terre Haute, IN], unknown original title, issue, or page. Reprinted as "Shall We Have Peace?" in *Social Democratic Herald,* vol. 4, no. 31, whole no. 183 (February 1, 1902), 2.

labor-fleecing is to be done, there always looms up a priest, who, sad, meek, and pious, rolls his eyes heavenward—and the job is done.

Archbishop Ireland is a millionaire.[4] His flocks have all their treasures in heaven. Verily, I am your shepherd and you are my mutton.

The archbishop is cheek by jowl with Jim Hill of the Great Northern. They collaborate and fix things in the Northwest. Ireland, making good use of his license as priest, is the smoothest of politicians, and Hill is not slow to catch on. Then Hill liberally "endows" as Ireland suggests, and between the two, nothing gets away.

Bishop Potter is another commanding figure in the neutral elements of the peace commission of the Civic Federation, the final tribunal of exploited workingmen.[5] Who is he? The spiritual advisor of John Pierpont Morgan. Every great tyrant, every colossal robber in history, had his spiritual advisor—his man of God to sanctify his crimes. The saintly bishop draws a princely salary. He rides in Morgan's palatial private car. He touches elbows with the upper capitalists and their salaried professional lackeys, and with no others. Every now and then, he drops a radical utterance. This is promptly snatched and spread by the capitalist press. The people are amazed, they hold their breath, applaud—and are fixed for another season.

On every vital issue, Bishop Potter is with the capitalist class. Their interests are secure in his custody.

Rather Morgan, Hanna, and Schwab straight than Cleveland, Ireland, and Potter by arbitration.

In the entire "neutral" element, there is not a single member whose material interests are not identified with and controlled by the capitalist class.[6]

A mighty class struggle is convulsing society. No living man is, or can be, "neutral" or "disinterested." He is on one side or the other—if not for freedom, he is for slavery of the working class. They are deadly opposites. A chemical law forbids fire and water to mingle, even at the bidding of a peace conference. By the same analogy, an economic law forbids peace between workers and capitalists. It is the law of development, and should it be suspended, the spinal cord of humanity would be severed and progress would be paralyzed.

I have had some experience with the Civic Federation and want to say to workingmen and women that if they would have homes built of gold bricks, the "civic" adjunct of the capitalist class will take the contract to house them all.

As for the American labor movement, it is being practically emasculated. Proportionate to its increasing impotency is its growth in numbers. In its present form it is encouraged, not resisted, by the masters.

The brotherhoods of railway employees have the complete sanction and support of the corporations, and their chief officers are dined by President Roosevelt.

By the way, the president is announcing the appointment of representatives of the United States government for the coming coronation of King Edward—also for posts of honor at the launching of Emperor Wilhelm's private yacht.

Now get ready your Sunday clothes, you sovereign sons of toil, for in these stately social functions, labor, the maker of all kings and presidents, will surely sparkle in the grand parade and carve the 'possum at the banquet.

But, as to the labor movement: the local unions have their political heelers and steerers. They sound the alarm when "politics" ventures in the anteroom. At the very mention of socialism, the heeler issues the warning note: "The goblins'll git ye if ye don't watch out."

The national officers, as a rule, are in close touch with the captains of industry, and guarantees are given that the trade union movement will stick to its time-honored policy of letting politics alone.

How Hanna and Ireland, Morgan and Schwab (fresh convert to union labor) must dig into each other's ribs and snort when they retire from the footlights.

Every labor union in the land ought to denounce and repudiate the New York scheme of peace at the price of slavery, and the whole labor movement must be rescued and readjusted to grapple with the conditions of today, or it is doomed to disintegration.

Peace, peace, there is no peace![7] There is no land in which capitalist masters and working slaves can abide in peace. The war is on, and the conflict will grow fiercer until the crash comes and wage-slavery is wiped from the earth.

Not until the last inch held by slavery is conquered by freedom can peace prevail. Then only will the multiplied millions who have subdued the earth and produced its wealth come to their own.

Onward, comrades, onward to the goal.

Battle Cry of Superstition†

March 10, 1902

Terre Haute, Ind., March 10 [1902]

The socialist movement encountered a great shock at Buffalo a few days ago. One Quigley, a Catholic bishop, and another Stauffer (Stuffer?) of the Protestant persuasion,[8] jointly and severally assailed social democracy, the latter gravely declaring that it was the "unhatched egg of anarchy"—in other words, a bad egg. The bishop vaulted into the arena, made due exhibition of his asininity, and in the name of the hierarchy proclaimed excommunication as the fate of all who cast their lot with the wicked socialists.[9]

No opposition to organized labor, declared the bishop, was intended, except insofar as it was tainted with the virus of socialism—a hint that union men would be wise to profit by.

It is not my purpose to write about religion, or to interfere with that of any man. I am trusting to the light and logic of the future to abolish creeds and dispel the darkness of superstition.

But we have those in the socialist movement who are so supersensitive that they rise in passionate protest when the church is even mentioned. They are doubtless honest and sincere, but their prejudice is such that if the orders and injunctions of such priests as Quigley and Stauffer could be and were obeyed, they would look on in silence and submission while the church, with iron boots, crushed out the socialist movement, and the sun of labor set in gloom to rise no more.

What has the church, as such, ever done for workingmen and women except to keep them in darkness, preach obedience to their masters, and promise them a future home in heaven as the reward of patience and submission in the present hell?

The fulmination of this precious combination at Buffalo reveals the true attitude of the church, which profanes the name of Jesus Christ. In all its pomp and power today, it stands for all he abhorred and against all he loved; and socialists would be worse than cowards, they would be base-born traitors not to

† Published in *Social Democratic Herald,* vol. 4, no. 38, whole no. 190 (March 22, 1902), 2.

speak the truth and challenge the enemy of the socialist movement in whatever form he may appear; and when the church consents to prostitute its functions in the service of the ruling class, its robes turn into rags, and every honest man should help to strip it naked and expose the whited sepulcher to the world.

For more than 25 years, I have watched the church in its attitude toward labor, and I know it is the enemy of the toilers and strives and strains to keep them in industrial bondage. The freedom of the working class will mean the end of the church as we know it today. It will simply be out of a job.

During the Chicago strikes, the priests and preachers grew hysterically violent in demanding the shooting and hanging of the strikers in the name of the meek and merciful Jesus. All denominations melted into one, and all the ministers were likewise a unit in defense of the corporations and denunciation and damnation of the strikers.

There is something almost melancholy in seeing a meek, sad-eyed, dyspeptic preacher suddenly grow fierce and bloodthirsty. It seems strange, but it is easily accounted for. The priest is simply the echo of the capitalist. If he declines the function, he ceases to preach.

In every labor strike I have ever known, the church and those who speak for it have lined up solidly with the corporations. This has been and must be the attitude of the church whose priests now direct its fiery fulmination against socialism at Buffalo.

Through all the centuries, the church has been the handmaid of tyranny and oppression—there she stands today, red with impotent rage because socialism has stripped her of her mask and challenged her to do her worst. Can the church extinguish the socialist movement? Can a bat snuff out the sun? It is high time the working class were opening their eyes, time that they were discarding the sacred (?) symbols of superstition and proclaiming their royal right to represent themselves without the vulgar and impertinent intervention of priests who are but the emissaries of their oppressors and exploiters.

They are no longer children to be scared by nursery goblins. They are growing up to manhood, and as they climb the heights, the dawn of socialism lights their way—its holy fires glow in their eyes, and they can see as never before the glorious goal of freedom.

They are now beginning to understand the reason why their enemies are deified and their friends are damned. They see the church as the fort and buttress of the ruling robbers of society.

They hear the preachers in one voice denounce George Herron—a man so pure of heart and lofty of conception and conviction that he walks barefooted through the fire rather than disobey the command of conscience. And yet the Christian clergy at the behest of their capitalist masters poured out a tirade of foul calumny that would have blushed the devil—and this for no other reason than he was a socialist, a true friend of the working class.

The Buffalo preachers may spare their subsidized wrath. The socialist movement scorns their puny protest and defies their tottering power. The dead ages of the past belong to the church—their living future belongs to socialism.

ᔓ

The Amalgamated Association of Iron, Steel, and Tin Workers are again showing signs of life and activity again. They have just effected a settlement in New York, according to press advices.

I have a question for members of that organization. When their strike collapsed last summer, their union was totally at the mercy of John Pierpont Morgan. Figuratively speaking, he had his heel on its neck. He could have crushed it as easily as the railroad corporations did the American Railway Union in 1894. He could have non-unionized every mill in the trust. He did not do it. Why?

Was he restrained by his love for labor or his fear of socialism?

The American Railway Union, created as a labor union, sprang up as the Social Democracy, now the Socialist Party.

The Amalgamated, as a labor union, votes the Republican ticket and is the bulwark of the steel trust.

Morgan profits by the experience of the past. He is a "union" man and will be until the union becomes class-conscious and its members vote as they strike.

Altgeld the Liberator†

March 18, 1902

John Peter Altgeld has joined Abraham Lincoln in the realm of the immortals.[10] His career was tempestuous and heroic, and the end tragic and sublime. The gods must have set the stage for the last earthly act of the intrepid warrior, and most nobly did he fill the leading role. When the last word of his impassioned plea for liberty died upon his eloquent lips, the climax came and the curtain fell upon another martyr in the great drama of humanity.

John Altgeld was born in the throes of revolt. A thousand years of feudal tyranny were culminating. The fateful year of 1848 had a violent temper. It rocked the cradle of the babe that was destined to become the tribune of the people.

The leader, now fallen, never took a backward step, never subordinated principle to policy, never sacrificed conviction to attain his end. He was fearless, he was determined, and he was incorruptible.

John P. Altgeld was in the highest sense a statesman; he was a daring leader and a fiery and intense orator whose eloquent and lofty appeals inspired the multitude.

His noblest and therefore greatest official act was the opening of dungeon doors to liberate innocent victims of corporate tyranny. If the gods have to do with politics, they ordained the election of John P. Altgeld for this incomparable service to humanity.

Through the rain of fire he walked with steady step to the hideous bastille's doors, nor faltered once until the captives walked forth men; his official robes turned to ashes in the ordeal, but lo! The flame of calumny to which our hero bared his head is even now become the aureole of his fame.

The robbers of the people, the stranglers of liberty, the foes of humanity feared and hated him; the fawning sycophants of wealth, the time-serving mercenaries of power slandered him; this was the measure of his greatness.

The few honest men who knew John P. Altgeld loved him. He was genuine; he was true; he could look God and man straight in the eye.

In the railroad strikes in 1894, he expanded to his true proportions. There he proved to be the fearless champion of the people. He stood upon the

† Published in *The Toiler,* March 21, 1902, unspecified page. Reprinted as "Tribute to Altgeld" in *Social Democratic Herald,* March 29, 1902.

boundary line of Illinois and protested against the military usurpation of the president, and though overwhelmed, he proudly vindicated his high honor, and he, more than any other man, retired Grover Cleveland and his pirate crew from American politics.

Altgeld was too great to become president; he will be remembered long after most presidents are forgotten.

How glorious the final scene! See him summon all his wasted strength. Note the transfiguration in the last superhuman effort—the light of liberty in his eye, the flush of dawn upon his brow, as he defiantly exclaimed:

> Again to the battle, Achaians!
> Our hearts bid the tyrants defiance!
> Our land—the first garden of Liberty's tree —
> It has been, and shall yet be, the land of the free; [11]

Workingmen and workingwomen never had a truer friend; he yearned to see them happy and consecrated all he had to make them free.

He paid the penalty of all the earth's redeemers. Socrates was poisoned, Christ crucified, John Brown strangled, Lincoln assassinated, and Altgeld stabbed by a million venomous tongues.

The grandchildren of his slayers will seek his works for knowledge and inspiration, and to the coming generations he will speak forever.

No Compromise with Slavery: May Day Speech in St. Louis† [excerpt]

May 1, 1902

It is indeed with great pleasure that I am before you here today. May Day sets my whole being afire, and upon its every recurrence, I consecrate again my life to the revolution which it holds in its meaning. It is with this spirit of revolution, new born, that I will say what I have to say.

The days of the reformer have gone, and those who would change our conditions today must be made of sterner stuff. In determining the liberty or the freedom of the slave, there is no room for reform, no room for compromise. If one man is to be denied the power to live off the labor of others, then slavery must be abolished. Its rigors cannot be mitigated by lessening the number of lashes or reducing the amount of the robbery. Robbery and lashes are not the lot of free men, and if we would be free men, we must put an end to both.

In the life of Wendell Phillips, the great emancipator of the black slave, there occurred an incident which showed the true worth of the man who seeks to compromise, who seeks to go step at a time. In the church in the city of Boston of which he was pastor, there was inscribed over the entranceway the words, "God bless this Commonwealth." Wendell Phillips had seen these words since his boyhood, and they had sunk deep into his brain. At one time during the worst days of Southern slavery, a little black girl who had run away from her masters in the South took refuge in this church, and at once there arose a question, what was to be done with her?

Some wanted to send her back, others wanted to deliver her to the officers, and still others declared that while they favored sending her back to the master whose property she was, they insisted that it should be done under condition that she should never again be mistreated.

After all others had given their views, Wendell Phillips arose and, in a voice without a falter, declared:

† Published as part of "The Enthusiasm on May Day Was Unbounded" in *St. Louis Labor,* vol. 2, whole no. 67 (May 10, 1902), 1.

> For many years have I entered this church, and every time I have seen that inscription over the doorway, but let me say that if in this place there is to be made a compromise with slavery, if we here do aught that will sanction ownership of flesh and blood, I will insist that that inscription be changed and instead of writing "God bless our Commonwealth," let us write it "God damn our Commonwealth."

Wendell Phillips is gone, and the slavery against which he fought has disappeared; no longer is human flesh and blood sold in the open market. But yet slavery still exists. Wendell Phillips never dreamed of the slavery of today, a slavery more awful than that against which he struggled, more awful because its helpless victims imagine themselves free.

There was no compromise with slavery in the '60s, and there will be none today. As the ownership of the man was at the root of chattel slavery, and as it was abolished only with the abolition of that ownership, so today the ownership of the machine is at the root of wage-slavery, and wage-slavery will come to an end only with the abolition of the ownership of the machine. Society itself must control the machine. Socialism is the only hope of the wage-slave.

Compromisers never destroyed chattel slavery, neither will they destroy wage-slavery, and those who advocate a step at a time in securing the emancipation of the working class would do well to remember the words of Wendell Phillips.

Through socialism alone will this be accomplished, and it is the duty of every workingman to align himself with the Socialist Party. Do not be discouraged if you are the only socialist in your precinct, you are a monument to the degeneracy of your neighbors. Join hands, fellow workers, join hands with your brothers of other lands, and when at last the glorious day comes, when there is no longer a master, no longer a slave, it will be your reward to know and feel the part you have played in its accomplishment. No grander reward could fall to any man.

The Pennsylvania Coal Strike Is On†

May 19, 1902

Terre Haute, Ind., May 19, [1902]

The miners' strike is on in the anthracite coal regions of Pennsylvania. The operators were defiant and eager for the fray. The miners pulled every wire to prevent the collision and finally voted to go out in the very last extremity. A large minority voted against the strike, and President [John] Mitchell,[12] all accounts agree, did his best to prevent it.

Most earnestly do I hope the poor devils will win, but there is no use trying to conceal the fact that they are up against it and that the coal and railroad companies have been preparing for the fight, openly courted it, and are determined to wipe out the union and run their mines to suit themselves.

At this writing, everything is quiet as a graveyard in the anthracite region, but nevertheless the Republican governor,[13] elected largely by the votes of coal miners who don't believe in going into politics, has already sworn in an army of special coal police, armed with Winchesters, to protect "property" and incidentally to perforate the hides of the striking miners if this becomes necessary to break up their strike and force them back into their holes through starvation tunnel, to dig for their masters.

That is all they are fit for; at least, that is what they themselves seem to think, for that is what they voted for under the direction of some of their district officers, who are simply the political pluggers of the gang of robbers that fleece the poor coal diggers when they work and have them murdered when they strike.

Pennsylvania, where hell is active as Mount Pelée[14] and slavery in full blast, has a Republican majority of 300,000, made up quite largely of the poor devils now on strike.

The governor is already making active preparation to return bullet for ballot in accordance with the invariable program of the capitalist class, whom the miners and other workingmen have made the ruling class of the country.

President Mitchell will do the best he can in a trying position. He has issued a request that miners abstain from the use of liquor during the strike,

† Published as "The Carnival of Capitalism" in *Social Democratic Herald,* vol. 4, no. 47, whole no. 199 (May 24, 1902), 1.

and, acting upon his advice, they thronged the churches on Sunday last and took the oath of total abstinence and the pledge to entirely keep out of saloons till the strike is settled.

As for the Civic Federation, it has already done its worst. It has delayed and dallied six weeks, taken the heart out of many of the strikers, and set them by the ears among themselves. Had the miners struck April 1, as they intended, they would have been far stronger than they are today.

My advice to you, striking miners, is to keep away from the capitalistic partnership of priest and politician, to cut loose from the Civic Federation, and to stand together to a man and fight it out yourselves. If you can't win, no one else can win for you; and if, in the end, you find that the corporations can beat you at the game of famine, you may, and it is hoped that you will have your eyes opened to the fact that your vote is your best weapon and that if the 140,000 miners of Pennsylvania will cast a solid vote for socialism, they will soon drive the robbers from the state and take possession of the mines and make themselves the masters of their industry, and the workingmen the rulers of the state.

As for the army of coal police already marshaled and armed by the governor to shoot the strikers upon the assumption that they are criminals, I advise that the miners in convention assembled unanimously resolve that, while they propose to keep within the law, they also propose to exercise all the rights and privileges the law grants them; and, furthermore, that the monstrous crime of Latimer shall not be repeated, and if any striker is shot down without good cause, the first shot shall be the signal for war, and the miners will shoot back; and if killing must be the program of the coal barons, let it be an operator for a miner instead of miners only, as in the past.

* * * 15

No Masters, No Slaves: Keynote Address to the Joint Convention of the Western Federation of Miners and Western Labor Union[†16]

May 26, 1902

Ladies and Gentlemen:—

The privilege of addressing you upon such an occasion as this imposes certain duties and responsibilities which I could not disregard without betraying your confidence, insulting your intelligence, and violating the sanctity of my own conscience. You have a right to expect that I shall be honest with you, that I shall be honest with myself, and in this respect, at least, you shall not be disappointed.

We are in the midst of the mightiest industrial revolution the world has ever known. Humanity is trembling upon the verge of the greatest organic change in all history. The capitalist competitive system is productive of industrial masters and industrial slaves. We have the fruit of this system before us for inspection. It has given us millionaires and mendicants, palaces and hovels, rogues and rags. It has reduced the workingman, the producer of all wealth, to the very deadline of degradation.

The importance of organization is so generally conceded that it need not be discussed. In every great contest, you have been divided, your members have been blacklisted, your unions have been destroyed, you have been left at the mercy of your masters. The time has come for the workingman in every department of industrial activity to realize that he has a class identity, that he has class interests, that if necessary for workingmen to combine upon the economic field where they are weakest, it is vastly more important that they shall combine upon the political field, where they are absolutely invulnerable. *[Applause.]*

Consider, briefly, the status of the workingman of this country. He has nothing but his labor-power in the very nature of the situation. If he succeeds in finding employment, he simply succeeds in selling himself into wage bondage. Take the most successful wage earner in Denver; he does not know when

---

† Published as "Mission of the Socialist Party" in *Butte Labor World,* June 2, 1902. Reprinted as "The Eloquent Debs" in *Miners' Magazine,* July 1902, 39–43.

some machine may be invented to displace him. He does not know where he can find another position if he loses this one. He goes up one street and down another. He leaves the city where he lives—perhaps goes on the trucks of a freight train. In due course of time, he becomes what they call a vagrant, a tramp; a victim of the existing economic system in which man's life is of absolutely no value; a system in which property alone is valuable; a system where private profit is more important than human life. *[Applause.]* He is idle, his wife may be in want, his children may be suffering. No matter; profit must be made. One hundred and forty-six thousand of these men are now on a strike in the East. Examine the reports of the Pennsylvania Bureau of Statistics for 1901 and you will find the average wage for the year of the Pennsylvania coal miner was 78 cents a day. They have been organized—they have been thoroughly organized. Some of them were foolish enough to imagine that they could, in that organization, conquer the capitalist. They were to strike on the first of April, but under the influence of the Civic Federation—a very useful annex to the capitalist class—failed to do so, and now after seven weeks, the Civic Federation acknowledges its helplessness.

Not long ago, I wrote a letter to the Eastern press in which I said:

> You miners ought to get together, 116,000 strong, and you ought unanimously to pass a resolution to the effect that you propose to obey the law, that you also propose to exercise all the rights and privileges granted you by that law, including the walking of the free man upon the highways of the state [*applause*]; and if it comes to pass that a miner is shot down, you ought to shoot back. If the mine operators of Pennsylvania insist upon a killing program, let it be an operator for a miner, and not miners only, as in the past.

These 146,000 miners have been voting the Republican ticket. They gave the present governor of the state his 280,000 majority, and he is rewarding them for their fidelity in the old-fashioned capitalist way. He is retuning bullets for ballots. When they learn to vote as they strike, when they assert their united power at the ballot box, when they vote their class into power, they will no longer have to starve upon the highways; they will no longer have for food the lead shot at them from the mouths of capitalistic guns. [*Applause.*]

My heart is with the strikers. I hope they will win. I would, if I could, give them all the support of all the organized and unorganized men of the city of Denver and the state of Colorado. *[Applause.]* I would try to teach them, however, the better way. A statement in a local paper, made by a mill owner, says: "The mill owners will not suffer." No, they will continue to eat three square meals a day. They can draw upon their bank accounts. The struggle is one between a human stomach and a steel bank vault. *[Applause.]*

The workingman no longer owns the tools with which he must work. The owners of the tools are the masters of the slaves who are compelled to use the tools. The whole battle is being fought about the tool of production. I would have you understand its great importance in this struggle. There was a time when the workingman owned the tool with which he worked. That tool was long since touched by the want of invention, and the machine is owned by a combination of capitalists. The workingman in this process lost control of the tool with which he worked. He still has his labor-power; he cannot work without his tools, and he is compelled to apply to the owner of his tool for permission to work—in other words, for permission to live. Not only this, this machine has become so perfect that it may be operated by the unskilled labor of a woman or the deft fingers of the child, so that they have to produce profit for their masters.

In this system, it is not a question of male labor or of female labor, of white labor or of black labor—it is a question of cheap labor. *[Applause.]* He who produces cheapest controls the market. The entire burden of the profit falls upon the working man. This is the tendency today in every department of activity.

I am no reformer. So far as I am concerned, I propose to end, not mend, this system. I don't like the term "reformer." It savors of suspicion. The most successful thieves I know pretend to be reformers. I like the term "revolution." There is something in it that stirs the blood. I enjoy it. I prefer agitation to stagnation. The time has come for action. I believe the conventions now in session realize it and the delegates will put themselves upon record in a way to give hope and inspiration to the working class of the entire country. *[Applause.]*

The Socialist Party is not a reform party. It proposes to abolish the capitalist system to transfer from private hands all the means of production and distribution and turn them over to the people in their collective capacity. If the coal, for instance, is not the people's, whose is it? *[A voice: "Mark Hanna's!"]* That seems to be the opinion of the workingmen, for they have been voting that way. Thousands of the workingmen have consented to make him a silent partner in the leadership of the American labor movement. *[Laughter.]* If I were a dove, I would as soon submit my case to a hawk for arbitration.

Now and then some splendid man occupying the pulpit dares speak out—it is not long before he is, like you, out of a job. You had a splendid example here in your midst in Myron Reed. *[Long, continued applause.]* It is gratifying to me it is a beautiful tribute, that he is remembered as he deserves to be, with gratitude and love. Myron Reed was a man of profound sympathies with the struggling and suffering poor. When the miners were on a strike in Colorado in '94, when they were besieged near Cripple Creek, and when the forces were being mustered to charge on them, Myron Reed stood in the presence of his fashionable congregation and said: "My heart is on Bull Hill. I have a deep sense that the miner was there first!" *[Renewed applause.]* From that moment, he was doomed. And he did not wait to be crucified, he crucified himself. He espoused the cause of the working class. The "respectables," so called, were turned against him. His former friends deserted him. He was in better company for it.

It takes a real man and a real woman to be a socialist. When great principles have been involved in history and the majority were always wrong, the minority have invariably been right; and in the majority of events, the minority have become the majority, and so it will be with the socialist movement. *[Applause.]*

I appeal to you workingmen to stand together today. Resolve that you will be true to your class. Then, in the spirit of Andrew Jackson, accept the consequences of your act. Emphasize every industrial conflict by political action. The ballot is the weapon. It was found after a thousand years of blood and tears. It is criminal not to make use of it, or, worse still, to use it to forge our fetters more securely. I appeal to you to read and think and study, and above all, if you have any prejudice against socialism, to dismiss it. You were told that it was a bad thing. Who says so? Trace the statement to its source, and you will find it is made by the man who lives out of your labor. *[Applause.]* Socialism is good for men. If it were not, he would not be the man to warn you against it.

A sane capitalist ought to embrace socialism. He does not do it for the reason that in this mad, insane strife, the strings of his heart have almost dried. His blood is no longer red. Through all his life he has been seeking to ruin the workingman because his salvation as a capitalist has compelled it.

When the work of the world is cooperatively done, there will be no masters, no slaves. He therefore has a right to work, for only by work can he maintain himself. He would work by divine right. The machinery of the world would be at his service. The machine is not yet ended. This will be its message:

> Come to me, you wageworkers; at your bidding I will work and I will produce; I will reserve from each day a certain number of hours that you

> may devote to moral and intellectual improvement; I will make it possible for you to live a complete life; I will make it possible for your soul to be emancipated from the domination of your stomach; I will make it possible for you to fertilize this earth; come to me. Work together cooperatively. I am at your service; I will produce not for profit, I will produce for use. I will produce to supply your physical wants; I will make it possible for every man to find the kind of work that nature intended that he should do; I will make it possible for every man to be an intelligent man. I will transform this miserable dungeon that covers you; I will make it a temple of sciences; I will make you workingmen the sovereigns of the earth. I will make the badge of labor the only badge of nobility.

[Applause.]

Go into Politics the Right Way: Speech to the Joint Convention of the Western Federation of Miners and Western Labor Union†[17] [excerpt]

May 31, 1902

Mr. President and Men and Women of the Cause of Labor:—

I yield to no man in the desire for unity of the working class. So far as I am concerned, I am willing to make any sacrifice to secure that unity save one, and that is principle and honor. *[Applause.]*

With the withdrawal of the Western Labor Union from the American Federation of Labor I had absolutely nothing to do. If, however, the withdrawal was justifiable at that time, the years that have since intervened have simply served to vindicate the wisdom of such action. *[Applause.]*

---

† Published as "Debs' Reply to Morrison and Kidd Before ALU Convention" in *American Labor Union Journal* [Butte, Montana], vol. 1, no. 10 (December 11, 1902), 2. The same "condensed report" published in *Official Report of the Proceedings of the American Labor Union in its Fifth Annual Convention, Denver, Colorado* (Denver: Western Newspaper Union, 1902), 42–7.

I wish to say in the beginning that I have been on terms of personal kindness with the two gentlemen who are your guests on this occasion, the two representatives of the American Federation of Labor, and if I am opposed to them today, it is because of certain fundamental differences in reference to the labor movement, and not from any personal consideration.

Mr. Morrison[18] asks: If there is anything wrong with the American Federation of Labor, why not remain within the federation and right the wrongs from within, instead of opposing it from without? Why, gentlemen, did not the founders of the American Federation of Labor remain within the organization of the Knights of Labor and right the wrongs from within? *[Applause.]*

Let us discuss another point—the president of the American Federation of Labor—and my only regret is that he is not present here today. When I have anything to say to a man, I like to meet him face-to-face and give him an opportunity to speak on his own behalf. The president of the American Federation of Labor is also the vice president of the [National] Civic Federation. Mark that, will you! You may say, "He is only acting in an unofficial capacity as an officer of the Civic Federation." Samuel Gompers, president of the American Federation of Labor, becomes "Sammy" Gompers, vice president of the Civic Federation. Mark Hanna is reported to have said, on leaving the council room, "We have forgotten Sammy!" and he was made vice president—or does anyone think he was because he was a cigarmaker? Don't you know, and don't I know, he was made vice president of the Civic Federation solely because he was and is the president of the American Federation of Labor?

You may tell me that ministers of the gospel are members of the Civic Federation, and I answer, so much the worse for the gospel. *[Applause.]*

Now, observe these ministers, these humble followers of the meek and lowly Jesus, the friend of the workingman, who, if living and here in Denver today, would stand for what I am advocating. *[Applause.]*

They appointed Bishop Potter to the Civic Federation; they did not appoint Father Hagerty.[19] They know their business; they are taking no chances.

Twenty thousand workingmen went on strike in the city of Boston recently, and the capitalists were very much alarmed. A class struggle was on exhibition. Secretary Easley[20] of the Civic Federation promptly consulted with the capitalists, and they sent their emissaries to consult with the leaders of the strike and asked them to order the men back to work and solemnly promised that justice would be done. The men returned to work, but their leaders were told there was no work for them. The strike was broken, the men were demoralized, and the manly men who had the courage to lead them were out of jobs.

Were I delegate to this convention, I would certainly favor the unity of the working class. But I would make some stipulations to the American Federation of Labor, and among the first would be, "When you cut loose from the Civic Federation, we will talk over matters looking to unity—but not until then." I would point to the fact that "your leading officers are members of the Civic Federation, and your executive council have not repudiated their action in joining and accepting offices. In this case, silence gives consent."

There is another matter to be considered. You may have been told what great things have been done for you. I am going to tell you what they have never done—what they never will do for you. It is conceded that the coal miners are thoroughly organized; they are also affiliated with the American Federation of Labor. We are told they are the most powerful organization in the world. What is the condition of these wageworkers? They live in miserable hovels, and their wives and children are half-clad and poorly fed. According to the official report of the Bureau of Labor Statistics of the state of Pennsylvania, there are 146,000 coal miners in that state. For the year 1901—the year in which they were supposed to enjoy the fruits of their great victory—their average wage, according to the official report, was 78 cents a day! What do you think of that? How do you like it?

What is the condition of the workers in the South today? It is true they have not been organized very long—some of them—but in some parts they are very well organized; but they will never materially better their condition under the present industrial system. Today, gentlemen, there is not one state in the South that has a child labor law. Capitalists from the North went to the South and said, "If you will agree to remove certain obnoxious restrictions, we will locate our cotton factories in the South." And today throughout the South, thousands of children in these cotton mills are being dwarfed in mind and deformed in body, debarred from the happy playtime and schooltime of childhood and youth, grinding out for their capitalist masters the profits to satisfy their greed. These are the conditions prevailing in the South today.

Now, to return to the coal miners—and my heart goes out to them—I would willingly give five years of my life, and I mean every word of it, if I could only bring any substantial relief.

Recently they met at Scranton and agreed to strike if their demands were not conceded. The strike was not called. On the first of April [1902] they were ready, but they were prevailed upon to submit their demands for arbitration and settlement to the Civic Federation. They asked for 30 days to consider, but they knew in advance the demands of the miners would never be granted. They knew this on the first day of April. Why was not the Civic Federation honest enough to say plainly and at once, "We can't do anything for you; you will have to fight your battle alone." When the 30 days expired, they asked for a few more days' time and, finally, the statement was made that the Civic Federation was powerless and could do nothing for them.

Do you suppose that Mark Hanna is an idiot? He is anything but that! He knew on the first day of April, as well as later, that the Civic Federation could not do anything for those struggling miners. What is the result of these delays? Every miner knows that on the first day of April they would have struck as one man. When finally the strike was declared, it was carried by a bare majority. They saw that they were betrayed, and many said, "The best thing to do is to go back to work."

These mines are mainly owned by a few plutocrats, and they say that they are going to run their mines as they choose. I tell you they haven't the right to own these mines and reduce workingmen to wage slavery. This slavery succeeds the black slavery of the South, and the boss succeeds the overseer with his whip and lash.

By the strike, these plutocrats suffer some inconveniences and loss of profit, but in the final results they will not lose anything. These coal barons live on the Nob Hills; have carriages and yachts and vaults filled with gold; they can live sumptuously, but the miners go hungry, and it would require the genius of a Dante to depict their haggard condition. These miners have not even the right to walk on the public highways! Their wives and children live in penury and want and misery. No sooner had the strike been declared when two thousand special police were sworn in, doubtless to guard the public highways "where even a dog has a right of way." Read the records of Homestead, Virden, Hazleton, and Coeur d'Alene—the story is ever the same!

Now, when the operators have stamped out this strike and crushed it, I want to know what the American Federation of Labor is going to do for them? What can it do for them? It is our right to know if they have still some relief in store—some balm in Gilead? If they have such, let them tell us what it is. If not, we will tell them what we have and what we propose to do. *[Applause.]* We are going to begin right here! We are going to begin right now in this western country. I tell you the day of trade unionism in its antiquated form is past. Not that I am opposed to trade unions, but I want them up to date; I want them equipped with a rapid-fire gun in this modern warfare instead of the old blunderbuss. They will have to change their methods before they can emancipate the downtrodden workingmen and women of the earth!

That is their true economic mission. I want the trade unions to organize thoroughly and to assert their rights upon the economic field and to do all they can to keep them there! *I want the trade unionists as such to stand together upon a political platform!*

I do not ask them to become a political organization; I wouldn't allow them to do so, if in my power to prevent. But I do want them to use their political power at the right time and the right place, and in the right way! *[Applause.]* The leaders of the American Federation do not want any political action; they advise trade unionists to keep out of politics while they use their official prestige to boost themselves into political jobs! The old parties are satisfied to have you keep out of politics. They know that without such action you have no power.

Did you see the injunction recently issued by Baker—Judge Baker[21] of Indiana? Well, he is an old man, almost worn out. Now, they have got to have some more of the same kind of judicial material, some more of the same kind of stuff, when old Baker shuffles off this mortal coil. This old corporation judge has a son precisely like himself. Now, Roosevelt has appointed to the federal bench of Indiana this son of baker—Judge Baker, the infamous tool of the corporations. Every time he had a chance, he attacked workingmen in the interest of the capitalists. The other day they had a local strike in Indianapolis when the employers rushed to Judge Baker for an injunction and he said: "I want you not only to ask for an injunction, but to ask for damages, and I will grand both the petition for injunction and damages." Think of a judge, when an injunction is asked for, asking the petitioners to also demand damages against half-fed working people! And the son of this man, another just like him, Roosevelt has appointed judge, and they are both on the bench of Indiana today; both ready to serve injunctions in the interest of the capitalist and corporations!

I am a socialist! That is to say, I am a "ripe" trade unionist. There are two kinds of trade unionists—those who are green and those who are ripe. I ought also, perhaps, to mention a third kind—those who have become rotten. *[Applause.]* Those are the fellows you want to keep your eye on.

To me, it is the most pitiful spectacle to see representatives of workingmen lobbying in legislative halls and begging to have some law for the alleged benefit of labor put on the statute books for some 2x4 judge to declare "unconstitutional." You don't want lobbyists in the outer halls; you want your members in the legislative seats to make laws for you.

"Just keep out of politics!" they insist, but I am here to tell you *to go into politics—but go in the right way!* In the matter of politics, it is safe to follow the example of the capitalists. A successful capitalist knows his business. Lobbyists and attorneys are not employed by individual capitalists, but by corporations. Labor must organize in the interests of labor and follow the political example set by the capitalists. These same capitalists organize a corporation and then push it into politics, and every one of them advises you to "keep out of politics." Mark Hanna has been in politics all his life, and he is worth $20 million, and the Pennsylvania miner, who is not in politics, gets 78 cents a day—and a grave in the potter's field.

* * *

What did the federation do for you in the strike at Leadville? You appealed for help and spent $100 in your efforts to obtain it, and after a dreary waiting you got a $5 contribution from the East. It is well enough for them to ask help from the West, but it is in order also to ask if the helping hand of the East has been visible in the western country. If it has, I do not think there are any witnesses to the fact, and it would take a magnifying glass to discover it.

* * *

I ask no man to be responsible for my words. I am not infallible, but I will simply say in conclusion, if I were a delegate, I would refuse the proffered official hand, and I would reduce to writing my cause for so doing, and if this is done, and I know you are able to do it, it will challenge the approval of any right-thinking men not only in the West, but all over the United States. I know that organized labor in the East is rife with discontent; I know that the most progressive trade union elements in the East are opposed to the reactionary policy of the American Federation of Labor, which you are not asked to endorse. If you take decided action, it will strengthen their hands. They have every reason to believe you will, and the report will echo from the Atlantic to the Pacific. But if you want to turn the hand back on the dial of labor; if you want to strike another blow at the heart of labor, subscribe to the present policy of the American Federation. If, on the other hand, you are keeping step with the inspired music of progress; if you can *see,* if you can *hear,* if you can *feel*—in other words, if you are not totally dead to all the appeals of your fellow men—adopt, by a unanimous vote if possible, but adopt, a vigorous and progressive policy, and after adopting that policy, fling your banner to the breeze and appeal to the workingmen of the country to rally beneath its folds. Wipe out the limitation implied by your name, and let the Western Labor Union become the American Labor Union.[22]

I admire the western spirit. I am with you in this and will face the East on this proposition. Now, if the American Federation of Labor really wants to unify, let it cut loose from labor's enemies; let it procure a divorce between Samuel Gompers and Mark Hanna! *[Applause.]* Let it declare for independent political action along class conscious lines and then—all hail!—we will then say the hour has struck for union. The East and the West will be wed, and we will have an all-embracing organization. We will conquer, grasp the reins of government, and establish the socialist republic! *[Prolonged applause.]*

Socialism on Every Tongue: Open Letter to the *Social Democratic Herald*†

June 6, 1902

Denver, Col., June 6 [1902]

To the *Herald*:—

The conventions will close today or tomorrow, and their work will be complete and glorious.[23] The old politicians and their henchmen who did all in their power to defeat political action on the part of organized labor are stampeded and thoroughly alarmed.

You would be surprised could you realize what a tremendous change has taken place during the past few days. In this city of 200,000, the one pervading theme, go where you may, is socialism. The red buttons of our party are in the churches, the stores, the restaurants, and everywhere; stranger meets stranger as comrade, and all are happy over the inspiring outlook.

The one danger that must be guarded against is too-rapid growth. There may be trouble from this source, but I am confident that we have a sufficient number of comrades scattered over the state who are well grounded to keep the ship true to her course and guide her safely to her destined port.

Eugene V. Debs

† Published in *Social Democratic Herald,* vol. 4, no. 50, whole no. 202 (June 14, 1902), 1. Not included in Constantine (ed.), *Letters of Eugene V. Debs, Vol. 1.*

Capitalism Has Nearly Reached Its Climax: Speech to a Mass Meeting Following the Joint Convention of the WFM and the WLU in Denver[†]

June 8, 1902

Ladies and Gentlemen and Comrades:—

I have said before, I wish to repeat it this evening, that it is impossible for me to understand how any sane human being can escape the logic of socialism. The economic development is so clearly toward social ownership that it is self-evident, and its culmination in the social republic is a foregone conclusion. It may be well enough to address oneself to the moral sense of man, to preach about the need of human brotherhood, but all time so spent is absolutely wasted so long as the present hard, stubborn, unyielding economic conditions exist. Only when we realize this, only when we united for the purpose of changing the economic basis of society, can we hope for improvement of social and spiritual conditions for the human race. If it were possible to arouse you all this evening by an appeal to your emotions, if all of your hearts were melted into one, and you were to leave this hall in that condition and under that influence, within 24 hours after leaving here, in the hard, merciless grind of the competitive system, all that influence would be dissipated. I would rather set one man thinking for himself than to arouse the maudlin sentiment of a million. *[Applause.]*

The socialist movement is essentially the movement of the working class, and allow me to say to you this evening that the heart of humanity throbs in the working class and the labor movement is the hope of the world. There are today but two classes. Some of you may imagine there are more, but you are mistaken. You are in one class or you are in the other; it is possible that you are in both—there are many men and women in the middle class who are exploiting themselves. There are but two classes, and when this competitive struggle shall have reached its climax, when the people who now constitute the middle element of society shall have been expatriated, the property of this and every other country will have gravitated into the hands of a very few. The great mass will have been totally stripped,

---

† Published as "Debs' Great Speech" in *Miners' Magazine,* August 1902, 26–35.

dispossessed, propertyless, with identical class interests that will bind them together as with hooks of steel.

There is a great deal of opposition to socialism in the middle class for the reason that the man who still has a little property fears that the socialist movement is to dispossess him. Why, my friend, you are laboring under a delusion. You are fighting for a system that will strip you naked and put you and your children on the street.

Not very long ago, I addressed a meeting on this subject in Terre Haute, where I reside, and a prominent merchant came forward at the close and said: "Mr. Debs, I believe you are sincere, but you are wasting your time. The world's all right. Every man has an equal chance with every other if he will only take advantage of it." I said: "Simply wait. In your present condition, my logic will not penetrate your armor, but it is only a question of a short time until you will be put where you properly belong by the logic of events." About two years after that, I addressed another meeting upon the same subject in the same town. At the close, the same ex-merchant came forward. He had aged very considerably within two years, his hair had become white, his cheeks were sunken, the luster had left his eye, and he spoke in almost a whisper. He said: "Two years ago, I told you that you were wrong. I have come forward tonight to tell you that you were right."

How did he happen to change his mind? Two years before, he was where you are now; he was in business, but he had some large competitors. It was an unequal struggle. He lost ground. His profits were reduced, his expenses were increased, until after a while, instead of making a little money, he lost, and he lost more and more until he failed, and when he was forced into bankruptcy and the sheriff took possession of his business and put him into the street, he then realized that a change of system was necessary. *[Applause.]*

So many of you who are in the middle class would, on account of your private purse, stop the march of this universe. Every proposition that presents itself to you is decided upon the basis of the probable effect it may have upon your pocketbook. Well, the time is coming when your pocketbook is to suffer, when your stock will be depleted, when you will find it impossible to make a living. The logic that fails to reach you tonight will penetrate you then, and will compel the conclusion that we have arrived at long ago, that we must have a change of system. So, while the socialist movement is today necessarily the movement of the working class, in the ultimate, it is the movement of all and for all humanity. The working class can only emancipate itself in one way, and this is by making the means of production common property, and this means the emancipation of the human race.

There are those who imagine that when the working class succeeds to power, they will at once proceed to subjugate, enslave, and exploit some other class. This has been the history of the past. It is not true of the present socialist movement, and in this very important respect, the present social revolution differs from every other in all past history.

Were I a sane, successful capitalist—pardon me, that is a contradiction of terms—if it were possible for me as a capitalist to amass a fortune and still remain normal, I would become a socialist from pure intellectual conviction. I would rather live in the very worst state of socialism that its bitterest enemies can charge upon it than to live in the very best state of capitalism that its warmest friends can claim for it. If I owned the earth, I could not enjoy it at the price of human slavery.

But the class struggle is going forward. It is a stern, unyielding fact. The socialist did not create this struggle. The socialist simply calls your attention to it. He points it out that you may clearly understand it, that you may note its tendency, that you may make the proper alignment. On the other hand, the capitalist who profits by this struggle seeks to cover and obscure it that it may be perpetuated. He cries out in protest against the socialist: "You are inflaming the minds of the people, you are trying to array class against class, and this is un-American and unpatriotic." I said last night, and I want to repeat it this evening, that in the capitalist system I am a rebel and not a patriot. *[Applause.]* I am doing all I can to array the working class against the capitalist class. I want the exploited workingman to know his master. *[Applause.]*

There are many in the middle class who know him, especially in the professions—the lawyer, for example, that great factor in capitalist society, almost a hundred thousand of whom produce nothing but trouble. *[Applause.]* Ninety-nine percent of the litigation that is in progress in this country today is traceable directly or indirectly to private ownership of the means of life. I never occupied a pulpit, but I know enough of scripture to make what I conceive to be an apt quotation: "The ox knoweth his owner; the ass, his master's crib."[24] The difference between the lawyer and the workingman is that the workingman produces wealth; he does useful work, is necessary to society and to civilization. The lawyer is a parasite. He simple absorbs wealth. He is leech upon the workingman. *[Applause.]*

And it pays far better, in the vulgar, material sense of the present day, to be useless than it does to be useful. It is possible to get rich by being useless, but it is scarcely possible to get rich by being useful. No workingman, no matter what his wage, no matter how long he lives, no matter how economical or miserly he may be, no workingman can get rich by his labor. The man who gets rich is he who coins the sweat and blood of the working class into profit for himself. *[Applause.]*

Now in the case of feudalism, the system that immediately preceded capitalism, this was done by the act of the feudal baron owning thousands, perhaps tens of thousands of serfs. During all the dark ages, all Europe constituted a feudal despotism. The feudal robbers had their palaces located among the cliffs, the ruins of which may yet be seen. They had vast landed estates, and these were peopled by millions of serfs that were chained to the soil. They were the chattel property of the lords. Five days in the week they worked for their masters, and one day weekly they were permitted to work for themselves, to produce just enough to keep themselves in working order.

Toward the close of the eighteenth century, by virtue of the ingenuity of the workingman, the simple, primitive tool of production began its wonderful transformation. The inventions, the discoveries that resulted in developing machinery and the application of machinery to industry so completely changed conditions that the interest of the feudal class was in conflict with social and industrial progress. With the application of machinery to industry and the increase of the productive power of labor which resulted, a surplus was produced, and then began the struggle for the market of the world that has steadily intensified from that day to this. Owners of the machinery were in competition with each other. Cheap labor was demanded. Women were forced to leave and enter into competition with men; children were withdrawn from school to supply the demand for cheaper and cheaper labor. When, finally, the feudal system had outlived its usefulness, the new class, the trader, the businessman, the incipient capitalist, supported by the serfs, arose in their might, overthrew the feudal system, and feudalism was swept forever from the earth.

From that time to this, the capitalist system has been steadily developing until it has almost reached its climax. Centralization and cooperation are the forces of this age. Competition has been almost extinguished. It is simply a question of days until individual initiative will be practically impossible. Production has been almost wholly socialized. When the evolution is complete, it will be entirely so. We have before our eyes the modern agencies of production in the form of syndicates and trusts. The evolution is only partial; we are just beyond the halfway point. The evolution must be pushed to its termination if civilization is to survive, and it is for this that we are organizing. At the present point of development, the trust is to many a veritable curse, and if the evolution were to cease here, it would be better that no labor-saving device had ever been invented; but fortunately it is not in the power of any human being, or of any class, nor of all combined, to check the evolutionary forces that have brought society to the present elevation and that are designed in the fullness of time to place all mankind upon an exalted plane of equality.

We are organizing to abolish the capitalist system, and to accomplish this object we require a certain well-defined political equipment. We must, as I have already stated, take control of the power of government. But let me call your attention to the fact that the party that succeeds to power, that seizes the reins of government, must be a class-conscious party. The present government corrupts everything it touches. It has already control of vastly too much. The present government is entirely coercive. It is simply a monumental policeman, and his chief duty consists in keeping the exploited victims of the capitalist in subjection and creating a new market for the sale of his surplus goods.

We must have socialist administration instead of capitalist government. To accomplish this, we must organize. We must succeed at the ballot box. We must sweep into power in every state and in the union as a whole. When we have so succeeded, we shall represent a majority of the people, those who have been expropriated during all these years. Some people ask with amazement how the people are to come in possession of the vast machinery of production. This is the simplest proposition I can imagine. How did the present owners come in possession of it? *[A voice: "Robbery."]* That is the plain term for it.

John D. Rockefeller owns all, or practically all, of the oil fields, oil refineries, sugar refineries, a vast portion of the railroads, telegraph, and telephone—and the Chicago Standard Oil University.[25] *[Laughter.]* What part of all this and these did he ever produce? Andrew Carnegie is scattering capitalist libraries abroad with a prodigal hand. He is hailed as the greatest benefactor of modern times. I want to concur very heartily with what our Comrade Wise has said in respect to the philanthropist: "Good Lord, save us from the philanthropist." The system in which the philanthropist flourishes is that which makes philanthropy a necessity. Andrew Carnegie, with all the millions he is scattering abroad, erecting monuments to his vanity, cannot spend the money as fast as it rushes in upon him from a thousand sources of exploitation. Carnegie is worth, as the capitalists put it, hundreds of millions of dollars. He accumulated this tremendous fortune, in the presence of which we stand bewildered, in the production of steel and in gaining control of steel markets of the world. Now, if a resident of Mars or Venus, by some modern appliance, were to wing his flight to earth and land in Denver, and you were to tell him about Carnegie, the wonderful steel magnate, he would at once infer that Carnegie was a manufacturer of steel; but instead of this, he is simply a stealer of manufacturing. *[Applause.]* Carnegie could not, if his soul depended upon it, make enough steel out of which to make a needle. Rockefeller, if his salvation were at stake, could not produce oil enough to grease a gimlet. *[Laughter.]*

Here is a vast deposit of coal, not the result of human labor, but of thousands of years of action of sunlight and heat upon decaying vegetable matter. The socialist declares that this coal, this deposit of the natural forces that ministers to the wants and needs of the children of men, should be, ought to be, the common property of all. If an individual had the right to take possession of this part of the earth, this storehouse of nature; if he has the right to place himself at the door and say: "All of you who want coal must pay tribute to me." If he has the right to do this, he has the right to own the entire earth. He has the right to monopolize the sun, if he can, and he would very promptly claim it if he could reach it, and if he could reach it, within a week there would be a meter on every sunbeam. Here are a hundred men who set to work; they develop a mine and produce a hundred tons of coal. What part of this coal, in your judgment, are they entitled to? [*A voice: "All of it."*] Certainly, and if they are not entitled to all of it, I would like to have you tell me what part anyone else is entitled to. If these hundred men are entitled to 100 percent of the product of their labor, it follows, logically, and there is no escape from the conclusion, that the working class at large are entitled to the full product of their toil.

Now, do you know what percent they are actually getting? The working class can today, with the aid of modern machinery, produce from 20 to 50 times as much as they could 60 years ago, but the very instrument of production, the machine, which has increased the productive capacity, has also, privately owned, increased the competition among the workers and lowered their wages. It used to require some years to learn a trade. The skill of the trade places the workingman above the level of indiscriminate competition. He then received practically the product of his toil. If he was a shoemaker and did not get the equivalent of his labor, he could quit the service of his employer. He could invest the $50 that he had saved in the few tools of his trade, the lapstone, hammer, knife, and a few pegs, rent a shop, and commence making shoes on his own account. This was true of the carpenter, the tailor, and other skilled workers. There were certain well-defined crafts, and when a man had mastered his trade, the tools were simple and cheap, and he could buy these and set to work and he was the master of what his labor produced.

In that day, there was no overproduction. Now, as I have said, the machine has increased the productive capacity to a marvelous degree. Why does not the worker have from 20 to 50 times as much of everything as he had 50 or 60 years ago? I will tell you: When the machine came, it absorbed the skill of the trade; that is to say, as the machine became more perfect, it could be operated by unskilled labor. The capitalist must have cheap labor to control the market. Here is a woman—the wage of her husband has gone down; he can no longer support his family; the woman must leave home and become a factor in industry. Millions of women are so employed, and millions of children are in competition with them. As a result, the wage steadily declines. The workingman produces in abundance, but he only consumes up to the point of the wage he receives. What is the wage he now receives? You have been told over and over again that the wage is higher today than it ever was, an untruth on the face of it, and I challenge contradiction. The wage of the worker in proportion to the production is smaller today that it ever was in the history of our country.

Let us get down to actual figures. In 1890, out of every $10 worth of finished product, the workingman received $2.22, according to the census reports. After a lapse of ten years, we find that instead of $2.22, he received but $1.77 in 1900, or a fraction over 17 percent of what his labor produced. As the machine multiplies, as the competition sharpens between men, women, and children, his wage diminishes in inverse ratio as his product increases.

Now, when the work was done by hand, the workingman, who is the consumer as well as the producer, furnished a market for what his labor produced. Everything was done by the slow and tedious process of hand labor. It took three or four days to make a suit of clothes, and now you can make one in a few minutes. Then men were, as a rule, well dressed; now thousands are in rags because we can make clothes too easily. When it took a long time to make a suit of clothes, the worker absorbed a good deal of the product of others while making the clothes. The workers also wore hats and clothes and shoes. They simply exchanged with each other, and every community supplied for its own wants. Overproduction and the struggle for a foreign market was practically unknown. But today the machine operated by a child produces these articles in abundance, but the machine does not wear hats and clothes and shoes. Do you see the point? The machine, in other words, does not provide the market for what it produces; and for many years we have produced not more than we can use, but more than we can sell, for the great body of the workers can only buy a small share of what they produce.

Now the capitalist class cannot absorb the surplus, and that is why our soldiers are in the Philippine Islands today. That is why it is patriotic for man to murder man. That is why it is necessary to transform this fair earth into a slaughterhouse. We are compelled to commit murder upon a gigantic scale to dispose of the surplus products that our own people here at home are suffering for the want of. I am not asking you to change this anarchistic, this utterly brutal system, from any merely moral consideration. I am making the deliberate statement here tonight that whether you will or not, this system will be changed. *[Cheers.]* In the eternal march of the race, one state of society follows another. The social organism, like the units that compose it, is subject to the inexorable laws of evolution. We are on the verge of a worldwide change. If you are unconscious of it, if you cannot see it, I advise you to consult an oculist; and if you see it and still withhold your support from the socialist movement, it is because you are an imaginary beneficiary of the slaughter, or because you are an intellectual coward. I say "imaginary" because the system has no real beneficiary. John Rockefeller serves as a warning, not an example. He succeeded at the price of imbecility and death. You can succeed if you are willing to pay the price, but you cannot succeed unless you are, and if you think you can, you are deceiving no one more than yourself. You will be obliged to settle by the books.

We come into this world without a dollar; we leave it the same way. Death is no respecter of persons; not even a multimillionaire can bribe him, nor can a federal judge enjoin him. *[Applause.]*

Just consider Rockefeller for a moment. The reason there is a big Rockefeller is because there are so many little Rockefellers. So many have the capitalist spirit, the ambition, and lack only the capacity and power. Rockefeller lives on the eighth or tenth floor of some office building. When you approach his office, you will find that you are halted by a guard. There is a lifesaving service station there. Just imagine yourself having to have yourself guarded against your fellow Christians. Rockefeller, like the Denver miner in this system, is a prisoner for life; like the miner, he has a keeper; like the miner, there is no pardoning power for him. The difference is that he occupies a gilded cell. He does not enjoy the life. He does not dare to reveal his identity when he appears upon the thoroughfares of New York; he is in dread of the flash of the dagger, the crack of the murderous pistol. He is in truth in fear of himself. He cowers before the specters in his vision. He knows that his vast fortune represents the skulls and bones of thousands and tens of thousands of his slaughtered victims, and when at night you are refreshing yourselves with slumber, he hears the wails of the victims far away, his brain reels, his nervous system is strained, his vitality is sapped, his constitution is undermined, he becomes a perverted human being. You may talk to him about Shakespeare—he may have heard of him—he has no more conception of this genius than the man who works in the ditch. He has a magnificent library, but examine the books; you will find the leaves uncut,[26] for the man who is engaged in accumulating a fortune has no time to nurture the intellect, no time to cultivate the heart, no time for the inspiration of his soul. He may sit in his palatial residence, surrounded by the luxuries of all climes; there may be music and dancing, but the festivities are never quite sufficient to drown the lamentations a few blocks from there in the wretched hovels, mingled with the despairing cry: "O God, that the bread should be so dear, and flesh and blood so cheap."

There is a collapse of his nervous organization and the most skilled specialists are hastily summoned. They make a careful examination of the patient and they find that all of their skill is fruitless, for the mark of death is already on him who so long unconsciously courted it. And after a while, the silent messenger enters there, as he does the hovel, with noiseless tread, and swiftly finds his way to the couch of pain, where the capitalist is drawing his last breath. In a twinkling, he is brought to a level with the victims of his cupidity.

He who enslaves his fellow beings simply forges fetters for himself. The master is as much less a man as his slave; and as much in need of emancipation. It is coming as certain as I stand in your presence, and the magnificent speeches that were made in advance of my own effort have made it clear to all.

We ask you, in justice to yourself, hold aloof no longer; come forward now, enroll your name, and take your place side by side with your comrades in this conquering movement. Take your place with us, and in the years to come, when at last the socialist movement has triumphed, your name will be inscribed upon the roll of the immortals.

The Inevitable War of the Classes†

June 21, 1902

In the present organization of society, the character of government is determined by the political party it represents, and the party is simply the political expression of the economic interests of the class it represents. For example, the Republican Party is essentially the party of the large and successful capitalist class; the Democratic Party is that of the smaller, struggling, and less successful capitalists, who in large measure consist of the middle class of society. The Socialist Party is the only party that is or can be truly representative of the interests of the working class, the only class essential to society and the class that is destined ultimately to succeed to political power, "not for the purpose of governing men," in the words of Engels, but "to administer things."[27]

The present form of government, based solely upon private property in the means of production, is wholly coercive; in socialism, it will be purely administrative. The only vital function of the present government is to keep the exploited class in subjection by their exploiters.

Congress, state legislatures, and municipal councils as a rule legislate wholly in the interest of the ruling capitalist class. Courts of justice, so called, decide cases of importance not upon their merit, but in the interest of the ruling class.

Ministers of the gospel are subject to the same influence, and their sermons are molded to serve the same purpose.

The owning class is necessarily the ruling class. It dictates legislation and, in case of doubt or controversy, has it construed in its own interest.

Less than 40 years ago, chattel slavery, a tragic phase in our economic development as well as a necessary part of it, was a perfectly respectable institution. The Southern plantation owners practically controlled the government, and even the Supreme Court of the United States was finally compelled to legalize the national iniquity.

Hundreds of able editors consecrated their talents to the perpetuation of the slave traffic. As many ministers of the gospel of Jesus Christ quoted passages from the scriptures to prove that it was ordained of God Himself. Statesmen were its tools, journalists its servants, ministers its apologists, lawyers its lackeys.

† Published in *Social Democratic Herald,* vol. 4, no. 51, whole no. 203 (June 21, 1902), 1.

This proves that Karl Marx was right in declaring that the economic basis of society determines the character of all social institutions and in proportion only as this basis changes, the institutions are modified. For instance, chattel slavery was legal and respectable as long as it was an economic necessity and no longer. When, in the march of the industrial revolution, accelerated so swiftly by the development and application of modern machinery, slavery was overthrown, it became immoral, unjust, and disreputable.

In other words, it was moral as long as it paid; it became immoral only when it ceased, because of changed economic conditions, to be profitable to the capitalist class.

What is here said is applicable in every detail to the present wage system in which one man is the servant and slave and at the mercy of another and in which those having antagonistic economic interests are ceaselessly at war, and this accounts for the present strike in Pennsylvania and the hundreds of strikes, boycotts, and lockouts which are continually disturbing the peace of society and reducing our vaunted civilization to a mere meaningless phrase.

This class struggle will not, cannot cease. It is simply the manifestation of the law of development. All of the forces of evolution are behind it. But for this same struggle in preceding ages, human beings would never have emerged from the jungles of savagery.

Through all the centuries of the past, man has enslaved and preyed upon his weaker fellow being. For thousands of years, there were lords and slaves; through all the Middle Ages, Europe constituted one vast feudal empire, ruled by barons and peopled with their serfs. In the closing years of the nineteenth century, after the feudal system had run its course, its countless and long-suffering victims arose in their might and swept it from the earth. The bourgeoisie, of which the modern capitalists are the offspring, were installed into power, and under the modifications of the new system, the relation between himself and the toiler was changed to the extent that he was called a wageworker and was free to choose his own master. Today we have capitalist masters and working slaves, who, although called sovereign citizens, are exploited of the fruit of their labor as completely under the present system as were their slavish predecessors in the dark centuries of the past.

The wage system, like the feudal system from which it sprang, will fulfill its mission and pass away. Upon every hand, we behold the unmistakable signs of decline and decay. Centralization is paving the way to the new society that is evolving from the present economic anarchy.

All capital, by the inexorable law of economic gravitation, will centralize in the hands of the few. Already, 80 percent of the American people are stripped of their possessions and constitute the dispossessed, propertyless class, whose historic mission it is finally, when concentration has completed its course, to dispossess the small possessing class in the name of the whole people.

To accomplish this, especially in the United States, where all men (and all women) should have the ballot, political organization is an absolute necessity, and hence the organization of the Socialist Party to represent the interests of the working class.

The prevailing economic system can only be abolished in two ways, namely, by securing control of government or by violent revolution. No sane man prefers violent to peaceful measures, and hence socialists rely upon the efficacy of a united class-conscious ballot to accomplish their end.

But few in number at present, comparatively speaking, their party will as certainly expand to continental and conquering proportions as did the Republican Party, whose mission it was, as a political organization, to espouse the cause of the black slaves of the Southern states, strike their fetters from their quivering flesh, and proclaim by the fiat of its immortal leader, Abraham Lincoln, their emancipation.

The Socialist Party is necessarily a revolutionary party in the sense above indicated, and its basic demand is the collective ownership of the means of production and distribution and the operation of all industry in the interest of all the people. This will mean an economic democracy, the basis of the real republic yet to be.

Economic freedom can result only from collective ownership, and upon this vital principle, the Socialist Party differs diametrically from every other party. Between private ownership and collective ownership, there can be no compromise. As well seek to harmonize fire and water. One produces for profit, the other for use. One produces millionaire and mendicant, the other economic equals. One gives us palaces and hovels, robes and rags, the other will secure to every man and woman the full product of his or her toil, abolish class rule, wipe out class distinction, secure the peace of society, and make of this earth for the first time a habitable sphere.

Politics—Democratic and Republican: Interview with the Spokane *Spokesman-Review*[†] [excerpt]

July 3, 1902

Mr. Debs talked entertainingly in an interview last night [July 3, 1902]. He has an infinite charm of manner and is essentially an enthusiast on the subject of socialism. He was asked for his views relative to the pending contest in the Democratic Party between Grover Cleveland and William J. Bryan and its probable outcome. In reply, Mr. Debs said:

In my judgment, the Democratic Party is on the eve of the greatest crisis in its history. The progressive or radical element is engaged in a bitter contest to maintain its supremacy against the Bourbon element. The Clevelands, the Gormans, and the Hills[28] are laying their wires to recapture the organization, and Mr. Bryan is stubbornly resisting their efforts.

Mr. Bryan's interviews and public declarations lead one to believe that he is not personally a candidate for president, and that he does not desire the nomination.[29] Therein lies the greatest source of weakness to the element which he represents. Bryan's hold on the masses of his party is so strong that as a candidate he would be irresistible; with him out of the running, the progressive Democrats are likely to be defeated because of their inability to concentrate upon any other man.[30]

The Bourbon element,[31] represented by Mr. Cleveland, is acting either upon a tacit or actual understanding with the leaders of the Republican Party. They must know that they cannot win, even if they control the party. Times are as prosperous now as is possible under competitive conditions, and the Republicans will doubtless win the next election. A country's political condition is invariably determined by its economic and industrial conditions.

Mr. Bryan would be the greatest man in America were he to take a bold stand for socialism. He says he does not believe in socialism, but in free competition, a thing that is absolutely impossible where the machinery—the tools

† Published in *Spokesman-Review* [Spokane, WA], July 4, 1902, original title and page unspecified. Reprinted as "Eugene V. Debs is Interviewed on Current Topics," *Social Democratic Herald,* vol. 5, no. 3, whole no. 207 (July 19, 1902), 1.

of labor—are in control of a few. Sooner or later, Mr. Bryan and the progressive element which follows him are bound to realize that the free competition which was possible in Jefferson's day is impossible now, by reason of a thousand and one conditions. Mr. Jefferson was the exponent of pure democracy in his day; but the democracy he taught is inapplicable to present conditions of industrial life.

Should the Bourbon faction control the next Democratic National Convention, the radical element of democracy, represented by Bryan, will slough off, and a very large proportion will find the way into the Socialist Party. What Mr. Bryan himself might do remains to be seen. My estimate of the man is that he is thoroughly honest, and that he will follow his convictions wherever they may lead him.

Personally, I hope that the Bourbon element controls. If it does, the issues of the next campaign will be presented in a fairly accurate light; not altogether so, perhaps, but still much better than if the Bryan element should win again.

Poor Opinion of Roosevelt

Mr. Debs was asked for his opinion of President Roosevelt's fight upon the trusts and said:

Before I take up Mr. Roosevelt's personality, permit me to say that I believe, with all socialists, that the trusts are essentially a product of industrial evolution. Combination has been forced by the exactions of the competitive system. It is as impossible to check its full development and fruition as to command the world to stand still. The socialists contend that the trusts should be operated for the benefit of all, not for the benefit of a favored few.

I regard Mr. Roosevelt's alleged antipathy to the trusts as a play to the galleries—a play dictated by party expediency and to satisfy public sentiment. Mr. Roosevelt's party is in power by virtue of trust support, and if he is reelected, which is his consuming ambition, it will be as a result of the same support. I do not anticipate any results from his fight on the trusts, partly because I believe him altogether insincere and partly because I believe any attempt to curb the growing power of combinations to be abortive.

In other ways, I dislike Mr. Roosevelt. The man is thoroughly imbued with the spirit of militarism. Under other conditions, he would be a despot. In some ways, I think he has shown himself devoid of the finer feelings of life. He is essentially arbitrary—almost tyrannical—by nature.

Another thought is pertinent to the trust fight of the administration. Mr. Knox, the attorney general, is the man who did the legal work in the creation of the steel trust.[32] Is it natural that one of the creators of the trust system should now act as its destroyer?

* * *

Progressive Trade Unionism†

August 2, 1902

The action taken by the three national conventions of labor organizations recently held in Denver in adopting a working-class political program has created widespread interest in every part of the country.[33] The reactionary elements predict for the new policy speedy and complete failure. So certain are they of this that they do not hesitate to misrepresent the action of the conventions and bear false testimony against those who took part in them. A number of misleading statements have appeared in the papers, and others are quietly circulated to bring the personnel of the conventions into disrepute, and this is engaged in by those who lack the courage to openly charge and face the men who led the movement which culminated in a new departure which promises to [revitalize] the entire labor movement of the country and bring it up to date in all its economic and political equipment.

The two men who led and inspired the conventions were Edward Boyce, president of the Western Federation of Miners, and Daniel McDonald,[34] president of the Western [Labor Union], now the American Labor Union.[35] McDonald was unanimously reelected upon that issue and holds his position by practically the unanimous confidence of the members of his great and growing organization. Edward Boyce retired from official life, honored by every true man and only hated by those who found him staunch and incorruptible, and utterly incapable of being swerved from his duty to his fellow workers. The name of this man will be honorably written in the history of trade unionism, as he has already written it in deeds of duty that live forever.

I need not, at this time, repeat the terms of the essential change which

† Published as "Progressive Trades-Unionism" in *Appeal to Reason,* whole no. 348 (August 2, 1902), 3.

has taken place in the western labor movement. It is all summed up in the simple statement that it has adopted a working-class political platform, and is now equipped for united action on the political field in every contest until the victory is finally won.

It has been charged that the trade union, under the new regime, has been converted into a political machine. This is not true. The essential economic features of the movement are as they were before. Indeed, if there is any change, these have been strengthened, and the national organization and all local bodies will proceed with their grievances and matters relating to wages, conditions, etc., as before. But when it comes to the use of the ballot, the organization is committed to the policy that it is the duty of union men to vote their class interests as well as to strike for them, and that the man who fails to do this is not in any true sense a union man, nor is he loyal to his fellow workers.

Objection has been made that the organization now controls a member's politics, and that it has as good a right to control his religion. This deduction will not hold. A man's religion is his own individual affair and does not concern his fellow man. But this is not true of his politics, for if he uses his vote to fasten a system of industrial slavery upon his fellows, they have a right to object, and they are at least justified in interfering to the extent that his action affects their interests.

When a man joins one of the old trade unions, he is expected to quit work when commanded to do so by the union. His employment may be entirely satisfactory to him, and he may be sorely in need of it to provide for wife and child. However this may be, if he refuses to quit when ordered to do so, and perhaps takes the chances of imposing starvation upon those he loves, he is kicked out without mercy and branded as a scab and pursued to the end of the earth. Perhaps this is not interfering with a man's "personal rights," as some of our critics would have us believe we are doing when we insist that a union man's best chance to show that he is such is by voting to emancipate his class instead of voting to perpetuate its slavery, and sink it to lower depths of degradation.

To have true power, the labor movement must be class conscious. Until it is so, the trade unions will be among the bulwarks of capitalism and wage-slavery. While the members strike against the consequences of the system, they steadily vote to perpetuate the system, and their leaders encourage them to adhere to, and not depart from, the ancient methods which, applied to present conditions, are marked with increasing impotency and are necessarily resulting in disappointment and failure.

The time is near at hand when the member of a union will be expelled just as promptly for casting a scab ballot, that is to say, for supporting the party of the enemy of labor, as if he took the place of a member while out on strike. Indeed, there may be some justification for the latter, but there can be none for the former act of treason, except alone that of ignorance, and this it is the duty of the true leader to use his best efforts to overcome, so that the workers on all occasions—economically, politically, and otherwise—can use their entire organized class power in resisting the capitalist system, and in charging it at every point until finally it is overthrown and the world's workers stand forth free men.

A Narrow Escape: Letter to the *Social Democratic Herald*†

August 8, 1902

Cañon City, Col., August 8 [1902]

Dear *Herald* and Comrades:—

My light came so near being snuffed out on Saturday [August 2, 1902] that I'm still wondering how it happened; and I about half conclude that the day of miracles has returned. I figured in a wreck on the Colorado & Southern Railway, in Alpine Tunnel, over 12,000 feet altitude, the highest steam railway pass in America, located between Gunnison and Buena Vista.

We were on a mixed train, all coal and other freight except one combination day coach and baggage, in which we rode. There were five passengers, two women and two men besides myself. We had four engines on the train to climb the steep mountain grade, two at head of train and two at rear, just ahead of our car. The road is rickety, and the rolling stock run-down, and it is criminal to rush that kind of a train through that kind of a hole. The continental divide is in the center of the tunnel, and with two engines at each end, the train is very

† Published as "Eugene V. Debs' Experience in a Western Railway Wreck" in *Social Democratic Herald*, vol. 5, no. 7, whole no. 211 (August 16, 1902), 1.

apt to break in two, and the tunnel is so dark that the engineer can't see a foot ahead of him after the first engines have filled it with smoke. The enginemen have often protested against running this kind of a train through the tunnel, but the company has paid no attention to it, for it's cheaper to get all the cars through in one train, for more trains would require more crews.

Well, we entered the tunnel going east at 1 p.m. Saturday, the 2nd, and just after we passed the red light in the center that marks the continental divide and were rushing down the other side, our train broke into three pieces, and our engine and car crashed into the engine ahead of us. The shock was terrific, and as the only dingy lamp in the car went out, we were left in blackest darkness. The scream of a woman, an unearthly shriek, pierced me to the marrow. Our car was derailed, seats smashed, baggage piled around us, engines off the track and jammed into each other. I picked myself together and felt that I wasn't seriously injured, although I found later that my leg was bruised and my back wrenched, from which I am still suffering acute pains.

I had some matches in my pocket,[36] and in the flickering light of these, we concluded that we must get out of the tunnel without delay. With the four engines in the tunnel, pouring out their dense volumes of smoke and gas, we began to suffocate, and the horrible thought came to us that we might be strangled to death before we could grope our way through the tunnel. At the same spot in the same tunnel, five men were suffocated to death in a previous wreck, they being unable to withstand the fumes of the gas, perishing there before help could reach them.

For a few minutes, I saw my doom, and the feeling began to settle over me that this black hole in the mountain peak was to be my tomb. I now understand how the unfortunate miner feels when he finds escape cut off and realizes himself buried alive. But we acted quickly and concluded to start for the other end of the tunnel.

There were some deep holes between the ties, and the walking and stumbling in the pitchy darkness was a trial not soon to be forgotten. I took one of the women by the arm, and our procession started, and after a weary march, the first ray of light greeted us around the curve, and it had all the glory of the primal fiat, "Let there be light!"[37] I shall never forget it. It was our good fortune that a stray current of wind was blowing in at the east end of the tunnel, or we would probably never have emerged from it alive.

Once out, we had to climb the steep mountain, over the tunnel, to reach the other side. On the very summit, I plucked a daisy and sent it to Mrs. Debs as a souvenir of the escape from the Alpine Tunnel. That daisy came near blooming over my grave.

We reached Buena Vista about 7 p.m., and I spoke there that night, although a far better subject for the hospital than the opera house.[38]

I am entirely satisfied and thanking my stars to have escaped so fortunately. I confess to a stray desire to remain on this side a while longer—long enough, indeed, to see how the folks enjoy the Cooperative Commonwealth.

My Near Escape: Letter to Julius Wayland of the *Appeal to Reason*†

August 23, 1902

Glenwood Springs, Colo.

My Dear Wayland:—

Came near crossing over to the other side recently. Was in a wreck in the Alpine Tunnel, and escaped as if by a miracle. Our train broke in two and the rear crashed into the front end. It was an awful smashup and we came near suffocating before we could get out of the tunnel. The wreck was due to the criminal practice of getting all the freight over the road in one train. It was a mixed train, chiefly freight, with four engines attached to it, and the tunnel is as dark as the black hole of Calcutta.

We were all shaken up and bruised. My leg and back were injured, but I hope to be about in a couple of weeks. Our calendar meetings are record-breakers.[39]

E. V. Debs

† Published as "Debs' Near Escape" in *Appeal to Reason,* whole no. 351 (August 23, 1902), 3. Not included in Constantine (ed.), *Letters of Eugene V. Debs.*

How He Stopped the Blacklist†

September 1902

It was on a mixed train on one of the mountain roads in the Western states. The conductor and both brakemen had already shown me their old ARU cards, which they treasured with almost affectionate tenderness. The soiled, illegible scraps were souvenirs of the "war," and revived a whole freight train of stirring reminiscences. The three weather-beaten trainmen were strangers prior to '94; they were off of three separate roads, and from three different states.

Each of the brakemen had told the story of his persecution after the strike. The companies had declared that no ARU striker should ever have another job on a railroad, and they were doing their level best to make good their brutal avowal. These two brakemen had to suffer long in the role of the "wandering Jew." Again and again they had secured jobs, under assumed names and otherwise, but as soon as they were found out, they were dismissed with the highly edifying information that the company no longer needed their services.

They were on the railroad blacklist. Only they know what this means who have been there. Many times had these brakemen been hungry, many times ejected from trains, often footsore after a weary walk to the next division point. But they bore it all and made no complaint. Fortunately, they were both single men, and their privations were at least free from the harrowing thought that wife and child were being tortured by their merciless persecutors. They finally conquered the blacklist and were once more allowed to become the slaves of the railroads.

∽

It was about noon when the conductor tapped me on the shoulder and invited me into the baggage end of the car to have dinner with the crew. They had their own kitchen and cooking utensils and had managed to dish up a most appetizing bill of fare. I was first served with a steaming platter of "mulligan," a popular dish with the mountain men.[40] Then followed cold meat, bread and butter, and hot coffee, topped off with a quarter section of pie.

† Published in *Wayland's Monthly* [Girard, Kansas], September 1902, 7–8. Reprinted as "Stopped the Black List" in *Debs: His Life, Writings, and Speeches* (Girard, Kansas: Appeal to Reason, 1908), 297–300.

The pipes were next lighted, and a lively exchange of reminiscence followed.

The conductor was obliged to leave us for a time, and while he was gone, the two brakemen told me how he had "stopped the blacklist." It is a short but immensely suggestive story. The conductor, like all brave men, was too modest to tell it himself. Here it is:

Bill, that was the conductor's name, was running a train on the S— Railway when the strike of '94 came. He was also chairman of the local grievance committee. He lost out with the rest and took his medicine without a whimper. When he left home to look for a job, his wife had the cheerful assurance that she and the two children would soon hear from him and that they would be united again at an early day.

Bill secured five jobs in straight succession. He was a first-class railroad man and could fill any kind of position. But as fast as he got a job, he lost it. The black demon was at his heels. He had offended his former master, and now he and his loving wife and innocent babes must die.

The last job Bill had held good for some days before he was spied out and discharged. He drew $15, but he did not send it to his wife, nor did he use it on himself. Bill had a grim determination written in every line of his swarthy face when he pocketed that $15 and his discharge, and started toward the city. He stopped short before a hardware store, and his eyes scanned the display in the window. In less than five minutes, he had entered, investigated, and emerged again.

With rapid strides, the blacklisted man hurried toward the railroad station.

We next see Bill on the streets of his old home. His friends, if any remained, would scarce have recognized him. Upon his wan features there was an ugly look that boded ill to someone, and in his hip pocket a loaded six-shooter was ready for action.

The superintendent turned deadly pale when Bill entered. He instinctively read his indictment in Bill's grim visage before a word was spoken.

"What can I do for you, Mr. ——?" tremblingly asked the pilloried official.

"Not a damned thing," replied Bill, in a strange, hoarse voice.

"You know what I'm here for," continued the victim of the blacklist, "and if you've got any prayers to offer before I make a lead mine of your carcass, you'd better begin at once."

While Bill spoke, the superintendent looked into the murderous pistol pointed at him by the desperate man, and an instant later, his office was turned into a prayer meeting. Such piteous pleas were rarely heard from such coward lips.

Bill's heart was touched; he would give the craven assassin another chance.

Withdrawing the weapon and shoving it into his pocket, Bill looked the official straight in the eye and in a steady voice said: "You have beaten me out of five jobs, and you are responsible for my wife and babies being homeless and hungry. You know that there is not a scratch upon my record as an employee, nor a stain upon my character as a man. You have deliberately plotted to torture and kill an innocent woman and two babies who depend upon my labor, and by God, you deserve to die like the dog you are. But I'm going to give you another chance for your life—mark me, just one. I shall get another job, and I shall refer to you as to my service record. If I lose that job, God damn your black heart, you'll do your blacklisting in hell, not here, for I'll send you there as sure as my name's Bill."

The superintendent drew a long breath of relief when Bill turned on his heels and left him alone. He did not doubt Bill's word. It is hardly necessary to say that the blacklist was ended. Bill got the job and holds it to this day. Not a man on the road is more respected than he, especially by the officials.

Bill did not appeal to the courts. He took no chances on a brace game. His nerve and his six-shooter settled the case, and there were no costs to pay.

Bill and his two brakemen are now socialists. The three hours I spent with those three men rolling over the western mountains I shall remember always with interest and satisfaction.

Jesse Cox: An Appreciation†

September 15, 1902

Terre Haute, Ind., September 15, 1902

Jesse Cox was a commanding figure in the socialist movement in America.[41] When the Nationalist movement was organized in Boston by Bellamy and others, Jesse Cox was one of the first to catch the spirit of it in the West; and it was largely through his efforts that a local Collectivist Club at Chicago was converted into a branch of the national organization. From the time the philosophy of collectivism first appealed to him until his great heart ceased to beat, he was an earnest, active, and uncompromising advocate of the movement.

Jesse Cox was in the completest sense a socialist. He had read the literature, and he understood the philosophy of socialism. But he wasted no time in quibbling or hairsplitting. He scorned the petty contentions that breed factions, and he had small patience with socialists who resort to the methods of capitalist politicians to gain their ends. Jesse Cox was clean-handed, open-minded, whole-hearted, and white-souled. There was nothing small and nothing mean about him. He was always frank, and there was never any doubt as to what he thought or where he stood.

For himself he wanted nothing—his only thought was to serve. He was ever contributing and never receiving. With him, socialism was the means and the end, and he stood upon the broad, open highway at the head of his column, pressing forward as he could—leaving the bypaths to others—his eye upon the goal and his heart throbbing for the march that kept his fellows in line.

For a long time, Jesse Cox stood almost alone. He was eminently successful in his profession, and people wondered that he turned to socialism and still more that he boldly avowed his belief in it. They did not know the man. With him, courage and conviction held equal sway. What he thought, he said and also acted. There was no taint of moral cowardice in his nature.

When the Social Democracy was organized, Jesse Cox was one of the most active, energetic, and helpful workers. His advice and counsel was invaluable. He was cool, dispassionate, and farseeing, and had his counsel always prevailed,

† Published as "An Appreciation" in *Social Democratic Herald,* vol. 5, no. 12, whole no. 216 (September 20, 1902), 2.

the socialist movement would be far more advanced in America than it is today.

While chairman of the National Executive Board, he vindicated his fealty to the cause and his right to leadership. From first to last, he was honest, unselfish, true. He was trusted, respected, and loved by every one of his colleagues. He was hated only by those who were too mean and small to know him.

The telegram from Seymour Stedman announcing the death of Jesse Cox touched and shocked me.[42] It had not been long since we had clasped palms, and the strains of his cheerful voice still lingered in my ears.

According to my reckoning, he died too soon by many years. But who can tell? If life be measured by good deeds, Jesse Cox lived full a century. Faithfully, he did all he could, and his works will endure, as his heart will continue to beat, in the socialist movement he loved so well.

Goodbye, Jesse! We loved you truly. We will forget you never.

The Barons at the White House†

October 4, 1902

Marion, Ky., October 4, 1902

I have just finished reading the statements of President Baer[43] and other official representatives of the railway magnates and coal barons at the White House conference held at the request and under the direction of President Roosevelt.[44]

Notwithstanding the president had expressly stipulated that he wished no discussion of the questions of right or wrong involved in the dispute—preferring to have the case considered upon the higher ground of "patriotism," whatever that may mean to a profit-pulling and labor-looting corporation—the coal and railway officials took advantage of the occasion, when they had an audience of 80 million eager listeners, to brand the great army of miners, whose labor pays their princely salaries and builds their marble palaces, as thugs, thieves, cutthroats, and assassins.

My blood leaped and boiled when I read this lying, vicious, brutal indictment penned by the bloated beneficiaries of the countless crimes that have crimsoned the green hills of Pennsylvania with blood drained from the veins of the coal diggers by the bullets and bludgeons of the mercenary hirelings in the service of the robber barons to keep their exploited slaves in subjection.

What stupendous gall! And what a deaf, dumb, and blind faith in the stupidity, cowardice, and everlasting servility of the working class!

Ah, gentlemen, you are woefully ignorant of the teachings of history. Little do you realize in your mad pursuit of profit that you are preparing the people to finally put you where you properly belong. You are sowing the wind and will reap the whirlwind, and when the hour finally strikes, it will fall like a knell upon your startled ears, and you may beg in vain for the arbitration you now scorn. And when your craven lips quiver with your last plea for mercy and it is denied you, remember that you granted none, and that inexorable justice demands that you shall atone to the last drop of blood and the last vain sigh for all the consequences of your atrocious acts.

And President Roosevelt, to whom the hired men of the barons read the riot act for daring to have them contaminated by meeting John Mitchell and

† Published in *The Toiler,* October 10, 1902, unspecified page.

the representatives of labor, what will he do now?

We have heard much about Roosevelt's wonderful nerve and indomitable will—his courage to act in the interest of the people in an emergency, even in the absence of law or precedent.

John Mitchell agreed to submit the whole case to the arbitration of a commission appointed by the president, the next thing to a flat surrender.

The corporation officials spurned Mitchell's proposition, defied the president, and commanded him to order out the federal troops to shoot the miners, crush their union, and starve their families as Cleveland had done in the railroad strike of 1894.

Here is your supreme opportunity, Mr. President! It is up to you, and you must act now in self-defense, unless you are willing to back down and surrender ignominiously to a handful of purse-proud, sodden plutocrats.

Are you an Andrew Jackson or a Grover Cleveland?

Eighty percent of the American people are with the struggling, starving coal miners of Pennsylvania. Their wish and their will ought to be law, even though the ruling class has not written it in the statute books of the country.

Granting that there is no law to empower the president to act in this extremity—neither is there any law to prevent him from acting.

Grover Cleveland acted in defiance of law to crush labor in the interest of capitalist tyranny and exploitation.

Theodore Roosevelt can, if he will, open the anthracite coal mines and avert the horrors of a coal famine. He has the power, and the people will stand by him.

It may also be urged that the president, being now a union man and having pledged his support to union principles at the Chattanooga convention of the Brotherhood of Locomotive Firemen,[45] is in duty bound to stand by the miners' union in its struggle, which has been endorsed by the brotherhood to which the president belongs; and failing in this, according to the ethics, rules, and principles to which he subscribed, the insufferable stigma of "scabbing" may blight his record as a union labor man.

I have no wish to hold any public office, and yet I confess that just at this juncture in the coal strike, I'd like to be president for just a week.

But the real good will come in the accessions to the socialist movement. The class war is revealed to the dullest and blindest of men.

To the ballot box, you working slaves, with the class-conscious ballots of socialism in your hands and the determination to be free men in your hearts.

ꟹ

Since the above was written, the report has come of the collapse of the conference. The operators swept the field, among the fallen and seriously wounded being the strenuous president of the United States.

Gods, what a spectacle! The coal Baerons[46] and Bullions[47] denouncing the miners' union for organizing a labor monopoly "in restraint of trade," in violation of law! This literally beats hell—these coal tsars, these red-handed, flint-hearted arch-anarchists with their steel and steal-clad monopoly that belches defiance, via the White House, of the government and the people, vomits its contempt upon the working class and rides roughshod over all law, human and divine—these are fine specimens to moralize about monopoly and conspiracy and law and order.

Oh, yes, the half-starved miners, and their half-naked wives and children, who have been robbed of all save the animal power required to dig coal and propagate their species, they are the lawbreakers and criminals, and ought to be shot dead in their tracks like wild beasts.

The picture is worthy of an old master and would make a masterpiece for the lurid gallery of Inferno, where devils might contemplate it for incitement to diabolical deeds.

If ever the barricades are thrown up in the streets of New York and Pennsylvania by an insurgent mob, and that bunch of coal barons find themselves tied back-to-back in the death cart on their way to the guillotine, they may seek comfort in the reflection that they are reaping the harvest sown by their own bloody hands.

What's the Matter with Chicago?†

October 15, 1902

Terre Haute, Ind., October 15, 1902

For some days, William E. Curtis,[48] the far-famed correspondent of the *Chicago Record-Herald,* has been pressing the above inquiry upon representative people of all classes with a view to throwing all possible light upon that vexed subject.

The inquiry is in such general terms and takes such wide scope that anything like a comprehensive answer would fill a book without exhausting the subject, while a review of the "interviews" would embrace the whole gamut of absurdity and folly and produce a library of comedy and tragedy.

Not one of the replies I have seen has sufficient merit to be printed in a paper read by grown folks, and those that purport to come from leaders of labor and representatives of the working class take the prize in what would appear to be a competitive contest for progressive asininity.

The leader, so called, who puts it upon record in a capitalist paper and gives the libel the widest circulation, that Chicago is all right, so far as the workers are concerned, that they have plenty and are prosperous and happy, is as fit to lead the working class as is a wolf to guide a flock of spring lambs.

It is from the wageworker's point of view that I shall attempt an answer to the question propounded by Mr. Curtis, and in dealing with the subject, I shall be as candid as may be expected from a socialist agitator.

The question is opportune at this season, when the "frost is on the pumpkin," and the ballot is soon to decide to what extent the people really know "what is the matter with Chicago."

First of all, Chicago is the product of modern capitalism, and, like all other great commercial centers, is unfit for human habitation. The Illinois Central Railroad company selected the site upon which the city is built, and this consisted of a vast miasmatic swamp far better suited to mosquito culture than for human beings. From the day the site was chosen by (and of course in the interest of all) said railway company, everything that entered into the building

† Published in the *Chicago Socialist,* vol. 4, whole no. 190 (October 25, 1904), 1–2. It is not known whether this piece first ran in the *Chicago Record-Herald* as part of its "What's the Matter with Chicago?" series or whether it was first published in the socialist press as an ironic aside.

of the town and the development of the city was determined purely from profit considerations and without the remotest concern for the health and comfort of the human beings who were to live there, especially those who had to do all the labor and produce all the wealth.

As a rule, hogs are only raised where they have good health and grow fat. Any old place will do to raise human beings.

At this very hour, typhoid fever and diphtheria are epidemic in Chicago, and the doctors agree that these ravages are due to the microbes and germs generated in the catch basins and sewers which fester and exhale their foul and fetid breath upon the vast swarms of human beings caught and fettered there.

Thousands upon thousands of Chicago's population have been poisoned to death by the impure water and foul atmosphere of this undrainable swamp (notwithstanding the doctored mortuary tables by which it is proven to prospective investors that it is the healthiest city on earth) and thousands more will commit suicide in the same way, but to compensate for it all, Chicago has the prize location for money-making, immense advantage for profit-mongering—and what are human beings compared to money?

During recent years, Chicago has expended millions to lift herself out of her native swamp, but the sewage floats back to report the dismal failure of the attempt, and every germ-laden breeze confirms the report.

That is one thing that is the matter with Chicago. It never was intended that human beings should live there. A thousand sites infinitely preferable for a city could have been found in close proximity, but they lacked the "commercial" advantages which are of such commanding importance in the capitalist system.

And now they wonder, "What is the matter with Chicago!"

Look at some of her filthy streets in the heart of the city, chronically torn up, the sunlight obscured, the air polluted, the water contaminated, every fountain and stream designed to bless the race poisoned at its source—and you need not wonder what ails Chicago, nor will you escape the conclusion that the case is chronic and that the present city will never recover from the fatal malady.

What is true of Chicago physically is emphasized in her social, moral, and spiritual aspects, and this applies to every commercial metropolis in the civilized world.

From any rational point of view, they are all dismal failures.

There is no reason under the sun, aside from the profit considerations of the capitalist system, why two million humans should be stacked up in layers and heaps until they jar the clouds, while millions of acres of virgin soil are totally uninhabited.

The very contemplation of the spectacle gives rise to serious doubt as to the sanity of the race.

Such a vast population in such a limited area cannot feed itself, has not room to move, and cannot keep clean.

The deadly virus of capitalism is surging through all the veins of this young mistress of trade, and the eruptions are found all over the body social and politic, and that's "what's the matter with Chicago."

Hundreds of the *Record-Herald's* quacks are prescribing their nostrums for the blotches and pustules which have broken out upon the surface, but few have sense enough to know and candor enough to admit that the virus must be expelled from the system—and these few are socialists who are so notoriously visionary and impracticable that their opinions are not worthy of space in a great paper printed to conserve the truth and promote the welfare of society.

This model metropolis of the West has broken all the records for political corruption. Her old rival on the Mississippi,[49] catching the inspiration doubtless, has been making some effort to crown herself with similar laurels, but for smooth political jobbery and fancy manipulation of the wires, Chicago is still far in the lead. In the "Windy City," ward politics have long been recognized as a fine art, and the collection is unrivaled anywhere.

From the millions of dollars filched from the millions of humans by the corporate owners of the common utilities, the reeking corruption funds flow like lava tides, and to attempt to purify the turbid stream by the "reform measures" proposed from time to time by the Republican-Democratic party in its internal conflict for the spoils of office, is as utter a piece of folly as to try with beeswax to seal up Mount Pelée

Chicago has plutocrats and paupers in the ratio of more than sixteen to one[50]—boulevards for the exhibition of the rich and alleys for the convenience of the poor.

Chicago has also a grand army of the most skilled pickpockets, artistic confidence operators, accomplished footpads,[51] and adept cracksmen[52] on earth. So well is this understood that on every breeze we hear the refrain:

> When Reuben comes to town,
> He's sure to be done brown—

And this lugubrious truth is treated as the richest of jokes, with utter unconsciousness of the moral degeneracy it reflects, the crime it glorifies, and the indictment of capitalist society it returns in answer to the *Record-Herald's* query: "What's the Matter with Chicago?"

Besides the array of "talent" above mentioned, fostered by competitive society everywhere, the marshy metropolis by the lake may boast of a vast and flourishing gambling industry, an illimitable and progressive "levee" district, sweatshops, slums, dives, bloated men, bedraggled women, ghastly caricatures of their former selves, babies cradled in rags and filth, aged children, than which nothing could be more melancholy—all these and a thousand more, the fruit of our present social anarchy, afflict Chicago; and worst of all, our wise social philosophers, schooled in the economics of capitalist universities, preach the comforting doctrine that all these are necessary evils and at best can but be restricted within certain bounds; and this hideous libel is made a cloak that theft may continue to masquerade as philanthropy.

It is at this point that Chicago particularly prides herself upon her "charities," hospitals, and eleemosynary endowments, all breathing the sweet spirit of Christian philanthropy—utterly ignorant of the fact, designedly or otherwise, that these very institutions are manifestations of social disease and are monumental of the iniquity of the system that must rear such whited sepulchers to conceal its crimes.

I do not oppose the insane asylum—but I abhor and condemn the cutthroat system that robs man of his reason, drives him to insanity, and makes the lunatic asylum an indispensable adjunct to every civilized community.

With the ten thousand "charities" that are proposed to poultice the sores and bruises of society, I have little patience. Worst of all is the charity ball. Chicago indulges in these festering festivals on a grand scale. Think of cavorting around in a dress suit because some poor wretch is hungry; and of indulging in a royal carousal to comfort some despairing woman on the brink of suicide; and finally, that in "fashionable society" the definition of this mixture of inanity and moral perversion is "charity."

Fleece your fellows! That is "business," and you are a captain of industry. Having "relieved" your victims of their pelts, dance and make merry to "relieve" their agony. This is "charity" and you are a philanthropist.

In summing up the moral assets of a great (?) city, the churches should not be overlooked. Chicago is a city of fine churches. All the denominations are copiously represented, and sermons in all languages and of all varieties are turned out in job lots and at retail to suit the market.

The churches are always numerous where vice is rampant. They seem to spring from the same soil and thrive in the same climate. And yet the churches are supposed to wage relentless warfare upon evil. To just what extent they have checked its spread in the "Windy City" may be inferred from the probing of the press into the body social to ascertain "what is the matter with Chicago."

The preachers are not wholly to blame, after all, for their moral and spiritual impotency. They are wageworkers, the same as coal miners, and are just as dependent upon the capitalist class. How can they be expected to antagonize the interests of their employers and hold their jobs? The unskilled preachers, the common laborers in the arid spots of the vineyard, are often wretchedly paid, and yet they remain unorganized and have never struck for better wages.

"What's the matter with Chicago?" Capitalism!

What's the cure? Socialism!

Regeneration will only come with depopulation—when socialism has relieved the congestion and released the people and they spread out over the country and live close to the grass.

The *Record-Herald* has furnished the people of Chicago and Illinois with a campaign issue.

If you want to know more about "what is the matter with Chicago," read the socialist papers and magazines; read the platform of the Socialist Party; and if you do, you will cut loose from the Republican-Democratic party, the double-headed political monstrosity of the capitalist class, and you will cast your vote for the Socialist Party and your lot with the international socialist movement, whose mission it is to uproot and overthrow the whole system of capitalist exploitation and put an end to the poverty and misery it entails—and that's "what's the matter with Chicago."

The Western Labor Movement[†]

November 1902

There seems to be considerable misapprehension, especially among socialists, in regard to the trade union movement of the western states, whose delegates, recently assembled in national convention, adopted the platform of the Socialist Party and pledged the support of their organizations to the international socialist movement. This radical departure from the effete and reactionary non-political policy of the American Federation of Labor, so long and so earnestly striven for by the western leaders, and so entirely compatible with the socialist conception of class-conscious and progressive trade unionism, should have been met with the prompt and hearty approbation of every unionist and every socialist in the land. That such was not the case, the lukewarm comment and half-approving, half-condemning tone of the Socialist Party press, with but one or two exceptions, bear convincing testimony, while the uncalled-for, unwise, and wholly unaccountable official pronunciamento of the St. Louis "Quorum," purporting to speak for the National Committee, capped the climax of unfairness and injustice to the western movement.[53]

Stripped of unnecessary verbiage and free from subterfuge, the Socialist Party has been placed in the attitude of turning its back upon the young, virile, class-conscious union movement of the West, and fawning at the feet of the "pure and simple" movement of the East, and this anomalous thing has been done by men who are supposed to stand sponsor to the party and whose utterance is credited with being *ex cathedra* upon party affairs.

They may congratulate themselves that upon this point at least they are in perfect accord with the capitalist press, and also with the "labor lieutenants," the henchmen, and the heelers, whose duty it is to warn the union against socialism and guard its members against working-class political action.

The writer takes issue with these comrades upon this vital proposition; and first of all insists that they (including the members of the Quorum) speak for themselves alone, as they undoubtedly have the right to do, and that their declaration in reference to the American Labor Union is in no sense a party expression, nor is it in any matter binding upon the party, nor is the party to be held responsible for the same.

† Published in *International Socialist Review,* vol. 3, no. 5 (November 1902), 257–65.

As a matter of fact, the rank and file of the Socialist Party, at least so far as I have been able to observe, rejoice in the action of the Denver convention, hail it as a happy augury for the future, and welcome with open arms the western comrades to fellowship in the party.

"Why didn't they stay in the Federation of Labor and carry on their agitation there? Why split the labor movement?" This is made the burden of the opposition to the western unionists, who refused to be assimilated by Mark Hanna's "Civic Federation"—the pretext for the scant, halfhearted recognition of their stalwart working-class organization and their ringing declaration in favor of socialism and in support of the Socialist Party.

And this objection may be dismissed with a single sentence. Why did not those who urge it remain in the Socialist Labor Party and carry on their agitation there? Why split the socialist movement?

It is not true that the western unionists set up a rival organization from geographical or sectional considerations, or to antagonize the Federation; and they who aver the contrary know little or nothing about the western movement, nor about the causes that brought it into existence. A brief review of these may throw some light on the subject.

In 1896, the annual convention of the American Federation of Labor was held in Cincinnati. The Western Federation of Miners, at that time an affiliated organization, was represented by President Edward Boyce and Patrick Clifford, of Colorado. The strike of the Leadville miners, more than three thousand in number, one of the bloodiest and costliest labor battles ever fought, was then in progress and had been for several months. The drain and strain on the resources of the Western Federation had been enormous. They needed help and they needed it sorely. They had always poured out their treasure liberally when help was needed by other organization, East as well as West, and now that they had reached their limit, they naturally expected prompt and substantial aid from affiliated organizations.

Boyce and Clifford appealed to the delegates. To use their own language, they were "turned down," receiving but vague promises which, little as they meant, were never fulfilled. At the close of the convention they left for home, disappointed and disgusted. They stopped off at Terre Haute to urge me to go to Leadville to lend a helping hand to the striking miners, which I proceeded to do as soon as I could get ready for the journey. It was here that they told me that the convention was a sore surprise to them, that three or four men had votes enough to practically control the whole affair,[54] and that the dilatory and reactionary proceedings had destroyed their confidence in the federation.

Afterward, I was told by the officers in charge of the strike that no aid of the least value, or even encouragement, had been rendered by the Federation of Labor, and that the financial contributions were scarcely sufficient to cover the expense of the canvass for same.

It was not long after this that the western miners withdrew from the federation, and a couple of years later, conceiving the necessity of organizing all classes of labor in the western states, which as yet had received but scant attention, the American Labor Union was organized, the Western Federation of Miners being the first organization in affiliation with the new central body.

But notwithstanding the withdrawal of the western miners from the American Federation, they continued loyally to support the eastern boycotts levied by the Federation, and it is a fact not to be gainsaid that while some of those boycotts were so feebly supported in the East, where they had been levied, as to be practically impotent, the union men of the West recognized them as scrupulously as if imposed by their own organization, and in Montana and other states drove the boycotted Eastern products out of the Western markets.

So far as I am able to inform myself, there is no instance on record where the American Federation of Labor, or any organization affiliated with it, ever sanctioned or supported a boycott levied by the western unions.

On the contrary, cases can be cited where the eastern organizations bluntly refused to recognize boycotts declared by the western organization.

Not only this, but the western unions have always contributed promptly and liberally to the financial support of all labor unions, East and West, North and South, affiliated and otherwise, Butte leading with thousands of dollars in support of all kinds of strikes, in all sections of the country, the liberality and loyalty of the Western Federation of Miners in such cases being proverbial—and yet I have never heard of an instance where the western unions received a dollar from any eastern organization since the withdrawal of the Miners' Federation.

At this very time, while the miners of the East are making a desperate struggle against starvation, the miners of the Far West, affiliated with the tabooed American Labor Union, are contributing from their hard earnings to the support of the Pennsylvania strikers, though they never expect to receive a penny from the East; and President [Charles] Moyer of the Western Federation of Miners is sending messages to President [John] Mitchell of the United Mine Workers. Still more—notwithstanding the bituminous miners of the middle states, members of the same organization as the anthracite strikers, decided not to strike in support of their anthracite brethren. President Moyer and Secretary [Bill] Haywood of the Western Federation wired President Mitchell that in their judgment all miners in the country should stand by the Pennsylvania strikers, and that the coal miners of the western union were ready to a man to lay down their tools until the anthracite strike was won.

This is the militant, progressive, liberal spirit of western unionism—now reinforced with a class-conscious political program—that could not brook the ultraconservative policy of the eastern movement, and seceded from it with motives as loyal to labor as ever prompted men to action.

The opponents of the Western Labor Union may search the annals of organized labor in vain, all the circumstances considered, for as noble an example of fidelity to the principles of union labor as that of President Moyer and Secretary Haywood of the Western Federation, speaking for the coal miners of the western states, having no grievance of their own and belonging to another organization, to which the East, if not hostile, was at least not friendly, voluntarily agreeing to lay down their tools and give up their jobs to help their fellow men more than two thousand miles distant, whom they had never seen and never expected to see.

Had the situation been reversed and the miners of Montana had gone on strike, would the eastern unions have sent any money out there, or would the eastern miners have volunteered to strike in sympathy with their western brethren?

The conventions of the Western Labor Union, the Western Federation of Miners, and the Hotel and Restaurant Employees' Union, held simultaneously at Denver in May last, attracted wide attention chiefly because of their declaration in favor of socialism and their adoption of an independent political program.[55] Prior to this, these organizations were rarely mentioned, in fact unknown in the eastern and middle states, and no reference to them was ever made by the capitalist press outside their own immediate jurisdiction. But the very moment they declared in favor of socialism, the capitalist press, the "pure and simple" union element, and, strange to say, some socialists, "Cry 'Havoc!' and let slip the dogs of war."[56] As for the socialists who joined in the outcry, or "damned with faint praise," they were perhaps persuaded, after a survey of the East and then the West, that it was wiser policy to curry favor with numbers than to stand by principles.

The impression prevails in some quarters that the American Labor Union was first instituted at the convention in Denver last May. This is erroneous, as the organization has been in existence several years, and at the late convention simply changed its name from the Western Labor Union to the American Labor Union to more properly describe its expanding jurisdiction.

Fault has been found because of the rival disposition shown by the convention of the American Federation and the purpose to invade other sections and organize rival unions, thereby dividing the movement and precipitating a factional labor war.

The delegates to the Denver convention considered this phase of question in all its bearings; they did not propose to antagonize the American Federation, nor to invade its jurisdiction, nor to set up rival unions, they simply proposed to protect their own movement in the Western states, and they did not propose to allow attacks to be made upon it without resenting them; and when they finally took action, even in the matter of changing their name, it was in self-defense, for from every quarter, even some of their own disgruntled element who sought to defeat the proposed adoption of socialism, came the threat that if the Western Union did not return to the American Federation, the latter would send a corps of organizers into the western states to institute rival unions and "wipe the western movement off the earth."

The "pure and simple" element in Denver and vicinity, affiliated with the American Federation, and not a few of the local politicians, who saw their doom in the socialist tendency of the convention, were loud and persistent in the threat of "annihilation" if the delegates refused to vote for affiliation with the American Federation. While there, I heard it frequently upon the street and elsewhere, and in fact Secretary Morrison, who, with Thomas I. Kidd of the executive council, represented the American Federation at the convention with the purpose of inducing the Western Labor Union to dissolve, and its affiliated organizations to join the American Federation, gave it out that if the delegates declined their overtures, the American Federation would proceed to organize in all the western states, as it acknowledged no boundary line to its jurisdiction in the United States.

The charge, therefore, of "invasion" and "rival unions" against the western movement falls to the ground. It can be proven beyond doubt that the western movement acted upon the defensive in this matter and that only when the threat to "wipe them out of existence" in their own territory was made, did they conclude to extend their jurisdiction to such sections as desired to embrace their organization.

If it is held that the American Federation had prior jurisdiction, it may be answered that George III and Great Britain had prior jurisdiction over the colonies, and that the jurisdiction of the Knights of Labor antedated that of the American Federation, and the National Labor Union that of the Knights of Labor, and so on back without end.

Whatever difference may have prompted the separation several years ago—and whether it was wise or otherwise, I shall not now consider, having no share in the praise or blame, as the action was taken by the western miners upon their own motion and they are entirely willing to accept the responsibility—it is certain that there is today a radical fundamental difference between the eastern and western wings of the American labor movement, and that in their present state and with their present conflicting policies and tendencies, they cannot be united, and even if they could be, factional and sectional strife would be at once engendered, and disruption would be inevitable.

The western movement could only have consented to go *back and backward* to the American Federation by stultifying itself and betraying and humiliating its thousands of progressive members who are far enough advanced to recognize the futility of labor organization without class-conscious political action and who will never retrace their steps to the fens and bogs of "pure and simple" unionism.

The western men want unity and they want harmony, but they will not go backward, they will not sacrifice progress to reaction to secure it.

They have declared their class-consciousness, and they cannot and will not snuff out that beacon light of emancipation.

They have committed their organization to the Socialist Party, and they cannot unite with an organization that is hostile to independent political action by the working class.

There is one way and one only to unite the American trade union movement. The American Federation of Labor must go forward to the American Labor Union; the American Labor Union will never go back to the American Federation of Labor. Numbers count for nothing; principle and progress for everything.

When the American Federation of Labor sheds its outgrown "pure and simple" policy; when it declares against the capitalist system and for union, class-conscious action at the ballot box, as the supreme test of union principles, as the American Labor Union has done; when it relegates "leaders" to the rear who secure fat offices for themselves in reward for keeping the rank and file in political ignorance and industrial slavery; when it shall cease to rely upon cringing lobbying committees, begging, like Lazarus at the gate of Dives, for a bone from a capitalist legislature and Congress it helped to elect, and marshals its members in class-array against their exploiters on election day to vote their own class into power, then unity will come, and the western men will hail with joy that day. And it is coming. It is simply bound to come.

In the meantime, there need be no quarrel between the East and West, and there will be none unless the threatened attempt to "snuff out" the West should materialize, in which case the "snuffers" will be entitled to the credit of having inspired a refreshing exhibition of the "staying" qualities of the class-conscious trade union movement of the western states.

The speaking tour of the national officers and executive council of the American Federation in the mountain states following the Denver convention, and widely heralded by the capitalist press as an "uprising of the conservative element of organized labor to squelch the Western radicals" can claim anything but a victory if that was the program of President Gompers and his colleagues. Some of their meetings, with all the advertising they received, scarcely amounted to a "corporal's guard," and where they had hundreds, the meetings held under the auspices of the Western Union had thousands in attendance without the aid of capitalist newspapers and in spite of the opposition of capitalist politicians.

As to whether the western movement is growing or declining since the Denver convention, it is sufficient to say that the reports show that during the month of September [1902], the organization affiliated with the American Labor Union added more than four thousand new names to their rolls of membership.

Passing through Denver recently, I noticed by the papers of that city in scarehead articles that the organizer of the American Federation, who had just been interviewed upon the subject, declared in emphatic terms that he had been instructed from headquarters at Washington to organize rival unions at every available point and where there was even one applicant, to admit him, totally regardless of the American Labor Union. If this is to be the policy of the eastern federation, it will have to be that of the western union, and as a result we shall have an era of unprecedented activity in the work of organizing the trade union movement of this country.

One thing is noticeable in this connection, and that is that the American Federation has evinced a greater interest in the western states, spent more money, and worked harder to organize them in the comparatively short time since the western union is in the field than in all previous years.

The rise of class-conscious trade unionism in the West was not the result of mere chance or personal design, but obedient to the rising tide of the revolutionary spirit of the proletariat of the rugged and sparsely settled mountain states, a composite population composed of pioneers, the most adventurous, brave, and freedom-loving men from all states of the American continent, and it is impossible that they, with their keen instinct and revolutionary tendency, could be long content to creep along in the creaking chariot of conservatism, even though it still bear traces of the union label.

The class-conscious union movement of the West is historic in origin and development, and every socialist should recognize its mission and encourage its growth. It is here that the tide of social revolution will reach its flood and thence roll into other sections, giving impetus where needed and hastening the glorious day of triumph.

I am the friend, not the enemy, of the American Federation of Labor. I would conserve, not destroy it. I am opposed, not to the organization or its members, many of whom are personal friends, but to those who are restraining its evolution and preventing it from fulfilling its true mission.

I would not convert it into a political organization, but simply bring it up to date and have it, as it must become if it is to survive, a class-conscious industrial union, its members recognizing the socialist ballot as the weapon of their class and using it accordingly, thus escaping the incongruities and self-contradictions of the present "pure and simple" union, whose members strike against and boycott the effects of the capitalist system while voting industriously to perpetuate the system.

It is true that there are elements of progress at work within the organization. Let them continue their efforts. Such men as Max S. Hayes, J. W. Slayton,[57] J. Mahlon Barnes,[58] and many others who have done and are doing excellent work on the inside have all help and no hindrance to expect from the western movement.

Certainly Max Hayes, elected delegate to the approaching convention of the American Federation of Labor by a popular vote of his organization, the International Typographical Union, upon the issue that he was a socialist, and now muzzled by an order of a delegate convention instructing him to vote against socialist measures, will not object to a little help from the outside.

In time, the two progressive forces will meet, and the work of redemption will have been accomplished.

Until then, as in the past, I shall support every boycott and every strike of the American Federation of Labor, and every organization affiliated with it, to the best of my ability, and when they lose in any of these struggles, no disheartening word from my lips shall darken their counsels or add to the bitterness of their defeat.

I have been plain and unreserved in my criticism, as I have a right to be. For many years, I have been an unofficial organizer for the Federation of Labor, and for all the trade unions connected with it, and in my travels, especially the past seven years in which I have been almost continuously traversing the country, I have organized and been the means of organizing hundreds of unions of all kinds. In the southern states, I held the first great labor meetings when there was little or no trace of organization, in many places not even a single member, and I at once set to work organizing each point with the result that when I covered the same territory shortly after, there were unions everywhere, and the movement spread rapidly over that section of the country. In view of these facts, I think I can consistently assert the right of candid criticism.

The attitude of the Socialist Party toward the trade union movement broadly endorsing and commending it, but stopping there, and allowing it to manage its own internal affairs is, without doubt, the correct one, as any intermeddling must result in harm with no possible hope of good. The party, as such, must continue to occupy this friendly yet non-interfering position, but the members may, of course, and in my judgment should join the trade unions East and West and North and South and put forth their best efforts to bring the American labor movement to its rightful position in the struggle for emancipation.

A Year of Trial for the Western Federation of Miners†

December 20, 1902

Cheney, Wash., December 20 [1902]

The radical departure of the Denver convention in May last [1902] makes this a year of trial for the Western Federation of Miners and for organized labor in general in the western states. The latter movement was lifted bodily out of the old ruts and grooves and placed upon a higher plane than it has hitherto occupied. The change was not accomplished without great effort, and the convention simply proved that it was equal to the task. It was this, and this alone, that

† Published as "A Year of Trial" in *Miners' Magazine*, vol. 4, no. 2 (February 1903), 37–9.

brought the convention into such bold prominence and that will ultimately give it an honored page in the history of industrial emancipation, and every delegate who had part in the work is entitled to the respect and approbation of the working class.

But the man who did more than all others to give the federation its rightful position in the labor world, who months before the convention, worked ceaselessly to that end, though he did so quietly and without display, was Edward Boyce, the retiring president, and one of the bravest men and truest souls that ever fought for labor's freedom. Arrested, clubbed, jailed, denounced, and persecuted, he was always calm, loyal, and at the front of his hosts. Ed Boyce led forward, not backward, as many "leaders" do. He understood his duty and performed it. Never once did he show the white feather.[59] Utterly forgetful of self, his one absorbing thought and controlling passion was the welfare of the western miners and the toiling mass. He accepted office under protest and avoided all display. He was heard no oftener than was necessary, but when he did speak it was with clearness, earnestness, and to the point.

I have traveled with him, worked and slept with him, and I know of no man of nobler character, purer integrity, loftier courage, or rarer common sense than Edward Boyce, the man who blazed the way to the highlands of duty and glory for the Western Federation and then, with characteristic modesty, retired to private life.

ꟹ

More than half the year is gone, and the next convention already looms in the future. The difficulties in adapting the organization to the changed conditions and carrying out the new policy have been by no means small, and yet they have been steadily conquered, and upon the whole the organization has made greater progress and is in a more healthful, vigorous, and promising condition than ever before. The new administration, like the old, has been a unit from the start, and the rank and file have given their energetic support in pushing the organization to the front and crowning its struggles with victory.

As I write, some battles are being fiercely contested in California, and the federation will be tried to the core. All the better is this for the organization. It will strengthen its stamina and develop its latent powers, and the final result is not in doubt for one moment. However long the battles may last, the ultimate victory will be with the organization. There will be no surrender to any "Civic Federation."

This is a good time, at the beginning of the new year, for each member to ask himself if he is doing his full duty as a member of the organization.

Are you active, alert, and thoroughly in earnest as a soldier in the federation army? Anyone can wear the badge, but it takes a good man to supply what the badge represents.

Every available mine worker in the West is to be brought into the organization; every point in the mining districts is to be organized; every local is to be strengthened; every possible subscriber is to be secured to the *Magazine,* and every other obligation, financial and otherwise, is to be met in the prompt and resolute spirit of true manhood.

The political program of the federation must not only be carried out but strengthened. The last vestige of opposition to it, whether through ignorance or corruption, must be overcome. The whole body of members must become conscious of their class interests and stand solid as a stone wall. They must vote as they strike. Election day is the supreme test of a man's unionism. If he votes the old party tickets to keep his class in chains, he is a traitor to his fellows. You can't be a trade unionist and a political non-unionist.

The old parties stand for the capitalist class—the mine owners and their hirelings. The Socialist Party is for the miners and the working class. They cannot compromise. It is all one or all the other. The union man of today has to understand the class struggle and be on the right side of it in a strike, at the ballot box, and at all other times and places.

Between now and the convention, every effort must be made to bring the federation into Denver in shape to do battle for its very life. Its greater work lies before it, and each member and local union should strain the last nerve in fitting and equipping the organization for its emancipating mission.

The *Magazine,* under the able and fearless editorial management of John O'Neill,[60] the wheelhorse of progressive unionism, has become a power in the labor movement. In every line there is a snap, and in every sentence fire. It is quoted and passed around. Workingmen are thrilled and inspired by its burning appeals; plutocrats damn it.

All the signs are cheering. On to victory!

Notes

1. Wire reports reprinting portions of this article broke on January 26, 1902, with an original report in the *New York Sun* datelined Terre Haute, January 24. *The Toiler* was published each Friday, making January 24 the most likely date of original publication.
2. A conference between leaders of labor and industry held under the auspices of the National Civic Federation was held in New York City from December 16–18, 1901. The "industrial peace conference" established an entity to be known as the Industrial Department of the National Civil Federation, featuring a 36-member "executive committee" that included equal representatives from corporations, trade unions, and "the public." The committee was "to do what may seem best to promote industrial peace" by arbitrating differences between employers and employees in an effort to prevent strikes and lockouts.
3. On December 24, 1901, former president Grover Cleveland accepted appointment to the Industrial Department of the National Civic Federation as a representative of "the public."
4. John Ireland (1838–1918) was the archbishop of St. Paul, Minnesota, from 1888 until his death.
5. Henry C. Potter (1834–1908) was bishop of the Episcopal Diocese of New York. He was active in the National Civic Federation from its establishment in 1900 and was an advocate of social peace between labor and capital.
6. In addition to Cleveland, Ireland, and Potter, the "neutral" members of the committee included Charles Francis Adams of Boston; former secretary of the interior Cornelius N. Bliss; Charles A. Bonaparte of Baltimore; former comptroller James H. Eckles; president of Harvard University Charles W. Eliot; John J. McCook, a New York City lawyer; Franklin McVeagh of Chicago, and John G. Milburn of Buffalo.
7. Adapted from Jeremiah 8:11.
8. Reverend Byron E. Stauffer (1870–1922) was the pastor of Grace Methodist Episcopal Church in Buffalo. Early in March 1902, he attacked socialism, arguing that "the socialist of today is the anarchist of tomorrow," destined to turn to the "violence and terrorism" of anarchism after society inevitably brushed aside his arguments.
9. Bishop James Edward Quigley (1854–1915) attracted headlines in February 1902 with his proclamation that "a workingman may be a union man and a good Catholic, but he cannot be both a social democrat and a Catholic."
10. John Peter Altgeld (1847–1902), governor of Illinois from 1893 to 1897, is best remembered for having pardoned the imprisoned Haymarket anarchists. He died on March 12, a few days before this piece was written by Debs for the local socialist newspaper.
11. Opening lines of the poem "Song of the Greeks" (1821) by Thomas Campbell (1777–1844).
12. John Mitchell (1870–1919) was president of the United Mine Workers of America

from 1898 to 1908 and a prominent member of the National Civic Federation along with Samuel Gompers. In 1904, Mitchell and Debs engaged in a bitter polemic over terms of a settlement of a strike of anthracite coal miners. See "The Coal Strike Surrender" (March 31, 1904), this volume.

13. Governor of Pennsylvania was William A. Stone (1846–1920), elected to office in 1898.
14. Mount Pelée, an active volcano on the island of Martinique, erupted in late April and early May 1902 in what was the worst volcanic disaster of the twentieth century. An estimated thirty thousand people were killed by lava, boiling water, and mud in a series of devastating eruptions.
15. An unrelated second part of the article offered commentary on the ascension to the throne of King Alfonso XIII of Spain.
16. Delivered at the Denver Coliseum. The joint convention ran from May 26 to June 8, 1902.
17. From May 26 through June 8, a joint convention of the Western Federation of Miners, Western Labor Union, and the Hotel and Restaurant Employees' Union was held in Denver, bringing together 300 delegates to form a broad new national labor organization, the American Labor Union. In an effort to forestall this effort, the American Federation of Labor dispatched two of its top officials to Denver—secretary Frank Morrison and Thomas I. Kidd, a member of the organization's executive council. For two hours, the pair attempted to make a case for keeping politics out of union activity and for affiliation of the ALU with the AF of L. With time at a premium, rather than hearing a protracted series of statements by delegates, the floor was yielded to Gene Debs, present on the floor as a guest of the convention. Debs delivered the following reply, speaking for about an hour. This condensed version of the speech is extracted from a stenographic report.
18. Frank Morrison (1859–1949), a member of the International Typographical Union and a close associate of Samuel Gompers, was secretary of the American Federation of Labor from 1897 to 1935 and secretary-treasurer from 1936 until his retirement in 1939.
19. Thomas J. Hagerty (1862–192X), a socialist "labor priest," addressed the Western Labor Union's joint convention immediately after Debs.
20. Ralph M. Easley (1856–1939) established the National Civic Federation in New York City in 1900 and served as chair of the group's executive council for the rest of his life.
21. John Harris Baker (1832–1915) was a Republican member of Congress from 1875 to 1881. He was appointed a federal judge by President Benjamin Harrison to fill the bench seat vacated by the promotion of Debs's nemesis William A. Woods in 1892.
22. The Denver convention to which Debs spoke changed the name of the Western Labor Union to the American Labor Union.
23. Debs refers to the joint conventions of the Western Federation of Miners and the American Labor Union, held in Denver.
24. From Isaiah 1:3.

25. The University of Chicago.
26. Many books were formerly made with large folded sheets bound into covers without being mechanically cut into individual pages, leaving the purchaser to cut open the individual leaves with a sharp device at the time of first reading. An uncut book was an unread book.
27. Apparently a very loose paraphrase from Frederick Engels, *Socialism: Utopian and Scientific.* London: Swan Sonnenschein & Co., 1892; 15–16 or 76–77.
28. David B. Hill (1843–1910) was a former governor and US senator from New York. A corporate attorney, Hill was loathed by progressive Democrats, although he was not directly associated with the corruption of Tammany Hall.
29. Although he ran for president of the United States in 1896 and 1900, Bryan did not run for the office in 1904. He would make his third and final run for the presidency in 1908.
30. Democrats nominated a conservative David Hill protégé, Alton Parker, in 1904. The progressive wing of the party had attempted to nominate William Randolph Hearst as its champion but failed to win sufficient support from Bryan to defeat the establishment nominee.
31. The conservative element.
32. Philander C. Knox (1853–1921) was an attorney for Carnegie Steel Corporation and sat with Andrew Mellon and Henry C. Frick on the board of the Pittsburgh National Bank of Commerce.
33. Reference to the joint conventions of the Western Federation of Miners, Western Labor Union, and Hotel and Restaurant Employees' Union held in late May and early June 1902. The gathering endorsed socialism.
34. Daniel McDonald, from Chicago, was the president of the Western Labor Union from its founding in 1888 until his resignation in March 1905.
35. The Western Labor Union changed its name to American Labor Union at the 1902 convention.
36. Debs was a cigar smoker.
37. From Genesis 1:3.
38. Opera houses were generally the largest public halls in each town and frequently were rented as the venue for Debs's speeches.
39. Debs was visiting the Cripple Creek district, where he was speaking to hard rock miners.
40. Mulligan stew was a community hot dish put together by individuals contributing what they had available.
41. Jesse Cox (1843–1902) was a well-to-do attorney and former chair of the executive board of the Social Democratic Party with headquarters in Chicago. Cox resigned this position in May 1900, bitterly opposed to what he foresaw as an inevitable drive toward unity with the Springfield SDP. He died on September 10, 1902, of pneumonia following surgery for removal of his appendix.
42. A telegram announcing the death datelined Chicago, September 11, 1902, had been squeezed onto the front page of the previous issue of *Social Democratic Herald.*

43. George F. Baer (1842–1914) was president of the Philadelphia and Reading Railroad and spokesman for the owners in the great coal strike of 1902.
44. The ill-fated presidential conference intended to negotiate an end to the ongoing coal strike was held in Washington, DC, on October 3, 1902. The gathering broke up abruptly with the representatives of the mine operators and railroads stating that they "decline to treat with President Mitchell."
45. The twenty-first convention of the Brotherhood of Locomotive Firemen opened in Chattanooga on September 8, 1902, with President Theodore Roosevelt addressing the gathering on its opening day. Roosevelt declared to the convention, "I believe emphatically in organized labor. I believe in the organization of wage workers." (See "The Eight Biennial Convention," *Locomotive Firemen's Magazine* [Peoria, IL], vol. 33, no. 4 (October 1902), 554.)
46. A play on George Baer's surname.
47. Inspiration for this pun is unclear.
48. William Eleroy Curtis (1850–1911) was a traveling correspondent for the *Chicago Inter Ocean* from 1873 to 1886 before moving to the *Record-Herald* in 1887. He would remain with that paper until the time of his death.
49. St. Louis, Missouri.
50. A play on the silver-to-gold value ratio advocated by William Jennings Bryan and other advocates of unlimited coinage of silver to boost the money supply.
51. Archaic slang term for a highwayman who traveled by foot rather than by horse; that is, a thief who preys on pedestrians.
52. Nineteenth-century slang term for burglars or safe-crackers.
53. Reference is to comments of the St. Louis Quorum of the National Committee—the de facto executive committee of the SPA—in its semi-annual report of September 12, 1902. The report declared that "while the Socialist Party . . . has solemnly pledged itself to the unification of the trade unions, yet a contrary policy has been set up in the West by comrades acting in a dual capacity as organizers of the American Labor Union and the Socialist Party, thus misrepresenting the attitude of our party and compromising it in their attempts to build up a rival organization to the American Federation of Labor." Unmentioned is the close connection of executive secretary Leon Greenbaum and other leaders in the St. Louis party organization with the AF of L and its affiliated unions in St. Louis, particularly the National Brewery Workers.
54. Delegates to conventions of the AF of L were allotted votes corresponding to the paid membership of their organizations, thus allowing a few big unions to control the outcome of all voting.
55. The joint convention of the Western Federation of Miners, Western Labor Union, and Hotel and Restaurant Employees' Union, held in Denver from May 26 to June 8, 1902, with more than 300 delegates in attendance. American Federation of Labor president Samuel Gompers did not attend, although the federation was represented by vice president Thomas I. Kidd and secretary Frank Morrison. The gathering endorsed socialism on June 4 by a vote of 230 to 73.
56 From *Julius Caesar* (1599) by William Shakespeare (1564-1616). "Havoc!" was a battle

command of the Middle Ages to the soldiery to engage in plunder and destruction.

57. John W. Slayton (1863-1935) was a carpenter and trade union activist who emerged as one of the leading socialists in the state of Pennsylvania. Slayton joined the Social Democratic Party soon after its formation and ran for Congress on the SDP ticket in 1900. In the summer of 1909 Slayton was one of the leaders of the McKees Rocks Strike, an action against the Pressed Steel Car Company, a manufacturer of railroad cars. In 1910 he headed the state ticket as the Socialist Party of Pennyslvania's candidate for governor.
58. J. Mahlon Barnes (1866–1934) was a cigar maker by trade and headed the Cigarmakers' Union in Philadelphia. Barnes was a committed activist in the Socialist Labor Party, leading the majority of Section Philadelphia out of the organization during the July 1899 split of the so-called "Kangaroos." Barnes would later serve as executive secretary of the Socialist Party of America from 1905 to 1911 and is credited with the idea for the "Socialist Red Special" campaign train that transported Debs around the country during the election of 1908.
59. "Show the white feather" was a nineteenth-century British expression for the demonstration of cowardice. The expression is believed to derive from cockfighting.
60. John M. O'Neill (1857–1936), a committed socialist, became the editor of the *Miners' Magazine,* official organ of the Western Federation of Miners, in 1901 and remained at the post for more than a decade.

1903

Auguries for the New Year†

January 3, 1903

The late congressional elections have truly been an eye-opener to the American people. Many a sneer of derision has been turned into a patronizing smile, while the politicians of all shades of the "old school" realize that of a sudden there is a pestiferous fly in their ointment and are wondering how it got there and by what means to get rid of it.

John Pierpont Morgan is quoted by the *Springfield Republican* as saying in substance that he and his coadjutors are simply organizing industry as a necessary part of our industrial and commercial development—which must eventuate in collective ownership of the competition-destroying modern agencies of wealth production and distribution.

If John is correctly quoted, he is not only clear-eyed in seeing the handwriting on the wall, but wise and sagacious in reading it aloud for the benefit of the class for whom he serves as prophet and guide. Comrade Morgan thus couples up with the revolution and fixes himself with and for the inevitable.

The *Chicago Chronicle,* Democratic organ, foe of monopoly, friend of the people, champion of freedom, etc., shows all its teeth and most of its interior anatomy in an editorial on the appalling "Despotism of Socialism," in which the startling discovery is proclaimed that, in socialism, free thought as we now enjoy it will be suppressed, for there is a conspiracy in the socialist movement that when the people get in power they will not allow themselves to think at all, and then despotism will strip off its mask, roll up its sleeves, and get in its deadly work on the people for a thousand years!

ഗ

At Cheney, Washington, in the State Normal School, on December 20 [1902], I gave my last lecture in the Northwest and am now speeding toward St. Paul on the Northern Pacific.

Since my engagement with the American Lyceum Union, I have been in Illinois, Wisconsin, Michigan, Ohio, Kentucky, Missouri, Colorado, Idaho, Oregon, and Washington. On the trip just close, I was obliged to cancel Eaton,

---

† Published in *Social Democratic Herald,* vol. 5, no. 28, whole no. 231 (January 3, 1903), 1.

Colorado, and Boise City, Idaho, on account of not being able to reach them in consequence of delayed trains—then entire service on the Union Pacific and Oregon Short Line being demoralized and trains running from 8 to 20 hours late, owing to dilapidated motive power and machinery resulting from the machinists' strike, which has been in progress almost a year and is bound to win in the end.

Since the beginning of the lecture season, I have spoken in colleges, high schools, and churches, though in most places the lecture is given at the opera house, under a variety of auspices, including women's clubs, YMCAs, college courses, school societies, church associations, debating clubs, etc.

But twice have I spoken under socialist auspices during this time, and but three or four times to less than a full house. As the lecture is given in the season course at almost every point, and the ticket for the season is sold in advance, a full house, rain or shine, is the rule.

The people everywhere are not only ready for the gospel of socialism, but receive it with every mark of enthusiasm, and the telling points in a speaker's argument are applauded just as heartily in a church or schoolroom as they are in a socialist propaganda meeting.

The trip in the Northwest was particularly gratifying in its evidences of substantial progress of the socialist movement since my previous visit to that section. At almost every place, I was received by "leading" citizens and called on by the "representative" men of the community, most of whom, a few years ago, would have joined in a tar-and-feather bee without a second invitation and then solemnly resolved that it was "the duty of all patriotic citizens to unite in stamping the curse of socialism and anarchy out of this great American republic."

At La Grande, Oregon, the school trustees called and invited me to the high school to address the pupils while the school was in session. The newspapers were uniformly fair and generally kind and even flattering. Oh, what a change!

In Oregon, J. Stitt Wilson[1] and Carl Thompson[2] have done splendid work. Their agitation has prepared that field for a great harvest. I heard their names spoken often by men and women who had been reached, brain and heart, by the social crusaders and are now at work spreading the light among their neighbors. Wilson and Thompson may congratulate themselves upon the results of their campaign in that state. Socialism is the all-absorbing theme; the average man has a good grip on the philosophy of it, and the movement is therefore free from maudlin sentiment and is bound to make steady and substantial progress in the right direction.

The one thing, however, that pleased me most of all was the great change in the railroad men of the Northwest. I was fairly "stumped" to find so many of them thorough socialists. At La Grande and Pendleton, Oregon, where the hotels were filled with engineers, conductors, firemen, brakemen, switchmen, telegraphers, car inspectors, shopmen, trackmen, etc., who came to pay their respects, nearly all were old ARU men and practically all were avowed socialists. At La Grande, it seemed like a reunion of the ARU. The old spirit was fanned into flame by the battle cry of socialism and now burns with more intensity than ever before.

ꟷ

The *Butte Miner* of December 22 [1902] contains a brief statement of the work of the Butte miners' union during the past year. Among other things, the report states that more than $10,000 was contributed by this local to strikes in various parts of the country, that it has $104,000 in its treasury, and that its property and assets aggregate almost $500,000. This is the work of the Butte union and of the Western Federation of Miners, the wealthiest, most resourceful, liberal, and progressive local labor union in the world.

ꟷ

My hearty good wishes to the *Social Democratic Herald* for a bright and prosperous New Year. As the stalwart exponent of social democracy and international socialism, you are doing valiant service and merit loyal and generous support.

The Arbitration Farce†

January 8, 1903

The performance at Scranton is proving the futility and folly of arbitration as a method of harmonizing the conflicting interests of capitalists and wageworkers.[3] Be the finding of this commission what it may, the condition of the mine workers remains the same, and there will be no appreciable change in those infernal regions. It goes without saying that the commission will "do something for the miners." Oh, yes, there's no doubt about that, and the capitalist press will exploit the "great victory" to the delight of many ignorant workingmen and all the capitalist politicians. But after the "victory" is celebrated, the slaves will return to their pits, and the strongest magnifying glass would reveal no difference in their condition before and after the arbitration.

They have lost more than five months of working time, and many of them are hopelessly in debt. The leaders are marked men, and if not already denied employment, they will have to go as soon as a pretext can be made to discharge them, and the blacklist will doubtlessly follow in their footsteps and see to it that they do not stop this side of famine or crime.

Those needed in the mines will receive a few pennies more a day by the grace of the commission, and twice the amount of increase thus allowed, or more, will be added to the price of coal. The operators remain on top and the miners at the bottom. Their relative positions remain precisely the same.

The operators get immediate returns from the increased price of coal. The miners will have to work steadily five years, assuming that they get an increase of 10 percent to make up the five months' loss of their wages.

Oh, the farce of "arbitrating" such a damnable crime! And yet we must pass through just this sort of thing to prove its hollowness, and so the Scranton show will eventually be worth its price.

Next to the operators—who had determined to make no concession, and having so declared themselves, had to resist arbitration—the chief beneficiary of the deal will be President Roosevelt. It was for him a capital political stroke, and the returns of the next national election will doubtless prove it.

† Published as "The Anthracite Arbitration" in *American Labor Union Journal,* vol. 1, no. 14 (January 8, 1903), 3. Reprinted as "The Arbitration Farce" in *Social Democratic Herald,* vol. 5, no. 31, whole no. 234 (January 24, 1903), 3.

Of course, there is not upon this commission—a purely capitalist device—a single representative of the working class. The specifications for the commission were provided by the operators, and the personnel by a president elected by them. Under such circumstances, the simple duty of the commission is to take considerable time in "investigating" this very complex case, taking particular pains to impress the open-mouthed millions with the gravity of the situation and the solemnity of the proceedings.

No wonder the lawyer who so far forgot the sanctity of the séance as to allude to the president as "Teddy" Roosevelt was so fiercely rebuked for his blasphemy.

If the commission really wanted to "investigate," they should have, after going through the hovels of the mine slaves, made a tour of the palaces of their masters. Why not? These are the parties to the contest, and if it is necessary to know how the coal diggers live in order to determine if they are sufficiently robbed, why not see how their exploiters live to arrive at the same conclusion.

Take the photographs of five of the miners' shacks and place them in a row with their occupants before them; then the photographs of the palaces of as many of the barons, with their imperial families in the foreground; place the latter above the former and you have a true picture of the issue involved, the nature of the struggle, and the utter farce of "arbitration."

The final settlement will be delayed, but not defeated, by such schemes. *We socialists are after those mines, and we will never rest until we have them and the parasites go to work and the workers are emancipated.*

That the long strike of the miners will be productive of far-reaching results, there is not the slightest doubt. It was an extraordinary contest and will be so chronicled in the history of the American class struggle. To my mind, the most wonderful thing about it was the "stickability" and discipline of this vast proletarian mass of all tongues, and for this, President [John] Mitchell and his colleagues deserve no small credit.

The fact that the working class, organized and unorganized, were back of the miners, and supplied them with the sinews of war; and the further fact that the middle class, who had been charged extortionate prices for coal, were in sympathy with the strikers, served to greatly strengthen the strike and increase its chances for success. Indeed, no other strike approaching this in magnitude ever had so little opposition and such general support. The time was opportune, and all the conditions were peculiarly favorable for the revolt; and my judgment is that under such circumstances the strike could have been won. This, however, would have necessitated a general strike of all the coal miners of the country, and had this occurred early in the beginning, there would have been no five months' game of freeze-out; there would have been far less suffering; the miners would have achieved a substantial victory; and it would have been all the better for the country at large. However, this is but my opinion, and the present outcome, the result of Mr. Mitchell's conservative policy, may work out all the better in the end. Still, I cannot but feel that a vigorous fight, backed up by all the resources at the command of labor, even though it had resulted in defeat, would have been better than the long-drawn game of endurance and final submission to the chloroforming process of arbitration.

For President Mitchell, personally, I have the highest regard. He is conscientiously devoted to the men who trust him, and his conduct during the strike, especially his unwavering fidelity and remarkable self-possession, merit the commendation of all men, but I think he will find in time that there is something wrong with a war policy—and every strike is a battle—that is hailed with satisfaction and elicits the hearty approval of the enemy.

President Mitchell and his policy have the unqualified approbation of the capitalist press—that is to say, the capitalist class who live out of the labor of the working class, and whose robbery of the anthracite miners has stripped and degraded them and their wives and children, until many of them are but ghastly remnants of the human species, and might properly be classified as hole-inhabiting human animals. I have been there often enough to be able to surround myself with the awful pictures when anthracite mining is the theme, and so it is easy to account for my contempt for "arbitration" of such hellish atrocities as are enacted in those worse-than-Siberian torture regions.

Walter Wellman,[4] the celebrated correspondent, in one of his letters to the Chicago press, quotes Mark Hanna as saying: "The operators are making a great mistake in not dealing with Mitchell. They ought to be thankful that he is where he is, and should be willing to contribute a million dollars to keep him there rather than risk having some radical agitator in his position."

This is certainly flattering to Mr. Mitchell from the capitalist point of view, but at least a doubtful compliment from the workers' standpoint. Mr. Hanna is one of the capitalistic friends of labor; he wants harmony—and the capitalist system; and he understands how to set about getting the one and prolonging the other.

The "sacredness of the contract" was permitted, in the critical hour, to paralyze the strike. Nothing was said about the sacredness of human life. The property of the capitalist must be regarded with reverential sanctity and awe, but the lives of the proletarian herd are of small consequence.

All honorable men live up to their contracts, but in certain exigencies, these lose their binding effect. A strike is war, and a measure of war has little regard for previous "contracts." If John Mitchell had backed up the anthracite strikers with all the miners in the country, he would have had a precedent in Abraham Lincoln. The proclamation of emancipation was wholly in violation of constitutional law and in utter contempt of millions of legal contracts entered into in good faith.

To return to the commission, the testimony of non-union miners, the dummies of the operators, about the "crimes" and "outrages" of the strikers is now being heard. The operators are having their inning, and Chairman [George] Gray[5] and his colleagues are in the clover.

The running comment of Chairman Gray and the minute description of his corrugated brow when he emphasizes the testimony against the strikers by interjecting his opinion of the "coward" who would engage in a boycott and the "criminal" who would interfere with the "honest workingman" who had taken his job, is doubtless very impressive to the man who has not the visual penetration to see the sham behind it all.

It also gives Chairman Gray, the well-fed corporation lawyer and capitalist judge, the inspiration to disport himself and give full play to his capitalist instincts. He has taken repeated advantage of his position as arbitrator and judge to denounce the "outrages" of the strikers, but has he had a single word to say about the outrages of criminal and law-breaking corporations that own the mines? Compared with the atrocities of the anthracite coal trust, the notorious law-defying combinations, in bribing judges, debauching legislatures, robbing the miners, starving their children, and holding up the public, the "outrages" of the strikers which so shock the judicial sensibilities of Chairman Gray are as a zephyr to a tornado or the ripple of a rivulet to the roar of the sea.

According to the published comment of Chairman Gray on the non-union testimony, the United Mine Workers is a criminal organization and its members are "cowards" and "scoundrels." Certain it is that the acts Chairman Gray denounces as "outrages" were the acts of union miners and in perfect accord with the policy of their organization.

A strike is simply war. The capitalists rely upon the power that private ownership of the means of production confers upon them to starve the strikers to death or defeat.

Of course, they are perfectly "law-abiding." They have the power of life and death over their slaves and act wholly within their "legal rights" in starving them and their families into submission. They would be idiotic indeed to use pistols or knives or clubs in slaying a few of their slaves, when they can slaughter them all by waiting until they are hungry.

From the workers' side, the case is wholly different. His condition and environment confer no special degrees for the refinement of ethics. Hunger looks him in the eye, and if he is a man instead of a vassal, as he thinks of wife and child, his blood begins to warm and his pulse to quicken, and he is ready to fight his enemy in any way he may have a chance, law or no law; and if Chairman Gray were a corporation slave instead of a judicial tool, he would understand this, and not make himself ridiculous in the eyes of every thinking man by expecting an anthracite miner to be as polite and suave as a Chesterfield[6] in dealing with the capitalist concern that robbed him and threatened with starvation his wife and child.

What a pity, indeed, that the American proletariat cannot imbibe the beautiful spirit of servility inculcated by Chairman Gray. In that case, they would never strike and always submit; but if in some evil hour they did strike, they would first buy a work on "law and order" and another on "morals and ethics," spray themselves with rosewater, cover their coarse paws with kid gloves, swear off swearing, and go to Sunday school and stay there until "public opinion" announced their "glorious victory" and the utter route of the capitalist enemy.

Lassalle said: "You can't produce a revolution with eau de cologne." Every labor strike is a battle in the class war, an outbreak in the social revolution.

We, too, deprecate violence, deplore misery, and abhor bloodshed, and this is why we are radical and aggressive in the struggle to put an end to the barbarous system whose normal estate is the oppression and suffering of the human race.

Socialism the Trend of the Times†

January 30, 1903

A convincing proof that the intellectual trend of the times is in astonishing channels has been brought most forcibly to my attention during my travels. I would have been tarred and feathered eight years ago in communities where now I am respectfully given appreciative attention. Sentiments uttered by me when it was my task to direct the fortunes of thousands of railroad workmen on strike were treated with scorn and contempt. Contumely was heaped upon me then.

Now these sentiments are accepted as the product of advanced thought, and I have so great a man as Pierpont Morgan admitting the truth of these "truisms." *Socialism, indeed, is the trend of the times.* I predict that soon after this remarkable period of high-tension railroad activity, there will come an era of strikes, compared to which the struggle of 1894 will be but a pygmy. Every available scrap-pile engine is now called into activity; the prodigious labor of the railroad men applied 24 hours a day does not suffice to keep down the congestion. But the reaction will lay bare the bolstered-up condition of things. The railroads are first to feel this reaction. Each great economic struggle is only another step toward socialism. Because I say this, I am not necessarily the advance agent of pessimism. J. J. Hill has said practically the same thing.

† Part of a syndicated plate published in various newspapers. As published in *The Sun* [Parsons, KS], vol. 24, no. 275 (January 30, 1903), 2.

The Social Crusaders†

February 4, 1903

The action recently taken by the State Executive Committee of Colorado relative to the comrades who have engaged in the propaganda of socialism in the name of "the Social Crusade" is ill-advised, in my opinion, and calculated not only to do injustice to the comrades in question, but to provoke resentment and introduce unnecessary discord in the party counsels throughout the state.

Although not a resident of Colorado and rarely obtruding myself in a matter of this kind, I have a special interest in the socialist movement in the Rocky Mountain states, and it has seemed to me that Colorado in particular presented a most inviting field for socialist propaganda and promised to be one of the first states, if not the very first, to win out for socialism.

It is in no spirit of dictation that I now write, but because I feel deeply upon the subject; and this must justify my motive in protesting against what I regard as an unfortunate precedent, as well as a great injustice to a body of men who have done more than any others in equal number to spread the light of socialism in the western states.

I am not impugning the honesty of the state committee, but I decidedly question their judgment in pronouncing "condemnation" upon a body of men whose only crime is that they propose to work for socialism in their own way. I do not understand that they have asked the state committee to endorse them; why should the committee feel called upon to condemn them?

All over Colorado there are socialists, clear-headed and class-conscious, who were first set to thinking and who first had their eyes opened by J. Stitt Wilson. Is it for this that the state committee "condemns" him?

If the state committee had anything against Wilson and his coworkers, would it not have been nearer right to call their attention to the fact and give them a chance to defend themselves?

The state committee errs in the first instance in declaring that the social crusade is organized in "opposition" to the Socialist Party. The Crusade has

† Published in *Colorado Chronicle,* February 4, 1903, unspecified title or page. Copy preserved on the *Papers of Eugene V. Debs* microfilm edition, reel 6, frame 1228. Reprinted as "The Crusaders" in *American Labor Union Journal,* vol. 1, no. 20 (February 19, 1903), 3.

from the start actively supported the Socialist Party, organizing locals, addressing meetings, distributing literature, and doing all that could be done to build up and make strong the party throughout the state.

There are scores of socialist clubs and independent societies all over the country, organized to aid in the socialist propaganda, thereby recruiting for the Socialist Party. Would the executive committee of Colorado wipe them all out because they choose their own way of working for socialism?

Now note the contradiction of the committee: After declaring against the crusaders for having an alleged "opposition" organization, they "condemn" them for "maintaining a separate organization within the state party." The committee was evidently confused. The Crusade, so called, is neither an opposition organization nor is it maintaining a separate organization within the state party. The Crusade simply consists of a few men with ideals who have become convinced that socialism is right and have resolved to consecrate their lives to it; and in my judgment these men have done more to dispel prejudice, get socialism rightly before the people, and build up the Socialist Party than any other equal number of men in the country.

These men happen to have served in the ministry. I am certainly not prejudiced in their favor on that account. But I have been in their footsteps, with and around and among them, and, knowing of their work, I would be mean indeed to see such an injustice done them without at least lifting my voice in protest.

It has been almost ten years since a minister called on me in Chicago and invited me to occupy his pulpit and tell his congregation something about the labor question.

The church never forgave him; I never forget him. His name was J. Stitt Wilson.

Five years ago, I was to speak on socialism in the quiet, conservative college town of Greencastle, Indiana. The people were all strangers, or their hands were raised against me. A young minister invited me to his home, and I ate bread with his family that evening. That was William H. Wise,[7] and I have loved him ever since.

There is not a crusader who could not occupy a pulpit and live a life of ease. Why do they give up position, leave home, part family ties, and take up the burden of their deep convictions? Because they are men of moral courage and intellectual honesty. Why should any socialist condemn them? Why?

Let us call the roll: J. Stitt Wilson, William H. Wise, Carl D. Thompson, Frank H. Wentworth,[8] Ben Wilson. What one of them is preaching "doubtful socialism?" What one of them does not stand squarely on the class struggle? What one of them is not working tooth and nail for the Socialist Party?

Let me make a proposition that I regard as a fair test of the case. To determine if the "doubtful socialism" is on the one side or the other, let the state committee call a meeting of socialists and invite one of the Crusade, say Carl D. Thompson, to appear on behalf of the crusaders. If he does not make it clear that he knows at least as much about the literature and science of socialism as his advisors, if he does not prove by the verdict of the audience that he is an able, eloquent, and altogether worthy advocate of the principles of international socialism, of which the movement has every reason to be proud, I will make my apologies to the state committee.

The trouble with some men is they must "judge" other men and "condemn" them if they don't conform to their contracted ideas. They talk about "revolutionary socialism" and "opportunism"; these and a few other stock phrases complete their vocabulary. Some of them have never read a standard work on socialism; do not understand its true philosophy—and yet presume to pronounce the decree of banishment upon others of clearer vision and larger grasp who don't happen to do things in ways to suit them.

Such men may organize a sect, but never a party; they may mean well, and usually do, but they are too fanatic and intolerant to develop a great movement. The worst of all is that they imagine themselves "revolutionary." They are in fact quite the reverse; such influence as they have is wholly reactionary.

I believe the socialists of Colorado will agree with me that the crusaders are men of brains, animated by the purest motives, and that their labors in and for the socialist movement have been as unselfish as any service ever rendered the cause by any other comrades; and this being true, they are entitled to the respect and goodwill of the party.

No comrade who knows William H. Wise as he is would condemn him or recommend that the party ignore his correspondence. He literally gave up all he had for the socialist movement, and privation has often been his lot and that of his family, for this reason purely and no other. He can forget himself as completely to serve a cause as any man I have ever known. He is a socialist to the core of his heart; not a sentimental one, but thoroughly scientific, and therefore revolutionary in the genuine sense of that greatly misused term. And so are all his coworkers.

In conclusion, I hope the state committee will, upon maturer consideration, rescind their decree. There is a better way to deal with this matter than with "condemnation proceedings."

Let the state committee invite the crusaders to meet with them and talk it over, and I am confident that there will be no difficulty in finding the right way out. Otherwise there will be factional strife and possibly party disruption.

The prospect in Colorado is too fine to be shattered. It would be a pity, if not a calamity.

Most earnestly do I hope that reasonable counsels may prevail; that justice may be done, and that the party in Colorado may press forward with unbroken columns to glorious victory.

Socialism and Civilization: Speech at Rochester, New York† [excerpt]

February 8, 1903

The labor question, broadly stated, is the question of all humanity, and upon its just solution depends the peace of society and the survival of civilization. The central and controlling fact of civilization is the evolution of industry.

A little over a century and a quarter ago, the American colonists were compelled to declare their political independence. The people were then engaged largely in agricultural pursuits, what they manufactured was produced in simple and primitive ways, and they used with their hands the tools with which they did their work. The problem of making a living was a comparatively easy one. Each man could, with the product of his own labor, satisfy his own wants.

Long ago the too-simple tool of those days was touched by the magic want of invention, until its mechanism has now become marvelously complex. In the great modern industrial evolution, the workingman has suffered, and because of his ignorance has allowed the tool of production to pass from his grasp. The cunning that was in the hand of labor has passed into the machine. As competition has become keen, handicraft has been succeeded more and more by the machine work, until skilled labor has become common labor; the

---

† Speech formally titled "Some Phases of the Labor Movement; or, Socialism and Civilization." Published in *Rochester Democrat and Chronicle*, vol. 71 (February 9, 1903), 10.

struggle for existence became so hard that woman was forced into the labor market and become a factor in industrial conditions.

As the evolution of machinery has continually progressed, it has been found that many of these could be operated by the deft touch of children, until now 3 million of these have been forced into the labor market in competition with men and women. This has resulted from the system that makes profit the all-important consideration and life of little importance. There must be cheap labor in spite of its effects on the lives of human beings.

The state of Alabama once had a law against child labor. The time is coming, however, when competition will force manufacturers to operate their factories where the raw materials are produced. This has already been done by the New England manufacturers. They went to the lawmakers of Alabama and said: "We must have cheap labor if we are to compete in the markets of the world, and in order to do this, we must employ the children in our mills. You have a law against the employment of children in this state. We should like it to come here, but, if this is enforced, it will compel us to go elsewhere."

What was the result? Today there is no law against the employment of children in Alabama.

We have seen how, under the prevailing system, the fortunes of the few mount to fabulous heights, while the great mass of the people are doomed to an existence of want, misery, and woe. There are some misguided persons who imagine that if the Democratic Party were in power, it would affect the decentralization of capital and bring back the former days of competition. If it were possible in some mysterious way to do this, it would be quite ineffective. With the development in modern machinery, capital would have combined again in within 20 years, and would be stronger than it has ever been in the past or is in the present.

The question is, shall this combination of capital crush us, or shall we take our place in line with this modern order of things and make it conform to our uses? We can't destroy the trust, the great combinations of capital, no more than we can go back to the days of the hand tool, the stagecoach, the canal barge, or the tallow candle.

This modern tool is a vast complex machine that needs an army of workingmen to operate it. If it belongs to one man, all the profits will accrue to one man. That man we call a capitalist. It takes 100,000 men to produce the steel manufactured in this country. This complex tool belongs to Andrew Carnegie, who, himself, if his life depended on it, could not produce enough steel to make a cambric needle, no more than John D. Rockefeller could produce oil to grease a gimlet. Despite these facts, to these men go the profits resulting from the labor of thousands of workingmen.

The workingman cannot get rich under the present system. It is only the man who exploits the labor of others who gets rich. In the old days, the only way a man could get rich was by owning the man. If the 4 million slaves who were emancipated 40 years ago were offered to the capitalists of today, they would not take them under any consideration. It is not necessary today that you should own slaves in order to become rich; it is only necessary that you should control the tools of production. It does not make any difference what other changes take place; so long as the tools of production are owned and controlled by individuals, the laboring man will be dependent, the slave of industrial conditions.

Society is being divided into two classes. There are those in our country today who do not like to hear anything said about classes. They say there is no such thing as classes in the United States. Among these is Chauncey Depew. He tells us that in the great American republic, every boy and young man has a chance of someday becoming president. Let me tell you that there are many of these same boys and young men who would at times willingly swap their chances of becoming president of the United States for a ham sandwich.

I stand in your presence this afternoon a socialist. I believe this earth is the inheritance of every human being who inhabits it. We have, however, today the capitalist class that owns the tools of production. They don't work with these tools themselves, but they buy the labor they need in the open market. While they don't use these tools, they lay claim to all the wealth produced by them, and those who use the tools can only live by selling their labor to those who own the tools.

We are in the midst of a great class struggle, a conflict which is shaking the foundations of society. Those who have read history carefully know that the great struggles of the world have been class struggles. In the impending revolution, the laboring class can only emancipate itself by bringing about the common ownership of the tools of production, then all humanity will be emancipated, even to J. Pierpont Morgan.

The only real reason for war today is that the capitalists may find foreign markets for their products. When it is decided by these that war is needed to open up a foreign market for the goods that those at home cannot buy, they induce the newspapers to serve to the people a diet of what is termed "patriotism," and through this, for some unaccountable reason, an insatiable desire to kill is produced in the minds of the people.

To me, war is a horrible thing. I think it is the prostitution of genius to glorify it.

In proportion to the value of what he produces, the American laboring man is paid less than his Japanese or Chinese competitor.

The purpose of socialism is not to reform. Its platform calls for a revolution now in present conditions.

We socialists don't want socialism now. The time is not ripe for it. We would not have it in Rochester tomorrow if we could. But the time for the ushering in of socialism is ripening very rapidly. What is needed to make the laboring people of the country ready for it is a well-developed panic. I am not desirous of posing as a prophet of evil, but this time is coming. Neither Republican nor the Democratic Party will guarantee that this period of false prosperity will last. A panic is coming, and the next panic will not be confined to America. It will be international in its effect, and then will be the time for the introduction of the coming order of things.

Socialism's Steady Progress†

March 7, 1903

The returns of the national election last fall revealed an unexpected factor, a new force, as it were, in American politics. The large and rapid increase in the socialist vote was a surprise to the nation. In the short space of two years, the voted leaped from about 130,000 to almost 400,000, and this at a time when "prosperity" was the dominant issue and "let well enough alone" the slogan of the campaign.

The significance of this vote lies not so much in its size as in its character, since the socialist movement is essentially revolutionary, and the Socialist Party, unlike the Greenback, Populist, and other parties, to which it has been likened and which sought simply to "reform" the present economic system, is unequivocally committed to the abolition of capitalist production and the substitution of the Cooperative Commonwealth.

† Published in *Social Democratic Herald,* vol. 5, no. 37, whole no. 240 (March 7, 1903), 3.

There are many who look upon the rapid rise of socialism as the ebullition of a passing hour, an ephemeral growth not at all calculated to menace the well-established political and economic regime of the time. They have not been critical students of the past, nor are they more than superficial observers of the present transition period in which industrial evolution is transmuting competitive small capital into centralized cooperative capital and recruiting isolated workers into industrial armies, the forerunner of a new economic system and a higher order of civilization than this earth has ever known. Such astute politicians as Mark Hanna see it. Said he: "The great political struggle of the future will be between the Republican Party and the Socialists." He is right.

Rev. Lyman J. Abbott,[9] the Brooklyn divine, can see it. Just after the last election, he said: "Socialism is inevitable."

J. Pierpont Morgan can see it. According to a late issue of the Springfield (Mass.) *Republican,* he said: "We are simply organizing industry for the people, and sooner or later they are bound to take possession."

This is the trend, and socialism, the political expression of it, can no more be restrained than the evolution that brought it into existence.

Where modern industry develops, socialism is bound to generate. This is as true of Indiana as of Massachusetts. Production on a large scale is the life preserver of the capitalist. This means centralization of capital, and this means the trust. It also means destruction to the small capitalists, and hence the vain cry against the combine—the protest of the past against the future.

Listen to what Karl Marx, the great economic philosopher and prophet, said 55 years ago:

> The essential condition for the existence, and for the sway of the bourgeois class, is the formation and augmentation of capital; the condition of capital is wage-labor. Wage-labor rests exclusively on competition between the laborers. The advance of industry, whose involuntary promoter is the bourgeoisie, replaces the isolation of the laborers, due to competition, by the revolutionary combination, due to association. The development of modern industry, therefore, cuts from under its feet the very foundation of which the bourgeoisie produces and appropriates products. What the bourgeoisie therefore produces, above all, are its own gravediggers. Its fall and the victory of the proletariat are equally inevitable.[10]

What we observe today upon every hand are simply signs of economic transformation, and socialists interpret them to mean that the present competitive system has about fulfilled its mission, and that, like the feudal system from which it sprang, it must soon give way to another, more compatible with the onward march of civilization.

A little over a century and a quarter ago, the colonists were compelled by the pressure of events to declare their political independence. The day is near when the people will be compelled to declare their industrial independence.

The combines and trusts are doing their work in converting competition into cooperation and laying the foundation for the industrial public. The vast army of workingmen are being forced into political and industrial solidarity, and every clash between them and their exploiters hastens the end of wage-slavery.

The recent strike of the miners brought the class struggle into bolder prominence than it had yet been revealed to the country. What the [coal strike] commission may or may not do is of little consequence to the miners, for, if the wage is increased, the amount will be added to the cost of production and the living expense will absorb the wage as before; but in the struggle, the eyes of hundreds of miners and other workmen were opened to the fact that they have identical interests as a class, just as the coal barons have identical class interests. And with this fresh-born conviction, they went to the polls on election day and voted for working-class candidates, standing on a working-class platform, and it is this that accounts in large measure for the rapid increase in the socialist vote in Pennsylvania and nearly all the other states of the Union.

Every combine increases the momentum and hastens the end. Every injunction is a lubricant to the machinery.

Industrial and commercial competition have had their day. The small tools used by individuals have become mammoth machines operated by armies. Production has been socialized; the means of production will have to be. Fifty thousand steelworkers will not forever permit Andrew Carnegie to take their product upon the pretext that the tool they use is his "private property," and that the product, therefore, belongs to him.

The coal mines of Pennsylvania are as necessary to modern life as the sunlight and atmosphere. So are the railroads and telegraph and telephone. So are the oil and sugar refineries, steel mills, tanneries, and all the rest of these agencies as soon as they have destroyed competition and monopolized the field.

Private ownership of the centralized means of production and distribution—an industrial despotism, or collective ownership and an industrial republic? It must be one or the other—which? History leaves no room for doubt.

What "the people" want, they take. The trouble is that they have been too patient and too modest, but they do finally act, and one of these days they are going to realize that this earth is theirs, and then they will take possession of it in the name of the human race.

If the triumphant and defiant capitalist insists upon precise and detailed information as to how the people are to come to their own, he may, with profit, consult the late feudal baron of Europe and the recent slave owner of the United States.

Socialism is the scientific and historic fulfillment of the law of social and economic progress. It is indeed inevitable, and the only danger, as Sprague has said, is in obstructing it.[11]

Victor Hugo uttered the noble prophecy that the twentieth century would abolish poverty. Socialism will fulfill that prophecy. Whatever may be said of the past, the present, with all its marvelous wealth-producing agencies, can plead no excuse for the poverty and misery that scourge the multiplied millions of the earth.

Industrial democracy will wrest the earth from its exploiters, and its vast and inexhaustible storehouse will yield abundance for all. The growth of socialism is the promise of freedom and brotherhood—the radiant herald of the dawn.

Frederic O. MacCartney Belongs to the Living[†]

June 1, 1903

Terre Haute, Ind., June 1, 1903

It is hard to write of the death of Frederic O. MacCartney.[12] He belongs to the living, not the dead, and it will be long before we can realize that his eloquent voice is hushed and his great heart stilled forever.

In the very spring of life—the ripening glory of his powers—he was cut down, and with such swiftness did the fatal blow descend that we who now stand over his prostrate flesh are so shocked and stunned that we cannot realize

---

† Published as "A Comrade's Tribute! Eugene V. Debs on the Tribune of the Proletaire, Frederic O. MacCartney," in *Social Democratic Herald,* vol. 6, no. 6, whole no. 253 (June 6, 1903), 1.

that death has come so near and snatched from us in all the flush of youth a comrade so loved and honored of us all.

Frederic MacCartney was an interesting, unique, and towering figure in the socialist movement. He had brain and heart, soul and conscience in large measure and fine proportion. He was a clear, clever, and versatile writer, a ready and resourceful debater, and as an orator had few equals in the movement.

MacCartney was born in Wisconsin, educated in Iowa, and received his theological training at Andover. It is fortunate that in his youth he came under the influence of George D. Herron, who then held the chair of Applied Christianity at Iowa College.[13] The bright, honest, warm-hearted youth was soon impregnated with the new social philosophy and progressive spirit which at that time permeated the institution.

With such qualities of head and heart, and such environment and training, it is not strange that soon after he entered the ministry, he concluded that creeds were cold and pulpits narrow. The more he thought about it, the less theology satisfied the hunger of his soul. He sorrowed with the poor and wept with the oppressed and heavy-laden. Something was surely wrong that this fair earth should be so scarred with misery. He investigated social conditions and studied economic science. Gradually the darkness in which he groped was dispelled. The scales fell from his eyes, and his vision was now clear. A new sun had risen for him. Henceforth his duty was plain, and he would apply himself to his task with all the strength he could summon to his command.

Too honest to profess what he was not, he made without fear the full avowal of his convictions and as a sequence cleared the pulpit that was too narrow and dogmatic to hold him.

From the beginning, he became a factor in the movement. He was filled to the brim with the spirit of international socialism. He felt himself aroused as if by Jehovah's own command. He burned with the social passion for freedom, equality, and brother-love, and from his own intensity scattered the sacred fire among his fellow men.

At Rockland, his home, MacCartney was the idol of the working class; they loved and laureled him as their own hero, and even those opposed to him were moved to pay to him the tribute of respect.

The legislative labors of our comrade need no notice here. The general assembly of Massachusetts will be poorer far without him, and the people may well feel that they have lost a friend. With his two socialist colleagues,[14] MacCartney was a tower of strength in the legislative halls of the old Bay State. From the day they entered, a new and distinctive power has been felt—a power with portent for the reign of capitalist corruption—the beginning of the end.

What pity, what pathos that such a brilliant career should be snuffed out at its very sunrise!

Ah, nature is forever the same—neither merciful nor vindictive—always inexorable.

Our dear comrade's zeal exceeded his discretion. He had no thought that powers of endurance have limitations. Early and late, in legislative debate and committee room, on the rostrum, the street corner, anywhere, everywhere, all the time at work, pleading, protesting, appealing, with tongue and pen in the name of oppressed and suffering humanity, his drafts upon nature were too deep and frequent, and the inevitable protest followed, the protest sealed by death.

We who knew and loved him, we who watched with pride his powers unfold each day and add fresh luster to his fame, will miss but will not mourn him. He died gloriously in the field of battle, and a thousand times rather that he was cut down prematurely from the strain and the wounds of conflict than that he lived to dotage in indifference and ease while the struggle rages for the overthrow of despotism and the enfranchisement of the human race.

MacCartney's character was crowned by all the manly virtues. He was pure in mind, tender at heart, lofty of soul. He had no mean desire, no selfish impulse, no groveling ambition, but from his large and luminous soul, there streamed the sacred aspiration to consecrate his life and service to his fellow man.

With uncovered heads and reverent hands, we place these flowers where our comrade sleeps.

Labor and the Race Question†

June 5, 1903

Terre Haute, Ind., June 5, 1903

The following letter, under date of May 23, 1903, has been received from Mr. Gurley Brewer,[15] editor of the *Indianapolis World:*[16]

> *The World* is investigating industrial conditions among colored people. Booker T. Washington advocates industrial education for the Negro. Is the attitude of our labor unions toward black labor compatible with the teachings of Washington? *The World* is a colored newspaper and would like to publish your views . . .

To this letter there was attached a clipping from the *World* containing an article from Mr. D. M. Parry,[17] president of the National Association of Manufacturers, in answer to the same question, the burden of which was that organized labor is a trust and that a majority of its members are opposed to the colored workingmen, especially in reference to the teachings of Washington. His arraignment of organized labor closed with the following remarkable paragraphs:

> Mr. Washington is doing more than merely teaching his fellow Negroes; he is emancipating the formal artificial conditions that act as a bar to their progressive development as a race . . .
>
> Driven from the opportunity of learning as artisans in the shops, their only hope is the technical schools such as Washington conducts . . . The chief hope of the younger generation of whites is also the technical school.

First, let me say that all my life I have opposed discrimination, political, economic, or social, against any human being on account of color or sex, regarding all such as relics of the ignorant, cruel, and barbarous past.

Next there was a time when organized labor in the main was hostile to the Negro, and it must be admitted in all candor that certain unions, such as

---

† Published in the *Indianapolis World,* June 20, 1903, unspecified page. Reprinted as "Debs on the Race Question," *New York Worker,* June 28, 1903. Excerpt reprinted as "Debs on the Color Question," *Appeal to Reason,* whole no. 39 (July 4, 1903), 2.

the railroad brotherhoods, still ignorantly guard the trades they represent, as well as their unions, against invasion by the colored man, and in this they have always had the active support of the corporation in whose interest it is to have workingmen at each other's throats, that they may keep them all, black and white, in subjection.

Indeed, it is a fact that wherever labor unions, now or in the past, opposed the Negro, such opposition was inspired, or at least encouraged, by the employing class represented by Mr. Parry, who now seeks so assiduously to place the responsibility on the poor ignorant dupes of his capitalistic master.

At Montgomery, Alabama, some years ago, a riot was almost precipitated at the instigation of the "upper class," because the labor union under whose auspices I spoke proposed the admission of Negroes to the opera house, on the floors reserved for white people, and the proprietor of the house declared that the house should be burnt to the ground before any "damned nigger" should have access to it.

The ignorant members of labor unions, and there are many such, thanks to the system of wage-slavery Mr. Parry so ably defends, who still oppose the Negro, unconsciously echo the interests of their industrial masters, while those who know better and fight the black man are spies and traitors in the service of the same masters.

The convention of the American Railway Union, which resulted in the great railroad strike of 1894, after a fierce and protracted debate, turned down the Negro, and it was one of the factors in our defeat. The leaders of the opposition, as I remember them, proved subsequently to have been traitors to the union, sent to the convention, doubtless, at the instigation of the corporations to defeat the unity of the working class.

Does not the logic of common sense and business sagacity which Mr. Parry, as a successful manufacturer. possesses in such an eminent degree confirm this view of the case?

But in spite of all such influence, the labor movement in general, in America and throughout the world, stands unequivocally committed to receive and treat the Negro upon terms of absolute equality with his white brother, and where this is not the case, the genius of unionism is violated, and investigation will disclose the fact that corporate power and its henchmen are at the back of it.

The Socialist Party, the political wing of the labor movement, is absolutely free from color prejudice, and the labor union, its economic wing, is rapidly becoming so, and in the next few years, not a trace of it will remain even in the so-called black belt of southern states.

The workers of the world, mainly through organized effort, are becoming conscious of their interests as a class, totally regardless of color, creed, or sex, and in time they will unite and act together upon a common basis of equality in spite of "the world, the flesh, and the devil" and the Manufacturers' Association.

The hypocritical plea of the industrial master for the education "of the poor Negro while he is living out of his labor," deceives no one except the ignorant and servile victims of the wage system.

The first requisite, Mr. Parry, in elevating the Negro is to get off his back.

From the tone of Mr. Parry's letter, I assume that he is a great friend of the Negro. Now there are any number of them capable of operating his factory and "bossing" it. How many does he employ, especially in the latter positions? To what extent does he make his professions good by associating with his black brethren and explaining to them, as Christ did, what they must do to be saved? Will Mr. Parry and his class pretend that their practice accords with their preaching? If they actually believe that the Negro is entitled to equal consideration with the white man, why do they not set the example by meeting and treating him as their brother?

That is my conviction as a union man, and I have the consistency and courage to practice it. Until Mr. Parry and his class do the same, no intelligent Negro will be deceived by their professions of friendship.

Now as to Mr. Booker T. Washington and the attitude of organized labor toward his scheme of industrial education.

Your question implies that you look upon Mr. Washington as the Moses of the black race, and his educational scheme as the sure means of their emancipation. To answer your question candidly, I feel gratified to be able to say that Mr. Washington's scheme is not at all compatible with organized labor.

Mr. Washington is backed by the plutocrats of the country clear up, or down, to Grover Cleveland. They furnish the means that support his institute, and if it were conducted with a view of opening the Negro's eyes and emancipating him from the system of wage-slavery which robs and debases him while it fattens his masters, not another dollar would be subscribed for the Negro's "industrial education."

Why is it that the plutocrats, the trust magnates of the country, are solidly in favor of Mr. Washington and his scheme? What faction of one-thousandth of 1 percent of the 11 million Negroes in the United States are to get the benefit of his industrial education? What are they to do with it when they get it?

If the answer is that they will compete with their white brethren, then is it not obvious that it means less wages and still lower depths of degradation for all?

Does not Mr. Washington advocate the meekness and humility of the Negro race and their respectful obedience to their exploiting masters? Would Wendell Phillips tolerate this scheme of saving the Negro through the charity of his master?

On what occasion did Mr. Washington ever utter one sentiment, one word in favor of emancipation? When did he ever advise his race to stand erect, to act together as one, to assert their united power, to hold up their heads like self-reliant, self-respecting men and hew out their way from the swamps of slavery to the highlands of freedom?

What has he ever done to show the Negro that in the present industrial system he is simply the slave of the capitalist and the prey of the politician? Why does he not tell the Negro that dependence upon charity is degrading, that robust self-reliance is a thousand times better, that he has 3 million votes to enforce his demand, and that he will be a slave as long as he listens to the siren song of his master and votes for capitalist parties that support wage-slavery?

Mr. Parry likes Mr. Washington, and Mr. Washington likes Mr. Parry better; better than Mr. Parry likes labor unions.

As between the two, Mr. Parry is the lesser enemy of the Negro. Washington lulls him to sleep with charity soothing-syrup while Parry stings him to action by attacking his unions.

I have much respect for Mr. Parry. He is a consistent capitalist and as such is far preferable to Mr. Hanna, who flatters labor unions for the votes of their members.

I also have great consideration for Mr. Washington, especially as he was born a slave. His motive is doubtless pure, but unfortunately for himself and his race, his blood is still tainted with reverence for and obeisance to the master, and he does not seem to realize that the auction block and slave pen differ in degree only from the "labor market."

What the Negro wants is not charity but industrial freedom, and then he will attend to his own education. There is no "Negro problem," apart from the general labor problem. The Negro is not one whit worse off than thousands of white slaves who throng the same labor market to sell their labor-power to the same industrial masters.

The workers, white and black, want land and mines and factories and machinery, and they are organizing to put themselves in possession of these means of production, and then they will be their own employers, they will get all they produce, and the problem will be solved.

The difference between their trust and Mr. Parry's present-day trust will be that it will embrace the whole population, and in the meantime Mr. Parry deserves our thanks for calling attention to it.

Class-Conscious Courts†

June 20, 1903

Terre Haute, Ind., June 20 [1903]

That the court of law is administered in the interest of the capitalist class as against the working class is one of the self-evident facts of modern society. It is of course conceded that now and then the workers get the benefit of a decision of no consequence and that on occasion even a case of seeming importance is decided in their favor, but this signifies little, as we shall see, and does not impeach the integrity of the general proposition.

Class rule is the fruit of class government, and class government is based upon class ownership of productive capital or private property in the sources and means of production.

Class rule of course implies class society and a class struggle. The class in power in modern civilized nations, the capitalists, rule in their own interest, and to this end the courts, the army and navy, the militia and police, the school and church, in short, all departments of government and all social institutions are simply the branches and offshoots of the tree of capitalism that is rooted in class ownership of the resources of life.

With the regularity and precision of clockwork, the "decisions" and "opinions" are ticked off and handed down by the courts to protect the interests and serve the purposes of the ruling class. This does not mean that judges are any more venal or corrupt than other men, but simply that, like the hands of the clock, they respond with automatic regularity to the machinery that controls their movements.

The lower courts, dependent directly upon the popular vote, are moved to vary the program with an occasional "glad hand" to labor, but if there is any substance in such an "off" decision, it is quickly snatched away by the Supreme

---

† Published in *Social Democratic Herald,* vol. 6, no. 10, whole no. 257 (July 4, 1903), 1.

Court, to which it is always appealed in the full confidence that the higher tribunal, far above the sway of popular passion, will quickly set aside the ruling of the inferior court, that there may be no friction between the capitalist machine and its judicial functions.

The favorable decision below vindicates the integrity of the court and satisfies "the people," while the action of the higher court safeguards the interests of the ruling class; and so all is serene, and the fleecing of the workers, legally sanctioned, continues as before.

The Kansas man, asked about the prohibition law in that state, said it worked like a charm. Said he: "The prohibitionists have the law, and the other fellows have the whiskey—what more do you want?"

In the meantime, the press, the politicians, and the preachers—the triple echo of the ruling class—roll their eyes heavenward and thank God for preserving the sanctity of our courts, the safeguard of the Republic.

The confidence of the workers in the purity of the courts of their exploiting masters must under all circumstances remain unshaken. The subject is really too sacred to be questioned. The solemn judge in his spotless ermine must not be profaned by the vulgar lips of the common rabble; and he who is base enough to assail the sanctity of the "bench" and question the infallibility of the wigs and gowns it shelters is guilty of treason and a menace to the country.

There is no greater sham, no more stupendous fraud than the alleged divinity of our present judicial institutions. Supported by the revenue wrung from the working class, they serve as instruments to keep that class in servile subjection to their masters.

The stinging arraignment of Charles Sumner[18] during the anti-slavery agitation, reciting the crimes of the courts in ancient as well as modern times, and showing that they had always been the bulwarks of tyranny and the obstructors of progress, is one of the classics of our language.

The courts, aye, the courts of the land must be held in reverence and awe by the workingmen who are shorn by them, or, at least, kept in law-abiding submission while the shearing is being done.

When the average workingman is brought into the presence of a judge, he approaches that august fetish with all the meekness and humility of a sinner at the bar of judgment.

An awful hush falls upon the scene. I have studied it closely, especially as the old bailiff, in convening the federal court, used to explain: "God save this honorable court." That settled it for the crowd, and they scarcely breathed during the solemn rites of the farcical performance.

Judges are elected mainly by the serfs of the capitalist class. What sensible man expects them to do other than serve their masters, precisely as do the serfs who elected them at the behest of the same masters?

The recent decision of the Circuit Court of Appeals in the celebrated "Merger" proceeding has been exploited by the capitalist press as a great victory for the people.[19] Roosevelt smiles and bows, the people applaud and throw up their hats, another term at the White House is insured, and Jim Hill and Archbishop Ireland wink the other eye.

Will the anti-merger decision, which, by the way, is not yet final, as the Supreme Court has still to pass upon it, compel the Pacific roads to "compete" against each other and lower passenger rates and freight tariffs in the interest of the people? Will not their owners cooperate in holding up the people just as if they were united under a single corporation title?

Of what possible interest is the decision to the working class, who own no railroad shares and have no hand in the stockholders' game of freeze-out? What crumb of comfort can they extract from this so-called crushing blow at corporate power? Isn't it all blow and no crush—fine bait to catch political suckers?

Every judge on the federal bench today—district, circuit, and supreme—with but a single exception, is a trained and successful corporation attorney, and instinctively subservient to corporate interests. That exception is Henry Clay Caldwell, the last surviving appointment of President Lincoln, and he is a socialist and has announced his determination to retire from the bench, I doubt not from scruples of integrity, for he is a pure and conscientious man.

And still, our trade union leaders, for the most part, sanction the labor lobby that hands around the ragged edge of capitalistic legislation to beg like a mendicant for what it ought to command like a man; and when now and then it receives a legislative crumb, it is snatched away by the judicial tentacles of the capitalist devilfish.

The Supreme Court of Indiana recently annulled the law providing for weekly payment of wages and also the law fixing a minimum wage in municipalities for city employees. The corporations and capitalistic interests objected, and that settles it. And yet the working class will elect the same legislature over and over again on the record they made as the "friends of labor."

Yet another thing about the courts: The poor man—and most men are poor in the capitalist system; that is its distinguishable characteristic—the poor man is shut out as completely as if he were an outlaw. The lower court is open to him, and that takes all the coin he can raise. If he wins, the case is appealed, and goes higher and higher until it is out of sight. The poor man is counted out in the first round. The corporations have their array of legal talent in court all the way up and all the time, and litigation is no extra expense to them. Thousands of crippled railway employees who have had "good claims" under the statutes have been ground out of the judicial mill with nothing left but their mutilated, crutch-propped bodies and their despair.

Workingmen, wake up! The time has come to open your eyes and see things as they are. You have been hoodwinked and robbed and enslaved long enough. Be a man and line up with your class in the great struggle for freedom. To train with the enemy, ignorantly or otherwise, as you have been doing, is treason to your fellow man. To be the ally on election day of the class that lives out of your labor and holds you in contempt is not only cowardly and contemptible, but criminal, and means death to your manhood and infamy to the name your bear.

The courts can be reached in just one way. The road is straight, and it has no connection with any of the side tracks. The Socialist Party unerringly points the way.

The courts to serve the people must be made free and untrammeled tribunals, and this they can only become in a Cooperative Commonwealth, a republic in fact as well as in theory, and when that time comes, courts will probably be in little demand, and they will make up in purity and in honor what they lose in prestige and power.

Capital and Labor: Parasites and Hosts†

July 3, 1903

Galusha A. Grow,[20] the aged politician and ex-speaker of Congress, is seriously disturbed about the "conflict between capital and labor," and is giving the closing days of his life to the solution of this vexed problem. In his public service, Mr. Grow is credited with having been a clean and honorable man, and it is a fitting climax to such a career that he should devote his last hours and his latest efforts to the cause of industrial peace.

But the trouble with Mr. Grow, like so many others of his advanced years, is that he lives in the past; he deals with conditions that have long since ceased to exist, seeming utterly oblivious of the industrial revolution which has wrought havoc with things as they were, and as he still sees them, and which is still in full swing and will not cease until industrial peace, the fruit of industrial freedom, has been conquered and the terms "capitalist" and "laborer," as we now understand them, lose their meaning as they merge in one and the same person, and every human being is at once capitalist and worker, employer and employed, as a unit of the socialist commonwealth.

In his recent article on "The Shortcomings of Arbitration,"[21] Mr. Grow very properly concludes that there is little hope for progress in that direction. And then, getting mixed in his terms, he falls into a succession of errors from which even his idealized "public opinion" cannot rescue him. Says he:

> There can be no war or even conflict between capital and labor when their real interests are rightly understood and fully appreciated. They are mutually dependent on each other, and *neither can accomplish any great results without the other*. Of what use is labor, beyond the supplying of mere physical wants by the cultivation of the soil, without capital to furnish transportation to market for the products of labors as well as for the development of industries? And of what use would capital be without labor? In the world's commerce, the locomotive is of no use without cars filled with the products of labor, and such cars would be of no use without capital to build the railroad and buy the locomotive.

† Published as "Let Us Get at the Right of It," *Colorado Socialist,* July 3, 1903, unspecified page. Reprinted as "Capital versus Labor" in *Social Democratic Herald,* vol. 6, no. 14, whole no. 261 (August 1, 1903), 1.

> The grievances of labor in free elective governments like ours are to be removed in the same way as other grievances are removed—*by an appeal to the intelligent judgment of public opinion*. In free elective governments—with free speech, free press, and universal ballot—there can be no excuse for a resort to lawless violence. No matter what the grievance complained of may be, a resort to lawless violence is an attack on the rights of every law-abiding citizen and upon organized society itself, and if successful it would be *the first step in the road that leads to anarchy* and national ruin.

Between "capital and labor," rightly understood, or wrongly understood, or not understood at all, there never was and never will be any conflict. Capital, except as to undeveloped natural resources, is the product of labor. There is no war between the worker and the machine. He made it and uses it, and now his very life and freedom depend upon it, but he does not own it, and this is where the "war" begins. He has no quarrel with the machine, but he is very decidedly in "conflict" with the capitalist who claims ownership of the machine and pockets what the worker and the machine produce.

The conflict, therefore, is not between labor and capital, but between labor and capitalists, a class who grow rich and defiant through their exploitation of the working class under the wage system.

It is true, as Mr. Grow says, that labor and capital "are mutually dependent on each other," but it is not true that workingmen and capitalists [must] sustain such mutual relations.

Workingmen could get along, and a thousand times better than at present, without the brood of capitalists to absorb their products, but the capitalists would perish from the earth but for the labor of the working class that sustains them.

Will Mr. Grow contend that William Waldorf Astor is a necessary factor, or any factor at all, in the production of wealth?

Mr. Astor is a highly developed capitalist, and it would be interesting to know in what way laborers are dependent upon him and other parasites that suck their lifeblood and yield absolutely nothing in return.

Is the leech essential to the life and health of the horse? Are they "mutually dependent on each other?"

Does Rockefeller produce a drop of oil, or Carnegie an ounce of steel, or Hill an inch of transportation? Were they and all their class to resign, would the spinal cord of these great enterprises be severed and humanity paralyzed?

Mr. Grow will have no difficulty in recalling the fact that only a few years ago there were thousands of "slave owners" in this boasted land of freedom, and that for two full centuries and a half they and their slaves were "mutually dependent on each other." That was the law and gospel of the land, and he who disputed it was mobbed like Lovejoy or hanged like John Brown. These slave owners not only robbed their Negroes of the fruit of their labor, but held them in sovereign contempt, while they constituted the aristocracy of the land.

They never dreamed that their slaves would one day be their political equals. Perish the ignoble, idiotic thought! They were the elect of the earth. They would rule forever—but they didn't.

The black slaves are getting along without their former plantation asters, and in the next great upheaval, all the slaves of the earth, white and black and brown and red and yellow, will abolish their industrial masters and stand forth the sovereign citizens of the world.

This is the mission of the socialist movement, and if Mr. Grow were informed as to its historic connection and relation, he would cease wasting his time and energy in the vain task of harmonizing antagonistic forces that are inexorably in conflict, working out the supreme problems of civilization.

The class struggle is the boundary line between man and beast—the glory of the human race and the sure promise of its final redemption.

Between workingmen and capitalists, there is conflict to extinction, war to the death.

The intervals of peace, or, rather, the cessation of hostility, are but the breathing spells for the renewal of the conflict.

The smaller capitalists are doomed to destruction, and their bloated conquerors, fully developed, become social parasites that will be abolished with the system that spawned them.

The owners of American railroads have nothing to do with their operation. They simply absorb their vast profits. They also bribe legislators, corrupt courts, and debauch politics. If the entire lot of them were to take a balloon for some other planet, they would never be missed. The trains would all run as usual.

The capital only is needed—the capitalists, as such, can go and will go—the sooner the better for all concerned, themselves included.

We are emerging from the darkness and moving grandly toward the dawn, as Carlyle said, "from competition in individualism to individuality in cooperation, from war and despotism in any form to peace and liberty."

Society Must Reap What It Sows: Interview with the *Terre Haute Gazette*†

July 11, 1903

If Captain Dudley is correctly quoted, he is an ass.[22] As a matter of fact, not a single socialist was connected, directly or indirectly, with the Evansville outrages.[23] The socialists are the only ones who recognize not merely the political and economic equality of the Negro, but his social equality as well. Among socialists, there is not the slightest trace of race prejudice, and to charge that they instigated the riotous crusade against the Negroes in Evansville is an infamous calumny.

Instead of the socialists, the fact is the rotten and vote-buying political party to which Dudley belongs is responsible for these crimes. In the late municipal election at Evansville, hundreds of Negroes were imported from Kentucky to help elect the present Republican mayor of that city.[24] The Negro whose murder of the policeman precipitated the conflict was one of these. He was a Republican, the policeman he murdered was a Republican, and the city officers for whom he acted as political plugger were also Republicans. After the election, this Negro felt that as one of the main props of the administration he could strut and swagger at will. This was the starting point of the present trouble which since then has been brewing and required only some spark to set it off. The whole trouble is the culmination of the Negro as a factor in politics and, as is notoriously true, a corrupting factor, since he finds ready sale for his votes in the political market of Evansville.

The socialists never purchased a Negro vote nor imported a Negro voter to debauch the politics and incite race war in Evansville. Can Will Dudley say the same for the party to which he belongs? . . .

Linton Affair Denounced

"Have you any observations to make on the Linton affair?" asked the Gazette reporter.

Very definitely. I regard the conduct of the mob at Linton in driving the Negro waiters of Alex Sanderson out of that town as cowardly and brutal

† Published as "'If Capt. Dudley is Correctly Quoted He Is an Ass'" in *Terre Haute Gazette,* July 11, 1903, unspecified page. Copy preserved in *Papers of Eugene V. Debs* microfilm edition, reel 10.

beyond the power of language to express, and they who are responsible for it should themselves be driven to the jungles where they belong, for they are wholly unfit to live in a civilized community.[25]

What had these Negroes done to merit such outrageous treatment? They were workingmen and were seeking simply to make an honest living. They went to Linton to do what they were employed to do and to molest or interfere with no one.

When the Negro is idle and shiftless, society has no patience with him and does not tolerate him. He is denounced and hunted down and lynched. When he seeks to make an honest living, he is driven out by the mob.

How would the cowardly crowd at Linton like to be subjected to that sort of treatment? In their case, it would be richly deserved, but this cannot be charged upon the Negro, since his antecedents were stolen away from their native land, brought to these shores, enslaved, brutalized, and robbed for three centuries.

Even the Negro pervert who is filled with an insane passion to commit a nameless crime is the spawn of the white man's violation of nature's law, and the crimes that now horrify humanity are the fruit of Anglo-Saxon misdeeds.

The Negroes of the South have been the victims of a thousand outrages in the name of our so-called civilization. They were kept in ignorance by design and brutalized under the forms of law while their daughters in their childhood became the prey of the white man's lust. The carnal maniac is the offspring of lust. Society, like the individual, must reap what it sows.

Miners Must Repudiate

It is generally understood that the mob at Linton was composed of union miners. I am not ready to believe this, but whoever it consisted of, they merit unqualified denunciation. I am opposed to all forms of violence, but do not hesitate to give my opinion that if, in the absence of any effort on the part of the state to protect them, the Negroes massed their forces and marched into Linton to resent the outrages perpetrated upon their people, they would be eminently justified in doing so. This, however, is not the way to proceed in such an extremity, and the Negroes do well to bear with patience and bide their time.

The miners' union cannot afford to bear the odium of such an outrage, and they owe it to themselves to disavow all connection with or responsibility for it. They can scarcely do less in view of the fact that their organization is appealing to the Negroes of Kentucky and West Virginia to help them fight their battles. At this very hour, President Mitchell is in Kansas assuring the Negroes that the miners' union is their friend and proposes to recognize them on terms of equality.

The Linton affair is an utter repudiation of the union's professions and, if unrebuked, the Negroes will have no reason to regard the union in a friendly light.

When the miners have another strike, can they blame the Negroes if they take their places? What claim have they on the Negro when they refuse to allow him to make a living? In this country, the Negro has the same rights as the white man, and if he can be driven from a community by a mob, the Civil War was fought in vain, and the boasted free institutions are a stupendous sham.

The Growth of Unionism in America†

September 3, 1903

While there has been more than a century of labor agitation and organization in the United States, the labor movement of today, in its economic mold, has developed it main proportions since the Civil War and its principal power and prominence during the last 20 years.

Eight years ago, I made an extensive agitation tour of the southern states,[26] and barring the few scattered unionists I met in my travels, there was not a healthy sign of organization in that entire section.

Today all the states of the South are organized, and in some of the industrial centers the agitation is as active, unionism as far advanced, and the movement as intelligent and progressive as in any other part of the country.

Ten years ago, the great West, especially the Rocky Mountain states, where the genius of unionism now towers above the crags, had but the merest shadow of the close-knit and powerful organization that now spreads over that vast territory and locks it fast in mighty embrace.

In 1886, Prof. Richard T. Ely[27] published his *Labor Movement in America.*[28] The work is now being revised and enlarged by the author to embrace

† Published as "Growth of Unionism in America" in *American Labor Union Journal* [Butte, MT], September 3, 1903, 5. Reprinted as "Ever Onward and Upward!" in *Social Democratic Herald,* vol. 6, no. 21, whole no. 268 (September 19, 1903), 1.

the last two decades, without which it lacks the most important chronicles of organized labor and is essentially incomplete.

The germs of American unionism were developed in the colonial period of our national life. The primitive state of industry prevented anything like a general spread of unionism in that early day, but here it had its inception, and as the agricultural community gave way to industrial society, the new growth, in all essential respects the same as its British progenitor, and, in fact, its direct transatlantic offspring, struck root, its tiny fibrils seeking nourishment in the industrial soil of the new nation.

For many years, the growth of unionism was necessarily slow and sporadic. The conditions from which it springs and in which it thrives were just beginning to develop after the war of the revolution, which also traced in shadowy outlines the approaching industrial revolution, since invention and discovery in the realm of physical science had already begun their miraculous mission, and the world was being awakened from its age-long torpor and inactivity.

The pulse of the new century was quickened and its heart thrilled by the magic touch of inventive genius. The Reign of Steam began, and this invisible monarch proved to be the greatest revolutionist of all the ages.

The closing years of the old century were illuminated by the discovery of the push-buttons of science; the opening years of the new century in turning on the light, building the machinery, and setting it into operation. The development and expansion of manufacture followed, and labor unionism "burst full-blossomed on the thorny stem of industrial society." The trades inspired the workers with the consciousness of their trade interests, and from this sprang the sentiment of solidarity, the pith and core of unionism.

The early form was a "pure and simple" trade union, consisting exclusively of the skilled mechanics of a given craft, limited to the local community in which they were employed. In its elementary state, the union was purely a local affair; this was the unit of organized labor, the cell composing the anatomy of the trade union movement. The workers were thus drawn together instinctively for purposes of self-defense, having scarcely a hint of industrial evolution and making little, if any, conscious attempt at a constructive program.

With the introduction of machinery, the subdivision of labor, the increase of production, the extension of the markets, the improved facilities for transportation afforded by the railroads, and the general development of industry, the local unions were united in district, state, and national bodies, and in time were knit into federations of international organizations.

There are still, curiously enough, many workingmen who, notwithstanding a century of industrial growth, the most phenomenal in all history, have profited nothing by experience and observation, and stand rooted to practically the same moss-covered spot their great grandfathers occupied in revolutionary days. Everything has been revolutionized except their hoary notions of union labor, and upon these not a patentable improvement has been made in a hundred years.

More curious still is the fact that these antiquated notions are embalmed by many of the leaders (!) as sacred relics, and any attempt to relegate them to the past where they belong is resented by these union guardians as high treason to the working class.

This simply shows that the ruling class are potent in the councils of organized labor as they are in other affairs.

It would seem that even a potato would open its eyes to this obvious fact. But the workingman sleeps on—or if he opens his eyes, he sees not. The machine he makes to lighten his task takes his job, pushes him into the street, and starves his child. And he knows not the reason why. But he *will* know, as certain as the sun shines, and that in the not distant future. He is waking up at last and beginning to see, and when his eyes are open wide and his vision has been clarified, there will be a mighty shaking up, and he will emerge unfettered, the master of the earth.

The labor movement is the nascent collective workingman. It is this giant who is to do battle with the collective capitalist for supremacy of the globe. In the preliminary engagements, he is meeting many a defeat, but he profits by them all, even by the doping of his own trainers, and in the final conflict, when he summons all his mighty powers, he will vanquish his antagonist, the tyrant of capitalism, and proclaim the triumph of light and freedom.

The one thing above all others for the workingman to see and understand is the class struggle. The very instant he grasps this fact, his feet are on the rock—he takes his place with his class and, come what will, he holds it, especially on election day.

This is the work to which the labor agitator must give himself with all the powers of his mind and body.

The American labor movement has come with a rush during the past few years; it is still largely in the hazy, nebulous state and is sure to bump and bruise itself severely before it develops the class-conscious solidarity, strength, and clearness it must have to triumph in the struggle and fulfill its historic mission.

The truly revolutionary labor movement which has sprung up in the West in the last 15 months is the most advanced and pronounced type of twentieth century unionism in America. Pure and simple unionism is splintering in the strain of the class conflict and Grover Cleveland, Mark Hanna, Archbishop Ireland, and Bishop Potter will try in vain to poultice it up with the bandages of capitalistic conciliation. The socialist philosophy for capitalist confusion; the class struggle for the middle-class muddle; revolution for reaction—that is the program.

The whole American labor movement, resist as it may, must be permeated with the spirit of class-conscious solidarity, the only kind that is fireproof and fakir-proof.

The American Labor Union,[29] the Western Federation of Miners, and affiliated bodies have made a tremendous start and are now on the main track under increasing pressure. The capitalists see it and are seized with frenzy and terror. Idaho Springs, Colorado City, and Denver are the sentry shots fired to arouse their army.

It is all magnificent. Nothing will give organization greater impetus—nothing more vividly reveal the class struggle and hasten the overthrow of industrial slavery and the triumph of the working class.

Wayland and the *Appeal to Reason*: From Obscurity to Fame†

September 5, 1903

In 1893, when the first number of *The Coming Nation* was issued at Greensburg, Indiana, by J. A. Wayland, I had just resigned as grand secretary and treasurer of the Brotherhood of Locomotive Firemen—an office I had held since 1880—with a view to organizing the American Railway Union so that the employees in every branch of the service, especially the unskilled and poorly paid, might get the benefits of organization. I was still editing the *Locomotive Firemen's Magazine,* the official journal of the brotherhood, and its files will attest my blissful ignorance at the time of the socialist philosophy and the class struggle, and my utter failure to grasp the significance, scope, and character of the socialist movement. From crown to foot soles I was a "pure and simple" trade unionist, and so completely was I absorbed in the vain task of getting all the workers organized and then securing "fair wages" and "decent treatment" by the power of numbers that I had no time to observe the trend of the industrial development or to note that new conditions were arising which necessitated corresponding changes in the forms and functions of the trade union movement.

As for socialism, I had a hazy conception that it was akin to anarchy and that it was not of sufficient importance to merit serious attention.

In the same year the "panic" broke out, and from the heights of "prosperity" the country was plunged headlong into the abyss of ruin and despair. The railroads were among the first to break for cover. The "association" scythe of the general managers at once cut great swaths in the wages of the employees, just as they will again in another year or two when the brotherhoods begin to think their work is done and "the fodder's in the shock."

The slaughter of slaves was fearful to contemplate. Thousands had their wages shockingly reduced, many were put upon half time, and still others in large numbers were thrown entirely out of employment. It was a great time for discontent, for agitation and organization. The old brotherhoods accepted the reductions. The ARU resisted them. The strikes followed in rapid succession, culminating in the Pullman contest in the summer of

† Published as "From Obscurity to Fame" in *Appeal to Reason,* whole no. 405 (September 5, 1903), 3.

1894; and when the smoke of battle cleared away, the scales had fallen from my eyes, and with many others I realized that socialism had been thrust upon me at the point of a capitalist bayonet and that the only alternative was to enlist in the socialist movement for the overthrow of the capitalist system and the abolition of wage-slavery.

I do not remember seeing *The Coming Nation* in 1893, the year of its birth, and I have but a dim recollection of seeing it in 1894. But in 1895 I became a reader of it, and I have a clear recollection of its rapid increase in circulation and of the stir it was creating in the conservative circles of capitalist thought.

What a profound change has taken place in this country and throughout the world in the ten years since *The Coming Nation* entered upon its wonderful crusade!

I doubt if Wayland himself, clear-sighted as he is, had any conception of the magnitude of the propaganda he was organizing—of the vast waste of capitalist combustibles to which he was applying the torch of social progress.

The Coming Nation was the first popular propaganda paper published in the interest of socialism in the United States. It may have been unscientific, but it was well adapted to that nebulous period. The short, sharp, pointed paragraphs of the editor pierced like darts. Wayland soon became known, his paper was in demand, and the people began to talk about socialism and *The Coming Nation.*

Wayland had a faculty of saying things in a way to arrest attention, stimulate thought, and provoke controversy. This is mainly why *The Coming Nation* "caught on," and why its successor, the *Appeal to Reason,* has developed such a phenomenal circulation.

With its present staff, the *Appeal,* while retaining its popular features, is thoroughly scientific and up-to-date, and is destined to be one of the few world publications to achieve the enviable distinction of commanding an international army of a million subscribers.

With a past of such historic interest and a future so luminous with glorious achievement, it is eminently fitting that this tenth anniversary year to be celebrated with a jubilee edition in honor of the triumphant march of Wayland and the *Appeal* from obscurity to fame.

Ten years ago, the socialist movement in the United States was small, weak, and but an insignificant factor in the politics of the country. Today we have an American party worthy in all regards of its place in the international socialist movement.

The Socialist Party is now organized from sea to sea, from the lakes to the gulf, its hundreds of local branches[30] spreading out over all the states and territories of the union.

Thousands of speakers and propagandists—men, women, and children—are in the field proclaiming the glad tidings of social redemption through the impending revolution and the triumph of the socialist movement.

Scores of papers, magazines, reviews, and other periodicals, constituting the socialist press, are doing yeoman service in arousing the working class and educating the people, and their number and influence is steadily increasing.

Socialist writers, authors, and teachers are springing up, and the American literature of socialism is now being written and taught to develop the class struggle and hasten the day of universal emancipation.

To our comrades in Europe and all other countries we send hearty greeting. We admire the intrepid socialist leaders abroad and applaud the rank and file in their brave struggle in our common cause, which in good time shall be crowned with victory for us all.

In conclusion: A million subscribers for the *Appeal* and more than a million votes for the Socialist Party in 1904![31]

Crimes of Capitalism†

October 6, 1903

Fort Worth, Texas, October [6], 1903

The frauds and other outrages perpetrated upon the few remaining Indians in the name of our vaunted civilization are shocking beyond expression. From the very first landing of the white man, the shameless crime of spoliation began. The "savage" must be civilized! And forthwith, deceit, duplicity, theft, and murder were enlisted in the conquest.

† Published in *Social Democratic Herald,* vol. 6, no. 26, whole no. 273 (October 24, 1903), 1.

The history of this conquest is crimson with crime.

The cruelest atrocities and most bloodthirsty vindictiveness of the American Indian were inspired and fanned into flame by the treachery and rapine of the marauding and plundering civilization.

It is this that has constituted "the white man's burden."

Voltaire once said, as nearly as I can recall his words: "William Penn was the only man who ever made a treaty with the American Indians not affirmed by an oath, and the only treaty that was never violated."[32]

The investigation of the Dawes Commission[33] and the wholesale robbery of Indians, squaws, and papooses by the government agents will furnish one of the concluding chapters in the history of civilization (?) of the savage (!) that will fitly climax four centuries of Christian conquest in the new world.

In this connection, the following dispatch clipped from the *St. Louis Globe-Democrat* of October 4 [1903] is highly edifying:

> Miami, Indian Territory, October 3—Grafters in the Indiana Territory are resorting to a unique method for making money. It has long been known that the Indian squaw readily falls in love with the first white man she meets who is willing to pay her any attention, and it does not matter very much whether he is handsome and stylish, or ugly; whether he is old or young, rich or poor. This makes easy sailing for the grafters of the territory, who have been making profitable use of the Indian maiden, by contracting with her to furnish a white husband with a cash consideration. Money has no value to the redskins, and it is said that in some cases they have been known to pay as much as $100 in cash for a husband.
>
> The brokers have no trouble in finding a husband, as the girls are to come into possession of some very valuable land. When the Choctaw allotment is made, every maiden in that nation will come into possession of 320 acres of land and about $2500 in cash as her share of the tribal funds on deposit in the United States Treasury.
>
> Some of these girls are very pretty, yet they could be readily picked as Indians. Many of them have received good education at the Indian schools, and most of them are willing to marry as soon as they get their allotment and the cash in hand. In many cases the brokers pull strings at both ends. They accept a contract from the girls to furnish her a husband at from $25 to $100 and then they advertise in some of the Eastern papers for the husband. They make him a proposition to furnish him with a pretty Indian girl for from $100 to $250. When the Eastern lad with a desire for the West learns that he is to get a bride with a fortune, and that

> he will have nothing to do for a year at least but spend her money, he becomes an easy customer for the marriage broker.

This is some of the "civilization" that socialism is to wreck; some of the "incentive" it is to destroy; some of the "individuality" it is to blot out; some of the "homes" it is to break up.

Yes, by the gods, that is the line of the social revolution, and when it has done its work, these vile abominations will be wiped from the earth.

The other day I met a full-blood Indian socialist. The light in his eye and the warm, eager pressure of his hand thrilled me through and through.

Welcome, indeed, red comrade!

ᔓ

The *Paris (Illinois) Gazette* recently had the following which was copied in the Terre Haute papers:

> Frizell Thompson, a 19-year old Negro youth en route from Chattanooga, Tenn., to St. Louis, fell or was knocked beneath a Big Four freight train in the Midland Yards at 3:30 o'clock Thursday morning [October 1, 1903] and his left leg so brutally crushed that amputation was found necessary. For four hours, the mutilated Negro lay on a truck at the downtown depot while the authorities were settling a dispute as to who was responsible for his care. His ragged clothes afforded little protection from the falling rain. A box served as a pillow.

Had the victim been rich instead of poor, even though black, the "authorities" would have had no dispute about his care.[34] A ragged white boy would have fared no better. The "authorities" under capitalism are out for the "stuff." They are also "patriotic" and for "the old flag."

What utter heartlessness this incident discloses! A man-eating tiger or shark could not be more destitute of mercy. It is enough to make a bronze statue shudder, and yet it is not an uncommon occurrence. It is said that "poverty is not a crime." It is a lie. Poverty is a crime, and the penalty is death by torture and neglect.

Socialism and only socialism will banish the gaunt monster poverty from the world.

Teddy's Stab at Unionism[†]

October 6, 1903

Fort Worth, Texas, [October 6, 1903]

I don't know why Mr. Roosevelt ought to be a friend to the workingman. His associations, his instincts and interests have always been wholly on the side of the capitalist class. As governor of New York, he sent the state militia to Croton Dam to shoot down workmen for protesting against the violation of the eight-hour law.[35] In his decision in the Miller case in the government printing office, he struck a staggering blow at organized labor, the effect of which is as yet but little understood.[36]

Upon the surface, the open shop would seem to be a fair proposition, but as a matter of fact it is an impossibility. Twenty-five years ago, when unionism was still weak, the open shop was one of the compromises, temporarily accepted. The economic development and progressive unionism swept the movement beyond that point and toward complete organization. A printing office today is either wholly union or wholly non-union. To declare that it shall be open is to non-unionize it. This would be the effect of President Roosevelt's order.

But today the "open shop" is practically impossible.

If part of the employees are union and part non-union they are not only in ceaseless conflict, but the employer in the open shop has a right to discharge an employee for any reason, or for no reason at all. Thus it becomes an easy matter to discriminate against union men and deprive them of the protection which they have worked so long and sacrificed so much to secure through their organization.

Any contract or agreement or regulation that the union may propose would be binding on its own members only; and it is admitted that separate contracts for union and non-union men would but serve to further complicate matters, the effect of which would be to virtually deprive the union of all its power, and thus destroy what it has taken years of organized effort to accomplish.

Here is the vital point involved in this affair. Other printing offices, and other employers generally, will point to the decision of President Roosevelt as

---

† Published in *Social Democratic Herald,* vol. 6, no. 25, whole no. 272 (October 17, 1903), 1.

precedent for assuming a similar attitude. The effect of this will be to non-unionize as many establishments as possible and render the union impotent as a factor in controlling wages and in determining the conditions of employment.

When a lawyer is employed by the government, he must be a member of the bar; that is to say, a member of the lawyers' union. Otherwise he is not considered competent or qualified to serve. The same is true of the physician, who must be a member in good standing of the medical association to secure an appointment in the public service.

The workingman alone is prohibited from making his union principles the basis of his acceptance in the government service.

I shall be mistaken if organized labor does not realize what the decision of President Roosevelt means in the Miller case and register a widespread protest that even the president of the United States may not ignore or disregard.

A Word to the Young†

October 10, 1903

Until recent years the young were not supposed to be wise enough to do much of anything except to follow in the footsteps of the old, the wrinkled and gray of hair. The physician, the judge, the lawyer, the author must all have the testimonials of Old Father Time before being accounted fit and proper to attain eminence in their respective professions.

While the world has lost none of its reverence for age, it nevertheless has changed in reference to the old notion that gray hairs are essential to wisdom and that physical infirmity is the beginning of mental maturity.

The young man and the young woman are in demand today as never before in the world's history, and an examination of its modern activities discloses the fact that in every field of endeavor they are achieving victories and winning the laurels of fame.

This does not signify that the aged are to be relegated to the rear or

† Published in *Social Democratic Herald,* vol. 6, no. 24, whole no. 271 (October 10, 1903), 1.

discarded—quite the contrary—their wisdom, gained from experience, their knowledge, the fruit of study are to be recognized at their true value, but in the intellectual and scientific era now dawning, mere age is no longer to be a guarantee of wisdom, nor callow youth the synonym of ignorance and folly.

The antiquated notions of the past are being discarded in these days of keen and searching investigation. Only that which bears the test of practical utility, of common sense, and of having the attributes of progress escapes the ruthless iconoclasm of this revolutionary age.

And this is as it should be. The past has had its day and its hoary traditions survive to tell us whence we came and help us determine whither we are tending.

The world today is aflame with the ardor of youth and trembles beneath its power of action. Old things are passing away. The new, the vital, the progressive are in demand. Ideas and ideals are swiftly changing.

It is glorious to be young and to have a hand, a heart, a brain, and a soul in this marvelous twentieth-century reformation.

Victor Hugo prophesied that the present century would abolish poverty. He was gifted with prescient vision. He foresaw the day when all the earth would be fair and beautiful and all mortals brethren, and the dawn gilded his noble brow, fired his soul with passion, and inspired his pen with immortality.

Victor Hugo was proud to avow himself a socialist. That is the noblest word in modern language and the proudest title mortal ever bore—a soldier in the Grand Army of Universal Peace!

Rulers will disappear, millionaires will sink into oblivion, or, like Dives, lift their eyes in hell imploring for a drop of water from the Lazarus they spurned,[37] titles will turn to dust, and the gilded trappings of our cruel commercial civilization will be spared as relics only, but the thoughts and deeds of the young and active, inspired evangels of the coming day, who are organizing the world's crusade to abolish the barbarous reign of capitalism and humanize the earth and glorify the race with brotherhood, will live and throb in the heart of humanity forever.

Graft vs. The Same Thing†

October 13, 1903

Galveston, Texas, [October 13, 1903]

In taking a general survey of the political situation on the eve of the various state and local elections that are to be held this month and next, we are struck with the mixed condition of things that prevails almost everywhere, and the curious alignments that are being made in the field of capitalist politics for the approaching raid upon the spoils of office.

Even the remnants of the Populist Party[38] that were supposed to be dead seem to have been only in a state of suspended animation and have come back to life again, and are now applying liniment to the stiff joints, and will soon be ready to limp back into the ring again and offer their "reform" nostrum for the salvation of the world.

In Colorado, Texas, and some other states, Populist conferences have been held and resolutions adopted that sound like a voice from the catacombs. What populism really needs is an undertaker with a long spade and an airtight concrete coffin that stays buried.

The sorry spectacle the Populists will present this year and the still sorrier figure they will carve will perhaps convince them that they are dead and ought not to be walking about in their grave clothes.

In Ohio, the situation is extremely attractive, equal to a hippodrome and as full of incident as a circus with a menagerie attached. The other day Mark Hanna, next to the greatest labor leader in America and candidate for reelection to the United States Senate, lost his temper, probably from sheer envy, in discussing Tom Johnson,[39] and declared the rich single-taxer "the anarchist leader of the socialists who were responsible for the assassination of President McKinley." This paragraph is a gem of the first water. It is also a true index of capitalist politics—rank idiocy with froth upon its craven lips.

There is no hyena that would be guilty of tearing his dead friend from his grave that he might expose his death wound as a plea for votes to secure an office for himself.

† Published in *The Worker* [New York City], vol. 13, no. 30 (October 25, 1903), 1.

While Hanna and Johnson and their allies are hammering each other around in the ring in their great one-act farce entitled "Stand Pat vs. Municipal Reform," the Socialist Party of the Buckeye State, led by that honest and fearless working-class advocate, Isaac Cowen,[40] their candidate for governor, are waging a vigorous and effective campaign throughout the state, and my advices lead me to believe that the results will be of the most gratifying character to themselves and the party at large.

ᔕ

The curious turn things have taken in New York City politics, and the complications resulting therefrom, combine to make that fight so unique as to attract the attention of the whole country. Of course, there is a monumental issue involved and the working class especially are vitally interested as to whether they shall be robbed under "McClellan's *partisan* administration or fleeced under Low's[41] *business* administration."

Great issue this is that appeals to the patriotic sons of America! More succinctly stated it is "Graft vs. The Same Thing." The pure and simple labor leaders of New York will doubtless find this a campaign rich with picking for the faithful who know when and where to keep out of politics.

Let the Tammany Tiger and the Low Gastrutis [*sic*] have it out. In either case, the worst will win. The only difference is the armor plate hypocrisy of the Low odorless machine.

The reform (!) administration of Low speaks for itself—it requires no special commendation—it is *low* enough.

If we have got to have one or the other, give us that without the "reform." We have tried all the capitalist parties and they are all alike—only more so when they have a moral spasm and hoist the banner of "reform." Then clap your hand on your pocketbook, if the "reformers" haven't already got it, and make for the tall timber.

The old parties take turns about "reforming" each other. The "reform" party is usually the one that has been turned out and wants to get back to the public cribs and troughs again.

The hubbub over the spoils in New York will doubtless absorb most of the interest lying around loose, and the din and roar may for the moment drown the clash of the class struggle, but it is only for the passing hour. These entanglements and collisions in the old parties will increase, and from each of them there will be jarred loose an element that is bound to gravitate toward the Socialist Party and take its place in the revolutionary army of international socialism.

The post office scandals, the shameless plunder and spoliation of the Indians by the Dawes Commission and other government agents paid and sworn to protect them against other thieves, and countless other cases of crime and corruption in the high offices of the state and nation, Republicans and Democrats alike, all serve to corroborate the socialist charge as to the essential rottenness of capitalist politics.

Private ownership of the means of production and distribution is the prolific source of political corruption. Workingmen do not debauch the politics of the nation. They have no incentive for so doing. With the capitalists it is otherwise. They have to buttress their private economic interests, in conflict with the collective interests of the community, with moral mire and political putridity, and to talk of "reforming" this sort of thing, à la Low, is like spraying a cesspool with eau de cologne.

In all this the socialist sees the working out of the social and economic forces, and his serenity is undisturbed, while his faith is increased and his determination intensified. The fall elections in the several states will register the rising tide of socialism and supply a new basis for comparison and calculation in determining the progress of the movement.

The Socialist Party is everywhere alert, active, and energetic, and the vote this fall will doubtless indicate a long stride toward the goal.

The Negro in the Class Struggle†

November 1903

It so happens that I write upon the Negro question in compliance with the request of the editor of the *International Socialist Review* [A. M. Simons] in the state of Louisiana, where the race prejudice is as strong and the feeling against the "nigger" as bitter and relentless as when Lincoln's proclamation of emancipation lashed the waning Confederacy into fury and incited the final and desperate attempts to burst the bonds that held the Southern states in the federal union. Indeed, so thoroughly is the South permeated with the malign spirit of

† Published in *International Socialist Review,* vol. 4, no. 5 (November 1903), 257–60.

race hatred that even socialists are to be found, and by no means rarely, who either share directly in the race hostility against the Negro, or avoid the issue, or apologize for the social obliteration of the color line in the class struggle.

The white man in the South declares that "the nigger is all right in his place"; that is, as menial, servant, and slave. If he dare hold up his head, feel the thrill of manhood in his veins, and nurse the hope that someday may bring deliverance; if in his brain the thought of freedom dawns and in his heart the aspiration to rise above the animal plane and propensities of his sires, he must be made to realize that notwithstanding the white man is civilized (?), the black man is a "nigger" still and must so remain as long as the planets wheel in space.

But while the white man is considerate enough to tolerate the Negro "in his place," the remotest suggestion at social recognition arouses all the pent-up wrath of his Anglo-Saxon civilization; and my observation is that the less real ground there is for such indignant assertion of self-superiority, the more passionately it is proclaimed.

At Yoakum, Texas, a few days ago, leaving the depot with two grips in my hands, I passed four or five bearers of the white man's burden perched on a railing and decorating their environment with tobacco juice. One of them, addressing me, said: "There's a nigger that'll carry your grips." A second one added: "That's what he's here for," and the third chimed in with "That's right, by God." Here was a savory bouquet of white superiority. One glance was sufficient to satisfy me that they represented all there is of justification for the implacable hatred of the Negro race. They were ignorant, lazy, unclean, totally void of ambition, themselves the foul product of the capitalist system and held in lowest contempt by the master class, yet esteeming themselves immeasurably above the cleanest, most intelligent and self-respecting Negro, having by reflex absorbed the "nigger"-hatred of their masters.

As a matter of fact, the industrial supremacy of the South before the war would not have been possible without the Negro, and the South of today would totally collapse without his labor. Cotton culture has been and is the great staple and it will not be denied that the fineness and superiority of the fiber that makes the export of the southern states the greatest in the world is due in large measure to the genius of the Negroes charged with its cultivation.

The whole world is under obligation to the Negro, and that the white heel is still upon the black neck is simply proof that the world is not yet civilized.

The history of the Negro in the United States is a history of crime without a parallel.

Why should the white man hate him? Because he stole him from his native land and for two centuries and a half robbed him of the fruit of his labor, kept him in beastly ignorance, and subjected him to the brutal domination of the lash? Because he tore the black child from the breast of its mother and ravished the black man's daughter before her father's eyes?

There are thousands of Negroes who bear testimony in their whitening skins that men who so furiously resent the suggestion of "social equality" are far less sensitive in respect to the sexual equality of the races.

But of all the senseless agitation in capitalist society, that in respect to "social equality" takes the palm. The very instant it is mentioned, the old aristocratic plantation owner's shrill cry about the "buck nigger" marrying the "fair young daughter" of his master is heard from the tomb and echoed and reechoed across the spaces and repeated by the "white trash" in proud vindication of their social superiority.

Social equality, forsooth! Is the black man pressing his claims for social recognition upon his white burden bearer? Is there any reason why he should? Is the white man's social recognition of his own white brother such to excite the Negro's ambition to covet the noble prize? Has the Negro any greater desire, or is there any reason why he should have, for social intercourse with the white man than the white man has for social relations with the Negro? This phase of the Negro question is pure fraud and serves to mask the real issue, which is not *social equality*, but *economic freedom.*

There never was any social inferiority that was not the shriveled fruit of economic inequality. The Negro, given economic freedom, will not ask the white man any social favors; and the burning question of "social equality" will disappear like mist before the sunrise.

I have said and say again that, properly speaking, there is no Negro question outside of the labor question—the working-class struggle. Our position as socialists and as a party is perfectly plain. We have simply to say: "The class struggle is colorless." The capitalists—white, black, and all other colors—on the other side.

When Marx said: "Workingmen of all countries unite," he gave concrete expression to the socialist philosophy of the class struggle; unlike the framers of the declaration of independence who announced that "all men are created equal" and then basely repudiated their own doctrine, Marx issued the call to all the workers of the globe, regardless of race, sex, creed, or any other condition whatsoever.

As a socialist party, we receive the Negro and all other races upon absolutely equal terms. We are the party of the working class, the whole working class, and we will not suffer ourselves to be divided by any specious appeal to race prejudice; and if we should be coaxed or driven from the straight road ,we will be lost in the wilderness and ought to perish there, for we shall no longer be a socialist party.

Let the capitalist press and capitalist "public opinion" indulge themselves in alternate flattery and abuse of the Negro; we as socialists will receive him in our party, treat him in our counsels, and stand by him all around the same as if his skin were white instead of black; and this we do not from any consideration of sentiment, but because it accords with the philosophy of socialism, the genius of the class struggle, and is eternally right and bound to triumph in the end.

With the "nigger" question, the "race war" from the capitalist viewpoint we have nothing to do. In capitalism, the Negro question is a grave one and will grow more threatening as the contradictions and complications of capitalist society multiply, but this need not worry us. Let them settle the Negro question in their way, if they can. We have nothing to do with it, for that is their fight. We have simply to open the eyes of as many Negroes as we can and bring them into the socialist movement to do battle for emancipation from wage-slavery, and when the working class have triumphed in the class struggle and stand forth economic as well as political free men, the race problem will forever disappear.

Socialists should with pride proclaim their sympathy with and fealty to the black race, and if any there be who hesitate to avow themselves in the face of ignorant and unreasoning prejudice, they lack the true spirit of the slavery-destroying revolutionary movement.

The voice of socialism must be as inspiring music to the ears of those in bondage, especially the weak black brethren, doubly enslaved, who are bowed to the earth and groan in despair beneath the burden of the centuries.

For myself, my heart goes to the Negro, and I make no apology to any white man for it. In fact, when I see the poor, brutalized, outraged black victim, I feel a burning sense of guilt for his intellectual poverty and moral debasement that makes me blush for the unspeakable crimes committed by my own race.

In closing, permit me to express the hope that the next convention may repeal the resolutions on the Negro question. The Negro does not need them, and they serve to increase rather than diminish the necessity for explanation. We have nothing special to offer the Negro, and we cannot make separate appeals to all the races.

The Socialist Party is the party of the working class, regardless of color—the whole working class of the whole world.

Reminiscences of Myron W. Reed†

November 1903

Who that ever looked into his kindly eyes and felt the touch of his honest hand does not remember him with mingled joy and sorrow?

Myron Reed was indeed a man!

His love was boundless as all space, and his sympathy as tender and profound as that of the man of Galilee. And his noble courage in defense of the weak blossomed into glorious heroism.

He despised sham, scored hypocrisy, ridiculed ceremony, laughed at what the dudes and dunces of society call "good form," trampled roughshod upon conventionality, wore a slouch hat, and gloried always in his natural self.

Many times, he shocked the prudes because he would not pretend, dissimulate—because, no matter who, or what, or where, he would be no other than just Myron Reed.

He had all the imperfections of a perfect man.

All who ever knew him loved him.

He was hated only by the ones so mean that they are punished with distorted vision that mistakes a man for a monster and a monster for a man.

James Whitcomb Riley once said to me: "Myron Reed is a real man—a brother to his fellow man."

One Sunday morning, the vast congregation at Broadway Temple in Denver, where Mr. Reed preached, was startled with the shortest, strangest, and sweetest sermon on record. The preacher was paler than usual, there were tears in his eyes, and his voice was tremulous with emotion.

"I can't speak to you today; the dog at our house is dead."

That, in my judgment, was one of Myron Reed's greatest sermons. There is more genuine religion in this utterance than in all the cold creeds and heartless theology of the world. Reed's very soul was in his speech as he declared his kinship with all breathing beings.

Walt Whitman, had he been present, would have understood. The great preacher's heart lay bare before his people. God had let them see a man—then crowned that man with immortality.

They who were too base to understand, and therefore hated Myron Reed,

---

† Published in *The Comrade* [New York City], vol. 3, no. 2 (November 1903), 34–5.

wondered why so many men and women and children loved him. How could any but the soulless help but love this big and generous man, who sobbed with aching heart because his faithful dog had died!

ᔕ

The most abandoned wretch was sure he had one friend at least. He could appeal to Myron Reed and warm his heart to life again.

A mutual friend at Denver once told me of an impecunious fellow who was always borrowing and always broke. One morning he dropped in to make the usual plea for a loan. He was hard-pressed and must have a five-dollar bill. But the story was stale, and he was turned down and out.

Half an hour later Reed sauntered in. "Let me have five dollars," said the preacher. The money was handed to him, and he walked out briskly and up the street. Around the corner waited our impecunious friend and into his outstretched hand was pressed the borrowed bill.

ᔕ

During the strike of the Leadville miners in the winter of '96, I arrived in Denver one Sunday morning,[42] being met by Edward Boyce, then president of the Western Federation of Miners. We were to leave for Leadville the same night. The Coronado mine had been attacked,[43] a terrific battle followed, and many were killed and wounded on both sides. Everybody was armed, and the feeling was intensely bitter against the strikers. The press was virulently denouncing organized labor in general and Boyce and myself in particular.

This was the state of affairs when I met Boyce in Denver, on the way to Leadville. Boyce suggested that we go to hear Myron Reed. I readily assented. The Broadway Theater was crowded. Reed had resigned his pastorate, and many of his people and a good many others followed him.

We had hardly entered when Mr. Reed arose and said: "I understand that Mr. Boyce and Mr. Debs are in the audience; will the gentlemen do me the honor to come forward and occupy seats on the platform?"

We were astounded, not dreaming that Mr. Reed knew that we were in the city. The effect was startling. Most of the audience looked upon us as red-handed murderers, and the announcement fairly stunned them. Mr. Reed hardly allowed them time to recover their breath. He introduced each of us to the audience as his personal and honored friend.

That was Myron Reed! I can see him yet—calm, serene, quietly exultant over one of his peculiar triumphs.

ᔕ

It was during the strike of the miners at Cripple Creek that Myron Reed displayed his Spartan heroism and proved for the thousandth time his devotion to the working class and his implacable hostility to their oppressors. At this time, he was still preaching to the largest church congregation in Denver and the elite of the city were well represented in his pews. They were attracted by the picturesque and brilliant preacher who spoke in a succession of electric flashes; whose epigrams blazed and sparkled with the living fire from his own genius.

Aesop taught in fables, Christ in parables, and Reed in epigrams.

Reed was at the very height of his popularity and power when the supreme test came. The state was being shaken to its foundations by the strike and revolt of the miners. The mining corporations had a horde of armed deputies in the field. The miners were besieged at Bull Hill. The state was on the brink of revolution, and the plutocrats were demanding the most despotic and repressive measures to crush out the rebellion.

Governor Waite was appealed to, but refused to allow the militia to be used as corporate hirelings and was threatened with impeachment.

Let it here be noted that Governor Waite stands solitary and alone as the only governor that ever used the military arm of the state government to protect the working class. This was his martyrdom. For steadfastly serving labor he was crucified—by labor.

It was in this crisis that Myron Reed expanded to heroic proportions. He had the ear and the heart of the people. Like a flash of lightning from a clear sky, his famous epigram burst from his soul. It was a thunderbolt hurled by Jove himself—"My heart is at Bull Hill!"

The fashionable congregation was horrified—the plutocracy for the moment was paralyzed.

The fate of the fearless preacher was sealed, Henceforth, he was a demagogue, and archenemy of law and order, and he must drain to the last drop the bitter cup of persecution and exile.

ఌ

Almost the last time I called on him, he said: "Debs, our friend Bellamy is here trying to recover his lost health. We must call on him and cheer him up and see what we can do for him."

The next morning, we had our visit with the author of *Looking Backward* and *Equality.* The finger of death had already traced his claim in his pallid features. Edward Bellamy, great soul, was marked for the tomb.

"Perhaps," suggested Bellamy, "I'd better go South."

"I wouldn't," answered Reed, "there isn't a heretic in the whole South."

As we withdrew, Mr. Reed turned to me and in a voice full of sadness said: "Poor fellow, he is hoping in vain; he'll soon be at rest."

As he said this and I looked into his own wasted features, I said to myself: "Alas, dear brother, and so will you."

Bellamy soon afterward entered the shadowy vale, and Reed was not long in following him.[44]

The recent visit of the delegates of the American Labor Union and the Western Federation of Miners to the tomb of Myron Reed, and the touching tribute paid to his memory by Edward Boyce, were fitting testimonials of Labor's gratitude and love.

The miners and their wives and children were loyal to him living and will venerate his memory though all coming years. Many others honored his high courage and stood nobly by him to the end.

When he fell asleep, thousands wept as they built monuments of flowers above his dust.

He was a Union soldier in the Civil War and a civil soldier in the union war. He was the tribune of the people, the friend of toil—a soldier, a socialist, and a man.

Myron Reed traced his name in deeds that live and coming generations will add fresh luster to his well-earned fame.

Fixed Conventions and Costly Courts†

November 24, 1903

Terre Haute, Ind., November 24 [1903]

The American Federation of Labor went on record against what purported to be socialism by an overwhelming majority at the Boston convention.[45] Three men control and cast the vote that controls the convention.[46] The socialist delegates cut a small figure in the meeting and were sat down upon hard, and now the pure and simple labor leaders and the pure and simple capital leaders

---

† Published as "Debs Comments of Current Events" in *Social Democratic Herald,* vol. 6, no. 32, whole no. 279 (December 5, 1903), 1.

join lustily in singing the doxology.

At the New Orleans convention last year,[47] the socialists compromised on a milk-and-water resolution to get the vote of the miners. This year on a resolution that meant but little more, the miners slammed them down good and plenty.

Instead of a dozen resolutions, the socialist delegates should, in my opinion, have united upon a single one committing the convention (1) to a recognition of the class struggle, and (2) in favor of working-class political action, forcing the pure and simple delegates to go on record against that plain proposition.

But as the federation convention is controlled absolutely by three or four delegates who have votes enough to do as they please, and as these will never change until they are forced to do so by their constituents, it is questionable if there is anything gained in going up against such a brace game. The same debates take place year after year, and what the pure and simple fellows say is put on the wires, while the speeches of the socialists die in the convention hall. As well might the socialists orate to a log of wooden Indians as seek to change the controlling clique of the convention, who are as impervious to socialist logic as flint is to feathers.

Just now the capitalist press is busy showing how much ground the socialists have lost in the federation since the New Orleans convention and commending the conservatism and sagacity of its leaders. Every labor skinner in the land is patting the federation on the back and spewing his fulsome flattery upon his pure and simple saviors.

The reason the leaders give for opposing socialism is that they "don't want the labor movement to be the tail end of a political party." Gods! Isn't that just what it is today? Is not the pure and simple trade union movement controlled largely by jackleg politicians and city hall henchmen? And is not the organization itself, under its present leadership, the tail end of the capitalist hybrid Republican Party? And do not these pure and simple leaders graduate into fat political jobs in this same capitalist party for keeping the working class at the tail end of it? Is it not the "tail end" of the labor movement that wags around . . . the same capitalist political party every time the legislature meets and begs like a dog for a bone? [It is] kicked into the gutter and howls until it meets in its own convention under a leadership that poultices its bruises with pure and simple plaster. Then the next legislature can apply another and more vigorous kick to the same tail end that has no business to emerge from its kennel until it is whistled for to elect fresh kickers to boot it back to the stern end where it properly belongs.

My conclusion is that socialists would better stop wasting their time on a convention controlled by three or four men who are dead set against socialism and progress, and who will never move an inch until they are lifted by the rank and file. Let them make the next convention unanimous against socialism, and that day they see their finish. Socialism is about the only thing that vitalizes the pure and simple movement enough to attract any considerable attention.

Instead of wasting time and money on a fixed convention, let us go among the rank and file and dare the pure and simple leaders to face us there. They can barricade themselves behind their majority at the convention, but out among the rank and file we can meet them upon equal ground and make them defend their pro-capitalist policies.

Between the pure and simple labor leaders and civic federationists and the socialist agitators, there is war, and the place to fight it out is not in an Alamo where they outnumber us a dozen to one, but out in the hearing of the working class, who shall know the truth and smite their misleaders to earth.

∽

The story is being circulated—for what reason may be surmised—that the American Railway Union and its president never paid a dollar of the court costs assessed against them during their trials and that they also left their attorneys' fees and other claims unpaid. The story is an absolute falsehood. The ARU and its president paid every court claim and every lawyer fee in full and owes neither the one nor the other a farthing.

In this connection, it may be said that it cost a fortune to reach the Supreme Court of the United States to be told there that the lower court had final jurisdiction in a contempt proceeding. The writer was opposed to making the effort, but was overruled, the plea being made, especially by the lawyers, that the decision would be of incalculable value as a precedent to the working class. The litigation cost many thousands of dollars—all the money we had in the treasury of the ARU, all we had personally, all we could beg, borrow, or raise in any other way went to satisfy the lawyers and courts—this was the price of our conviction.

It is true that we agreed to pay some of the lawyers still more in case the ARU recovered financially, but it was distinctly understood that if the organization did not recover its financial standing, there should be no claim, and the large fees already paid were to be accepted as payment in full.

The ARU did not recover, for all the railroad corporations combined to crush it. Therefore, the contingent fees were not due and were never claimed. The lawyers were well paid, and every dollar due them was settled in full according to agreement, and every dollar due on every other claim was paid in full.

Neither the ARU nor its president owes any court or any lawyer a dollar, and any assertion to the contrary is a lie and a calumny.[48]

ꕥ

How grand these lines of Longfellow:

> The world rolls into light;
> It is daybreak everywhere.[49]

There is light ahead and all about us, and the sun of socialism will soon rise to meridian glory.

As to True Brotherhood: An Open Letter to the United Brotherhood of Railway Employees†

December 5, 1903

Terre Haute, Ind., December 5 [1903]

To the United Brotherhood of Railway Employees[50]:—

You are having, and will continue to have, for some time, an uphill work, but this is the kind strong men undertake and the kind that develops their best qualities and gives their names to history. The opposition you have will serve a beneficent purpose if your members meet it with an unconquerable determination to overcome it and reach their goal.

The railway corporations are all against you for the same reason that they were opposed to the ARU, and they are not to be blamed for looking out for their own interests. They are *against* any organization that attempts to *unite* their employees. They are *for* every organization that *divides* them. The grand officers of the several special class "brotherhoods" travel on annual passes. The officers of your organization pay their fare. It is such an advantage to belong

† Published as "As to True Brotherhood" in *Social Democratic Herald,* vol. 6, no. 40, whole no. 287 (January 30, 1904), 1.

to the former in the way of securing corporation favors and privileges that an army of men keep up their membership in them, though they have not for years been employed in the railway service. While they declare their hostility toward your brotherhood because of what they call its "mixed" membership, every one of them have every branch of the service represented in their own membership, from a conductor to a wiper, and beyond that, from a preacher to a policeman.

For many years I have seen and felt the necessity of a united organization of railway employees. The reason for this, in this day of capitalist concentration, is so obvious as to be self-evident. The railroad corporations are, of course, against it. A large number of salaried labor leaders are also against it, notwithstanding their organizations fail every time they are subjected to the supreme test. They failed in 1873,[51] they failed in 1877,[52] in 1888,[53] and in 1894.[54] They will fail again when the crucial test comes in the next twelvemonth, more or less.

During the "boom" times of the last three or four years, the railroads have been "making" an army of new railroad men. The signs of depression are already beginning to appear. The letdown is inevitable, and among the first things that will happen will be sweeping reductions of wages. The army of surplus men will be available in case of a strike, and the leaders will doubtless advise their followers, as they have in the past, that "half a loaf is better than no bread." If under such conditions they strike, they will be beaten, and if they don't strike, their wages will go down, and the fruit of their boasted victories will turn to ashes. This has happened over and over again. Must it continue to happen for another century before the eyes of the working victims are opened to the fact that they must unite from end to end of the service and present a solid front to protect their interests?

In their present form, the railroads can and do use the brotherhoods against each other, and as for any actual federation, it will never be accomplished, for at that point the railroads will fight them, and that is not in harmony with their policy of "identical interests."

The simple, effective way—and only way—to unite railway employees is within a single organization, each class within its own sub-jurisdiction and in control of its own affairs, subject only to the supervision of the general organization. The United Brotherhood recognizes and acts upon this fundamental principle. Sooner or later the railway employees will have to come to it. It is simply a question as to how long they prefer division to unity, defeat to victory. Your organization is in the critical period of its development, and it remains to be seen if your leaders and rank and file are of the fiber that defies failure and which the coming organization must have to fulfill its mission. Judging from those I have met and know, your membership will stand firm, however severe the tempest may rage, until victory is assured.

The next few months will bring you your great opportunity, and I shall hope that, being familiar with the lessons of the past, you will profit by them. When the "panic" comes and thousands are thrown out of work and wages begin to sink, the need of unity will be felt far more than you can teach it and preach it in peaceable times.

The time demands a united brotherhood with a class-conscious political program. Without the latter, it is not much more than a plaything of corporate capital. Teach your members the necessity of working-class political action, so that while striking against the encroachments of the corporation they will at the same time be lining up to abolish capitalism and make the workers, instead of the parasites, the masters of the earth.

Yours fraternally,
Eugene V. Debs

How Long Will You Stand It? Speech at Chicago Coliseum† [excerpt]

December 6, 1903

A few days ago, the editor of a Chicago paper, discussing the returns of the recent state elections in the editorial column of his paper, concluded that the socialist movement had received its death blow, that in fact socialism was dead in America. Well, then, this must be the resurrection.[55]

I stand in your presence this afternoon a socialist—class-conscious, revolutionary, uncompromising. I have little time and no use for what is commonly called reform. You cannot reform rottenness. The only reform of the capitalist system which is possible is overthrow and destruction. Capitalist politics are essentially corrupt and demoralizing. Pick up your daily newspaper—it is a chronicle of crime. What is the status of the workingman in the present government? Has he a voice loud enough to be heard? As a matter of fact, he is completely ignored for the reason that he is not yet conscious of his conquering power.

The Republican Party is in absolute power in the interest, we are told, mainly of the working class, the producers of wealth. The Democratic Party is not only dead, but in an advanced state of decomposition. But it will not be permitted to disintegrate entirely. It still has a mission. The time has come to shove in a Democratic administration because a panic is due, and the panic must of course fall upon the Democratic jackass, and then we will hear the old stereotype cry, "That is what you get for turning out the Republican Party. Give us eight more years of Republican rule."

But there is an ever-increasing number of workingmen in this country who can no longer be deceived. The workingmen are beginning to realize that if they would emancipate themselves from the degrading thralldom of the ages, they must unite upon the economic field and upon the political field, but

† Published as "Ten Thousand at the Coliseum; Stupendous Socialist Success," *Chicago Socialist,* vol. 5, whole no. 249 (December 12, 1903), 1. Same stenographic report used but paragraph sequence changed for republication as "The Great Game of Politics" in *Social Democratic Herald,* vol. 6, no. 35, whole no. 282 (December 26, 1903), 1 and "It Appeals to the Intelligence," whole no. 283 (January 2, 1904), 1. Best guess at original sequence appears here.

above all things they must unite. The solidarity of the working class is the supreme demand of the hour.

There are some so-called leaders of labor who favor solidarity upon the economic field, but who are opposed to it on the political field. They are not in fact union men. They lack the vital, essential principle of true unionism. They lead the working class backward, not forward. They are in alliance, active or passive, with the capitalist class.

Samuel Gompers, president of the American Federation of Labor, said the other day that he had read socialism in two languages. He had better have understood it in one. He is opposed to politics in the union. He knows very well that when politics comes into the union, he will go out of the union. He and Mark Hanna will solve the labor question if you workingmen will let them alone, but when it is solved in their way, it will not be solved in your way.

ꟹ

Your grandfather made a pair of shoes, and they were his own. You make a thousand pairs of shoes where he made one. You do not own a single one of them. You can produce wealth in fabulous abundance, but you have not got it. Why not? Because you work with tools that belong to your master, and what you produce belongs to him. Ownership of the tools implies ownership of the product. Your grandfather owned and enjoyed the fruit of his labor because he worked with tools that belonged to himself. Your employer goes to Europe or goes around the world in his private yacht, or enjoys what is called exclusive society, because he is the proprietor of the tools with which you work.

The politician on the eve of any election tells you that you are a sovereign citizen. You are nothing of the kind. In the present system, you are simply labor-power, merchandise, bought in what they call the labor market as if you were hair, hide, bone, or any other commodity subject to the law of demand and supply. The more labor-power and the less demand, the lower your wages. The lower your wages, the less you can consume. You are always in competition with each other—men, women, and children—to sell your labor-power to the owners of the machinery. You cannot compete against them with your bare hands. You have got to sell them your labor-power.

At this point it is pertinent to ask, what is labor-power? Labor-power is human energy. Labor-power is life, or as sacred as life itself. Looking backward over the past 40 years, we read of the auction block and the slave pen. We see a human being with a throbbing heart and an immortal soul; we see him placed upon the auction block in public, his teeth inspected and his body examined to see if he is sound. He is then torn from his wife and children and sold to the highest bidder.

We stand aghast as we contemplate the fact that this auction block existed for 200 years upon American soil. The time will come when the world will again take a backward look and stand horrified as it contemplates the harder spectacle of the entire working class flung between what is called the labor market, where the labor-power of human beings is sold every day and every hour, year in and year out, by the lowest bidder.

You expect to reform such a system. I ask you: How? You punish crime, but you produce it a hundredfold. We socialists do not propose to mend this system; we propose to put an end to it, and that is the reason we are appealing to you this afternoon, not to accept our philosophy unthinkingly, not to subscribe to our principles without investigation.

We are appealing to you to preserve your mental integrity, your moral rectitude; we are appealing to you to think for yourselves. You have been satisfied to do your thinking by proxy. It is a thousand times better for you workingmen and workingwomen to spend your time in cultivating self-reliance. Stop crawling in the dust. Stand erect. See how tall you are in the sunlight. Brush the dust of servitude from your knees. Hold high communion with yourself.

You are a worker. The first thing necessary for you to understand is that you are bound irrevocably to every other worker in the country. As individual workingmen, you are ground to atoms, you are reduced to slavery, and you are at the mercy of the masters. When you unite, however, there will be twelve of you for every capitalist. You are fighting them with your stomachs. We socialists want you to fight them with your brains.

ɞ

The average workingman is an abject slave. I would rather be a dog and bay at the moon than to be that kind of a sovereign citizen. I love to think of a sovereign citizen. The term appeals to me strongly. But in the present system, it is a hollow mockery. Think of a sovereign citizen looking for a boss, going to the factory, quivering at the knees, taking off his hat in the presence of a 2x4 boss and announcing himself for sale.

Chattel slavery would be impossible in the present development of the capitalist system. Free competitive labor is cheaper than slave labor. The capitalist's responsibility ceases when the wages are paid.

It is said that socialism is impracticable. Socialism is the only system that is practical. It is the present system that has shown itself impracticable.

I am a socialist. I am one of several hundred thousand in the United States who absolutely refuse to shoulder a gun at the command of Roosevelt or any other man and shoot down workingmen. If he wants any killing of human beings done, he will do it himself, so far as I am concerned.

You outnumber your oppressors twelve to one. You can not only relieve yourselves from the consequences of this accursed system, you can absolutely abolish it. You can put yourselves in control of the government, take possession of your own, and emancipate yourself from slavery.

The average workingman is satisfied with so little. Give him a steady job, enough wages to keep his passive soul within his half-dressed body, and he wants to thank somebody. He is looking about for the benefactor. He wants to pass resolutions thanking some politician, some priest, some parasite of some description. I am doing what little I can to augment the discontent of the working class, to direct that discontent properly and give it intelligence, give it solidarity to press forward, and in due time the working class will reach the heights of economic emancipation. I may not live to see it. The socialist does not stop to consider whether the change is coming next week or next month or next century. He knows that it is coming, that it is inevitable. He has taken his place as a class-conscious socialist, and he never can become anything else.

You hear a man who voted the socialist ticket last month. If he is not going to vote it next month, it is because he never was a socialist. So we wait and watch and work because our movement is in alliance with the revolutionary forces, and as certain to triumph as that the rivers roll to the sea. It is but a question of time, and we can afford to bide that time.

ꟹ

Can you tell the difference between the quality and effect of an injunction issued by a Republican judge and one issued by a Democratic judge? [*A voice: "The brass molders know it."*] When the labor movement goes into politics, the injunction will cease, the system under which the workingman is simply a piece of labor-power will be abolished.

Is it by chance that every member of the United States Supreme Court is a trained and successful trust and corporation attorney? Don't you workingmen know that when you do succeed in pushing some law through the state legislature or even the national Congress which is designed to inconvenience the capitalist class, they have state and national supreme courts to declare the laws unconstitutional? And what are you going to do about it? Submit until the next election, and then vote the Republican or Democratic ticket and have a repetition of it.

As Abraham Lincoln once said, "If you want that sort of thing, why, that's the sort of thing you want." It is simply a question as to how long you can, or rather how long you will, stand it. Organize as thoroughly as you choose, they will have a mortgage on your leaders. If the rank and file in Chicago would do a little excavating they would find wires between City Hall and the Federation of Labor. And because there are wires underground, there are overhead policemen's clubs for your heads.

∽

You had a great strike recently on the Chicago City Railway. The press announced that the union had achieved something of a victory. I would like to have a photograph. [*A voice: "Get one of the buttons that they daren't wear."*]

The Chicago City Railway employees were organized as thoroughly as they can be if they wait a century. But they lost. Why? Because there is a vast body of men always out of work under the capitalist system. It is called the reserve army of capitalism and can be drawn on at will. If a hundred thousand or two hundred thousand men lay down their tools and give up their places of employment, there are the same number always ready to take their places.

I want all trade unionists of Chicago to take the affairs of their unions into their own hands and make it impossible for the fakir and fraud labor leader to flourish in the labor movement. The reason a labor leader is popular today and has office and salary is because he is not true to the working class. I do not want Mark Hanna to bear testimony to my efficiency as a labor leader.[56]

∽

The capitalist press united in pronouncing the coal strike the greatest victory ever achieved by the working class. It is true that their wages were increased 10 percent. It is also true that their living expense increased from 15 to 20 percent. The board created by the commission made Carroll D. Wright, the national labor commissioner, umpire. Every single solitary question submitted to that tribunal was decided against the striking miners with but one exception, and that but a nominal exception.

The corporations are in absolute control in those coal fields—bleak, barren, desolate beyond the power of language to describe. There is an army of 150,000 human beings, miners of coal, in a state of abject slavery, from which there is no escape under the capitalist system. I have been in those mines again and again, and I know whereof I speak. I have heard the echo of the pit that sounded like muffled drums beating funeral marches.

∽

They say the socialists are trying to destroy the labor unions. I like to use plain words: They lie. I would enjoy the opportunity of meeting President Gompers or President Mitchell on this platform before this audience, in the presence not of socialists, but of their own trade unionists, in discussing this question.

They tell you that we propose to destroy the movement. We propose nothing of the kind. We propose to vitalize the movement and make it fulfill its historic mission. We do not propose that Mark Hanna, Archbishop Ireland, or Bishop Potter shall run the trade union movement in the interest of the capitalist class. We propose that the trade union movement shall run itself in the right channel and in the right direction. We do not propose to make a socialist party of the trade union movement. We simply propose that the trade unions shall recognize the class struggle. We want the trade unions to say, "Yes, our eyes are open. We recognize the fact that there is a mighty struggle in progress between capital on the one hand and the working class on the other hand. We realize that we must organize, unite, and act together; that we must strike when there is no other recourse, levy the boycott, and do what we can on the economic field."

Every time you engage in a battle of that kind, I will guarantee that you can rely upon the support of every socialist. Two years ago, after they had been telling the trade unions that we socialists were trying to wipe out the trade union, a streetcar strike came, and a boycott was declared. It was not a great while afterward until the leaders of the Central Labor Union began to dicker with the capitalists to sell out that strike. In spite of our opposition, it was not long until they arranged a settlement, declared the strike off, and left the entire body of union men out of jobs. We, the socialists, are still walking in the city of Terre Haute, and we are the only ones who are.

Notes

1. J. Stitt Wilson (1868–1942) was a Canadian-born Methodist minister and Christian socialist who joined the speakers' bureau of the utopian socialist Brotherhood of the Cooperative Commonwealth in 1897. Active in the Socialist Party from the time of its establishement, Wilson served as mayor of Berkeley, California, from 1911 to 1913.
2. Carl D. Thompson (1870–1949) was a preacher and Christian socialist, closely affiliated with J. Stitt Wilson's Social Crusade from 1901. Thompson later moved to Milwaukee and was prominent in the socialist movement there, winning election to the Wisconsin legislature in 1906. He split with the Socialist Party in 1917 over its opposition to World War I, becoming active in the liberal Committee of 48.
3. An extended strike of anthracite coal mines was called off in October 1902 in favor of the decision of a seven-member arbitration committee appointed by President Theodore Roosevelt. From November through the following January, the committee heard testimony in Scranton, Pennsylvania. Clarence Darrow, lead attorney for the miners, bringing a series of 125 witnesses to the stand to state the workers' case, with the operators following with their own barrage of testimony.
4. Walter Wellman (1858–1934) was the Washington correspondent of the *Chicago Herald* who engaged in adventures for his readers such as attempting to locate the exact landing place of Christopher Columbus and taking part in an expedition attempting to reach the North Pole.
5. George Gray (1840–1925) was a former Democratic United States senator and judge of the US Court of Appeals who chaired the coal strike investigating committee of 1902. Gray's name was twice placed into nomination for president of the United States at the Democratic National Convention, with his best result a second-place finish to William Jennings Bryan in 1908.
6. "Suave as a Chesterfield" was a commonly used turn of phrase alluding to the fourth Earl of Chesterfield, Philip Stanhope (1694–1773), whose posthumous book *Letters to His Son on the Art of Becoming a Man of the World and a Gentleman* (1774) collected 400 erudite and nuanced letters dealing with the social code of the day and how a gentleman should behave.
7. William H. Wise was a minister of the Methodist-Episcopal Church.
8. Franklin H. Wentworth was the son of a prominent Chicago newspaper editor, mayor, and member of Congress who became active in the socialist movement in 1899. Wentworth edited *The Social Crusade* from 1901 to 1903 and was a leading Christian socialist speaker and writer during the first decade of the twentieth century.
9. Lyman J. Abbott (1835–1922) was a Congregationalist minister, a Christian theologian, and a longtime magazine editor. A prolific writer, Abbott was editor of *The Christian Union,* later better known as *The Outlook,* from 1881 until the time of his death.
10. Karl Marx and Frederick Engels, *Manifesto of the Communist Party* [1848] (Terre Haute, IN: Debs Publishing Co., July 1901), 23. Reprinted in *Marx-Engels Collected Works: Volume 6: Marx and Engels, 1845–1848.* (New York: International Publishers, 1976), 496.

11. In the preface to *Socialism from Genesis to Revelation* (1893), Reverend Franklin Monroe Sprague (1841–1926) wrote: "Socialism being the product of social evolution, the only danger lies in obstructing it. Evolution is a normal development, a growth; revolution is a creation. To obstruct evolution is to invite revolution."
12. Massachusetts state representative Frederic O. MacCartney (1864–1903), a Unitarian minister, died on May 26, 1903, of bronchial pneumonia. A former partisan of the Social Democratic Party with headquarters in Chicago, MacCartney was just 38 years old at the time of his death.
13. Iowa College is today known as Grinnell College, located in Grinnell, Iowa.
14. James F. Carey (1867–1938) and Louis M. Scates (1863–1954) were the two other Social Democratic Party candidates elected to the legislature in the fall of 1898.
15. Gurley Brewer (1866–1919) was an attorney, publisher, and Republican Party political activist who was regarded as one of the top African-American public speakers in the state of Indiana.
16. The *Indianapolis World* was a black-owned newspaper writing for an African-American audience.
17. David M. Parry (1830–1915) was an Indianapolis industrialist who was president of the National Association of Manufacturers (NAM) at the time. In his April 14 keynote to NAM's 1903 convention in New Orleans, Parry called organized labor "a despotism, springing into being in the midst of a liberty-loving people" and declared it to be an institution based on force and violence and "commanded by leaders who are at heart disciples of revolution." His nationally reprinted remarks received multiple standing ovations from the gathering's 600 delegates.
18. Charles Sumner (1811–1874) was a US senator from Massachusetts for nearly a quarter century. A radical Republican, Sumner was a leader of anti-slavery forces in Congress. Sumner is remembered for being the victim of a physical assault on the floor of the Senate in 1856 by pro-slavery Democrat Preston Brooks of South Carolina, an event that galvanized sentiment on the slavery issue, culminating in the American Civil War.
19. In April 1903, the Northern Securities Company, a holding company headed by transportation tycoon James J. Hill that sought increased monopoly power in the railroad industry through the merger of two leading roads, was declared by the US Circuit Court of Appeals for the Eighth District to be an illegal combination in restraint of trade. The company was enjoined from exercising control over the Northern Pacific and Great Northern railways, and those companies were prohibited from paying dividends to Northern Securities. The case was immediately carried to the US Supreme Court, which in March 1904 affirmed the ruling of the lower court in a 5–4 vote.
20. Galusha A. Grow (1823–1907) of Pennsylvania was first elected to Congress in 1850, switching parties in 1856 in protest of President Franklin Pierce's signing of the Kansas-Nebraska Act. Grow is remembered for his role in an 1858 fight on the floor of the House of Representatives, during which he was physically attacked by Laurence M. Keitt, a reactionary Democrat from South Carolina. While serving as speaker of the House, the radical Republican Grow was defeated in a bid for

reelection in 1862. He did not return to Congress until 1894.

21. "The Shortcomings of Arbitration" was a short syndicated piece published in various newspapers in July 1893.
22. Debs was sought for comment on an interview with Captain A. W. Dudley, Company B, Indiana National Guard published in the *Terre Haute Gazette* on July 10, 1903. In the interview, Dudley laid the blame for race riots in Evansville, Indiana, upon socialists.
23. On July 3, 1903, a black man walking out on a bar debt was halted by a white policeman and the two exchanged gunfire, resulting in the death of the gut-shot police officer. During the night, a lynch mob formed, but the arrested shooter was shuttled out of jail via a tunnel to an awaiting train to a neighboring town before the mob, consisting of several thousand people, broke into the jail using a telephone poll as a battering ram. A day of racial violence followed, with a dozen people killed by gunfire before Republican governor Winfield T. Durbin declared martial law and locked down the city with a force of 300 members of the National Guard.
24. The mayor of Evansville was Charles G. Covert (1863–1953), a former country sheriff who was later criticized for his tardiness in alerting the governor to the emergency.
25. On July 6, 1903, Terre Haute caterer Alex Sanderson and eight black employees appeared in Linton, Indiana, to provide food service at a banquet opening a new Elks lodge in the town. A mob of several hundred miners formed and threatened to dynamite the hall, riotously chasing the food workers from town in a cab.
26. Debs began his first tour of the South, a six-week journey that took him to Alabama, Georgia, Florida, South Carolina, and Missouri during the second week of February 1896.
27. Richard T. Ely (1854–1943), a de facto Christian socialist, was one of the leading scholars of the progressive era. He was for more than three decades a professor of economics at the University of Wisconsin and was the author of a number of books on the history of socialism, the labor movement, and economic theory.
28. Richard T. Ely, *The Labor Movement in America.* New York: Thomas Y. Crowell & Co., 1886.
29. The Western Labor Union changed its name to the American Labor Movement at its Fifth Annual Convention, held in Denver from May 26 to June 8, 1902.
30. Debs uses an incorrect term here. The primary party unit of the Socialist Party of America was the "local," sometimes split into subdivisions based on common language or tighter geographical range called "branches." The Social Democratic Party with headquarters in Chicago made use of primary party units called "local branches." The Springfield SDP followed the Socialist Labor Party in calling their primary party units "sections."
31. This piece was written for a special twelve-page edition of the *Appeal to Reason* with an advertised print run of 1 million copies.
32. Allusion to *Letters on the English: Letter IV, On the Quakers* (1733) by François-Marie Arouet de Voltaire (1694–1778). The common translation reads: "The first step [Penn] took was to enter into an alliance with his American neighbors, and this is the

only treaty between those people and the Christians that was not ratified by an oath, and was never infringed."

33. The Dawes Commission of 1893 conducted registration of tribal members with a view to the expropriation of the treaty lands ceded to the so-called "Five Civilized Tribes" in today's Oklahoma. Communal lands were platted into privately held individual lots with the federal government "claiming" any surplus land following the process of allotment to individuals.
34. The dispute was between the Cleveland, Cincinnati, Chicago & St. Louis Railway, the so-called "Big Four," and Edgar County, Illinois, over which entity was financially responsible for the victim's care. Thompson later attempted to sue the railroad for $15,000 for the injury he sustained when he was pushed out of a train, but he settled his case out of court for a reported $500.
35. On April 5, 1900, about 400 Italian immigrant quarry workers supplying material for a new dam near Croton-on-Hudson, New York, went on strike in a wage dispute. The project to improve the water supply of New York City was disrupted, with nearly a thousand workers idled. On April 15, a formal call was made for the state militia to restore order, which was rapidly granted by Governor Roosevelt. During the night of April 16, one of these militiamen was killed by an assassin, causing the insertion of more troops, who ultimately numbered 1,350. Arrest warrants were issued for strike leaders and 26 arrests made, which together with the show of military force caused the collapse of the strike at the end of the third week of April.
36. William A. Miller, a veteran foreman in the US Government Printing Office whose abusive management style had alienated the union book binders working there, was fired from his job on May 18, 1903. This termination was overturned by President Theodore Roosevelt on July 27, and Miller returned to his former position. The incident, which simmered throughout the summer and early fall as Miller sued for back pay due to illegal termination; the union, which had expelled Miller for his behavior, simultaneously fought for his firing for cause due to non-membership in the union and personal fitness for the job. The incident was used as a fulcrum against trade unionism in the printing industry by its opponents, a drive bolstered by Roosevelt's September 29 statement after meeting with Samuel Gompers and four other labor leaders that "in the employment and dismissal of men in the government service, I can no more recognize the fact that a man does or does not belong to a union as being for or against him than can I recognize the fact that he is a Protestant or a Catholic, a Jew or a gentile, as being for or against him."
37. Allusion to the story of Lazarus in Luke 16.
38. That is, the People's Party.
39. Tom L. Johnson (1854–1911), a former member of Congress, was the Democratic mayor of Cleveland from 1901 to 1909. Johnson became a national figure as a civic reformer and prominent advocate of Henry George's single-tax economic scheme.
40. Isaac Cowen, a former prohibitionist and member of the Amalgamated Iron and Steel Association of Cleveland, was business agent of the Cleveland Central Labor Union. Cowen headed the Socialist Party of Ohio's ticket as its candidate for governor in the

elections of 1903 and 1905, finishing a distant third each time. He was regarded as a skilled public orator and was briefly a national organizer for the Socialist Party in 1907.

41. Seth Low (1850–1916) was a progressive Republican who was a former mayor of Brooklyn and president of Columbia University who won election as mayor of the consolidated city of New York in 1901. He was defeated by Democrat George B. McClellan, Jr. in the 1903 campaign.
42. Debs arrived in Denver on Sunday, January 10, 1897.
43. The Coronado mine attack took place during the early morning hours of September 21, 1896.
44. Edward Bellamy died of tuberculosis on May 22, 1898. Myron Reed died of chronic colitis on January 30, 1899.
45. The 23rd Annual Convention of the American Federation of Labor was held in Boston at Faneuil Hall from November 9–23, 1903.
46. Unions were allocated votes in proportion to their paid memberships, with the largest organizations casting the most votes.
47. The 22nd Annual Convention of the American Federation of Labor was held at Odd Fellows' Hall, New Orleans, from November 13–22, 1902.
48. Debs clearly indicates here that the ARU's debt was paid in full by this date in 1903.
49. Closing lines of "The Bells of San Blas" (1882), by Henry Wadsworth Longfellow (1807–1882).
50. The United Brotherhood of Railway Employees (UBRE) was launched in San Francisco in the spring of 1901 in an effort to pick up the banner of the American Railway Union. President of the organization was George Estes, of Roseburg, Oregon. The UBRE had a membership located almost exclusively in the West. Wire reports detailing the organization's launch in May 1901 moved reporters to track down Debs for his comment. Debs declared: "I have decided to hold aloof from the organization for the present, because I have other matters to attend to. Probably when the railway men of the entire country are ready to enter into such a movement I shall assist them." The UBRE, which was based in Chicago from 1902, conducted a strike against the Canadian Pacific Railroad in March 1903 and survived at least through 1905 before fading from the historical record.
51. Year of financial panic resulting from the collapse of Jay Cooke & Company, a firm heavily invested in railroad construction.
52. Year of the "Great Strike."
53. Year of the start of the Burlington Strike.
54. Year of the American Railway Union's strike against the Pullman Palace Car Company.
55. This speech was delivered to a crowd of ten thousand at Chicago Coliseum, a mass meeting called by the Socialist Party. One commentator noted of Debs that "although his voice was far-reaching and his endurance marvelous, the speaker could not make himself heard by all of the people who were so eager to listen . . ."
56. A potshot at Samuel Gompers of the American Federation of Labor and John Mitchell of the United Mine Workers of America, who sat together with Hanna as leading members of the National Civic Federation.

1904

The Negro and His Nemesis[†]

January 1904

Since the appearance of my article on "The Negro in the Class Struggle" in the November *Review* I have received the following anonymous letter:

> Elgin, Ill., November 25, 1903
>
> Mr. Debs:—
>
> Sir, I am a constant reader of the *International Socialist Review*. I have analyzed your last article on the Negro question with apprehension and fear. You say that the South is permeated with the race prejudice of the Negro more than the North. I say it is not so. When it comes right down to a test, the North is more fierce in the race prejudice of the Negro than the South ever has been or ever will be. I tell you, you will jeopardize the best interests of the Socialist Party if you insist on political equality of the Negro. For that will not only mean political equality but also social equality eventually. I do not believe you realize what that means. You get social and political equality for the Negro, then let him come and ask the hand of your daughter in marriage, "for that seems to be the height of his ambition," and we will see whether you still have a hankering for social and political equality for the Negro. For I tell you, the Negro will not be satisfied with equality with reservation. It is impossible for the Anglo-Saxon and the African to live on equal terms. You try it, and he will pull you down to his level. Mr. Lincoln, himself, said that "There is a physical difference between the white and the black races, which I believe will forever forbid them living together on terms of social and political equality."
>
> If the Socialist leaders stoop to this method to gain votes, then their policy and doctrine is as rotten and degraded as that of the Republican and Democratic parties, and I tell you, if the resolutions are adopted to give the African equality with the Anglo-Saxon, you will lose more votes than you now think. I for my part shall do all I can to make you lose as many as possible, and there will be others. For don't you know that just a little sour dough will spoil the whole batch of bread. You will do the

---

† Published in *International Socialist Review*, vol. 4, no. 7 (January 1904), 391–7.

Negro a greater favor by leaving him where he is. You elevate and educate him, and you will make his position impossible in the USA.

Mr. Debs, if you have any doubts on this subject, I beg you for humanity's sake to read Mr. Thomas Dixon's *The Leopard's Spots,* and I hope that all others who have voiced your sentiments heretofore will do the same.[1]

I assure you, I shall watch the *International Socialist Review* with the most intense hope of a reply after you have read Mr. Thomas Dixon's message to humanity.

Respectfully yours,
So far a staunch member of the Socialist Party

The writer, who subscribes himself "a staunch member of the Socialist Party," is the only member of that kind I have ever heard of who fears to sign his name to, and accept responsibility for, what he writes. The really "staunch" socialist attacks in the open—he does not shoot from ambush.

The anonymous writer, as a rule, ought to be ignored, since he is unwilling to face those he accuses, while he may be a sneak or coward, traitor or spy, in the role of a "staunch socialist," whose base design it is to divide and disrupt the movement. For reasons which will appear later, this communication is made an exception and will be treated as if from a known party member in good standing.

It would be interesting to know of what branch our critic is a member and how long he has been, and how he happened to become a "staunch member of the Socialist Party." That he is entirely ignorant of the philosophy of socialism may not be to his discredit, but that a "staunch member" has not even read the platform of his party not only admits of no excuse, but takes the "staunchness" all out of him, punctures and discredits his foolish and fanatical criticism and leaves him naked and exposed to ridicule and contempt

The Elgin writer has all the eminent and well-recognized qualifications necessary to oppose Negro equality. His criticism and the spirit that prompts it harmonize delightfully with his assumed superiority.

That he may understand that he claims to be a "staunch member" of a party he knows nothing about I here incorporate the "Negro Resolutions" adopted by our last national convention, which constitute a vital part of the national platform of the Socialist Party and clearly defined its attitude toward the Negro:

Negro Resolution

> *Whereas,* The Negroes of the United States, because of their long training in slavery and but recent emancipation therefrom, occupy a peculiar position in the working class and in society at large; and
>
> *Whereas,* The capitalist class seeks to preserve this peculiar condition, and to foster and increase color prejudice and race hatred between the white worker and the black, so as to make their social and economic interests to appear to be separate and antagonistic, in order that the workers of both races may thereby be more easily and completely exploited; and
>
> *Whereas,* Both the old political parties and educational and religious institutions alike betray the Negro in his present helpless struggle against disfranchisement and violence, in order to receive the economic favors of the capitalist class. Be it, therefore,
>
> *Resolved,* That we, the Socialists of America, in national convention assembled, do hereby assure our Negro fellow worker of our sympathy with him in his subjection to lawlessness and oppression, and also assure him of the fellowship of the workers who suffer from the lawlessness and exploitation of capital in every nation or tribe of the world. And be it further
>
> *Resolved,* That we declare to the Negro worker the identity of his interests and struggles with the interests and struggles of the workers of all lands, without regard to race or color or sectional lines; that the causes which have made him the victim of social and political inequality are the effects of the long exploitation of his labor-power; that all social and race prejudices spring from the ancient economic causes which still endure, to the misery of the whole human family, that the only line of division which exists in fact is that between the producers and the owners of the world—between capitalism and labor. And be it further
>
> *Resolved,* That we, the American Socialist Party, invite the Negro to membership and fellowship with us in the world movement for economic emancipation by which equal liberty and opportunity shall be secured to every man and fraternity become the order of the world.

But even without this specific declaration, the position of the party is so clear that no member and no other person of ordinary intelligence can fail to comprehend it.

The Socialist Party is the congealed, tangible expression of the socialist movement, and the socialist movement is based upon the modern class struggle in which all workers of all countries, regardless of race, nationality, creed, or sex, are called upon to unite against the capitalist class, their common exploiter and oppressor. In this great class struggle, the economic equality of all workers is a foregone conclusion, and he who does not recognize and subscribe to it as one of the basic principles of the socialist philosophy is not a socialist, and if a party member must have been admitted through misunderstanding or false pretense, and should be speedily set adrift, that he may return to the capitalist parties with their social and economic strata from the "white trash" and "buck nigger" down to the syphilitic snob and harlot heiress who barters virtue for title in the matrimonial market.

I did not say that the race prejudice in the South was more intense than in the North. No such comparison was made, and my critic's denial is therefore unnecessary upon this point. Whether the prejudice of the South differs from that of the North is quite another question and entirely aside from the one at issue, nor is it of sufficient interest to consider at this time.

The Elgin writer says that we shall "jeopardize the best interests of the Socialist Party" if we insist upon the political equality of the Negro. I say that the Socialist Party would be false to its historic mission, violate the fundamental principles of socialism, deny its philosophy, and repudiate its own teachings if, on account of race considerations, it sought to exclude any human being from political equality and economic freedom. Then, indeed, would it not only "jeopardize" its best interests, but forfeit its very life, for it would soon be scorned and deserted as a thing unclean, leaving but a stench in the nostrils of honest men.

Political equality is to be denied the Negro, according to this writer, because it would lead to social equality, and this would be terrible—especially for those "white" men who are already married to Negro women and those "white" women who have long since picked the "buck nigger" in preference to the "white trash" whose social superiority they were unable to distinguish or appreciate.

Of course the Negro will "not be satisfied with equality with reservation." Why should he be? Would you?

Suppose you change places with the Negro just a year, then let us hear from you—"with reservation."

What now follows it is difficult to consider with patience: "You get social and political equality for the Negro, then let him come and ask the hand of your daughter in marriage."

In the first place, you don't get equality for the Negro—you haven't got it yourself. In the present social scale, there is no difference between you and the Negro—you are on the same level in the labor market, and the capitalist whose agent buys your labor-power doesn't know and doesn't care if you are white or black, for he deals with you simply as labor-power, and is uninterested save as to the quality and quantity you can supply. He cares no more about the color of your hide than does Armour about that of the steers he buys in the cattle market.

In the next place, the Negro will fight for his own political and economic equality. He will take his place in the Socialist Party with the workers of all colors and all countries, and all of them will unite in the fight to destroy the capitalist system that now makes common slaves of them all.

Foolish and vain indeed is the workingman who makes the color of his skin the stepping-stone to his imaginary superiority. The trouble is with his head, and if he can get that right, he will find that what ails him is not superiority but inferiority, and that he, as well as the Negro he despises, is the victim of wage-slavery, which robs him of what he produces and keeps both him and the Negro tied down to the dead level of ignorance and degradation.

As for "the Negro asking the hand of your daughter in marriage," that is so silly and senseless that the writer is probably after all justified in withholding his name. How about the daughter asking the hand of the Negro in marriage? Don't you know that this is happening every day? Then, according to your logic, the inferiority and degeneracy of the white race is established, and the Negro ought to rise in solemn protest against political equality, lest the white man ask the hand of his daughter in marriage.

"It is impossible," continues our critic, "for the Anglo-Saxon and the African to live upon equal terms. You try it and he will pull you down to his level." Our critic must have tried something that had a downward pull, for surely that is his present tendency.

The fact is that it is impossible for the Anglo-Saxon and the African to live on unequal terms. A hundred years of American history culminating in the Civil War proves that. Does our correspondent want a repetition of the barbarous experiment?

How does the Anglo-Saxon get along with the Anglo-Saxon—leaving the Negro entirely out of the question? Do they bill and coo and love and caress each other? Is the Anglo-Saxon capitalist so devoted to his Anglo-Saxon wage-slave that he shares his burden and makes him the equal partner of his wealth and joy? Are they not as widely separated as the earth and sky, and do they not fight each other to the death? Does not the white capitalist look down with contempt upon the white wage-slave? And don't you know that the plutocrat would feel himself pretty nearly, if not quite as outrageously, insulted to have his Anglo- Saxon wage-slave ask the hand of his daughter in marriage as if that slave were black instead of white?

Why are you not afraid that some Anglo-Saxon engine-wiper on the New York Central will ask the hand of Vanderbilt's daughter in marriage?

What social distinction is there between a white and a black deckhand on a Mississippi steamboat? Is it visible even with the aid of a microscope? They are both slaves, work side by side, sometimes a bunch of black slaves under a white "boss" and at other times a herd of white slaves under a black "boss." Not infrequently, you have to take a second look to tell them apart—but all are slaves and all are humans and all are robbed by their "superior" white brother who attends church, is an alleged follower of Jesus Christ, and has a horror of "social equality." To him "a slave is a slave for a' that"—when he bargains for labor-power he is not generally concerned about the color of the package, but if he is, it is to give the black preference because it can be bought at a lower price in the labor market, in which equality always prevails—the equality of intellectual and social debasement. To paraphrase Wordsworth:

A wage-slave by the river's brim
A simple wage-slave is to him
And he is nothing more.[2]

The man who seeks to arouse race prejudice among workingmen is not their friend. He who advises the white wageworker to look down upon the black wageworker is the enemy of both.

The capitalist has some excuse for despising the slave—he lives out of his labor, out of his life, and cannot escape his sense of guilt, and so he looks with contempt upon his victim. You can forgive the man who robs you, but you can't forgive the man you rob—in his haggard features, you read your indictment, and this makes his face so repulsive that you must keep it under your heels where you cannot see it.

One need not experiment with "sour dough" nor waste any time on "sour" literature turned into "Leopard Spots" to arrive at sound conclusions upon these points, and the true socialist delights not only in taking his position and speaking out, but in inviting and accepting without complaint all the consequences of his convictions, be they what they may.

Abraham Lincoln was a noble man, but he was not an abolitionist, and what he said in reference to the Negro was with due regard to his circumscribed environs, and, for the time, was doubtless the quintessence of wisdom, but he was not an oracle who spoke for all coming ages, and we are not bound by what he thought prudent to say in a totally different situation half a century ago.

The Socialist platform has not a word in reference to "social equality." It declares in favor of political and economic equality, and only he who denies this to any other human being is unfit for it.

Socialism will give all men economic freedom, equal opportunity to work, and the full product of their labor. Their "social" relations they will be free to regulate to suit themselves. Like religion, this will be an individual matter, and our Elgin Negro-hater can consider himself just as "superior" as he chooses, confine his social attentions exclusively to white folks, and enjoy his leisure time in hunting down the black specter who is bent on asking his daughter's hand in marriage.

What warrant has he to say that the height of the Negro's ambition is to marry a white woman? No more than a Negro has to say that the height of a white woman's ambition is to marry a Negro. The number of such cases is about equally divided, and it is so infinitesimally small that anyone who can see danger to society in it ought to have his visual organs treated for progressive exaggeration.

The normal Negro has ambition to rise. This is to his credit and ought to be encouraged. He is not asking, nor does he need, the white man's social favors. He can regulate his personal associations with entire satisfaction to himself, without Anglo-Saxon concessions.

Socialism will strike the economic fetters from his body, and he himself will do the rest.

Suppose another race as much "superior" to the white as the white is to the black should drop from the skies. Would our Illinois correspondent at once fall upon his knees and acknowledge his everlasting inferiority, or would he seek to overcome it and rise to the higher plane of his superiors?

The Negro, like the white man, is subject to the laws of physical, mental, and moral development. But in his case, these laws have been suspended. Socialism simply proposes that the Negro shall have full opportunity to develop his mind and soul, and this will in time emancipate the race from animalism, so repulsive to those especially whose fortunes are built up out of it.

The African is here and to stay. How came he to our shores? Ask your grandfathers, Mr. Anonymous, and if they will tell the truth you will, or should, blush for their crimes.

The black man was stolen from his native land, from his wife and child, brought to these shores, and made a slave. He was chained and whipped and robbed by his "white superior," while the son of his "superior" raped the black child before his eyes. For centuries he was kept in ignorance and debased and debauched by the white man's law.

The rape-fiend? Horrible!

Whence came he! Not by chance. He can be accounted for. Trace him to his source, and you will find an Anglo-Saxon at the other end. There are no rape-maniacs in Africa. They are the spawn of civilized lust.

Anglo-Saxon civilization is reaping and will continue to reap what it has sown.

For myself, I want no advantage over my fellow man, and if he is weaker than I, all the more is it my duty to help him.

Nor shall my door or my heart be ever closed against any human being on account of the color of his skin.

Mayor Jones and "All the People"†

January 1904

Mayor Jones, the prophet of the golden rule, denies the class struggle and proclaims himself "for all the people." He is for the exploiting capitalist as well as the exploited wageworker. Naturally he could not be against the one or the other and still be "for all the people." He declares his opposition to the wage system, but just how he can be *against* the system and *for* the class who uphold and get rich out of it and will fight for it to the last ditch, he has not yet explained.

Perhaps Mayor Jones expects the capitalists themselves to abolish the wage system and go to work for a living. As well expect spring pullets to pick themselves of their last pinfeather and walk into the kitchen and ask to be fricasseed.

From a man who in the present struggle is "for all the people," that is to say, for both sides, for master as well as slave, the following excerpts certainly sound strange and require a little explanation:

> The struggle for more wages will ever continue while the wage system lasts, until by an awakened social instinct and a more enlightened con-

† Published in *Wilshire's Magazine* [Toronto, ON], vol. 6, no. 1 (January 1904), 19–20.

> ception of our relation to each other we shall come to see that we are really brothers and must learn to live brotherly.
>
> * * *
>
> Workingmen must not only make common cause with the workingmen of their craft, but with every other craft under the shining sun. They must learn not only to make common cause with the workingmen of their nationality and their color, but with all colors.
>
> The capitalist will not hesitate to take his moneybags and go to the Orient if he can and make more money out of a Chinaman there than out of a white man here . . .
>
> It is the capitalistic spirit—the spirit that would separate man from man and brother from brother—which must be overcome, and to this end, let labor make its contribution and to the development of the idea of unity, of equality, liberty, and fraternity, if we hope to see the American ideal wrought out and democratic American conditions prevail, where every man can stand as an equal and a brother.[3]

The question is, what is Mayor Jones doing to abolish this wage system? At the last election, he supported the Democratic Party, that is, he is pledged in every fiber of his corrupt being to perpetuate wage-slavery.

Mayor Jones keeps telling us that he is a man without a party; that he has no use for a party; and yet when the campaign is on and election day rolls around and he has a chance to vote for the abolition of wage-slavery, we find him regularly in the field, whooping it up for a party which this partyless patriot knows will defend the wage system, with its robbery of the working class, while there is a breath in its moribund body.

It may be pertinent to ask Mayor Jones what "struggle" he has reference to? And if he is on both sides of it? Or if it has but one side?

Manifestly, the mayor sees a "struggle." If it is not a class struggle, what kind of a struggle is it? Will the mayor please explain if both sides of this struggle are opposed to the wage system? Is it not a fact that one side is fighting *for* that system and the other *against* it? Which side is Mayor Jones on?

If he is on the side of the working class, and a bona fide opponent of the wage system, then he is *against* the capitalist class; and if *against* the capitalist class, he is not for *all the people,* unless in his golden rule encyclopedia he finds that capitalists are in the mineral instead of the animal kingdom. However, that may be just at present the capitalists are *the people* by a good working majority, and if Mayor Jones is *for* them in the "struggle" he admits is going to abolish the wage system, he is not a socialist, nor is he for the working class, nor is he opposed to wage-slavery.

Mayor Jones makes out a tough case against the capitalist in the paragraph quoted above. All wage-slaves are alike to him. The Chinaman is as good as the American sovereign (?). Simply a question of price with the capitalist, and yet Mayor Jones is for him, for he is "for all the people."

Since Mayor Jones is for the capitalist, and the capitalist is for the wage system—in fact is its incarnation and will perish with it—it follows that he is also for wage-slavery, his disavowal to the contrary notwithstanding.

Mayor Jones, in the name of the working class, defends their exploiters; in the name of economic freedom votes for wage-slavery; in the name of a "free untrammeled soul," a "man without a party," he is cheek by jowl with a gang of machine politicians and supports the decrepit and corrupt Democratic Party.

According to Mayor Jones, it is the "capitalistic spirit" that is doing all the mischief. But how are we to extract the "capitalistic spirit" from the capitalist? And if we could extract the "spirit," the capitalist would be dead.

We socialists perfectly understand the "capitalistic spirit," but we are not wasting any time on the "spirit."

The only way to destroy the "capitalistic spirit," the breath of capitalism, is to destroy capitalism. And this means fight, and no living man or dead deity can be on both sides of this fight any more than he can go up on one elevator and down on another at the same time.

I feel a special interest in Mayor Jones because it was a speech of mine, delivered in Toronto in 1895, which started the mayor off, as he afterward admitted to me, on his career of agitation. I would like to see him take his stand where all doubt as to his allegiance to the working class would be removed. His present attitude is not only hazy, equivocal, and uncertain, but since he trains with and supports a capitalist party, he must be set down as the friend of the capitalist class and the enemy of the working class.

Personally, I have a kindly feeling toward Mr. Jones. Not only this, but I have such a friendly interest in him that I would like to see him make the record he has the brain and heart to make in the great struggle for emancipation from the cruelty and crime, the slavery and horror of capitalist despotism.

The eccentricities of Mayor Jones will not always amuse the people of Toledo and keep him in the mayor's office.

He is dallying on a foundation of shifting sand, and he will have to get on the rock or be swallowed up in oblivion.

Why Peabodyism Exists†

February 13, 1904

The name of Colorado ought to be changed to Colorussia. Not a vestige of democratic government is left there. The rule of military despotism is absolute. And this is as it should be. The working class of Colorado ordered it so, and their will is and shall and must always and everywhere be law. In the state elections last fall, all the workingmen of Colorado, organized and unorganized, with the exception of less than three thousand voters who voted the Socialist ticket—and many of these were not workingmen—voted for precisely what they are now getting. They have not the excuse of having been misled or betrayed by false leaders. The officers and leaders of the ALU and WF of M are class-conscious stalwarts in the labor movement. They are men of intelligence, courage, and honor, and this applies also to the press of the Western movement. These leaders were deserted early by the whole rank and file, who rushed pell-mell into the shambles and are now being mercilessly slaughtered for their treason.

The election returns of last fall show that an overwhelming majority of the members of the ALU and the WF of M voted for capitalist despotism in preference to social democracy—and this in defiance of the fact that their national organizations, through their delegates in convention assembled, had repudiated the Republican, Democratic, and Populistic sections of the capitalist party, and had declared unequivocally in favor of the Socialist Party. Following this, the state was canvassed over and over again by socialist agitators and speakers, but when election day came, the union men, so called, deserted the standards of their organizations, repudiated the action of their representatives, betrayed their union principles, and insulted their brave and conscientious leaders by supporting almost solidly the candidates of the mill- and mine-owning plutocracy.

This is the noted fact and Peabodyism is simply the fruit of that fact. Colorado workingmen are reaping exactly what they have sown.[4] It is good for them, galling as the crop may be, for it will make union men of them on election day, and it would seem that nothing else on earth would teach them their class interests and make them quit scabbing on their class at the polls.

† Published in *Social Democratic Herald,* vol. 6, no. 42, whole no. 289 (February 13, 1904), 1.

They knew that Peabody was the candidate of the mill and mine owners—that he would govern the workers and that the mine owners would govern the governor. Most of the workers of Colorado voted for him. All of them have got him. (Is it the concern of a union man how another votes?

Most of the rest went to the Populist graveyard and dug up its corpse and hugged it convulsively to their bosom. Those who voted for Peabody to govern them did so to please their economic masters. The rest voted for a "good man" to save them. Anything except confidence in, and support of, the one and only party that stood for and whose candidates were fighting for their class!

In 1894, they crucified Governor Davis H. Waite, because he stood by them instead of their masters. In 1904, they are crucified by retributive justice.

I thank whatever gods are entitled to their credit for Governor Peabody. He suits me in everything, except that he does not go far enough. He ought to make a bull pen of the whole state. An overwhelming majority of the workingmen voted for it and he ought not—and in fact cannot, without violating his official oath—disregard their wishes.

As an eye-opener for the working class, we are forced to yield the palm to Peabody. He is making more socialists than all the agitators combined. It almost seems as if Peabody is a socialist spy in the camp of the enemy. In any event, he is doing the business—teaching workers just what it means to elect capitalist candidates to govern them—"a consummation devoutly to be wished."[5]

The fight in Colorado is the result of the betrayal of the working class by the workers themselves on election day. They are in for it, and no power on earth can relieve them of the consequences of their acts.

To pour out sympathy on them is time wasted. To fight for them and while fighting to *tell them the truth, especially about themselves,* is the duty of those who are with them in the struggle.

The innocent suffer with the guilty, but the final outcome will be good for all. The guilty will learn better, and the innocent will be vindicated and strengthened.

May the strikers win, and above all may they learn to remember election day and keep it class-conscious.

ᔕ

President Gompers and President Mitchell declare that a union man has a right to vote as he pleases. Has he? Let us see. Before unions were organized, men claimed the right to work when they pleased. Most of them still claim it and keep out of unions. Parry says they have that right and that is his pivotal objection to unionism. Gompers and Mitchell say that a union man cannot work when he pleases—that he cannot work if by doing so he lowers the wages or otherwise injures his fellow men, that he must merge his individual interest as a worker in the larger interest of his class, that through the prosperity of his class his own is advanced. In other words, the union decides whether a man shall work or not. This vital principle of the individual, which involves his very life, he is compelled to surrender in the interest of his class.

Are men united in the trade unions that they may be divided at the polls?

Is it the *United Mine Workers* the day before the election and the *Divided Mine Workers* on election day?

Is not the labor question a political question?

Parry says a man has the right to work as he pleases. Gompers and Mitchell say a man has the right to vote as he pleases. Their position is essentially the same and leads to the same results.

The workingman has the ballot. Election day comes. He has now to decide if all the workers shall be ruled and robbed by a capitalist government, or whether they shall rule themselves as free men and enjoy the fruit of their labor.

That is the question the workingman is called upon to decide every election day.

Has he a right to vote as *he* pleases? And if he *pleases* to betray his class and vote for their masters, is he a union man, or is he a scab?

Has my fellow unionist the right to vote me into wage-slavery and still claim to be a union man? Is it not in fact the rankest kind of scabbing?

Gompers and Mitchell say it is none of the union's business how a member votes. I say that the union based upon this principle, or rather lack of principle, in this year 1904, is not a *union* at all in any intelligent sense—it is a *disunion* and promotes division where it is most fatal—at the ballot box.

The man who votes against his class is not a union man. He may wear a union badge as big as a mule-shoe, he may be ignorant, but whatever else he may be or not be, he is a scab. He betrays, like Judas, his fellow worker to his capitalist master, robs him of what his labor produces, impoverishes his family, starves his wife, deforms his children, and all this he does because, according to Gompers and Mitchell, "he can vote as he pleases," and the unions of his fellows have no right to object to his unalienable right to vote them into wage-slavery and still strut and swagger as a "union man."

Hell is full of such union (?) men. Give me the union man who is true to his class politically as well as economically, 365 days in the year, and 366 days in the leap year. That kind of a union man knows his duty and performs it and does not have to have it "forced down his throat" that it is treason to labor to vote for slavery.

The Coal Strike Surrender†

March 31, 1904

Terre Haute, Ind., March 31, 1904

Now that the threatened coal strike has ended in a tame surrender of a two years' scale at a reduction of wages virtually forced upon the miners by a coalition of their leaders with the operators, a certain small and obscure press dispatch—a mere word to the wise, yet sufficient at the time—takes on immense interest in its prophetic significance.

The delegates to the late Indianapolis convention of miners whom I had occasion to address will no doubt remember my words, and those who were angered because I told them in plain terms what has since come true almost to the letter will perhaps be willing to forgive me.

But to the dispatch. Here it is just as it was sent out by the Associated Press from Pittsburgh under date of March 6 [1904] and just as it appeared in the morning dailies of March 6:

> PITTSBURGH, Pa., March 6—The *Post* tomorrow will say:
>
> There was by no means a hopeless spirit among the returning coal operators from the Indianapolis convention with the miners which closed Saturday [March 5] with a disagreement.
>
> From the best of authority, the *Post* was informed yesterday that the break in the negotiations between the two interests is not a permanent one and that, by March 21, another meeting of joint subcommittees will be held quietly. The whole matter will again be discussed among them and a solution to the present difficulty sought. It was further said that there was every reason for believing that the ultimate end of the whole matter would be the acceptance of the lower rate by the miners, or the 85 cents a ton base for pick-mining, for the next two years.

Here we have it that the operators *knew in advance* that there would be *no strike* and that the miners would accept the reduction and this they knew

† Published as "Were the Coal Miners Headed Off!" in *Social Democratic Herald,* vol. 6, no. 50, whole no. 297 (April 9, 1904), 1. Reprinted as part of the pamphlet *Reply to John Mitchell* (Terre Haute: Standard Publishing Co., 1904), 5–9.

notwithstanding the fact that the convention, by a solid vote of the state, had refused to accept the reduction and virtually declared for a strike.

Let us examine the question a moment. The joint convention of miners and operators adjourned *sine die* March 5. No agreement had been reached. All negotiations were ended. A strike, so the papers declared, was inevitable. Only a miracle could prevent it.

The miners and operators returned to their homes. Preparations began for war. It was at this juncture that the above dispatch went out from Pittsburgh. It was doubtless intended as a "tip" to the capitalists and stock gamblers of the country, and was issued immediately upon the return of the Pennsylvania operators from the Indianapolis convention.

Pittsburgh, be it remembered, is the home of President Robbins of the Pittsburgh Coal Co. and floor leader and spokesman of the operators in all joint conventions with the miners. It is quite evident, therefore, that *"the best of authority"* quoted in the above dispatch was none other than Robbins, and it is equally evident that he knew what he was talking about for his prediction of surrender, made in face of the fact that the national convention had virtually declared for war, was fulfilled to the letter.

The question is, did Robbins, chief of the operators, have an understanding with Mitchell, president of the miners? It must be admitted that it looks that way. Proof may be lacking, but the circumstances combine to make that conclusion almost inevitable.

When the miners first met in convention, President Mitchell and the other leaders were quite aggressive. They were going to sweep all opposition before them and get what they wanted, for they had an organization that could and would carry the day.

A set of demands, including increased wages, was at once formulated, and the performance began. Mitchell, taking the floor for the miners, proved by the facts and figures that they were asking only what was reasonable, that the financial reports of the coal companies showed *large increases in profits* over the preceding years, that the operators could well afford to make the concessions, and that they, the miners, were "terribly in earnest" and that the United Mine Workers of America would under no possible circumstances "take a backward step."

As the fight progressed, the leaders of the miners made one concession after another until they had finally surrendered everything. But the operators were not satisfied. They had come with love in their hearts and a made-to-order, warranted-to-fit reduction of wages in their grips, just because they were all in the same economic class and their interests were therefore identical, and to prove it they permitted their own leaders to scale down the bulging wages of the opulent coal diggers.

But the delegates, having given up everything, balked at least. Even Mitchell's "masterful effort" on behalf of the operators fell flat.

The reduction would not go down.

The convention voted to fight, and the delegates went home to prepare for hostilities.

Now read the dispatch again in the light of what followed.

As soon as the convention adjourned, the leaders of the miners began to work upon the rank and file, very many of whom are so pitifully ignorant that they look upon a union official as a Chinaman does upon his joss.[6]

President Mitchell, from being "terribly in earnest" on behalf of the miners, became the special pleader of the operators.

Oh, what a transformation!

Mitchell, the labor leader, and Robbins, the labor exploiter, pooling issues and joining hands to force down the wages of mine slaves!

Oh, what a spectacle!

With all possible haste, the national and state leaders made the rounds among the faithful. The "dangerous" locals and districts were all visited and mass meetings held to save the operators.

The slaves had instinctively rebelled against the wage cut, and the rebellion must be put down by their own leaders if they expected the plaudits of the capitalist exploiters and the "well done" of the pulpit, press, and "public."

Alternate pleas, warnings, and threats were turned on until the fires were put out and the day was saved for the operators.

Only a little while ago, Gompers warned the capitalists that reductions of wages would not be tolerated, and solemnly enjoined his followers to resist them to the last.

Mitchell, Shaffer, and other lieutenants of Gompers are the active allies of the capitalists in enforcing reductions.

Watch the developments!

To conclude: The United Mine Workers of America have been struck by lightning.[7]

Darrow, Hearst, and the Democrats†

April 1, 1904

There has been a decided misunderstanding as to Mr. Darrow's political affiliations.[8] It is true that he has at times publicly addressed and temporarily affiliated with Republicans, Democrats, Populists, anarchists, single-taxers, and socialists; it is not true, however, that he has ever been a socialist, that he has ever pretended to be, or that he ever had any connection with the Socialist Party. It is therefore quite evident that there is no ground for the assumption that the socialists are surprised or disappointed because of Mr. Darrow's espousal of the Hearstocratic section of the Democratic Party. The Socialist Party has never claimed Mr. Darrow, and Mr. Darrow, beyond his well-known socialistic tendencies, has shown no sign of joining or supporting the socialist movement.

As a matter of fact, Mr. Darrow has always plumed himself upon being a freelance, and he has certainly given himself unlimited scope in his political maneuvering; and in this respect, at least, he is admirably fitted to address the Democratic Party, composed as it is of all the various and incongruous elements necessary to attract Mr. Darrow's versatile genius, and he should be at his best in that capacity.

Mr. Darrow was elected to the last legislature of Illinois as a Democrat. Great things were expected of him, but he seemed to have little influence with the "practical politicians" of the Sucker state. So far as I know, Mr. Darrow has always been a Democrat. While, as I have said, he has for the moment been identified with men and movements of all political castes, and of no political caste at all, when it has come down to action instead of mere play, he has always been a Democrat and never in a single instance a Socialist.

He has been Mayor Harrison's chief supporter, twice followed Bryan to defeat, and in every election, national, state, and municipal, has cast his lot with the Democratic Party.

Personally, I have always had the friendliest feelings for Mr. Darrow. Nor have I forgotten that during our trials he served us loyally and to the full extent of his splendid legal ability. But politically, I have not the slightest sympathy

† Published in an unspecified Terre Haute daily on April 1, 1904. Reprinted as "A Politician Rightly Labelled" in *Social Democratic Herald,* vol. 6, no. 51, whole no. 300 (April 30, 1904), 1.

with him, and in the light of certain advanced positions he has taken in the past, I cannot understand, nor can I help but regret his present political attitude.

As for the Democratic Party of today, it is writhing in the throes of disintegration; torn asunder by conflicting tendencies which cannot be harmonized. Its plutocratic wing and its democratic wing will not flap at the same time.

In such a chaotic state of affairs, the only hope lies in the nomination of a candidate for president who has no convictions at all, or who is so obscure that his convictions are totally unknown. A campaign based upon such a nomination will hardly inspire any extraordinary enthusiasm.

What is known as the Hearst movement has sprung from the wide and deep antipathy of the people to the plutocracy and the trusts. Hearst and his element are smart enough to see the drift and are in politics because they believe they can ride into power on the popular wave of anti-trust sentiment. The Hearst movement represents no vital principle whatever. Its pretended democracy is a sham. No such movement would be possible were it not for the dense ignorance of the people. With childlike faith, they believe that Mr. Hearst, as president, would, like a modern Goliath, slay the trust octopus and lead his children triumphantly into the promised land.

The papers of Mr. Hearst have shrewdly catered to the socialist sentiment just far enough to appeal to its available support and, having done this, they coolly wash their hands of all interest in or connection with the socialist movement.

The socialist understands Hearst and his office hunt to a nicety. If he is nominated, he will serve them the good purpose of purging the socialist movement of all the muddle-brained element who are with it one day and against it the next, and who will find congenial company in the middle and muddle class following of the latest Moses.

The fact that Mr. Hearst has not only a "barrel" but a vat is making his campaign, especially the preliminary stages of it, a carnival of 16 to 1 glory.[9]

Crimes of Capitalism in Colorado†

April 9, 1904

The arrest and deportation of Mother Jones and the arrest and imprisonment of Charles H. Moyer,[10] the lion-hearted president of the Western Federation of Miners, are among the latest outrages in the daily budget of crime reported from Colorado.

The crimes of the capitalists and their henchmen under the law-and-order administration of their executive utensil multiply so rapidly that it requires a swift pen to keep the record.

And the record must be kept to the minutest detail, for when the day of final accounting comes, as come it will as surely as the green earth rolls sunward, the capitalist class will settle by the books to the last cry of agony and the last groan of despair wrung from the misery of their crucified and exiled victims.

The midnight assault of the brutal soldiery upon Comrade Floaten[11]—than whom a truer comrade does not live—the beastly insult to his pleading wife, the violent deportation of Guy Miller, president of the Telluride union and his comrades; the lashing of a union man to a telephone pole solely because of his being a union man; the jailing of inoffensive citizens, and the outrages upon defenseless females are all charged up in red letters in the book of remembrance.

Governor Peabody and his accessories will answer to the last line of the last indictment drawn by an awakening justice at the bar of an aroused working class.

The coming day of judgment is slow, but it is sure.

And the memory of the working class is long—they do not forget.

At times the blood boils with indignation, but we must keep cool, keep calm—cool and calm and resolute.

The talk about armed attack by the unarmed worker is criminal folly—worse still, it is suicide.

The time may come for that, but it is not now. That is the program of Peabody and his mercenary hirelings to incite attack that the blood of union men may flow like mountain streams.

Have you forgotten how the working class in Colorado voted but a few months ago? Well, that is the way they will shoot today.

---

† Published in *Chicago Socialist,* vol. 6, whole no. 266 (April 9, 1904), 1.

Should armed collision now ensue in consequence of excited councils, the brave and brainy union men would pay the forfeit with their lives, and the movement in the state would be crushed and paralyzed.

These are the days to preach the class struggle in Colorado. Every day makes it clearer; every outrage confirms and emphasizes its commanding truth. The real danger comes with the cry to "bury Peabody beneath an avalanche of votes."

The unthinking will rush from the frying pan into the fire. In their eagerness to bury Peabody, they will forget Peabodyism. To bury Peabody will be time wasted if capitalism, of which he is but the spawn, is overlooked.

The Democratic Party will freely proffer its services in the burying of Peabody and passionately proclaim its sympathy and friendship.

Trust it no more than you would the Republican Party.

The only difference from the workingman's point of view is that one is run in the interest of a small number of large exploiters, and the other in the interest of a large number of small exploiters.

They are both against the working class.

The Republican Peabody will be duplicated, if the workers so will it, by a Democratic Nobody. The capitalist class will rule as before, and bull pens will do business at the old stands.

The Socialist Party is the party to support, the working-class party, the deadly and uncompromising foe of capitalism and wage-slavery.

Arouse, ye workingmen!

Open your eyes to the class struggle!

Join and support the only party that stands squarely upon the class struggle as the basis of its revolutionary character. The Republican, Democratic, and Populist parties are all capitalist parties, all for wage-slavery, all against the working class.

Mother Jones in exile, Charles Moyer, your brave leader, in jail!

Have you red blood in your veins?

Has you manhood rotted into cowardice?

Wake up and take your place in the class struggle!

For the desecration of the flag, your leader is in jail. What flag? The flag of the capitalist class—the flag that floats above the bull pens of Colorado. The wholesome truths he stamped upon its stripes are your shame and your masters' crime.

Rally to the red standard of international socialism, the symbol of proletarian revolt, and the workers of Colorado and all the world shall yet be free.

An Ideal Labor Press[†]

May 1904

The primal consideration in the present industrial system is profit. All other things are secondary. Profit is the lifeblood of capital—the vital current of the capitalist system—and when it shall cease to flow, the system will be dead.

The capitalist is the owner of the worker's tools. Before the latter can work, he must have access to the capitalist's tool house and permission to use the master's tools. What he produces with these tools belongs to the master, to whom he must sell his labor at the market price. The owner of the tools is therefore master of the man.

Only when the capitalist can extract a satisfactory profit from his labor-power is the worker given a job or allowed to work at all.

Profit first; labor, life, love, liberty—all these must take second place.

In such a system, labor is in chains, and the standard of living, if such it may be called, is cornerstoned in crusts and rags. Under such conditions, ideas and ideals are not prolific among the sons and daughters of toil. Slavery does not excite lofty aspirations nor inspire noble ideals.

The tendency is to sodden irresolution and brutish inertia. But this very tendency nourishes the germ of resistance that ripens into the spirit of revolt.

The labor movement is the child of slavery—the offspring of oppression—in revolt against the misery and suffering that gave it birth. Its splendid growth is the marvel of our time, the forerunner of freedom, the hope of mankind.

Ten thousand times has the labor movement stumbled and fallen and bruised itself, and risen again; been sized by the throat and choked and clubbed into insensibility; enjoined by courts, assaulted by thugs, charged by the militia, shot down by regulars, traduced by the press, frowned upon by public opinion, deceived by politicians, threatened by priests, repudiated by renegades, preyed upon by grafters, infested by spies, deserted by cowards, betrayed by traitors, bled by leeches, and sold out by leaders; but, notwithstanding all this, and all these, it is today the most vital and potential power this planet has

† Published in the *International Metal Worker* [Chicago], May 1904, unspecified pages. Reprinted in *The Worker* [New York], vol. 14, no. 8 (May 22, 1904), 4. Included in *Debs: His Life, Writings, and Speeches* (1908), 239–42, in which it is wrongly attributed to *The Metal Worker,* a different publication.

ever known, and its historic mission of emancipating the workers of the world from the thralldom of the ages is as certain of ultimate realization as the setting of the rising sun.

The most vital thing about this world movement is the educational propaganda—its capacity and power to shed light in the brain of the working class, arouse them from their torpor, develop their faculties for thinking, teach them their economic class interests, effect their solidarity, and imbue them with the spirit of the impending social revolution.

In this propaganda, the life breath of the movement, the press is paramount to all other agencies and influences, and the progress of the press is a sure index of the progress of the movement.

Unfortunately, the workers lack intelligent appreciation of the importance of the press; they also lack judgment and discrimination in dealing with the subject, and utterly neglect some good papers, and permit them to perish, which others that are anything but helpful or beneficial to the cause they are supposed to represent are liberally patronized, and flourish at the expense of the ignorance and stupidity that support them.

The material prosperity of a labor paper today is no guarantee of its moral or intellectual value. Indeed, some of the most worthless labor publications have the finest mechanical appearance and are supported by the largest circulations. Such a press is not only not a help of labor, but a millstone about its neck that only the awakening intelligence of the working class can remove.

How thoroughly alive the capitalists are to the power of the press! And how assiduously they develop and support it, that it may in turn buttress their class interests. The press is one of the most valuable assets, and, as an investment, pays the highest dividends.

When there is trouble between capital and labor, the press volleys and thunders against labor and its unions and leaders and all other things that dare to breathe against the sacred rights of capital. In such a contest, labor is dumb, speechless, it has no press that reaches the public, and must submit to the vilest calumny, the most outrageous misrepresentation.

The lesson has been taught in all the languages of labor and written in the blood of its countless martyred victims. Labor must have a press as formidable as the great movement of the working class requires to worthily represent its dignity and fearlessly and uncompromisingly advocate its principles.

Every member of a trade union should feel himself obligated to do his full share in the important work of building up the press of the labor movement; he should at least support the paper of his union, and one or more of the papers of his party, and, above all, he should read them and school himself in the art of intelligent criticism, and let the editor hear from him when he has a criticism to offer or a suggestion to make.

The expense of supporting the labor press is but a trifle to the individual member—less than the daily outlay for other trifles that are of no benefit and can easily be dispensed with.

The editor of a labor paper is of far more importance to the union and the movement than the president or any other officer of the union. He ought to be chosen with special reference to his knowledge upon the labor question and his fitness to advocate and defend the economic interests of the class he represents.

The vast amount of capitalist advertising some labor publications carry certifies unerringly to the worthlessness of their literary contents. Capitalists do not, as a rule, advertise in labor papers that are loyal to working-class interests. It is only on condition that the advertising colors and controls the editorial that the capitalist generously allows his patronage to go to the labor paper.

The workingman who wants to read a labor paper with the true ring, one that ably, honestly, and fearlessly speaks for the working class, will find it safer to steer clear of those that are loaded with capitalist advertising and make his selection from those that are nearly or quite boycotted by the class that lives and thrives upon the slavery of the working class.

The labor press of today is not ideal, but it is improving steadily, and the time will come when the ideal labor press will be realized; when the labor movement will command editors, writers, journalists, artists of the first class; when hundreds of papers, including dailies in the large cities, will gather the news and discuss it from the labor standpoint; when illustrated magazines and periodicals will illuminate the literature of labor and all will combine to realize our ideal labor press and bless the way to victory.

Speech Accepting the 1904 Presidential Nomination of the Socialist Party of America†

May 6, 1904

In the councils of the Socialist Party, the collective will is supreme. *[Applause.]* Personally, I could have wished to remain in the ranks, to make my record, humble though it might be, fighting unnamed and unhonored side by side with my comrades. I accept your nomination, not because of any honor it confers—because in the socialist movement no comrade can be honored except as he honors himself by his fidelity to the movement. *[Applause.]* I accept your nomination because of the confidence it implies, because of the duty it imposes. I cannot but wish that I may in a reasonable measure meet your expectations; that I may prove myself fit and worthy to bear aloft in the coming strife the banner of the working class *[applause]*; that by my utterances and by my conduct, not in an individual capacity, but as your representative, I may prove myself worthy to bear the standard of the only party that proposes to emancipate my class from the thralldom of the ages. *[Applause.]*

It is my honor to stand in the presence of a very historic convention, and I would that Karl Marx might be here today *[applause]*; I would that Lassalle and Engels, the men who long before the movement had its present standing wrought and sacrificed to make it possible for me to stand in this magnificent presence—I wish it were possible for them to share in the glories of this occasion. We are on the eve of battle today. We are ready for the contest. *[Applause.]* We are eager for the fray. *[Applause.]* We depart from here with the endorsement of a convention that shall challenge undisputed the approval of the working class of the world. *[Applause.]* The platform upon which we stand is the first American utterance upon the subject of international socialism. *[Applause.]* Hitherto we have repeated, we have reiterated, we have followed. For the first time in the history of the American movement we have realized

† Published as "Debs' Speech of Acceptance" in William Mailly (ed.), *National Convention of the Socialist Party held at Chicago, Illinois, May 1 to 6, 1904: Stenographic Report by Wilson E. McDermut* (Chicago: National Committee of the Socialist Party, 1904), 254–5. Reprinted as part of the pamphlet *Speeches of Acceptance of Eugene V. Debs and Ben Hanford* (Chicago: National Committee of the Socialist Party, 1904).

the American expression of that movement. There is not a line, not a word in that platform which is not revolutionary, which is not clear, which does not state precisely and properly the position of the American movement. We leave this convention standing on this platform, to throw down the gauntlet to the capitalist enemy *[applause]*, to challenge the capitalist oppressor to do battle for the perpetuation of a system that keeps in chains those in whose name we meet today. *[Applause.]*

There is a Republican Party; the dominant capitalist party of this time; the party that has its representative in the White House; the party that dominates both branches of the Congress; the party that controls the Supreme Court; the party that absolutely controls the press; the party that gives inspiration to the subsidized pulpit; the party that controls every force of government; the party that is absolutely in power in every department of our activity. And as a necessary result we find that corruption is rampant; that the Congress of the United States dare not respond to the demands of the people to open the sources of corruption from which the lava stream flows down the mountain sides; that they adjourned long before the hour struck for adjournment in order that they might postpone the inevitable. *[Applause.]*

There is a Democratic Party—*[A Voice: "Where?"]*—a party that has not stock enough left to proclaim its own bankruptcy *[laughter and applause]*; an expiring party that stands upon the crumbling foundations of a dying class; a party that is torn by dissension; a party that cannot unite; a party that is looking backward and hoping for the resurrection of the men who gave it inspiration a century ago; a party that is appealing to the cemeteries of the past *[applause]*; a party that is trying to vitalize itself by its ghosts, by its corpses, by those who cannot be heard in their own defense. *[Applause.]* Thomas Jefferson would scorn to enter a modern Democratic convention. He would have as little business there as Abraham Lincoln would have in a modern Republican convention. *[Applause.]* If they were living today, they would be delegates to this convention. *[Tremendous applause.]*

The Socialist Party meets these two parties face to face, without a semblance of apology, without an attempt at explanation, scorning to compromise, it throws down the gage of battle and declares that there is but one solution of what is called the labor question, and that is by the complete overthrow of the capitalist system. *[Applause.]*

You have honored me in the magnitude of the task that you have imposed upon me, far beyond the power of my weak words to express. I can simply say that obedient to your call I respond. *[Applause.]* Responsive to your command, I am here. I shall serve you to the limit of my capacity. My controlling ambition shall be to bear the standard aloft where the battle waxes thickest. *[Applause.]* I shall not hesitate as the opportunity comes to me to voice the emancipating gospel of the socialist movement. I shall be heard in the coming campaign *[applause]* as often, and as decidedly, and as emphatically, as revolutionarily *[applause]*, as uncompromisingly *[applause]* as my ability, my strength, and my fidelity to the movement will allow. I invoke no aid but that which springs from the misery of my class *[applause]*; no power that does not spring spontaneous from the prostrate body of the workers of the world. Above all other things, I realize that for the first time in the history of all the ages there is a working-class movement *["Hear, hear!" and applause]*—perfectly free from the sentimentality of those who riot in the misery of the class who are in that movement. On this occasion above all others, my comrades, we are appealing to ourselves, we are bestirring ourselves, we are arousing the working class, the class that through all of the ages has been oppressed, crushed, suffered, for the one reason that through all the centuries of the past this class has lacked the consciousness of its overmastering power that shall give it control and make it master of the world. *[Applause.]* This class is just beginning to awaken from the torpor of the centuries *[applause]*, and the most hopeful sign of the times is that from the dull, the dim eye of the man who is in this class, there goes forth for the first time in history the first gleam of intelligence, the first sign of the promise that he is waking up and that he is becoming conscious of his power; and when he, through the inspiration of the socialist movement, shall become completely conscious of that power, he will overthrow the capitalist system and bring the emancipation of his class. *[Great applause.]*

To consecrate myself to my small part of this great work is my supreme ambition. *[Applause.]* I can hope only to do that part which is expected of me so well that my comrades, when the final verdict is rendered, will say, "He was not a candidate for president; he did not aspire to hold office; he did not try to associate his name with the passing glories, but he did prove himself worthy to be a member of the Socialist Party *[applause]*; he proved his right to a place in the international socialist movement of the world." *[Applause.]* If when this little work shall have been completed, this can be said of me, my acceptance of your nomination will have been so much more completely made than I could hope to frame it in weak words, that I close not with the decided utterance, but with the wish and the hope and the ambition that when the fight has been fought, when the task you have imposed upon me has been performed so far as it lies in the power of an individual to perform that task, that my acceptance of the honor you have conferred upon me will have been made and that your wisdom and your judgment will have been vindicated by the membership of the party throughout the country.

From the depths of my heart, I thank you. I thank you and each of you, and through you I thank those you represent. I thank you not from my lips merely. I thank you from the depths of a heart that is responsive to your consideration. We shall meet again. We shall meet often, and when we meet finally, we shall meet in much larger numbers to ratify the coming of the Socialist Republic. *[Great and prolonged applause.]*

Our First National Campaign: Interview with the *Terre Haute Sunday Tribune*†

May 15, 1904

No definite plans for the campaign have as yet been formulated, and the National Executive Committee will not begin actual work until about the first of July. Then will follow the first real national campaign the Socialists have ever conducted. In the convention last week in Chicago, every state was represented, and every state now has an active party organization.

Since the national election four years ago, there has been an unceasing propaganda of education in every part of the country, and the party has now assumed national proportions and will be recognized as the campaign proceeds as a factor in the politics of the country.

As to the plans and methods to be adopted, much will depend on the outcome of the Democratic convention at St. Louis.[12] It is conceded, of course, that Roosevelt will be the Republican nominee. Assuming that Parker[13] will be nominated by the Democrats, I take it that there will be a decided defection on the part of the radical element of that party. The leaders of the Democratic Party are now attempting to harmonize the party organization, which, to me,

---

† Originally published in the *Terre Haute Sunday Tribune,* May 15, 1904, original title and page unknown. Reprinted as "Debs Gives His Views of the Coming Campaign," *Social Democratic Herald,* vol. 7, no. 3, whole no. 303 (May 21, 1904), 1.

appears to be an impossible task.

In the last two campaigns, the radical element secured control and lost. It now seems to be clear that the conservative section will secure the upper hand, and to effect as far as possible a reconciliation of the conflicting factions, a compromise candidate, or at least one who has not been prominently identified with either section, will likely be chosen in the person of Mr. Parker or Mr. McClellan.[14] Allowing that this will be the outcome of the St. Louis convention, it seems quite probable that those who are demanding the nomination of Mr. Hearst will refuse to support the nominee, and that many of them will drift into the socialist movement. Then, in that case, the vote of the Socialist Party will be augmented in a degree that will prove a surprise to the country.

The *St. Louis Globe-Democrat,* in an editorial a few days ago, made substantially this forecast and issued notice to the politicians of both the old parties to keep their eyes on the socialists.

Another factor of decided importance in the approaching campaign will be the decline in industrial activity. The state of industry is always a controlling influence in national politics. Four years ago, industry was at high tide and the Socialist vote was comparatively small. This year the tide is running out, notwithstanding the efforts that are put forth to hold it in abeyance, and the party slogan, "Let well enough alone" will not have the effect it had four years ago, when labor generally was employed and workingmen were measurably satisfied with their conditions.

Many of the large industrial enterprises, including the steel mills, the barometers of trade, are already compelled to curtail their working forces and reduce wages, the immediate effect of which will be to create discontent among the workers, and this will find expression in a largely increased vote for the Socialist Party. Taking advantage of this, they will place thousands of speakers in the field.

It is always venturesome to guess in the game of politics, but I would not be at all surprised to see the vote of the Socialists run into seven figures. My personal plans are not yet arranged. I expect, however, to speak in all the important cities, closing the campaign in Terre Haute.

The candidate for the vice presidency on our ticket is Mr. Ben Hanford, a printer in the employ of the *New York Journal,* and a man well-enough known all over the country for his eloquence and effectiveness on the rostrum. He will make a thorough canvass.

Stray Leaves from an Agitator's Notebook†

June 1904

Twenty-nine years ago, on February 27 last, I first joined a labor union. On that day, my name was enrolled as a member of the Brotherhood of Locomotive Firemen, and the very hour of my initiation I became an agitator. It seemed to be the very thing I had been looking for—and I was ready for it. The whole current of my life was changed that day. I have a distinct recollection of the initiation and can still see the faces of the 21 "tallow pots" who made up the group of charter members, nearly all of whom, in the mutations of railroad life, have since gone over the range. A new purpose entered my life, a fresh force impelled me as I repeated the obligation to serve the "brotherhood," and I left that meeting with a totally different and far loftier ambition than I had ever known before.

I had served my apprenticeship in the railroad shops and, being the only "cub" at the time, knew what it was to have a dozen bosses at once and all the grievances I could carry without spilling.

Later, as a locomotive fireman, I learned something of the hardships of the rail in snow, sleet, and hail, of the ceaseless danger that lurks along the iron highway, the uncertainty of employment, scant wages, and the altogether trying lot of the workingman, so that from my very boyhood I was made to feel the wrongs of labor, and from the consciousness of these, there also sprang the conviction that one day they would all be righted.

On the day I became a member of the union, I was also elected one of its officers, and for 21 years without a break, official position in some capacity claimed my service.

It was during this time that I organized the Brotherhood of Railroad Brakemen, now the Brotherhood of Railroad Trainmen, and helped to organize the Switchmen's Mutual Aid Association and a number of other organizations. The American Railway Union was the best of them all. It united all the workers in the service. That is why the railroad corporation declared it to be the worst of all.

For two years after the Pullman strike, I was shadowed by railroad detectives, east, west, north, and south. The companies were determined to break up

† Published as "Stray Leaves from the Notebook of an Agitator" in *The Comrade,* vol. 3, no. 9 (June 1904), 187–9.

the union. We tried organizing in secret. It would not work. The spy could not be kept out. At Providence, Rhode Island, I organized at midnight in my bedroom at the hotel. The men had come from different directions, one at a time. The next morning, they all were called into the office, paid off, and discharged. At New Decatur, Alabama, we had 111 members obligated in secret, one at a time. A member so admitted was not supposed to know who else belonged. One morning, 18 of the more prominent of these were summoned to the office. The roll of the 111 offenders was read off to them. For the first time, they knew who their fellow members were. The officials had ferreted out the information and gave it to them from the company records. The 18 leaders were discharged outright. The remaining 88 were ordered to produce their final withdrawal cards from the American Railway Union within ten days. Hundreds of similar instances might be cited.

The railroad managers of the whole country were up in arms to annihilate the organization. From Maine to Arizona, from Florida to British Columbia, their bloodhounds were sniffing for the scent. At Williams, Arizona, two of them who had followed me from Albuquerque attempted to break into my room, and in trying to force the door the bolt was sprung so the door could not be opened, and I had to arouse the hotel attendants by a succession of yells, one of whom climbed over the transom armed with a screwdriver and removed the lock and bolt so as to release me in time to catch the four o'clock morning train for The Needles. The landlady was up, and all was excitement. She knew the detectives and despised them. Her parting words were: "Watch out for the scoundrels or they'll get you yet." When the train pulled in, I got aboard, and so did the sleuths. One of them, the smaller of the two, who, as I observed, had a game leg, was quite friendly and offered me an "eye-opener" from a quart bottle. The other, who was tall and had but one eye and the most murderous countenance I ever saw, which he kept shaded with the brim of an enormous slouch hat, had nothing to say. At Needles, an incident occurred which will make another story.

The railroad managers had a mortal dread of the ARU. They feared its very ghost. As the train stopped at Las Vegas on the return trip, the editor of one of the papers got aboard for an interview. He imparted some quiet information he had obtained. Said he: "The wires here have been busy with your name. Not an employee will dare to come near you. The officials have prepared for any possible emergency. The fact is they are quite alarmed. They fear they may have it all over again, and even your shadow passing over the line would scare them."

There was not the least bit of danger. The ARU was riddled with bullets and breathing its last as a railroad union.

The railroads were determined to stamp it out and forever. It was a dastardly conspiracy against vested interests! Its chief object was not to bury the dead, but to unite and emancipate the living.

But instead of stamping it out, they stamped it into the living labor movement. The American Railroad Union became the Social Democracy. Thanks to the railroad companies for driving the union into politics, working-class politics! Most of this power is still latent, but the start has been made, and the rest are bound to come.

∽

A little less than two years ago, at Trinidad, Colorado, I was the guest of the railroad boys. I slept at their boardinghouse, ate at their table, and was once more one of them. Two of them were known for their Damon and Pythias friendship.[15] This is the story briefly told:

Jack had been a local leader in the ARU strike, and when it was over was blacklisted and hunted with relentless fury. One night, far from his former home, ragged, half-starved, and shivering with cold, he sat crouched in the corner of a boxcar loaded with machinery and rattling over the rough joints of a western road. Along toward morning, he discovered that he was not the sole occupant of the car. His private car had evidently been invaded during the night. He hailed the intruder.

"Hello, there!"

"Hello, back at you!"

The cut and fashion of their clothes and the general style of their outward appearance were near enough alike to mark them as twins.

"How're you fixed?"

"Not a sou."

"Same here."

"Shake."

Both were traveling under assumed names, and both had good cause to be suspicious. But after a while, their mutual misery dissolved the restraint. They warmed to each other, and they needed to, for they had hunger of the heart as well as the body.

"So, you're an old railroad man, eh?"

"That's right!"

"Anything to show for it?"

"Only this, partner, but hobo though I be, I wouldn't take a farm for it."

Saying this, Jack's companion reached into his rags and pulled out a traveling card of the ARU that looked as far gone as its owner.

The two tramps embraced and vowed their mutual fidelity as the train reached its destination.

Then followed weeks of tramping, privation, and hunger pangs. The two became one, sleeping in the same straw-stack at night, covered by the same rags as they plodded wearily along, and sharing the same "handout" along the highway.

Finally, Jack, through the influence of an old friend, struck a job. The "pie-card" he bought, his first investment, was for both. When payday came, every cent was shared. Jack and his friend once more had decent clothes, and with Jack's influence his partner soon had a job.

From that day these tramps have been as brothers. Their attachment for each other is beautiful, almost pathetic. The love they bear each other is holy love born of bruised and bleeding hearts crushed beneath the iron hoof of despotic power.

And thus are they who suffer for righteousness rewarded!

What Rockefeller has wealth enough to buy such a royal possession as the priceless heritage of these two tramps?

ꟹ

Not long ago, I stopped at Salamanca, New York, the first time in 26 years. My first visit was not for my health. I was put off there, and it was two days before I managed to get out of town in the caboose of a freight train. I had the same experience several times before finally reaching Port Jervis, the Mecca of my pilgrimage, where Joshua Leach, the grand master of the Brotherhood of Locomotive Firemen, then had his headquarters.

My late visit was different. I was escorted to the opera house with the trade unions and many others in the cheering procession while the band was playing "There'll Be a Hot Time in the Old Town Tonight."

My impression of Salamanca was altogether more favorable than that I received some five and twenty years ago when I started out in callow youth without scrip in my purse to save the world.

ꟹ

For just one night, I was general manager of a great railroad, though I never received any salary for the service I rendered in that capacity.

The strike on the Great Northern, extending from St. Paul to the coast, was settled on the evening of May 1, 1894. It was a complete victory for the ARU.

President James J. Hill and I had shaken hands and declared the hatchet buried. He said he was glad it was over and assured me that he had no feeling of resentment. As we stood chatting in his office, he said: "By the way, Debs, you'll have to be my general manager tonight, for the men won't go to work except by your orders." I said: "All right, sir, I'll guarantee that by morning the trains will all be running on schedule time." He seemed to be nettled, and I did not blame him when he said: "How about my wages? I too am an employee of the Great Northern Railway. And since everybody gets a raise, where do I come in?" He laughed heartily when I answered: "Join the American Railway Union and we'll see that you get a square deal."

And then I assumed the duties of general manager. The men all along the line were extremely suspicious. They had been betrayed before and were taking no chances. The chief operator sat at the keys while I dictated the orders. The messages were soon speeding over the wires. At some places, there was no trouble. At others there was no little trouble to convince the men that there was no trickery about it and that the orders bearing my signature were genuine.

At last we had every point on the line started except one, and the answer from there was: "The whole town is drunk and celebrating. Will be ready for duty in the morning." Nor did they cease celebrating until daylight, and then all hands reported for duty.

When I left the Great Northern headquarters, all the trains were moving, the shops, yards, and offices were throbbing with activity, and everybody was happy.

My service as general manager of the Great Northern was entirely satisfactory to President Hill, as he assured me when I left there, but I never applied for membership in the General Managers' Association.

✥

It was not long after this before President Hill and our own members wired me as to my interpretation of certain clauses of the agreement. It was evident that trouble was brewing again. I went to St. Paul on the first train. Our committee was promptly convened, but Mr. Hill could not be found. No one knew where he was. It struck me that delay was dangerous, and that prompt action was necessary. We at once summoned Charles A. Pillsbury, the millionaire miller, since deceased, and a personal friend of Mr. Hill who had taken an active interest in the previous strike and settlement. Mr. Pillsbury and some of his associates came to the hall.

Mr. Pillsbury said if the agreement had been violated, he did not know it. He did not know where Mr. Hill was and suggested that we would better wait patiently until he returned. He hoped we would not be rash and that there would be no trouble. When he took his seat, I got up. "Mr. Pillsbury," said I, "if Mr. Hill is not here, or if there is not someone here to act for him within 30 minutes, we will tie up the Great Northern from end to end." The hall rang with applause. Within 15 minutes, Mr. Hill was in the hall, we went into a back room, and in about 30 minutes more everything was adjusted, and for the second time the victory of the ARU was complete.

ᔓ

In the fall of 1896, I addressed a great political gathering at Duluth, Minnesota.[16] The trade union banners were for the first time in a political procession. It was a red-letter day. The crowd was immense. No hall was large enough, and as it was too chilly for outdoors, arrangements were made to hold the meeting in the old streetcar stables. The roof was low, but there was ample room, and this was what we needed. Just after I got started, some man interrupted. Not understanding what he said, I paused and asked him to repeat his remark. "I said you're all right," he exclaimed. Within a few feet of him towered a fellow who seemed seven feet tall. His eyes blazed daggers at the first party as he growled, "By God, you'd better!" The crowd cheered and there was not further interruption that night.

ᔓ

An introduction I once received is good for a hearty laugh every time I recall the incident. There was intense prejudice against me, and the young man who had been selected to introduce me to the audience concluded he would try to disarm it. The house was jammed. This was his first experience. He got along quite well till he forgot his lines. And then he closed somewhat abruptly after this fashion: "Mr. Debs is hated by some people because he has been in strikes. This is not right. It is the law of nature to defend yourself. Only a coward will refuse to stand up for his rights. Why, even a dog will growl if you try to deprive him of the bone he is gnawing, a cat will scratch in self-defense, a bee will sting to protect itself, a goat will butt you if you get in his way, while you all know what a jackass will do if you monkey with him. Ladies and gentlemen, this is Mr. Debs, who will now address you."

He brought down the house and was immensely pleased with his first effort on the public platform.

Unionism and Socialism: A Plea for Both†

circa June 15, 1904

The labor question, as it is called, has come to be recognized as the foremost of our time. In some form, it thrusts itself into every human relation, and directly or indirectly has a part in every controversy.

A thousand "solutions" of the labor question find their way into print, but the question not only remains unsolved, but steadily assumes greater and graver proportions. The nostrums have no effect other than to prove their own inefficiency.

There has always been a labor question since man first exploited man in the struggle for existence, but not until its true meaning was revealed in the development of modern industry did it command serious thought or intelligent consideration, and only then came any adequate conception of its importance to the race.

Man has always sought the mastery of his fellow man. To enslave his fellow in some form and to live out of his labor has been the mainspring of human action.

To escape submission, not in freedom, but in mastery over others, has been the controlling desire, and this has filled the world with slavery and crime.

In all the ages of the past, human society has been organized and maintained upon the basis of the exploitation and degradation of those who toil. And so it is today.

The chief end of government has been and is to keep the victims of oppression and injustice in subjection.

The men and women who toil and produce have been and are at the mercy of those who wax fat and scornful upon the fruit of their labor.

The labor question was born of the first pang of protest that died unvoiced in the breast of unrequited toil.

The labor movement of modern times is the product of past ages. It has come to us for the impetus of our day, in pursuit of its worldwide mission of emancipation.

Unionism, as applied to labor in the modern sense, is the fruit and flower of the last century.

---

† Published as a pamphlet by Debs (Terre Haute: Standard Publishing Co., 1904).

In the United States, as in other countries, the trade union dates from the beginning of industrial society.

During the colonial period of our history, when agriculture was the principal pursuit, when the shop was small and work was done by hand with simple tools, and the worker could virtually employ himself, there was no unionism among the workers.

When machinery was applied to industry, and mill and factory took the place of the country blacksmith shop; when the workers were divorced from their tools and recruited in the mills; when they were obliged to compete against each other for employment; when they found themselves in the labor market with but a low bid or none at all upon their labor-power; when they began to realize that as toolless workingmen they were at the mercy of the tool-owning masters, the necessity for union among them took root, and as industry developed, the trade union movement followed in its wake and became a factor in the struggle of the workers against the aggressions of their employers.

In his search for the beginnings of trade unionism in our country, Prof. Richard T. Ely, in his *Labor Movement in America,* says:

> I find no traces of anything like a modern trade union in the colonial period of American history, and it is evident on reflection that there was little need, if any, of organization on the part of labor at that time.
>
> * * *
>
> Such manufacturing, as was found, consisted largely in the production of values-in-use. Clothing, for example, was spun and woven, and then converted into garments in the household for its various members. The artisans comprised chiefly the carpenter, the blacksmith, and the shoemaker, many of whom worked in their own little shops with no employees, while the number of subordinates in any one shop was almost invariably small, and it would probably have been difficult to find a journeyman who did not expect, in a few years, to become an independent producer.[17]

This was the general condition from the labor standpoint at the close of the eighteenth century. But with the dawn of the new century and the application of machinery and the spread of industry that followed came the beginning of the change. The workers gradually organized into unions and began to take active measures to increase their wages and otherwise improve their condition. Referring to this early period in the rise of unionism, the same author records the incident of one of the first strikes as follows:

> Something very like a modern strike occurred in the year 1802. The sailors in New York received ten dollars a month, but wished an increase of four dollars a month, and endeavored to enforce their demands by quitting work. It is said that they marched about the city, accompanied by a band, and compelled seamen, employed at the old wages, to leave their ships and join them. But the iniquitous combination and conspiracy laws, which viewed concerted action of laborers as a crime, were then in force in all modern lands, and the constables were soon in pursuit, arrested the leader, lodged him in jail, and so ended the earliest of labor strikes.[18]

This sounds as if it had been the occurrence of yesterday, instead of more than a hundred years ago. The combination and conspiracy laws have been repealed, but the labor leader fares no better now than when these laws were still on the statute books. The writ of injunction is now made to serve the purpose of the master class, and there is no possible situation in which it cannot be made to apply and as swiftly and surely strike the vital point and paralyze the opposition to the master's rule.

We need not at this time trace the growth of the trade union from its small and local beginnings to its present national and international proportions; from the little group of hand-workers in the service of an individual employer to the armies of organized and federated workers in allied industries controlled by vast corporations, syndicates, and trusts. The fact stands forth in bold relief that the union was born of necessity and that it has grown strong with the development of industry and the increasing economic dependence of the workers.

A century ago, a boy served his apprenticeship and became the master of his trade. The few simple tools with which work was then done were generally owned by the man who used them; he could provide himself with the small quantity of raw material he required and freely follow his chosen pursuit and enjoy the fruit of his labor. But as everything had to be produced by the work of his hands, production was a slow process, meager of results, and the worker found it necessary to devote from 12 to 15 hours to his daily task to earn a sufficient amount to support himself and family.

It required most of the time and energy of the average worker to produce enough to satisfy the physical wants of himself and those dependent upon his labor.

There was little leisure for mental improvement, for recreation or social intercourse. The best that can be said for the workingman of this period is that he enjoyed political freedom, controlled in large measure his own employment, by virtue of his owning the tools of his trade, appropriated to his own use the product of his labor, and lived his quiet, uneventful round to the end of his days.

This was a new country, with boundless stretches of virgin soil. There was ample room and opportunity, air and sunlight, for all.

There was no millionaire in the United States; nor was there a tramp. These types are the products of the same system. The former is produced at the expense of the latter, and both at the expense of the working class. They appeared at the same time in the industrial development, and they will disappear together with the abolition of the system that brought them into existence.

The application of machinery to productive industry was followed by tremendous and far-reaching changes in the whole structure of society. First among these was the change in the status of the worker, who, from an independent mechanic or small producer, was reduced to the level of a dependent wageworker. The machine had leaped, as it were, into the arena of industrial activity, and had left little or no room for the application of the worker's skill or the use of his individual tools.

The economic dependence of the working class became more and more rigidly fixed—and at the same time, a new era dawned for the human race.

The more or less isolated individual artisans were converted into groups of associated workers and marshaled for the impending social revolution.

It was at this time that the trades union movement began to take definite form. Unorganized, the workers were not only in open competition with each other for the sale of their labor-power in the labor market, but their wages could be reduced, and their hours of labor lengthened at will, and they were left practically at the mercy of their employers.

It is interesting to note the spirit evinced by the pioneers of unionism, the causes that impelled them and the reasons they assigned for banding themselves together in defense of their common interests. In this connection we again quote from Professor Ely's *Labor Movement in America,* as follows:

> The next event to attract our attention in New York is an address delivered before "The General Trades Unions of the City of New York" at Chatham Street Chapel, on December 2, 1833, by Eli Moore, president of the union. This General Trades Union, as its name indicates, was a combination of subordinate unions "of the various trades and arts" in New York City and its vicinity and is the earliest example in the United States, so far as I know, of those Central Labor Unions which attempt to unite all the workingmen in one locality in one body, and which have now become so common among us. The address of Mr. Moore is characterized by a more modern tone than is found in most productions of the labor leaders of

> that period. The object of these unions is stated to be "to guard against the encroachments of aristocracy, to preserve our natural and political rights, to elevate our moral and intellectual condition, to promote our pecuniary interests, to narrow the line of distinction between the journeyman and employer, to establish the honor and safety of our respective vocations upon a more secure and permanent basis, and to alleviate the distresses of those suffering from want of employment."[19]

This is a remarkably clear statement of the objects of unionism in that early period, and indicates to what extent workingmen had even then been compelled to recognize their craft interests and unite and act together in defense thereof.

So far, and for many years later, the efforts of trade unions were confined to defensive tactics, and to the amelioration of objectionable conditions. The wage system had yet to develop its most offensive features and awaken the workers to the necessity of putting an end to it as the only means of achieving their freedom; and it was this that finally forced the extension of organized activity from the economic to the political field of labor unionism.

As the use of machinery became more general, and competition became more intense; as capital was centralized and industry organized to obtain better results, the workers realized their dependence more and more, and unionism grew apace. One trade after another fell into line and raised the banner of economic solidarity. Then followed strikes and lockouts and other devices incident to that form of warfare. Sometimes the unionists gained an advantage, but more often they suffered defeat, lost courage, and abandoned the union, only to return to the scene of disaster with renewed determination to fight the battle over again and again until victory should at last perch upon the union banner.

Pioneer Agitators

Oh, how many there were, whose names are forgotten, who suffered untold agonies to lay the foundation of the labor movement, of whose real mission they had but the vaguest conception!

These pioneers of progress paved the way for us and deserve far more at our hands than we have in our power to do for them. We may at best rescue their nameless memory from the darkness of oblivion, and this we undertake to do with the liveliest sense of obligation for the service they rendered, and the sacrifices they made in the early and trying stages of the struggle to improve the condition and advance the welfare of their fellow toilers.

The writer has met and known some of these untitled agitators of the earlier day, whose hearts were set on organizing their class, or at least their branch of it, and who had the courage to undertake the task and accept all the bitter consequences it imposed.

The union men of today have little or no conception of what the pioneer unionists had to contend with when they first started forth on their mission of organization. The organizer of the present time has to face difficulties enough, it is true, but as a rule the road has at least been broken for his approaching footsteps; the union has already been organized, and a committee meets him at the station and escorts him to the hotel.

Far different was it with the pioneer who left home without "scrip in his purse," whose chief stock consisted in his ability to "screw his courage to the sticking point" and whom privation and hardship only consecrated more completely to his self-appointed martyrdom.

Starting out, more than likely, after having been discharged for organizing a local union of his craft, or for serving on a committee, or interceding for a fellow, or "talking back" to the boss, or any other of the numerous acts which mark the conduct of the manly worker, distinguishing him from his weak and fawning brother, and bringing upon him the reprobation of his master—starting out to organize his fellow workers, that they might fare better than fell to his lot, he faced the world without a friend to bid him welcome or cheer him onward. Having no money for railroad fare, he must beat his way, but such a slight inconvenience does not deter him an instant. Reaching his destination, he brushes up as well as his scanty toilet will allow and then proceeds with due caution to look up "the boys," careful to elude the vigilance of the boss, who has no earthly use for a worthless labor agitator.

We shall not attempt to follow our pioneer through all his tortuous windings, nor have we space to more than hint at the story of his cruel persecution and pathetic end.

Our pioneer, leaving home, in many an instance, never saw wife and child again. Repulsed by the very men he was hungering to serve, penniless, deserted, neglected, and alone, he became "the poor wanderer of a stormy day," and ended his career a nameless outcast. Whatever his frailties and faults, they were virtues all, for they marked the generous heart, the sympathetic soul who loves his brother and accepts for himself the bitter portion of suffering and shame that he may serve his fellow man.

The labor agitator of the early day held no office, had no title, drew no salary, saw no footlights, heard no applause, never saw his name in print, and fills an unknown grave.

The labor movement is his monument, and though his name is not inscribed upon it, his soul is in it, and with it marches on forever.

Trade Unionism

From the small beginnings of a century ago, the trade union movement, keeping pace with industrial development, has become a tremendous power in the land.

The close of the Civil War was followed by a new era of industrial and commercial activity, and trade unions sprang up on every hand. Local organizations of the same craft multiplied and were united in national bodies, and these were in time bound together in national and international federation.

The swift and vast concentration of capital and the unprecedented industrial activity which marked the close of the nineteenth century were followed by the most extraordinary growth in the number and variety of trade unions in the history of the movement; yet this expansion, remarkable as it was, has not only been equaled, but excelled, in the first years of the new century, the tide of unionism sweeping over the whole country, and rising steadily higher, notwithstanding the efforts put forth from a hundred sources controlled by the ruling class to restrain its march, impair its utility, or stamp it out of existence.

The history of the last 30 years of trade unionism is filled with stirring incident and supplies abundant material for a good-sized volume. Organizations have risen and fallen, battles have been fought with varying results, every device known to the ingenuity of the ruling class has been employed to check the movement, but through it all the trend has been steadily toward a more perfect organization and a more comprehensive grasp of its mighty mission. The strikes and boycotts and lockouts which occurred with startling frequency during this period, some of them accompanied by riots and other forms of violence, tell their own tragic story of the class struggle which is shaking the foundations of society, and will end only with the complete overthrow of the wage system and the freedom of the working class from every form of slavery.

No strike has ever been lost, and there can be no defeat for the labor movement.

However disastrous the day of battle has been, it has been worth its price, and only the scars remain to bear testimony that the movement is invincible and that no mortal wound can be inflicted upon it.

What has the union done for the worker? Far more than these brief pages will allow us to place on record.

The union has from its inception taught, however imperfectly, the fundamental need of solidarity; it has inspired hope in the breast of the defeated and despairing worker, joining his hand with the hand of his fellow worker and bidding them lift their bowed bodies from the earth and look above and beyond the tribulations of the hour to the shining heights of future achievement.

The union has fought the battles of the worker upon a thousand fields, and though defeated often, rallied and charged again and again to wrest from the enemy the laurels of victory.

The union was first to trace in outline the lesson above all others the workingman need to learn, and that is the collective interest and welfare of his class, in which his own is indissolubly bound, and that no vital or permanent change of conditions is possible that does not embrace his class as a whole.

The union has been a moral stimulus as well as a material aid to the worker; it has appealed to him to develop his faculties and to think for himself; to cultivate self-reliance and learn to depend upon himself; to have pride of character and make some effort to defend himself; to sympathize with and support his fellow workers and make their cause his own.

Although these things have as yet been only vaguely and imperfectly accomplished, yet they started in and have grown with the union, and to this extent the union has promoted the class-conscious solidarity of the working class.

It is true that the trade union movement has in some essential respects proved a disappointment, but it may not on this account be repudiated as a failure. The worst that can in truth be said of it is that it has not kept up with the procession of events, that it lacks the progressive spirit so necessary to its higher development and larger usefulness, but there are reasons for this, and they suggest themselves to the most casual student of the movement.

When workingmen first began to organize unions, every effort was made by the employing class to stamp out the incipient rebellion. This was kept up for years, but in spite of all that could be done to extinguish the fires of revolt, the smoldering embers broke forth again and again, each time with increased intensity and vigor; and when at last it became apparent to the shrewder and more far-seeing members of the capitalist family that the union movement had come to stay, they forthwith changed their tactics, discarding their frowns and masking their features with the most artful smiles as they extended their greeting and pronounced their blessing upon this latest and greatest benefaction to the human race.

In fewer words, seeing that they could not head it off, they decided to take it by the hand and guide it into harmless channels.

This is precisely the policy pursued, first and last, by the late Marcus A. Hanna, and it will not be denied that he had the entire confidence of the capitalist class and that they clearly recognized his keen perception, astute diplomacy, and sagacious leadership in dealing with the union movement.

Mr. Hanna denominated the national leaders of the trade unions as his "lieutenants"; had the "Civic Federation" organized and himself elected president, that he and his lieutenants might meet upon equal ground and as often as necessary; he slapped them familiarly on the back, had his picture taken with them, and cracked jokes with them; and all the time he was doing this he was the beau ideal of Wall Street, the ruling voice in the capitalist councils, and all the trusts, syndicates, and combines; all the magnates, barons, lords, and plutocrats in one voice proclaimed him the ruler of rulers, the political prophet of their class, the cornerstone and central pillar in the capitalist system.

Mr. Hanna did not live to see his plan of "benevolent feudalism" consummated, nor to be elected president of the United States, as his Wall Street admirers and trade union friends intended, but he did live long enough to see the gathering clouds of the social revolution on the political horizon; and to prevent the trade union movement from becoming a factor in it, he taxed the resources of his fertile brain and bended all the energies of his indomitable will. Clearer-sighted than all others of his class, he was promptly crowned their leader. He saw what was coming and prepared to meet and defeat it, or at least put off the crisis to a later day.

The trade union movement must remain a "pure and simple" organization. It must not be subject to the laws of evolution; it must be securely anchored to its conservative, time-honored policy, hold fast to its good name, and preserve inviolate all the traditions of the past. Finally, it must eschew politics as utterly destructive of trade union ends, and above all, beware of and guard against the contamination of socialism, whose breath is disruption and whose touch is death.

That was the position of Senator Hanna; it is that of the smaller lights who are serving as his successors. It is this position that is taken by the press, the pulpit, and the politician; it is this position that is reflected in the trade union movement itself, and voiced by its officials, who are at once the leaders of labor and the lieutenants of capital, and who, in their dual role, find it more and more difficult to harmonize the conflicting interests of the class of whom they are the leaders and the class of whom they are the lieutenants.

It is not claimed for a moment that these leaders are corrupt in the sense that they would betray their trust for a consideration. Such charges and intimations are frequently made, but so far as we know, they are baseless and unjust in almost every instance; and it is our opinion that an accusation of such gravity is never justified, whatever the circumstances, unless the proof can be furnished to support the charge and convict the offender.

But the criticism to which these leaders are properly subject is that they fear to offend the capitalist class, well knowing that the influence of this class is potential in the labor union, and that if the labor lieutenant fails of obedience and respect to his superior capitalist officers, he can soon be made to feel their displeasure, and unless he relents, his popularity wanes, and he finds himself a leader without an office.

The late Peter M. Arthur, of the Brotherhood of Locomotive Engineers, was a conspicuous example of this kind of leadership. There was frequently the most violent opposition to him, but his standing with the railway corporations secured him in his position, and it was simply impossible to dislodge him. Had he been radical instead of conservative, had he stood wholly on the side of the engineers instead of cultivating the good offices of the managers and placating the corporations, he would have been deposed years ago and pronounced a miserable failure as a labor leader.

The capitalist press has much to do with shaping the course of a labor leader; he shrinks from its cruel attacks and he yields, sometimes unconsciously, to its blandishments and honeyed phrases, and in spite of himself becomes a servile trimmer and cowardly time-server.

The trade union movement of the present day has enemies within and without, and upon all sides, some attacking it openly and others insidiously, but all bent either upon destroying it or reducing it to unresisting impotency.

The enemies of unionism, while differing in method, are united solidly upon one point, and that is in the effort to misrepresent and discredit the men who, scorning and defying the capitalist exploiters and their minions, point steadily the straight and uncompromising course the movement must take if it is to accomplish its allotted task and safely reach its destined port.

These men, though frequently regarded as the enemies, are the true friends of trade unionism and in good time are certain to be vindicated.

The more or less open enemies have inaugurated some startling innovations during the past few years. The private armies the corporations used some years ago, such as Pinkerton mercenaries, coal and iron police, deputy marshals, etc., have been relegated to second place as out of date, or they are wholly out of commission. It has been found after repeated experiments that the courts are far more deadly to trade unions, and that they operate noiselessly and with unerring precision.

The rapid-fire injunction is a great improvement on the Gatling gun. Nothing can get beyond its range, and it never misses fire.

The capitalists are in entire control of the injunction artillery, and all the judicial gunner has to do is to touch it off at their command.

Step by step, the writ of injunction has invaded the domain of trade unionism, limiting its jurisdiction, curtailing its powers, sapping its strength, and undermining its foundations, and this has been done by the courts in the name of the institutions they were designed to safeguard but have shamelessly betrayed at the behest of the barons of capitalism.

Injunctions have been issued restraining the trade unions and their members from striking, from boycotting, from voting funds to strikers, from levying assessments to support their members, from walking on the public highway, from asking non-union men not to take their places, from meeting to oppose wage reductions, from expelling a spy from membership, from holding conversation with those who had taken or were about to take their jobs, from congregating in public places, from holding meetings, from doing anything and everything, directly, indirectly, or any other way, to interfere with the employing class in their unalienable right to operate their plants as their own interests may dictate, and to run things generally to suit themselves.

The courts have found it in line with judicial procedure to strike every weapon from labor's economic hand and leave it defenseless at the mercy of its exploiter; and now that the courts have gone to the last extremity in this nefarious plot of subjugation, labor, at last, is waking up to the fact that it has not been using its political arm in the struggle at all; that the ballot which it can wield is strong enough not only to disarm the enemy, but to drive that enemy entirely from the field.

The courts, so notoriously in control of capital, and so shamelessly perverted to its base and sordid purposes are, therefore, exercising a wholesome effect upon trade unionism by compelling the members to note the class character of our capitalist government, and driving them to the inevitable conclusion that the labor question is also a political question and that the working class must organize their political power that they may wrest the government from capitalist control and put an end to class rule forever.

Trade unionists for the most part learn slowly, but they learn surely, and fresh object lessons are prepared for them every day.

They have seen a Democratic president of the United States send the federal troops into a sovereign state of the Union in violation of the Constitution, and in defiance of the protest of the governor and the people, to crush a body of peaceable workingmen at the behest of a combination of railroads bent on destroying their union and reducing them to vassalage.

They have seen a Republican president refuse to interpose his executive authority when militarism, in the name of the capitalist class, seized another sovereign state by the throat and strangled its civil administration to death while it committed the most dastardly crimes upon defenseless workingmen in the annals of capitalist brutality and military despotism.

They have seen a composite Republican-Democratic Congress, the legislative tool of the exploiting class, pass a military bill which makes every citizen a soldier and the president a military dictator.

They have seen this same Congress, session after session, making false promises to deluded labor committees; pretending to be the friends of workingmen and anxious to be of service to them, while at the same time in league with the capitalist lobby and pledged to defeat every measure that would afford even the slightest promise of relief to the working class. The anti-injunction bill and the eight-hour measure, pigeonholed and rejected again and again in the face of repeated promises that they should pass, tell their own story of duplicity and treachery to labor of the highest legislative body in the land.

They have seen Republican governors and Democratic governors order out the militia repeatedly to shoot down workingmen at the command of their capitalist masters.

They have seen these same governors construct military prisons and "bull pens," seize unoffending workingmen without warrant of law, and thrust them into these vile quarters for no other reason than to break up their unions and leave them helpless at the feet of corporate rapacity.

They have seen the Supreme Court of the nation turn labor out without a hearing, while the corporation lawyers, who compose this august body, and who hold their commissions in virtue of the "well done" of their capitalist retainers, solemnly descant upon the immaculate purity of our judicial institutions.

They have seen state legislatures, both Republican and Democratic, with never an exception, controlled bodily by the capitalist class and turn the committees of labor unions empty-handed from their doors.

They have seen state supreme courts declare as unconstitutional the last vestige of law upon the statute books that could by any possibility be construed as affording any shelter or relief to the labor union or its members.

They have seen these and many other things and will doubtless see many more before their eyes are opened as a class; but we are thankful for them all, painful though they be to us in having to bear witness to the suffering of our benighted brethren.

In this way only can they be made to see, to think, to act, and every wrong they suffer brings them nearer to their liberation.

The "pure and simple" trade union of the past does not answer the requirements of today, and they who insist that it does are blind to the changes going on about them and out of harmony with the progressive forces of the age.

The attempt to preserve the "autonomy" of each trade and segregate it within its own independent jurisdiction, while the lines which once separated them are being obliterated, and the trades are being interwoven and interlocked in the process of industrial evolution, is as futile as to declare and attempt to enforce the independence of the waves of the sea.

A modern industrial plant has a hundred trades and parts of trades represented in its working force. To have these workers parceled out to a hundred unions is to divide and not to organize them, to give them over to factions and petty leadership and leave them an easy prey to the machinations of the enemy. The dominant craft should control the plant or, rather, the union, and it should embrace the entire working force. This is the industrial plan, the modern method applied to modern conditions, and it will in time prevail.

The trade autonomy can be expressed within the general union, so far as that is necessary or desirable, and there need be no conflict on account of it.

The attempt of each trade to maintain its own independence separately and apart from others results in increasing jurisdictional entanglements, fruitful of dissension, strife, and ultimate disruption.

The work of organizing has little, if any, permanent value unless the work of education, the right kind of education, goes hand in hand with it.

There is no cohesiveness in ignorance.

The members of a trade union should be taught the true import, the whole object of the labor movement, and understand its entire program.

They should know that the labor movement means more, infinitely more, than a paltry increase in wages and the strike necessary to secure it; that while it engages to do all that possibly can be done to better the working conditions of its members, its higher object is to overthrow the capitalist system of private ownership of the tools of labor, abolish wage-slavery, and achieve the freedom of the whole working class and, in fact, of all mankind.

Karl Marx recognized the necessity of the trade union when he said:

> . . . the general tendency of capitalist production is not to raise, but to sink the average standard of wages or to push the *value of labor* more

> or less to its *minimum limit*. Such being the tendency of things in this system, is this saying that the working class ought to renounce their resistance against the encroachments of capital, and abandon their attempts at making the best of the occasional chances for their temporary improvement? If they did, they would be degraded to one level mass of broken wretches past salvation.
>
> * * *
>
> By cowardly giving way in their everyday conflict with capital, they would certainly disqualify themselves for the initiating of any larger movement.[20]

Marx also set forth the limitations of the trade union and indicated the true course it should pursue as follows:

> At the same time, and quite apart from the general servitude involved in the wage system, the working class ought not to exaggerate to themselves the ultimate working of these everyday struggles. They ought not to forget that they are fighting with effects, but not with the causes of those effects; that they are retarding the downward movement, but not changing its direction; that they are applying palliatives, not curing the malady. They ought, therefore, not to be exclusively absorbed in these unavoidable guerrilla fights incessantly springing up from the never-ceasing encroachments of capital or changes of the market. They ought to understand that, with all the miseries it imposes upon them, the present system simultaneously engenders the *material conditions* and the *social forms* necessary for an economic reconstruction of society. Instead of the *conservative* motto, "*A fair day's wages for a fair day's work!*" they ought to inscribe on their banner the *revolutionary* watchword, "*Abolition of the wage system.*"
>
> * * *
>
> Trade unions work well as centers of resistance against the encroachments of capital. They fail partially from an injudicious use of their power. They fail generally from limiting themselves to a guerrilla war against the effects of the existing system, instead of simultaneously trying to change it, instead of using their organized forces as a lever for the final emancipation of the working class, that is to say, the ultimate abolition of the wage system.[21]

In an address to the Knights of St. Crispin, in April 1872, Wendell Phillips, the eloquent orator and passionate hater of slavery in every form, said, "I hail the labor movement for the reason that it is my only hope for democracy."

Wendell Phillips was right; he spoke with prophetic insight. He knew that the labor movement alone could democratize society and give freedom to the race.

In the same address he uttered these words, which every trade unionist should know by heart: "Unless there is a power in your movement, industrially and politically, the last knell of democratic liberty in this Union is struck."

The orator then proceeded to emphasize the urgent need of developing the political power of the movement; and it is just this that the trade unionist should be made to clearly understand.

The cry, "no politics in the union," "dragging the union into politics," or "making the union the tail to some political kite," is born of ignorance or dishonesty, or a combination of both. It is echoed by every ward-heeling politician in the country. The plain purpose is to deceive and mislead the workers.

It is not the welfare of the union that these capitalist henchmen are so much concerned about, but the fear that the working class, as a class organized into a party of their own, will go into politics, for well they know that when that day dawns, their occupation will be gone.

And this is why they employ their time in setting the union against the political party of the working class, the only union labor party there ever was or ever will be, and warning the members against the evil designs of the socialists.

The important thing to impress upon the mind of the trade unionist is that it is his duty to cultivate the habit of doing his own thinking.

The moment he realizes this, he is beyond the power of the scheming politician, the emissary of the exploiter, in or out of the labor movement.

The trade union is not and cannot become a political machine, nor can it be used for political purposes. They who insist upon working-class political action not only have no intention to convert the trade union into a political party, but they would oppose any such attempt on the part of others.

The trade union is an economic organization with distinct economic functions and as such is a part, a necessary part, but a part only of the labor movement; it has its own sphere of activity, its own program, and is its own master within its economic limitations.

But the labor movement has also its political side, and the trade unionist must be educated to realize its importance and to understand that the political side of the movement must be unionized as well as the economic side; and that he is not in fact a union man at all who, although a member of the union on the economic side, is a non-unionist on the political side; and while striking for, votes against the working class.

The trade union expresses the economic power, and the Socialist Party expresses the political power of the labor movement.

The fully developed labor unionist uses both his economic and political power in the interest of his class. He understands that the struggle between labor and capital is a class struggle; that the working class are in a great majority, but divided, some in trade unions and some out of them, some in one political party and some in another; that because they are divided, they are helpless and must submit to being robbed of what their labor produces, and treated with contempt; that they must unite their class in the trade union on the one hand and in the Socialist Party on the other hand; that industrially and politically, they must act together as a class against the capitalist class, and that this struggle is a class struggle, and that any workingman who deserts his union in a strike and goes to the other side is a scab, and any workingman who deserts his party on election day and goes over to the enemy is a betrayer of his class and an enemy of his fellow man.

Both sides are organized in this class struggle, the capitalists, however, far more thoroughly than the workers. In the first place the capitalists are, comparatively, few in number, while the workers number many millions. Next, the capitalists are men of financial means and resources, and can buy the best brains and command the highest order of ability the market affords. Then again, they own the earth and the mills and mines and locomotives and ships and stores and the jobs that are attached to them, and this not only gives them tremendous advantage in the struggle but makes them for the time the absolute masters of the situation.

The workers, on the other hand, are poor as a rule, and ignorant as a class, but they are in an overwhelming majority. In a word, they have the power but are not conscious of it.

This then is the supreme demand: to make them conscious of the power of their class, or class-conscious workingmen.

The working class alone does the world's work, has created its capital, produced its wealth, constructed its mills and factories, dug its canals, made its roadbeds, laid its rails and operates its trains, spanned the rivers with bridges and tunneled the mountains, delved for the precious stones that glitter upon the bosom of vulgar idleness, and reared the majestic palaces that shelter insolent parasites.

The working class alone—and by the working class, I mean all useful workers, all who by the labor of their hands or the effort of their brains, or both in alliance, as they ought universally to be, increase the knowledge and add to the wealth of society—the working class alone is essential to society and therefore the only class that can survive in the worldwide struggle for freedom.

We have said that both classes, the capitalist class and the working class, are organized for the class struggle, but the organization, especially that of the workers, is far from complete; indeed, it would be nearer exact to say that it has but just fairly begun.

On the economic field of the class struggle the capitalists have their Manufacturers' Association, Citizens' Alliance, Corporations' Auxiliary, and—we must add—Civic Federation, while on the political field they have the Republican Party and the Democratic Party, the former for large capitalists and the latter for small capitalists, but both of them for capitalists and both against the workers.

Standing face to face with the above named economic and political forces of the capitalists, the workingmen have on the economic field their trade unions and on the political field their working-class Socialist Party.

In the class struggle, the workers must unite and fight together as one on both economic and political fields.

The Socialist Party is to the workingman politically what the trade union is to him industrially; the former is the party of his class, while the latter is the union of his trade.

The difference between them is that while the trade union is confined to the trade, the Socialist Party embraces the entire working class, and while the union is limited to bettering conditions under the wage system, the party is organized to conquer the political power of the nation, wipe out the wage system, and make the workers themselves the masters of the earth.

In this program, the trade union and the Socialist Party, the economic and political wings of the labor movement, should not only not be in conflict but act together in perfect harmony in every struggle, whether it be on the one field or the other, in the strike or at the ballot box. The main thing is that in every such struggle, the workers shall be united, shall in fact be unionists and no more be guilty of scabbing on their party than on their union, no more think of voting a capitalist ticket on election day and turning the working class over to capitalist robbery and misrule than they would think of voting in the union to turn it over to the capitalists and have it run in the interest of the capitalist class.

To do its part in the class struggle, the trade union need no more go into politics than the Socialist Party need go into the trades. Each has its place and its functions.

The union deals with trade problems, and the party deals with politics.

The union is educating the workers in the management of industrial activities and fitting them for cooperative control and democratic regulation of their trades—the party is recruiting and training and drilling the political army that is to conquer the capitalist forces on the political battlefield; and having control of the machinery of government, use it to transfer the industries from the capitalists to the workers, from the parasites to the people.

In his excellent paper on "The Social Opportunity," published in a recent issue of the *International Socialist Review,* Dr. George D. Herron, discussing trade unions and their relation to the Socialist Party, and the labor movement in general, clearly sees the trend of the development and arrives at conclusions that are sound and commend themselves to the thoughtful consideration of all trade unionists and socialists. Says Dr. Herron:

> On the one side, it is the trade unionist who is on the firing line of the class struggle. He it is who blocked the wheels of the capitalist machine; he it is who has prevented the unchecked development of capitalist increase; he it is who has prevented the whole labor body of the world from being kept forever at the point of mere hunger wages; he it is who has taught the workers of the world the lesson of solidarity, and delivered them from that wretched and unthinking competition with each other which kept them at the mercy of capitalism; he it is who has prepared the way for the Cooperative Commonwealth. On the other hand, trade unionism is by no means the solution of the workers' problem, nor is it the goal of the labor struggle. It is merely a capitalist line of defense within the capitalist system. Its existence and its struggles are necessitated only by the existence and predatory nature of capitalism.
>
> * * *
>
> Organized labor has an instinct that far outreaches its intelligence, and that far outreaches the intelligence of the preaching and teaching class—the instinct that the workers of the world are bound up together in one common destiny; that their battle for the future is one; and that there is no possible safety or extrication for any worker unless all the workers of the world are extricated and saved from capitalism together.
>
> * * *
>
> Until the workers shall become a clearly defined socialist movement, standing for and moving toward the unqualified Cooperative Commonwealth, while at the same time understanding and proclaiming their im-

> mediate interests, they will only play into the hands of their exploiters, and be led by their betrayers.
>
> It is the socialist who must point this out in the right way. He is not to do this by seeking to commit trade union bodies to the principles of socialism. Resolution or commitments of this sort accomplish little good. Nor is he to do it by taking a servile attitude toward organized labor, nor by meddling with the details or the machinery of the trade unions. Not by trying to commit socialism to trade unionism, nor trade unionism to socialism, will the socialist end be accomplished. It is better to leave the trade unions do their distinctive work, as the workers' defense against the encroachments of capitalism, as the economic development of the worker against the economic development of the capitalist, giving unqualified support and sympathy to the struggles of the organized worker to sustain himself in his economic sphere. But let the socialist also so build up the character and harmony and strength of the socialist movement as a political force, that it shall command the respect and confidence of the worker, irrespective of his trade or his union obligations. It is urgent that we so keep in mind the difference between the two developments that neither shall cripple the other. The socialist movement, as a political development of the workers for their economic emancipation, is one thing; the trade union development, as an economic defense of the workers within the capitalist system, is another thing. Let us not interfere with the internal affairs of the trade unions or seek to have them become distinctively political bodies in themselves, any more than we would seek to make a distinctive political body in itself of a church, or a public school, or a lawyer's office. But let us attend to the harmonious and commanding development of the socialist political movement as the channel and power by which labor is to come to its emancipation and its commonwealth.[22]

We have quoted thus at length to make clear the position of the writer who has given close study to the question and in the paper above quoted has done much to light the way to sound tactics and sane procedure.

It is of vital importance to the trade union that its members be class-conscious, that they understand the class struggle and their duty as union men on the political field, so that in every move that is made they will have the goal in view, and while taking advantage of every opportunity to secure concessions and enlarge their economic advantage, they will at the same time unite at the ballot box, not only to back up the economic struggle of the trade unions but to finally wrest the government from capitalist control and establish the working-class republic.

Socialism

There are those who sneeringly class socialism among the "isms" that appear and disappear as passing fads and pretend to dismiss it with an impatient wave of the hand. There is just enough in this great world movement to them to excite their ridicule and provoke their contempt. At least they would have us think so, and if we take them at their word, their ignorance does not rise to the level of our contempt but entitles them to our pity.

To the workingman in particular, it is important to know what socialism is and what it means.

Let us endeavor to make it so clear to him that he will readily grasp it, and the moment he does, he becomes a socialist.

It is our conviction that no workingman can clearly understand what socialism means without becoming and remaining a socialist. It is simply impossible for him to be anything else, and the only reason that all workingmen are not socialists is that they do not know what it means.

They have heard of socialism—and they have heard of anarchy and of other things all mixed together—and without going to any trouble about it, they conclude that it is all the same thing and a good thing to let alone.

Why? Because the capitalist editor has said so; the politician has sworn to it, and the preacher has said amen to it, and surely that ought to settle it.

But it doesn't. It settles but one thing, and that is that the capitalist is opposed to socialism and that the editor and politician and preacher are but the voices of the capitalist. There are some exceptions, but not enough to affect the rule.

Socialism is first of all a political movement of the working class, clearly defined and uncompromising, which aims at the overthrow of the prevailing capitalist system by securing control of the national government and by the exercise of the public powers, supplanting the existing capitalist class government with socialist administration—that is to say, changing a republic in name into a republic in fact.

Socialism also means a coming phase of civilization, next in order to the present one, in which the collective people will own and operate the sources and means of wealth production, in which all will have equal right to work and all will cooperate together in producing wealth and all will enjoy all the fruit of their collective labor.

In the present system of society, called the capitalist system, since it is controlled by and supported in the interest of the capitalist class, we have two general classes of people; first, capitalists and second, workers. The capitalists are few, the workers are many; the capitalists are called capitalists because they own the productive capital of the country, the lands, mines, quarries, oil and gas wells, mills, factories, shops, stores, warehouses, refineries, tanneries, elevators, docks, wharves, railroads, streetcars, steamships, smelters, blast furnaces, brick and stone yards, stock pens, packing houses, telegraph wires and poles, pipe lines, and all other sources, means, and tools of production, distribution, and exchange. The capitalist class who own and control these things also own and control, of course, the millions of jobs that are attached to and inseparable from them.

It goes without saying that the owner of the job is the master of the fellow who depends upon the job.

Now why does the workingman depend upon the capitalist for a job? Simply because the capitalist owns the tools with which work is done, and without these, the workingman is as helpless as if he had no arms.

Before the tool became a machine, the worker who used it also owned it; if one was lost or destroyed, he got another. The tool was small; it was for individual use, and what the workingman produced with it was his own. He did not have to beg someone else to allow him to use his tools—he had his own.

But a century has passed since then, and in the order of progress, that simple tool has become a mammoth machine.

The old hand tool was used by a single worker—and owned by him who used it.

The machine requires a thousand or ten thousand workers to operate it, but they do not own it, and what they produce with it does not go to them, but to the capitalist who does own it.

The workers who use the machine are the slaves of the capitalist who owns it.

They can only work by his permission.

The capitalist is a capitalist solely for profit—without profit, he would not be in business an instant. That is his first and only consideration.

In the capitalist system, profit is prior to and more important than the life or liberty of the workingman.

The capitalist profits first, last, and always. He owns the tools and only allows the worker to use them on condition that he can extract a satisfactory profit from his labor. If he cannot do this, the tools are not allowed to be used—he locks them up and waits.

The capitalist does no work himself; that is, no useful or necessary work. He spends his time watching other parasites in the capitalist game of "dog eat dog," or in idleness or dissipation. The workers who use his tools give him all the wealth they produce, and he allows them a sufficient wage to keep them in working order.

The wage is to the worker what oil is to the machine.

The machine cannot run without lubricant, and the worker cannot work and reproduce himself without being fed, clothed, and housed; this is his lubricant, and the amount he requires to keep him in running order regulates his wage.

Karl Marx, in his *Wage Labor and Capital,* makes these points clear in his own terse and masterly style. We quote as follows:

> The free laborer . . . sells himself, and, indeed, sells himself piecemeal. He sells at auction eight, ten, twelve, fifteen hours of his life, day after day, to the highest bidder, to the owner of the raw materials, instruments of labor, and means of subsistence, that is, to the capitalist. The worker belongs neither to an owner nor to the land, but eight, ten, twelve, fifteen hours of his daily life belong to he who buys them. The worker leaves the capitalist to whom he hires himself whenever he likes, and the capitalist discharges him whenever he thinks fit, as soon as he no longer gets any profit out of him, or not the anticipated profit. But the worker, whose sole source of livelihood is the sale of his labor-power, cannot leave the *whole class of purchasers, that is, the capitalist class,* without renouncing his existence. *He belongs not to this or that capitalist, but to the capitalist class,* and it is his business to dispose of himself, that is to find a purchaser within this capitalist class.[23]

Coming to the matter of wages and how they are determined, Marx continues:

> Wages . . . are the *price* of a definite commodity, of labor-power. Wages are, therefore, determined by the same laws that determine the price of every other commodity.
>
> The question, therefore, is *how is the price of a commodity determined?*
>
> By what means is the *price* of a commodity determined?
>
> By means of competition between buyers and sellers, by the relation of inquiry to delivery, of demand to supply.
>
> * * *
>
> Now, the same general laws that regulate the price of commodities in general of course also regulate *wages*, the *price of labor.*
>
> Wages will rise and fall according to the relation of demand and supply, according to the turn taken by the competition between the buyers of labor-power, the capitalists, and the sellers of labor-power, the workers.

> The fluctuations in wages correspond in general to the fluctuations in prices of commodities. *Within these fluctuations, however, the price of labor will be determined by the cost of production, by the labor time necessary to produce this commodity—labor-power.*
>
> *What, then is the cost of production of labor-power?*
>
> *It is the cost required for maintaining the worker as a worker and for developing him into a worker.*

* * *

> The *price of his labor* will, therefore, be determined by the *price of the necessary means of subsistence.*[24]

This is the capitalist system in its effect upon the working class. They have no tools but must work to live. They throng the labor market, especially when times are hard and work is scarce, and eagerly, anxiously look for someone willing to use their labor-power and bid them in at the market price.

To speak of liberty in such a system is a mockery; to surrender is a crime.

The workers of the nation and the world must be aroused.

In the capitalist system, "night dropped her sable curtain down and pinned it with a star,"[25] and the great majority grope in darkness. The pin must be removed from the curtain, even though it be a star.

But the darkness, after all, is but imaginary. The sun is marching to meridian glory, and the world is flooded with light.

Charlotte Perkins Stetson, the inspired evangel of the coming civilization, says:

> Ye shut your eyes and call it night,
> Ye grope and fall in seas of light—
> Would ye but understand![26]

Not for a moment do we despair of the future. The greatest educational propaganda ever known is spreading over the earth.

The working class will both see and understand. They have the inherent power of self-development. They are but just beginning to come into consciousness of their power, and with the first glimmerings of this consciousness, the capitalist system is doomed. It may hold on for a time, for even a long time, but its doom is sealed.

Even now, the coming consciousness of this worldwide working-class power is shaking the foundations of all governments and all civilizations.

The capitalist system has had its day and, like other systems that have gone before, it must pass away when it has fulfilled its mission and make room for another system in harmony with the forces of progress and compatible with the onward march of civilization.

The centralization of capital, the concentration of industry, and the co-operation of workingmen mark the beginning of the end. Competition is no longer "the life of trade." Only they are clamoring for "competition" who have been worsted in the struggle and would like to have another deal.

The small class who won out in the game of competition and own the trusts want no more of it. They know what it is and have had enough. Mr. John D. Rockefeller needs no competition to give life to his trade, and his pious son does not expatiate upon the beauties of competition in his class at Sunday school.

No successful capitalist wants competition—for himself—he only wants it for the working class, so that he can buy his labor-power at the lowest competitive price in the labor market.

The simple truth is that competition in industrial life belongs to the past and is practically outgrown. The time is approaching when it will be no longer possible.

The improvement and enlargement of machinery, and the ever-increasing scale of production, compel the concentration of capital, and this makes inevitable the concentration and cooperation of the workers.

The capitalists—the successful ones, of course—cooperate on the one side; the workers, who are lucky enough to get the jobs, on the other side.

One side get the profits, grow rich, live in palaces, ride in yachts, gamble at Monte Carlo, drink champagne, choose judges, buy editors, hire preachers, corrupt politics, build universities, endow libraries, patronize churches, get the gout, preach morals, and bequeath the earth to their lineal descendants.

The other side do the work, early and late, in heat and cold; they sweat and groan and bleed and die—the steel billets they make are their corpses. They build the mills and all the machinery; they man the plant, and the thing of stone and steel begins to throb. They live far away in the outskirts, in cottages, just this side of the hovels, where gaunt famine walks with despair and "*Les Misérables*" leer and mock at civilization. When the mills shut down, they are out of work and out of food and out of home; and when old age begins to steal away their vigor and the step is no longer agile, nor the sinew strong, nor the hand cunning; when the frame begins to bend and quiver and the eye to grow dim, and they are no longer fit as labor-power to make profit for their masters, they are pushed aside into the human drift that empties into the gulf of despair and death.

The system, once adapted to human needs, has outlived its usefulness and is now an unmitigated curse. It stands in the way of progress and checks the advance of civilization.

If by its fruit we know the tree, so by the same token do we know our social system. Its corrupt fruit betrays its foul and unclean nature and condemns it to death.

The swarms of vagrants, tramps, outcasts, paupers, thieves, gamblers, pickpockets, suicides, confidence men, fallen women, consumptives, idiots, dwarfed children; the disease, poverty, insanity, and crime rampant in every land under the sway of capitalism rise up and cry out against it, and hush to silence all the pleas of its mercenaries and strike the knell of its doom.

The Ancient and Middle Age civilizations had their rise, they ruled and fell, and that of our own day must follow them.

Evolution is the order of nature, and society, like the units that compose it, is subject to its inexorable law.

The day of individual effort, of small tools, free competition, hand labor, long hours, and meager results is gone, never to return. The civilization reared upon this old foundation is crumbling.

The economic basis of society is being transformed.

The working class are being knit together in the bonds of cooperation; they are becoming conscious of their interests as a class and marshaling the workers for the class struggle and collective ownership.

With the triumph of the workers, the mode of production and distribution will be revolutionized.

Private ownership and production for profit will be supplanted by social ownership and production for use.

The economic interests of the workers will be mutual. They will work together in harmony instead of being arrayed against each other in competitive warfare.

The collective workers will own the machinery of production, and there will be work for all, and all will receive their socially due share of the product of their cooperative labor.

It is for this great work that the workers and their sympathizers must organize and educate and agitate.

The socialist movement is of the working class itself; it is from the injustice perpetrated upon and the misery suffered by this class that the movement sprung, and it is to this class it makes its appeal. It is the voice of awakened labor arousing itself to action.

As we look abroad and see things as they are, the capitalists entrenched and fortified and the workers impoverished, ignorant and in bondage, we are apt to be impressed with the magnitude of the task that lies before the socialist movement, but as we become grounded in the socialist philosophy, as we understand the process of economic determinism and grasp the principles of industrial and social evolution, the magnitude of the undertaking, far from daunting the socialist spirit, appeals to each comrade to enlist in the struggle because of the very greatness of the conflict and the immeasurable good that lies beyond it, and as he girds himself and touches elbows with his comrades, his own latent resources are developed, and his blood thrills with new life as he feels himself rising to the majesty of a man.

Now he has found his true place, and though he be reviled against and ostracized, traduced and denounced, though he be reduced to rags and tormented with hunger pangs, he will bear it all and more, for he is battling for a principle, he has been consecrated to a cause and he cannot turn back.

To reach the workers that are still in darkness and to open their eyes, that is the task, and to this we must give ourselves with all the strength we have, with patience that never fails and an abiding faith in the ultimate victory.

The moment a worker sees himself in his true light, he severs his relations with the capitalist parties, for he realizes at once that he no more belongs there than Rockefeller belongs in the Socialist Party.

What is the actual status of the workingman in the capitalist society of today?

Is he in any true sense a citizen?

Has he any basis for the claim that he is a free man?

First of all, he cannot work unless some capitalist finds it to his interest to employ him.

Why not? Because he has no tools and man cannot work without them.

Why has he no tools? Because tools in these days are, as a rule, great machines and very costly, and in the capitalist system are the private property of the capitalists.

This being true, the workingman, before he can do a tap of work, before he can earn a dime to feed himself, his wife, or his child, must first consult the tool-owning capitalist; or, rather, his labor-buying superintendent. Very meekly, therefore, and not without fear in his heart and trembling in his knees, he enters the office and offers his labor-power in exchange for a wage that represents but a part, usually a small part, of what his labor produces.

His offer may be accepted or rejected.

Not infrequently, the "boss" has been annoyed by so many job-hunters that he has become irritable and gruffly turns the applicant away.

But admitting that he finds employment, during working hours he is virtually the property of his master.

The bell or the whistle claims him on the stroke of the hour. He is subject to the master's shop regulations, and these, of course, are established solely to conserve his master's interests. He works, first of all, for his master, who extracts the surplus value from his labor, but for which he would not be allowed to work at all. He has little or no voice in determining any of the conditions of his employment.

Suddenly, without warning, the shop closes down or he is discharged, and his wage, small at best, is cut off. He has to live, the rent must be paid, the wife and children must have clothing and food, fuel must be provided, and yet he has no job, no wages, and no prospects of getting any.

Is a worker in that position free?

Is he a citizen?

A man?

No! He is simply a wage-slave, a job-holder, while it lasts, here today and gone tomorrow.

For the great body of wageworkers there is no escape; they cannot rise above the level of their class. The few who do are the exceptions that prove the rule.

And yet there are those who have the effrontery to warn these wage-slaves that if they turn to socialism, they will lose all incentive to work, and their individuality will fade away.

Incentive and individuality forsooth! Where are they now?

Translated into plain terms, this warning means that a slave who is robbed of all he produces, except enough to keep him in producing condition, as in the present system, has great incentive to work and is highly individualized, but if he breaks his fetters and frees himself and becomes his own master and gets all his labor produces, as he will in socialism, then all incentive to work vanishes, and his individuality, so used to chains and dungeons, unable to stand the air of freedom, withers away and is lost forever.

The capitalists and their emissaries who resort to such bungling attempts at deception and imposture betray the low estimate they place on the intelligence of their wageworkers and also show that they fully understand to what depths of ignorance and credulity these slaves have sunk in the wage system.

In the light of existing conditions, there can be no reform that will be of any great or permanent benefit to the working class.

The present system of private ownership must be abolished, and the workers themselves must be made the owners of the tools with which they work, and to accomplish this they must organize their class for political action, and this work is already well underway in the Socialist Party, which is composed of the working class and stands for the working class on a revolutionary platform which declares in favor of the collective ownership of the means of production and the democratic management of industry in the interest of the whole people.

What intelligent workingman can hold out against the irresistible claim the socialist movement has upon him? What reason has he to give? What excuse can he offer?

None! Not one!

The only worker who has an excuse to keep out of the socialist movement is the unfortunate fellow who is ignorant and does not know better. He does not know what socialism is. That is his misfortune. But that is not all, nor the worst of all. He thinks he knows what it is.

In his ignorance he has taken the word of another for it, whose interest it is to keep him in darkness. So he continues to march with the Republican Party or shout with the Democratic Party, and he no more knows why he is a Republican or Democrat than he knows why he is not a Socialist.

It is impossible for a workingman to contemplate the situation and the outlook and have any intelligent conception of the trend and meaning of things without becoming a Socialist.

Consider for a moment the beastly debasement to which womanhood is subjected in capitalist society. She is simply the property of man to be governed by him as may suit his convenience. She does not vote; she has no voice and must bear silent witness to her legally ordained inferiority.

She has to compete with men in the factories and workshops and stores, and her inferiority is taken advantage of to make her work at still lower wages than the male slave gets who works at her side.

As an economic dependent, she is compelled to sacrifice the innate refinement, the inherent purity and nobility of her sex, and for a pallet of straw marries the man she does not love.

The debauching effect of the capitalist system upon womanhood is accurately registered in the divorce court and the house of shame.

In socialism, woman would stand forth the equal of man—all the avenues would be open to her, and she would naturally find her fitting place and rise from the low plane of menial servility to the dignity of ideal womanhood.

Breathing the air of economic freedom, amply able to provide for herself in socialist society, we may be certain that the cruel injustice that is now perpetrated upon her sex and the degradation that results from it will disappear forever.

Consider again the barren prospect of the average boy who faces the world today. If he is the son of a workingman, his father is able to do little in the way of giving him a start.

He does not get to college, nor even to the high school, but has to be satisfied with what he can get in the lower grades, for as soon as he has physical growth enough to work, he must find something to do, so that he may help support the family.

His father has no influence and can get no preferred employment for him at the expense of some other boy, so he thankfully accepts any kind of service that he may be allowed to perform.

How hard it is to find a place for that boy of yours!

"What shall we do with Johnnie—and Nellie?" is the question of the anxious mother long before they are ripe for the labor market.

"The child is weak, you know," continues the nervous, loving little mother, "and can't do hard work; and I feel dreadfully worried about him."

What a picture! Yet so common that the multitude do not see it. This mother, numbered by thousands many times over, instinctively understands the capitalist system, feels its cruelty, and dreads its approaching horrors which cast their shadows upon her tender, loving heart.

Nothing can be sadder than to see the mother take the boy she bore by the hand and start to town with him to peddle him off as merchandise to someone who has use for a child-slave.

To know just how that feels, one must have had precisely that experience.

The mother looks down so fondly and caressingly upon her boy; and he looks up into her eyes so timidly and appealingly as she explains his good points to the businessman or factory boss, who in turn inspects the lad and interrogates him to verify his mother's claims, and finally informs them that they may call again the following week, but that he does not think he can use the boy.

Well, what finally becomes of the boy? He is now grown, his mother's worry is long since ended, as the grass grows green where she sleeps—and he, the boy? Why, he's a factory hand—a hand, mind you, and he gets a dollar and a quarter a day when the factory is running.

That is all he will ever get.

He is an industrial life prisoner—no pardoning power for him in the capitalist system.

No sweet home, no beautiful wife, no happy children, no books, no flowers, no pictures, no comrades, no love, no joy for him.

Just a hand! A human factory hand!

Think of a hand with a soul in it!

In the capitalist system, the soul has no business. It cannot produce profit by any process of capitalist calculation.

The working hand is what is needed for the capitalist's tool, and so the human must be reduced to a hand.

No head, no heart, no soul—simply a hand.

A thousand hands to one brain—the hands of workingmen, the brain of a capitalist.

A thousand dumb animals, in human form; a thousand slaves in the fetters of ignorance, their heads having run to hands—all these owned and worked and fleeced by one stock-dealing, profit-mongering capitalist.

This is capitalism!

And this system is supported alternately by the Republican Party and the Democratic Party.

These two capitalist parties relieve each other in support of the capitalist system, while the capitalist system relieves the working class of what they produce.

A thousand hands to one head is the abnormal development of the capitalist system.

A thousand workingmen turned into hands to develop and gorge and decorate one capitalist paunch!

This brutal order of things must be overthrown. The human race was not born to degeneracy.

A thousand heads have grown for every thousand pairs of hands; a thousand hearts throb in testimony of the unity of heads and hands; and a thousand souls, though crushed and mangled, burn in protest and are pledged to redeem a thousand men.

Heads and hands, hearts and souls, are the heritage of all.

Full opportunity for full development is the unalienable right of all.

He who denies it is a tyrant; he who does not demand it is a coward; he who is indifferent to it is a slave; he who does not desire it is dead.

The earth for all the people. That is the demand.

The machinery of production and distribution for all the people. That is the demand.

The collective ownership and control of industry and its democratic management in the interest of all the people. That is the demand.

The elimination of rent, interest, and profit, and the production of wealth to satisfy the wants of all the people. That is the demand.

Cooperative industry in which all shall work together in harmony as the basis of a new social order, a higher civilization, a real republic. That is the demand.

The end of class struggles and class rule, of master and slave, of ignorance and vice, of poverty and shame, of cruelty and crime—the birth of freedom, the dawn of brotherhood, the beginning of *man*. That is the demand.

This is socialism!

The Independence Depot Bombing: A Case of Capitalist Infernalism†

June 25, 1904

If the railroad platform recently blown up at Victor, Colorado, resulting in the death of a score of workingmen, was the result of a deliberate plot to commit murder, I will stake my reputation that it was instigated by the mine owners or their hirelings.[27] To me the case is clear as daylight. Of course, the mine owners are too foxy to be connected with the crime in any way that could be proved, but it is safe to assume that their hirelings understood what they were engaged for and earned their pay by performing their hellish duties.

When murder is committed in the dark, the first question is always: Who benefited by it? The question is peculiarly applicable to this case. Who benefited by this crime? The mine owners, of course. At whose expense? The strikers, of course.

The mine owners had everything to gain; the strikers everything to lose. The very instant the explosion occurred, hell broke loose *against the strikers.*

† Published as "Capitalist Infernalism" in *Chicago Socialist,* vol. 6, whole no. 277 (June 25, 1904), 1.

This was a foregone conclusion. Not a question was allowed. No ifs or ands or explanations. *Wipe out the Western Federation of Miners and crush the strikers to the earth!* That is what the explosion was plotted for, and to conceal their tracks, the mine owners and their lickspittle Citizens' Alliance at once force the sheriff and other officers of the law to resign and by violence took the machinery of law into their own hands so that they might conduct the investigation, cover up the corporation criminals, and convict innocent union men.

They will have any number of paid character assassins on the ground to swear to anything that may be necessary to carry out their diabolical program. But it will fail! No matter how cunningly devised or how skillfully they do their work, the truth will out at last, and the real conspirators will come to light. It has been so in the past, and it will be so again.

All the powers of Peabody, Bell,[28] and the horde of bloodthirsty labor exploiters they represent, all the powers of hell and capitalism cannot prevail against the truth.

During the Pullman strike, hundreds of instances occurred to prove the allegations herein contained. In California, the sleuthhounds of the Southern Pacific laid a net and caught a weak-minded member of the ARU to join a plot to wreck a train. The ARU member was caught, of course, and sentenced. The capitalist press howled down the ARU, and the whole state arose in arms against it, even the members of the order being misled, many of them turning upon their former associates, who remained loyal in spite of the criminal conspiracy to destroy the organization.

In Utah, the Union Pacific detectives got a couple of members of the ARU drunk and hauled them out of town to a point along the line where they found some tools and set to work to pull up a rail about the time a train was due. But the whole thing was so carefully arranged that before the rail was lifted, the train came to a stop, and at the same moment the sheriff and his deputies stepped out from the bushes and placed the alleged train wreckers under arrest.

Of course, the press had screaming headlines an hour later, announcing the fiendish conspiracy of the ARU, and demanded that all the powers of the state be invoked to crush it out of existence. Of course, the politicians and preachers and other patriots (?) all joined heartily in the chorus, with the result that the strike was broken up, the order disrupted, and the poor devils sent to the penitentiary.

In due time their innocence was admitted by the decent people of Salt Lake City, including officers of the law, and they were pardoned.

Were it necessary, I could tell of hundreds of instances, and produce absolute proof, where detectives and spies and spotters and sneaks in the service of the corporations instigated violence, set fires, and committed numberless other crimes to make strikers appear as rioters, incendiaries, and murderers that injunctions might be issued against them to restrain them of their liberty, that soldiers might be called out to massacre them, and that the people of the country might turn upon them as if they were monsters seeking to devour their fellow beings instead of half-starved workingmen mildly protesting against the crimes they could no longer bear.

The union miners of Colorado are not guilty. I will put my word against that of Sherman Bell, who has already announced, according to the press dispatches, that 40 or 50 of them would swing for the crime. He has unmasked his animus and revealed his spirit. He has given his case away. In the exultation of the moment, he has laid bare the plot to fasten the guilt of crime upon union men before they have been tried.

Just at this moment he has the power of a petty despot, but he would better beware. If he and his law-defying, crime-inciting pals bring innocent men to the gallows, they may live to feel the noose around their own necks, and they certainly will live to see the blood of these victims of capitalist robbery and military anarchy washed away in a torrent of retributive justice.

O, workingmen of Colorado, this is the supreme hour of your lives. You have been tried by fire and sword, by dungeon and by devils. You have not lowered your colors, and I appeal to you not to lower them now. They have done their worst and you have stood it all, and you can and will stand the rest.

Stand solid as a granite wall in this fight, and you will render the cause of labor a service that generations yet unborn will thank and honor you for.

Don't surrender! Die rather!

They can no more crush out the spirit of unionism than they can expel the mountains or snuff out the sun.

You are fighting for humanity, and every day of the struggle hastens the day of liberation.

If they deport you, return again and again and again.

You represent an internal principle that they will battle against in vain.

Their petty temporary victories will but hasten the day of their own crushing and everlasting defeat.

It is the class struggle you are engaged in. You are the workers, they are the capitalists; you are the producers, they are the parasites; you are the victims, they are the robbers.

You are in the majority, overwhelmingly. Unite! Close up the ranks!

Every true man is with you. Swear that by the eternal you will hold your ground to the bitter end.

This year you have your supreme opportunity. The national election gives you your chance.

Strike, I appeal to you, a blow on election day that will shake the capitalists of Colorado and the nation out of their boots.

Would you strike terror to the craven souls of the class who are murdering and starving you? Would you have all opposition to unionism withdrawn and have those who now smite you smile fawningly upon you? Would you restore law and order and go back into the mines as union men? Would you strike a blow in the interest of the working class that will be felt throughout the length and breadth of the land? Would you see Peabody cower in abject fear and Sherman Bell turn pale as the victims of his military hyenaism? Would you revive hope in the breasts of despairing toilers, cheer their desponding wives, and comfort their terror-stricken children? Would you strike at the black heart of tyranny, rebuke its murderous minions, repudiate its cringing apologists, and have the handwriting blaze upon the wall where every capitalist and every coward may read their inevitable doom? Would you assert your own manhood, hold your head erect, and feel the throb of coming freedom?

If you would see these things and more to follow along the same lines, you have one thing to do. In November next, march to the polls from end to end of the state in one solid phalanx and deposit a round hundred thousand votes for revolutionary socialism.

One hundred thousand votes at least for the Socialist Party and emancipation. This will strike terror to Peabody and raise hell in Wall Street.

Do it and you will have answered the challenge of the mine owners on their own ground.

Do it and you will vitalize and inspire the labor movement of America and the world.

Do it and you are triumphant, and the enemy will disappear before your march like chaff before the cyclone.

Do less than this and you are defeated, broken, humiliated, in the dirt with the spurred heel of a military satrap on your neck.

If after what you have seen and felt and suffered under a capitalist administration; a Democratic governor in Idaho, a Republican governor in Colorado; injunctions, soldiers, bull pens, deportations, and numberless crimes committed everywhere under Republican rule and Democratic rule, the twin rule of capitalist tyranny; if after all this you go to the polls and vote the Republican ticket or the Democratic ticket, you ought to be damned and you will be, as surely as servile submission to slavery has always been damned throughout all the centuries of the past.

But you will not be guilty of such foul treason to principle, such cowardly betrayal of your class. You will be men and you will do your duty while the world looks on and awaits your revolutionary verdict.

The Anniversary of Class War in Colorado†

June 25, 1904

Almost a year has passed since the strikes were precipitated in Colorado.

What caused them and who is responsible for the consequences?

Let the naked facts be stated.

The legislature of Colorado passed an eight-hour law in 1899 exactly like the eight-hour law of Utah, which the United States Supreme Court had declared constitutional.

The Supreme Court of Colorado, owned bodily by the Mine Owners' Association and Smelter Trust, declared the law unconstitutional.

In 1902, a constitutional amendment was submitted to the people of the state, commanding the legislature in express terms to pass an eight-hour law. *This was carried out by a popular majority of more than 40,000 votes.*

The legislature met and was bought outright by the mine and mill owners with scarcely an attempt to conceal the damnable crime. The members of the legislature, with the gold of the capitalists bulging in their breeches, refused to pass the law demanded by a majority of more than 40,000 of the people.

These are the absolute facts. No one can deny them. These foul facts caused the present strike.

The mine, mill, and smelter workers, inhaling the poison fumes and gases which undermined their health and destroyed their lives, struck only after the mine and mill owners had debauched the Supreme Court, bought the legislature,

---

† Published as "Debs on Colorado!" in *Social Democratic Herald,* vol. 8, whole no. 308 (June 25, 1904), 1.

and trampled roughshod over the legally expressed will of the people.

The miners struck for their lives.

They struck as the very last resort.

Who are the criminals, the lawbreakers, the killers of men, the corrupters of the body politic, the debauchers of the nation?

Who but the capitalist anarchists who compose the Mine Owners' Association, the Colorado Fuel and Iron Company, and the American Smelting and Refining Company?

These are the brazen brigands who have the flint face to talk about law and order.

"To hell with the constitution" has been their murderous motto from the start, and their trail is red with the blood of the working class.

The latest crime in their desperation to crush the Western Federation of Miners was the blowing up of the depot platform at Victor,[29] filled with workingmen. Note that not a mine owner, nor any other capitalist, or member of the Citizens' Alliance, or detective, or other corporation hireling was on the platform. Only poor, dumb workingmen were blown up to cover up the crimes of capital and bring down the wrath of the nation upon the union miners.

The mine owners charge the union miners instigated the crime.

It is a foul and damnable lie.

If these capitalist conspirators, these dressed-up footpads, were not substitute of conscience as cobras, this vile and abominable lie would stick in their throats, turn their faces black, and strangle them to death.

They will have character assassins in plenty to swear away the lives of men their blood-blotched gold could not buy.

Sherman Bell has already announced they would swing—this without evidence and before being tried—and this in the name of law and order.

Who benefited from the crime? The mine owners. Who are its victims? The union miners.

Who compelled the sheriff and other officers of the law, under threat of hanging, to resign their offices and filled them with corporation hirelings? The mine owners. Who were bound and gagged and clubbed and bull-penned and deported and shot dead without a hearing? The union miners.

Let them dare hand one of these innocent men and by the gods of retribution, hell will crack about their own ears before the curtain falls on the last scene of their gory revelry.

In 1859, the slave owners of Virginia hung old John Brown, the criminal agitator.

In 1860, Abraham Lincoln was elected president of the United States.

In 1861, the earth shook beneath the tread of armed legions and millions were singing:

> John Brown's body lies a moldering in the ground,
> But his soul goes marching on.

In 1863, the proclamation of emancipation was issued.

In 1865, less than six years after John Brown was murdered, as the mine owners of Colorado now threaten to murder union leaders, the slave owners were annihilated, and chattel slavery was wiped from the earth in a storm of iron and a deluge of blood.

Then it was chattel slavery. Now it is wage-slavery. Then it concerned a few Negroes. Now it embraces all the workers of the world.

"Whom the gods would destroy they first make mad."[30]

The gods made the slave owners mad and smote them to death.

The gods are making the Colorado capitalists mad, and in their blind fury they are rushing to their doom.

Let them hand an innocent union man in Colorado. Let them sow the wind! Let them put their own necks in the nooses!

They will reap the crop they are sowing to the smallest seed of injustice.

And now a vital question: Why are the capitalists of Colorado and the nation waging a war of extermination upon the Western Federation of Miners and the American Labor Union?

Why? Why?

Because they declared for socialism.

That is the reason—the only reason.

Their assault, therefore, is not upon labor unionism, but upon socialism.

This makes it our fight—the fight of the whole working class.

Let us recognize this fact and support our comrades in Colorado to the bitter end.

We see our comrades in the Rocky Mountains murdered in cold blood by hired mercenaries, driven from home, forced out of the state, and dumped on the desert to die like lepers, crowded like cattle in festering pens and fed on vermin; bludgeoned, bayonetted, insulted, and outraged in a thousand other ways.

We see the governor as the servile tool of the mine owners, the Supreme Court their fawning sycophants, and the legislature their bought-and-paid-for lickspittles.

We see President Roosevelt smiling serenely upon this bloody scene, as

Peabody blows out the Constitution and Sherman Bell struts the state an armed bully. Would Roosevelt lack the power to act if Moyer and Haywood were in the roles of Peabody and Bell?

Not a word from Roosevelt. Not a word from Judge Parker, from Gorman, McClellan, Hill, or Hearst. Not one. Not one.

These are the national representatives of the Republican Party and the Democratic Party. Their silence proclaims their attitude. They and their parties are with the capitalist anarchists of Colorado, who are strangling law and assassinating labor.

The Socialist Party alone is the party of the union men of Colorado. The mine owners are well aware of this, and their hostility to the union is but the pretext for their determination to stamp the Socialist Party out of Colorado.

That is the issue.

The mine owners understand it clearly, and all the capitalists are lined up accordingly.

Let us face the issue and fight it out.

They may win the skirmishes. The ultimate victory is ours. We can stand ten thousand defeats. The working class cannot be vanquished.

The capitalist mine-owning class have got to go. The working class are bound to come.

And now for action! We, the socialists of America, should appoint a Colorado Day to hoist aloft the banner of revolt.

The National Committee of the Socialist Party, it is suggested, should issue a proclamation to all the socialists of the land. Let the first Sunday in August or some other suitable day be appointed as Colorado Day and celebrated throughout the land as the anniversary of the class war in the Rocky Mountains in which our comrades are so valiantly engaged.

Let the socialists rally in every village, town, and city. Let them gather outdoors and tell the story of the struggle of the people.

Let them recite the crimes of capitalism in Colorado and indict the ruling class at the bar of justice.

Let them proclaim the principles of socialism and point the way to freedom.

Let them also appeal to each and every listener in every audience to add his mite to the collection, make it large as possible, and send the amount to William D. Haywood, national secretary, Western Federation of Miners, 625 Mining Exchange Building, Denver, Colorado.

If immediate steps are taken, the day can be made memorable in the annals of the class struggle. The people are already aroused, and a thousand socialist orators can move them to action.

Let us unite from end to end of the land and across the Canadian border in celebration of the anniversary of the Colorado class struggle, and on that day the mine owners of Colorado and the coupon-clippers of Wall Street and the exploiters of labor everywhere will distinctly hear the rumblings of the social revolution.

The American Movement[†31]

August 1904

The twentieth century, according to the prophecy of Victor Hugo, is to be the century of humanity.

In all the procession of the centuries gone, not one was for humanity. From the very first, tyranny has flourished, freedom has failed; the few have ruled, the many have served; the parasite has worn the purple of power, while honest industry has lived in poverty and died in despair.

But the eternal years, the centuries yet to come, are for humanity, and out of the misery of the past will rise the civilization of the future.

The nineteenth century evolved the liberating and humanizing movement; the twentieth century will doubtless witness its culmination in the crash of despotisms and the rise of worldwide democracy, freedom, and brotherhood.

It was while in exile, in 1864, that Hugo wrote:

> The transformation of the crowd into the people—profound task! It is to this labor that the men called socialists have devoted themselves during the last 40 years. The author of this book, however insignificant he may be, is one of the oldest in this labor. If he claims his place among these philosophers, it is because it is a place of persecution. A certain hatred of socialism, very blind, but very general, has raged for 15 or 16 years, and

---

† Published as a pamphlet by Debs *The American Movement* (Terre Haute, IN: Standard Publishing Co. 1904), Reprinted as a pamphlet by Charles H. Kerr & Co.

> is still raging most bitterly among the influential classes. Let it not be forgotten that true socialism has for its end the elevation of the masses to the civic dignity, and that, therefore, the principal care is for moral and intellectual cultivation.[32]

If, as we are quite ready to believe, the twentieth century realizes the prophecy of the French poet and "bursts full-blossomed on the thorny stem of time" as the century of humanity—it will be the denouement of the socialist agitation that began in the preceding century—the fruition of the international socialist movement.

In the closing years of the last century, following in the wake of the French Revolution, the tendencies in Europe were unmistakably toward what has since developed into modern socialism. Of course, the early stages were nebulous and vague, and the trend was not yet strongly marked or clearly disclosed.

But as the inventive genius of man asserted itself in the industrial world; as the use of steam as motive power expanded and machinery was introduced and its application to industry became more general, with its inevitable effects upon artisans, laborers, and small tradesmen, the movement was accelerated in varying forms, chiefly utopian, until many years afterward, toward the middle of the nineteenth century, when it was crystallized by the genius of Marx, Engels, Lassalle, and others, who caught the revolutionary current, clarified it, and sent it circling round the globe on its mission of freedom and fraternity.

The earliest traces of socialism in the United States had their origin in the stream of immigration that flowed from the old world to the new and bore upon its bosom the germs of discontent warmed into life in the effete feudalism of European civilization. We shall not here undertake to chronicle the many attempts, covering more than half a century, or until about 1840, to spread socialism or semi-socialistic doctrine among the American people and thus turn the tide of labor agitation in that direction. The times were fruitful of industrial and social unrest and the many schemes and plans that were proposed, utopian, impractical, impossible though they undoubtedly were, were at the same time the signs and symptoms of social gestation, the forerunners of the mighty change that was laying hold of governments and institutions and destined to revolutionize them all and level the human race upward to the plane of all-embracing civilization.

Almost 80 years ago, Robert Owen,[33] dreamer, enthusiast, and humanitarian, came from England to America to make the new continent blossom with utopian splendor. His series of experiments in communism, doomed to disappointment and failure, are an interesting study in the early years of the

American movement; and although in the light of our present knowledge of industrial evolution his undertaking may seem visionary and foolish to some, he rendered invaluable service in clearing away the brush and dispelling the fog; and the history of socialism cannot be written without his name.

Decidedly less utopian and more practical and promising were the developments in the '40s when what is known as Fourierism played its interesting and historic role in America. Many of the most intellectual men and women of the day were attracted to the movement. The most ardent enthusiasm seized the devotees, and they set to work with hand and heart to convert the American wilderness into the promised land of milk and honey. Of course, the dominant strain was emotional and sympathetic, but there was nevertheless a solid substratum of scientific soundness in the undertaking, as is proved conclusively by the writings of the men who so heartily gave it support.

Brook Farm, a beautiful reminiscence, tinged with disappointment, was founded near Boston in 1841. Among the many illustrious names associated with Brook Farm, the following have peculiar interest after 60 years: George Ripley,[34] Ralph Waldo Emerson,[35] Horace Greeley, James Russell Lowell, John Greenleaf Whittier, William Cullen Bryant, Albert Brisbane,[36] Ellery Channing,[37] James Freeman Clarke,[38] Theodore Parker,[39] A. Bronson Alcott,[40] John Thomas Codman,[41] Henry D. Thoreau,[42] Nathaniel Hawthorne,[43] George Bancroft,[44] Charles A. Dana,[45] and George William Curtis.[46]

The Brook Farm Association, organized by "intellectuals" who had no knowledge of the laws of economic determinism or of the historic evolution of society, was ideal in conception and breathed the air of equality and brotherhood. The association declared its object to be "a radical and universal reform, rather than to redress any particular wrong . . ." In the "preliminary statement," the members announced that the work they had undertaken was not a "mere resolution, but a necessary step in the progress which no one can be blind enough to think has yet reached its limit."

They said, furthermore:

> We believe that humanity, trained by these long centuries of suffering and struggle, led onward by so many saints and heroes and sages, is at length prepared to enter into that universal order toward which it has perpetually moved. Thus . . . we declare that the imperative duty of this time and this country, nay, more, that its only salvation, and the salvation of civilized countries, lies in the reorganization of society according to the unchanging laws of human nature and of universal harmony . . .

These passages are indicative of a clear perception for that time and would require but little remodeling to adapt them for incorporation into a modern scientific socialist platform.

The closing paragraph, which follows, is worthy to be preserved in socialist literature. It voices in lofty strain the conviction of the Brook Farmers in the ultimate realization of their hope for something like a Cooperative Commonwealth. They say:

> And whatever may be the result of any special efforts, we can never doubt that the object we have in view shall be finally attained; that human life shall yet be developed, not in discord and misery, but in harmony and joy, and that the perfected earth shall at last bear on her bosom a race of men worthy of the name.

This was written in January 1844, and the whole document bears evidence of socialistic thought and tendencies.

Ralph Waldo Emerson wrote: "And truly, I honor the generous ideas of the socialists, the magnificence of their theories, and the enthusiasm with which they have been urged."

Albert Brisbane, Parke Godwin,[47] and Horace Greeley, the latter unique and in some respects the most clear-sighted and practical of them all, were commanding figures in that day. All of them had human blood in their veins—all had democratic instincts and perceived more or less clearly the drift of the time, the tendency toward collective society, industrial freedom, and social justice.

In the meantime, Marx and his coadjutors were clearing the murky atmosphere of the old world. They were dissecting the prevailing mode of production and capitalist society in general, and in their researches discovered the fundamental law of social development in the "materialistic conception of history," the scientific basis of socialist thought and activity throughout the world. From this time forward, the working-class movement had a scientific foundation, the scattered and contentious factions were gradually united and harmonized, and socialism became a distinct and recognized factor in the industrial and political destiny of the race.

Following the example and taking inspiration from the pioneers of the old world, and reinforced by the socialists who crossed the water and at once began the proselyting inherent in the revolutionary spirit, the Americans took heart; they entered upon their labors with renewed zeal, scattered the seed of the socialist philosophy, and it struck root in American soil.

Albert Brisbane was one of the commanding figures in inspiring and directing the American movement. He was a pronounced socialist and as early as 1840 set forth his views in a volume entitled *Social Destiny of Man: or, Association and Reorganization of Industry.*[48] In this work, Brisbane made a strong plea and cogent argument in favor of cooperative industry and "an equitable distribution of profits to each individual."

Going to Europe in 1848, Brisbane for the first time met Karl Marx at Cologne, of whom he afterward wrote as follows:

> I found there Karl Marx, the leader of the popular movement. The writings of Marx on labor and capital and the social theories he then elaborated have had more influence on the great socialistic movement of Europe than that of any other man. He it was who laid the foundation of that modern collectivism which at present bids fair to become the leading socialist doctrine of Europe. He was then just rising into prominence; a man of some thirty years, short, solidly built, with a fine face and bushy black hair. His expression was that of great energy, and behind his self-contained reserve of manner were visible the fire and passion of a great soul . . .
>
> Briefly stated, as represented by the collectivism of today, his doctrine demands the abolition of individual ownership of the natural wealth of the world—the soil, the mines, the inventions and creations of industry which are the means of production, as well as of the machinery of the world. This wealth, furnished by nature, or created by the genius of humanity, is to be made collective property, held by the state (collectively) for the equal advantage of the whole body of the people. Governments are to represent the collective intelligence of the nation; to manage, direct, and supervise all general operations and relations of an industrial character . . .

Brisbane traveled extensively in Europe, met the men of note in the principal countries, and studied the industrial and social conditions with a view to propagating the collectivist movement in the United States. On his return, filled with the spirit of enthusiasm, he vigorously entered upon his work of agitation and is fairly entitled to the credit of having rendered great service in the pioneer work of starting the socialist movement in America.

Without desire to disparage any of the men of that time by invidious comparison, the immense personality and rustic simplicity, coupled with the keen perception, rugged honesty, and intense earnestness of Horace Greeley, command special admiration. The power of Greeley's influence in the early history of the socialist movement in America, when hate and persecution were aroused by the mere mention of it, has never yet been fairly recognized. He has been called "our later Franklin" and deserves the title.

Parton, the biographer of Greeley, said:

> The subject of Greeley's oratory is one alone; it is ever the same; the object of his public life is single. It is the "emancipation of labor," its emancipation from ignorance, vice, servitude, insecurity, poverty. This is his chosen, only theme, whether he speaks from the platform or writes for the *Tribune*.[49]

Horace Greeley was in the true sense a labor leader. He was the first president of Typographical Union No. 6 of New York City and took advanced ground on every question that affected not only the printers but the whole working class. There was nothing conservative about the views of Greeley on the labor question. He was, above all else, radical and progressive, that is to say, revolutionary, and the labor leaders of today could, with credit to themselves and benefit to their organizations, study his character and writings and follow his example.

The upheaval in Europe in 1848 forced many of the radicals and socialists into exile; and the general tide that set in toward the Western world bore many of these restless spirits to our shores; and no sooner were they landed before they began to sow the revolutionary seed and organize the propaganda they had been compelled to abandon on the other side.

The German socialists who came over were the very men needed here at that time. They were trained and disciplined in the "old guard"; they had the rugged bearing and fearlessness of army veterans, and they knew no such word as discouragement or failure. Among these sturdy agitators, Wilhelm Weitling[50] bore a conspicuous part in preparing the way for organization and for action along political lines.

From this time the propaganda became more active and also clearer and more definite in character. The movement was gradually evolving from the haze of communism that clung to it through all its early years and was beginning to take form as an independent political organization with the central object of conquering the powers of government as a means of emancipating the working class from wage-slavery. Labor unions, turner bunds, and singing societies were organized all through the '50s, all tending in the same direction and, though not all pronounced, having substantially the same end in view.

In this brief sketch, we have not the space to record in detail the many attempts that were made to organize a national working-class political movement in the United States. This must be the work of the historian, and fortunately for the reader and student, he has recently appeared. The first authentic volume upon the subject is the *History of Socialism in the United States,* by Morris Hillquit,[51] a book of over 350 pages, written in excellent style and treating ably and exhaustively the various stages of the development from its inception to the large and growing movement of our day.

The little volume entitled *A Brief History of Socialism in America,* by Frederic Heath,[52] editor of the *Social Democratic Herald,* a valuable collection of historical data to which has been added much original matter, both interesting and instructive, is also well worthy of perusal.

Professor Richard T. Ely, in his *Labor Movement in America,* discussing the "Beginnings of Modern Socialism," says in reference to the period we are now considering:

> The socialism of today may be said to date from the European revolutions of 1848, all of which soon terminated disastrously for the people as opposed to their rulers. Many German refugees sought our shores, and some of them were ardent socialists and communists, who endeavored to propagate their ideas. Wilhelm Weitling, a tailor, born in Magdeburg in 1808, was prominent among these . . . became one of the first to scatter those seeds of economic radicalism which have brought forth such large increase in the social democracy of our own times.[53]

The first large society to adopt and propagate socialism in America was composed of the German gymnastic unions (Turnverein).[54] The Socialist Turnverein of New York drew up a constitution for an association, to be composed of the various local gymnastic unions, and published it in 1850. A preliminary gathering of a few delegates was held in New York in the Shakespeare Hotel, then the headquarters of the "progressive" elements among the Germans. It was finally decided to call a meeting of delegates, to be held in Philadelphia, on October 5 of the same year, to effect a permanent organization. Several Turnverein acted on the suggestion, and among others, delegates were present from New York, Boston, and Baltimore. The first name adopted was "Associated Gymnastic Unions of North America" which was, however, changed the following year to "Socialistic Gymnastic Union."

Through the '60s and '70s, the agitation steadily increased, local organizations were formed in various parts of the country, but they were chiefly for the passing day and, after serving their temporary purpose, disappeared.

The American Civil War and the emancipation of the Negro race which followed, resulting in millions of "free" Negroes being thrown upon the "labor market," had its effect in developing capitalist production.

The years following the war marked an era of extraordinary industrial and commercial activity. Inventive genius was taxed to provide machinery and the power necessary to operate it in factory, mill, and mine. Manufacturing developed at an enormous rate. The railroads were penetrating the great West, and the population spread over the vast domain. Then came the symptoms of congestion, the glutted markets and the clogging of the productive machinery. The "good times" had come to a sudden end; factories and workshops closed down; railroads reduced wages and discharged thousands. The country swarmed with unemployed workingmen; everybody was ominously discussing the "panic" and the "hard times." Discontent was brewing, and strikes were threatened by the idle workers.

The railroad strikes and many others broke out in the financial crisis of 1873. It was a period of financial bankruptcy, industrial stagnation, and general gloom. The sheriff's hammer was heard everywhere beating the dolorous funeral marches of departed prosperity. It was during this panic that the "tramp" era was inaugurated in the United States and the tramp became a recognized factor in our social life.

The trade union movement had organized rapidly during the years of industrial prosperity. Many of the trades had formed national organizations, and when the crash came, the strikes followed in rapid order.

In July 1877, the railroad strikes, supported by the railroad brotherhoods, notably the Brotherhood of Locomotive Engineers and Brotherhood of Locomotive Firemen, waged with intense severity and resulting in widespread rioting, bloodshed, and destruction of property, spread over a vast area of the country and threatened the direst consequences if the grievances of the strikers were not adjusted. This was among the first strikes in which the writer had an active part, and many incidents and scenes are remembered which would make an interesting chapter of proletarian history.[55]

The story of these strikes was written by Allan Pinkerton, the detective, in a curious volume *entitled Strikers, Communists, Tramps, and Detectives.*[56] The volume has the portrait of the late P. M. Arthur, grand chief of the Brotherhood of Locomotive Engineers, who was then regarded as a radical labor agitator, as the frontispiece. It also contains a complete exposé of the brotherhood, illustrated with diagrams and including its ceremony of initiation, signs, passwords, and all of its secret inner workings.

The strikes spread rapidly east and west and were followed by rioting and violence in most of the railroad centers. The Pittsburgh riots were the most disastrous in the loss of life and destruction of property. In his account of it, Allan Pinkerton, describing the charge of the militia upon the mob, says:

> Suddenly a little puff of smoke shot out from a second-story window, followed by a ringing report and a quick cry from a soldier who had been struck, but not dangerously wounded.
>
> Back along the column came the officers, exhorting the men to be patient and not return the fire.
>
> The speed of the troops increased. The energy of the mob redoubled. The pistol shot from the window seemed almost a signal, for instantly afterward, from along the crowd's front, several more shots were fired, and but a few minutes more had elapsed, until from behind every lamppost, over every hydrant head, and from out every door and window, shot the flame, the smoke, and the bullets.
>
> Soldiers fell; and now their comrades returned the fire, while, as in every other instance, the disorganized, howling mob received far the worst punishment. Some of the wounded soldiers would escape with their lives through the devices, and at the personal risk of humane people along the street who gave them help and shelter. Others, not so fortunate, were heartlessly murdered when too helpless for defense.
>
> * * *
>
> At one point near where a good deal of killing had been done the previous day . . . a building at the corner of the streets not only was completely riddled with bullets, but bore evidence of the earnest efforts on behalf of religion by the Young Men's Christian Association in the shape of a poster upon which was placarded the startling warning: "Prepare to Meet Thy God!"[57]

The strikes were finally crushed out and the leaders driven out and blacklisted.

It was in this struggle that the powers of the federal courts were first invoked to break a railroad strike. The strike leaders and committees were arrested by order of the federal judges, sitting at Indianapolis, Indiana, and committed to jail upon various trumped-up charges.

The late president Benjamin Harrison had the exclusive distinction of having served the railway corporations in the dual capacity of lawyer and soldier. He prosecuted the strikers in the federal courts, securing prison sentences for them, and he also organized and commanded a company of soldiers during the strike, and made speeches denouncing the strikers.

Ten years later he was elevated to the presidency of the United States.

The loss of the strike was a staggering blow to organized labor, and many unions passed out of existence. Upon the railroads the mere suspicion of belonging to a union was sufficient ground for instant discharge.

In time, however, the ban was removed, the corporations feeling themselves the masters of the situation, and with returning financial and industrial activity, the work of organization was resumed with greater energy and determination than ever before.

In the events that followed swiftly during these years, it will be noted that the United States had become entirely Europeanized in respect to the suppression of exploited and discontented workingmen.

It is scarcely necessary to observe in this connection that capitalism is the same everywhere, that like causes produce like results.

Wherever capitalism appears, in pursuit of its mission of exploitation, there will socialism, fertilized by misery, watered by tears, and vitalized by agitation, be also found, unfurling its class-struggle banner and proclaiming its mission of emancipation.

During all these years of strikes and strife, of occasional victory and frequent defeat for labor, the socialist agitation was kept up as far as conditions and means would allow. Under the most unfavorable circumstances the comrades did what they could, held their ground, and patiently waited for a more favorable turn in the situation.

Following the Paris Commune in 1871 and its tragic ending, many French radicals came to our shores and gave new spirit to the movement. Referring to these, Professor Ely, in his *Labor Movement in America,* says:

> In 1871 a new impulse was received from the French refugees who came to America after the suppression of the uprising of the commune of Paris and brought with them a spirit of violence, but a more important event in this early period was the order of the congress of the International held in the Hague in 1872, which transferred to New York the "general council" of the association. Modern socialism had then undoubtedly begun to exist in America. The first proclamation of the council from their new headquarters was an appeal to workingmen "to emancipate labor and eradicate all international and national strife."
>
> In the spring of 1872, "an imposing demonstration" in favor of eight hours took place in New York City. The paper before me estimates the number of those taking part in the procession through the principal streets at 20,000, and among the other societies were the various New York sections of the International Workingmen's Association bearing a banner with their motto "Workingmen of All Countries, Unite!" The

> following year witnessed the disasters in the industrial and commercial world . . . and the distress consequent thereupon was an important aid to their propaganda. The "Exceptional Law" passed against socialists by the German Parliament in 1878, drove many socialists from Germany to this country, and these have strengthened the cause of American socialism through membership in trade unions and in the Socialist Labor Party.
>
> There have been several changes among the socialists in party organization and name since 1873, and national conventions or congresses have met from time to time. Their dates and places of meeting have been Philadelphia, 1874; Pittsburgh, 1876; Newark, 1877; Allegheny City, 1880; Baltimore and Pittsburgh, 1883; and Cincinnati, 1885. The name "Socialist Labor Party" was adopted in 1877 at the Newark convention. In 1883, the split between the moderates and extremists had become definite, and the latter held their congress in Pittsburgh and the former in Baltimore.[58]

In 1876, the Workingmen's Party was organized, and in 1877, at the convention held at Newark, it became the Socialist Labor Party. The course of the party was marked by bitter internal dissension. While the membership was largely made up of radicals, they were elementally inharmonious and at cross purposes.

The common point of union was hostility to the prevailing regime; beyond that the trouble began, for the anarchists and communists were still in the same movement with the socialists, having yet to be differentiated in the subsequent industrial and social development.

The socialists were intent upon building up a working-class party for independent political action; the anarchists repudiated the ballot and advocated the overthrow of capitalist rule by any means, including force.

August Spies, who was afterward executed for his alleged complicity in the Haymarket riots, was at this time a prominent member of the party. He used anarchism and socialism as synonymous terms. He said: "Anarchism, or socialism, means the reorganization of society upon scientific principles and the abolition of causes which produce vice and crime."

George Engel, who shared the same cruel fate, said:

> Anarchism and socialism are as much alike, in my opinion, as one egg is to another. They differ only in their tactics. The anarchists have abandoned the way of liberating humanity which socialists would take to accomplish this, I say: Believe no more in the ballot, and use all other means at your command.

These differences in tactics alluded to by Engel not only created violent dissensions in the party but resulted in the withdrawal of the anarchists into groups of their own, followed later by the execution and imprisonment of their leaders because of their alleged participation in the Haymarket riots.

But with all the difficulties that confronted it on every hand and the fierce factional contention within its own ranks, the Socialist Labor Party, composed of thoughtful, intelligent men, aggressive and progressive, of rugged honesty and thrilled with the revolutionary spirit and the aspiration for freedom, became from its inception a decided factor in the labor movement. It first appeared upon the scene when the country was seething with discontent, the result of the prolonged period of financial and industrial depression that began in 1873 and like a scourge spread rapidly over the country, leaving desolation and gloom in its wake. To the working class it was an ordeal of fire, but the suffering and sacrifice were not in vain. Economic necessity determined the course of events, and the workers, some of them at least, had their eyes opened to the cause of their misery and were thus impelled to action looking to the abolition of the existing industrial order, based upon wage-slavery, rather than giving themselves wholly, as they had hitherto done, to the fruitless task, as it now appeared, of ameliorating its effects and consequences. It was these men, led by the foreign radicals, who had long before been scourged by the capitalist masters in their own lands, who rallied to the revolutionary standard of the new working-class party.

That such a party was born to a tempestuous career was, of course, a foregone conclusion. Its early trials and struggles tested the dauntless spirit of the comrades who engaged in them and constitute a thrilling chapter—which one day will be adequately understood and appreciated—in the labor movement of the United States.

The busy, ignorant world about this revolutionary nucleus knew little or nothing about it; had no conception of its significance and looked upon its adherents as foolish fanatics whose antics were harmless and whose designs would dissolve like bubbles on the surface of a stream.

Looking backward, it is not difficult to see what importance attaches to this beginning of the political organization of the working class, as a class, for the distinct purpose of conquering the public powers and emancipating the toilers from the inhumanity of wage-slavery.

Discussing this period and the work covered by it, Morris Hillquit, in his *History of Socialism in the United States,* says:

> The Socialist Labor Party was the dominant factor in the socialist move-

> ment of this country for more than 20 years, and its variegated career forms the most intricate and interesting part of the history of American socialism.
>
> At the first glance it appears a series of incoherent events, ill-considered political experiments, sudden changes of policy, incongruous alliances, internal and external strife, and a succession of unaccountable ups and downs, with no perceptible progress or gain.
>
> But the confusion is only apparent. On closer analysis we find a logical thread running all through the seemingly devious course of the party, and a good reason for every one of its seemingly planless moves.
>
> The difficulties which beset the path of the Socialist Labor Party were extraordinary. As one of the first socialist parties organized in this country on a national scale, it had to cope with the usual adversities which attend every radical reform movement at the outset of its career—weakness and diffidence in its own ranks, hostility and ridicule from the outside.[59]

These were stirring times. The trade union movement was entering upon a period of unprecedented activity. The Knights of Labor were in the ascendant, and other labor unions were multiplying and rapidly increasing their membership. Everywhere the voice of the agitator was heard. In March 1885 was inaugurated the strike of the Knights of Labor on the Gould Southwestern Railway system, to be followed by the greater strike on the same system in 1886, which spread rapidly over the states of Missouri, Illinois, Arkansas, Kansas, and Texas, and threatened to involve the railway traffic of all the western and southwestern states. It was one of the most notable labor strikes and brought the Knights of Labor conspicuously before the whole country. The Knights were finally beaten, although the fight was so stubbornly contested, and the public was so thoroughly aroused, that Congress was prevailed upon to investigate the trouble and the committee issued a detailed report in two parts containing about 1100 pages.

On May 1 of the same year, the general strikes for the eight-hour work day broke out in various parts of the country, involving several hundred thousand organized workers, most of whom met with disappointment and failure.

The agitation carried on during this time for the shorter work day, known as the eight-hour movement, culminated on May 4, 1886, in the Haymarket riots at Chicago and the outrageous execution of the anarchists on November 11 of the following year, a foul blot on our capitalistic civilization that will remain to damn it forever.

The murderous assaults upon peaceable meetings and the brutal clubbing of orderly workingmen by the police of Chicago at the behest of their political superiors, the tools of the capitalist class, goaded the leaders almost to desperation and led to the Haymarket massacre, a fiendish plot to silence the agitation and crush the movement for an eight-hour workday which was spreading over the country; and. it must be confessed, it served for a time at least the malign purpose of the pretended supporters of "law and order." But as certain as retributive justice pursues her course, the dragon's teeth sown by the capitalist hand in the Haymarket tragedy, taking root in the blood of innocent workingmen, will yet spring from the pregnant soil of freedom to avenge the crimes of plutocratic tyranny and misrule.

In 1884, Laurence Gronlund[60] published his *Cooperative Commonwealth* and he was doubtless right when he claimed, six years later, that this work had contributed its full share to the spread of socialism. Gronlund said that as late as 1880 he could count all the native American socialists on the fingers of one hand. When the patient labors, the bitter poverty, and the shocking privations of this pioneer socialist are taken into account, his untimely and almost tragic death seems to have been, after all, a blessed balm to his weary soul. He gave his life to civilize the world and was rewarded with suffering and death.

Four years after Gronlund's *Cooperative Commonwealth* appeared, in 1888, Edward Bellamy published his *Looking Backward,* and it had a most wonderful effect upon the people. He struck a responsive popular chord and his name was upon every tongue. The editions ran into the hundreds of thousands, and the people were profoundly stirred by what was called the vision of a poetic dreamer. Although not an exposition of scientific socialism, Bellamy's social romance, *Looking Backward,* with its sequel, *Equality,* were valuable and timely contributions to the literature of socialism and not only aroused the people but started many on the road to the revolutionary movement. The quick and wide response to the author's plea for a new social arrangement evinced not only the discontent of the people, but their eager readiness to grasp at anything that might give promise of escape from the poverty, the insecurity, the daily horrors of the existing order. Thousands were moved to study the question by the books of Bellamy and thus became socialists and found their way into the socialist movement.

In February 1888, the strike occurred on the Burlington system involving all its engineers and firemen and some of its brakemen and switchmen. P. M. Arthur, then grand chief of the Brotherhood of Locomotive

Engineers, was threatened with federal court proceedings on account of a boycott which had been placed upon CB&Q cars and was so effective that it looked as if a complete tie-up of traffic would result from it. The boycott was raised, and the strike began to wane. But the contest continued almost a year, and it cost the brotherhoods fully $2 million. At last, however, the strikers were exhausted and compelled to yield to total defeat.

Thus was it proved by the loss of another great railroad strike—not one of which was ever won by the brotherhoods—that when the supreme test of strength comes, the railway unions are always crushed by the railway corporations.

The defeat of this and other strikes, together with the fact that most railway employees were ineligible to the then-existing brotherhoods, led to the organization of the American Railway Union in 1893, which embraced all the employees in railway service. The new union grew rapidly. Soon after it was organized, it engaged in and won several minor strikes. In April 1894, the strike on the Great Northern, involving all the employees of the entire system, was fought and resulted in a complete victory for the union in less than three weeks. A short time later, another strike was threatened, owing to disagreement growing out of the construction of the agreement. For the second time, thousands were pouring into the union all over the country. Then followed the Pullman strike, in the latter part of June. The Pullman Company, backed by the combined railway corporations represented by the General Managers' Association, resolved to crush the union. They not only failed, but the union paralyzed their traffic and defeated them all. Seeing that the union was triumphant, they changed their tactics. They had the United States marshal of Illinois swear in an army of deputies, ostensibly to protect property, but in fact to incite tumult. In his official report to the council of Chicago, the chief of police said that these "deputies" consisted of thieves, thugs, and ex-convicts, the worst element that had ever been turned loose on any city. As soon as the deputies began to operate, as directed by their leaders, and under cover of night, trouble began, and this is what the corporations wanted. Peace and order were fatal to them as turbulence and violence were fatal to the union. They understood this perfectly. Hence the deputies and disorder. Immediately these thugs began to perform, the capitalist papers and Associated Press flashed broadcast the falsehood that the strikers were on the warpath and threatened destruction to every living thing. The falsehood caught on like magic. Far and wide the cry went up: "Down with the ARU!" "Down with anarchy!" The tide turned. The triumphant union and defeated corporations changed places. With practically the whole population aroused against the ARU, every outrage upon it was not only possible, but perpetrated with enthusiasm in the name of patriotism. The ARU had no press, no way of getting its side before the people, and thousands of the very workers on whose behalf it was fighting and had staked everything, turned upon it and joined in the flood of angry denunciation that was launched upon it.

Injunctions by the hundred were issued and served by all the courts between the Ohio and the Pacific. A half dozen burly ruffians, by order of the federal authorities—precisely who could never be learned—backed up a cart at the union headquarters, forced their way into the offices, sacked them, taking records, books, private papers, and unopened letters, without warrant of any description, nailing up the headquarters and hauling the booty to the federal building.

How is this for a specimen of "law and order" the capitalist class and their brood of hirelings so ceaselessly harp about?

In violation of law and precedent and in defiance of the protest of the governor of Illinois, the mayor of Chicago and an overwhelming majority of the people, Grover Cleveland, then president of the United States, forced the federal troops into the state for the sole purpose of aiding the corporations to crush the union and defeat the strike, and when history shall be truthfully written, this crime will make the name of Cleveland the synonym of infamy forever.

Thousands of falsehoods were coined and circulated by the capitalist press, shifting the blame for lawlessness and crime from the instigators to innocent men; the leaders were arrested without charges and jailed without trial, headquarters were broken up, a special grand jury was sworn in expressly to indict, a notorious capitalist union-hater being made foreman, and a hundred other flagrant violations of the law and outrages upon justice were committed in the name of law to defeat justice and enthrone corporate rapacity. The venality of capitalist government never made so bold an exhibition of itself. It was scandalous beyond expression and shocking to the last degree. Every department of the federal government was freely placed at the service of the railroad corporations, and Republican and Democratic officials vied with each other in cheerful and servile obedience to their masters.

When the government and its capitalist lackeys had completed their service as corporation scavengers, General Miles, the military satrap, like a vulture stuffed with carrion, pompously exclaimed at a plutocratic banquet in honor of his gallant services: *"I have broken the backbone of this strike."*

Such sublime heroism in such a holy cause, Grover Cleveland, Nelson Miles, et al., will not be forgotten nor remain unrewarded.

The Coming Nation, started at Greensburg, Indiana, by J. A. Wayland, in 1893, was the first popular propaganda paper to be published in the interest of socialism in this country. It reached a large circulation and the proceeds were used in founding and developing the Ruskin Cooperative Colony in Tennessee. Later Mr. Wayland began the publication of the *Appeal to Reason,* and it now numbers its subscribers by the hundreds of thousands. It is not saying too much for the *Appeal* that it has been a great factor in preparing the American soil for the seed of socialism. Its enormous editions have been and are being spread broadcast, and copies may be found in the remotest recesses and the most inaccessible regions. The propaganda thus organized by Mr. Wayland, for which he has peculiar genius, and carried forward and enlarged constantly with the aid of a corps of able comrades, has been and is a source of incalculable strength in promoting education among the workers and building up the general movement.

The periodical and weekly press, so necessary to any political movement, is now developing rapidly, and there is every reason to believe that within the next few years there will be a formidable array of reviews, magazines, illustrated journals, and daily and weekly papers to represent the movement and do battle for its supremacy.

The last convention of the American Railway Union was the first convention of the Social Democracy of America, and this was held at Chicago in June 1897, the delegates voting to change the railway union into a working-class political party.

The Railway Times, the official paper of the union, became the *Social Democrat* and later the *Social Democratic Herald* and is now published at Milwaukee in the interest of the Socialist Party.[61]

The Social Democracy, the evolution of unionism crushed by the weight of despotic power, was the logical extension and expansion of the American Railway Union, and the direct outgrowth of the great industrial uprising known as the Pullman strike and the brutal tyranny and relentless persecution that followed it. The General Managers' Association pursued the American Railway Union with fiendish ferocity, determined to stamp out the last spark of its life, and as a result, when the few surviving delegates met in national convention in the year named, the last they ever held as a railway labor union, the American Railway Union, loved and respected by labor, and feared and hated by capital, was metamorphosed into the Social Democracy.

At the national convention which followed a year later, in June 1898, a split occurred, one wing adhering to the colonization scheme, making that the chief end of their movement while the latter abandoned the colonization feature and struck out for political action as a working-class party. The latter was known as the Social Democratic Party and progressed rapidly from the start, while the former soon exhausted its resources and passed out of existence.

The Socialist Labor Party, in which internal dissension had been brewing for some time, divided into separate factions in July 1899, the anti-administration faction uniting with the Social Democratic Party in the following year, giving the united party the name of the Socialist Party, the name it bears today.

In the brief summary of the development of the American movement much has had to be omitted for the want of space. To sketch in outline merely, with the hope of stimulating to further reading and study of the history and literature of the Socialist movement, has been the purpose of this brief treatise.

Scarcely, however, can reference be omitted to the helpful influence of the popular pen of Robert Blatchford, the author of *Merrie England* and other works and one of the most simple, attractive, and convincing writers on socialism in all the world. Hundreds of thousands of copies of *Merrie England* have been sold and given away, and the demand still continues. The work of Mr. Blatchford is specially adapted to beginners. He has the rare faculty of making himself interesting to the workingman and working woman, addressing himself to them in their own simple language and illustrating his argument in the same simple and convincing fashion. Robert Blatchford and his writings have contributed materially to the spread of socialism in this country and are justly entitled to the grateful acknowledgment of the American movement.

Reference to Karl Marx, Ferdinand Lassalle, Frederick Engels, Wilhelm Liebknecht, and August Bebel, the titans of revolutionary socialism, and their contemporaries and successors, need not be made in these brief pages, nor to the socialist classics which are so well known and may be read in all languages.

The immortal shibboleth of Marx: "Workingmen of all countries unite! You have nothing to lose but your chains—you have a world to gain" is the rallying cry of the class struggle, the inspiration of the working class, and is heard echoing and re-echoing around the world.

The socialist vote in the United States shows a steady and, all things considered, satisfactory progress of the movement.

In the national election of 1898, the socialist vote was 21,164.

In 1900, the Socialist Party cast 87,814 votes, and the Socialist Labor Party 39,739 votes, a total of 127,553 votes.

Since the election of 1900, there has been greater activity in organizing and a more widespread propaganda than ever before. In the elections of the past, it can scarcely be claimed that the socialist movement was represented by a national party. It entered these contests with but few states organized and with no resources worth mentioning to sustain it during the campaign.

It is far different today.

The Socialist Party is organized in almost every state and territory in the American union. Its members are filled with enthusiasm and working with an energy born of the throb and thrill of revolution. The party has a press supporting it that extends from sea to sea and is as vigilant and tireless in its labors as it is steadfast and true to the party principles.

The Socialist Party stands upon a sound platform, embodying the principles of international socialism, clearly and eloquently expressed, and proclaims its mission of conquest on the basis of the class struggle. Its tactics are in harmony with its principles, and both are absolutely uncompromising.

Viewed today from any intelligent standpoint, the outlook of the socialist movement is full of promise—to the capitalist, of struggle and defeat; to the worker, of coming freedom.

It is the break of dawn upon the horizon of human destiny, and it has no limitations but the walls of the universe.

What party strife or factional turmoil may yet ensue we neither know nor care. We know only that the principles of socialism are necessary to the emancipation of the working class and to the true happiness of all classes and that its historic mission is that of a conquering movement. We know that day by day, nourished by the misery and vitalized by the aspirations of the working class, the area of its activity widens, it grows in strength and increases its mental and moral grasp, and when the final hour of capitalism and wage-slavery strikes, the socialist movement, the greatest in all history—great enough to embrace the human race—will crown the class struggles of the centuries with victory and proclaim freedom to all mankind.

Moving Toward Socialism†

August 30, 1904

A few years ago, the socialist philosophy was spurned as irrational and impossible, and its exponents were looked upon as foolish fanatics by thoughtful men in the United States.

During the last decade a profound change has taken place with reference to socialism. Many thousands who once rejected it with scorn are now among its staunchest supporters. Newspapers, magazines, and periodicals are discussing it; rulers, statesmen, and politicians are worried about it; ministers, teachers, and moralists are descanting upon it, and every day it becomes more and more apparent that a new and vital problem has presented itself.

The change in the popular mind in regard to socialism is not due solely, or even mainly, to mental processes. The many "converts" to the socialist philosophy may not credit their intellectual faculties alone for seeing the light, but are indebted primarily, as a rule, to economic necessity, the growing insecurity in the means of making a livelihood as the result of the concentration of capital and other changes in the economic structure of society that are rapidly transforming our boasted republic into an industrial despotism.

No greater mistake was ever made than to suppose that socialism is a dream and that "human nature" must be excluded before it can be realized. It is just because "human nature" is as it is that socialism is inevitable.

Socialism is neither a dream nor a scheme, but a theory of society based upon the principles of social evolution, the trend of which is so clearly indicated in the changes daily taking place before our very eyes that the wonder is that any man with the ordinary power of observation can fail to see that the economic foundations of society are shaping for a superstructure of socialism, and that it will be socialism because it can be nothing else.

*

Not long after the congressional elections of 1902, the Rev. Lyman Abbott, taking notice of the great increase in the socialist vote, said: "Socialism is

† Published in *Chicago News* (August 30, 1904), unspecified original title or page. Reprinted as "Moving Toward Socialism" in *Social Democratic Herald,* vol. 7, no. 19, whole no. 319 (September 10, 1904), 1.

inevitable." In a lecture recently delivered, the same eminent divine rudely disturbed the calm in conservative circles by saying:

> Our industries must be democratized; if different small bodies of men are to control all our domestic necessities, where goes our democracy? The democratizing of industry means the distribution of wealth. The labor problem can never be solved as long as one set of men owns the tools (machinery) and another set uses them. When all those connected with one industry become together owners and users, then will come the harmony and union which have been so long striven for.

The economics of socialism are embodied in this revolutionary utterance. Production of wealth is now a social function, and the means of production must be socially owned unless society is to disintegrate and civilization to turn backward toward barbarism.

The toolless worker is an industrial slave.

The tool-owning capitalist is an industrial master.

They are the dominant types of commercial society. They represent two powerful and antagonistic classes. There can be no permanent peace between them. The intervals of quiet are but breathing moments between outbreaks. Their economic interests are irreconcilable.

The violent and bloody upheaval in Colorado proves it.

The gruesome packing trades strike in Chicago bears witness to it.[62]

The Citizens' Alliance and the trade union movement are the incarnation of it.

There is war between them to the death.

ɕɔ

Workers at last are waking. The cry that there are "no classes" in this country deceives them no longer. It is true that President Roosevelt anathematizes the demagogues who "array class against class in the American republic," but it is barely possible that within a generation of two the demagogues and demigods of this day may exchange places.

The mine slaves of Pennsylvania are not in the same class with Harry Lehr[63] and William Waldorf Astor,[64] President Roosevelt to the contrary notwithstanding.

The development of the capitalist system has produced economic classes and arrayed them against each other in every civilized land on earth, be it autocratic Russia, monarchic Germany, or free America. They differ only in degree of development. In the presence of this worldwide evolution, to charge individuals with arraying these two classes against each other is like accusing the whitecaps on the crests of stirring up the mighty deep.

David M. Parry is doing as much to array class against class as any other individual, though he aims at the opposite effect.

The slave owners of the South were the chief instrumentalities in their own overthrow. The tool owners of capitalism are being shaped for similar ends.

The late Senator Hanna was discerning enough to foresee what was coming when he predicted that the great struggle of the future would be between the Republican Party and the socialists. It requires rare discrimination to choose between the Republican and Democratic parties. Ninety percent of the voters could not tell the platforms apart. There is scarcely an issue between them and certainly none, nor the shadow of one, so far as the working class is concerned.

Political parties express the economic interests of classes. The Republican Party represents the dominant capitalist class, the Democratic Party the small capitalists. The latter are being worsted as a class, and their party is tottering on its foundations. It is today in all essential respects a Republican party. This is all that holds it together, and even in spite of this it is disintegrating.

As the middle class crumbles, the Democratic Party tumbles.

In the coming phases of the class struggle there will be room for but two parties—namely, a working-class party and a capitalist class party. The capitalists know that this political alignment is fatal to them and are doing all in their power to prevent it. But they are pitted against the inexorable laws of industrial evolution, and sooner or later the alignment will be made, and the working classes will triumph over their exploiters.

The Republican and Democratic parties have united at every point where the one or the other was menaced by Socialist success. These are infallible signs of the coming political alignment based upon economic class interest. The capitalists will go to the Republican Party and the workers to the Socialist Party. The Democratic Party will go out of business.

The waked-up workers of the country say it is a class struggle. The capitalists deny it. Every day's development emphasizes it. It is so clearly revealed in the packinghouse strike that only the purblind fail to see it. The capitalists are one. So are the workers. Their opposing economic interests separate them. What one gains is at the loss of the other.

Upon that basis, they will sooner or later meet on the political battlefield.

ᔓ

Every defeat on economic grounds recruits the army on the political field. Trade unionists take their final degree in the Socialist Party.

Capitalists are shortsighted when they rejoice over the success of a lockout or the defeat of a strike. When the capitalists have won strikes enough, the socialists will have votes enough to retire them from business.

The armies of workers are becoming organized not only as a union of labor but, what is more, as a party of the working class. They need only to become conscious of their power as a class to abolish every form of servitude and rule the world.

The workers are just learning to vote as they strike—as a class and against the class that exploits them. They are being forced by economic necessity into consciousness of their class interests, and in that ratio the Socialist Party is growing. Four years ago, the Socialist Party was credited with less than 100,000 votes. There will be an extraordinary increase this year.

Capitalist prosperity has reached its limit. Hard times are setting in. The vast surplus that labor produces, and that labor needs but cannot buy, periodically congests the market and then labor has to go idle, hungry, and naked until the surplus can be worked off. Production for use verses production for profit is the only remedy.

Men are better than millionaires and mendicants. Homes are better than castles and hovels. Freedom is better than despotism; and freedom for all is the mission of the socialist movement.

Capitalism has almost run its course. The old system is breaking down. The Colorado and Chicago[65] eruptions are symptoms of the degeneration that has attacked the body economic of the capitalist system, and these eruptions are apt to spread over the entire body.

There is no cause for alarm. Society is but reconstructing itself, and the process is eternal. These are transition days—eventful, stirring, and full of promise for the working class and all mankind.

As long as there is a "working class" and a "labor market," there will be class conflict that will preclude social peace. When all are useful workers and all have equal opportunity to produce wealth and enjoy it, there will be no classes and no animal struggle for existence.

This will be only when the workers own the tools and secure wealth for themselves. To procure these, they must first secure control of government, and this is why the labor question is essentially a political question. When the working class succeeds to political power, it will be easy to put the workers in possession of their tools and emancipate them from wage-slavery.

Industrial self-government is necessary to political self-government, and both are vital to a free nation.

Face to Face†

September 1904

No voter, however ignorant, need be deceived as to what the two great national parties stand for this year. The workingman who votes for Roosevelt or Parker does so knowing that he is voting for capitalist rule and working-class slavery; he is satisfied with things as they are and wants no change; he does not take the trouble to think and that is where is trouble begins.

Eight years ago, and again four years ago, the situation differed decidedly from that of today. The Democratic Party, having kicked over its Wall Street traces, was braying lustily as the champion of the "common people." With Bryan as the Moses of the "common people," the trusts would be uprooted, monopoly destroyed, the gold bugs put to flight, and the trusting children led triumphantly into the promised land.

It apparently did not occur to most of those who voted for Bryan that there are two kinds of "common people," viz., capitalists and wageworkers; nor did the workingmen who rallied with the "common people" understand that they were being buncoed and that the triumph of the "common people" could mean wage-slavery for them and nothing more.

Four years ago, it was difficult to make the workers understand that there was no fundamental difference between the two old parties. They were taken in by the delusive slogan about "the masses and the classes," and they were sure that with Bryan's election the day of jubilee would dawn and they would cavort in the Elysian fields forever.

Amidst such din and confusion, such ignorance and bliss, the Socialist Party,[66] standing serenely on its scientific principles, was given but scant attention, and it had only to await the reaction when the rushing mob should butt its unthinking head against the inevitable wall.

† Published in *Wilshire's Magazine,* whole no. 74 (September 1904), 385–6.

The Democratic Party did not succeed in breaking into office, its paramount issue, as the champion of the "common people," so it bolted back to Wall Street and is again in the tried old traces, with Grover Cleveland at the ribbons and Alton Parker on the box.[67] The only thing democratic about this moribund aggregation is its name. The harmonizer in its chameleon councils is its chronic appetite for spoils.

The Republican Party has great solicitude for its Democratic dummy. If anything should happen to its sharing partner, what would become of the quadrennial sham battle that divides labor and insures capitalist supremacy?

The Republican leaders and Democratic leaders want to defeat each other only to get the rich picking on the inside, but neither of them wants anything serious to happen to the other. Each of these capitalist parties knows that the other party is necessary to its business. They must be kept evenly matched or the game is off.

Socialism will drive both of them into the same party in the near future, and they will then look alike to all workingmen as they do now to socialists who see them as they are.

It would save considerable expense if Roosevelt and Parker would shake the dice for the presidency. Both men are precisely alike in their qualifications to serve the capitalist class and that is all they have been nominated for. Their principles are the same, and only an imaginary line and a real appetite divide their parties.

The workingman who supports either Roosevelt or Parker renounces his reason, abdicates his manhood, surrenders his self-respect, and grovels in the dirt at the feet of his chosen master, who will reward his fawning cowardice with kicks of contempt.

In this campaign, the Republican-Democratic Party is avowedly the party of the capitalist class, of the trusts, the gold-grabbers, coupon-cutters, brokers, sharks, confidence operators, private yachts, Seeley dinners,[68] high life and low morals, decrepit dudes, feathered and bejeweled dunces, international bargain-counter marriages, plutocratic revelry, wage-slavery, poverty, misery, prostitution, suicide, bull pens, injunctions, riots, clubbings, deportations, boodle, quackery, mental servility and moral depravity, frenzied finance and putrefied politics, Roosevelt and Davis, Parker and Fairbanks, Cleveland and Bryan, Belmont[69] and Tillman,[70] Peabody and Parry.

Standing against this political aggregation is the Socialist Party, the party of the working class, the only party that stands for industrial freedom, political equality, and social justice, and this party, revolutionary to the core, will conquer capitalism and emancipate man.

The Socialist Party and the Working Class: Opening Campaign Speech in Indianapolis[†71]

September 1, 1904

Mr. Chairman, Citizens, and Comrades:—

There has never been a free people, a civilized nation, a real republic on this earth. Human society always consisted of masters and slaves, and the slaves have always been and are today the foundation stones of the social fabric.

Wage-labor is but a name; wage-slavery is a fact. The 25 million wageworkers in the United States are 25 million twentieth-century slaves. This is the plain meaning of what is known as the labor market. And the labor market follows the capitalist flag.

The most barbarous fact in all Christendom is the labor market. The mere term sufficiently expresses the animalism of commercial civilization. They who buy and they who sell in the labor market are alike dehumanized by the inhuman traffic in the brains and blood and bones of human beings.

The labor market is the foundation of so-called civilized society. Without these shambles, without this commerce in human life, this sacrifice of manhood and womanhood, this barter of babes, this sale of souls, the capitalist civilizations of all lands and all climes would crumble to ruin and perish from the earth.

Twenty-five million wage-slaves are bought and sold daily at prevailing prices in the American labor market. This is the paramount issue in the present national campaign.

Let me say at the very threshold of this discussion that the workers have but the one issue in this campaign, the overthrow of the capitalist system and the emancipation of the working class from wage-slavery.

The capitalists may have the tariff, finance, imperialism, and other dust-covered and moth-eaten issues entirely to themselves. The rattle of these relics no longer deceives workingmen whose heads are on their own shoulders. They know by experience and observation that the gold standard, free silver,

† Published in *International Socialist Review,* vol. 5, no. 3 (September 1904), 129–42. Reprinted as a pamphlet by the National Committee of the Socialist Party (1904); Standard Publishing Co. (1904); Charles H. Kerr & Co. (1904).

fiat money,[72] protective tariff, free trade, imperialism and anti-imperialism[73] all mean capitalist rule and wage-slavery. Their eyes are open and they can see; their brains are in operation and they can think.

The very moment a workingman begins to do his own thinking he understands the paramount issue, parts company with the capitalist politician, and falls in line with his own class on the political battlefield.

The political solidarity of the working class means the death of despotism, the birth of freedom, the sunrise of civilization.

Having said this much by way of introduction, I will now enter upon the actualities of my theme.

The Class Struggle

We are entering tonight upon a momentous campaign. The struggle for political supremacy is not between political parties merely, as appears upon the surface, but at bottom it is a life-and-death struggle between two hostile economic classes, the one the capitalist and the other the working class.

The capitalist class is represented by the Republican, Democratic, Populist, and Prohibition parties, all of which stand for private ownership of the means of production and the triumph of any one of which will mean continued wage-slavery to the working class.

As the Populist and Prohibition sections of the capitalist party represent minority elements which propose to reform the capitalist system without disturbing wage-slavery, a vain and impossible task, they will be omitted from this discussion with all the credit due the rank and file for their good intentions.

The Republican and Democratic parties, or, to be more exact, the Republican-Democratic Party, represents the capitalist class in the class struggle. They are the political wings of the capitalist system, and such differences as arise between them relate to spoils and not to principles.

With either of these parties in power, one thing is always certain, and that is that the capitalist class are in the saddle and the working class under the saddle.

Under the administration of both these parties, the means of production are private property, production is carried forward for capitalist profit purely, markets are glutted and industry paralyzed, workingmen become tramps and criminals while injunctions, soldiers, and riot guns are brought into action to preserve "law and order" in the chaotic carnival of capitalistic anarchy.

Deny it as may the cunning capitalists who are clear-sighted enough to perceive it, or ignore it as may the torpid workers who are too blind and unthinking to see it, the struggle in which we are engaged today is a class struggle, and as the toiling millions come to see and understand it and rally to the political standard of their class, they will drive all capitalist parties of whatever name into the same party, and the class struggle will then be so clearly revealed that the hosts of labor will find their true place in the conflict and strike the united and decisive blow that will destroy slavery and achieve their full and final emancipation.

In this struggle the workingmen and women and children are represented by the Socialist Party, and it is my privilege to address you in the name of that revolutionary and uncompromising party of the working class.

Attitude of the Workers

What shall be the attitude of the workers of the United States in the present campaign? What part shall they take in it? What party and what principles shall they support by their ballots? And why?

These are questions the importance of which are not sufficiently recognized by workingmen or they would not be the prey of parasites and the servile tools of scheming politicians who use them only at election time to renew their master's lease of power and perpetuate their own ignorance, poverty, and shame.

In answering these questions I propose to be as frank and candid as plain-meaning words will allow, for I have but one object in this discussion and that object is not office, but the truth, and I shall state it as I see it if I have to stand alone.

But I shall not stand alone, for the party that has my allegiance and may have my life, the Socialist Party, the party of the working class, the party of emancipation, is made up of men and women who know their rights and scorn to compromise with their oppressors; who want no votes that can be bought and no support under any false pretenses whatsoever.

The Socialist Party stands squarely upon its proletarian principles and relies wholly upon the forces of industrial progress and the education of the working class.

The Socialist Party buys no votes and promises no offices. Not a farthing is spent for whiskey or cigars. Every penny in the campaign fund is the voluntary offering of workers and their sympathizers, and every penny is used for education.

What other parties can say the same?

Ignorance alone stands in the way of socialist success. The capitalist parties understand this and use their resources to prevent the workers from seeing the light. Intellectual darkness is essential to industrial slavery. Capitalist parties stand for slavery and night. The Socialist Party is the herald of freedom and light.

Capitalist parties cunningly contrive to divide the workers upon dead issues. The Socialist Party is uniting them upon the living issue: Death to wage-slavery!

When industrial slavery is as dead as the issues of the Siamese capitalist parties, the Socialist Party will have fulfilled its mission and enriched history.

And now to our questions: First, every workingman and woman owe it to themselves, their class, and their country to take an active and intelligent interest in political affairs.

The Ballot

The ballot of united labor expresses the people's will, and the people's will is the supreme law of a free nation. The ballot means that labor is no longer dumb, that at last it has a voice, that it may be heard and if united must be heeded.

Centuries of struggle and sacrifice were required to wrest this symbol of freedom from the mailed clutch of tyranny and place it in the hand of labor as the shield and lance of attack and defense.

The abuse and not the use of it is responsible for its evil.

The divided vote of labor is the abuse of the ballot, and the penalty is slavery and death.

The united vote of those who toil and have not will vanquish those who have and toil not and solve forever the problem of democracy.

The Historic Struggle of Classes

Since the race was young, there have been class struggles. In every state of society, ancient and modern, labor has been exploited, degraded, and in subjection. Civilization has done little for labor except to modify the forms of its exploitation.

Labor has always been the mudsill of the social fabric—is so now and will be until the class struggle ends in class extinction and free society.

Society has always been and is now built upon exploitation—the exploitation of a class, the working class—whether slaves, serfs, or wage-laborers; and the exploited working class have always been, instinctively or consciously, in revolt against their oppressors.

Through all the centuries, the enslaved toilers have moved slowly but surely toward their final freedom.

The call of the Socialist Party is to the exploited class, the workers in all useful trades and professions, all honest occupations, from the most menial service to the highest skill, to rally beneath their own standard and put an end to the last of the barbarous class struggles by conquering the capitalist government, taking possession of the means of production, and making them common property of all, abolishing wage-slavery and establishing the Cooperative Commonwealth.

The first step in this direction is to sever all relations with capitalist parties. They are precisely alike, and I challenge their most discriminating partisans to tell them apart in relation to labor.

The Republican and Democratic parties are alike capitalist parties—differing only in being committed to different sets of capitalist interests—they have the same principles under varying colors, are equally corrupt, and are one in their subservience to capital and their hostility to labor.

The ignorant workingman who supports either of these parties forgets his own fetters and is the unconscious author of his own misery. He can and must be made to see and think and act with his fellows in supporting the party of his class, and this work of education is the crowning virtue of the socialist movement.

The Republican Party

Let us briefly consider the Republican Party from the worker's standpoint. It is capitalist to the core. It has not and cannot have the slightest interest in labor except to exploit it.

Why should a workingman support the Republican Party?

Why should a millionaire support the Socialist Party?

For precisely the same reason that all the millionaires are opposed to the Socialist Party, all the workers should be opposed to the Republican Party. It is a capitalist party, is loyal to capitalist interests and entitled to the support of capitalist voters on election day. All it has for workingmen is its "glorious past" and a "glad hand" when it wants their votes.

The Republican Party is now and has been for several years in complete control of government. What has it done for labor? What has it not done for capital?

Not one of the crying abuses of capital has been curbed under Republican rule. Not one of the petitions of labor has been granted.

The eight-hour and anti-injunction bills, upon which organized labor is a unit, were again ruthlessly slain by the last Congress in obedience to the capitalist masters. David M. Parry has greater influence at Washington than all the millions of organized workers.

Read the national platform of the Republican Party and see if there is in all its bombast a crumb of comfort for labor. The convention that adopted it was a capitalist convention, and the only thought it had of labor was how to extract its vote without waking it up. In the only reference it made to labor, it had to speak easy so as to avoid offense to the capitalists who own it and furnish the boodle to keep it in power.

The labor platforms of the Republican and Democratic parties are interchangeable and non-redeemable. They both favor "justice to capital and justice to labor." This hoary old platitude is worse than meaningless. It is false and misleading and so intended. Justice to labor means that labor shall have what it produces. This leaves nothing for capital.

Justice to labor means the end of capital.

The old parties intend nothing of the kind. It is false pretense and false promise. It has served well in the past. Will it continue to catch the votes of unthinking and deluded workers?

What workingmen had part in the Republican national convention or were honored by it?

The grand coliseum swarmed with trust magnates, corporation barons, money lords, stock gamblers, professional politicians, lawyers, lobbyists, and other plutocratic tools and mercenaries, but there was no room for the horny-handed and horny-headed sons of toil. They built it but were not in it.

Compare that convention with the convention of the Socialist Party, composed almost wholly of workingmen and women and controlled wholly in the interest of their class.

But a party is still better known by its chosen representatives than by its platform declarations. Who are the nominees of the Republican Party for the highest offices in the gift of the nation, and what is their relation to the working class?

First of all, Theodore Roosevelt and Charles W. Fairbanks,[74] candidates for president and vice president, respectively, deny the class struggle, and this almost infallibly fixes their status as friends of capital and enemies of labor. They insist that they can serve both; but the fact is obvious that only one can be served and that one at the expense of the other. Mr. Roosevelt's whole political career proves it.

The capitalists made no mistake in nominating Mr. Roosevelt. They know him well and he has served them well. They know that his instincts, associations, tastes, and desires are with them, that he is in fact one of them and that he has nothing in common with the working class.

The only evidence of the contrary is his membership in the Brotherhood of Locomotive Firemen, which seems to have come to him coincident with his ambition to succeed himself in the presidential chair. He is a full-fledged member of the union, has the grip, signs, and passwords, but it is not reported that he is attending meetings, doing picket duty, supporting strikes and boycotts, and performing such other duties as his union obligation imposes.

When ex-president Grover Cleveland violated the Constitution and outraged justice by seizing the state of Illinois by the throat and handcuffing her civil administration at the behest of the crime-sustained trusts and corporations, Theodore Roosevelt was among his most ardent admirers and enthusiastic supporters. He wrote in hearty commendation of the atrocious act, pronounced it most exalted patriotism, and said he would have done the same thing himself had he been president.

And so he would and so he will!

How impressive to see the Rough Rider embrace the Smooth Statesman! Oyster Bay and Buzzard's Bay![75]

> Two souls with but a single thought,
> Two hearts that beat as one.[76]

There is also the highest authority for the statement charging Mr. Roosevelt with declaring about the same time he was lauding Cleveland that if he was in command, he would have such as Altgeld, Debs, and other traitors lined up against a dead wall and shot into corpses. The brutal remark was not for publication but found its way into print, and Mr. Roosevelt, after he became a candidate, attempted to make denial, but the distinguished editor who heard him say it pinned him fast, and the slight doubt that remained was dispelled by the words themselves, which sound like Roosevelt and bear the impress of his warlike visage.

Following the Pullman strike in 1894, there was an indignant and emphatic popular protest against "government by injunction," which has not yet by any means subsided. Organized labor was, and is, a unit against this insidious form of judicial usurpation as a means of abrogating constitutional restraints of despotic power.

Mr. Roosevelt, with his usual zeal to serve the ruling class and keep their protesting slaves in subjection, vaulted into the arena and launched his vitriolic tirade upon the mob that dared oppose the divine decree of a corporation judge.

"The men who object to what they style 'government by injunction,'" said he, "are, as regards the essential principles of government, in hearty sympathy with their remote skin-clad ancestors, who lived in caves, fought one another with stone-headed axes, and ate the mammoth and woolly rhinoceros. They are . . . dangerous whenever there is the least danger of their making the principles of this ages-buried past living factors in our present life. They are not in sympathy with men of good minds and good civic morality."[77]

In direct terms and plain words, Mr. Roosevelt denounces all those who oppose "government by injunction" as cannibals, barbarians, and anarchists, and this violent and sweeping stigma embraces the whole organized movement of labor, every man, woman, and child that wears the badge of union labor in the United States.

It is not strange in the light of these facts that the national Congress, under President Roosevelt's administration, suppresses anti-injunction and eight-hour bills and all other measures favored by labor and resisted by capital.

No stronger or more convincing proof is required of Mr. Roosevelt's allegiance to capital and opposition to labor, nor of the class struggle and class rule which he so vehemently denies; and the workingman who, in the face of these words and acts can still support Mr. Roosevelt, must feel himself flattered in being publicly proclaimed a barbarian, and sheer gratitude, doubtless, impels him to crown his benefactor with the highest honors of the land.

If the working class are barbarians, according to Mr. Roosevelt, this may account for his esteeming himself as having the very qualities necessary to make himself chief of the tribe.

But it must be noted that Mr. Roosevelt denounced organized labor as savages long before he was a candidate for president. After he became a candidate, he joined the tribe and is today, himself, according to his own dictum, a barbarian and the enemy of civic morality.

The labor union to which President Roosevelt belongs and which he is solemnly obligated to support is unanimously opposed to "government by injunction." President Roosevelt knew it when he joined it, and he also knew that those who oppose injunction rule have the instincts of cannibals and are a menace to morality, but his proud nature succumbed to political ambition, and his ethical ideas vanished as he struck the trail that led to the tribe and, after a most dramatic scene and impressive ceremony, was decorated with the honorary badge of international barbarism.

How Theodore Roosevelt, the trade-unionist, can support the presidential candidate who denounced him as an immoral and dangerous barbarian he may decide at his leisure, and so may all other men in the United States who are branded with the same vulgar stigma, and their ballots will determine if they have the manhood to resent insult and rebuke its author, or if they have been fitly characterized and deserve the humiliation and contempt.

The appointment of Judge Taft to a cabinet position is corroborative evidence, if any be required, of President Roosevelt's fervent faith in government by injunction. Judge Taft first came into national notoriety when, some years ago, sitting with Judge Ricks, who was later tried for malfeasance, he issued the celebrated injunction during the Toledo, Ann Arbor & North Michigan railroad strike that paralyzed the Brotherhoods of Locomotive Engineers and Firemen and won for him the gratitude and esteem of every corporation in the land. He was hauled to Toledo, the headquarters of the railroad, in a special car, pulled by a special engine, on special time, and after hastily consulting the railroad magnates and receiving instructions, he let go the judicial lightning that shivered the unions to splinters and ended the strike in total defeat. Judge Taft is a special favorite with the trust barons, and his elevation to the cabinet was ratified with joy at the court of St. Plute.

Still again did President Roosevelt drive home his arch-enmity to labor and his implacable hostility to the trade union movement when he made Paul Morton,[78] the notorious union-hater and union-wrecker, his secretary of the navy. That appointment was an open insult to every trade unionist in the country, and they who lack the self-respect to resent it at the polls may wear the badge, but they are lacking wholly in the spirit and principles of union labor.

Go ask the brotherhood men who were driven from the CB&Q and the striking union machinists on the Santa Fe to give you the pedigree of Mr. Morton, and you will learn that his hate for union men is coupled only by his love for the scabs who take their places.

Such a man and such another as Sherman Bell, the military ferret of the Colorado mine owners, are the ideal patriots and personal chums of Mr. Roosevelt, and by honoring these, he dishonors himself and should be repudiated by the ballot of every working man in the nation.

Mr. Fairbanks, the Republican candidate for vice president, is a corporation attorney of the first class and a plutocrat in good and regular standing. He is in every respect a fit and proper representative of his party, and every millionaire in the land may safely support him.

The Democratic Party

In referring to the Democratic Party in this discussion, we may save time by simply saying that since it was born again at the St. Louis convention, it is near enough like its Republican ally to pass for a twin brother.

The former party of the "common people" is no longer under the boycott of plutocracy since it has adopted the Wall Street label and renounced its middle-class heresies.

The radical and progressive element of the former democracy have been evicted and must seek other quarters. They were an unmitigated nuisance in the conservative counsels of the old party. They were for the "common people," and the trusts have no use for such a party.

Where but to the Socialist Party can these progressive people turn? They are now without a party, and the only genuine Democratic Party in the field is the Socialist Party, and every true Democrat should thank Wall Street for driving him out of a party that is democratic in name only and into one that is democratic in fact.

The St. Louis convention was a trust jubilee. The Wall Street reorganizers made short work of the free silver element. From first to last it was a capitalistic convocation. Labor was totally ignored. As an incident, two thousand choice chairs were reserved for the Business Men's League of St. Louis, an organization hostile to organized labor, but not a chair was tendered to those whose labor had built the convention hall, had clothed, transported, fed, and wined the delegates and whose votes are counted on, as if they were so many dumb driven cattle, to pull the ticket through in November.[79]

As another incident, when Lieutenant Richmond Hobson[80] dramatically declared that President Cleveland had been the only president who had ever been patriotic enough to use the federal troops to crush union labor, the trust agents, lobbyists, tools, and claqueurs screamed with delight, and the convention shook with applause.

The platform is precisely the same as the Republican platform in relation to labor. It says nothing and means the same. A plank was proposed condemning the outrages in Colorado under Republican administration, but upon order from the Parryites it was promptly thrown aside.

The editor of *American Industries,* organ of the Manufacturers' Association,[81] commented at length in the issue of July 15 [1904] on the triumph of capital and the defeat of labor at both Republican and Democratic national conventions. Among other things he said: "The two labor lobbies, partly similar in makeup, were, to put it bluntly, thrown out bodily in both places." And that is the simple fact and is known of all men who read the papers. The capitalist organs exult because labor, to use their own brutal expression, was kicked bodily out of both the Republican and Democratic national conventions.

What more than this is needed to open the eyes of workingmen to the fact that neither of these parties is their party and that they are as strangely out of place in them as Rockefeller and Vanderbilt would be in the Socialist Party?

And how many more times are they to be "kicked out bodily" before they stay out and join the party of their class, in which labor is not only honored but is supreme, a party that is clean, that has conscience and convictions, a party that will one day sweep the old parties from the field like chaff and issue the Proclamation of Labor's Emancipation?

Judge Alton B. Parker corresponds precisely to the Democratic platform. It was made to order for him. His famous telegram in the expiring hour removed the last wrinkle and left it a perfect fit.

Thomas W. Lawson,[82] the Boston millionaire, charges that Senator Patrick McCarren,[83] who brought out Judge Parker for the nomination, is on the payroll of the Standard Oil Company as political master mechanic at $20,000 a year, and that Parker is the chosen tool of Standard Oil. Mr. Lawson offers Senator McCarren $100,000 if he will disprove the charge.

William Jennings Bryan denounced Judge Parker as a tool of Wall Street before he was nominated and declared that no self-respecting Democrat could vote for him, and after his nomination he charged that it had been dictated by the trusts and secured by "crooked and indefensible methods." Mr. Bryan also said that labor had been betrayed in the convention and need look for nothing from the Democratic Party. He made many other damaging charges against his party and its candidates, but when the supreme test came he was not equal to it, and instead of denouncing the betrayers of the "common people" and repudiating their made-to-order Wall Street program, he compromised with the pirates that scuttled his ship and promised with his lips the support his heart refused and his conscience condemned.

The Democratic nominee for president was one of the supreme judges of the state of New York who declared the eight-hour law unconstitutional, and this is an index of his political character.

In his address accepting the nomination, he makes but a single allusion to labor, and in this he takes occasion to say that labor is charged with having recently used dynamite in destroying property and that the perpetrators should be subjected to "the most rigorous punishment known to the law." This cruel intimation amounts to conviction in advance of trial and indicates clearly the trend of his capitalistically trained judicial mind. He made no such reference to capital, nor to those ermined rascals who use judicial dynamite in blowing up the Constitution while labor is looted and starved by capitalistic freebooters who trample all law in the mire and leer and mock at their despoiled and helpless victims.

It is hardly necessary to make more than passing reference to Henry G. Davis,[84] Democratic candidate for vice president. He is a coal baron, railroad owner, and, of course, an enemy to union labor. He has amassed a great fortune exploiting his wage-slaves and has always strenuously resisted every attempt to organize them for the betterment of their condition. Mr. Davis is a staunch believer in the virtue of the injunction as applied to union labor. As a young man he was in charge of a slave plantation, and his conviction is that wage-slaves should be kept free from the contaminating influence of the labor agitator and render cheerful obedience to their master.

Mr. Davis is as well qualified to serve his party as is Senator Fairbanks to serve the Republican Party, and wageworkers should have no trouble in making their choice between this precious pair of plutocrats, and certainly no intelligent workingman will hesitate an instant to discard them both and cast his vote for Ben Hanford, their working-class competitor, who is as loyally devoted to labor as Fairbanks and Davis are to capital.

The Socialist Party

In what has been said of other parties I have tried to show why they should not be supported by the common people, least of all by workingmen, and I think I have shown clearly enough that such workers as do support them are guilty, consciously or unconsciously, of treason to their class. They are voting into power the enemies of labor and are morally responsible for the crimes thus perpetrated upon their fellow workers, and sooner or later they will have to suffer the consequences of their miserable acts.

The Socialist Party is not, and does not pretend to be, a capitalist party. It does not ask, nor does it expect the votes of the capitalist class. Such capitalists as do support it do so seeing the approaching doom of the capitalist system and with a full understanding that the Socialist Party is not a capitalist party, nor a middle-class party, but a revolutionary working-class party whose historic mission is to conquer capitalism on the political battlefield, take control of government, and through the public powers take possession of the means of wealth production, abolish wage-slavery, and emancipate all workers and all humanity.

The people are as capable of achieving their industrial freedom as they were to secure their political liberty, and both are necessary to a free nation.

The capitalist system is no longer adapted to the needs of modern society. It is outgrown and fetters the forces of progress. Industrial and commercial competition are largely of the past. The handwriting blazes on the wall.

Centralization and combination are the modern forces in industrial and commercial life. Competition is breaking down, and coöperation is supplanting it.

The hand tools of early times are used no more. Mammoth machines have taken their places. A few thousand capitalists own them, and many millions of workingmen use them. All the wealth the vast army of labor produces above its subsistence is taken by the machine-owning capitalists, who also own the land and the mills, the factories, railroads, and mines, the forests and fields and all other means of production and transportation.

Hence wealth and poverty, millionaires and beggars, castles and caves, luxury and squalor, painted parasites on the boulevard and painted poverty among the red lights.

Hence strikes, boycotts, riots, murder, suicide, insanity, prostitution on a fearful and increasing scale.

The capitalist parties can do nothing. They are a part, an iniquitous part of the foul and decaying system. There is no remedy for the ravages of death.

Capitalism is dying and its extremities are already decomposing. The blotches upon the surface show that the blood no longer circulates. The time is near when the cadaver will have to be removed and the atmosphere purified.

In contrast with the Republican and Democratic conventions, where politicians were the puppets of plutocracy, the convention of the Socialist Party consisted of workingmen and women fresh from their labors, strong, clean, wholesome, self-reliant, ready to do and dare for the cause of labor, the cause of humanity.

Proud indeed am I to have been chosen by such a body of men and women to bear aloft the proletarian standard in this campaign, and heartily do I endorse the clear and cogent platform of the party which appeals with increasing force and eloquence to the whole working class of the country.

To my associate upon the national ticket I give my hand with all my heart. Ben Hanford typifies the working class and fitly represents the historic mission and revolutionary character of the Socialist Party.

Closing Words

These are stirring days for living men. The day of crisis is drawing near, and socialists are exerting all their power to prepare the people for it.

The old order of society can survive but little longer. Socialism is next in order. The swelling minority sounds warning of the impending change. Soon that minority will be the majority and then will come the Cooperative Commonwealth.

Every workingman should rally to the standard of his class and hasten the full-orbed day of freedom.

Every progressive democrat must find his way in our direction, and if he will but free himself from prejudice and study the principles of socialism, he will soon be a sturdy supporter of our party.

Every sympathizer with labor, every friend of justice, every lover of humanity should support the Socialist Party as the only party that is organized to abolish industrial slavery, the prolific source of the giant evils that afflict the people.

Who with a heart in his breast can look upon Colorado without keenly feeling the cruelties and crimes of capitalism? Repression will not help her. Brutality will only brutalize her. Private ownership and wage-slavery are the curse of Colorado. Only socialism will save Colorado and the nation.

The overthrow of capitalism is the object of the Socialist Party. It will not fuse with any other party and it would rather die than compromise.

The Socialist Party comprehends the magnitude of its task and has the patience of preliminary defeat and the faith of ultimate victory.

The working class must be emancipated by the working class.

Woman must be given her true place in society by the working class.

Child labor must be abolished by the working class.

Society must be reconstructed by the working class.

The working class must be employed by the working class.

The fruits of labor must be enjoyed by the working class.

War, bloody war, must be ended by the working class.

These are the principles and objects of the Socialist Party, and we fearlessly proclaim them to our fellow men.

We know our cause is just and that it must prevail.

With faith and hope and courage, we hold our heads erect and with dauntless spirit marshal the working class for the march from capitalism to socialism, from slavery to freedom, from barbarism to civilization.

The Pressing Need[†]

September 17, 1904

Comrades and Friends:—

We are in the heat of the greatest socialist campaign ever waged in the United States. The conditions of the country all combined to give us our long-sought opportunity to organize our propaganda on a national scale and build up a militant national party of the working class.

Now has the time arrived. The workers everywhere are moving toward socialism, and the people of all classes want to hear what socialism is and what it proposes to accomplish.

The crowds that attend our meetings are enormous and the enthusiasm intense, and at these meetings many new supporters are won to the party and the movement.

The party is in excellent working order, the members in excellent spirit, and the outlook is all that could be desired. There is but one element and weakness of our campaign: *we lack funds.*

The harvest is ripe for the reapers, but they come not.

Comrades, there ought to be a thousand speakers in the field from now until election day. The people are hungering for the message of socialism.

Now, right now, is the time to bring it to them in all its splendid meaning and awakening power. To fail at this time is to turn our backs upon the supreme opportunity and set back the movement instead of pushing it forward with united energy.

Comrades, the insignificant campaign fund of less than $5,000 is not creditable to us as a national party, nor is it eloquent of the fealty of our membership to the international movement.

There are a million socialists and sympathizers in the United States who would average a ten-cent contribution to the national campaign fund. This would give us a fund of *one hundred thousand dollars,* and this is what we should have, and with such a fund we could attack the capitalist strongholds all along the line and arouse and enthuse our rank and file while striking terror to the capitalist enemy and their army of political mercenaries.

† Published in *Socialist Party Official Bulletin* [Chicago], September 1904, 1.

Comrades, the money can be raised. It is simply a question of making a thorough canvass of every crossroad, hamlet, village, town, and city in the land.

Do it now.

Appoint a committee or go at it single-handed, and give every socialist, semi-socialist, and sympathizer a chance to chip in a dime or more to the campaign fund to be used to send our speakers and spread literature to rouse the people and strike capitalism a body blow in November.

Comrades, every one of us must count this year. Let not one stand back or wait for another to take the lead. If ever the time was when the best we had and all we had was needed by the socialist movement, that time is now.

The badge we wear is not a decoration merely. It represents obligation, and no true comrade will shirk it in the hour of battle.

Every fiber of our bodies, every particle of our energy, every atom of our united capacity must be strained this year.

The battle is raging as never before, and we must rally with our combined power for the assault upon the bulwarks of the enemy.

Let each and every comrade be a volunteer in the service of the campaign fund. Send what you can to the national secretary, collect what you can and then send that, and then collect and send more, and for every penny you manage to turn in, the propaganda will be strengthened and you will have added to the great working-class victory awaiting us in November.

Eugene V. Debs

Approved by the National Quorum,[85]

September 17, 1904

Note:— All remittances should be sent direct and made payable to William Mailly, National Secretary, 269 Dearborn Street, Chicago, Il. Contributions acknowledged in the socialist press.

The Tragedy of Toil[†]

October 1904

Work is joy; labor is pain; toil is tragedy.

We hear much about the "dignity of labor," especially from those who do not labor. They have inherited the notion of the feudal barons of the Middle Ages. The laborer should be contented with his lot. God knows what is best for him. Even the scavenger should fill the sewer with song and work overtime from pure joy.

To create discontent in the mind of the menial, to tell him that his lot is a beastly one and that he should rise above it, is and always has been regarded as wicked and harmful, and such mischievous offenders are known to us as agitators and demagogues.

The toil of the scavenger is necessary to present society, but that does not make it honorable. It is the reproach of society. If the human scavenger were necessary and society were civilized, every man would take his turn in that repulsive role. To shirk his share of the necessary social service would be as abhorrent to the mind and morals of a civilized being as to impose upon his fellow men in any other way.

By what moral right is the health of one citizen conserved by destroying that of another?

If Edison had to do his share of the "dirty work" of commercial society—and unless it is done, he could not do his—there would soon be mechanical appliances for such service, and scavengers would rise to the dignity of human beings.

This is preeminently a commercial age. Almost everything is viewed from the commercial standpoint, and to have any value at all it must have commercial value. This is as true of the human being as of any other animal, or any other commodity.

If this fundamentally true proposition can be denied, let the "labor market" be explained.

How do those who expiate the "horny-handed sons of toil" a few days before election reconcile the "dignity of labor" with the "labor market?" The one is a denial of the other.

† Published in *Wayside Tales* [Chicago], vol. 8, no. 8 (October 1904), unspecified page. Reprinted in *Santa Cruz Evening Sentinel*, vol. 9, no. 123 (October 24, 1904), 4, and later in the socialist press as "The 'Dignity' of Labor."

The term "labor market" expresses the fact that in capitalist society labor is merchandise that is bought and sold at market prices. This is the status of the 25 million wageworkers in the United States, and to talk about the "dignity of labor" in the presence of such a condition is to belie the fact, and the public men, such as politicians, professors, and parsons, who engage in this sort of thing are enemies of labor in the disguise of friends, whose wise and conservative sayings are commended by the papers owned by labor's exploiters and whose influence is all given for pay, or position, or other consideration, to perpetuate the slavery of the children of toil.

Society today has two commanding types, namely, capitalists and workers. The workers only are merchandise. The "labor market" silences all doubt upon this point. The laborer goes with this labor-power, and when he sells that, as he is now compelled to do or starve, his industrial bondage is sealed, and rarely is there any escape from it.

To plead in extenuation that certain millionaires were once bootblacks and errand boys is beside the point and begs the question. These are the rare exceptions that owe their rise to fortuitous circumstances, and they but serve to prove the rule.

The great mass of wageworkers live and die wageworkers. There is no release from them except as a whole, and this is the fundamental tenet of the modern labor movement, the mission of which is to emancipate the whole mass of wage labor by abolishing the wage system, and to make the workers themselves the owners of the means of production, so that they, and they alone, shall control their labor and enjoy its fruit.

In that hour, labor rises from the low level of merchandise to the exalted plane of manhood.

If it be true, as some affirm, that capitalists are also laborers and in the same category with laborers, then why do we not hear of a "capital market" as well as a "labor market?" The fact is that there is no such market for the simple and sufficient reason that there is no such merchandise. The capitalist is the buyer of labor-power, the expression of the laborer's energy and life, at the market price. He deals in that commodity, that kind of merchandise, but he himself, as a capitalist, is not for sale at any price. Perish the thought!

The "labor market" has upon it the everlasting seal of social execration. The useful have always been detested by the useless. The parasite scorns the gudgeon he preys upon.

In this classless land of democratic institutions where all are free and therefore equal, the working millions are barred from breaking in, by statutory enactment under penalty of fine and imprisonment. Of course, they are all right "in their place," but their place is in their class and their class is in the labor market.

The line is drawn between the classes by social custom, which, after all, is the court of final resort.

No workingman, though pure as Christ and wise as Socrates, not though his character were adorned with every virtue, would be admitted to the exclusive circle of the famed Four Hundred.[86] He would still be a workingman—plebeian, inferior, vulgar, repulsive. Such is the social standard of capitalist society, and to protest against it is almost a crime. If a man belongs to the "working class," his social status is fixed. He must not aspire to associate above his class.

"Oh, dear," said a "society" lady in the hearing of the writer, "it is too bad that laboring people can't live off by themselves; they are such coarse creatures and out of place among refined and well-bred people."

The innocent woman should not be blamed. She but voiced society's barbarous verdict. She did not know that labor's degradation is society's shame and crime and that the penalties are blazoned in every issue of every paper and periodical in every civilized land on earth.

This good woman and the thousands like her do not dream that the "coarse creatures" they despise provide them with food and raiment and shelter; that without these "coarse creatures" they would be stripped nude of their fineries, live upon roots, and lapse into savagery.

Nor does "society," as the small and useless section of it is called, know better than the misguided sister I have quoted, and so far as "society" is concerned, labor will not only remain unappreciated, but will wear forever the badge of degradation, and its menial servility will continue to excite the world's contempt.

Society needs to be reconstructed upon a new foundation, and the working class—the only class without which society would die and the race perish—the working class alone is equal to the task. The change is needed not only to end the tragedy of toil but the tragedy of idleness.

Pure morals wither in the exclusive upper atmosphere of the Four Hundred as certainly as they do in the depths of the social cellars of the slums.

The social revolution now in progress will end only when the means of wealth production and the natural resources have been secured to all for the use of all and wealth is produced by all for the enjoyment of all. The working classes are the motive power in that revolution, for they know at last that they never can be free until they are free themselves.

The labor question, intelligently understood, embraces the whole program of human emancipation.

The working class is the power and a united ballot the means to end the tragedy of toil.

In collective society organized upon an industrial basis, all will work; none will toil. Modern machinery will be the only slavery. Freedom will be the heritage of all.

The tragedy of toil will have ended, and man will be civilized.

Use Your Brains in Your Own Interest†

October 1904

O, workers of America, use your brains in your own interest, instead of being satisfied with deforming your bodies to enrich your masters!

You were born to noble manhood, not to serve as beasts of burden.

Be men enough to think and act for yourselves, and if you do, the mission of the Socialist Party will appeal to your intelligence and claim your allegiance and support.

To conquer capitalism, to abolish slavery, to put an end to poverty, to overcome injustice, to be free men, to have the right to work, to secure what your labor produces, to see your wives and children glad in the joys of home and health, peace, and plenty—you have to do one thing, and that can be expressed in one word: Unite!

You are a vast majority of the earth and ought to rule it.

You are lacking in intelligence only, and this you have the means and opportunity to cultivate.

The mission of the Socialist Party is to free your minds from prejudice, cultivate your intelligence, develop your brains, that you may become the slaveless masters of the earth.

When you succeed to power, all humanity will be free and civilized, and the

† Published in *Labor,* October 1, 1904, unspecified page. Copy preserved in *Papers of Eugene V. Debs* microfilm edition, reel 7.

exercise of power to silence the discontent of slaves will be no longer necessary.

To the working class the Socialist Party makes its appeal. The Socialist Party is the working class, insofar as it has awakened to its class interests and become conscious of its class power.

To organize the working class into a political party to battle for and achieve their own emancipation is the mission of the Socialist Party, and every worker in the land should hail with joy its glorious advent and join with all his heart the swelling chorus of the social revolution.

Socialists Making Unprecedented Gains: Telegram to the *St. Louis Post-Dispatch*†

October 1, 1904

Wallace, Idaho, October 1 [1904]

That the Socialist Party is a factor of increasing importance in the present campaign is becoming more apparent every day. Such meetings as the socialists are holding are not only unprecedented in third-party movements, but the leaders of the old parties have become positively alarmed and find themselves compelled to revise their calculations and put forth the most strenuous efforts to resist the encroachments of the socialist propaganda.

The rapid rise of socialism is not surprising to the socialists themselves. Since the last national campaign, an unceasing propaganda of education has been carried on in every part of the country. Millions of leaflets, tracts, and pamphlets, translated into every language spoken by the working class, have been systematically distributed. A score of socialist papers, aggregating 2 million readers, are now published, while hundreds of speakers, both men and women, are canvassing the country in the interest of the Socialist Party and its candidates.

The accessions this year are accelerated largely by the hostile attitude of the capitalist class toward the trade union movement. The persecution of

† Published as "Debs Predicts Great Gains by the Socialists" in *St. Louis Post-Dispatch,* vol. 57, no. 42 (October 2, 1904), 5.

organized labor in Republican Colorado and anti-boycott law in Democratic Alabama, the uniform decisions of the courts against labor, the use of soldiers to protect capitalist property and crush organized labor, the breaking of the strikes in the packing trades, the textile strikes and other industrial strikes, the defiant declarations of the Citizens' Alliance and the Manufacturers' Association have all combined to drive workingmen from both the old parties with the determination to build up a party of their own and meet the capitalists on the political battlefield, where they outnumber them a dozen to one. This is one of the principal causes of the exodus to the Socialist Party.

New York is the leading state in the revolutionary movement of the working class. The Empire State this year will poll an enormous increase and possibly cast as large a vote as was cast in all the United States four years ago.

Other industrial states will follow with corresponding increases. Massachusetts and New Jersey in the East; Ohio, Indiana, Illinois, and Wisconsin in the Middle West; and California, Oregon, and Washington on the Pacific coast will make a phenomenal showing, while all other states will develop such an increase over four years ago that the returns will be a revelation to the whole country. As to the pivotal states, it is difficult to foretell in what manner or to what extent the results will be affected.

The Republican workingman yields as readily as the Democratic workingman to the logic of socialism. It is a question of economic self-interest, and the working class are driven by the logic of events to independent political action. As capital concentrates, labor is forced to organize, and as its efforts fail on the economic field, it rallies on the political field, and thus the capitalists themselves are promoting the political organization of the working class for the overthrow of the wage system and the inauguration of cooperative industry as the basis of the coming republic.

In estimating the probable showing of the Socialist Party, we do not venture to use figures. We leave this to the leaders of the parties that must figure out in advance the apportionment of the spoils. It is sufficient to say that when the smoke of battle clears from the political battlefield in November, the whole world will know that there is a national Socialist Party in the United States.

It Ought Not Be Difficult to Decide: Campaign Speech at Chicago Auditorium†

October 17, 1904

Ladies and Fellow Workingmen:—

I thank you heartily for this demonstration, and it inspires one to feel the thrill and throb of the sources that underlie society and move the world.[87] This demonstration marks an epoch in the awakening of the working class—in the development of the socialist movement, the greatest movement known to history.

We are in the midst of a worldwide industrial, political, and social revolution. The capitalist system, with its extreme wealth upon the one hand, its abject and widespread poverty on the other, and its political corruption, its industrial slavery, and its social demoralization has about run its course and will soon pass away to make room for one in harmony with the forces, progress, and onward march of civilization. Regardless of all that we hear of liberty, this land is not yet truly civilized and free. Through all the centuries of the past, the many have been the slaves of the few. The great masses have borne the burdens of the race and for the most part living in poverty and dying in despair. The world today trembles upon the verge of the greatest organic change in history.

Benjamin Franklin, that great philosopher, once said that man is a tool-using animal, and without tools man would lapse into savagery.

In the earlier days, the needs were few, and with primitive tools man could easily fill all his wants, but since that time there has been a century of industrial revolution. The tool has become a mammoth machine—a great social instrument. Production has become socialized, but the worker has lost control of the tool. The worker must now sell his labor-power to the capitalist class, which owns and controls the machine. And how is this controlled? By the law of supply and demand. Labor-power is in the market for sale. You don't hear of a capital market because there is no such market. The capitalist buys labor-power. He buys as cheaply as possible, and between these two classes there is an economic and political struggle, and strikes and lockouts, injunctions and bloodshed.

† Published as part of "Debs and Hanford on Class Struggle and the Working Class" in *Chicago Socialist*, vol. 6, whole no. 294 (October 22, 1904), 1–2.

The politician sometimes seeks to obscure this class struggle. The socialist points out that this class rule must be abolished and human freedom shall be established, freedom for all humanity. The politician believes in keeping you in darkness. You are too intelligent to hear. He calls you the "horny-handed sons of toil," but he really means you "horny-headed sons of toil." The socialist tells you not to be interested in nor to follow his leadership but insists upon opening your eyes that you may see, that you may understand and candidly tells you how ignorant you are.

You produce by your labor all the wealth of the country. You have little or nothing to show for it. You build all the palaces and live in cottages and shanties. You support this government, but you are oppressed and suppressed by it. You support the state and the militia and the regular troops, and when they are called out, it is always and everywhere for the one purpose of draining your veins of your blood. You make millions of guns, but you contrive to be at the wrong end of them. You build Pullman palace cars and walk. You produce everything and have practically nothing, while the other class produces nothing and has everything.

This does not prove your intelligence. If you were intelligent, you would produce wealth, not for your masters but for yourselves. If you could get along without King George, you can get along without King John Rockefeller. Political liberty without economic freedom is a myth. Political liberty is rooted in economic freedom. The man who controls and owns the means that sustain my life, owns and controls me. I am his slave and in no sense a free man.

You are divided at the ballot box upon alleged issues, issues in which you have not the slightest interest. The politicians talk to you about the flag—the flag, by the way, that floats over the bull pen in Colorado.

I was speaking a few days ago out West where Senator Dolliver[88] of Iowa was stumping. He was appealing to the working class to vote the Republican ticket because that party had placed a protective tariff on wool. The working class are just beginning to understand the wool issue. The wool they are interested in is not the kind these politicians have been pulling over their eyes lo! these many years. They are beginning to understand whether the tariff is high, or whether it is low; whether we have the gold standard, free silver, or fiat money; whether we favor or oppose expansion and imperialism; the fact remains that the working class has no tools, and we want those tools and we want to use them for ourselves. The Republican Party does not propose that the working class shall have the tools; neither does the Democratic Party. Both these parties propose that the working class shall be tools—the tools of the capitalist class. The Republican Party is the party of the capitalist class.

Against Mr. Roosevelt I have nothing personal. Not one word to say against either Mr. Roosevelt or Mr. Parker, personally; nor against Mr. Fairbanks or Mr. Davis. But I propose to prove that they are the enemies of the working class. Those men insist that they can serve both the working class and the capitalist class. This is impossible. The men who serve one class serves that class at the expense of the other class.

ဢ

Let us see what Mr. Roosevelt's record is. There was a strike on at Croton Dam, in New York, with the workingmen trying to have the eight-hour law enforced, but Mr. Roosevelt sent the militia there to shoot them down if it had been necessary in order to protect the capitalist class who were violating the law.

Now, all of you workingmen remember well the stand Mr. Roosevelt took in the open-shop policy in the government printing office at Washington not long ago. Grover Cleveland sent the federal troops into the state of Illinois in violation of the Constitution of the United States—snuffed it out, so to speak, and, effectively speaking, handcuffed John P. Altgeld in order to break the strike in progress at that time. When Mr. Cleveland committed this crime, he had no more ardent admirer than Theodore Roosevelt, and if Mr. Roosevelt had been in Cleveland's position, he would have done the same thing. Read the way Mr. Roosevelt eulogizes in his book the acts of Mr. Cleveland.

Secretary of War William Howard Taft is the anointed son of the capitalist class. He issued the first injunction in this country, on the Toledo & Ann Arbor Railway. The employees had that strike won, but Judge Taft's decision lost it for them, and ever since then Judge Taft has been the most glorified being in the eyes of the capitalist class.

Not long ago, President Roosevelt found it necessary to appoint a new secretary of the navy, and whom did he choose? One Paul Morton, who is well known here in Chicago, especially by the engineers and firemen who were employed in the Burlington system in 1888, when they went out on strike and when Mr. Morton filled the columns of the daily press with calumnies calculated to destroy their standing as a labor organization. He was the strikebreaker of the Burlington system and won promotion by his service in that capacity.

It is such men as Judge Taft, Paul Morton, and Sherman Bell—the military bully and blackguard of the state of Colorado—who have become the chums and official associates of President Roosevelt. Each and all of them have proved every time they have had an opportunity that they are the subservient tools of the capitalist class and the implacable enemies of the working class. *[Applause.]*

ℰ𝒮

The Democrats had a convention in the city of St. Louis. This convention was surrounded by the same private cars and the same railway magnates, with a different set of politicians. That party is simply the political expression of the economic interests of a class. The Republican Party is the party of the dominant capitalist class, but the Democratic St. Louis convention was the representative of the middle class, the small capitalist class. The large capitalists concluded that the middle class was crumbling, that its economic power was vanishing, that it no longer amounted to anything as a party, and so this class reached out under the domination of Wall Street and seized the Democratic Party and took possession in broad daylight. And now we have two Republican Parties and no Democratic Party—except the Socialist Party, the most democratic party, the only really democratic party the world has ever known. *[Applause.]*

You common people of the Democratic Party are not under the necessity of leaving that party. It has saved you the trouble. It has left you—out in the cold. You better come in out of the elements.

The very first thing the convention did, representing the Democratic Party, the alleged party of the common people, the champion of the working class, the foe of monopoly and enemy of the trusts—the first thing this convention did was to place two thousand reserved chairs at the disposal of the Business Man's League, the Citizens' Alliance of St. Louis, an organization deadly hostile to organized labor; but not a single chair was placed at the disposal of labor, organized or unorganized. When Captain Hobson, the hero of the *Merrimac*—and of the merry smack *[laughter]*—arose and declared that Grover Cleveland had been the only president who had ever used the powers of his great office to crush labor in the interest of capital, that convention rang with applause. This incident clearly demonstrated the fact that this convention was in sympathy with Grover Cleveland and the capitalist class, since Grover Cleveland was such a faithful servant of that class.

There is not the slightest difference between the two parties so far as the working class is concerned. They both stand for the capitalist system, for the private ownership of the means of wealth production and the operation of industry in the interest of the capitalist class. They are both committed to the perpetuation of wage-slavery, and whether one or the other wins, you lose. *[Applause.]*

This convention nominated Judge Parker, who within 12 months was wholly unknown to the American people. As if by magic the Democratic politicians east and west, north and south, arose and exclaimed, "Eureka, we have discovered the Moses who is to lead the people out of the wilderness into a land flowing with milk and honey." How did this come about? Mr. Thomas W. Lawson, who is writing a series of articles in *Everybody's Magazine,* who is not a socialist, but because he has been up against the Standard Oil Company and he is under the necessity of explaining in the interest of those who have been fleeced—Thomas W. Lawson, on the eve of the Democratic convention, declared that Patrick McCarren, the political manager of Judge Parker, was on the payroll of the Standard Oil Company at $25,000 a year, and he furthermore declared his willingness to send Mr. McCarren a certified check for $100,000 if he disproved the statement. He has not attempted to disprove it, and by his silence pleads guilty to this very grave charge. The Democratic machine is lubricated with Standard Oil. *[Applause.]*

Just prior to the St. Louis convention Mr. Bryan came to this city, engaged a hall, delivered an address, and tried to stem the current of Wall Street in the Democratic Party. He declared that Judge Parker was the tool of the trusts and that no self-respecting Democrat could vote for him. After Judge Parker was nominated, Mr. Bryan said that his nomination was secured by crooked and indefensible methods. If this be true, and there is no doubt about it, Judge Parker must be a crooked and indefensible candidate, for a straight candidate does not need a crooked nomination. *[Applause.]*

The Republican convention nominated for vice president Charles W. Fairbanks, a capitalist and millionaire. If you are in his class, you can safely vote for him and he is entitled to your most favorable consideration. How many of you are there in this class?

The Democratic convention nominated for vice president Henry G. Davis, also a capitalist and a multimillionaire, the owner of a large part of the state of West Virginia, a railroad magnate, a coal baron who does not permit the men in his employ to organize. In his biography you will note that in his youth he was a slave driver; and he is yet; he has simply exchanged a small number of black slaves for a large number of white slaves. *[Applause.]* He has the old notion that a working man ought to be exceedingly grateful that he is tolerated at all, that he is permitted to remain upon earth, that he ought to work faithfully for his master all day long and when evening comes, that he ought to pass a resolution of thanks that he has a master who robs him of nearly all that his labor produces; that if he makes any attempt to better his condition, he ought to be suppressed by law. *[Applause.]*

ൾ

There was another convention, national in scope and character, held in the city of Chicago, but not very widely reported in the press. It was the convention of the Socialist Party, the party of the working class. *[Applause.]* No private cars were in evidence. The delegates had paid their fare going and returning to their homes. They had met not to exalt some individual as a subject for hero worship, but to devise ways and means of emancipating and exalting the working class of the world. *[Applause.]*

This convention consisted of workingmen and workingwomen *[applause]*, wholesome, high-minded men and women who had but one object, and that is the emancipation of the working class. They adopted a platform consisting of but a single plank, a labor plank. It declares against the capitalist system, against wage-slavery, and in favor of the socialist republic.

First of all, it proposes the organization of the working class into a party representing the economic interests of the working class. *[Applause.]* For every capitalist in the United States, there are a dozen workingmen. They are overwhelmingly in the majority, and when they are politically organized as a class and become conscious of their power as a class, they will conquer the public powers and sweep into office in this state and every state of the Union and in the nation at large. They will take possession of the industries, put the working class in possession and control of the machinery of production and distribution, and then will capitalism fall, never to rise again. *[Applause.]*

This convention nominated for vice president a workingman, a member of a trade union, who, if he had used the ability he has in his own interest, could long since have been rich in the worldly sense; who years ago in his very youth consecrated himself completely to the working class; who has used his time, energy, and ability to elevate and improve the condition and emancipate that class from the degrading thralldom of the ages.

It ought not to be difficult for you workingmen to decide which of these three candidates is your candidate. Do you know of any millionaire who is going to vote for Ben Hanford and myself? I do not—and I do not blame them. They know that we are not their candidates. Unfortunately, a great many workingmen do not know that we are their candidates. We are perfectly willing that Roosevelt and Fairbanks and Parker and Davis shall have all of the votes of the capitalists. We will be satisfied with all of the votes of the workers. And if we get the votes of all of the workers, you can visit us at the White House after the fourth day of next March.[89] *[Applause.]*

We may not be elected this fall. If so, it will not be our fault; it will be your fault, and you will have to accept the consequences of your act. You will get what you voted for. So far as we are concerned, defeat means but little, because we are but individuals. But it means a great deal so far as you are concerned, for it will mean for you four more years of wage-slavery. But we are not in the least discouraged; quite the contrary. As we look abroad, we note that the working class here and there and everywhere are massing their forces beneath the conquering banner of economic freedom, and to the extent that they are crushed on the industrial field, they rally their forces on the political field. *[Applause.]*

On the industrial field, they are under a thousand disadvantages. The capitalists have resources, are organized, and have control of the opportunities of employment. They are also but few in number. On the other hand, the workers are many. They work for wages, but they have no resources. If they cannot be suppressed in one way, the injunction can be issued and the soldiers brought out, and all the powers of government can be invoked to crush them. But on the political field they meet the capitalists face to face upon equal ground. It is only necessary that they shall understand that their interests as a class are absolutely identical, that they ought to be bound together as by hoops of steel, that they must unite and act together; and when they do this, as they will in time, they will sweep into power, they will get possession of government, and when once they have possession of government, they will also take possession of industry and operate it in their own interest. *[Applause.]*

Many of you in the middle class are opposed to socialism. You still think there is some chance for you under capitalism, and you fear that the socialists will take what little you have and divide it among the shiftless and thriftless. You need not have the slightest fear. The socialist has no use for your small capital; it would do him not the least good. He is after the earth, the trusts, and the machinery of production. *[Applause.]* Besides, soon you will have nothing to divide. When the big capitalists get through with you, you will be ready for us. You may not be ready yet, but you are ripening very rapidly. When you have been stripped of what you have, when you have become proletarians, when you have become expropriated, you will be ready to join us in expropriating the expropriators. *[Applause.]*

Let centralization go forward steadily until it is complete and industry is organized and competition has been practically eliminated. Every system that has appeared has first had birth, has developed to maturity and declined to decay and death. Every system fulfills its historic mission, outlives its usefulness, and passes away. Every such system develops a class whose economic necessity compels them to put an end to that system. The working class realize that there is no hope for them under the present system; that they have no tools, and can only work by permission; that they therefore live by permission; that the wealth they produce goes to the master who owns the tools with which they work, and that they receive in exchange a wage barely sufficient to keep them in working order. They are beginning to realize that their interests are identical, and to the extent that they become conscious of their interests as a class, so the Socialist Party increases in number, power, and influence; and although it may lose its skirmishes, the ultimate victory is with the Socialist Party without a shadow of a doubt. *[Applause.]*

∽

The two old parties, the hyphenated party, the capitalist party, draw their campaign funds from the same source. According to the press dispatches, more than $6 million has already been subscribed to the Democratic Party, and more than $10 million to the Republican Party. These funds are paid by the American trusts in advance, and if these parties succeed, they will serve those trusts. Upon the other hand, the Socialist Party does not receive a penny in the way of contribution from a trust or corporation. It has not as many thousands in its campaign fund as they have millions of dollars, and every penny in its fund is used to open the eyes of and educate the working class. The Socialist Party is the only party that does not want a vote unless the man who casts that vote has the intelligence to know what he is voting for. *[Applause.]* It has not a penny to spend for whiskey to influence the vote; not a penny to haul you to the polls on election day so that you can walk the other 364 days of the year. *[Applause.]*

The Socialist Party is the party of the whole working class—men and women. It proposes that women shall have every right that man enjoys. *[Applause.]* At present, woman is not merely economically enslaved, but she is politically mute and dumb. The Socialist Party proposes that woman shall be economically free. In the present society she must be provided for, must be supported. What does this mean? It means that she is a dependent, in economic servitude. In a sane state of society, rationally organized, woman would be able to provide for herself. She would stand erect in the innate purity of her sex, and she would not be compelled, if she happened to be the daughter of poverty, to exchange her womanhood for shelter. *[Applause.]* In marriage, love would be the only consideration, and then we would not have 65,000 divorces in a single year in the United States.[90] *[Applause.]*

The Socialist Party proposes absolutely to abolish child labor. Not only is there no excuse for child labor, but it is a rebuke to our alleged and vaunted Christian civilization, a crime that defies the power of language to properly describe. *[Applause.]* In the present system, capitalists must buy labor-power as cheaply as possible. Machinery has become so perfect that it may be operated by children. They can, they do, they must work more cheaply than women and men, and so in their early tender years, when they ought to be upon the playground or at school, scourged by their poverty, they are forced into the industrial dungeon. They stand at the machine and feed it; they become cogs in the revolving wheels. Their lives are ground into profit for their masters. They are dwarfed, stunted, deformed. Their lives are broken. They have no fair chance in life. The little girl who is driven into industrial mills at seven, eight, nine, or ten years of age, and feeds the machine until she is old enough to approach the marriage state, if she lives, and assume the functions of motherhood, is wholly unfit for them. Her offspring are born tired. Their tissues are born tired. Their nerves are exhausted. They have no fair chance in life, no sunshine, no atmosphere, no wholesome foods. Deprived of education, their lives are wrecked while they perform labor for their economic masters. *[Applause.]*

Our so-called commercial supremacy is built upon broken lives. It is a result of the use of cheap labor so that we can undersell our foreign competitors, also that we may export the greater share of what we produce. And this fact is sometimes glorified by the capitalist politicians. In this system, highly developed, there is a period of industrial activity, followed inevitably by a period of industrial depression. Next winter in Chicago will be a very hard winter, and when multiplied, thousands of you workingmen will find yourselves out of employment. It may be some consolation to you to know that we are the greatest exporting nation on the face of the globe. *[Applause.]*

ೞ

We live in the most favored land beneath the bending skies. We have raw materials in overwhelming abundance, the most wonderful machinery the world has ever known, and millions of eager and anxious workers stand ready to apply their labor to the machinery to transmit the raw materials into finished products. But, on the other hand, the working class do not consume. Production is limited by consumption, consumption is limited by wages, wages by competition. Machinery has intensified competition among the millions of men, women, and children. The sharper and fiercer that competition, the smaller the wage. The smaller the wage, the less of what their labor produces they can buy. What follows? The working class constitute the great bulk of the population. They cannot buy what their labor produces, the surplus cannot be absorbed by the capitalist class, who are comparatively small; and hence we must export this surplus to foreign countries. The workers cannot consume their products in modern industry. Therefore, the market is glutted, the surplus is forced back upon us. Then comes the reaction, and the country is in a state of panic, industry is paralyzed, the factory, mill, mine, shop, and forge close down. Hundreds of thousands of workingmen are flung out of employment. Their labor-power is no longer required. They have produced more than their masters can consume, and so they must pay the penalty of their overproduction.

All of the signs of the depression are developing. The great plants are beginning to cut down the working force, reducing wages, breaking the strike. They are holding this condition in abeyance as best they can until after the next election. Then, when it comes, there will be an army of workingmen looking for work. Some will leave Chicago, some will come to Chicago; all will be in enforced idleness. Some of them become vagrants, some of them tramps, some of them criminals. It is in this way that crime is made to graduate in the capitalist system, all the way from petty larceny to homicide. *[Applause.]*

There was a time in this country 60 years ago when you might look in the dictionary and you could not find the word "tramp." There is an army of these unfortunates today, not because human nature has undergone a transformation, but because there has been an industrial revolution. According to the annual tabulation of the *Chicago Tribune,* there are about 600,000 thieves and gamblers in the United States; more than half a million fallen women, the most melancholy objects in our so-called civilization; 125,000 convicts; all of our insane asylums crowded and our penitentiaries overflowing. Suicide is increasing at an alarming rate. All these were the fruits of the capitalist system. It has outlived its usefulness. It is an unmitigated curse and ought to be abolished in the interest of all the human race. *[Applause.]*

In this system, absolutely no man is secure, and you instinctively know it. You have $10,000, but you have not the slightest assurance that you will not die in an almshouse and sleep at last in a potter's field. *[Applause.]* You do not know; you cannot tell. It is impossible to draw aside the curtain of the future. You are straining every nerve to educate your son and give him some advantages. Over whom? Over the son of your neighbor. They are told everlastingly that there is room on top. On top of whom? On top of your fellow man. *[Applause.]*

In the capitalist competitive society, men are pitted against men in every department of activity, and the struggle has become so sharp, so fierce, so brutal, that it develops and appeals to all that is cold and cruel and dehumanizing in man. The real difficulty is, how shall we get food, clothing, and shelter? In every vision, there is the specter of want, the possibility of failure. You do not know what is finally to become of you. Leave your son $10,000, and you do not know that he will have 10 cents six weeks after you go to your final resting place. He may have to sell the power of his two hands, his labor-power, and when someone advertises for hands, he will be one of those who will respond.

By the way, in the capitalist system, when men are wanted, "hands" are advertised for. When the capitalist sees an advertisement for hands, he does not respond. He knows that that does not mean him. He is not for sale. He is head; he is not hands. *[Applause.]* The capitalist uses his head. He allows 50 workingmen to apply their hands to his machinery and convert raw materials into wealth. He becomes rich, and they remain poor. Some of them live in cottages, still others in hovels, and some in lairs that are wholly unfit for human habitation. You see this division in every city in the land; here in Chicago notably, where capitalism is quite fully developed. The fashionable boulevards are lined with palaces. The larger districts embrace the comfortable houses of the middle class. In the still larger territory poverty dwells, and beyond that you see the red light glimmering in the distance.

You have a son. Look into his blue eyes and think of the possibilities before him, and think of the solicitude that you feel as to his possible future, and the uncertainties of our present system will give you no little concern.

You have a little daughter. She may be forced to enter a department store and work in her early, tender years, for two and a half or three dollars a week. Do you know what that means? It means that at a time when she ought to be at home under the influence of her mother, she is subjected to a thousand temptations. She must be respectably clad and present a neat and tidy appearance. She is compelled to work early and late. She makes a misstep; she starts on the downward road. It is because in the capitalist system the department store is the source of that broadening and ever-deepening stream which leads into the red-light district. *[Applause.]*

It is said that these things are inherent in and inseparable from our civilization. I repudiate the charge as a libel upon the human race, as a slander upon civilization.

∽

In the competitive system, we are pitted against each other. Our economic interests are in conflict. We make war upon each other. We do not develop those qualities that dignify and glorify human nature. We do develop tooth and fang and claw, cunning at the expense of conscience. No one understands this better than the businessman. No one mistrusts the businessman more than the businessman. It is his rule to treat every man as a rogue until he proves himself otherwise, and never to give him a chance to prove otherwise, for that might be his own undoing. *[Applause.]*

It was Emerson who once said that if you will trace to its other end the chain that fetters the slave, you will find that it is riveted to the wrist of his master. Morally speaking, the master cannot rise far above the level of his slave. He may . . . wear good clothes and fare sumptuously, but he is in no true sense a civilized human being. His brain is thronged with problems: how to make larger dividends, how to secure greater profit. The more he gets, the hungrier he grows. He fails and falls at last a victim to the capitalist system. He gets rich in the worldly sense; in every other sense he remains a pauper. Do the capitalists lead complete lives? What do they know outside of the rules of exploitation? How many capitalists are there in the city of Chicago who can give a scientific definition of the term "capital?" How many can intelligently define themselves, or have ever read a standard book on political economy, or know anything about the history of their own country or anything about literature, science, art? How many of them have time to contemplate the stars or the myriad wonder of the universe? How many of them rise above the animal plane, stand erect in the majesty of true manhood, and give expression to their own honest convictions? A very small part of them. They go to their homes, but they do not hear the loving voice of the wife, the prattle of the child, the crooning of the baby—sweeter music than the minstrelsy of the most gifted musician. They are engaged in this beastly, brutalizing struggle for mastery over their fellow men.

We appeal to the moral sense. We know that man is in an economic condition in which he is compelled to fight his fellow man for bread. We are concerned with the environment. We do not propose a mere change of party—we propose a change of system. *[Applause.]* We are not reformers—we are revolutionists. *[Applause.]* We do not fuse with any other party, and we would a thousand times rather die than compromise. *[Applause.]*

We are moving forward on a straight line, day by day becoming conscious of our power, realizing that as Samson was shorn of his locks, the secret of his power, so the working class have been shorn of the tools with which they work, and these tools are the secret of their power. We are marching forward, keeping step to the inspiring music of the new emancipation; keeping step with the forces of evolution, in league with them, knowing that the same forces that have brought man to his present plane are still in operation and will continue so until at last mankind are civilized and free.

And so we wait, we watch, and we work. We appeal directly to the working class, and through the working class to that class which is rapidly recruiting the working class, to organize a party that represents their economic interest, the revolutionary party of the working class who have done the work through all of the centuries, and who have been in slavery since the beginning of time.

In the ancient civilization men were abject slaves; in the Middle Ages they were serfs; in modern times they are wage-slaves of capital. The next stage will be socialism. We are looking forward to that time, and as we strain our vision just the slightest we behold the dawn, the glorious sunrise, and when the sun of socialism has marked the meridian of its glory, it will look down upon a nation in which there is no master and no slave. *[Applause.]*

So we wait until this minority becomes the majority. If you believe in these conquering principles, if you esteem human life of greater value than material profit, we ask you to join this party, to give this movement your support. It is not yet popular. When it becomes so, it will not need you. If you want to write your name in letters that will live, join it now. Take the advice that Beecher[91] gave a young man when he said, "Young man, in your youth join some righteous and unpopular cause."[92]

The socialist movement is that cause. It is spreading over the world. It proposes to humanize the human race. We are engaged in the last of a long series of class struggles. Socialism will put an end to the animal conflict for existence. It will civilize the world. And, among other things—and let me emphasize it, if I can, in closing—it will put an end to war. *[Applause.]*

Every Christian nation on the face of the globe is armed to the teeth today, with a powerful navy and a large standing army ready at the word of command to blow Christian brains into the froth, to send the souls of millions to the bar of the Almighty because profit is vastly more important than human life in the capitalist system. War is the prostitution of genius, the brutalizing of the human race. You invent an explosive by which you can snuff out a hundred thousand human lives in the twinkling of an eye, and take it down to Washington, and your fortune is made. Under socialism, genius will be exalted in order to dignify manhood. The nations of the earth will be drawn into close, harmonious, sympathetic relations with each other. No more will the workingmen of one country be arrayed in deadly conflict with the workingmen of another. Under socialism, war will be forever ended. The interests of the working class of one country will be the same as the interests of the working class of all other countries.

I am one of those who absolutely refuse to shoulder a death-dealing gun at the behest of any capitalist murderer whatever. If he wants to commit murder, he must commit it himself, so far as socialism is concerned. With the end of capitalism comes the end of war. Capitalism is war. With the beginning of socialism comes the inauguration of peace, the beginning of the march of advancing civilization.

Then machinery will be the only slave. At the touch of man, it will produce in abundance for all. The industrial dungeon will become the temple of science. The badge of labor will be the only badge of aristocracy. Then work will be joy. Every man will gladly do his share of the world's useful work. Every man will have leisure and can cultivate his mind and give his heart and soul an opportunity. Men will rise from the rule of capitalism, from the kingdom of necessity, to the atmosphere of freedom. The army of tramps will be dispersed. The penitentiaries will be vacant. The insane asylums will be depopulated, the shadow of the gallows will no longer fall upon the land.

If you believe in the conquering principle of the socialist movement that will put an end to capitalism and establish the socialist republic, we ask you to join us in marshaling the working class for the grand international march from capitalism into socialism, from slavery to freedom, from merchandise to manhood, from barbarism to socialism.

I thank you each and all. *[Great applause.]*

Advice to First Voters†

October 25, 1904

Answering your two interrogatories,[93] viz: "Why should the first voter cast his ballot for the Socialist Party?" and "Why should the first voter ally himself with or become a member of the Socialist Party?" I have to say:

First, that the Socialist Party is the only party that squarely meets the living issues of the day; the only party that stands for pure democracy.

The tariff, finance, and collateral relics belong to the past. The first voter, unless he happens to be of the few who inherit a fortune, has not interest in these fossilized issues.

Under a high protective tariff or free trade, the gold standard or free silver, the condition of the first voter, if he has nothing but his labor-power to support him, remains the same.

What chance has the poor young man of today to rise above the dead level of wage-slavery? About one in a hundred. And even then, he may lose all and tumble down to where he started from or make his exit from the competitive carnival through the back door of suicide.

The Republican and Democratic parties are one in their allegiance to Wall Street and capitalist supremacy; they draw their campaign funds from the same source and are severally and jointly mortgaged in advance to the trusts and syndicates that constitute, in the present system, the economic masters of the working class and the political rulers of the nation.

A vote for either of these parties is a vote for plutocratic misrule and wage slavery.

The Socialist Party is essentially the party of the working class; and it appeals also to the middle class who are being driven from the competitive field and forced into the working class.

The working class, the only class without which society could not exist, is the coming ruling class, and its emancipation, which will follow the abolition of the wage system, will mean the freedom of humanity, based upon cooperative industry; and it will also mean the end of the animal struggle for existence in human society and the beginning of the first real civilization the world has ever known.

---

† Syndicated to various papers by the Newspaper Enterprise Association. Published as "Advice to First Voters" in *Pittsburgh Press,* vol. 21, no. 296 (October 25, 1904), 6.

The Socialist Party, therefore, is the coming party, and the young man who wants his first vote to count against the private ownership of the earth and the tyranny of class rule and for industrial democracy and the freedom of the race will cast that vote for the Socialist Party with all his heart.

Second: The Republican and Democratic parties are the twin tools of Wall Street, and their candidates are equally acceptable to Rockefeller, Morgan & Co., the throneless monarchs of the American people.

The Socialist Party stands diametrically opposite to this hybrid political aggregation.

Every millionaire in the land is in the Republican Party or the Democratic Party. Not one of them is in the Socialist Party.

Rockefeller is the enemy of socialism for the very reason that socialism is the enemy of Rockefellerism.

The first voter whose ambition it is to become a Rockefeller should not vote the Socialist ticket, but the young man who aspires to become a free man among free men should join the Socialist Party, the only party that believes that the people have capacity for industrial as well as political self-government, the only party that proposes to make this in fact a government of and by and for the people.

Shall the trusts rule the people, or shall the people rule the trusts? That is the only issue in this campaign.

The Republican and Democratic twins are for the trusts and against the people.

But the Socialist Party does not intend to "smash" the trusts. It took too long and cost too much, and they are too useful and necessary to destroy.

The Socialist Party, when it gets into power, will take over the trusts and have them owned and operated by all the people to produce wealth for all the people. Then there will be work for all and wealth for all who are willing to work for it.

In other words, the Socialist Party proposes to transfer the sources, means, and machinery of production and distribution from the private hands to the collective people, so that wealth may be produced in abundance, not to enrich a small class, but for the comfort and enjoyment of all.

This is the overshadowing issue, notwithstanding the capitalist attempts to obscure it by juggling with galvanized dummies to divert the attention of the people, and upon this great issue every first voter in the land who prefers freedom to slavery, intelligence to ignorance, peace to war, love to hate, plenty to poverty, happiness to wretchedness, man to mammon, should cast his lot with the Socialist Party.

The Swing of Victory†

November 9, 1904

Terre Haute, Ind., November 9 [1904]

The Socialist[94] vote in every part of the country has been enormously increased. My advices are that Cook County, Illinois, will give us at least 45,000 votes. The state of Illinois alone will probably cast a larger Socialist vote this year than was cast in all the United States four years ago.

We have made remarkable gains in Milwaukee and elected worthy comrades to the legislature. It is too early to make an estimate of the total national vote, but enough is known to warrant the statement that from this time forward the Republicans will have the Socialist Party to reckon with, and that the coming alignment will be between the Republican Party representing the capitalistic interests, and the Socialist Party representing the working classes. As for the Democratic Party, the Eastern capitalists hit harder than they intended, and it can hardly be pulled together again to serve as a twin to the Republican Party to divide the working classes.

Twice has the Bourbon Democracy of the South coupled up with the radical Western wing of the party and gone down to defeat. It then quit the radical element and embraced the conservative element of the East and has now been knocked in the head harder than before, and this ought to finish this moribund aggregation that has no principles and is only held together by its appetite for spoils.

We will not see Mr. Roosevelt extract the fangs and silence the rattles of the trusts, and we will also see with what effect he will wave the wand of prosperity in the face of the impending industrial depression.

From now on, every move on the political chess board, whether so designed or not, will be in the interest of socialism and promote the growth of the socialist movement, and it is entirely possible that in four years more the Socialist Party may sweep the United States.

† Untitled letter published in *Social Democratic Herald,* vol. 7, no. 28, whole no. 328 (November 12, 1904), 1. Reprinted as "The Swing of Victory" in *The Vanguard, vol. 3, no. 3, whole no. 23* (November 1904), 6.

The Lessons of the 1904 Election†

November 10, 1904

Terre Haute, Ind., November 10 [1904]

Two distinct and opposing tendencies are revealed in the late election. One is the overwhelming triumph of capitalistic interests; the other is the advent of the working class in national politics, shown by the enormous increase in the Socialist Party's vote. The Democratic Party, as the representative of middle-class interests, has been practically eliminated, and no sort of reorganization can save it from disintegration, for the simple reason that the middle class, upon which it is mainly built, is being wiped out of existence.

The trust is doing its work in spite of the hue and cry against it. The next few years will see the climax of trustification, and it is this that will control the new political alignment which will admit no middle-class party or halfway policy.

The truth is that it is the fight between capital and labor, which the politicians of the capitalistic parties have in the past been able to obscure and confuse, but the trusts are removing all doubt, and in the near future the control must narrow down to that, and there can be no escape from it.

Senator Hanna foresaw it clearly when, shortly before his death, he said, "The next great political struggle in the United States will be between the Republicans and the Socialists."

The Republicans are chagrined at this great victory It involves responsibility that they can never meet. They have absolute power to deal with trusts. Thoughtful men know they can do nothing. Trusts defy Republican restriction. They will increase in scope and power until they absorb everything. The beginning of the end has been passed. The transition will be swift.

Industrial depression is almost upon us. Socialism grows amazingly. Within four years it is possible the Socialists will sweep the country. Women are taking an active part in the propaganda. They are in revolt against the system which damns them. Industrial cooperation must be the basis of the coming republic.

† Statement to the press published under multiple titles, November 11, 1904 and after. See, for example: "Debs on the Trusts," *Allentown [PA] Morning Call,* vol. 29, no. 112 (November 12, 1904), 6.

The Democratic Party Has Been Practically Eliminated: Telegram to the *St. Louis Post-Dispatch*†

November 11, 1904

Terre Haute, Ind., November 11 [1904]

Two distinct and opposing tendencies are revealed in the late election. First, the overwhelming triumph of the capitalistic interests, represented by the Republican Party, and the other, the advent of the working class in national politics, shown by the enormous increase of the "socialistic" vote.

The Democratic Party as the representative of the middle-class interests has been practically eliminated. No sort of reorganization can save it from disintegration. It was a middle-class party, and that class is being wiped out of existence.

The trust is doing its work despite all hue and cry. The next few years will see the climax of trustification, and political realignment will follow. Capitalist politicians can no longer obscure issues. The trusts have removed doubts. Senator Hanna prophesied truly when he said shortly before his death: "The next great political struggle will be between the Republicans and the Socialists."

Republicans are chagrined at their huge victory. It brings responsibilities they cannot meet. Their power is absolute.

The trusts are beyond restriction.

The outcome is known.

The trusts will own America—economically, politically.

Then will come transition, swiftly. Socialism may sweep the country four years from now. Womanhood seeks escape from capitalistic thralldom. Women are active in the propaganda. They are in revolt.

The nation will soon see clearly. The people would take the trusts and have them run by and for the people. Industrial cooperation must be the basis of the coming republic.

Eugene V. Debs

† Published as "'Democratic Party Eliminated'—Debs" in *St. Louis Post-Dispatch,* vol. 57, no. 82 (November 11, 1904), 3. A free-standing excerpt from the pamphlet *Unionism and Socialism: A Plea for Both.*

Known by Its Fruits†

December 24, 1904

If by its fruit we know the tree, so by the same token do we know our social system. Its corrupt fruit betrays its foul and unclean nature and condemns it to death.

The swarms of vagrants, tramps, outcasts, paupers, thieves, gamblers, pickpockets, suicides, confidence men, fallen women, consumptives, idiots, dwarfed children; the disease, poverty, insanity, and crime rampant in every land under the sway of capitalism rise up and cry out against it, and hush to silence all the pleas of its mercenaries and strike the knell of its doom.

The ancient and Middle Age civilizations had their rise; they ruled and fell, and that of our own day must follow them. Evolution is the order of nature, and society, like the units that compose it, is subject to its inexorable law.

The day of individual effort, of small tools, free competition, hand labor, long hours, and meager results is gone, never to return. The civilization reared upon this old foundation is crumbling.

The economic base of society is being transformed.

The working class are being knit together in the bonds of cooperation; they are becoming conscious of their interests as a class and marshaling the workers for the class struggle and collective ownership.

With the triumph of the workers, the mode of production and distribution will be revolutionized. Private ownership and production for profit will be supplanted by social ownership and production for use.

The economic interests of the workers will be mutual. They will work together in harmony instead of being arrayed against each other in competitive warfare. The collective workers will own the machinery of production, and there will be work for all, and all will receive their socially due share of the product of their cooperative labor.

It is for this great work that the workers and their sympathizers must organize and educate and agitate.

The social democratic movement is of the working class itself; it is from the injustice perpetrated upon and the misery suffered by this class that the

---

† Published in *Social Democratic Herald,* vol. 7, no. 34, whole no. 334 (December 24, 1904), 1.

movement sprung, and it is to this class it makes its appeal. It is the voice of awakened labor arousing itself to action.

As we look abroad and see things as they are, the capitalists entrenched and fortified and the workers impoverished, ignorant, and in bondage, we are apt to be impressed with the magnitude of the task that lies before the socialist movement, but as we become grounded in the socialist philosophy, as we understand the process of economic determinism and grasp the principles of industrial and social evolution, the magnitude of the undertaking, far from daunting the socialist spirit, appeals to each comrade to enlist in the struggle because of the very greatness of the conflict and the immeasurable good that lies beyond it, and as he girds himself and touches elbows with his comrades, his own latent resources are developed, and his blood thrills with new life as he feels himself rising to the majesty of a man.

Now he has found his true place, and though he be reviled against and ostracized, traduced and denounced, though he be reduced to rags and tormented with hunger pangs, he will bear it all and more, for he is battling for a principle, he has been consecrated to a cause, and he cannot turn back.

To reach the workers that are still in darkness and to open their eyes, that is the task, and to this we must give ourselves with all the strength we have, with patience that never fails and an abiding faith in the ultimate victory.

The moment a worker sees himself in his true light, he severs his relations with the capitalist parties, for he realizes at once that he no more belongs there than Rockefeller belongs in our party.

Notes

1. Thomas Dixon, Jr., *The Leopard's Spots: A Romance of the White Man's Burden—1865–1900* (New York: Doubleday, Page & Co., 1902). The novel was the first part of a trilogy that included *The Clansman: A Historical Romance of the Ku Klux Klan* (1905) and *The Traitor* (1907), racist historical fiction about the Reconstruction South that served as background material for D. W. Griffith's white supremacist epic film *The Birth of a Nation* (1915).
2. Adapted from "Peter Bell: A Tale" (1798) by William Wordsworth (1770–1850). The original reads: *"A primrose by a river's brim / A yellow primrose was to him, / And it was nothing more."*
3. From Samuel M. Jones's contribution to the symposium "Labor Day: The Day We Celebrate," *American Federationist* [Washington, DC], vol. 10, no. 9 (September 1903), 811. Debs's quotation silently inserts numerous italics, deleted here.
4 James H. Peabody (1852-1917) was the Republican governor of Colorado who intervened militarily to crush the Cripple Creek miners' strike of 1903-04.
5. From *The Tragedy of Hamlet, Prince of Denmark* (c. 1602), Act III, Scene I, by William Shakespeare.
6. Idol of worship.
7. This article was followed by a lengthy letter of protest dated May 7, 1904, by John Mitchell, T. L. Lewis, and William B. Wilson, attacking Debs for propagating a series of "falsities," published in the *Social Democratic Herald* of May 21, 1904. The polemic was joined by Debs with letters to the *Herald* dated May 28 (published June 4) and June 24 (published July 2). All four of these documents were republished by Debs as the pamphlet, *Reply to John Mitchell* (Terre Haute: Standard Publishing Co., 1904).
8. Clarence S. Darrow (1857-1938) was one of the leading trial attorneys of the era and was familiar to Debs as his counsel during his legal travails of 1894-5. Darrow spoke in Terre Haute on March 30, 1904, in support of Democratic presidential aspirant William Randolph Hearst (1863-1951). A local newspaper incorrectly reported that the Socialist Party was disappointed in this defection of Darrow from its ranks. A rival Terre Haute paper solicited Debs's views on the matter, which generated this article.
9. Translated: The fact that Hearst has not only a pile of money, but a whole swimming pool full is making his campaign as big a circus as the Bryan campaign of 1896.
10. Moyer had been pursued since March 1904 for the circulation of leaflets and posters bearing the form of the Stars and Stripes including caricatures of former members of the Western Federation of Miners who had quit to become strikebreakers. The alleged offense was one of desecration of the flag, a violation of state statutes.
11. A. H. Floaten was manager of a cooperative department store in Telluride, Colorado, and a member of the Socialist Party's governing National Committee. During the night of March 14–15, a group of armed men from the Citizens Alliance burst into Floaten's home, drove his wife from the house, pistol-whipped him, and "deported" him in his bloody nightshirt along with 70 or 80 striking union miners and their sympathizers. Forced to relocate to Denver for some months, Floaten would be

the nominee of the Socialist Party of Colorado for governor in 1904. Floaten later handled literature distribution from the Socialist Red Special during the Debs presidential campaign of 1908.

12. The 1904 Democratic National Convention was held July 6–10 at the coliseum housed in the old St. Louis Exposition and Music Hall. The gathering nominated Judge Alton B. Parker, a conservative, for president.
13. Alton B. Parker (1852–1926) was chief judge of the New York Court of Appeals.
14. George B. McClellan, Jr. (1865–1940), son of the famous Civil War general, was a former four-term member of Congress and then currently mayor of New York City.
15. The legend of Damon and Pythias is a tale of ideal friendship from ancient Greece. In this story, Pythias, convicted of the capital crime of plotting against the autocrat, persuades the authorities to be allowed to return home one last time to settle his affairs, with his friend Damon held as a hostage to be executed in his stead if he fails to return. Pythias does return to meet his fate, an act of honor and loyalty that moves the ruler to free the pair.
16. On October 21, 1896, Debs was joined by ARU secretary-treasurer Sylvester Keliher in Duluth on behalf of Democratic-People's Party fusion presidential nominee William Jennings Bryan. The pair spoke before a crowd estimated at five thousand people.
17. Richard T. Ely, *The Labor Movement in America* [1886]. New edition (New York: Thomas Y. Crowell, 1890), 36–7.
18. Ely, *Labor Movement*, 38.
19. Ely, *Labor Movement*, 43–44.
20. Karl Marx, *Value, Price, and Profit* [1865]. In *Marx-Engels Collected Works: Volume 20: Marx and Engels, 1864–68* (New York: International Publishers, 1984), 148.
21. Marx, *Value, Price, and Profit*, 148–9.
22. George D. Herron, "The Social Opportunity," *International Socialist Review,* vol. 4, no. 10 (April 1904), 588–90
23. Karl Marx, *Wage Labor and Capital* [1849, revised 1891], in *Marx-Engels Collected Works: Volume 9: Marx and Engels, 1849* (New York: International Publishers, 1977), 203.
24. Marx, *Wage Labor and Capital*, 204–5, 209.
25. From "Death in Disguise," by McDonald Clarke (1798–1842).
26. Concluding lines from "Songs" [1893], by Charlotte Perkins Stetson Gilman (1860–1935).
27. During the evening of June 6, 1904, a railway platform in Independence, Colorado, occupied by strikebreaking miners from the Deadwood mine awaiting a train to return them to home in Victor was destroyed by a bomb, killing 13 and wounding nine others, at least one of whom subsequently died. The bomb, which was estimated to contain between 150 and 300 pounds of black powder, was detonated by the report of a revolver attached to the powder, the trigger of which was pulled by a long wire. At his June 1907 trial, convicted assassin Harry Orchard confessed to committing the Independence platform bombing at the direction of Western

Federation of Miners officials, a claim that some still dispute.

28. Brigadier general Sherman M. Bell was adjutant general in command of the Colorado National Guard during the labor wars that swept the state in 1903 and 1904. The former Rough Rider Bell has been described by one historian as "an arrogant megalomaniac who thought that all labor problems involving the WFM were susceptible to a military solution." See: George G. Suggs, Jr., *Colorado's War on Militant Unionism.* Detroit: Wayne State University Press, 1972; 81.
29. The bomb was actually detonated in the neighboring hamlet of Independence, killing strikebreaking miners waiting to board an arriving train for their return home to Victor.
30. A line assigned to Prometheus in "The Masque of Pandora" (1875) by Henry Wadsworth Longfellow (1807–1882).
31. This is a revised and substantially expanded version of Debs's article "The Socialistic Movement in America," *Social Democratic Herald,* vol. 4, no. 43, whole no. 195 (April 26, 1902), 1. It borrows substantially from Morris Hillquit's research.
32. From *William Shakespeare* (1864), by Victor Hugo (1802–1885).
33. Robert Owen (1771–1858) was a millionaire philanthropist and the owner of a large textile mill in New Lanark, Scotland. A socialist philosopher and experimenter, Owen sought to reduce working hours and improve conditions through cooperation in sizable production units that made provision for public housing, food preparation, and education. In 1825, Owen established a model cooperative colony in New Harmony, Indiana.
34. George Ripley (1802–1880) was a Unitarian minister and journalist. Brook Farm, a utopian socialist colony, was started through Ripley's volition in 1841.
35. Ralph Waldo Emerson (1803–1882) was a poet, philosopher, lecturer, and essayist known for developing and popularizing transcendentalism.
36. Albert Brisbane (1809–1890) was a pioneer American socialist, the author of the influential book *Social Destiny of Man* (1840) and co-editor of the Fourierist journal *The Phalanx* (1843–1845).
37. William Ellery Channing (1818–1901) was a poet and the first biographer of Henry David Thoreau.
38. James Freeman Clarke (1810–1888) was a Unitarian minister and writer.
39. Theodore Parker (1810–1860) was a Unitarian minister and prominent abolitionist. He suffered a premature death from tuberculosis.
40. Amos Bronson Alcott (1799–1888) was a reform-minded educator and writer and the father of renowned novelist Louisa May Alcott (1832–1888).
41. John Thomas Codman (1827–1907), a youthful member of Brook Farm, is best remembered for his book *Brook Farm: Historic and Personal Memoir.* New York: Arena Publishing Co., 1894.
42. Henry David Thoreau (1817–1862), an essayist and poet, is regarded as the leading figure of Transcendentalism and holds an iconic place in the world of American literature.
43. Nathanial Hawthorne (1804–1864) was a popular novelist and short-story writer

best remembered for his 1850 work *The Scarlet Letter.*

44. George Bancroft (1800–1891), son of a Unitarian minister, was a prominent historian who authored a massive multivolume history of the United States.
45. Charles A. Dana (1819–1897) was a prominent journalist and newspaper editor who was the right-hand man of Horace Greeley at the *New York Tribune*. Dana met Karl Marx while covering the revolutions of 1848 in Europe and was influential in bringing Marx aboard as a correspondent to the paper, for which he wrote for more than a decade.
46. George William Curtis (1824–1892) was a writer and public speaker.
47. Parke Godwin (1816–1904) was a journalist and advocate of the ideas of François Marie Charles Fourier (1772–1837).
48. Albert Brisbane, *Social Destiny of Man; or, Association and Reorganization of Industry.* Philadelphia: C. F. Stollmeyer, 1840.
49. James Parton, *The Life of Horace Greeley, Editor of the New York Tribune* (Boston: Fields, Osgood & Co., 1869), 334–5.
50. Wilhelm Weitling (1808–1871), an émigré to the United States after the failure of the revolutions of 1848, was one of the earliest exponents of socialism in the United States. He launched a monthly journal, *Die Republik der Arbeiter* [The Republic of the Worker], in 1850.
51. Morris Hillquit, *History of Socialism in the United States* (New York: Funk and Wagnalls Co., 1903).
52. Frederic Heath, *Socialism in America.* Paperback title: *Social Democracy Red Book* (Terre Haute, IN: Debs Publishing Co., January 1900).
53. Ely, *Labor Movement,* 219–20.
54. Local German-American gymnastic clubs that also served the function of social and political societies.
55. It is disingenuous at best for Debs—who last worked as a locomotive fireman in October 1874 and was then employed by a grocer wholesaler—to intimate that he played any part whatsoever in the strikes of 1877. Debs was anti-strike in this period.
56. Allan Pinkerton, *Strikers, Communists, Tramps, and Detectives* (New York: G. W. Carleton & Co., 1882).
57. Pinkerton, *Strikers* 257–8, 267–8.
58. Ely, *The Labor Movement in America,* 227–8.
59. Hillquit, *History of Socialism in the United States,* 213.
60. Laurence Gronlund (1846–1899) was one of the most influential American socialist writers of the nineteenth century. Gronlund's 1884 book *The Cooperative Commonwealth* did much to popularize the basic economic ideas expounded by Karl Marx for an English-speaking audience. In subsequent years, Gronlund was deeply influenced by the evolutionary ideas of the Fabian Society in England, adapting its ideas to American conditions in his final book, *The New Economy: A Peaceful Solution of the Social Problem* (1898).
61. This is an inaccuracy. *The Railway Times* did in fact rename itself as *The Social Democrat* on July 1, 1897; however, that paper stayed with the pro-colonization element in the June 1898 split that formed the Social Democratic Party. It

terminated publication after just three more issues due to financial difficulties. The *Social Democratic Herald* was launched in July 1898 as a rival publication by the political actionists, initiating a new issue numbering series. The latter paper served as the official organ of the Chicago SDP until the formation of the Socialist Party of America in the summer of 1901, at which time it was taken over by publisher Victor L. Berger and moved from Chicago to Milwaukee to become an independent publication. The *Social Democratic Herald* was ultimately succeeded in December 1911 by a new daily newspaper published by Berger, the *Milwaukee Leader*.

62. Slaughterhouse workers and meat processing workers went on strike on July 12, 1904. Twenty thousand workers walked out on Armour, Swift, and five other large meatpacking concerns in Chicago, joined by nearly 13,000 in Kansas City and 23,000 others across the Midwest. An attempt at speedy settlement of the work stoppage through arbitration failed, and the battle continued through the entire month of August and into September, with strikebreakers employed and the cost of meat to consumers escalating as available supplies dwindled.
63. Henry Symes "Harry" Lehr (1869–1929) was a prominent Baltimore socialite known for his staging of elaborate parties.
64. William Waldorf Astor (1848–1919), a New York Republican politician and philanthropist, was the only child of millionaire financier John Jacob Astor III (1822–1890).
65. That is, the packinghouse strike.
66. The Socialist Party of America was not established until the summer of 1901 and thus is a name used anachronistically here. The 1900 campaign was a coalition effort of two independent parties, the Social Democratic Party with headquarters in Chicago and the Social Democratic Party with headquarters in Springfield, Massachusetts.
67. Nineteenth-century slang for a horse-drawn carriage; one who was "at the ribbons" held the reins, one "on the box" sat beside the driver.
68. The "Seeley dinner" was a legendary stag party held December 20, 1896, at a New York club called Sherry's for socialite Clinton B. Seeley. According to a newspaper feature story published a quarter century later, the Seeley bachelor party "left a permanent name in the annals of New York wickedness." The cause of shock to polite society was an exotic dancer named "Little Egypt," who "unclad, save for a few almost superfluous pieces of gauze," danced the lascivious "hootchy kootchy" for the event's champagne-swilling guests, prompting a sensational police raid that ended in her arrest. (See "Shadows of the Famous Seeley Dinner," *Philadelphia Inquirer*, April 11, 1920, 7.)
69. Apparently a reference to August Belmont II (1853–1924), a New York financier. His younger brother Oliver Belmont (1858–1908) was a one-term member of Congress.
70. Benjamin Tillman (1847–1918) was a racist and reactionary Democratic United States senator from South Carolina.
71. This speech officially launched the second campaign of Eugene V. Debs for president of the United States. A ten-week public tour followed, with Debs speaking nightly to packed houses from California to Massachusetts, Alabama to Michigan. Three

distinct pamphlet editions of this speech were issued in conjunction with the 1904 campaign, and the title remained in print through Chicago publisher Charles H. Kerr & Co. for more than a decade. It was thus one of the basic pieces of American socialist propaganda literature of the era.

72. Money without intrinsic value, such as paper money or coins made of base metals.
73. The concept of imperialism (and its antithesis, anti-imperialism) was developed around the turn of the twentieth century. It was initially regarded by many American radicals of the day as a diversionary issue of liberal reformers, shifting attention from the fundamental question of capitalism vs. socialism.
74. Charles W. Fairbanks (1852–1918), an attorney from Indianapolis, was a one-term member of the US Senate from Indiana, succeeding Democrat Daniel W. Voorhees in the position from 1897 until his inauguration as vice president in 1905.
75. Oyster Bay, New York, and Buzzard's Bay, Massachusetts, were the locations of the posh summer homes of presidents Roosevelt and Cleveland, respectively.
76. A ubiquitous romantic couplet frequently misattributed in the internet age to John Keats (1795–1821). The lines are actually derived from a translation of the poem "Mein Herz, ich will dich fragen," by Friedrich Halm (pseudonym of Eligius Franz Joseph von Münch-Bellinghausen, 1806–1871).
77. Theodore Roosevelt, "The Three Vice-Presidential Candidates and What They Represent," *Review of Reviews,* vol. 14, no. 3 (September 1896), 295.
78. Paul Morton (1857–1911) was a businessman and railroad official serving as vice president of the Santa Fe Railroad. Morton was forced out as secretary of the Navy in 1905 when news of illegal rebates granted by the Santa Fe to favored shippers under Morton's regime was made public.
79. Debs is correct in his assertion that 2,000 of 11,000 total seats at the 1904 Democratic National Convention held in July had been reserved for the Business Men's League of St. Louis—a number only slightly less than the 2,020 seats reserved for delegates and alternates themselves and the 2,288 gallery tickets allocated for distribution by delegates.
80. Lieutenant Richmond Hobson was a hero of the Spanish-American War, having led a dangerous mission of eight volunteers to attempt to sink the steamship *USS Merrimac* as a blockship in the entrance of Santiago harbor in order to entrap the Spanish fleet. The ship was sunk by the Spanish without accomplishing its object, and Hobson and his seven compatriots were made prisoners of war. The *Merrimac* was the only ship sunk by the Spanish during the brief 1898 conflagration.
81. That is, the National Association of Manufacturers.
82. Thomas W. Lawson (1857–1925) was a Boston multimillionaire who made his fortune as a partner of the Amalgamated Copper Mining Co., extracting profit from mines of Montana. Lawson later disavowed his earlier commercial activities and became a reform advocate, authoring the book *Frenzied Finance, Volume 1: The Crime of Amalgamated* (1905) and running as an independent candidate for the United States Senate in 1918.
83. Patrick Henry McCarran (1849–1909) served a number of terms as a Democratic

member of the New York State Senate.

84. Henry G. Davis (1823–1916), a millionaire and former member of the US Senate from West Virginia, was 80 years old at the time of his nomination for vice president, making him the oldest major party nominee for top office.
85. The National Quorum was an elected committee of five living in proximity to the Socialist Party's headquarters city. The Quorum held frequent physical meetings as an executive committee in charge of the daily affairs of the party, supervising the national secretary.
86. The most elite circle of the ruling class, a term derived from the assertion by social arbiter Ward McAllister (1827–1898) that there were only 400 people that really mattered in fashionable New York society.
87. Speaking before a packed house at the Chicago Auditorium, a crowd estimated at 4,000, Debs was greeted by a massive ovation that "swept over the vast audience, subsided, grew again, and again, and again."
88. Jonathan Prentiss Dolliver (1858–1910) was a Republican member of Congress who joined the United States Senate in August 1900 to fill a vacancy caused by the death of John Henry Gear (1825–1900).
89. Until 1937, the inauguration of the new presidential administration took place on March 4 of the year following the general election. Inauguration day was subsequently moved to January 20. In the event that either of these two dates landed on a Sunday, the inauguration ceremony was held the following day.
90. By way of comparison, there were an average of more than 1.1 million divorces per year in the United States during the 1990s. Owing to a decline in the marriage rate in the twenty-first century, this number stood at about 825,000 per year during the 2010s.
91. Henry Ward Beecher (1813–1887) was a noted Congregationalist minister and abolitionist.
92. Numerous variations of this frequently quoted directive exist, usually attributed to abolitionist Wendell Phillips (1811–1884).
93. These same questions were also asked of representatives of the Democratic, Republican, Prohibition, and People's parties, as well as of Lincoln Steffens (1866–1936) as an independent advocate of the policies of good government.
94. The published version has "Social Democratic Party" throughout, doubtlessly an editorial change made by *Social Democratic Herald* editor Fred Heath for his Wisconsin readership—the Socialist Party being officially known by that name in that state.

Appendix

Special Convention Forthcoming: From ARU Circular Letter No. 3 (1897)[†] [excerpt]

April 1, 1897

April 1, 1897

Official Circular No. 3[1]

* * *

A special convention will be held, probably in June. The board of directors now have the matter under advisement, and the official announcement will be made at an early day. The convention will, without doubt, take advance ground and adopt a new policy fully abreast of the progressive spirit of the times. It will be a most interesting and important gathering. The veterans will be in line again, and upon the scene.

* * *

Eugene V. Debs,
President
Sylvester Keliher,
Secretary

† Published as part of "City Labor Notes," *Los Angeles Herald,* vol. 26, no. 201 (April 19, 1897), 10.

To Members of the Social Democracy of America: A Circular Letter from the Social Democratic Party of America†

June 16, 1898

The Social Democratic Party of America
Address Communications and Remittances to
Theodore Debs, 519 E. 66th Street,
Chicago, Ill.

Chicago, June 16, 1898

To Members of the Social Democracy of America

Comrades:—

There has been a division of the delegates who met in annual convention in this city in the name of the social democracy, beginning June 7 and ending June 11, and the result has been the formation of a new party, known as the **Social Democratic Party of America.**

To report the truth respecting the withdrawal of the undersigned delegates from the convention, and the causes which led thereto, and to the formation of a new party, is the purpose of this address, and we bespeak for it the calm and serious consideration its importance demands.

Soon after the convention was called to order, it became apparent that the delegates were divided into two factions, and as the deliberations proceeded, the breach which separated them grew wider, and all hope of bringing them into harmonious alliance vanished.

The prime factor in the disruption of the social democracy was the appearance in the convention of a number of delegates representing Chicago branches which were reported to have been organized within two or three days of the time the convention met, and these delegates were sufficient in number to control the convention. As a matter of fact, they were chosen for that purpose and for that purpose alone, and it can be proved that the branches they

† Typeset circular letter mailed to party members. Copy preserved in *Papers of Eugene V. Debs* microfilm edition, reel 6, frames 1064–5.

were alleged to represent had not, and have not now, any existence.

That there was an undercurrent to defeat independent political action, especially in some sections in which certain delegates were personally interested, was too plainly evident to admit of doubt. The intense activity of certain other persons who are known to be violently opposed to political action emphasized the conviction that "colonization" was made the pretext for defeating the independent political program of the organization.

Another factor in the separation was the colonization department. Upon this feature there were and are no doubt honest differences, but that the work done, or rather not done, by the commission during the past year is a sore disappointment as well as a flat failure is a fact so painfully evident as to silence all controversy. The constitution authorized the commission to select some state for colonization, with a view to securing control, political and otherwise, but this mandatory duty had been totally disregarded, and instead of this, all kinds of schemes were proposed and abandoned, and absolutely nothing accomplished. There was undoubtedly a radical departure from the original design to decide upon a state and colonize it to secure political control; and on the lines followed by the commission, which the convention was determined to continue, failure and ruin are, we are convinced, inevitable, as time will demonstrate.

From time to time the commission reported in the columns of *The Social Democrat* that they were on the eve of launching great enterprises, raising the hopes of members to the highest pitch, and as nothing materialized from these glowing promises, the disappointment and dissatisfaction of delegates was intense, and when the reports of the commission showed that almost $2500 had been received and spent, and that there was nothing tangible to show for it, the feeling found expression in bitter opposition.

A third cause of the trouble grew out of the fact that a certain number joined the social democracy, avowing their faith in the colonization department, who are not social democrats, are opposed to political action, and are, in fact, opposed to the fundamental principles of the organization.[2]

Under these circumstances, and realizing that the various elements alluded to were utterly and hopelessly irreconcilable, the undersigned withdrew from the convention at the adjournment of the session of Friday night, 2:30 a.m., and proceeded at once to the Revere House, where it was unanimously decided to organize a new socialist party, composed exclusively of socialists who subscribe to the principles and program of international socialism.

Comrade Frederic Heath of Wisconsin presided, and Comrade F. G. R. Gordon of New Hampshire acted as secretary. The following proceedings were had:

The platform reported by the majority of the committee in the Uhlich Hall convention was approved.

The name "Social Democratic Party of America" was adopted.

A temporary national committee composed of delegates from the various cities and states was chosen.

An address to the membership of the social democracy, setting forth the causes which led to the separation, was ordered issued and signed by the delegates representing the seceding branches. The meeting adjourned at 4:00 a.m. to meet again to perfect the organization at Hull House at 10:00 a.m.

Thus, at the dawn of a new day, the new organization was born.

The delegates met at Hull House pursuant to adjournment, Jesse Cox of Illinois in the chair and William Mailly of Tennessee acting as secretary. The following executive committee was chosen: Jesse Cox, Seymour Stedman, Eugene V. Debs, Victor L. Berger, and Frederic Heath. The executive committee was authorized to carefully revise the platform, prepare a suitable constitution, and submit the same to the membership for approval by a referendum vote.

The resolutions respecting organized labor, and also the resolutions in memory of Edward Bellamy and Paul Grottkau adopted by the Uhlich Hall convention, were readopted.

A. S. Edwards of Tennessee was chosen national organizer.

Jacob Winnen, representing the Social Democratic Federation, appeared before the body, expressing his approval of the new organization and declaring that he had no doubt the members would ratify the action and ally themselves with the Social Democratic Party at an early day.

(Note: E. V. Debs was prevented by illness from attending the Revere House and Hull House meetings but was in accord with their object, and his name therefore appears with the rest.)

The executive committee deem it advisable to continue headquarters at Chicago for the preset. The place for holding the next annual convention will be determined hereafter.

The publication of an official paper will be begun at the earliest possible moment.

The constitution fixes the dues at 25 cents per quarter, payable quarterly in advance, and the first quarter's dues is payable on July 1, and each branch is requested to send this amount for each member as soon as possible, together with a list of the names and addresses of members.

Herewith is forwarded to each branch a copy of the platform and constitution and, in accordance with the action of the meeting held by the withdrawing delegates, each branch is requested to have the same voted on by the members and advise us of the approval or rejection of same as early as possible. It is hoped that the constitution will be promptly approved, even though some defects may be apparent, in order that the organization can be perfected. Such defects as may appear can be remedied later by a referendum vote.

As we are entirely without funds and require office equipment, printing, supplies, etc., we earnestly appeal to each branch and each member to send at once such an amount, however small, as can be spared to meet immediate demands.

The officers of the executive board for the present are as follows:

Chairman, Jesse Cox, 95 Fifth Avenue, Chicago.

Secretary, Seymour Stedman.

The temporary national secretary and treasurer is Theodore Debs and his address is 519 East 66th Street, and all correspondence and remittances will be addressed to him until otherwise ordered.

Immediately on receipt of this address, branches are requested to notify us if they approve of our action and are with us in the new organization. Branches deciding to ally themselves with the Social Democratic Party will have charters issued to them and cards of membership issued to their members as soon as these can be provided.

The motto of the Social Democratic Party is pure socialism and no compromise. The party stands for united political action and proposes to enter the national field this fall by nominating candidates for Congress in every district in which the organization has a foothold. Candidates for municipal and state offices will also be nominated wherever possible and a thorough campaign made for a united socialist vote throughout the country.

Comrades, we feel that the Social Democratic Party is the party of the American socialist movement. It stands for international socialism and appeals for support on its merits as a class-conscious, revolutionary social organization. The convention which resulted in separation has not weakened but strengthened the movement. There are now no longer warring factions, conflicting elements, but absolute unity and harmony, which are bound to bring success.

Every loyal supporter of socialist principles should promptly come to the front and join the Social Democratic Party of America. Never was the outlook more promising. East, West, North, and South, comrades are with us, and ringing messages of approval cheer us on the course we have taken. There is cause for neither doubt nor despondency. The cause of socialism has again given evidence that it cannot be sidetracked, that it is a living force in human affairs, and that in due course of time it will abolish the slavery of capitalism and give us the Cooperative Commonwealth.

With socialist greetings and awaiting your reply, we subscribe ourselves

Yours fraternally,
James F. Carey, Massachusetts
Margaret Haile, Massachusetts
Anna Ferry Smith, California
Eugene V. Debs, Indiana
Theodore Debs, Indiana
Hugo Miller, Indiana
Sylvester Keliher, Illinois
Jesse Cox, Illinois
Seymour Stedman, Illinois
George Koop, Illinois
M. Winchevsky, New York
Louis E. Miller, New York
I. A. Hourwich, New York
I. Phillips, New York
Joseph Barondess, New York
William Butscher, New York
Samuel Levine, New Jersey
G. A. Hoehn, Missouri
C. F. Meier, Missouri
Mary G. Jones, Missouri
William Mailly, Tennessee
A. S. Edwards, Tennessee
Victor L. Berger, Wisconsin
Frederic Heath, Wisconsin
Charles G. Kuhn, Wisconsin
George Moerschel, Wisconsin
Jacob Hunger, Wisconsin
John Doerfler, Wisconsin

Oscar Loebel, Wisconsin
F. G. R. Gordon, New Hampshire
Charles R. Martin, Ohio
W. J. Carberry, Ohio
Walter H. Miller, Pennsylvania

Manifesto of the National Executive Board to the Members of the Social Democratic Party†

April 2, 1900

Chicago, Ill., April 2, 1900

Comrades:—

Certain facts having come to the knowledge of your national committee concerning the New York conference through the reports to the board on the part of three of their members representing our party, and through a perusal of the press of the Socialist Labor Party, we deem it our duty at this time on behalf of the cause of socialism to issue to you a statement regarding the actions of the New York conference and to give to you a review of the facts relating to the union of these two socialist forces.[3]

Before taking up such a review, however, it should be stated that the official paper of the party, the *Herald*, was for many months prior to the convention open to discussion of the subject of union. During that time not less than 23 communications were published, 13 being in favor of union, three qualifiedly favorable, and seven opposed. It should also be stated here, since attempts have been made to create the impression that the national officers of the organization were opposed to union, that said officers went to Indianapolis favorable to an honorable union, with perhaps a single exception.[4]

The committee of 18 in New York[5] failed of performing its true work in two salient and vital points, viz.:

---

† Published in *Social Democratic Herald*, vol. 2, no. 42, whole no. 92 (April 7, 1900), 1.

First—As regards name, involving the violation of pledges given to your comrades at Indianapolis by members of the committee of the Socialist Labor Party, Messrs. Harriman, Hillquit, Hayes, and Benham;

Second—As regards the referendum vote, involving the question of whether there should be a majority vote of each party voting separately or of both parties voting as one.

Now, we desire to discuss with you, first, the question of the name. It has been recognized all through this discussion of unity that our stand for the name Social Democratic Party has not been based upon a blind allegiance to a symbol. We have stood by the name Social Democratic because of the history which it symbolizes, the spirit of our movement, and the methods which have been used in building up the party, which have given it a standing among the political movements of our time; and further, because of its international significance and the splendid achievements accomplished under it during the 20 months of our existence as a party.

The Compact Made

It cannot be denied that the overwhelming majority of the members of the Social Democratic Party was and is in favor of retaining the present name. This was clearly manifest in the Indianapolis convention. The convention, it must be remembered, was essentially a mass convention, over 2,100 individual credentials handed in.[6] The only thing which apparently stood in the way of the definite perfecting of the union at Indianapolis was this very question of name. The difficulties in the way in this respect were removed by a solemn compact entered into by Messrs. Harriman, Hillquit, and Hayes, and members of our party at a conference held in the Occidental Hotel, Indianapolis, on the evening of Thursday, March 9.

As regards Mr. G. B. Benham's attitude concerning the name, comrades present at the conference of March 9 will agree that he pledged himself to unequivocally and aggressively support the name Social Democratic on the condition that Harriman and Hayes were accepted by our party as candidates.[7] Mr. Benham distinguished himself at New York by presenting a labored argument against the name.

Mr. Job Harriman also stated plainly to Comrade Stedman that he would support the name. Stedman announced on the floor of the convention that he changed his vote from the majority to the minority report because Harriman and Hayes had given him the promise to support the name.

We incorporate herein two statements regarding this compact by Comrades F. G. R. Gordon and A. S. Edwards:

Edwards's Statement and Affidavit

On the evening of March 8 at the New Occidental Hotel, Indianapolis, a meeting was held for the purpose, if possible, of arriving at an agreement. There were present as representatives of the Socialist Labor Party Morris Hillquit, Job Harriman, and G. B. Benham; and F. G. R. Gordon, William Mailly, C. R. Martin, A. S. Edwards, J. C. Chase, J. F. Carey, V. L. Berger. Gordon stated that since E. V. Debs declined to accept the nomination, it had been deemed advisable to hold a meeting of a few members of the SDP and the SLP delegates to see if an agreement honorable to both parties could not be made. He said the delegates to the convention were willing to accept Harriman and Hayes as the candidates, and if that was done, he thought the delegates of the SLP should be asked to give some assurance that the name Social Democratic would be accepted.

Morris Hillquit was the first to respond. He said, in substance, that if the convention on the following day nominated Harriman and Hayes, there would be no difficulty about the name; that he would give his personal pledge (which he then and there did) that so far as he was concerned the name Social Democratic would be the only one submitted by the joint conference committee; further, he said that he would give those present the moral assurance that the name Social Democratic would be accepted by the committee of nine representing the SLP.

The next to speak was G. B. Benham. He said that he agreed fully with Mr. Hillquit, that the name was an acceptable one, and that such an arrangement as was proposed would be satisfactory and settle the question of name. He gave his personal pledge.

Job Harriman followed with the explicit and unqualified statement that he was in full accord with Hillquit, gave his personal pledge, and added that he would write to the sections of the SLP urging acceptance of the name Social Democratic Party.

Then Victor L. Berger said, in substance: "If Debs can be induced to accept, and the ticket nominated is Debs and Harriman, will you then stand by the name and will your pledges be good? I have some personal influence with Debs and am willing to make another effort. I do not know that I can succeed, but I will try, and if he does accept, will you recommend only the name Social Democratic Party?"

To this Hillquit was first to reply. This he did in precise terms, declaring as on the first proposition, that he would stand for the one name, Social Democratic Party.

Benham declined to commit himself as he had done on the Harriman-Hayes proposition.

Harriman expressly declared that he accepted the proposition and would stand by the agreement on the name if the ticket were Debs and Harriman.

Hayes being absent, the question was asked whether he would approve and accept the action of the meeting. Both Hillquit and Harriman stated that Hayes's endorsement and pledge could be relied upon and any agreement made there would be sanctioned by him.

To the foregoing I wish to add that no other conditions or provisions whatever were suggested or agreed upon, that the members of the SDP on their part accepted the conclusion arrived at in good faith, and that it was the distinct understanding when the meeting adjourned that if the convention nominated Debs and Harriman no other name than that of the Social Democratic Party would be submitted by the joint conference.

A. S. Edwards

Subscribed and sworn to before me,
this third day of April, AD 1900.

Charles H. Soelke,
Notary Public.

Gordon's Statement and Affidavit

Milwaukee, Wis., April 2, 1900

I believe it to be in the interest of truth and justice that a statement be made in reference to the peace conference held on Thursday, March 8, at the Occidental Hotel. The convention had adjourned in confusion and considerable bad feeling. Comrade Mailly requested me to talk to certain comrades who were pretty "hot under the collar." On the way to the hotel I suggested to Comrades Hillquit and Mailly that we get a half dozen of the warring comrades into a room and see if we could not effect some kind of peace that would be honorable to all. This was agreed to, and I lost no time in bringing it about. I sought Victor L. Berger, who had been especially anxious to retain the name and spirit of the Social Democratic Party, and asked him to attend. He at first flatly refused, stating he was afraid of trickery, but finally consented after much urging upon the part of Comrade Mailly and myself and also upon an invitation of Comrade

Carey. Comrade Berger had been invited to attend a conference of the oldest friends of Comrade E. V. Debs for the purpose of prevailing upon Debs to accept the nomination, but upon the urgent demands and appeals of Comrades Mailly, Carey, and Gordon, he consented to attend the peace conference instead.

I made the proposition at the peace conference that in case Debs would not accept the nomination the SDP nominate Harriman and Hayes for the standard bearers of the united party and that the SLP on their part pledge themselves to accept and work for the name Social Democratic Party as the official name of the united party. Comrades Hillquit and Harriman agreed to this, Comrade Harriman pledging himself to write to all SLP sections, appealing to them to vote for the name Social Democratic Party.

Comrade Berger then put this question: "How would it be about the name then in case Debs will run, do you still agree in that case to the name Social Democratic Party?" After some discussion, the point was made by Comrade Mailly that Debs was the choice of all, that we, the SDP, were to accept Harriman, and the SLP, on their part, accept the name of the SDP. This was agreed to by both Harriman and Hillquit. Comrade Benham did not agree to this.

The peace conference adjourned to meet at 11:30 p.m. In the meantime, the other conference had succeeded in gaining Debs's consent to accept the nomination; he (Debs) giving his consent at almost the very minute that the peace conference adjourned. Things having been settled to the satisfaction of all, the 11:30 conference was not called simply because Debs's acceptance had settled everything.

F. G. R. Gordon

Subscribed and sworn to before me,
this 3rd day of April, 1900.

James A. Sheridan,
Notary Public, Wisconsin.

Mr. Morris Hillquit, in his first address to the convention on Wednesday, March 7, declared that the Rochester convention[8] had purposely refrained from adopting a name in order that they might be free to adopt any name that might be agreed upon.

Friday afternoon [March 9], at a meeting of the joint committee, in support of the plan to hold the conference at New York, and in support of his wish to have the conference put off two weeks in order that he might win over his people to the acceptance of the name, Mr. Hillquit again indirectly but nevertheless clearly re-avowed his allegiance to the name.

Mr. Max Hayes, on the floor of the convention Thursday afternoon [March 8], announced his personal choice of the name Social Democratic and in strong terms pledged himself and his paper, the *Cleveland Citizen,* to the name.

The Compact Broken

We now come to the painful part of our statement—a record of broken promises. However hard or repugnant it may be, we hereby make the charge that in the New York conference the compact described above was ruthlessly violated by Hillquit, Harriman, and Hayes, all of whom opposed the name Social Democratic Party.

For one whole day the name was discussed, and they stated when charged with a violation of their pledges that they did not feel bound to keep their word because Eugene V. Debs had accepted the nomination before the pledges were given. The personal pledge of Harriman to Stedman the former evaded by stating that he did not make the promise but "with concessions." This latter statement Stedman positively denied. No other conditions were asked for or agreed upon save those contained in the sworn statements of Comrades Gordon and Edwards given above. Harriman in committee never mentioned that qualification until charged with a breach of faith. We call your special attention to the fact, as stated in Comrade Edwards's affidavit, that while the agreement at Indianapolis was that only one name would be submitted to the referendum of the parties, the entire committee representing the SLP (excepting Hayes, who did not vote) went direct and solidly against the name and voted for the submission of two names.

It must be noted also that while Mr. Max Hayes, as heretofore described, had pledged himself to work for the name, nevertheless he evaded the responsibility by absenting himself from the conference while the question of name came under discussion. He promised Comrade Leonard D. Abbott in New York that he would attend a session and speak in favor of the name. This he failed to do.

A most significant fact connected with this New York conference is that on motion of Sieverman (SLP), seconded by Stone (SLP); the joint committee prohibited any minority report except by permission of a majority of either committee. Sieverman said in this connection that they (the minority) can get their report to the members in the best way they know how, but any action by a minority should be no part of these proceedings.

It was said by the members of the committee of the SLP in the New York conference that inasmuch as Comrade Berger was not instrumental in gaining Comrade Debs's acceptance of the nomination, they were absolved from their pledges. It is also charged that Comrade Berger knew of Debs's acceptance at the time he was treating with them in the "peace conference." Comrade Debs has affirmed to us that when Comrade Berger left him to attend what Gordon calls the "peace conference," he could not have known at that time of his acceptance, for the good and sufficient reason that he (Debs) had not decided to accept.

Convention Instructions Disregarded

We come now to our second point regarding the referendum vote. One of the most important considerations in deciding on the name by the two parties was the character of the referendum.

Your convention decided that the referendum vote should be taken by each party voting separately.

Notwithstanding these definite instructions, the joint committee by a majority vote deliberately violated the specific directions of your convention, which it must be remembered was the sovereign power creating the committee which swept aside the wishes of the convention. They did this by deciding to submit a contrary proposition to the parties, as follows: "In case the party name voted for by you fails to obtain the concurrent majority of both parties, shall the name receiving the majority of the total vote of both parties be adopted?"

It must not be overlooked that our party has an enrolled and paid-up membership in charge of a national secretary. On the contrary, the SLP does not know its membership and has studiously evaded giving any definite information concerning it. With these facts confronting us, it will be seen that their vote would depend upon the returns made by the secretaries of local sections. Under such conditions, while we do not claim that the returns would be fictitious, yet we contend that said returns might be so in the case of the SLP. Hence a majority of both parties, voting as one, might be a fictitious majority so far as the SLP is concerned.

It will be noticed that Comrade E. V. Debs's name is not affixed to this statement, although he is a member of the National Executive Board. His attitude, however, upon the information herein contained, is in entire accord with the rest of the board. He was present at our conference and heard this read. The purpose of the board to preserve the Social Democratic Party has his unqualified approval. From the fact that he is a candidate and has received a telegram on behalf of the majority of the committee asking him to suspend judgment until he sees the majority report, his name is withheld.

We submit to you, comrades, that union with a knowledge of the foregoing facts cannot be honorably consummated.

Is Union Possible?

It may be asked, why has the national executive taken immediate action before reading the official majority report? In reply, we say that promptness on our part will alone save disintegration and disastrous disaffection. Prompt action is demanded by the exigencies of the case and because the spirit of revolt is already thundering at our doors.

Comrades, the social democratic movement has been built upon the altar of sacrifice. Toil and hardship, poverty and privation, have been the lot of its pioneers. Shall months and years of arduous service to establish a revolutionary working-class party in this country come to naught? United in spirit, agreed as to methods, harmoniously we have gone forth to the achievement of victories. Shall these results, this normal growth, be turned to defeat and dissolution? Political unity formed upon diplomacy, tainted with bad faith and double-dealing, can never stand. The enduring socialist movement must be founded upon unsullied honor and integrity. It must be a movement, not a sect. Union in which all the essential elements of unity are lacking is impossible. A united socialist party cannot be built upon a basis of broken pledges.

You, comrades, are the arbiters. This momentous question must be decided. Loyalty to the cause of socialism in this crisis calls for fidelity and unflinching support of the Social Democratic Party.

Referendum

In view of the facts above stated, the National Executive Board submits the following to the members for a referendum vote:

"Is union between the Social Democratic Party and the Socialist Labor Party faction desirable?"

VOTE YES OR NO.

Jesse Cox,
Victor L. Berger,
Frederic Heath,
Seymour Stedman

❧

Comrades, Take Notice

Members are requested to at once take up the Referendum submitted by the executive board, canvass the whole question, and return their votes through branch secretaries to the national secretary not later than May 7 [1900].

Notes

1. No copy of the original document is currently known to exist.
2. An allusion to a number of anarchists involved in the activities of the Social Democracy in the Chicago area.
3. A conference bringing together the two nine-member unity committees of the Social Democratic Party and the Socialist Labor Party was held in New York City on April 20, 1900. Although not himself a member of the elected SDP committee, the meeting was also attended by Eugene V. Debs.
4. Reference is to the Indianapolis convention of the SDP, held from March 6–9, 1900. Of the five members of the National Executive Board, four would ultimately stay with the SDP through the process of its merger with the dissident faction of the SLP, with chairman Jesse Cox resigning over the matter later in April. Victor L. Berger was also a consistent opponent to the merger.
5. Both the SDP and the SLP dissidents appointed nine-member committees to negotiate the merger of the two organizations.
6. This assertion is deceptive. There were actually a total of 67 delegate mandates ultimately approved, each voting multiple proxies signed by party members. The hall in which the convention was held seated 200.
7. Job Harriman of California and Max S. Hayes of Ohio had been nominated as the presidential ticket of the dissident SLP at their convention held at Rochester, New York, from January 27 to February 2, 1900.
8. The insurgent anti-DeLeon faction of the Socialist Labor Party held its "Tenth Convention" in Rochester, New York, from January 27 to February 2, 1900. The regular SLP held a "Tenth Convention" of its own in New York City from June 2–8, 1900.

Index

About the Editors

Tim Davenport is involved with several online radical history projects, including his Early American Marxism website, Marxists Internet Archive, and Wikipedia. He is a member of the Historians of American Communism, the Organization of American Historians, the Society for Historians of the Gilded Age and Progressive Era, and the Labor and Working-Class History Association. He is coeditor with Paul LeBlanc of *The "American Exceptionalism" of Jay Lovestone and His Comrades, 1929–1940* (Haymarket Books, 2018).

David Walters is a lifelong socialist and trade unionist. He was one of the founders of the Marxists Internet Archive and remains with the MIA as a volunteer, managing the site's Eugene V. Debs archive. He is the past director of the Holt Labor Library in San Francisco.

About Haymarket Books

Haymarket Books is a radical, independent, nonprofit book publisher based in Chicago. Our mission is to publish books that contribute to struggles for social and economic justice. We strive to make our books a vibrant and organic part of social movements and the education and development of a critical, engaged, international left.

We take inspiration and courage from our namesakes, the Haymarket martyrs, who gave their lives fighting for a better world. Their 1886 struggle for the eight-hour day—which gave us May Day, the international workers' holiday—reminds workers around the world that ordinary people can organize and struggle for their own liberation. These struggles continue today across the globe—struggles against oppression, exploitation, poverty, and war.

Since our founding in 2001, Haymarket Books has published more than five hundred titles. Radically independent, we seek to drive a wedge into the risk-averse world of corporate book publishing. Our authors include Noam Chomsky, Arundhati Roy, Rebecca Solnit, Angela Y. Davis, Howard Zinn, Amy Goodman, Wallace Shawn, Mike Davis, Winona LaDuke, Ilan Pappé, Richard Wolff, Dave Zirin, Keeanga-Yamahtta Taylor, Nick Turse, Dahr Jamail, David Barsamian, Elizabeth Laird, Amira Hass, Mark Steel, Avi Lewis, Naomi Klein, and Neil Davidson. We are also the trade publishers of the acclaimed Historical Materialism Book Series and of Dispatch Books.

Also available from Haymarket Books

The American Socialist Movement, 1897–1912
Ira Kipnis

The Bending Cross: A Biography of Eugene Victor Debs
Ray Ginger, introduction by Mike Davis

Lucy Parsons: An American Revolutionary
Carolyn Ashbaugh

The Labor Wars: From the Molly Maguires to the Sit Downs
Sidney Lens

A Short History of the U.S. Working Class: From Colonial Times to the Twenty-First Century (Revolutionary Studies)
Paul Le Blanc